AF413741

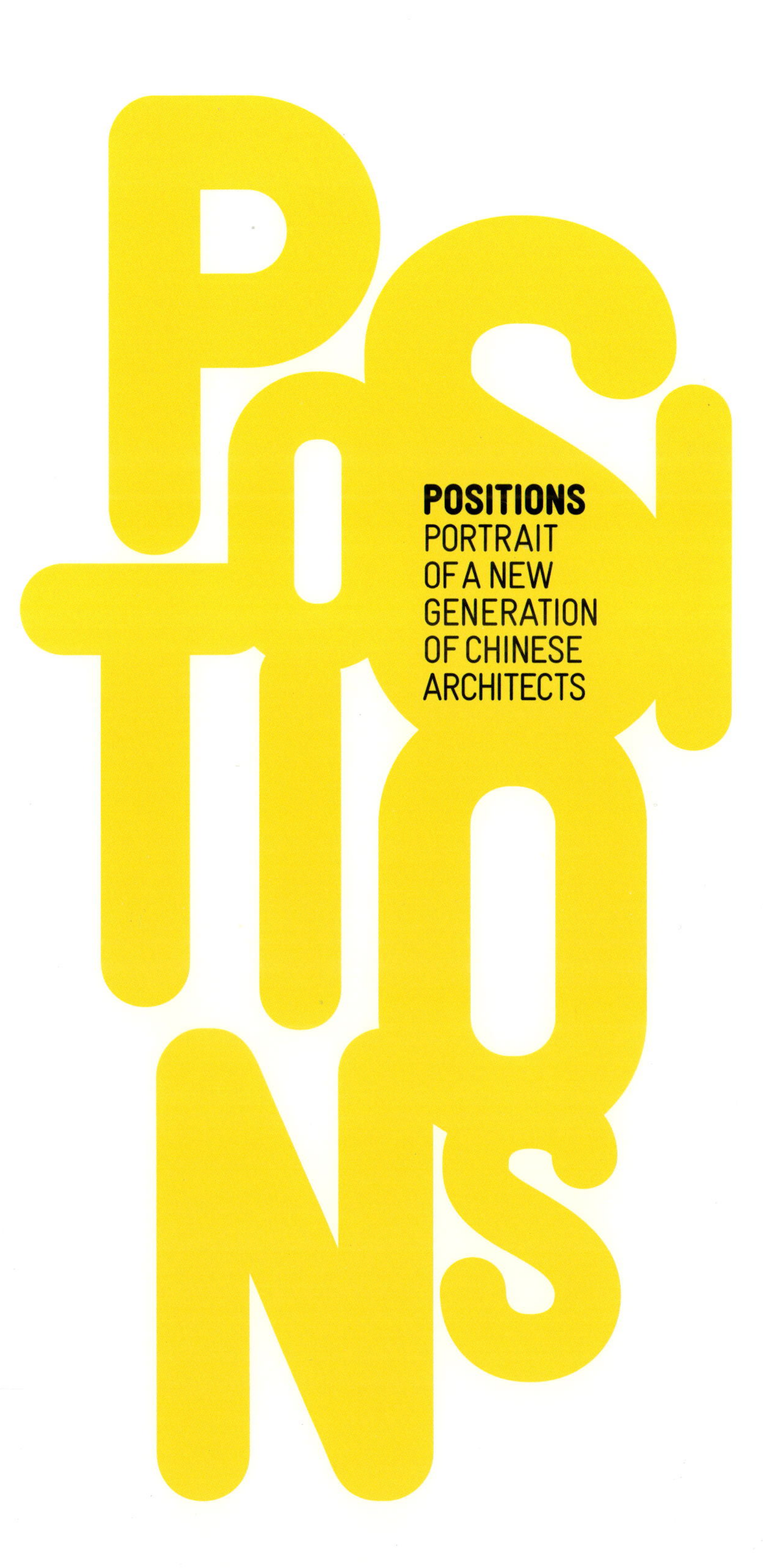
POSITIONS
PORTRAIT
OF A NEW
GENERATION
OF CHINESE
ARCHITECTS

CHINA ARCHITECTURE DESIGN & RESEARCH GROUP

JIAKUN ARCHITECTS

DESHAUS

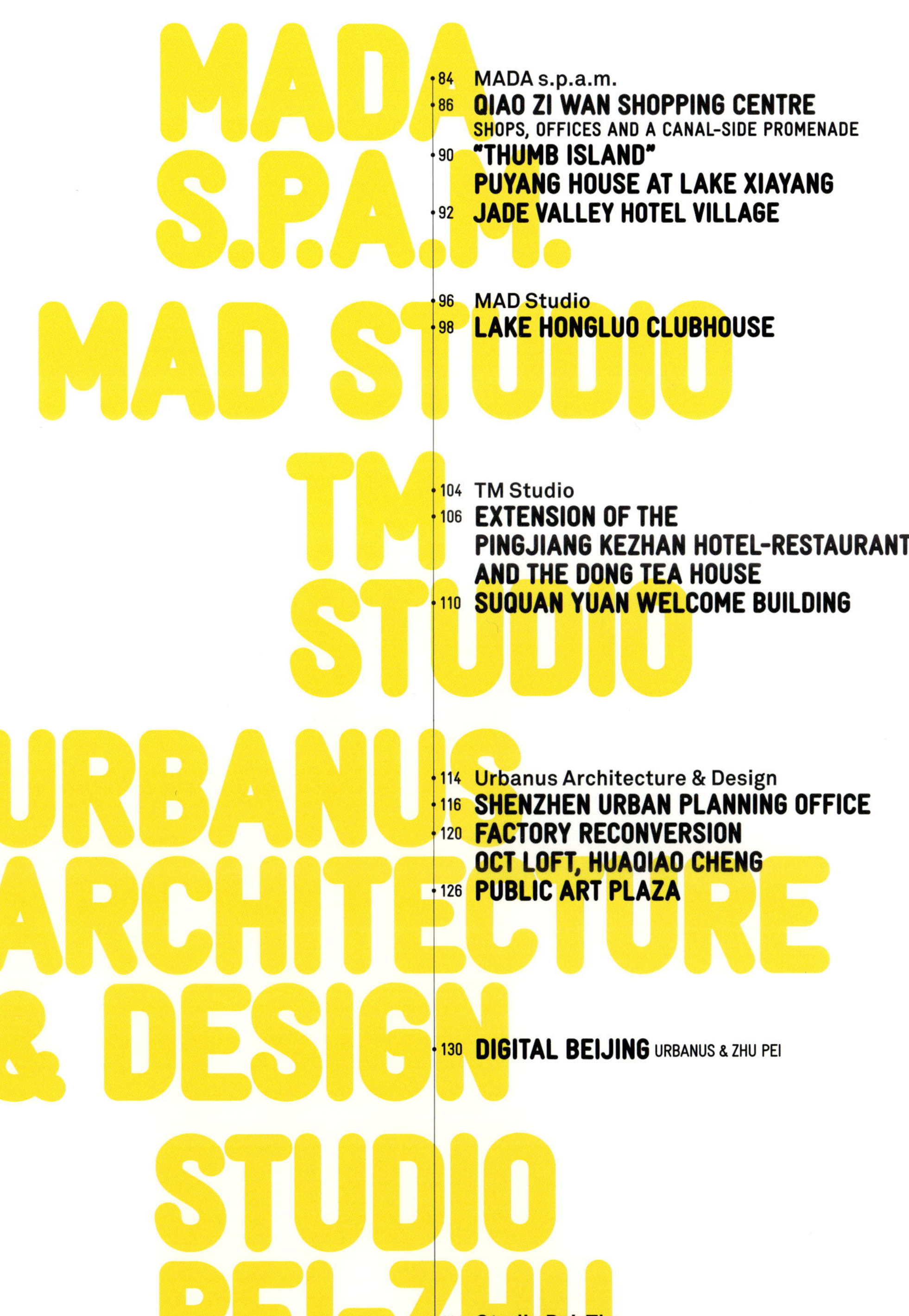

MADA
S.P.A.M.
MAD STUDIO
TM
STUDIO
URBANUS
ARCHITECTURE
& DESIGN
STUDIO
PEI-ZHU

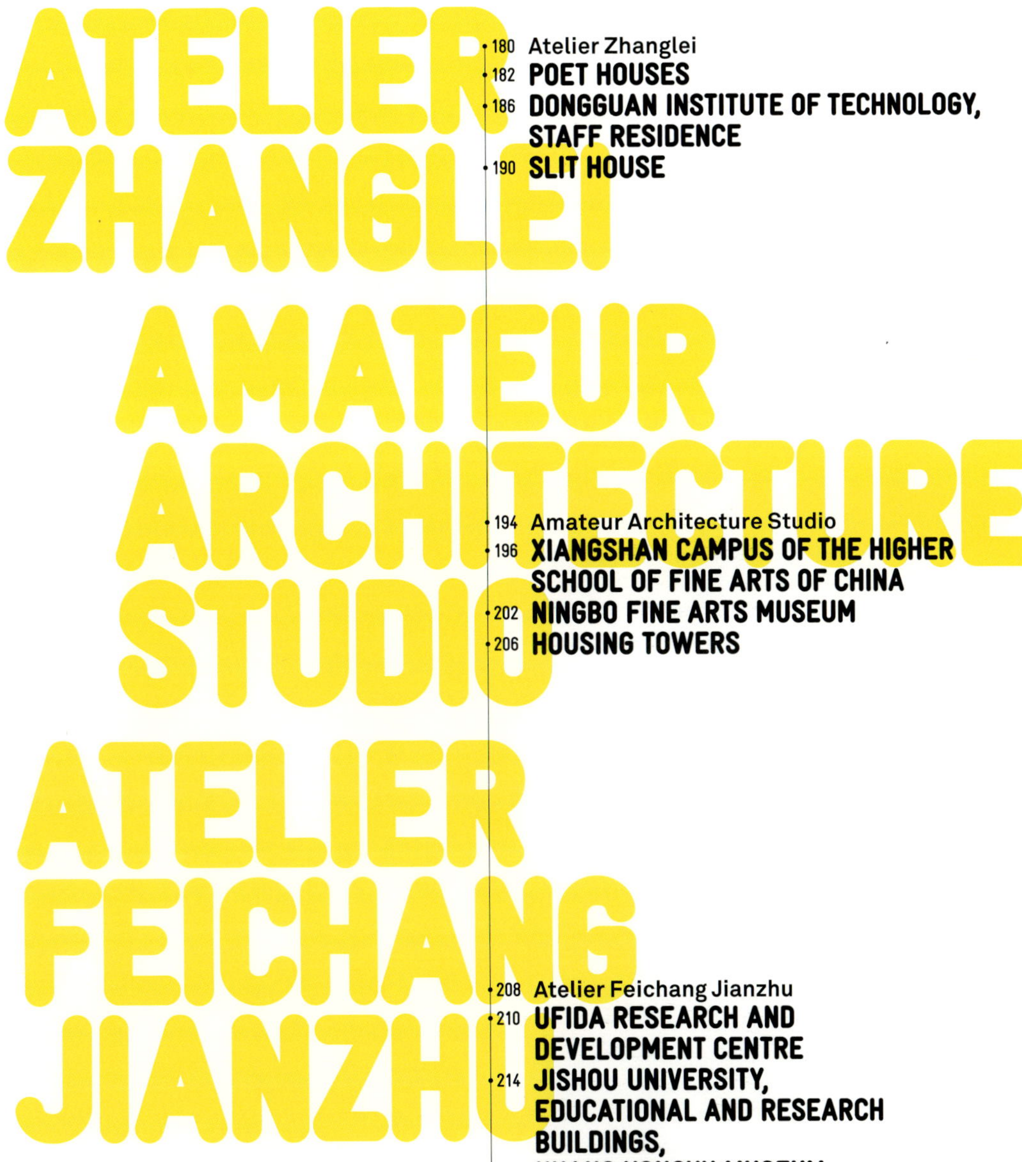

Introduction
It is no easy task to go out from our borders, to preserve our capacity of
amazement, and to open ourselves to other practices of the professions linked to
architecture, to urban planning and to the landscape.

With "Positions", the twin sister of the big thematic exhibition "In the Chinese
City. Perspectives on the transmutations of an Empire", the aim is quite naturally
for the Cité de l'architecture & du patrimoine to defend its ability to place
architecture at the heart of the contemporary issues of the city and heritage, and
to recall the emotion which may be aroused by a composed landscape, the dignity
of a site, the elegance of proportions, the propensity of a place to make us happy...

A few dozen architectural models, the portraits of the architects, the photographs
of constructed edifices (some fifty buildings selected from several hundred which
were visited), recorded interviews with architects and urban planners who are
building today's city and are seeking to protect yesterday's heritage... all this
is the result of the patient task of a surveyor in the field. If, for the uninformed
observer, it could all appear to be but a drop of water in the immensity of the
Chinese production in this sector, we see rather the evidencing of remarkable
personalities and a founding event in Europe as in China since it rests on the
in-depth researches of a decade in a particularly shifting landscape.

The cornerstone of this prospective edifice was laid at the colloquium of 1999 on
the role of architectural criticism, at Tsinghua University in Beijing, which included
the participation of some of our "guides" (Francis Rambert, today director of the
French Institute of Architecture, and Frédéric Edelmann, critic for the newspaper
Le Monde). The colloquium was organised by Diana Chan Chieng, president of
A3-Art Architecture Association, with Françoise Ged at the Observatory of the
Architecture of Contemporary China (OACC). At the end of 2000, an exchange
between French and Chinese critics, of the journal *Time + architecture* published
in Shanghai, gave a substantial continuation to these preliminary meetings.
This means that for ten years the gaze of our pilots has been honed in these
vast estuaries of Chinese construction, where they guide us today to chosen
viewpoints. That is to say, what is involved here is an in-depth job, already
punctuated by meetings like the conference organised at the halls of the Regional
Council of the Order of Architects of Île-de-France by the OACC in the autumn
of 2003, with some of these young Chinese architects who were hardly known in
their own country at that time, and like the gathering of May 2005, on the occasion
of the Shanghai Meetings, which we were proud to conduct with our privileged
partners of Tongji University.

To observe, to understand, to compare and to dare to surpass the programmed viewpoints, this is the journey which we propose here with this handful of courageous, endearing and talented personalities, who belong to two already distinct generations, with a fifteen-year interval: those, to use a Chinese popular expression, who have tasted the "bitter food" of the dark periods of the Great Leap Forward and the Cultural Revolution, and then the reopening of the universities, the first trips abroad and the explosion of urban consumption of the last two decades; and those whose first memories begin with the opening to the market and to the West. Material consumption, consumption of spaces, consumption of natural resources, condemnation of traditional societies, rehabilitation of Confucian values… there we have individualities who have lived in the space of a few years what is experienced perhaps over the long course of what is called a "very full" life. Their pathways cross or complement each other, they are witnesses and creator of our times. In the mirror of their convictions and proposals, can we refine our own knowledge and perceptions?

These were especially the aims of the presidential programme of welcome, exchanges and training of "150 Chinese architects, urban planners and landscape architects in France", which unfolded from 1997 to 2005. This interesting initiative, implemented and coordinated by the Observatory of the Architecture of Contemporary China, was concretised thanks to the unfailing engagement of the Ministry of Foreign Affairs alongside the Directorate for Architecture and Heritage, and it represents a success unanimously applauded in China as well as France.

To conclude, let us mention these Chinese urban planners whom the filmed interviews of the exhibition allow us to discover: on the initiative of the National Centre of Research on the Chinese Historic Cities, they have chosen to take up the challenge of keeping active and alive the old city centres ravaged by disparate but formidably efficient factors formed, there as well as here, by land pressure, real estate speculation, mass tourism facilities… These are the same questions posed in our so-called temperate latitudes. We are confident that the cooperation commenced on these topics with our partners of Tongji University and the Directorate for Architecture and Heritage will prove fruitful for a new decade.

François de Mazières
President of Cité de l'architecture & du patrimoine

The Foam on the Ocean

Nothing is lost, everything is imported, everything is recycled. In a country with over one hundred million internauts, real estate projects are caught in an incessant flow of images. The icons, models and other concepts from all over the planet are cheerfully "taken up".

Likewise, the transformation of the Chinese landscape has led to the emergence of a class which is highly focused on consumption. New wealth, new quarters, new urban identities. China loves to develop "theme cities", borrowing its styles from Europe in this way (here a Spanish city, there an Italian town, and there again an English city...). Gated communities also find fertile soil for growth there. But where is architecture concealed in all this?

In the ocean of structures which is unrolling across Chinese territory, quality architecture has something of foam to it... refreshing, bubbling, elusive...

"Positions", an indispensable complement to the exhibition devoted to the Chinese city, seeks to define the contours of a production which is linked to small and medium scales, making the elements of the everyday in this way.

But who are these acknowledged architects who, on firm positions, refuse to yield to the powerful grinder of globalised generic production?

They were still students, some of them merely schoolchildren, when Norman Foster finished his celebrated tower in Hong Kong, then a British colony, in the mid-1980s. That was the period when, on the continent, China launched its urban economic reform which aimed to open fourteen coastal cities, including Shanghai and Guangzhou (previously Canton). These young architects are in a position today to take orders and they are at work in a climate of hypermodernity.

In the 1990s, one observed the first signs of a new expression. Today it is clear, an architecture is emerging, a generation is appearing. The architects are between 35 and 50 years old. They are trained in China and often subsequently in the United States or sometimes in France (Qi Xin, Zhang Bin...), although in some cases these architects are the product of a one hundred per cent Chinese training (Cui Kai, Deshaus, Liu Jiakun, Wang Shu, Tong Ming...). This raises the question of the identity of this architecture which is more and more globalised, and of the interplay of influences.

Frédéric Edelmann and Françoise Ged, the curators of the exhibition, set themselves a rule aimed to protect them from the inflation of projects for which, in the currently overheated real estate climate, there is no true certainty of eventual completion. These experts made it a point of honour to visit each of the buildings presented in the exhibition.

Marked positions, distinctive attitudes... the debate is rich in this extensive territory of possibilities. The distance is great between a Wang Shu who loves to revisit traditional architecture and a Ma Yansong who, after conceiving megastructures for the Ground Zero site in New York, has developed his schema of Beijing with a variant aimed to

vegetalise the whole Tian'anmen site, including Paul Andreu's titanium opera house...
The distance is even greater between Cui Kai, who having mastered large work sites,
was in fact the ideal partner for Jean-Marie Dutillheul (and would sign some large
projects with him, such as the Shanghai station, that immense intermodal wheel
erected to the south of the city) and signatures such as Ma Qingyun or Zhu Pei.
The author of an impressive floating dragon in Qinqpu (with its very trendy vegetalised
fifth façade), Ma Qingyun, the accomplice of Rem Koolhaas and today the dean of
an architecture university in Los Angeles, is one of the most Westernised Chinese
architects. Despite that, he is not cut off from his roots, as is witnessed by his
contextual work for his father's house or the tourism ensemble which he is building
around a vineyard in Jade Valley.
Zhu Pei, for his part, signs buildings which are as graphic as they are unitary, in the
manner of the blind monolith of the Olympic complex (Digital Beijing Center) or the
hotel built just a stone's throw away from the Forbidden City, with its fibre-glass skin
of honeycomb cells. As in Europe, the "skin" becomes in China the interface of the
dialogue between heritage and the contemporary.
In this photograph of a new generation of architects, Ai Wei Wei stands out for his
singularity. The author of radical buildings, he intervenes both as architect and artistic
director at the Jinhua architecture and sculpture park, when he is not busy working
with Herzog & De Meuron on the weaving of the Olympic "Nest".

The venerable Ieoh Ming Pei will have finally opened the path ... The architect of the
National Gallery in Washington, of the Louvre Pyramid in Paris and of the tower of
the Bank of China erected in Hong Kong on the principle of the growth of bamboo,
has recently made a fine return to the country by signing the elegant Suzhou museum,
with a gentleness of scale and of tonality in grey and white.
By definition, emblematic architectures have something exceptional to them. By the
Great Wall of China, the so-called Commune operation, an architecture park crowned
by a Golden Lion at the Venice Biennale, is emblematic of the architectural policy of
a real-estate group which has opted for "signed" architecture as its trade mark.
There, in this mythical and highly touristic frame, experimentation has been carried
out on the theme of the house, with a selection of Asian architects (the "suitcase"
house by Gary Chang, the "bamboo" house by Kengo Kuma...).
Another exception in Qingpu, in the suburbs of Shanghai where, under the impulse of
a far-seeing mayor, one reads clearly the effects of a quality policy carried out with
such architects as Deshaus, Liu Jiakun and Ma Qingyun. In this way, an administrative
building, a chamber of commerce, a school and a cultural centre find a writing which
is not lacking in rigour or refinement. So now let's surf on the foam...

Francis Rambert
Director of the Institut français d'architecture

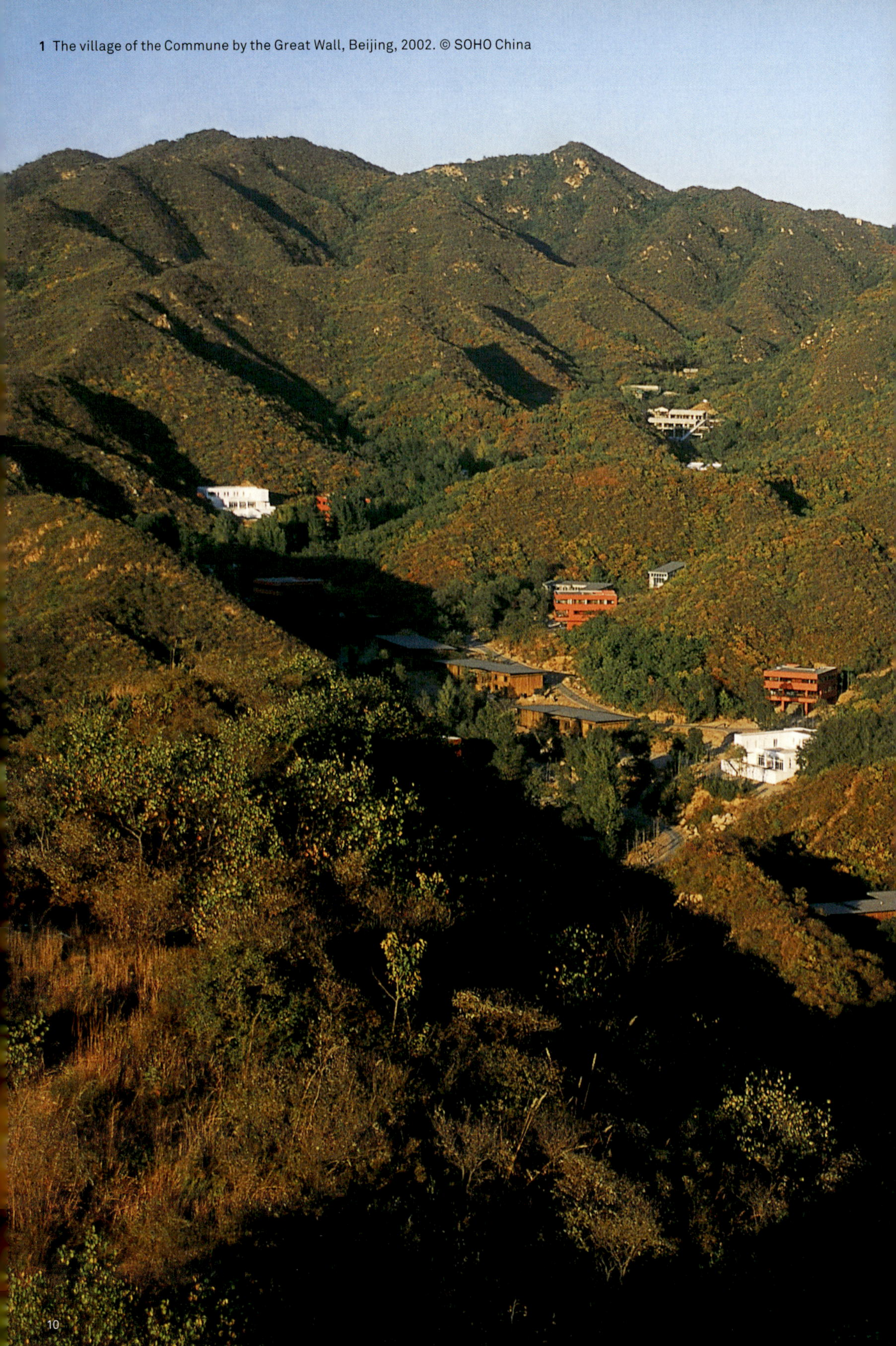

1 The village of the Commune by the Great Wall, Beijing, 2002. © SOHO China

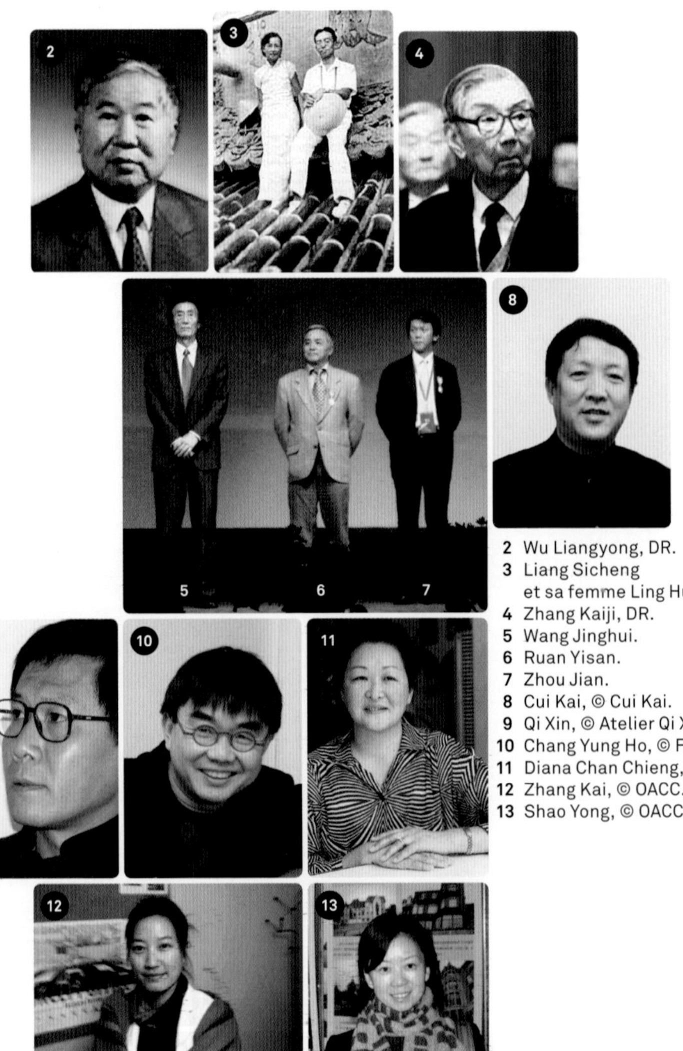

2 Wu Liangyong, DR.
3 Liang Sicheng
  et sa femme Ling Huiyin, DR.
4 Zhang Kaiji, DR.
5 Wang Jinghui.
6 Ruan Yisan.
7 Zhou Jian.
8 Cui Kai, © Cui Kai.
9 Qi Xin, © Atelier Qi Xin.
10 Chang Yung Ho, © FCJZ.
11 Diana Chan Chieng, © DCC.
12 Zhang Kai, © OACC.
13 Shao Yong, © OACC.

Positions

To report on architecture in the People's Republic of China at the time of the
Beijing Olympics resembles *a priori* a puzzle. An intense labour of clearing the field
allows the history of literature, painting and cinema to be grasped with a relative
continuity, even if it means excluding (or including, as there may be some cases)
the sombre hours of the Cultural Revolution and the periods dominated by the
imperatives of propaganda. In China, however, architecture is often disconnected
from its history, from its natural, economic, social and, now and always, political
environment, while in the West, the university system and the classically solitary
dimension of research make a comprehensive approach difficult. The sources,
even in Chinese, remain hardly accessible when they exist, and we must limit
ourselves to fragmented views.

More recent architecture is better documented, while remaining dependent
mainly on the increasingly numerous journals. *Time+Architecture* ⓮, published
by Tongji University in Shanghai, which includes English summaries of its articles
published in Chinese, has played a pioneering role in this respect.

In this book we present some forty projects by fifteen architects between 30
and 55 years of age. Some of them (in our "circle", a good third) have carried out
all their studies in China and have only made an occasional trip abroad to attend
conferences or to present their work. Others, on the other hand, have built their
know-how in the United States or Europe (one third in the US and a little less
than one third in Europe) after a classic curriculum in China, benefiting from
specialisations of the schools or sometimes from internships in big or less than
big international studios. The work of most of them has already been exhibited
and all of them, in one way or another, have been published in Chinese journals,
while two or three among them, such as Ma Qingyun, Chang Yung Ho and Ma
Yansong, even have a prestigious audience and devote part of their time to their
colleagues and to courses at the elite schools of America and Europe. Are they
well known for that account?

The Observatory of the Architecture of Contemporary China ⓯, created by the
Directorate for Architecture in 1997 with Bruno Fayolle Lussac, Jean-Paul Loubes,
and Françoise Ged as director, has proven to be a precious support. It has allowed
us to verify on site and in detail, project by project, realisation by realisation,
what really existed and what was based on big hopes in the exhibitions on China.
Some projects presented as having been realised or as being on the verge of
realisation have in fact remained on paper. Other projects, just as numerous,
proved on site to be quite different from the photographs and 3D projections with
which the Western experts on architecture have embellished their picture rails
over the course of recent years.

It is true that the visit to the projects included in this book, which form but a
fraction of all those which we went to see, benefited from a set of exceptional
conditions. For example, the support of the Ministry of Culture to the Observatory,
the essential assistance of the Ministry of Foreign Affairs, and the support of
a unique exchange programme: "150 Chinese Architects, Urban Planners and
Landscape Architects in France", have permitted us to carry out a true labour
of criticism and verification, mainly in the urban China but also on its margins.
Why fifteen architects and only these forty projects? This may seem quite little
with respect to the hundreds of millions of square metres built annually in

China and the impressive forest of new cities, representing a protean colossal
production. We ourselves wondered about the reason for such a small harvest,
considering that our information network has all but no equal. It relies mainly
on Tongji University (Shanghai) and on the exceptional personality of Zhou Jian,
the director of the school of architecture; on the school of architecture of Tsinghua
University (Beijing), and on the generous and efficient personalities of Cui Kai and
Zou Huan; as well as on the directors of the schools of architecture of Chongqing,
Guangzhou, Tianjin and Nanking, and on a number of other structures, mostly at
the universities. Likewise, several directors of Chinese architecture studios also
showed themselves to be friends and precious guides, such as Feng Yueqiang,
Qi Xin, and Diana Chan Chieng. It is thanks to this network that we are in a position
to present here the latest works carried out by a new generation of Chinese
architects, even if we cannot provide an overall report on architecture in China.
For the recent period, we would be led to present in the latter hypothesis
some works as prestigious as the National Television ⓰ (CCTV) Tower designed
by Rem Koolhaas in Beijing and the Olympic stadium ⓱ of the Swiss architects
Herzog & de Meuron. We would also have to present daring works which are
intellectually less ambitious but spectacular for their size, their finishes and
a certain elegance: the Jinmao tower ⓲ (by the American studio SOM) and its
neighbour the World Financial Center (KPF studio on behalf of the Japanese
group Mori), the big south station of Shanghai ⓳ by the design studio of the
French railway station agency (AREP), Andreu's National Theatre in Beijing, and
an impressive number of office complexes, conference halls and airports signed
by the world's most powerful studios (GMP, ADPi, Isozaki, Kurokawa...).
Are not the Chinese themselves present on site? They are indeed, but the system
which emphasizes the "project institutes" or "construction institutes", with
a practice of hierarchical consensus for the major decisions, has eliminated up
to now the essential features of creativeness. The architects of these institutes
often follow their work sites from a distance and delegate to other local institutes
the realisation of the designs. When they are associated with foreign architecture
studios, some of them resign themselves to imitating these firms by a game
of cut-and-paste. When a specifically Chinese design emerges at one of these
institutes, it is treated the same as the designs coming from Asia or Europe,
that is to say, simplifying them, fragmenting them and repeating them to the point
where there is an initial loss of sense and of the project itself.
Nevertheless, everyone will be able to observe that in recent years the quality
of construction, of materials and of implementation has not ceased to improve,
especially in the housing towers which, *grosso modo,* have no longer anything
to envy the condominiums of the United States or of South America, without
assuring, for that account, a happy and peaceful future life for the inhabitants
of the cities. All this production has its own story and in order to understand what
may be the great value of the little group of pioneers whom we have assembled
here, the effort must be made to project oneself into a painful past and to make
some still little-encouraging affirmations about the contemporary situation.
What was this past like?

The birth of modern architecture in a destabilised China
At the opening of the 20th century, the urban and rural construction in China
had practically remained immobile for seven centuries and Beijing was a perfect
example of this. The inputs in this field came essentially from the modernisation
tied to the violent birth, because it arose from treaties justly qualified as
"unequal", of the foreign concessions and legations, and of the trading posts
and factories. The laying of telegraph lines and railways, the issue of the speed
of exchanges within the country, collided, according to the tradition of *feng
shui,* against the "veins of the dragon", that is to say, nature, a nature that was
nevertheless constantly modelled by the hand of man and already punctuated
with remarkable works. Also at stake was the legitimacy of an imperial power
undecided about making the shift called for by the reformers, and the empress
Cixi was not wrong, immersed in unbearable anxieties by the arrival of the railway
and the construction of the first station in Beijing. Aside from that, the evolution
of the county seemed to follow the construction of the railway lines, in Hong
Kong, in Guangzhou, with the ambition peculiar to the colonising ideal all along
the Yangzi to Nanking, in Hankou (today's Wuhan), or in the northern provinces:
Tianjin, Moukden (now Shenyang), Changchun, Harbin… It is also true, however,
that it is the path followed at the same time by the first photographers, outside
the hazardous explorations of brave-hearted archaeologists and Sinologists,
who drew up the repertory of memorable monuments worthy of interest.
With the opening to foreign trade and the economic development of the coastal
cities (starting with Shanghai) architects and engineers began to arrive in China,
via Hong Kong, such as the Palmer & Turner studio, to propose the standards
of a new splendour, thoroughly Neo-classical like the Bund of Shanghai, where
the studio signed most of the buildings up to the 1930s. Others followed more
innovative criteria, such as the Hungarian architect Hudec, the Swiss Minutti
or the French Léonard and Veyssère. In the same city, factories and warehouses
emerge, including some non-standard realisations such as the Piranesian meat
packing plants in the Hongkou quarter **❷⓪**, attributed to the English architect
Balfour and built by Sun Deshui. Within these buildings there is little exoticism,
which does not exclude the incorporation of some Chinese motifs or materials,
from the return to the country of the first architects trained abroad, or more
rarely, Chinese interpretations such as the large roofings by the American Murphy
on all the new programmes, which were then the university campuses.
Indeed, the sons of Mandarins or of merchants converted to the virtues of
Western civilisation sent their children to the American schools, since it was
mainly in the US that the model was to be found, the ideal of Chicago or New York,
although some were also sent to Japan or Europe. Curiously enough, the ties with
France and fine arts education passed through the University of Pennsylvania,
where the department of architecture was directed by Paul Cret, welcoming
a large number of Chinese students, including the one who was to become the
celebrated Liang Sicheng (1901-1972) and several of those who would open studios
in Shanghai, Shenyang, Nanking or Tianjin in the 1930s. The promoters of the
time disseminated models of housing estates with landscape villas featuring

eye-catchers in the Île-de-France, Bavarian or Spanish style, contributing in this way to an eclectic view of Western modernity.

The Chinese genius, even if strongly Westernised on the façade, took refuge in the repetition and variation of the model of the *lilong* (the Shanghai housing estate habitat) ㉑, which may be found all along the Yangzi and even in Tianjin. It forms a very urban typology which is distinct from the ensembles of courtyard houses of the *hutong* of Beijing and the North.

Neither the first waves of destruction linked to the invasions of foreign powers, the Boxer Rebellion nor even the violence of the Japanese bombardments (Nanking, Shanghai, Chongqing...) brought about any fundamental change in the coexistence in the cities of Western standards, of buildings under reciprocal influences and of edifices in the Chinese tradition. The effervescence of the years 1920-1930 in Shanghai was reflected in the professional associations of architects and of engineers, with divergent or complementary objectives, now lauding the progress of civil engineering, now valuing Chinese art and architecture or presenting modern architecture abroad and in China.

While Ieoh Ming Pei was leaving for the United States on the eve of the Sino-Japanese War, the few rare Chinese architects who succeeded in imposing themselves in the country had to forge a body of thought with no other reference than the knowledge already acquired, depending to a large extent on their instinct of preservation. The heritage dimension would never be forgotten. It would be embodied by personalities rich with all the culture of the country, such as Liang Sicheng ❸ and Liu Dunzhen, by others facing the ideal of a modernity which would be peculiar to the country. This would be the case of Zhang Kaiji ❹ or Wu Liangyong ❷. All these figures have been concealed by recent history, but they have crossed the tragic 20th century with a real strength of spirit.

The historical study of Chinese architecture unfolded mainly during the first half of the century. Here we are speaking of study, that is to say, of a reflection on the evolution of models through history, on the basis of field surveys and not on the perpetuation of the principle of practical or theoretical building manuals. As in the West but with a distance of several decades, the notion of monuments to be preserved lay at the heart of the concerns of the Society of Studies on Chinese Constructions, active from 1930 to 1946. What became known as "heritage" in the West by the end of the 1970s, in China was termed "historic monuments" and they emerged thanks to the contribution of Liang Sicheng and Liu Dunzhen with the support of their students, in part as a reaction to the destructions which the country suffered.

The Japanese violence does not mix well with projects for the future, but that did not prevent the appearance of some buildings which are more or less marked by the Japanese influence and by the collaborative relations with a history which remains largely to be written. The birth of the People's Republic in 1949 did not simplify, properly speaking, the revival of Chinese architecture. The urgencies lay elsewhere and the influences would arrive from elsewhere as well. Soon the Soviet advisers and their experts would come to contribute a new layer to the landscapes of the big cities. The Maoist ideal then joined up with the Stalinist ideal, using it only in part.

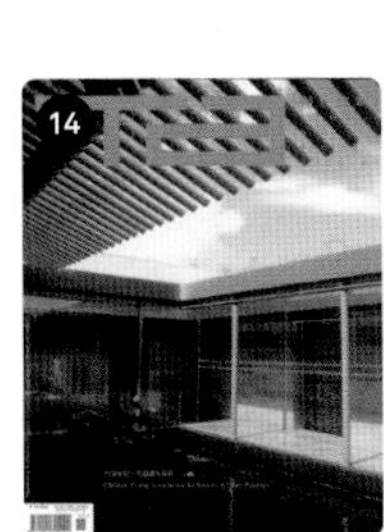
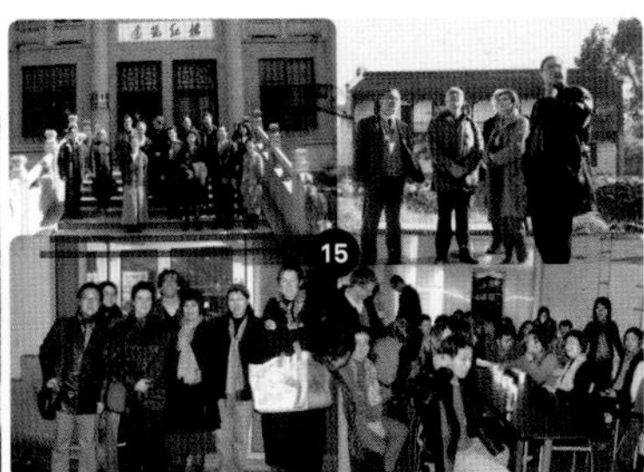
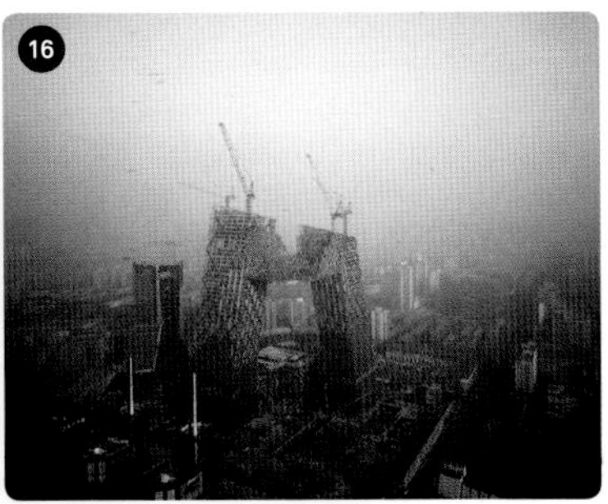
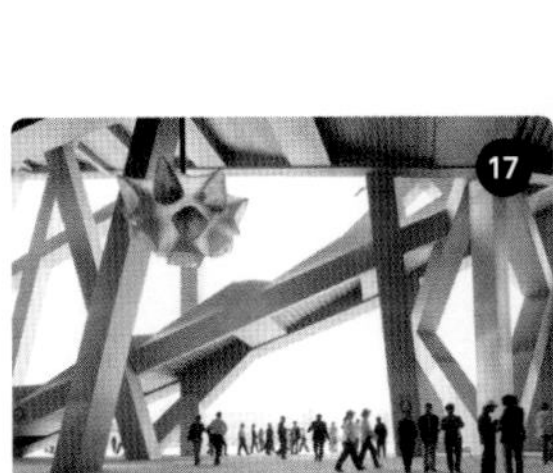
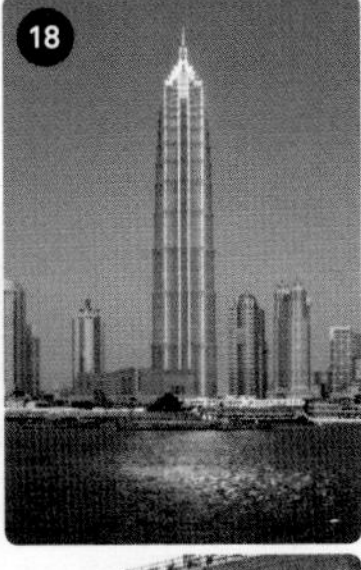
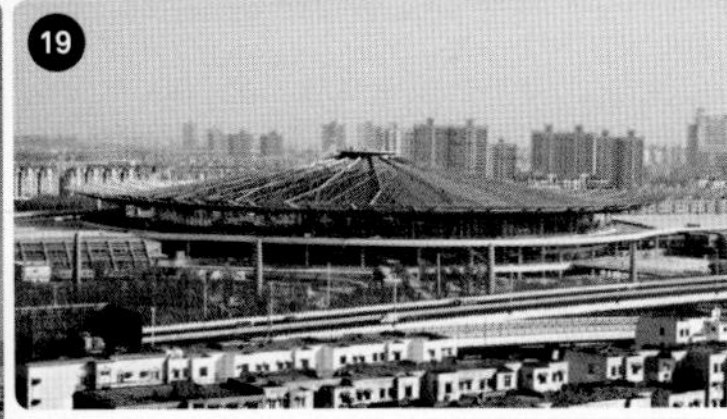
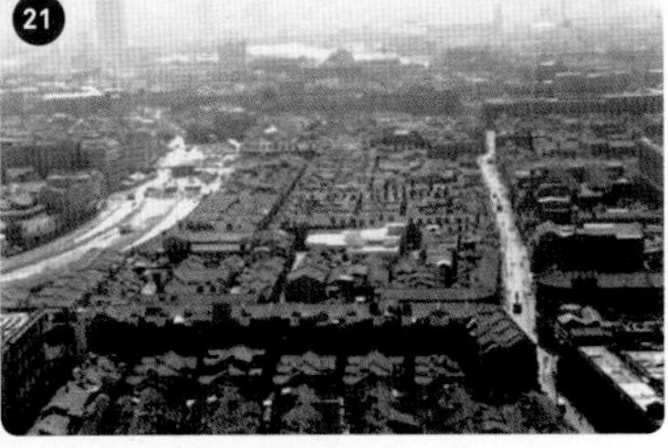
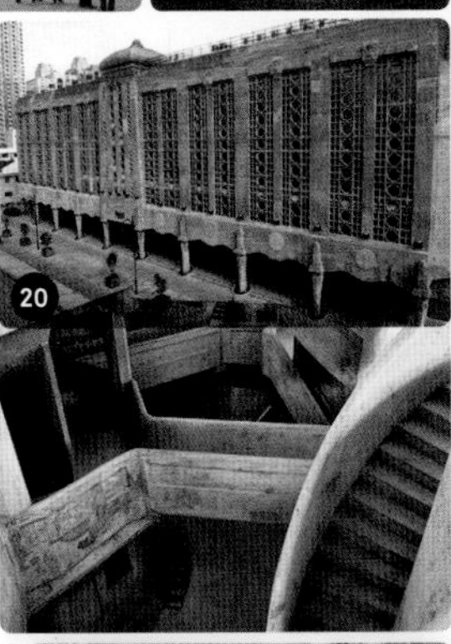
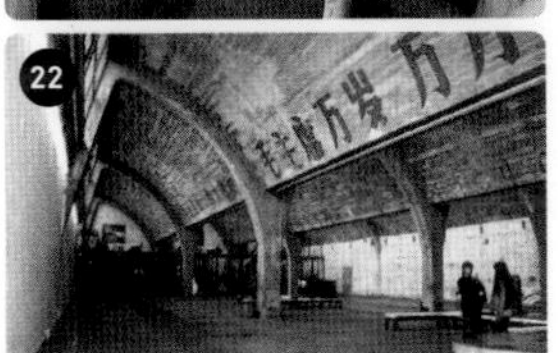
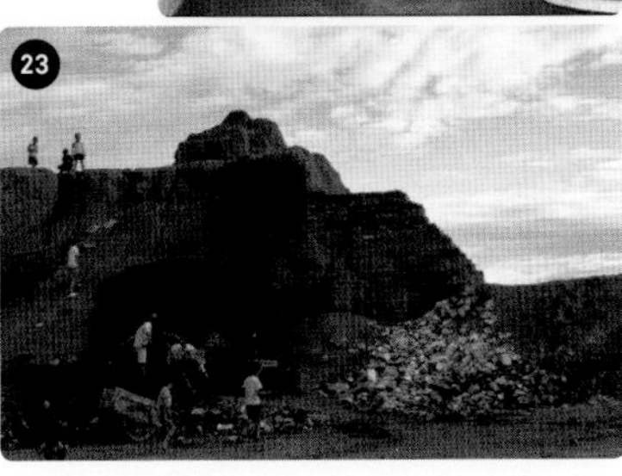

14 Cover of the journal
Time + Architecture,
"The Young Generation of Chinese
Architects and their Practices",
Tongji University, June 2005

15 Missions in China of the Observatory of
the Architecture of Contemporary China

16 Headquarters of Chinese Television,
(CCTV-TVCC) Beijing. Architects: OMA
(Rem Koolhaas, Ole Scheeren),
© Philippe Ruault.

17 Olympic Stadium, Beijing
Architects: Herzog & de Meuron,
© Iwan Baan.

18 Jinmao Tower, Shanghai.
Architects: SOM (Skidmore, Owings
& Merrill LLP), © SOM.

19 South Station of Shanghai .
Architects: AREP, © T. Chapuis.

20 Old Abattoirs of Shanghai, 1933.
© Gilles Sabrie.

21 *Lilong* in Shanghai, DR.

22 Contemporary art gallery, Dashanzi,
Beijing, DR.

23 Old walls of Beijing, 1966.
© Solange Brandt

In 1959, Chang'an Avenue in Beijing, 100 metres wide in its central part and
40 kilometres long, was planned on a typically Soviet model, bordered by major
buildings erected to celebrate the regime's first ten years. These structures
included celebrated buildings like the People's National Assembly and the Museum
of History and the Revolution, and a number of headquarters buildings of ministries
and government services (aviation, post office...), of which the architecture
(today almost entirely disappeared) revealed the great quality of the design and
of the know-how of the Chinese project management. Nevertheless, it is difficult
to put into perspective the intelligence of the local project management and the
exterior inputs, as is revealed by the large industrial quarters of the times, such as
Dashanzi ㉒, celebrated today for its contemporary art galleries – which are
installed beneath the vaults of factories attributed to East German architects.
As from the 1960s, after the scathing failure of the Great Leap Forward
(1958-1961), and even more singularly as from the Cultural Revolution, it was
the selfsame spirit and culture of China which remained long paralysed.

The annihilation of culture and knowledge
The opening of Chang'an Avenue, the construction of Tian'anmen Square and the
big buildings which surround it, still bore witness to a constructive intelligence,
contestable but marked by a concern for organisation and the idea of a coherent
future. It was also contested because as of February 1950, Liang Sicheng sought
to persuade Mao to save the totality, still homogeneous, of the old Beijing.
With Chen Zhanxiang, it was proposed to establish the capital outside the walls,
occupied subsequently by the path of the 2nd ring road ㉓.
Not long after, even before the Great Leap Forward the first purges gave the
intellectuals a preliminary taste of the nightmare which was forming. Under the
cover of rapid industrialisation, the Great Leap Forward replaced all forms of
initiative in the country with famine and terror. To build or rebuild must have
seemed to be of little importance when the question was to survive and to have
something to eat. The structures erected in this period leave one perplexed.
They are the blast furnaces and the rudimentary shelters which one finds in the
temples and palaces of the big cities. Meanwhile, the rupture with the USSR in
the year 1960 had a decisive impact on the deliveries of industrial products and
doubtless on the dissemination of these prototypes of collective dwellings,
five-level blocks, standardised and normalised ㉔ to be erected quickly from the
north to the south of the country. The lodging of the people of the already very
densely populated cities was not yet at the heart of the priorities.
As from 1966, the Cultural Revolution added a new tragic dimension. The closing
of the universities, which would not reopen their doors until ten years later,
destroyed in depth the professions tied to construction, for these are the
professions – engineers and architects – for which the training time and the
consolidation into teams, doubtless demand the longest duration. In this respect,
the cultural dimension of architecture proves to be an extra handicap from the
moment that it is opposed by nature to the imperatives of the regime. The death
of the Great Helmsman in 1976, and then the arrival of Deng Xiaoping in 1978,
after the brief interval of Hua Guofeng, would no doubt lead to the progressive
release of economic energies.[1] But the distance was great, if not to say immense,

1 The magazine *L'Architecture d'aujourd'hui* publishes, in February 1979 (n. 201), a very richly illustrated
and heavy documented on the history of Chinese architecture from 1949 to 1979.
A remarkable issue, which covers two periods.

between the then still formless new ideal of the new China and the urgencies,
the inadequacy of the infrastructures and of the industrial tool... the capacity of
reaction, in short, of a country with a population which had by then reached one
thousand million inhabitants.

Investment went first to the essential: the construction of dwellings and
infrastructures. From the end of the 1980s, the financial resources began to be
constituted through diverse mechanisms of speculation, doubtless an iniquitous
process but inevitable. The CPC brought together at that time a large part of the
last tatters of the intelligentsia, as well as all those who organised the national
and local authority. That is to say, it would prove difficult to dissociate
the interests of the nation from this if nothing else heterogeneous grouping.
Since the aim was to resume the construction of cities, the roles were
distributed with a good-natured simplicity.

Borough mayors or district chiefs are responsible for finding the necessary land
for urban renewal. Land remains State property, but its use value is auctioned
and its prices often rise even before it has been developed. The returns on
investments are quicker than the enactment of regulations alleged to temper
these bouts of fever. If a quarter in the city centre is concerned, the absence of
rights of the tenants and of the rare owners leaves an open field for the promoters,
who are usually close to the city managers. In keeping with the precepts of the
previous century, in the early days of the country's industrial modernisation,
the public and private sectors were closely tied in setting up operations,
real estate operations in this case, in which the public sector contributes its part
in land while the private sector makes its contribution by building, and the two
share the profits from the new leases. Suddenly, the commercialisation of real
estate in some cities, firstly, and later across the country, freed the public sector
from the heavy twofold burden of the construction and upkeep of the dwellings,
generating indeed enrichments as fulgurant as they were disparate.

Similar mechanisms were reproduced within the great corps of the State such
as the army, the urban administration, education, and health, and in this way
a landscape was re-created in the last twenty years of the 20th century, which
is dominated locally by the development of a new wealth, the tastes of which
show themselves perhaps to be close to those of the West's nouveaux riches.

At national level, architecture became a matter of tics. Throughout the country
one found in the same periods the same blue glazing, the same white tiles,
coverings which seemed then as precious as they were protective.

Or else, grouped in the fields transformed into housing estates, with the untiringly
repeated model of the scaled-down White House, inherited from the serials
broadcast on omnipresent screens, by builder-peasants who prefer the yield
of concrete to that, more ungrateful, of market-gardening.

In Beijing itself, mayor Chen Xitong, before being condemned for corruption in
1995, had imposed on all new structures the installation of a little roof "Chinese
style" ㉕. Some years later, in Shanghai, it was the turn of the terraced roofs of the
housing blocks to invent a "fifth façade", as seen from the urban viaducts. The old
blocks with which one cannot yet make a clean sweep will be covered with little
sloped roofs alleged to add a touch of coquetry to the cities' profile. Where was
there room for the architects' work in such a panorama?

During the Maoist years, one of the only anchorage points of individual talent had been the toilets which were imposed, not without reason, at intervals of every fifty to one hundred metres in the interior of big cities such as Beijing. It is striking to see how the bridled imagination can manage to awaken in the most minuscule projects and, years later, this type of micro-architecture would remain a place of exercise for young talents in quest of freedom. One sees this as well in the parks of Shenzhen as in the proximity of Yuanmingyuan, where the architects invent successively the most comical or elegant sanitary ware.

The explosion of architecture in the liberal economy period
If the Mao years had represented a time of petrification, the Deng Xiaoping years (1980-1997), for their part, would be marked at once by inertia and *laisser-faire*. The inertia involved architecture and new constructions. It was not truly a *laisser-faire*, which affects, on the other hand, the heritage, nor even a "make-shift *laisser-faire*". The project institutes, tied to the cities or the universities, function in fact in a very hierarchical way. This hierarchy, which was itself marked by the cultural decline of the Maoist period, entertained itself by reproducing the models prescribed by the project chiefs, still under the influence of their old education in the USSR, or even of the latest post-modern images taken from the Western journals. The Chinese publications then presented the novelties under the name of the institute in charge of the design, without giving a thought to mentioning the architects or engineers responsible for the project, and much less the teams in charge of their realisation. Buildings would not start to be identified under the signature of their designers until the 1990s.
The students learned how to build and erect different types of edifices – schools, stations, stadiums, dwellings – or quarters in the case of urban planners, and the professionals repeated the models which were held to be the best and which evolve relatively little from year to year. The project institutes inscribed themselves in a hierarchy according to which one had or did not have access to tenders and to construction in the province, the country or even abroad, a hierarchy which likewise established categories according to the complexity of the buildings to be erected, which is as much as to say that these threshold effects and successive exclusions hardly favoured the appearance and realisation of new ideas.
The major buildings and especially the stations and the administrative headquarters of the regions or cities, have long been under-calibrated with respect to the development of the population and to a new need for social organisation, founded on priority over the quantitative diktats of the five-year plans rather than on realities analysed on site. These standards appeared there like a considerably fatigued transposition of the Soviet heritage, mixed with a spiritless submission to stereotypes supposed to conjugate "Chineseness" and modern language.
It is truly difficult to put into perspective the influences behind the buildings which then arose with economic development. The cities sprawled, the mayors gained in autonomy, and the headquarters of the authorities erected in haste in

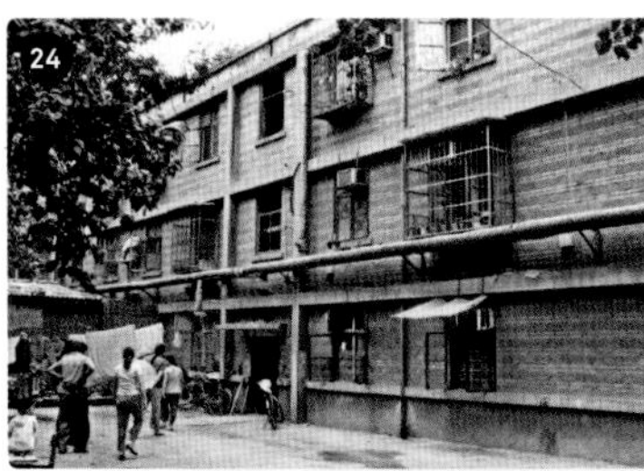

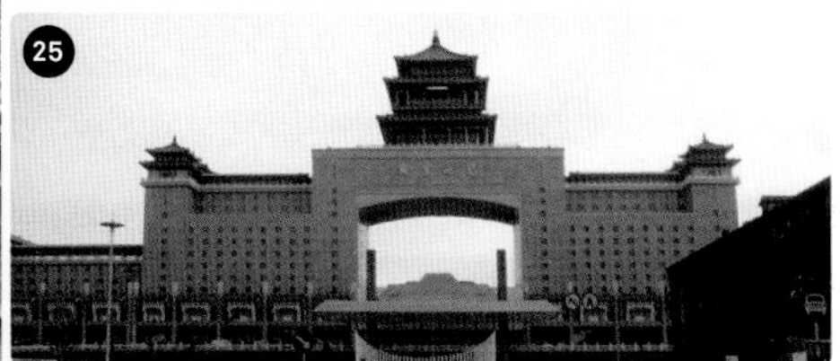

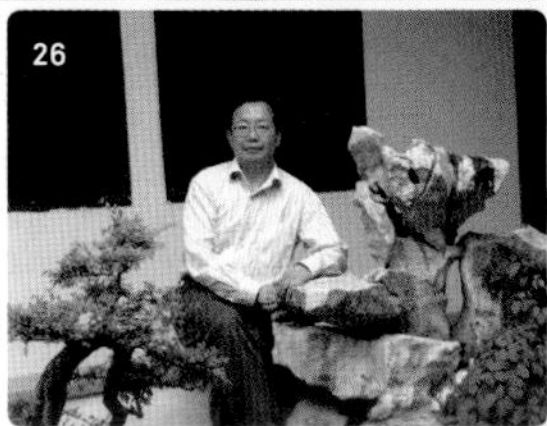

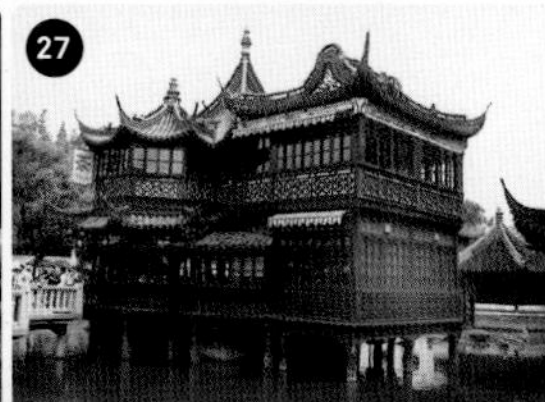

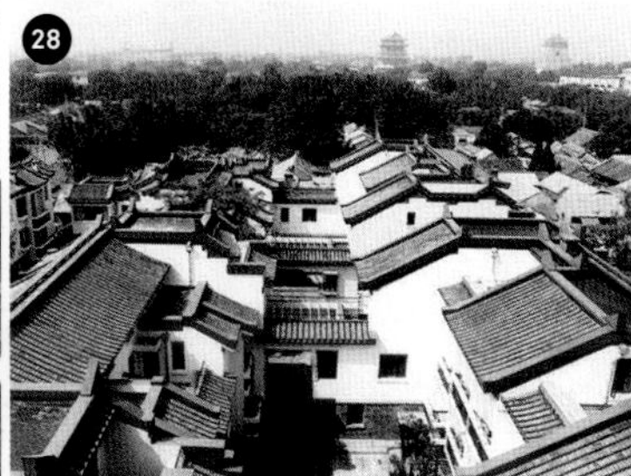

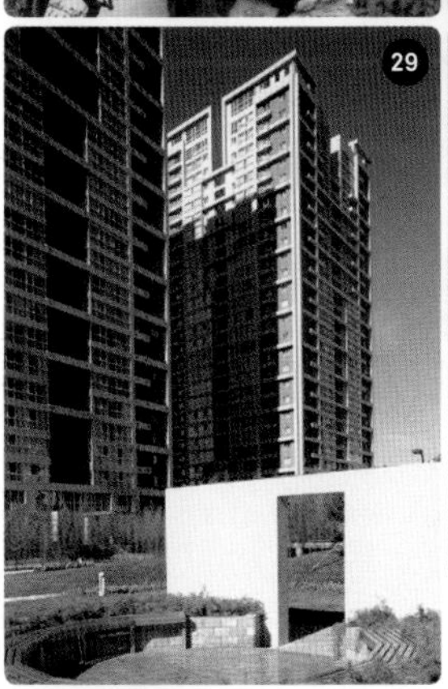

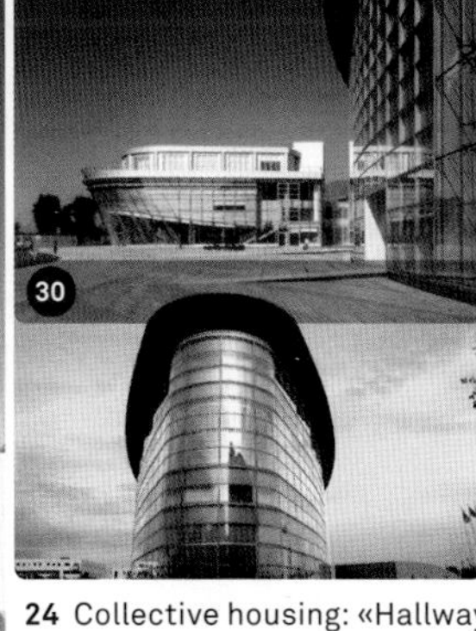

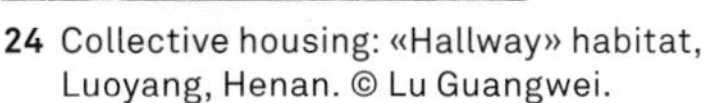

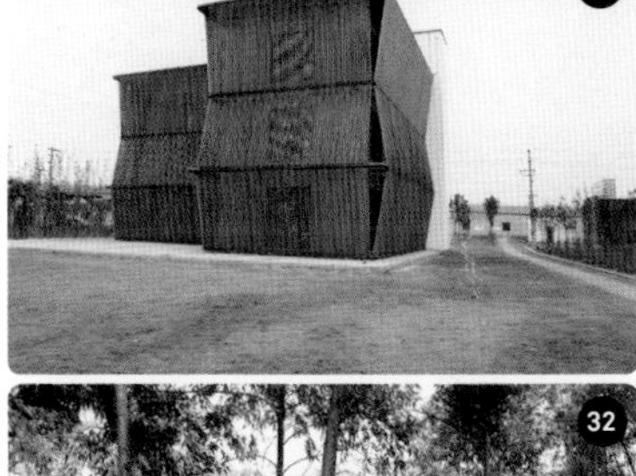

24 Collective housing: «Hallway» habitat,
Luoyang, Henan. © Lu Guangwei.
25 West Station in Beijing, a new structure
with a little Chinese-style roof, DR.
26 Ruan Yongsan, © RY.
27 Huxinting Tea House, Suzhou, DR.
28 Ju'er hutong, Beijing, DR.
29 Soho Tower, Beijing. Architect: Cui Kai, © Cui Kai.
30 Training Institute for officials of the Ministry
of Finance, Beijing Architects: Qi Xin Architects
& Engineers. © Atelier Qi Xin.
31 Qing Song Wai Yuan Garden, Qingpu (Shanghai)
Architects: Scenic Architecture. © OACC.
32 Toilets at Lianhuashan Park, Shenzhen
Architects: X-urban. © OACC.
33 Central Business District, Beijing. © OACC.

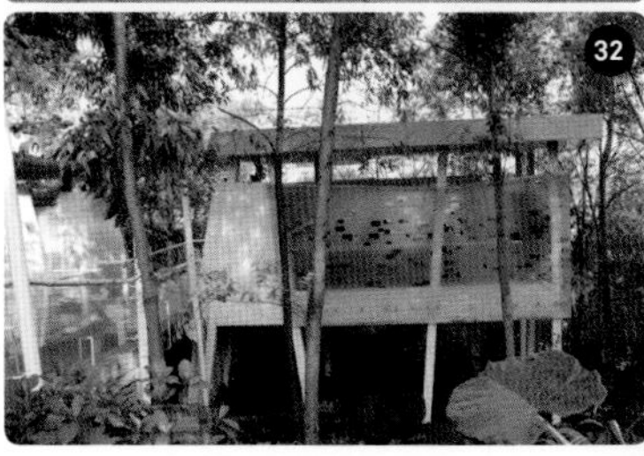

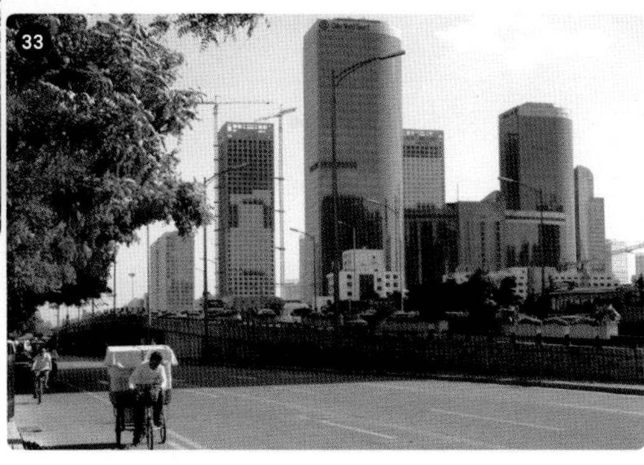

the new suburbs rivalled each other in the sad proportions of their showy façades.
The buildings, broad and massive, are endowed with monumental stairways,
grandiose colonnades, caryatids and atlantes, and when one wishes to signal,
as a reality or a nod, that one remembers tradition, to the structure are added
imitation *feng shui* partitions or vast courtyards which are hard put to recall the
order of the square courtyards.
Since the 1990s, all big cities have loved to generate the first embryos of the
skyscraper and a smoked glass which is fairly close to what one sees in the worst
of American or Western décor. It may be added to the picture that, in the interior
of the buildings, the decoration rules obey quite wisely the flow of the stocks of
the produced materials, whether it is a case of partitions, ceilings, doors, lighting
fixtures... and of course the sanitary blocks.
The method does not differ completely from what one finds in the standard
production of all the poor countries, in this case in a still poor country.
What strikes one the most, however, is the development of paradoxical methods
in project design. The institutes, already well-stocked with standard models
which are rather similar to the patterns used in sewing, stock themselves
now, depending on the arrivals of the book dealers but also on interuniversity
exchanges, with works which deliver, on an equal footing, practically all of the
Western (American, European, Australian) or Japanese products. Elements
of these models are taken up, transformed and adapted, without considering
too closely the changes in function and without the least concern for the
original scales. The customer who has become the king, a demanding but
not very qualified client, places these easily available images in competition.
It is the architects' task to propose to him assemblies and combinations,
even contradictory ones, in order to avoid the risk of losing the contract at the
project institute and the personalised bonuses or advances, henceforth tied
to the number of projects carried out.
On the occasion of a colloquium in Shanghai in 2004, two groups of young Chinese
architects were formed: those of one group had gone to carry out their studies or
part of their studies at foreign schools or had simply gone to see what was being
done elsewhere, just as we once sent our architects to Rome, Athens or Cairo.
Within this group, each person presented his work. It was clear that, beyond
the plastic or cultural qualities of each client, the mastery of scales, from the
largest dimension to the treatment of details, was admitted as a skill and a
necessity of the profession. In the second group, the professionals (who were
generally younger), had not all had the occasion to travel. They were brasher,
often compensating their intellectual withdrawal by a somewhat unpleasant
but touching nationalism, which placed the achievement of the institutes, large
or small, on the pinnacle of Chinese architectural glory. The presented projects,
without exception, stood apart from all urban or social reflection, or else they
were purely formalist and, as one thing leads to another, perfectly out of scale,
with their corridors resembling the halls of palaces and their roofs being
placed with as little concern as in a children's construction toy.

The heritage, victim of laisser-faire
Laisser-faire puts in place tools of destruction of the heritage. The last decade
of the 20th century would be marked by the complete disappearance of numerous
historic cities, such as Zhengzhou and Taiyuan, or the still partial disappearance
of others, such as Lhassa, Xi'an, Nanking…
1998, however, marked the holding of the first colloquium on historic cities
organised by Unesco-World Heritage Centre, with the Chinese Ministry of
Construction and the city of Suzhou. The colloquium was conceived for the mayors
of Chinese cities, giving them the opportunity to meet their counterparts of the
European Union. This would represent for some personalities and some mayors
a more or less intense sensitisation with respect to the issue of the preservation
of ancient cities, strengthened by the conviction of Chinese academics, who were
finally requested for these international festivities. In Suzhou itself, while the
colloquium was unfolding, the bulldozers continued to open large gashes in the
wise fabric of the channels and shady streets of the Chinese Venice. Unesco's
world heritage division would raise a challenge which was already lost essentially
in Suzhou, a city which found itself "punished": only four celebrated gardens of
the city would be included on Unesco's list, while the city as a whole could have
been catalogued just as legitimately as Lijiang (Yunnan) or Pingyao (Shanxi),
classified the previous year.
In fact, it was after an astonishing acceleration movement, right at the end of the
1990s and in the opening years of the new-born 21st century that the bulldozers
and the machines of destruction really began to work at full steam. On the
mechanisms of this destruction, we will refer here to the book accompanying
the exhibition "In the Chinese City. Perspectives on the transmutations of an
Empire", presented from June to September 2008 at the Cité de l'architecture & du
patrimoine.
It should be noted here, however, that these destructive forces, which would have
annihilated the essence of Beijing and many other towns, have only too late been
subject to an urban reflection which was already being made by some academics
and professors, and to the rebirth of architectural history. For this reason the
architects, whatever their talent or potential, work in levitation. The low level
of fees and the shortness of the design and construction lead-times make it an
acrobatic exercise to abandon mass construction and depart from the institutes'
production methods. The demand for new construction, considering all fields
as a whole (housing, education, offices, factories, shops, leisure…) became
all the more pressing with the arrival of the 21st century and the construction
professions found there an enviable position. The mechanisms of corruption
or appropriation which were the mark of numerous works in the 1980s, express
themselves in a different context in which the rules, the urban management
services and all the new owners' associations proved increasingly efficient.
At the end of the 20th century it was clear that the urban heritage in a city such as
Beijing was seriously threatened in different way than that of Shanghai. It could
also be seen that the ancient fabric of the *hutong*, inside the layout inherited

from the Mongol imperial edict and its method of subdivision of plots, which they shelter from ancient residences of prestige or from modest houses, was not the object of a dynamic reflection. Precise measurements were made, on the other hand, allowing the publication in 2002 of the detailed illustrated catalogue of twenty-five historic areas of the old Beijing intended to be an object of regulatory protection. This catalogue of almost four hundred pages in length, available in the majority of the large bookstores, is obsolete today. The proposed projects have not drawn sufficient attention, although it is also true that the precise maps of the quarters of the city and the municipality did not provide any further pertinent information with respect to the urban evolution and future. Consequently, it is only the personal knowledge of architects or the work undertaken by teams such as that of the Observatory of the Architecture of Contemporary China which permit, on foot or by taxi, the exploration of the significant traces of the cities' evolution. In Shanghai, the commercial energy as well as the strong personalities of academics and practitioners such as Zhou Jian ❼, who was initially more involved in urban actions but is perfectly aware of the issues linked to architectural quality and to the perennity of the heritage, join up with the long-term work of Professor Ruan Yisan ❻ or of his brother Ruan Yongsan ㉖ in Suzhou. A large part of the territories resulting from the old international and French concessions were thus declared "protected sectors" in 2004, thanks to the combined actions of the Office for Urban Action and of the professors; these are the people who were in charge of the analysis of the urban landscape and of construction in order to propose the rules of control applicable to the future building permits. It was almost too late for the fragments of the old so-called Chinese town, which had resisted the incendiary attacks of the Taiping or their affiliates in the middle of the 19th century; all around these ancient streets and canals filled in with the first steps of modernisation, rich courtyard houses and strata of more popular dwellings have been devastated by the shopping centres which encircle Yuyuan and the Huxinting ㉗ tea house neighbouring this beautiful garden, with the commercial enthusiasm of the 1990s. The bulldozers abandoned themselves to veritable ravages in a fabric which was composite and therefore all the more fragile, where street markets alternated with all sorts of stalls surmounted by transverse dwellings and little courtyards hidden from view to the passers-by. Beijing, for its part, appears more hesitant. Is it still possible to believe in the validity of the twenty-five quarters promised for preservation? Many boroughs are already undergoing the fast violent experience of the bulldozer, beginning with the best-built ones, which leads to a some what greater devaluation of the quarters which by tradition have been a good deal less divided into plots. Two operations have called attention: the Ju'er *hutong* ㉘ is by far the most subtle. The operation was carried out in two phases from 1989 to 1992 by the architect Wu Liangyong (who was a student of Liang Sicheng). It consisted of conceiving, on a sector of eight hectares, the improvement of the living conditions of some forty families who amply doubled their living area, swapping their 25 square metres for one or two rooms of 60 square metres, in the Shishahai quarter. To do this, the architect declines, on three to four levels as a maximum, the renovated principle of traditional lanes and tree-planted courtyards which are interconnected and, at least until recently, allowed the free passage of the population. Nevertheless, Wu Liangyong's project was short-lived, since the commercialisation of the housing which then developed in all the big cities, propelling the land and real-estate values to the top of the list of concerns, reduced to nothing the generous ambition of proposing a comfortable dwelling in an ancient fabric to modest populations. For that matter, these are the first people to profit from their stylish apartments, renting them out to cheerful expatriates or entertainers. The success of the Ju'er *hutong* has never been denied, however, since it proved that the densification and modernisation of the traditional city were possible, as was the serious preservation (without pastiche) of the old quarters.

The second, more recent, operation is more mysterious. It was situated a little farther to the south at Beiheyan Avenue. This was a purely promotional and fairly luxurious operation, carried out in the opening years of the 21st century. It imitated rather than interpreted the tradition of lanes for a highly favoured clientele. Behind the façades of a tempered modernism, the Yujing Garden, financed by a Hong Kong group, promised dwellings of high standing, which seem not to have had any takers yet.

To finish up with this dilly-dallying on the thwarted virtues of the city's old fabric, it would be well to mention the Liulichang quarter, where most of the antiquarians of the Chinese city were gathered. The façades on the street were renewed at the end of the 1980s and then again every ten years, according to the rules of a poor pastiche, the golds and reds of which continue to rejoice the eyes of tourists who are naturally little informed, with the new porticoes of badly painted concrete hardly distinguishing themselves from the old *pailou* of Beijing's crossroads.

This manner of building, or rebuilding, a Chinese urban landscape is known in China under the name of *fengmao*. It passes for the rule although it is an exotic phenomenon which is hardly assured of the support of local history (the latter considerably mistreated by the official history) and, much less, of the decoding of the technical know-hows or of the regional cultures, condemned among the four pieces of bric-a-brac denounced in less prosperous periods. Above all, it lets the Westerners who doubtless inspired this strategy to act as if the Chinese people did not have any interest in their heritage and in the quality of the craftsmen and artists who strove to create it.

Lastly, this phenomenon induces a false or true question as to what may be derived from idiosyncrasies peculiar to the Middle Kingdom in contemporary architecture. Why is this question posed more in China than in the West?

Each architect has his own answer today, but the unprecedented intensity of the destruction of the big cities, which increased in the course of the 1990s, can in itself prompt such a query. This is a question containing both anguish and vertigo: should really nothing remain of China's physical past to witness its history?

The will of modernisation inherited in a perhaps legitimate, perhaps dramatic way from the Western models threatens in any case to drown China in a sea of towers, punctuated here and there by pastiche quarters devoted to tourism. Very few cities and quarters have resisted up to now, aside from Shanghai, but it is also in the universities of Shanghai and, in a less desperate manner, in those of Beijing that one sees the birth of a fragile renovation and of new practices aimed to preserve the heritage dimensions of the cities.

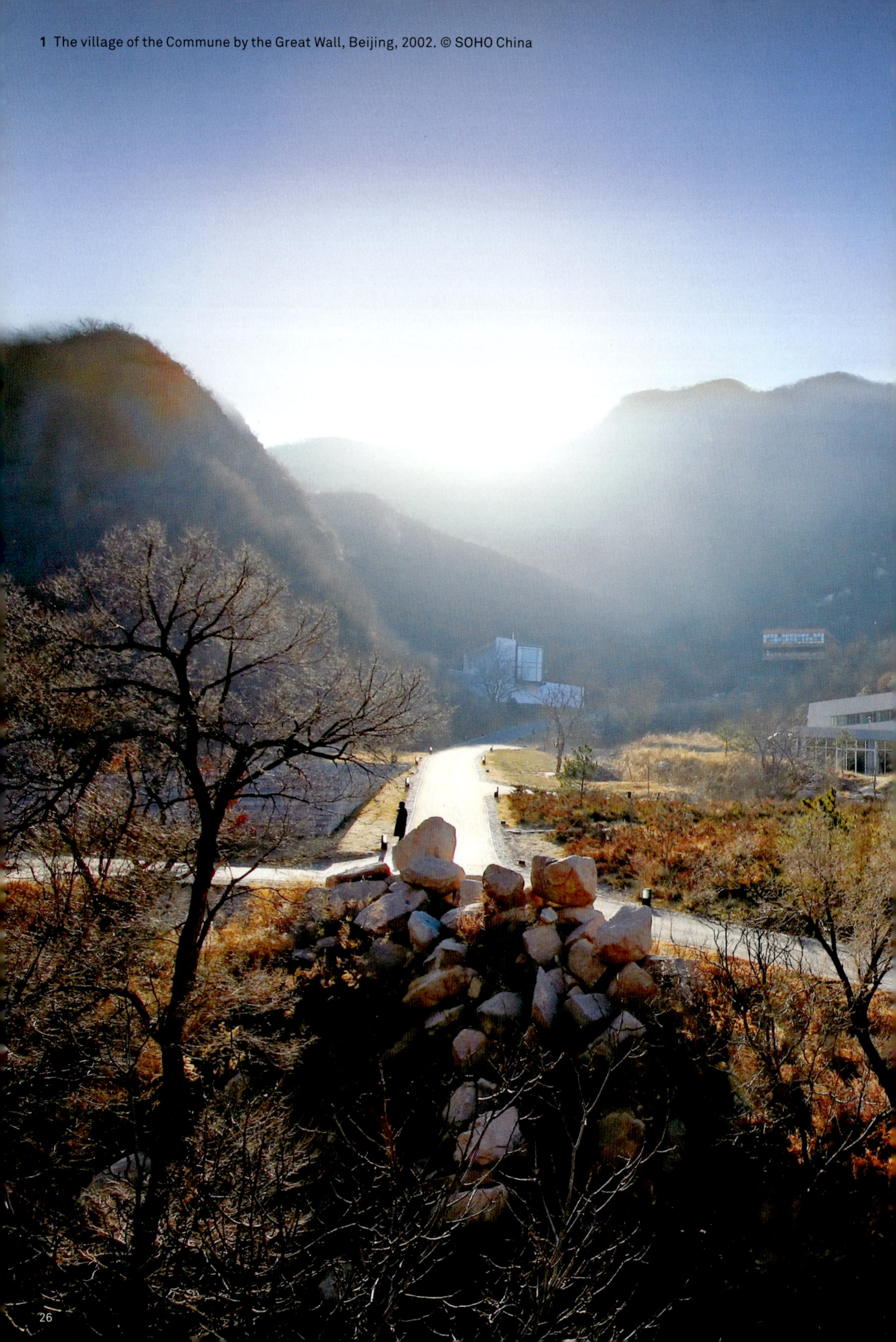

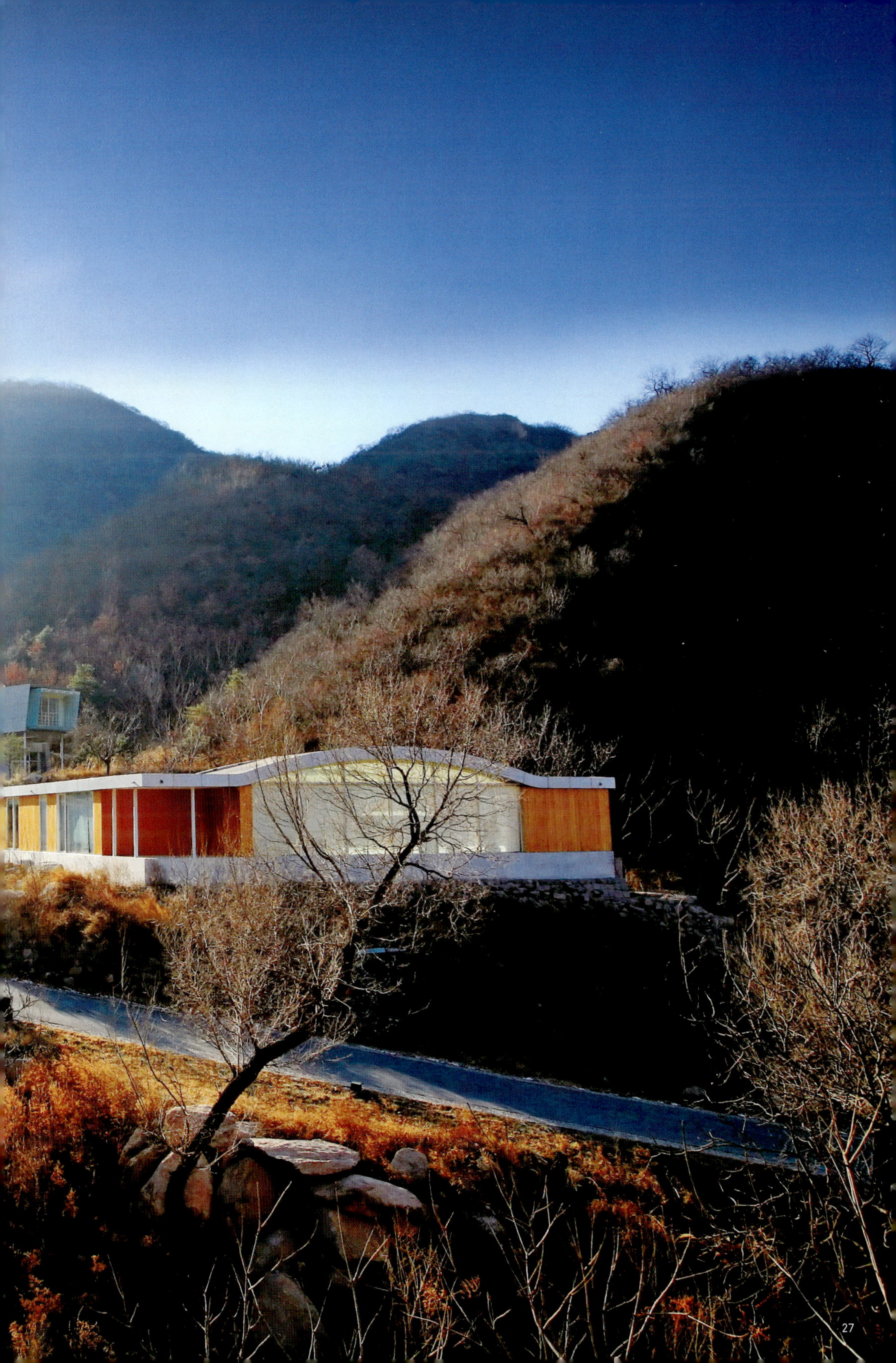

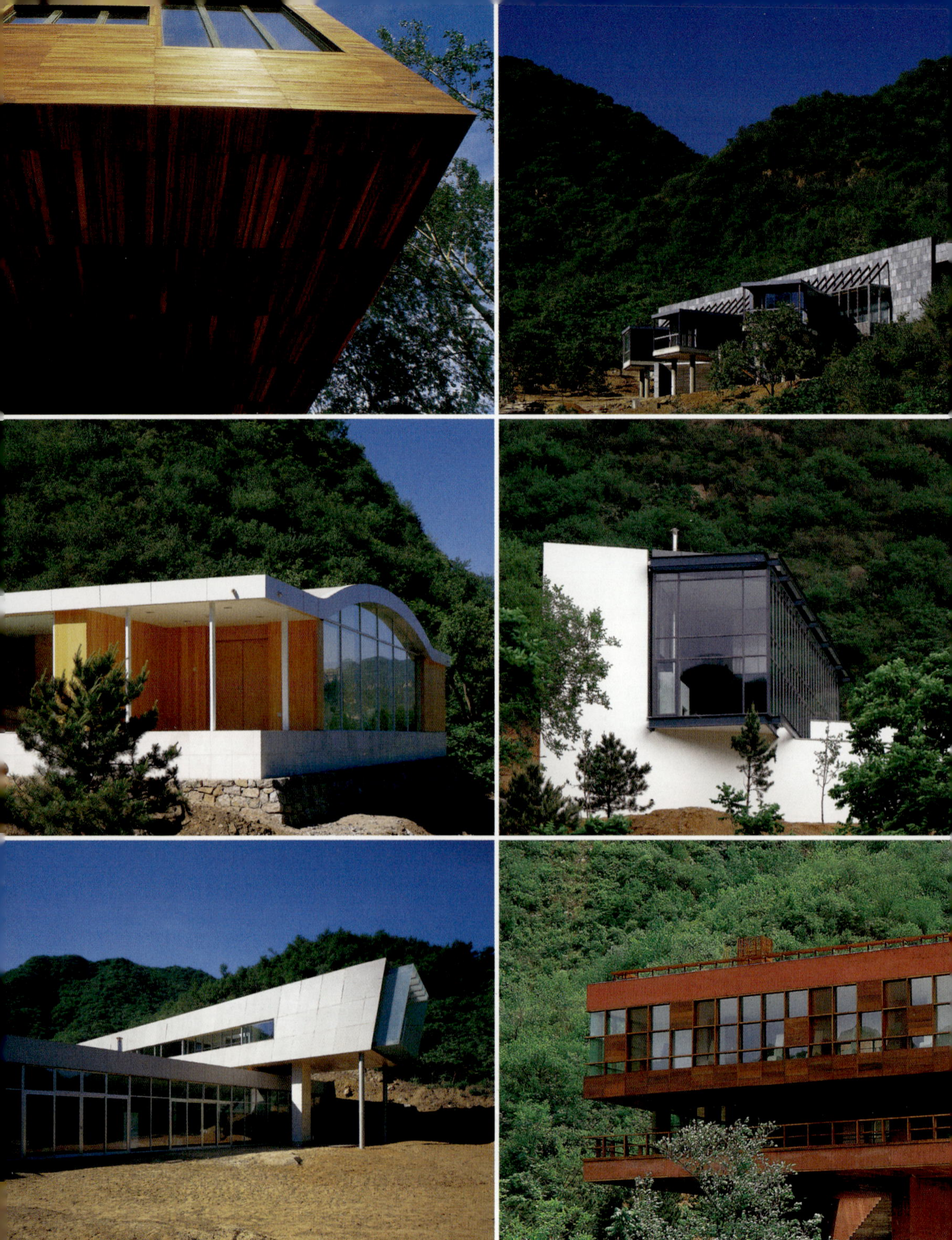

1 **The village of the Commune by the Great Wall, Beijing, 2002.** © SOHO China

Suitcase House, Gary Chang (*Hong Kong*)
Furniture House, Shigeru Ban (*Japan*)
"See" and "Seen" House, Cui Kai (*China*)

"Airport", Chien Hsueh Yi (*Taiwan*)
Distorted Courtyard House, Rocco Yim (*Hong Kong*)
Cantilever House, Antonio Ochoa (*China*)

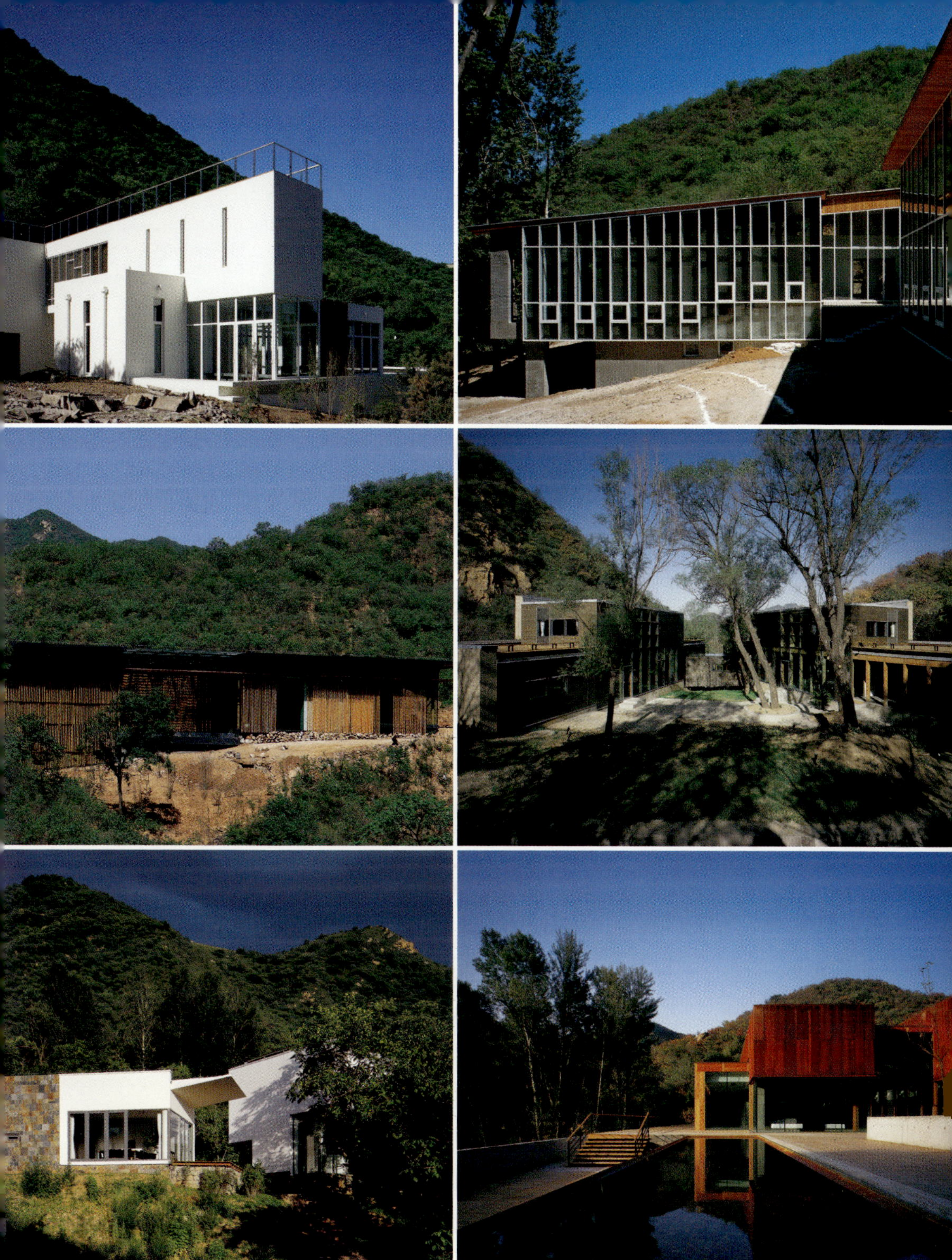

The Shared House, Kanika R'kul (*Thailand*)
Bamboo Wall, Kengo Kuma (*Japan*)
The Twins, Kay Ngee Tan (*Singapore*)

Forest House, Nobuaki Furuya (*Japan*)
Split House, Chang Yung Ho (*China*)
Clubhouse, Seung H-Sang (*South Korea*)

The re-invention of the profession
The series of fifteen portraits which forms this work would have to be
substantially increased if one were to consider all the efforts undertaken
across China to bring about the rebirth of a quality architecture, with or without
taking heritage issues into account. These are often singular personalities
who have prevented the extinction of the flame of this culture in the course
of the 20th century.
After Liang Sicheng, the baton of the heritage and urban planning was taken up
by figures of a different nature, such as professor Wu Liangyong in Beijing, public
officials of the Ministry of Construction such as professor Wang Jinghui [5] and,
for contemporary architecture, by Cui Kai [8] , now aged 51 years. Cui Kai is one
of the most mysterious and endearing personalities on the current architectural
scene: a professor, organiser, architect and project manager, he acts like a
generous orchestra conductor, like the protector of a generation of which he has
been one of the foremost representatives. Indeed, in the course of the 1990s
there were several persons who asked themselves what the meaning of their
profession should be. Cui Kai was one of the first to visit to his construction sites
in person, to follow the details of the work and the concerns which his younger
colleagues come across. Of the professional complicity shared with the founders
of the first private architecture studios, there has remained a common tie and
passion bringing together project managers isolated by their demanding spirit,
which endures as a result of the quantitative disproportion between their limited
production and the fulgurant explosion of the cities throughout the country.
We have seen the field of ruins without quality where the architect's profession
was to be reconstituted. We have seen how they have had to accommodate the
disappearance of a heritage on which they had no voice, at least until recent
times. We have seen how the schools of architecture disappeared in the tempest
of the Cultural Revolution and how difficult it was for this profession to learn
again to accommodate a reality devoid of ideal. In short, we have seen how trips or
studies abroad have progressively allowed this generation to measure better the
validity of its work, to find the points of comparison necessary for the exercise of
any profession.
The intellectual machine is almost back in motion. Two categories are
reconstituted. One, in an embryonic way, corresponds to project management
as it is practised for the better in all the countries in the world. It is there above
all where the artistic dimension of the profession is found, it is there where the
good students who appear in the journals and who win the most prestigious prizes
are recruited. The other category, in the image of what is happening elsewhere
in the world, responds more docilely to the orders of clients who have but partly
awakened from the long Chinese sleep. It is they who will provide the essential
aspect of the construction of dwellings or offices, shopping centres, urban
infrastructures, etc.
In the beginning, one and the other continue to follow the same rules, the
same sharing of work inherited from the project or construction institutes,
organised during the Communist period. The architect produces a design,
which is immediately withdrawn from him and entrusted to hundreds of pencil-

pushers and engineers of the institute, where it is crumbled down and naturally loses its form and originality. The passage from the project institutes to the construction institutes and then on to the State enterprises will long assure the repetitive mediocrity of the works carried out.

For this reason, it is the institutes tied to the schools of architecture and of urban planning, schools which are themselves integrated in the country's major universities, which will allow the chaotic but progressive return of a veritable quality. Right at the end of the 1990s and the beginning of the 2000s, there appeared the first significant projects in which one finds the mark of the universities of Tsinghua (Beijing) and Tongji (Shanghai) as well as of Chongqing (Guangzhou). This concern translates into quite little: the use of brick in large structures, the quest for large spans, recourse at times to strange prototypes without known ancestry outside of science fiction. It is a way like any other to move out of the cubical metaphors which continue to be the rule, even if this rule tends to become attenuated in the development areas of the south. In the economic areas under development, especially Shenzhen and soon Shanghai, the major international architecture studios disembarked in the same period. These are the big American or Australian firms followed by the German offices, for which the economic penetration in Chinese territory proves singularly decomplexified with respect to the other Europeans. Notable among them is GMP, which is for Germany the private equivalent of the French Arep, with its more ambiguous status, linked to the SNCF agency. Before the latter, there arrived above all Aéroports de Paris, where Paul Andreu was still the head architect. The point in common of all these studios, independently of their nationality, is a structure which, in terms of the number and diversity of the assembled professions, is fairly close to those of the Chinese institutes. The local clients may have the feeling of being on familiar territory. Moreover, the tradition of bribes and corruption, inherent to the reconstruction of the means of production in China, is naturally maintained by these enormous studios where the kickbacks are usually included in the margins. There exists, nevertheless, if one may say so, an air of heroics in these foreigners who come to try their luck in China. While remunerations range from 7 to 12% of the price of the works depending on countries, in China they hardly reach 3 to 4%. A justified compensation: once their project has been delivered, the architects no longer have to follow it. It is even sometimes expressly requested that they should not set foot on the building sites. An unfortunate compensation: this is also the way in which the projects are betrayed and the architect's responsibility becomes diluted at the same time as the quality expected from their attentive surveillance.

A handful of architects resumes its work with style
Faced with a wave which is at once ridable, encouraging and doubtless somewhat disquieting, the new generations of architects have been under formation, the latest one qualified as the "fifth generation", which means nothing in professional terms but has the advantage of identifying it with its counterparts of the same age in the field of cinema. Cui Kai, Qi Xin ❾ and Chang Yung Ho ❿ were the first to leap into the adventure, with Cui Kai embodying a form of Beijing stability,

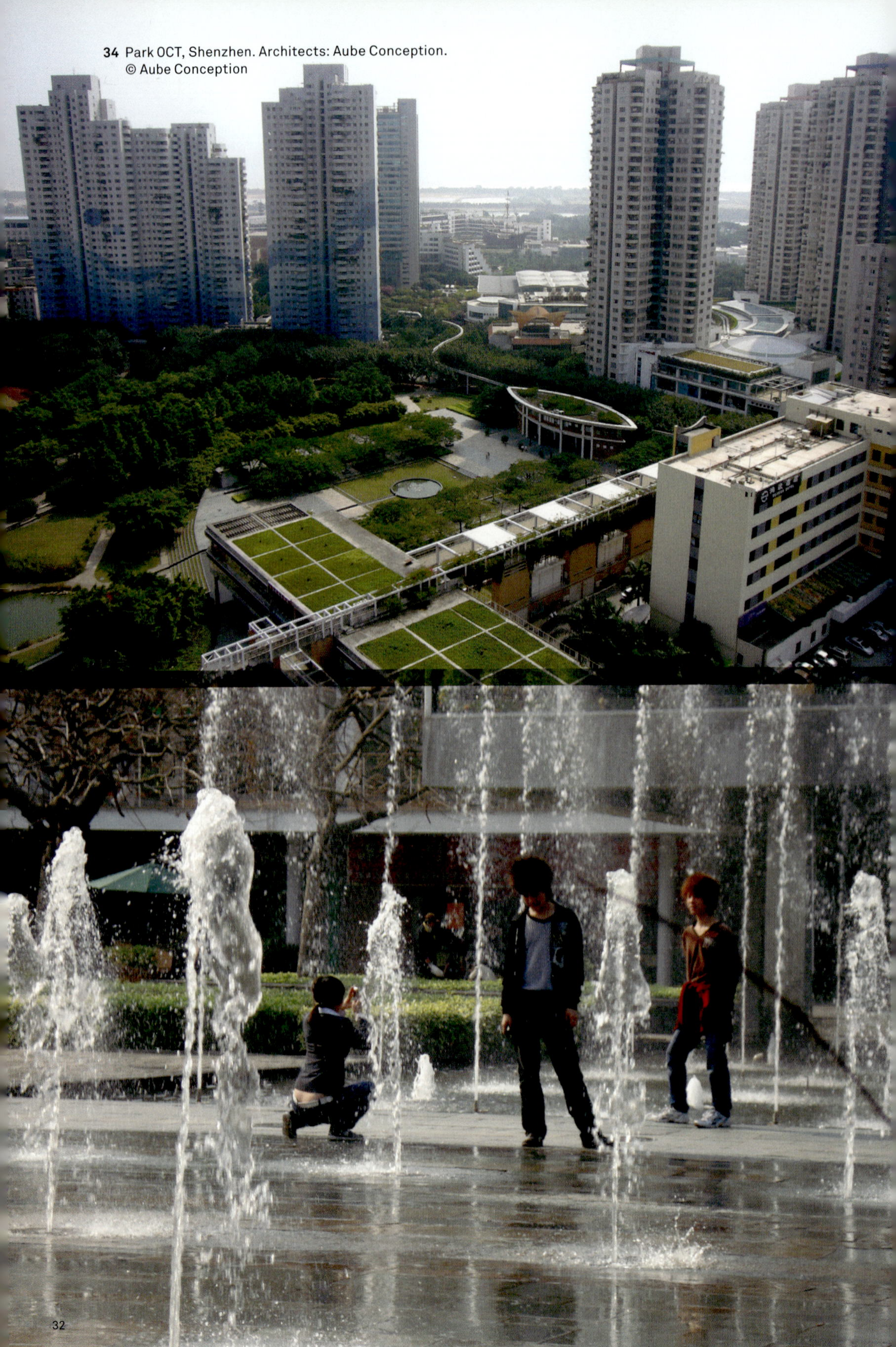

34 Park OCT, Shenzhen. Architects: Aube Conception.
© Aube Conception

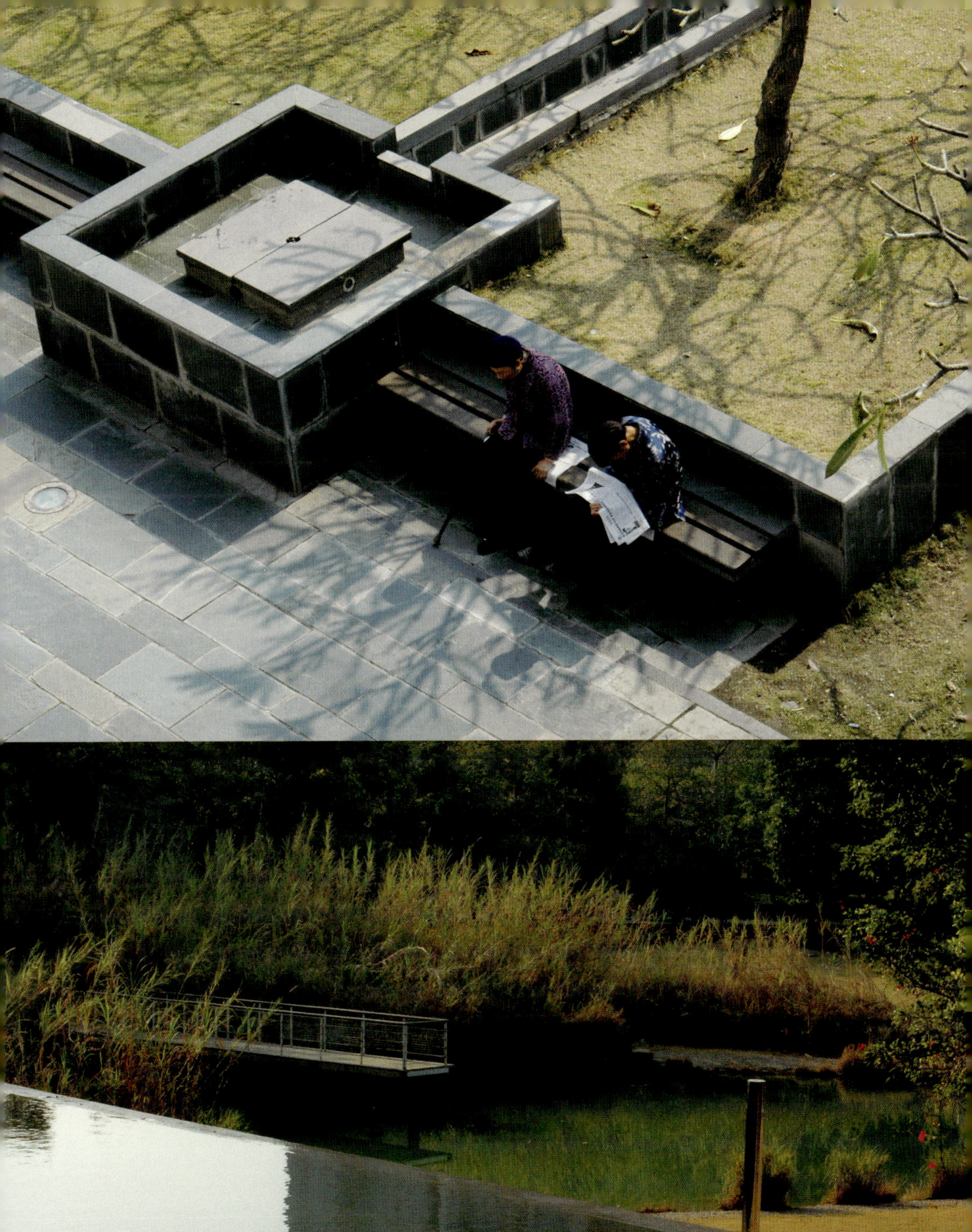

Chang importing the ideal of the American theorising and practising architect, and Qi Xin offering the discreet virtues of the little French-style structures.
In this generation which was formed in the course of the 1980s, there are also some figures such as Diana Chan Chieng **⑪**, who would contribute notably to the exchanges between China and the rest of the world, including first of all France, where she carried out part of her studies with Qi Xin and the language and culture of which she masters. It was around these precursors that the very first private architecture studios of the 1990s were organised, each one adopting different methods of operation according to the countries, most often America, where the architects had completed their studies. The structural disparities were accompanied by marked financial disparities and an extremely varied approach to the profession, and each of the studios could moreover lend its style to the theoretically most contradictory trends.
What are these trends and what are their ingredients? The first one consists of accepting as unavoidable the evaporation of the old fabric, of adopting the Western models such as towers, and of attempting to introduce into them some elements of traditional structures which lent rhythm to the life of the families and the family clans. In this respect, the first set of towers built by Cui Kai for the Soho group **㉙**, near Jianguomen Avenue in Beijing, appears to mark a turning point. These are towers (480,000 square metres) within the imposed maximum height of 100 metres, but in their interior he conceived large courtyards at each four levels, like superimposed spaces where the tradition of the *siheyuan* (courtyard houses) could be reconstituted. The tower ensemble, of which the commercialisation began in 1998, was completed in 2001 and has undergone several mutations since contemporary structures have some difficulty in replicating the gentleness and silence of the open-air courtyards.
In the same period, Qi Xin for his part conceived a training institute for officials **㉚** of the Ministry of Finance in the north-east of Beijing. For this competition he preferred the sobriety of a model to a profusion of 3D images, a sufficiently rare choice for it to be mentioned, with a client presided over by Prime Minister Zhu Rongji. On this little campus, he brought together a contemporary vocabulary, which was at that time rather poorly mastered by the Chinese construction companies, and a series of small dwellings arranged symmetrically around a vast space, forming a delicate transposition between the monumentality attached to the client's prestige and the everyday nature of the building's uses.
Cui Kai's tower ensemble was the fruit of an order from the Soho group, a real estate promotion enterprise dominated by two figures: Pan Shiyi and Zhang Xin. From the end of the 1990s, these two promoters undertook an unprecedented project which would bear the name of Commune by the Great Wall **❶**. The site is located, in effect, near the tourist inferno into which the Badaling portion of the Great Wall has become converted. Consequently, it benefits from motorway infrastructures, which were still rare at that time. The promoters have called on twelve architects of Asian origin or living in Asia, including three Chinese professionals: Cui Kai, Yung Ho Chang , and Chien Hsueh-Yi from Taiwan.
Likewise, arriving in China for the first time were such figures as Kengo Kuma and Shigeru Ban, from Japan; Rocco Yim and Gary Chang, from Hong Kong, and Kanika R'kul from Thailand.

The model of such a collection of architecture (the goal of which is firstly to expose and hence highlight the dynamism of the real-estate group, and secondly to speculate since the unlimited reproduction of these luxury villas is already envisaged) takes on an undeniable added value thanks precisely to the quality of the projects. The process, associating several notable architects in a project of large territorial scale, would be repeated in a somewhat different form in several cities of China. One finds it in the urban mode at Qingpu, one of the districts of the municipality of Shanghai, where the personality of Sun Jiwei, its deputy mayor and an urban planner by profession, played a decisive role. The model is also found in the unfinished museum cluster of Anren (near Chengdu) where, at the request of the collector and promoter Fan Jianchuan, the architects Chang Yung Ho and Liu Jiakun, surrounded by several other "new wave" professionals, have conceived an exceptional ensemble devoted to the Cultural Revolution and the war against Japan. For the time being it remains to be completed.

The journal *Time + Architecture,* published by Tongji University, would run in 2006 several articles by its editor-in-chief Zhi Wenjun, and by Cai Yu, who explain how the network of this generation (with ages ranging from 35 years to a little over 50 years) is organised. On 14 December 2003, several of these people met at a Beijing gallery, not far from the Ministry of Construction, to exhibit their work and above all to exchange their views. Cui Kai was not present on that occasion but Qi Xin was there in his role as a discreet rallier, as well as Liu Yichun of the Deshaus group with his look of a young dreamer (although he is one of the keenest observers of his generation), Chang Yung Ho and Zhu Pei. These are the same people, and some thirty others, whom one finds at work throughout the country in configurations which are always different but marked by a complicity which struggles to be put to use.

Zhu Pei did not separate from his partners of Urbanus (Wang Hui, Meng Yan, Liu Xiaodu), while others such as the foursome of Standardarchitecture had not yet shown up. Was Ma Qingyun there or was he busy organising the links of this "quality circle" Chinese-style with his American or European counterparts? No one expected to see the sombre Liu Jiakun or the poet Wang Shu... they are always on some other planet and if they ever wish to make an appearance they usually arrive alone before everyone else.

The fifteen names which we have gathered in this volume do not belong in reality to this network which is, moreover, an informal one. They are the most representative or the most flamboyant. Nevertheless, for one reason or another, their paths do cross. For example it would be Ai Weiwei, the venerable sage of the Group of the Stars, who would advise Herzog & de Meuron to call on Cui Kai for the construction of the Grand Stadium. Liu Yichun, for his part, makes known systematically the work of his colleagues while he guides one about Shanghai. It was he who acquainted us with the Scenic Architecture studio of Zhu Xiaofeng and with an ensemble at Qingpu called the Qin Song Waiyuan Garden ㉛, with its façades of wooden slats which have since appeared in all the European publications and exhibitions.

Mention should also be made of professors or urban designers such as Zou Huan (Beijing), two female professionals as differently resolute as Zhang Kai ⑫ and Shao Yong ⑬, or the almost more French than Chinese architect Feng Yueqiang (of the Aube studio, based in Shenzhen and Paris), whose eclectic career comes close to the universalism of Cui Kai. He is associated at the time of this writing with Frédéric Edme, one of the authors of the OCT Park in Shenzhen ㉞, which is a remarkable landscape ensemble to which each passing year lends a greater spatial and, naturally, vegetal quality.

One point in common of this whole generation is the almost obliged passage through what one may call micro-architecture, a term which refers to the size of the buildings, such as the toilets at Lianhuashan Park ㉜ in the same city of Shenzhen, or the Mima Café, on the edge of the Yuanmingyuan in Beijing, by Wang Hui, a homonym in pinyin of one of the leading partners at Urbanus. However, it may also involve provisional buildings as have been produced by the hundreds amid the transformations of Beijing, serving as sales offices for the large programmes of dwellings or offices. The fact is that the work of our "quality circle" cannot be compared to the immensity of the urban phenomenon throughout contemporary China. In the institutes, it is not rare for an architect to be led to "produce" the equivalent of one million square metres per year, which quite obviously means that he neither follows the details of his projects nor visits the work sites. Likewise, programmes reaching close to one million square metres are not rare in the big metropolises, such as Beijing, Shanghai, Shenzhen, Guangzhou and Chongqing.

Some certainties in an ocean of disquiet
In this universe in which the towers and immense residential areas designed from scratch have become the rule, the qualitative improvement under way in recent years is not a negligible phenomenon. The fantastical futuristic image of Shenzhen conveyed by the students of Rem Koolhaas who were sent on a sacrificial mission to the Pearl River delta, remains in part a reality, but it is confronted by new ensembles which are singularly better designed, with details of manufacture and operation which no longer have anything to envy their far-off cousins in America.

It is true that throughout China, the problem of energy resources, of the distribution of electricity and that of water and its evacuation have become major concerns which are little in keeping with the harmonious development of these strictly supervised cities. The temporary cut-offs and restrictions of water, however, while they are particularly acute in Chine, stem now from a world phenomenon: never a day goes by without the national or local authorities recalling, even if it is only to keep up appearances or for propaganda purposes, the urgency of reconsidering development on a sustainable basis.

This was not the situation of the towers erected at the beginning of the 1990s and 2000s. There was probably quite a gap between, on the one hand, the available techniques and materials, and on the other, the level of engineering required for the smooth running of buildings with futuristic images, or in the eyes of the Chinese of those times, concrete forests of the megapolises of the future that showed little concern for more prosaic realities.

Independently of financial bubbles, a large number of skyscrapers have remained vacant in Shanghai, although doubtless in smaller numbers in Beijing, because they had become unsuitable for sale as the carcassing was completed. Others have been sold and are occupied, but with difficulties of use for the inhabitants, including absurd deserts of lifts and circuits of drinking water and waste water which have led to some quite strange surprises. The problems are so numerous and so severe that working groups have been formed in the construction institutes to study the transformation or reconversion of these big skeletons with ill-finished bodies.

The best of the very large works, especially those of the Beijing Summer Olympics but also in Shanghai, Guangzhou and Chongqing, have more often than not been tendered to foreign architecture studios (in practice, it is a question of calls for tenders of the big public construction companies, even if some portions are possibly taken on by foreign firms). While one may be surprised by the brutal character of the urban development and by the disappearance of the heritage, a phenomenon which affects each and every one of the cities to a very high degree, other considerations, fortunately enough, must also be made.

In Shanghai several of the towers, such as the Jinmao or its new neighbour, the World Financial Tower (commissioned to the American studio KPF by the Japanese firm Mori), and several others in Pudong and in Puxi (the new and the old banks of the Huangpu), have nothing to envy their American or Australian models, and one would be happy if, on the same scale, such architectural feats were to appear in the catalogues of buildings of France or even Europe at large, where this type of constructions generally continues to be conceived as an isolated mark and not a structuring element of cities.

This means that if the client, essentially Asian (Hong Kong, Taiwan, Singapore and Japan, which are at least just as present as the promoters from the People's Republic of China) proves audacious and generous in its choices, the majority of the decision-makers of the big cities remain all the more fascinated by gigantism, that is, by structures out of scale, a fairly typical phenomenon in countries where the culture has been long and deeply altered.

Accordingly, in contrast to the micro-architectures in which the country's young talents seek to express themselves, the mega-structures tend to crush the landscape. The search for a balance between the quantity of materials used and the profile of the building not being an objective, what is then represented by this battalion which we have gathered under the term of "new architecture" or "quality circle"? If one considers the Qingpu district or such cities as Ningbo and to a lesser extent Hangzhou, it is clear that, as elsewhere, only the political will paired with a cultured lucidity is capable of making medium-sized urban ensembles evolve towards a very high level of quality. Most of the big cities seem to have lost the match. The awareness of this has unfortunately arisen too late in Beijing, despite some superb achievements linked to the Olympic Games or to the birth of the Central Business District ㉝. The essence of the city takes its pace from the multiplication of the motorways and ring roads, with all the disquiet which this may induce, beyond the question of urban forms in a world marked by pollution and the decrease of resources.

Guangzhou and Shenzhen are fortunate to lie near the delta, where by the landscape compensates the uncertainties which still revolve around the

megalopolis[2] which, beyond these two cities, includes Dongguan, Zhuhai and
even Hong Kong. Chongqing benefits from its extraordinary relief and, while the
bombardments and destructions of the promoters have not been a gift for it,
and while the air and water pollution remains a short-term menace, one may still
imagine a spectacular metropolis in a more distant future.
Lastly, it is only in Shanghai that the heritage issues have been able to be taken
into consideration on time, even if they only comprise very little what one calls the
Chinese city, within the perimeter of the old walls from the 16th century, involving
much more the area of the old concessions. The site of this town and its anchorage
in history tend to attribute it the role of a beacon city, which Beijing has been
able to assume thanks to its rich heritage until the beginning of this millennium.
Most of the other big cities have been severely mutilated, and it appears difficult
from now to fill the trench between the uniformisation of the Chinese cities and
the light provided by this excessively limited "quality circle".
Consequently, through their work and their activity, this handful of architects
and urban planners whom we have found, poses the true questions and allows one
to imagine for the future a denser, more present generation to compensate the
effects of an overly rapid modernisation on such a scale.
A question which crosses most of the works of most of these architects remains
that of a permanence of a specifically "Chinese" dimension, form or culture.
Several of them refuse explicitly to integrate this reference and call for a radical
rupture which would place them in a both timeless and international universe.
This is the case of the youngest professionals, but not necessarily of all, including
those who, like Ma Yansong, have studied under Zaha Hadid and reproduce
in their country the models with which they have filled their spiritual baggage.
Nevertheless, even these people who are the most averse to the Chinese tropism
from the standpoint of the Western critique, may also be those who integrate
themselves most willingly into the contemporary dimensions of China. When Ma
Yansong makes his skyscrapers glide at 400 metres in height, it is within this logic
of the grandeur and arrogance which is demanded by the clients who are the most
"disconnected" from tradition and closest to the contemporary giddiness.
Others make a more nuanced and sometimes more adaptable reflection.
Some object to any tie to any tradition whatsoever. Would this also be the case
of the Deshaus practitioners who, building in a Chinese context and adapting
their constructions to it, affirm that they can charge themselves with the air of
the times and with the spirit of the places? One sees clearly, however, in the work
of such a figure as Ma Qingyun, how much the urban reflection, as it arises from
the Chinese practices, can influence the work of this new generation. The density,
the omnipresence of commercial functions, the capacity of life to infiltrate each
fragment of space up to the moment when the walls of rites or of money come to
be raised... all this forms part of the materials which these architects use when
they come to make a fragment of city. The Chinese order and the Western order
in this respect appear to obey almost opposite schemas, even if the result may
engender apparent similarities.

2 This term designates a conurbation such as that of the Pearl River delta or Chongqing,
while "megapolis" means a single very large agglomeration with several million inhabitants.

A third group of architects, to which Ma draws closer on occasion, the same as Chang Yung Ho, finds its standard-bearer in the person of Wang Shu, who uses traditional materials or, to be more exact, recovers the materials freed from their structures by the passing of the bulldozers. In a more spiritual mode, he takes up classic structures: that of the central courtyard, that of the great wood roofs, and that, in short, of a dialogue with the landscape. But just as he makes use of the materials according to the innovative directives of his intelligence (roof tiles can become sun-screens), he takes up the spatial traditions of China according to codes compatible with the demands of the most outright modernity. Indeed, what is modernity today if not the taking into consideration of sustainable development, the capacity to master the sunlight and the shade without taking recourse to additional energy?

In all cases, the architects are more resistant to this idea of a link with the history of Chinese architecture, even if they can integrate it in their practice. Is this a final rupture or is it rather a reaction to the terrible hot spells and cold which have been the result of the cruel games of politics with nationalism and with culture? In order truly to understand one day what moves the spirit of this generation, if at least it survives the urban explosion of China, it will be necessary to act as the historians of each family, or of the ties which join them beyond the common experience of the universities, the project institutes and the trips abroad. While many universities and many schools have seen their education halted, or at least greatly restricted, the violence of the 20th century has affected each family and each individual in the same proportions. By sincere conviction, by opportunism or by necessity, numerous fathers of architects or sons of architects have had to join the ranks of the Communist party, which was paradoxically, in certain periods, the only refuge against the cultural devastations of the Red Age, as one now demurely calls the Maoist period in China.

When Lao She wrote *Four Generations under One Roof*, he was putting into perspective fractures which did not cease to grow after his death, in 1966, when the Cultural Revolution was just beginning. An architect will never – for that matter the same as most of the Chinese – express himself on the political dimensions of his existence. Likewise, it is only very exceptionally that one or the other may make a fragmentary statement on the current situation. Indeed, the discourse of the whole profession is limited to a professional rhetoric since, in China as elsewhere, few professions are less free of political and economic ties than that of the architect.

Frédéric Edelmann

CHINA ARCHITECTURE DESIGN & RESEARCH GROUP
1 Desheng Shangcheng office building
2 Yinxu Archaeological Museum

JIAKUN ARCHITECTS
3 Luyeyuan Sculpture Museum
4 Museum of the Red Age (maoist period)
  Fan Jianchuan museum cluster
5 Qingpu Urban Planning and Exhibition Centre

DESHAUS
6 Xiayu nursery school
7 Shanghai Business Association, Qingpu branch office
8 Dongguan Institute of Technology, departments of information
  technology, electronics, and human sciences
9 Clubhouse of the Renhengyunjie residential ensemble

MADA S.P.A.M.
10 Qiao Zi Wan shopping centre
   Shops, offices and a canal-side promenade
11 "Thumb Island", Puyang house at lake Xiayang
12 Jade Valley Hotel Village

MAD STUDIO
13 Lake Hongluo Clubhouse

TM STUDIO
14 Extension of the Pingjiang Kezhan hotel-restaurant
   and the Dong Tea House
15 Suquan Yuan welcome building

URBANUS ARCHITECTURE & DESIGN
16 Shenzhen urban planning office
17 Factory reconversion OCT Loft, Huaqiao Cheng
18 Public Art Plaza
19 Digital Beijing (Urbanus & Zhu Pei)

STUDIO PEI-ZHU
20 Blur Hotel or Mumianhua Hotel
21 Bookstore and office of the Beijing Publishing Group

ATELIER Z+
22 Tongji University, French-Chinese Exchange Centre
23 Tongji University, School of Architecture and Urban Planning,
   Building 3

FAKE DESIGN
24 Development of the banks of river Yiwu

STANDARDARCHITECTURE
25 Yangshuo shopping centre
26 Wuhan French-Chinese Art Centre
27 Backyard bookstore

QI XIN ARCHITECTS AND ENGINEERS
28 Siheyuan, Promenade and shopping area at the Olympic Games site
29 Yuniaoliusu, Liangzhu cultural village

ATELIER ZHANGLEI
30 Poet houses
31 Dongguan Institute of Technology, staff residence
32 Slit House

AMATEUR ARCHITECTURE STUDIO
33 Xiangshan Campus of the Higher School of Fine Arts of China
34 Ningbo Fine Arts Museum
35 Housing towers

ATELIER FEICHANG JIANZHU
36 UFIDA Research and Development Centre
37 Jishou University, educational and research buildings, and Huang Yongyu Museum
38 Villa Shizilin

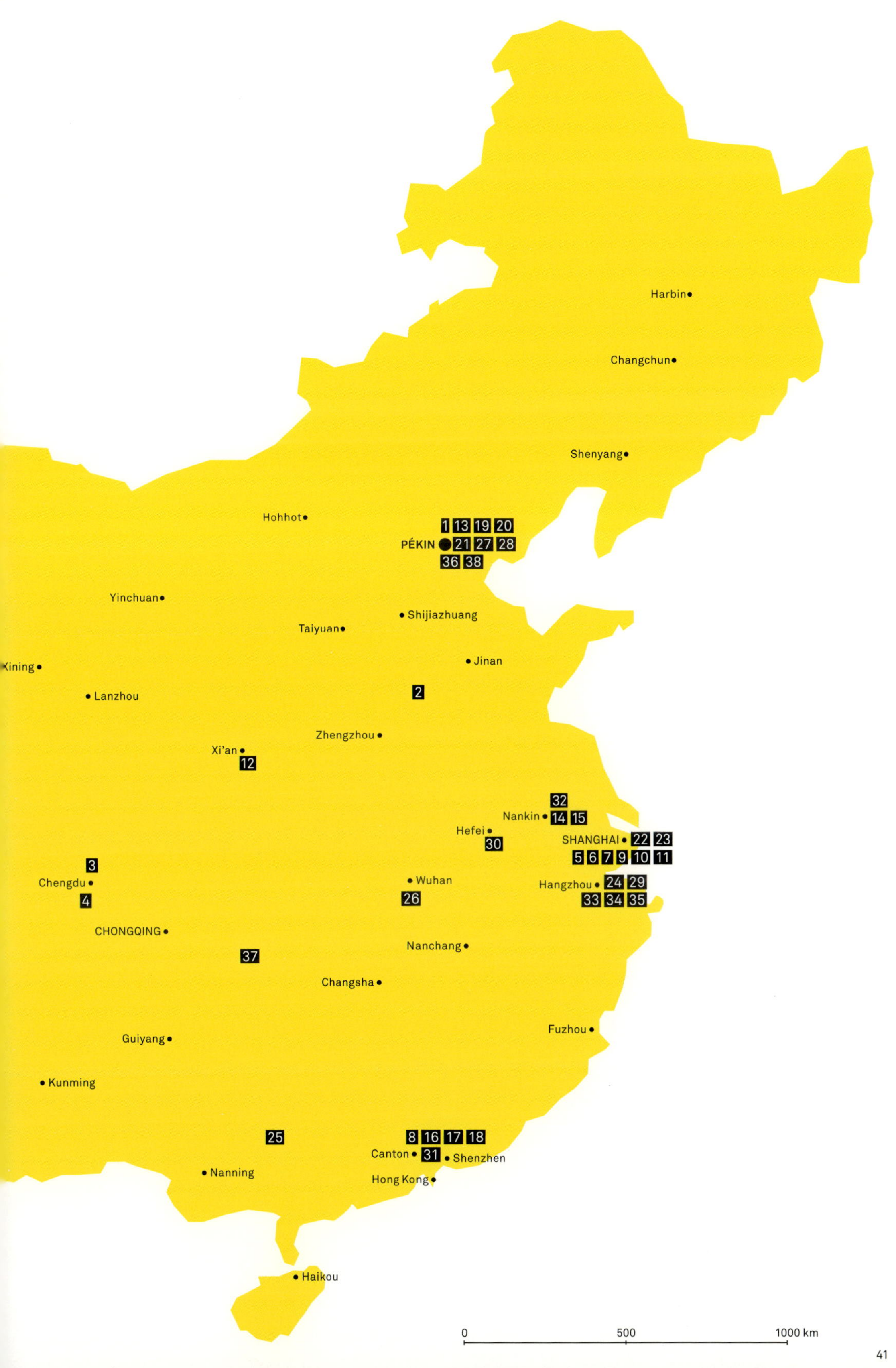

Harbin•
Changchun•
Shenyang•
Hohhot•
1 13 19 20
PÉKIN ● 21 27 28
36 38
Yinchuan•
• Shijiazhuang
Taiyuan•
Xining•
• Lanzhou
• Jinan
2
Zhengzhou•
Xi'an•
12
32
Nankin • 14 15
Hefei •
SHANGHAI • 22 23
30
5 6 7 9 10 11
3
Chengdu •
• Wuhan
Hangzhou • 24 29
4
26
33 34 35
CHONGQING •
37
Nanchang •
Changsha •
Guiyang •
Fuzhou •
• Kunming
25
8 16 17 18
Canton • 31 • Shenzhen
• Nanning
Hong Kong•
• Haikou
0   500   1000 km

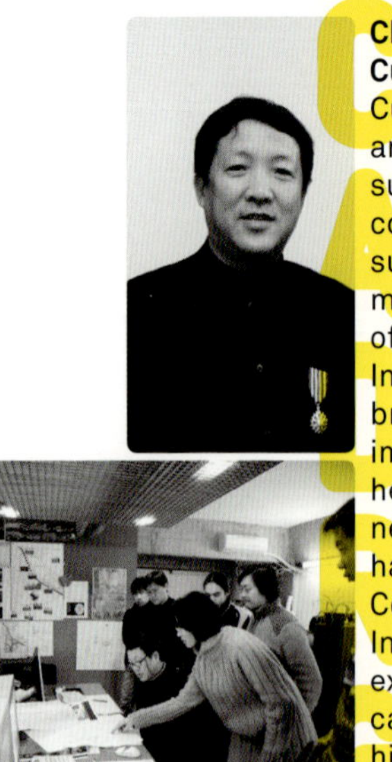

China Architecture Design & Research Group 中国建筑设计研究院
Cui Kai 崔恺

Cui Kai is one of the most likeable figures on the Chinese architectural scene. Neither the best known nor the first to have succeeded in standing out, Cui Kai is always the first to give his colleagues an opportunity and to give projects a hand in reaching success. Born in 1957, he has established himself as a decision-maker and as a team captain whose own talent and achievements often remain in the background.

In Beijing, he was not yet ten years old when the Cultural Revolution broke out and although he never speaks of that period, one may imagine that his was an agitated or perturbed adolescence before he carried out his studies at the University of Tianjin, the great port neighbouring the capital. After that he returned to Beijing, where he has worked at the Design and Research Institute of the Ministry of Construction from 1989 to the present.

In contrast to most of his young colleagues, Cui Kai has never made extended stays abroad but this man of influence is known in his capacity as vice president of the China Architecture Society and as his country's representative in the International Union of Architects (UIA). Proposed as vice minister of Construction, he preferred to continue his work as an architect and indeed he is always among the first at the work sites each morning.

A professor at Tianjin and at Nanking, since the year 2000 he has been the respected head of the China Architecture Design and Research Group (CAG) – the new name of the China Architecture Society – to which Herzog & de Meuron looked for support on establishing themselves in the Middle Kingdom.

As an architect Cui Kai is known above all for the Soho ensemble (four hundred and eighty thousand square metres), distributed in some ten towers in the south of the Central Business District and for the same Soho group he has built one of the houses of the Commune by the Great Wall. Like other figures with his training, Cui Kai could have stayed anchored in the models of the 1980s, a rather heavy type of building marked by the attempt to prolong the stereotypes of the Revolution. In reality, he has breathed in so much that he has let himself be influenced by the young colleagues of his studio whom he has spontaneously placed in the forefront, which makes it difficult to judge what corresponds specifically to him in each of the group's projects. From the numerous batches of recent works, we have focused here on two in particular, one in Beijing near the Deshengmen Gate and the other in Yinxu near Anyang.

Cui Kai 崔恺
Born 1957
Master in architecture, Tianjin
University, 1984
Project Institute, date of foundation: 1952
Number of employees: 4 000

Contact
China Architecture Design
& Research Group
19 Chegongzhuang Street
Beijing 100044
P. R. China
T: +86-(0)10-6830 2910
F: +86-(0)10-6834 3967
Cuik@china.com
www.cadreg.com

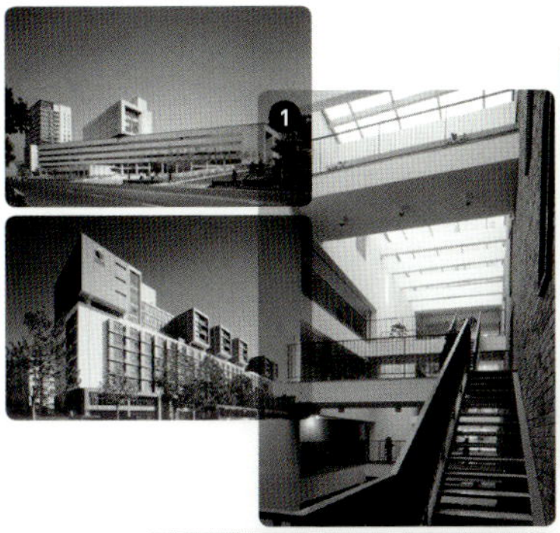

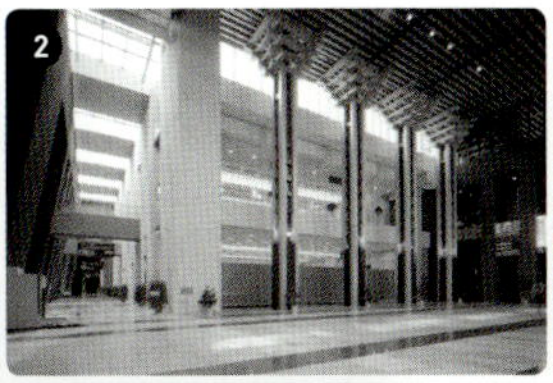

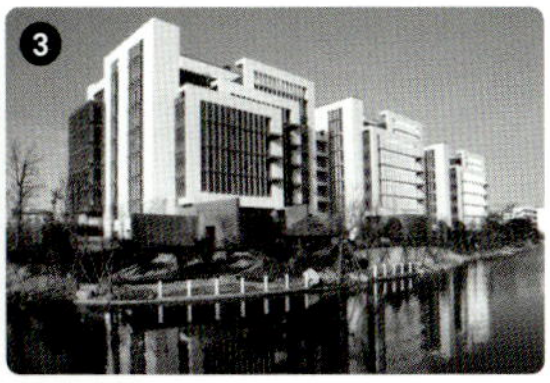

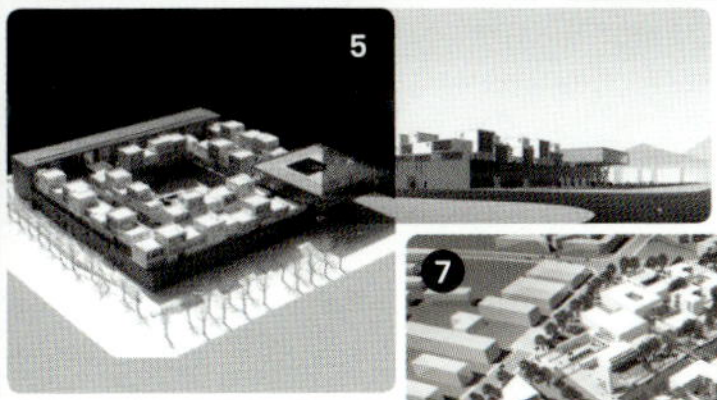

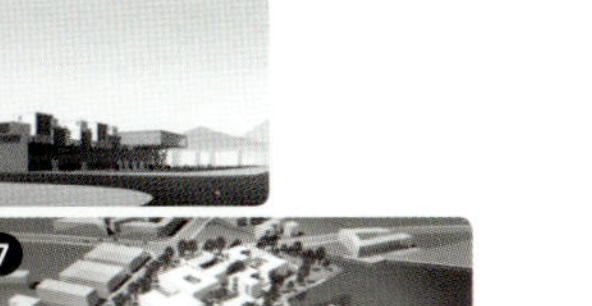

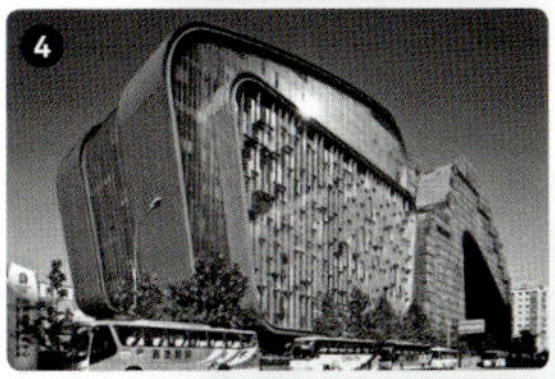

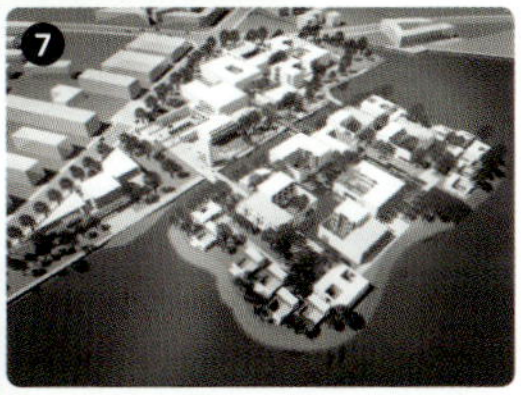

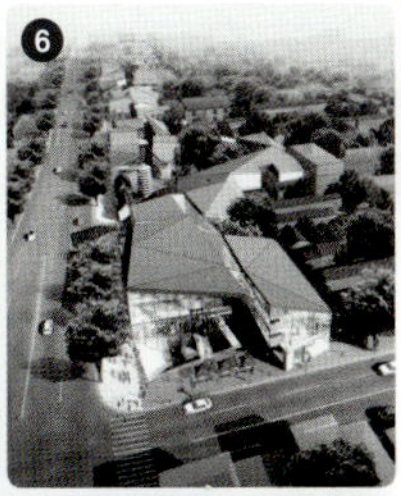

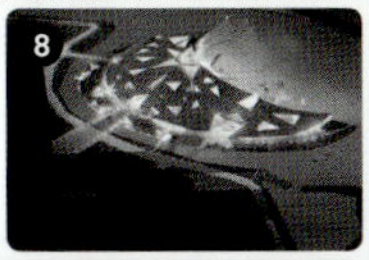

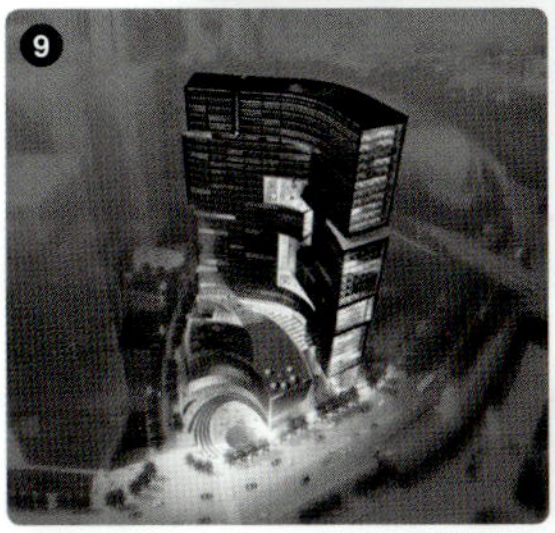

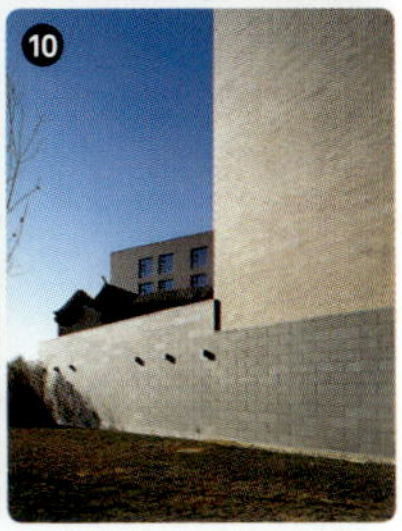

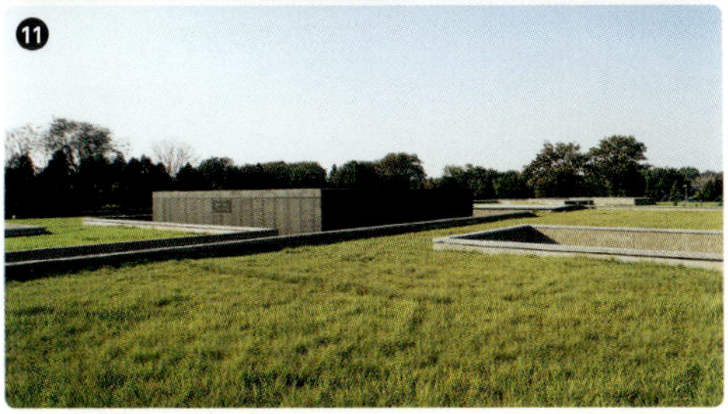

1 Apartments for computer engineers in Dalian (Liaoning), 2005.
2 Lhassa Station (Tibet), 2006.
3 Office building Bobo de Ningbo (Zhejiang), 2006.
4 Offices and printing house of Beijing Digital-Telecom, 2005.
5 Residences/artists workshops in Xishan, Beijing, 2007.
6 Urban redevelopment of Avenue South Xisi, Beijing, 2007.
7 Zhujiajiao hotel on the water, Shanghai, 2008.
8 Island of the moon, multi-purpose complex, Tianjin (Hebei), 2008
9 Tower B18-1, Chongqing, 2008.
10 Desheng Shangcheng Office building, Beijing, 2005.
11 Yinxu Archaeological Museum, Anyang, 2005.

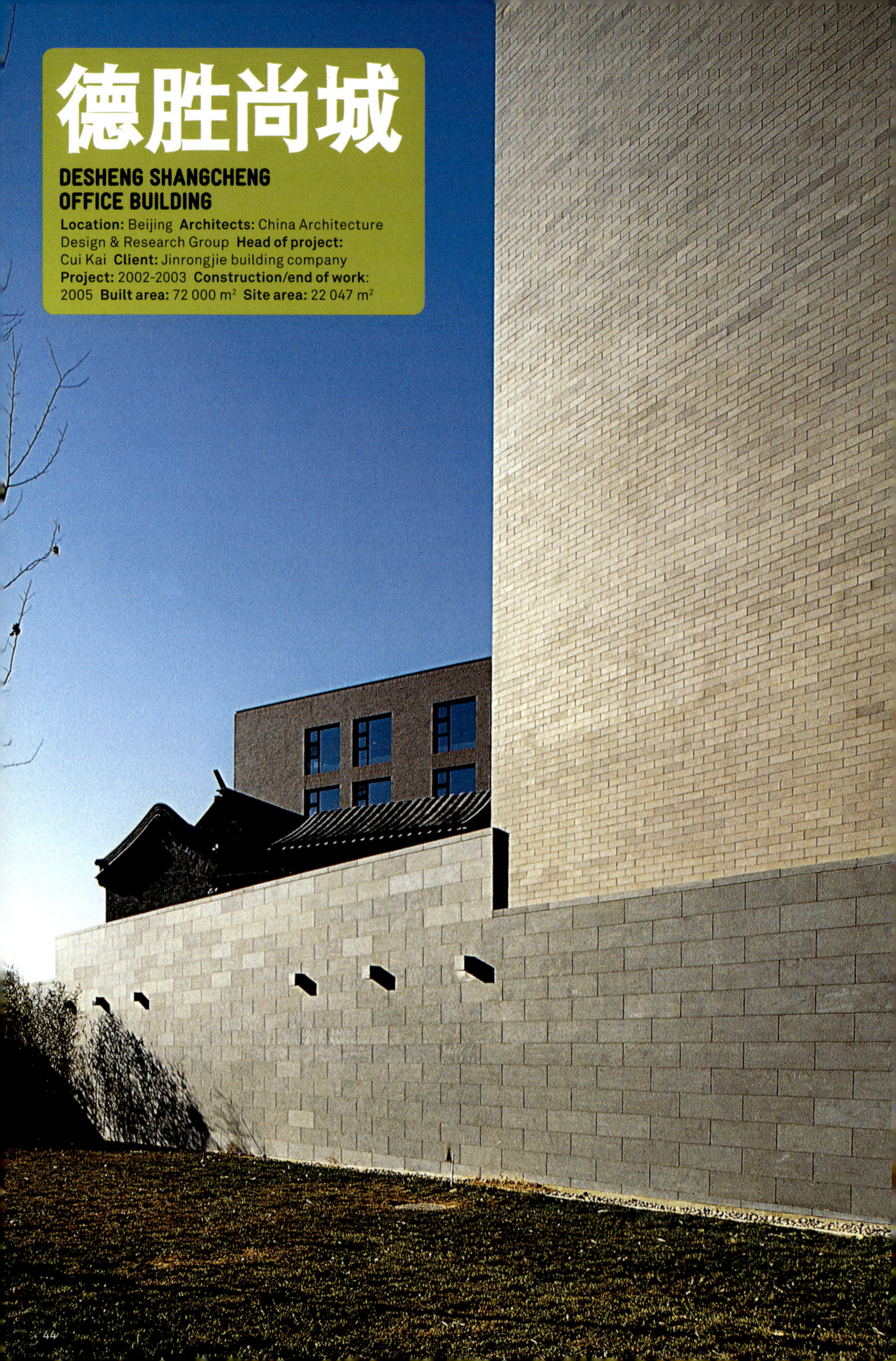

德胜尚城

DESHENG SHANGCHENG
OFFICE BUILDING

Location: Beijing Architects: China Architecture
Design & Research Group Head of project:
Cui Kai Client: Jinrongjie building company
Project: 2002-2003 Construction/end of work:
2005 Built area: 72 000 m² Site area: 22 047 m²

The Desheng Shangcheng ensemble, on the
north-west edge of the second ringroad, is one
of the most beautiful urban projects carried
out by the Cui Kai team, under the direction of
Pang Guo Wei. This is the first office complex of
this scope to depart from the paths of Western-
style corporate architecture or from the heavy
spiritless symmetrical structures which are
produced by so many institutes. This set of
buildings did not emerge on virgin soil. Less
than fifty years ago it would have found itself
confronting the wall of the Inner City between
the Desheng and Xizhi gates.
Indeed, farther back in time it would even have
been situated inside that wall, before the Ming
dynasty took the initiative of tightening its hold
on Beijing. To keep from being situated
excessively close to the very dense motorway
networks which converge at this point where
University Avenue and the second ringroad meet,
Cui Kai and his team designed a substantially
elevated ensemble which would be at once
a defensive gate, a street and a protective wall,
as well as a museum, since they have recovered
on site all that they could of the quarter's
historical elements, setting them both
charmingly and picturesquely on the office
buildings' roofs and terraces. The grey
brick bonding also recalls Beijing's past as do
the courtyards and lanes which arise here from
functional needs.

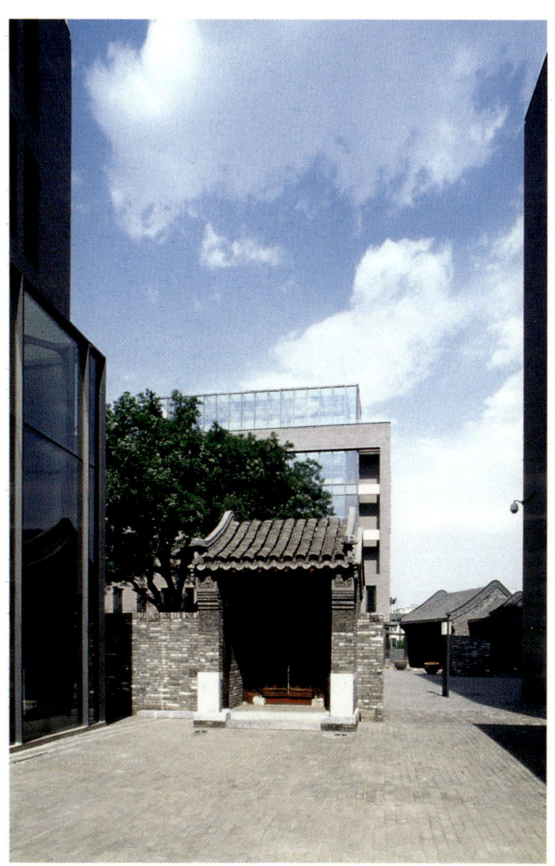

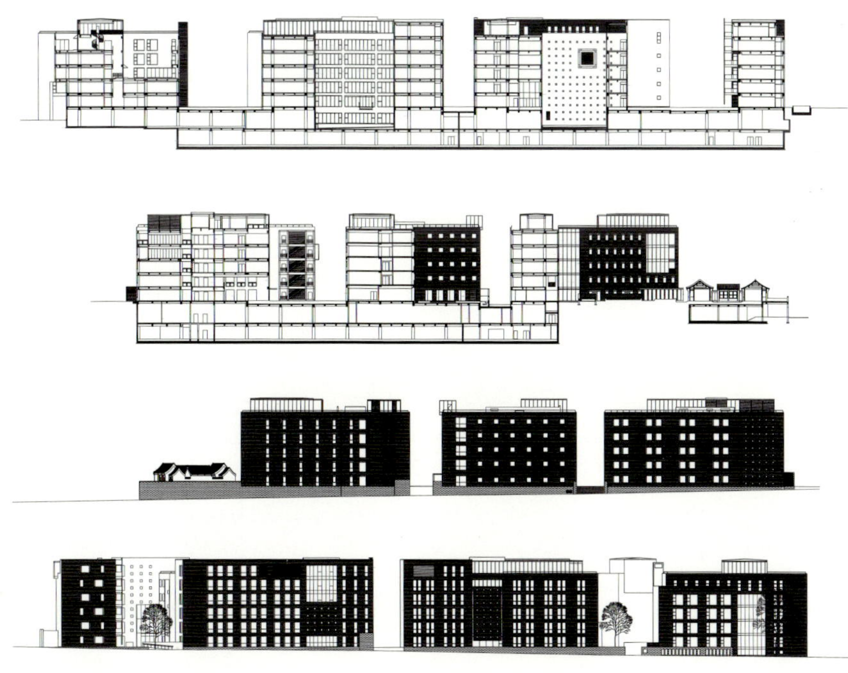

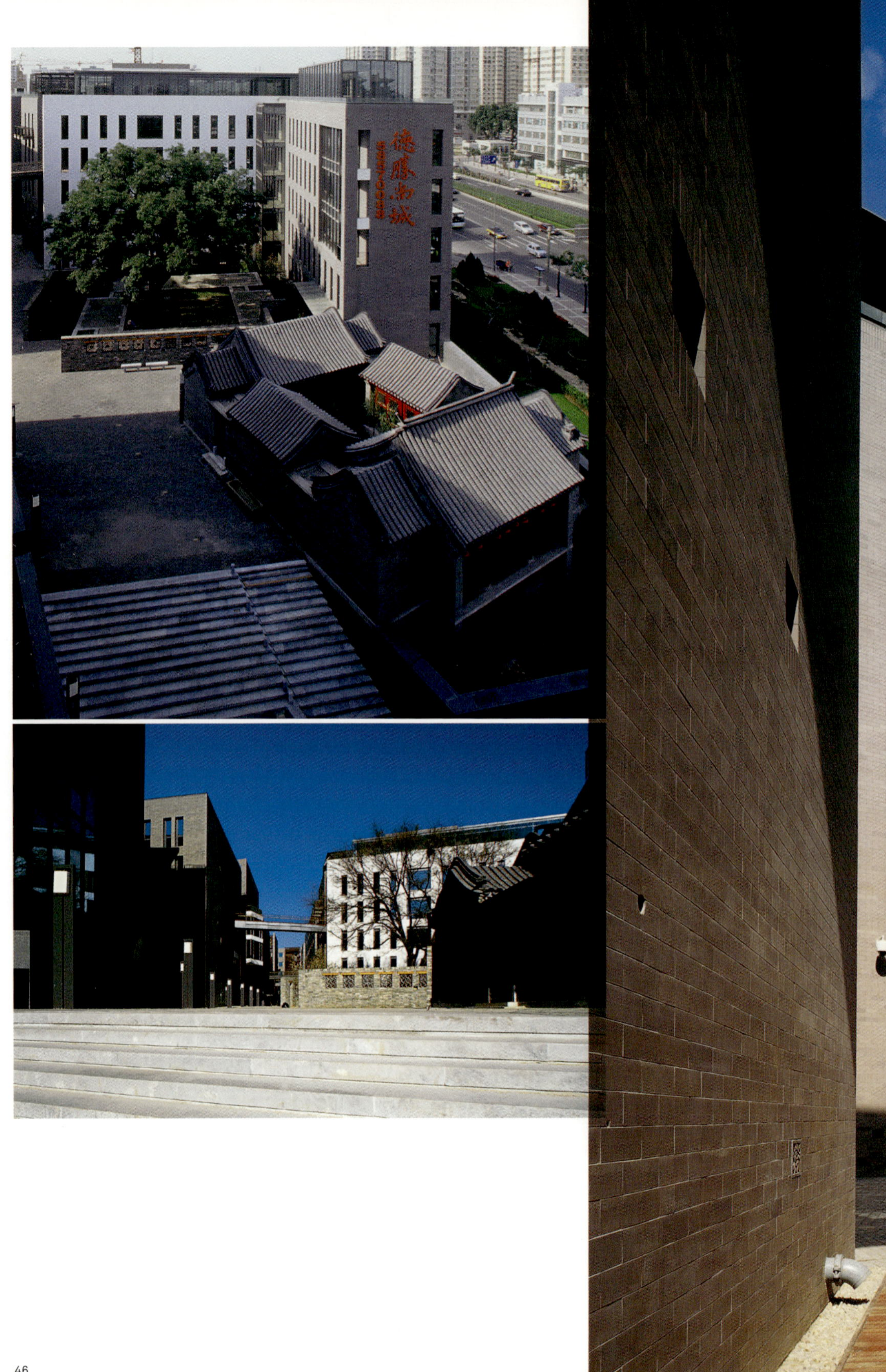

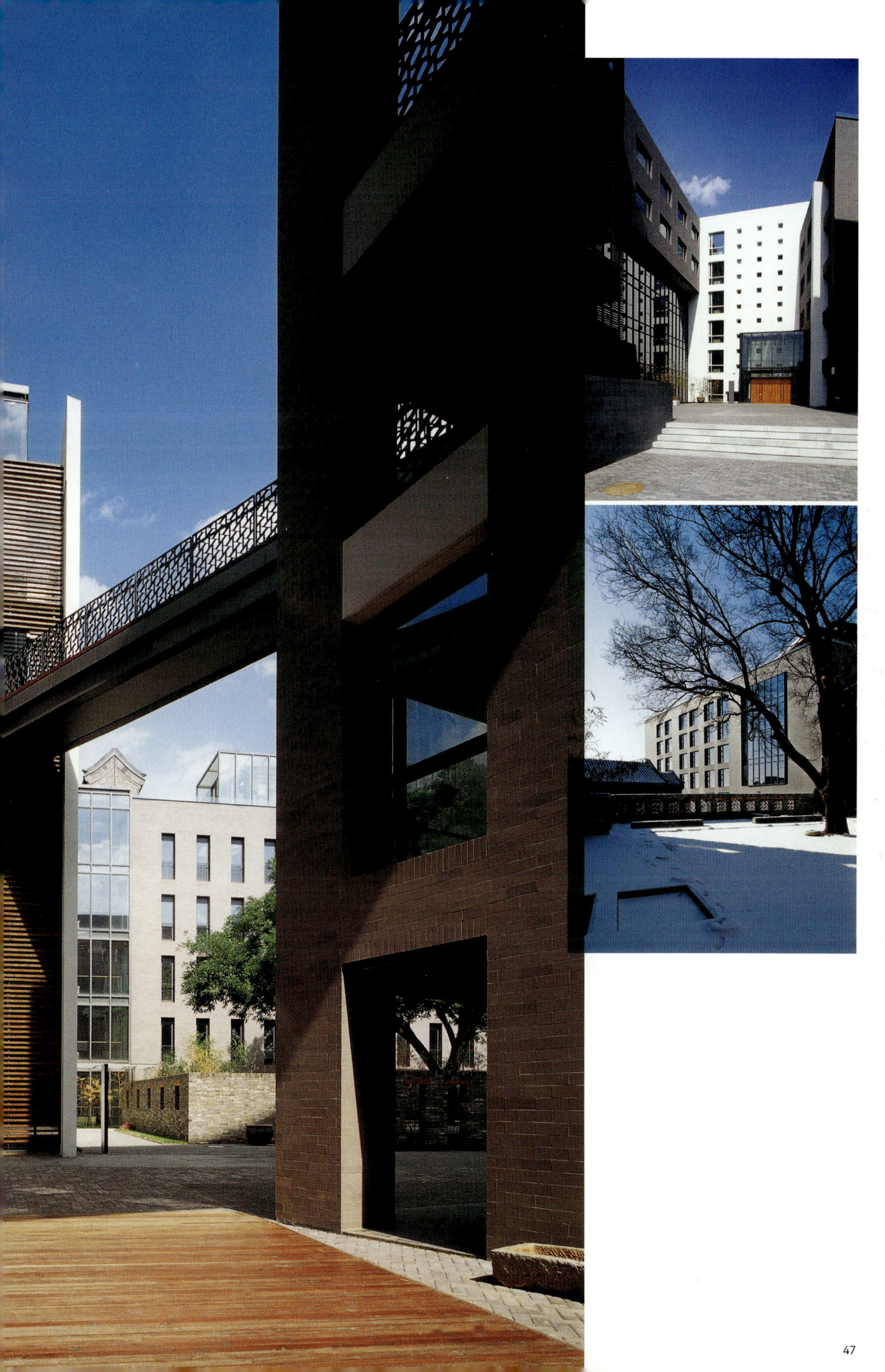

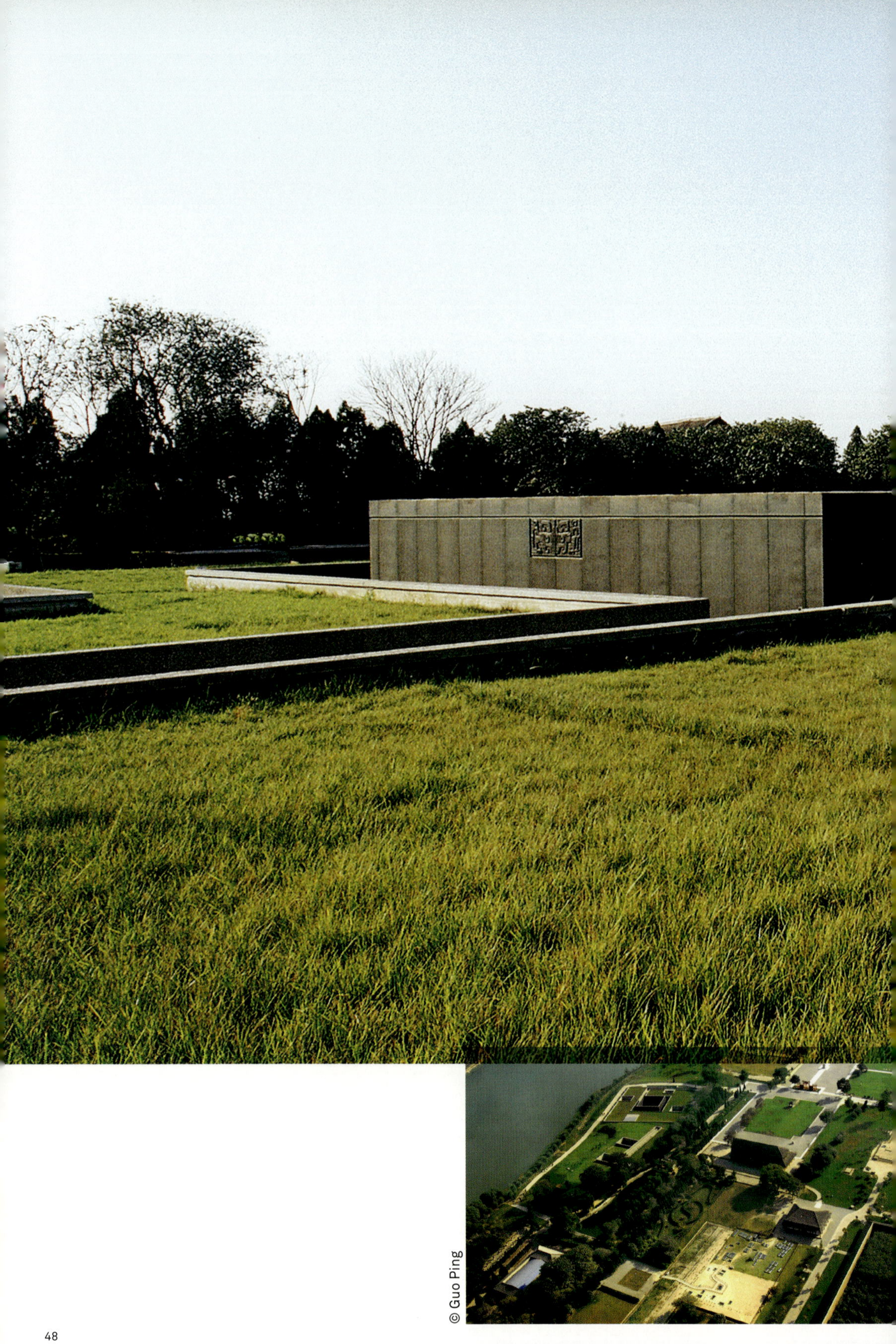

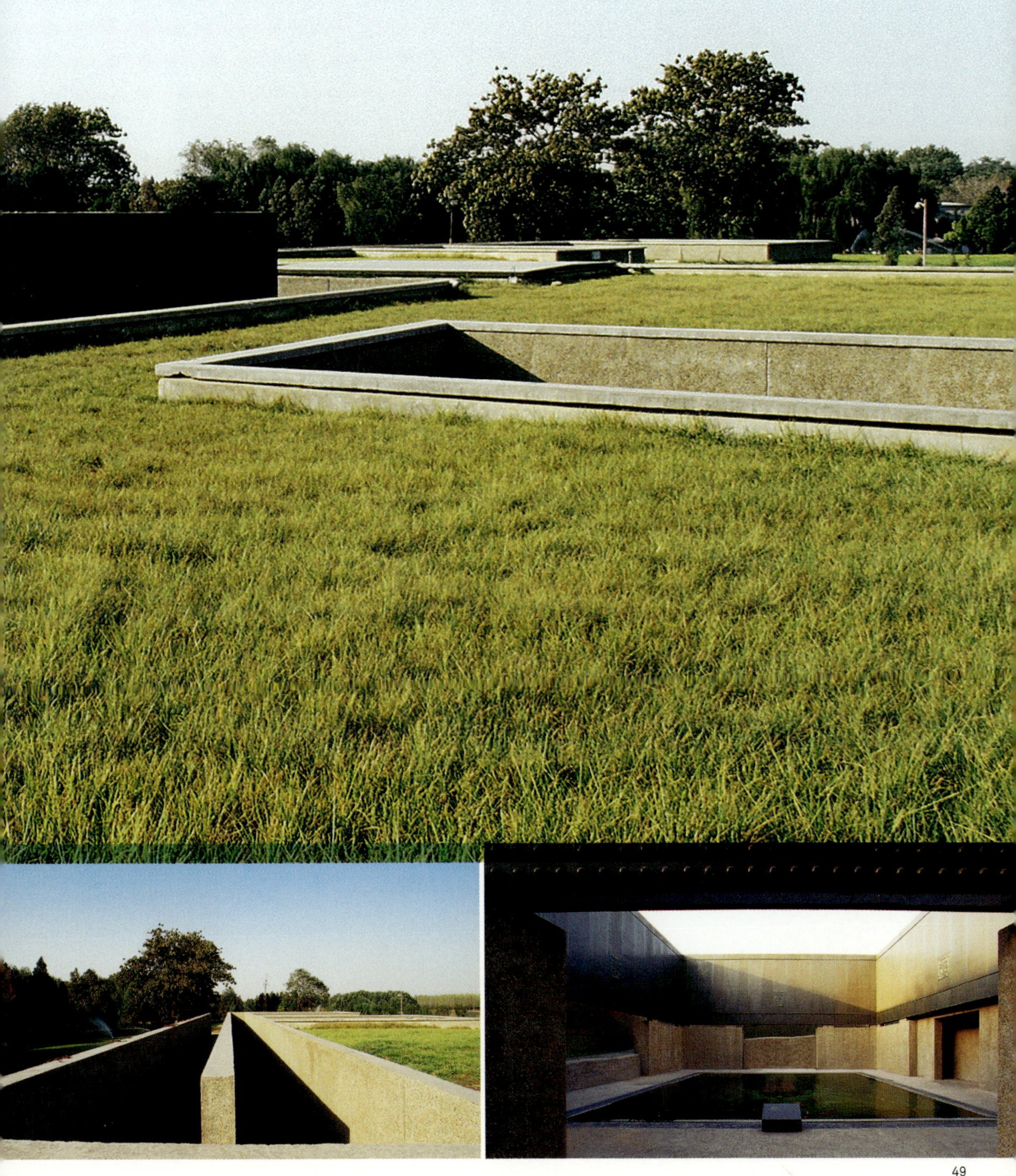

殷墟博物馆 YINXU ARCHAEOLOGICAL MUSEUM
Location: Anyang (Henan) Architects: China Architecture Design & Research Group
Head of project: Cui Kai Client: City of Anyang Project: April 2005 Construction/end of work:
September 2005 Built area: 3 525 m² Site area: 6 520 m² Cost: 190 million euro

We have almost had to rummage through Cui Kai's offices and file cabinets to find a trace of this building. It was extremely innovative for China, even though the museums of archaeological sites have since multiplied there in inverse proportion to the protection that the cities' heritage would deserve.

The museum of Yinxu, near Anyang (Henan province), hardly rises above the ground, as one perceives only the top of the walls and the entrance of a labyrinth or, more precisely, of a tomb. Taking a bird's-eye view, these protruding structures allow half a dozen courtyards to be seen in addition to a path which is all the more mysterious because it is only really concretised underground.

Faced with an archaeological site like this one, which is composed essentially of the ruins of palaces and tombs, in the West one would have probably avoided the architectural gesture, perhaps preferring a presentation under glass slabs accompanied by a solid museum in which the relics would be assembled.

The Chinese architect, however, has chosen to create a combined space, both palatial and sepulchral, in which the pieces, which are among the most precious relics of ancient China, are presented as if in situ. Nevertheless, the real and the symbolic parts being clearly designated, here one avoids the strange impression which such a mixture produces for example at Knossos, on Crete.

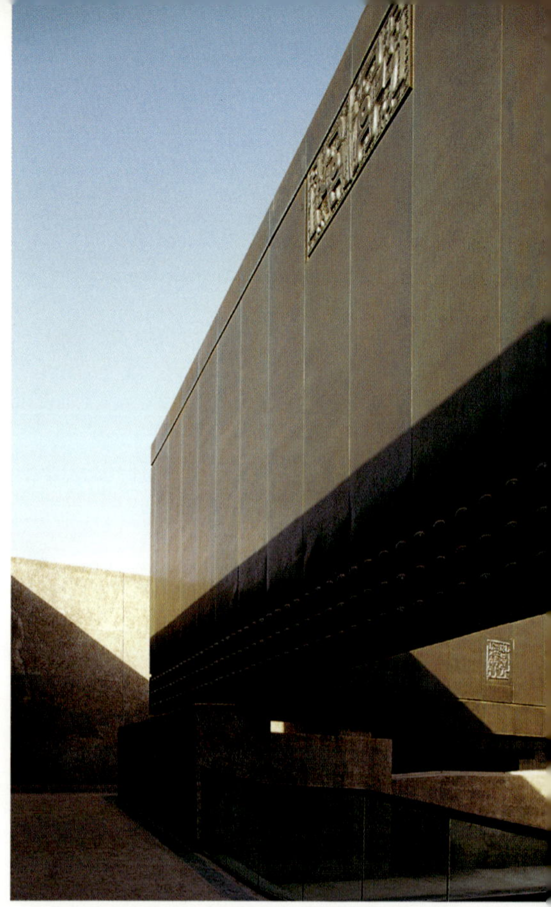

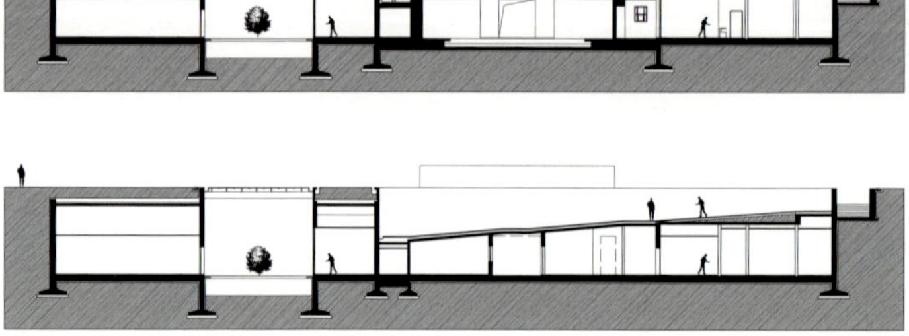

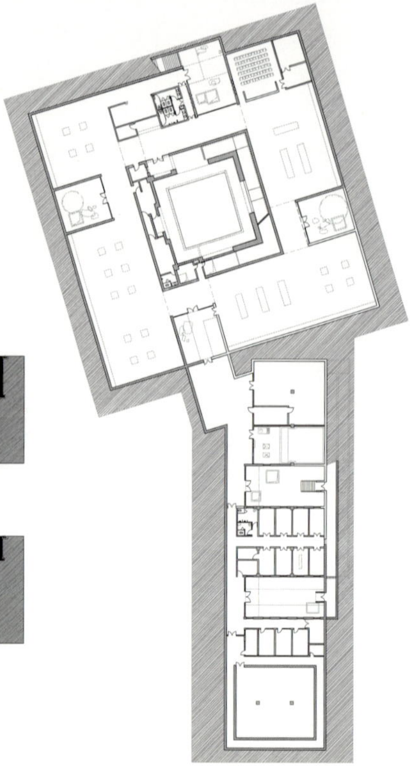

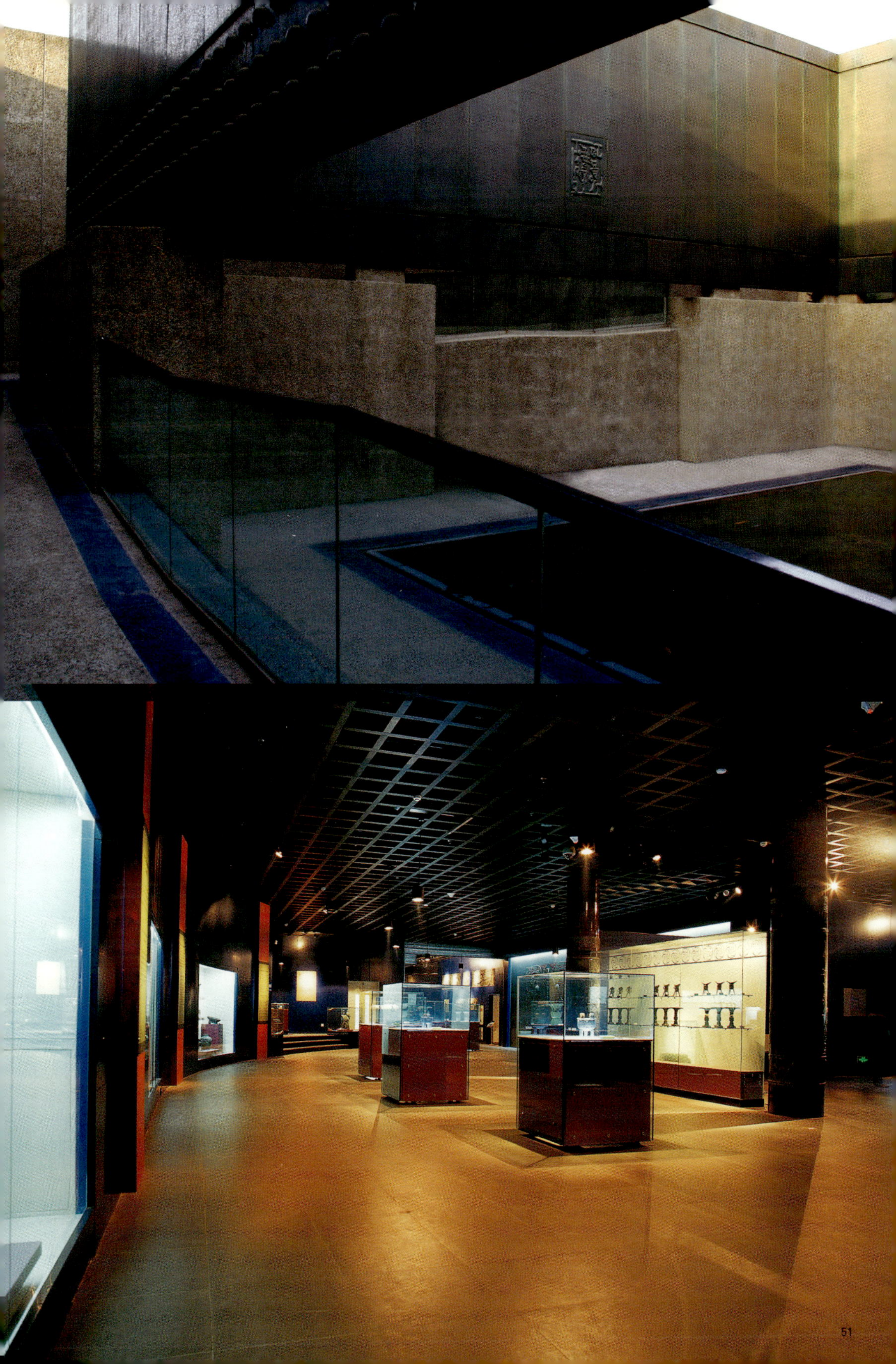

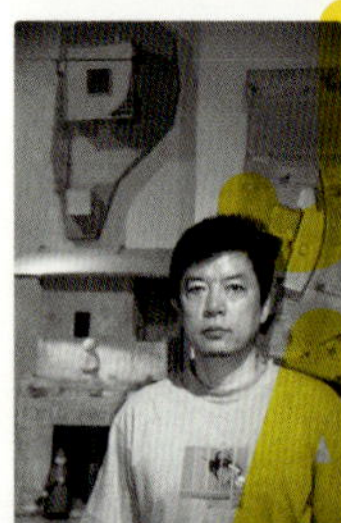

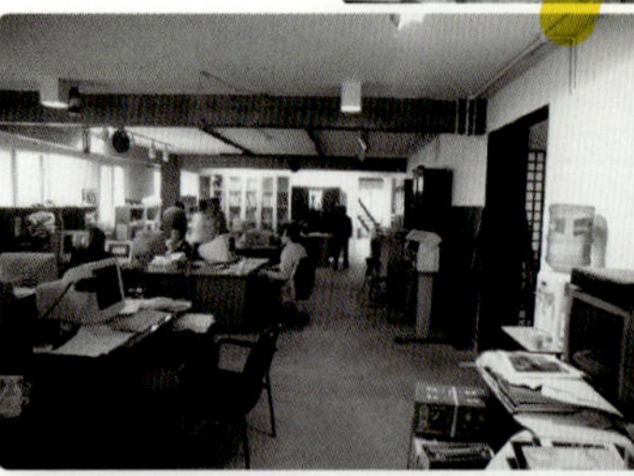

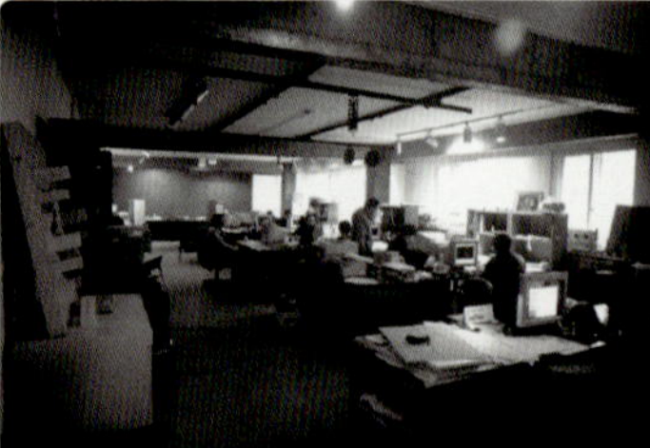

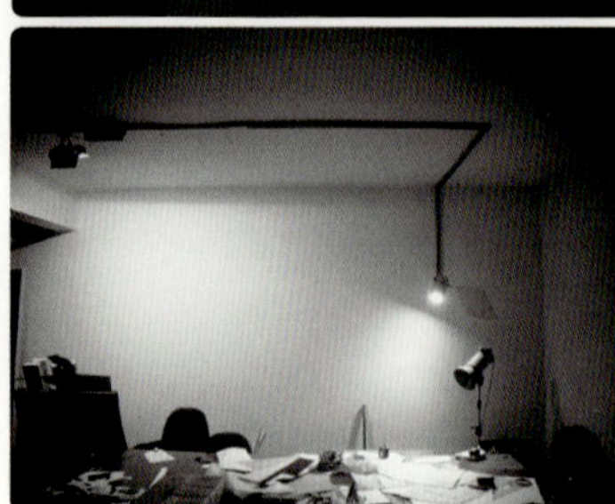

Jiakun Architects 家琨建筑设计事务所
Liu Jiakun 刘家琨

Liu Jiakun, born in 1956, is a full-blooded native of Sichuan, the great plain at the foot of the Himalayas which was the scene of the struggles of the kingdoms of Shu and Wei. The kingdom of Shu had Chengdu as its capital, which is precisely where the architect was born. The capital of the kingdom of Ba was Chongqing, and it was in this city that Liu carried out his studies before starting to work in Tibet. Until 1990, however, Liu Jiakun's profession was that of a writer. Indeed, from all these periods, he has formed a personality which is at once sombre, determined or closed – ready to open itself when his cultural universe finds an attentive ear.

He is the person behind of one of contemporary China's most emblematic buildings, a much-published and coveted museum located one hundred kilometres from Chengdu: the Luyeyuan Stone Sculpture Museum (2001/2004).

In Chongqing he uses stone with less finesse at the Fine Arts Institute at one of the city's universities. In this building one can clearly see the tensions which move this creator, caught between the contradictory fires of his own culture. The Institute expresses violence, while the Sculpture Museum adopts a serene language.

Liu is prolific and he has built numerous structures across the whole country. These buildings are always different, always ingenious, and the observer capable of defining this architect's style has yet to be born.

The simplest thing would be to say that he combines, with the temperament of a poet who is irascible and a dreamer by turns, the vocabulary of modernity and the immense variety of materials offered by today's China. In Qingpu (Shanghai), he delivered a long horizontal building which shelters the city's Urban Planning Office. It is in an international style and its Chinese colours are in their sombre, almost black version. Here we will halt at the building which he has erected for the museum cluster of Anren, which is also situated not far from Chengdu. It forms the link between the sculpture museum of Luyeyuan (the grey of concrete), the government building of Qingpu (the suspicious black of the public administration) and the ambitious reading of traditional red brick. Liu Jiakun affirms the opposite, stating that he is independent of his architectural readings.

Whatever the case may be, on completing a visit to his buildings one feels tempted to pronounce some of architecture's most magical names: Le Corbusier, Simounet, Kahn, Siza... not bad at all as implicit references.

Liu Jiakun 刘家琨
Born 1956
Degree in Architecture
School of Chongqing, 1982
Studio founded in 1999
Number of employees: 26

Contact
Jiakun Architects
2-7F, block11, 3# Yulin Nanlu
610041 Chengdu, Sichuan, China
T: +86 28 85 56 88 99
F: +86 28 85 58 94 91
jkads@263.net
www.jiakun.com

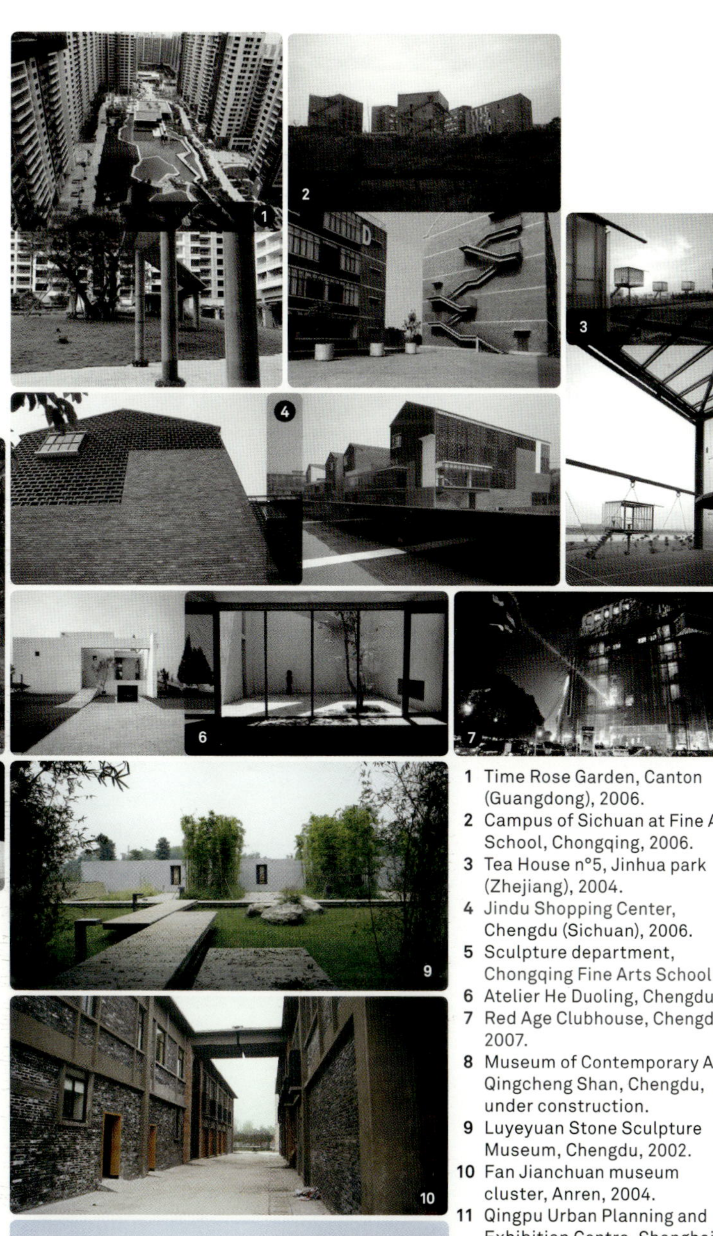

1 Time Rose Garden, Canton (Guangdong), 2006.
2 Campus of Sichuan at Fine Arts School, Chongqing, 2006.
3 Tea House n°5, Jinhua park (Zhejiang), 2004.
4 Jindu Shopping Center, Chengdu (Sichuan), 2006.
5 Sculpture department, Chongqing Fine Arts School, 2004.
6 Atelier He Duoling, Chengdu, 1997.
7 Red Age Clubhouse, Chengdu, 2007.
8 Museum of Contemporary Art Qingcheng Shan, Chengdu, under construction.
9 Luyeyuan Stone Sculpture Museum, Chengdu, 2002.
10 Fan Jianchuan museum cluster, Anren, 2004.
11 Qingpu Urban Planning and Exhibition Centre, Shanghai, 2006.

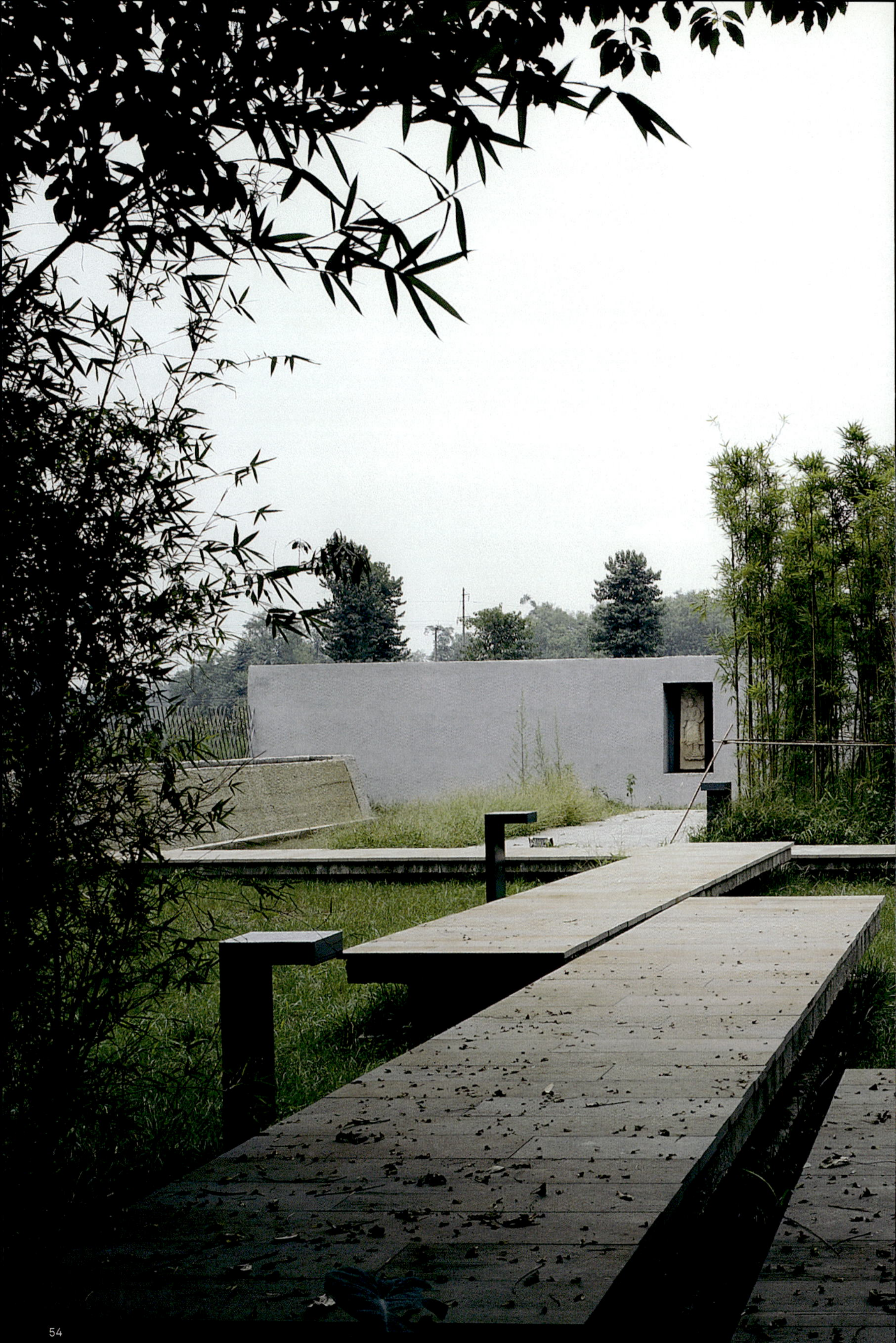

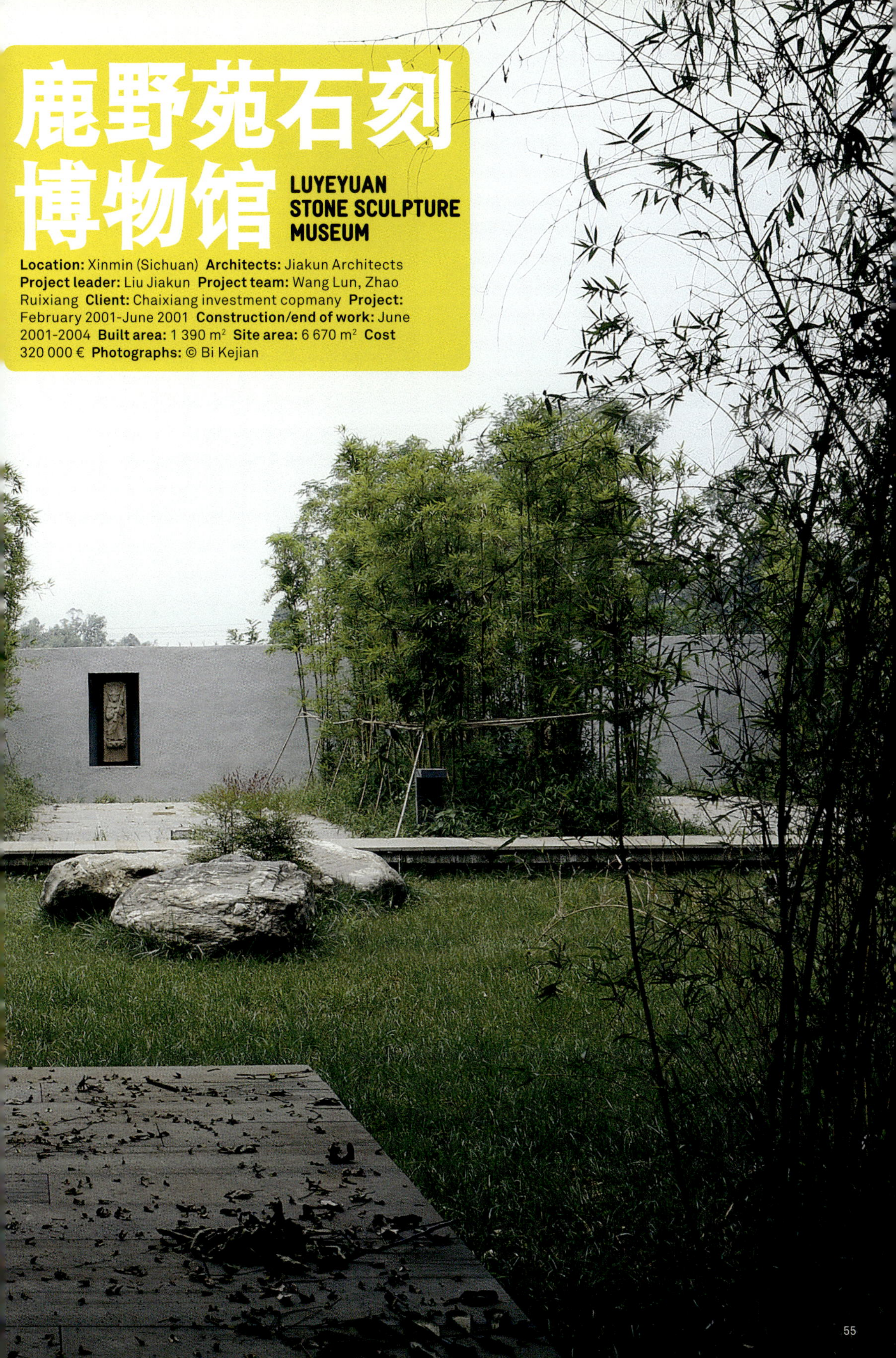

鹿野苑石刻
博物馆

LUYEYUAN
STONE SCULPTURE
MUSEUM

Location: Xinmin (Sichuan) Architects: Jiakun Architects
Project leader: Liu Jiakun Project team: Wang Lun, Zhao
Ruixiang Client: Chaixiang investment copmany Project:
February 2001-June 2001 Construction/end of work: June
2001-2004 Built area: 1 390 m² Site area: 6 670 m² Cost
320 000 € Photographs: © Bi Kejian

The Luyeyuan Stone Sculpture Museum in Ximmin (Sichuan province) has been financed by a private patron. It is formed by a set of buildings in raw concrete, on the limit of the coarseness which appears to mark the spontaneity of the local masons, little accustomed to working material in this way.

The first of these buildings was finished in 2001 and the remainder were completed on several occasions up to 2004, although it is not really possible to note any formal ruptures between the various phases. The ensemble forms an exciting promenade through the flora of Sichuan where the water, agitated and serene by turns, helps to set one in a timeless and even placeless universe, as if all the Buddhas of Cambodia, China and Japan were bent on making a stopover here. It is a sort of vast "work in progress" in which the architect deploys a feverish inventiveness to find the most appropriate location for each piece, outside or in, and when the figures are installed indoors, to provide each one the most precise, purest and most suitable staging to express their religious sentiment. Liu styles himself as an atheist but he must surely have some dealings with the celestial regions to succeed as he does, with little or no electricity and often in an atmosphere made gloomy by the fog, in capturing exactly the right lighting. A rare sentiment of permanence arises from modernity in this way.

French observers will be reminded of Roland Simounet's archaeology museum at Nemours and of certain aspects of Gaudin's Guimet Museum, while Indians will be meeting up again with the rough inspiration of Le Corbusier's concrete at Chandigarh, and Japanese visitor may think for a moment that they are at one of the pre-modern sites of Kyoto. People from Sichuan, for their part, will be seeing contemporary China's first "Neobrutalist" site.

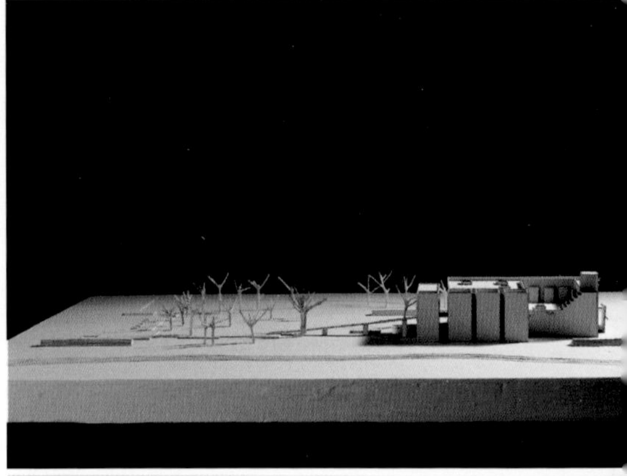

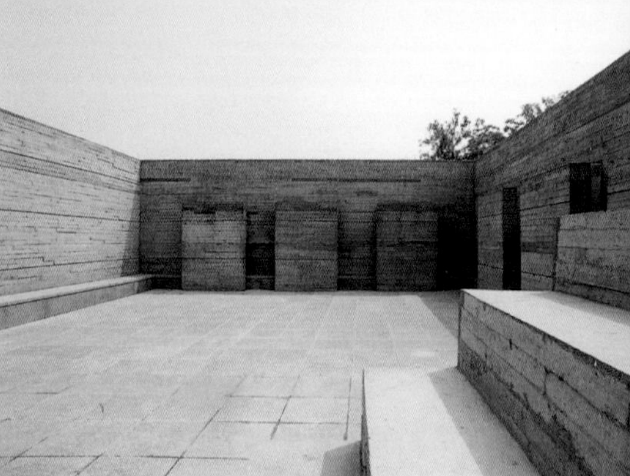

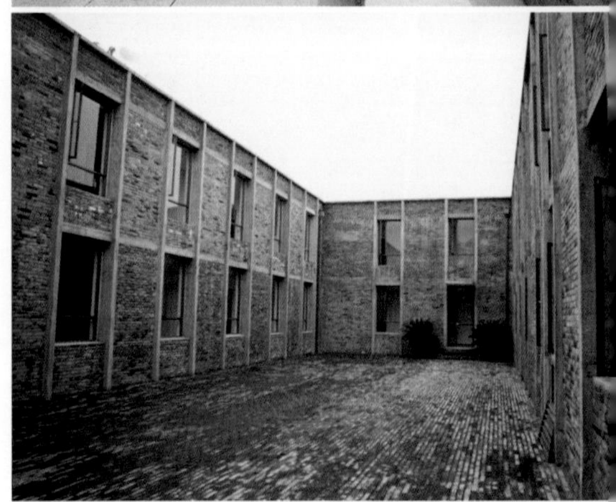

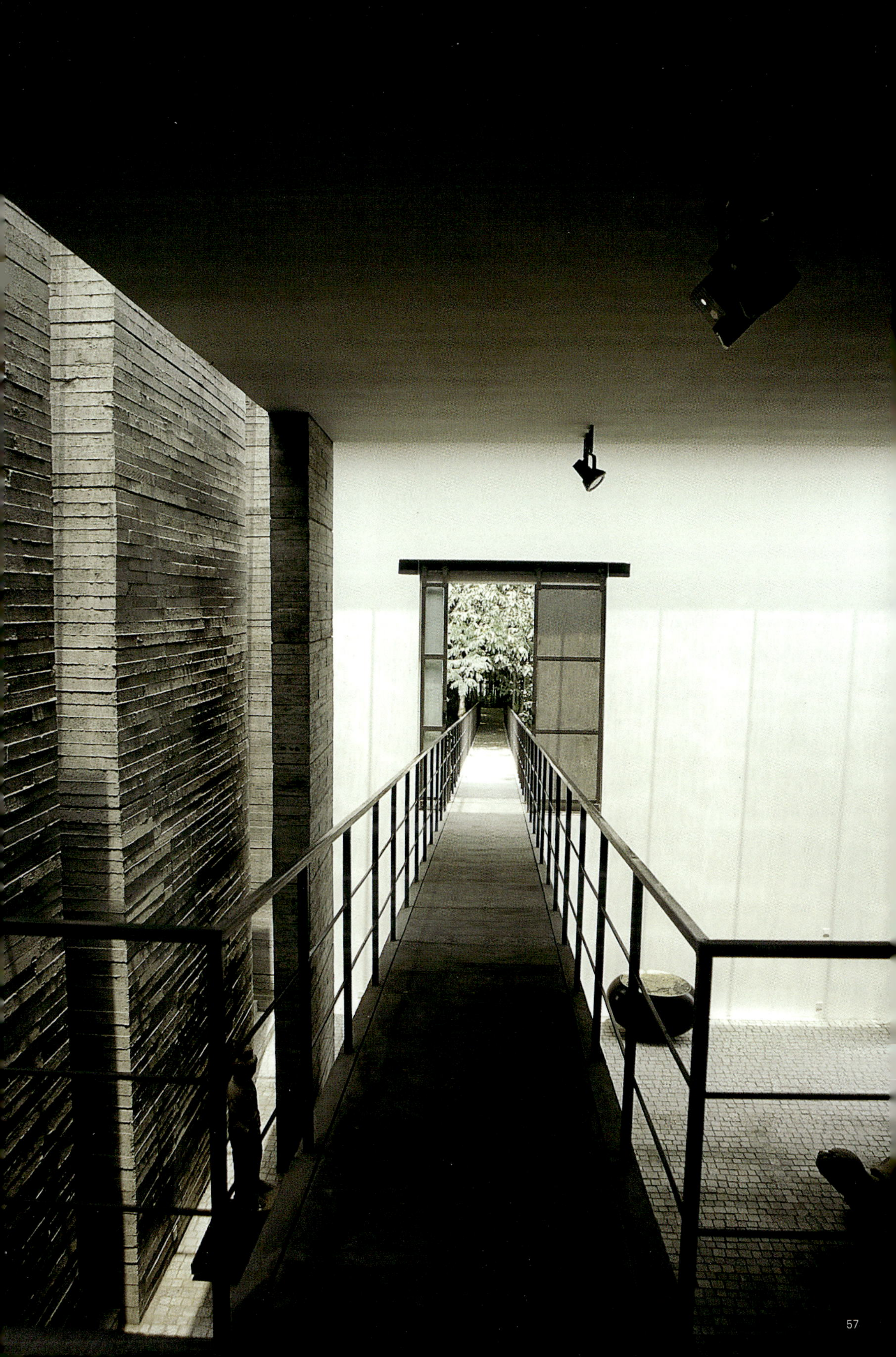

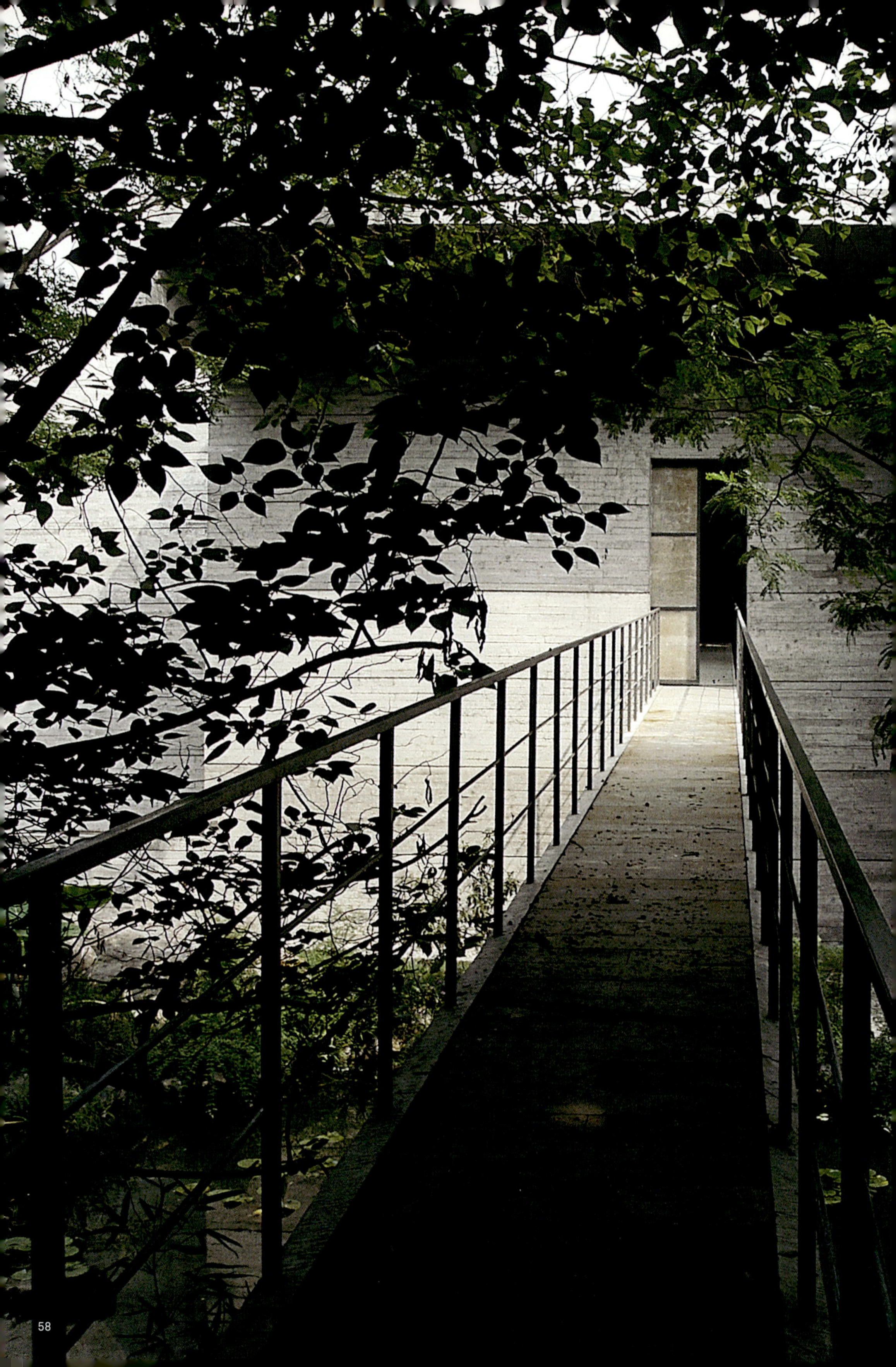

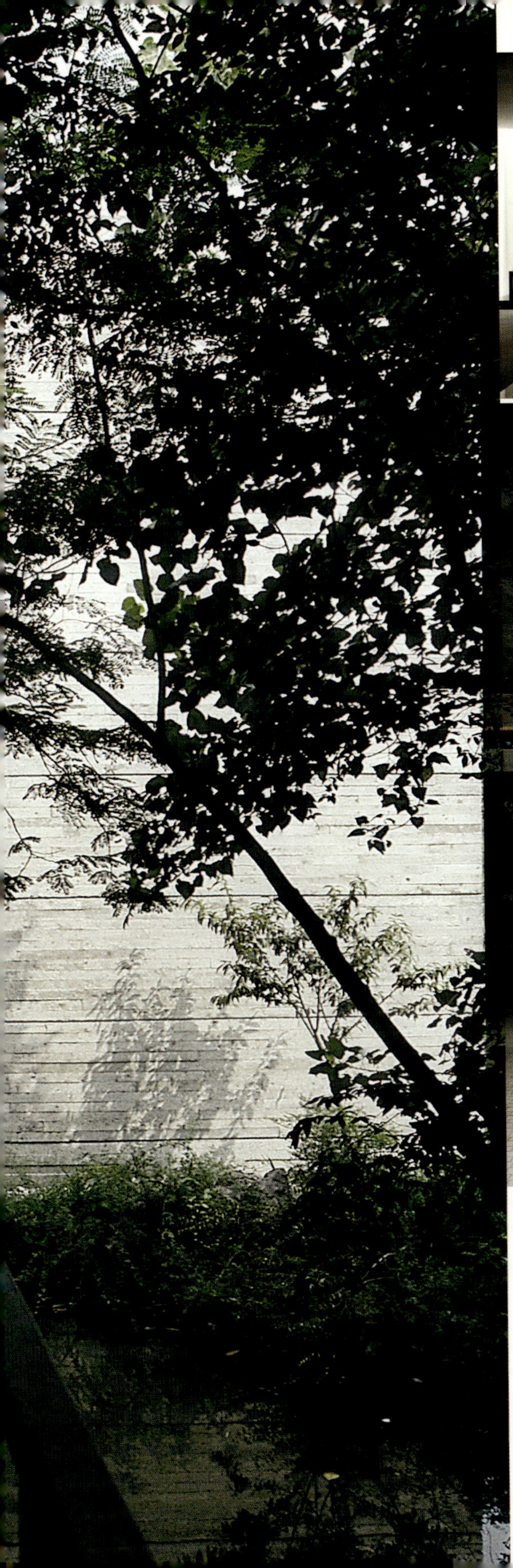

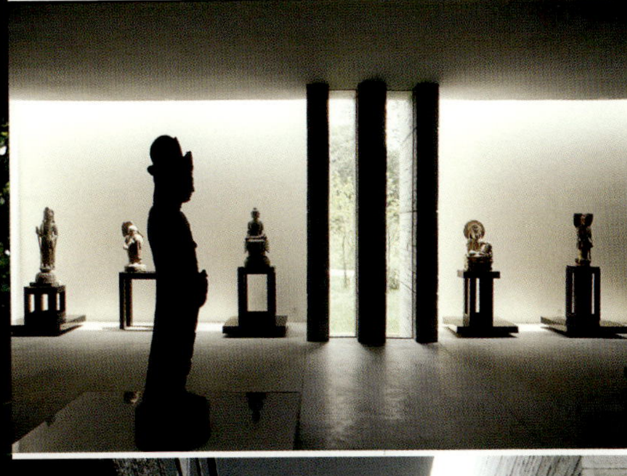

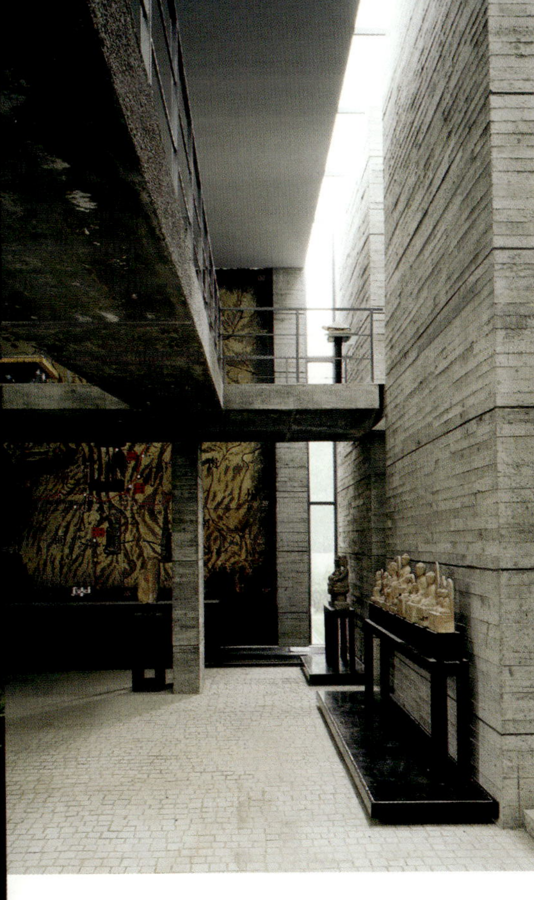

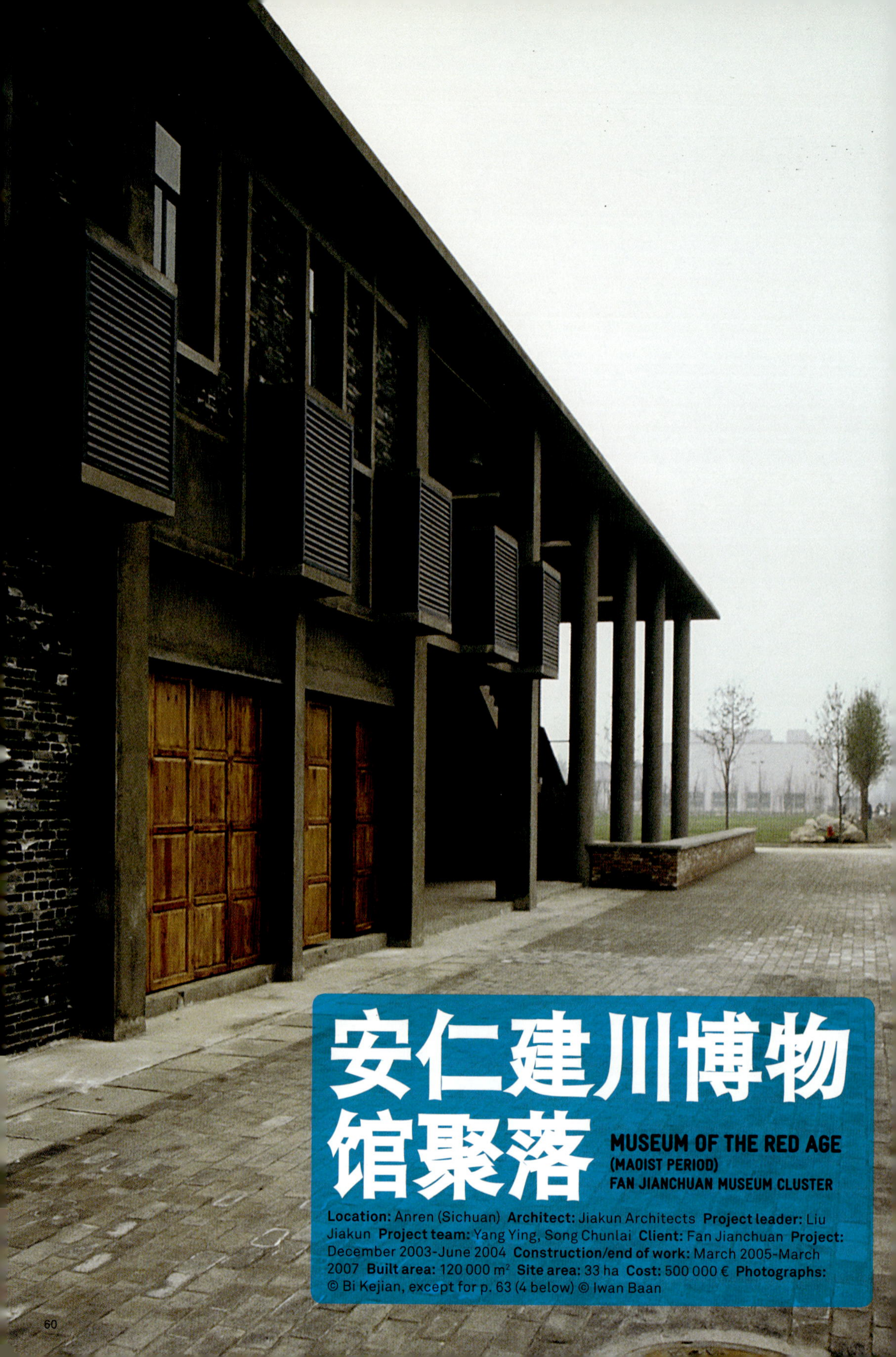

安仁建川博物
馆聚落

MUSEUM OF THE RED AGE
(MAOIST PERIOD)
FAN JIANCHUAN MUSEUM CLUSTER

Location: Anren (Sichuan) Architect: Jiakun Architects Project leader: Liu Jiakun Project team: Yang Ying, Song Chunlai Client: Fan Jianchuan Project: December 2003-June 2004 Construction/end of work: March 2005-March 2007 Built area: 120 000 m² Site area: 33 ha Cost: 500 000 € Photographs: © Bi Kejian, except for p. 63 (4 below) © Iwan Baan

At the request of Fan Jianchuan, the cluster of museums in Anren has been organised by Yung-Ho Chang, an architect who has become here the urban planner of the ineffable. Twenty architects were to work on this project devoted to the War of Resistance against Japan, the Cultural Revolution and popular traditions, an apparently heterogeneous cluster which responds, in fact, to the sponsor's three main sets of personal collections.

One of the major buildings, the one commemorating what is called here the "Red Age", has been entrusted to Liu Jiakun.

Some of the elements of this museum cluster having never been built before, it will come to shelter almost all that the Maoist period produced in the way of propaganda items, diverse testimonies of the personality cult of the leader, etc. There will be few explanations or none at all in this building where what will speak for itself is the accumulation of thousands of badges, hundreds of clocks, chamber pots, newspapers and so on, all carefully arranged in a perhaps rather obsessed and oppressive manner.

Indeed, in this respect Liu's building reveals some amazing scenographic capabilities. Knowingly or not, he even succeeds in reflecting the constructive obsession of Mao Zedong who, at his numerous dwellings throughout China, had made it a principle to forbid the direct entry of light into the rooms. In effect, overhead lighting is used almost systematically at the Jianchuan Museum.

There is little relation between the volumes of the various halls and the copious collections which they shelter. The architecture, in which brick sets the keynote, ends up by accepting and serving this plethora of objects, of which each visitor is now free to make his or her own reading.

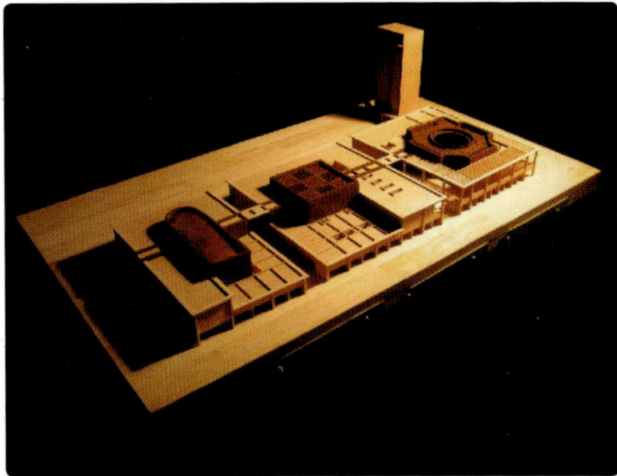

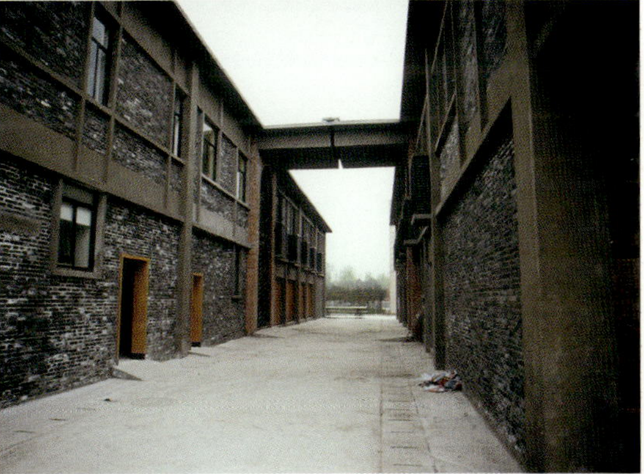

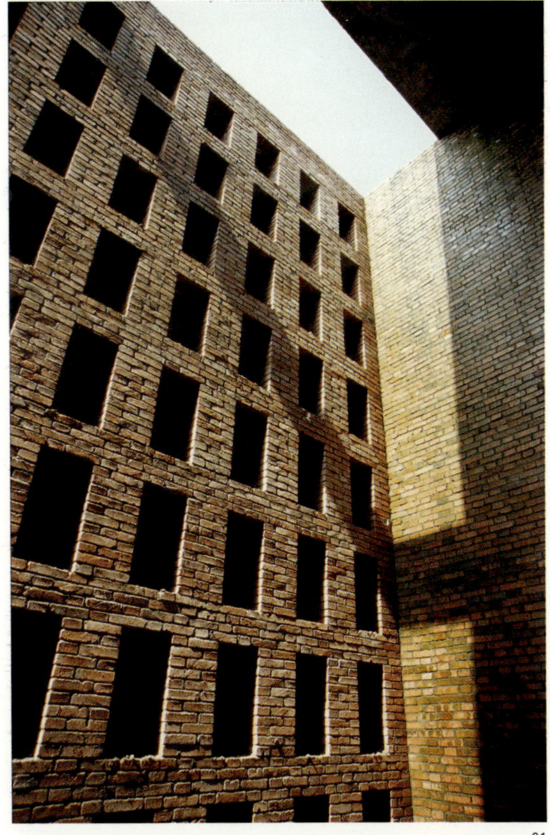

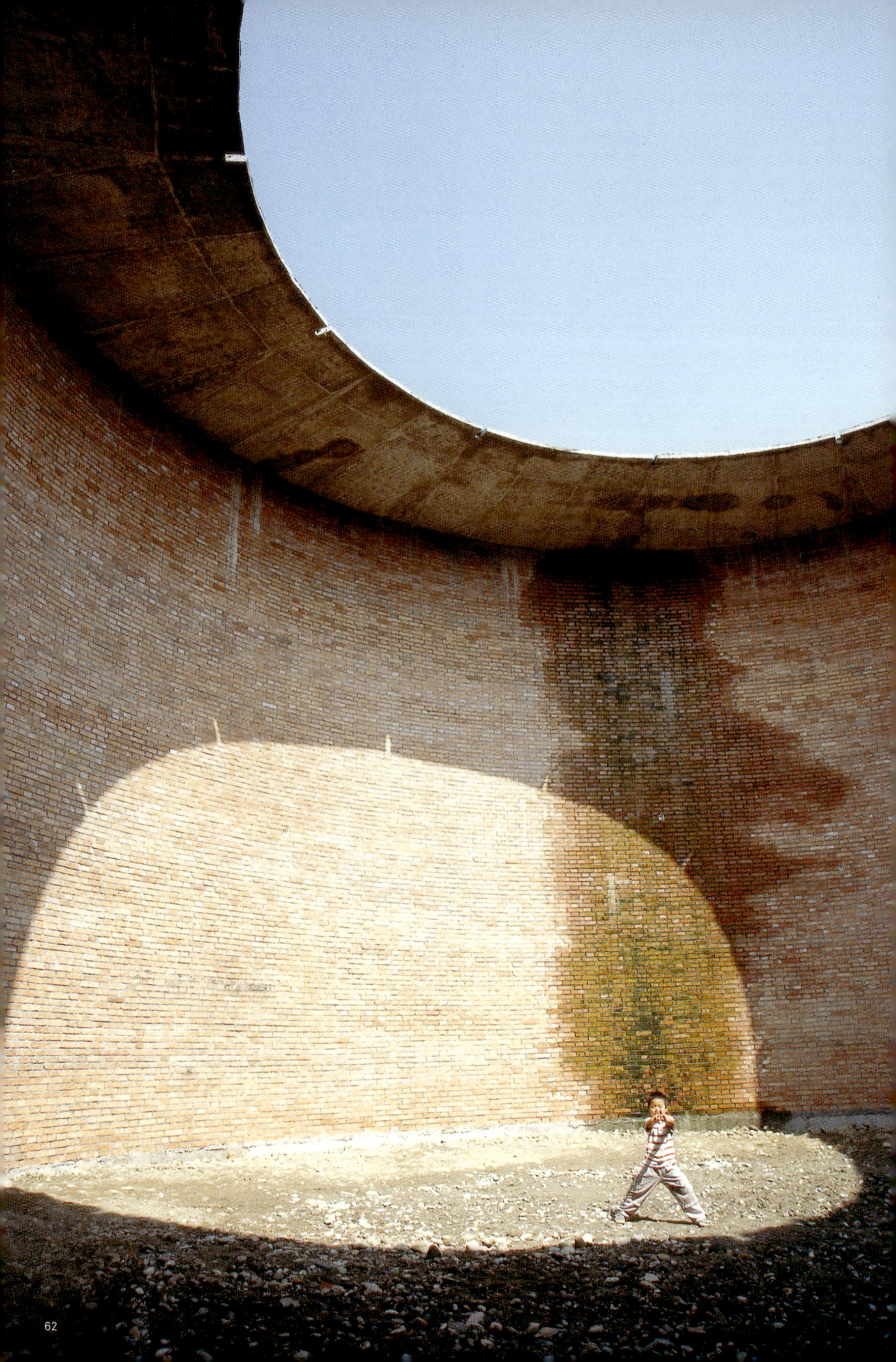

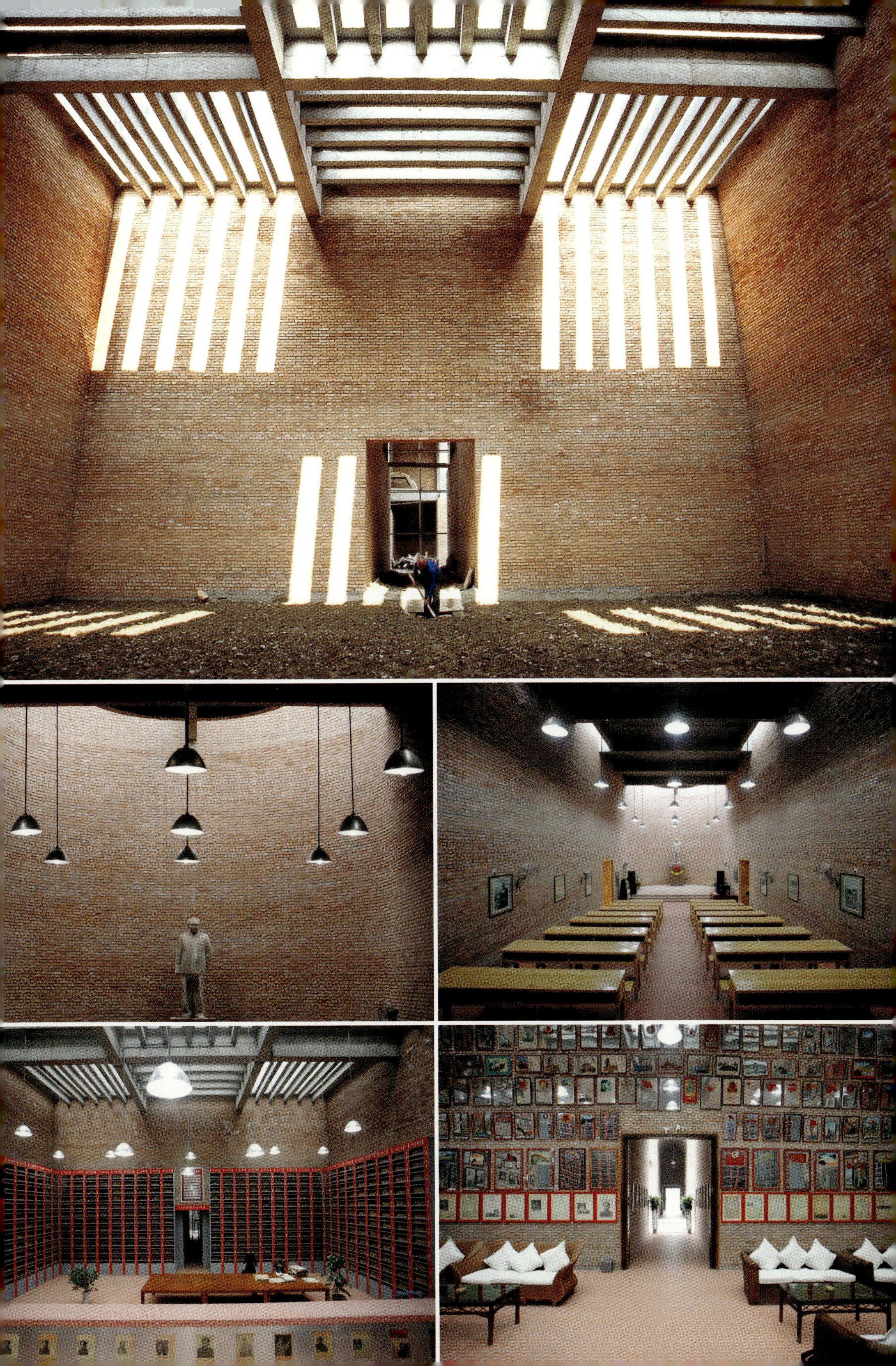

青浦新城展示中心

QINGPU URBAN PLANNING AND EXHIBITION CENTRE

Location: Qingpu (Shanghai) **Architect:** Jiakun Architects **Project leader:** Liu Jiakun **Project team:** Cai Kefei **Client:** Centre d'exposition et d'urbanisme de Qingpu **Project:** August 2003-June 2004 **Construction/end of work:** June 2004-June 2006 **Built area:** 10 155 m² **Site area:** 20 974 m² **Cost** 4.2 million euro **Photographs :** © Bi Kejian

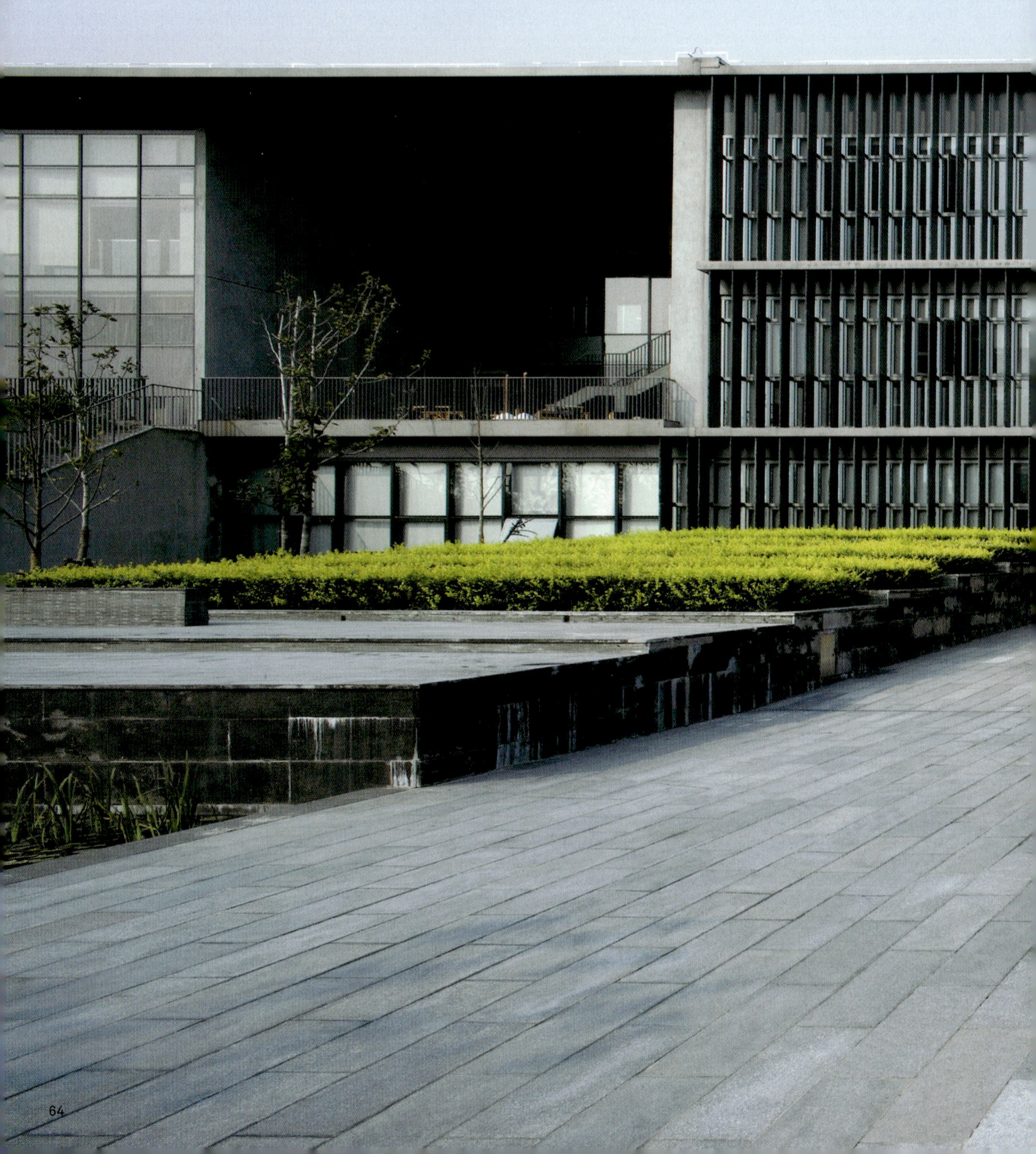

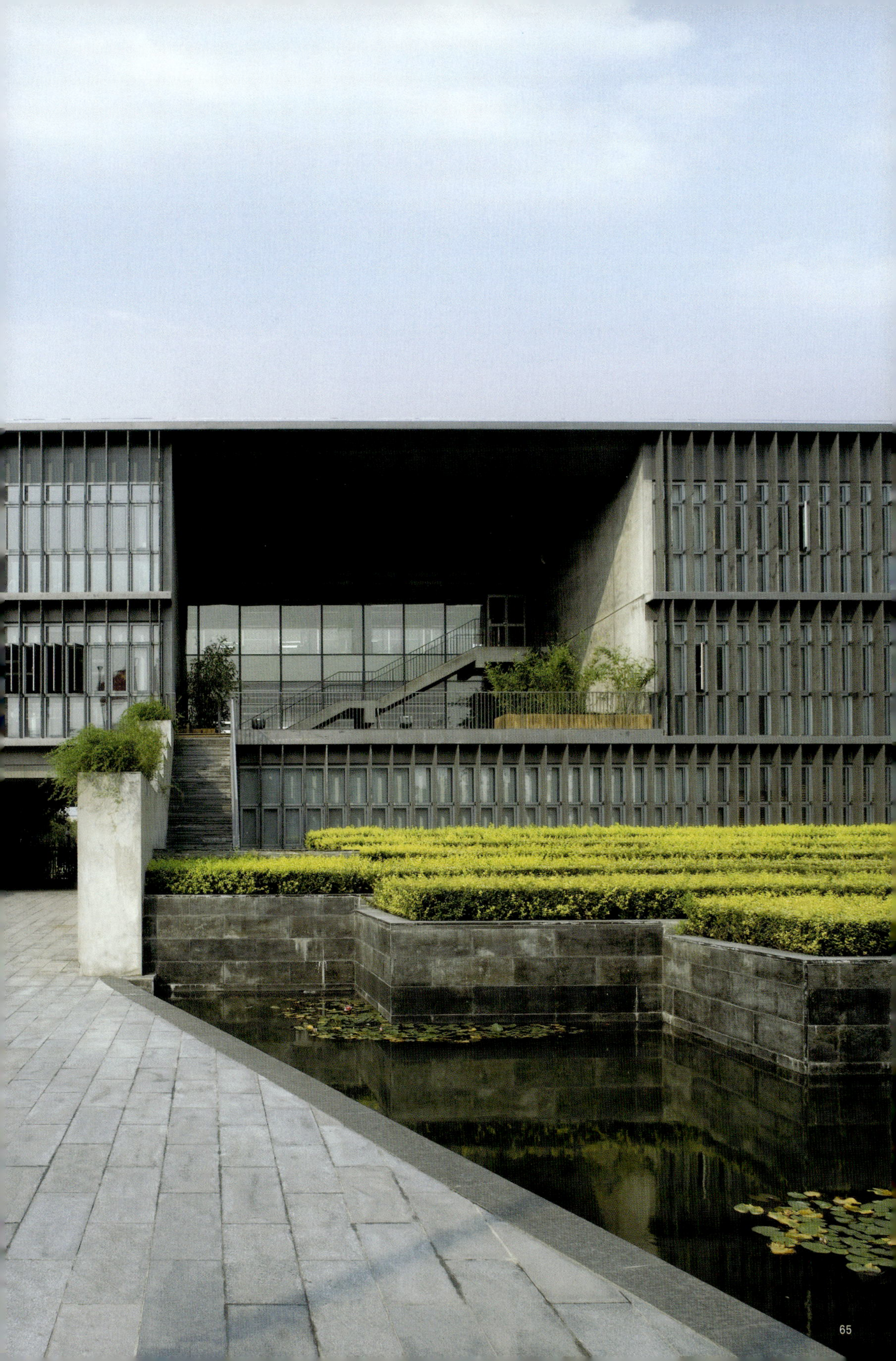

The style is international and the site is Chinese, between the city and the water. This building by Liu Jiakun overlooks a composite site in progress in the municipality of Qingpu next to Shanghai.

The former mayor, Sun Jiwei, who is an urban planning graduate of Tongji University, called on Liu Jiakun to work in his city just as he called on some of the other most prestigious contemporary Chinese architects such as Ma Qingyun and the Deshaus studio. This is a universe of towers with no other logic than their view of little Lake Xiayang. Ma Qingyun's serpentine building has a cultural calling, a little farther on lies the colourful nursery school by Deshaus, and then comes the long low block designed by Liu Jiakun: which of these buildings came first? The speed of construction here has perhaps led the Sichuan architect to conceive this long building as a protective wall, as a snake-mountain which can provide a feng shui favourable to the composite landscape.

This is quite logical since it is here that building permits are issued, here that the city exhibits its projects and here, as in all the cities of the country, that a very small number of civil servants manage the urban planning of a town as large as a medium-sized city in Europe.

The façade is sombre, almost black. In reality, it forms a succession of full and empty spaces, the full ones bordered by dark glass façades or sunshades of vertical stones. The empty spaces create shadows, courtyards of sorts or secret gardens from which arises perhaps the impression that an almost-black grey is the dominant colour here.

In the interior, the circulations prove to be rather linear and horizontal and are interrupted by baffles. In the exterior, the main façade of the building overlooking the lake is separated from the road system by a long trench and a broad swathe of lawn which lends an unexpected majesty to this temple of urban paperwork.

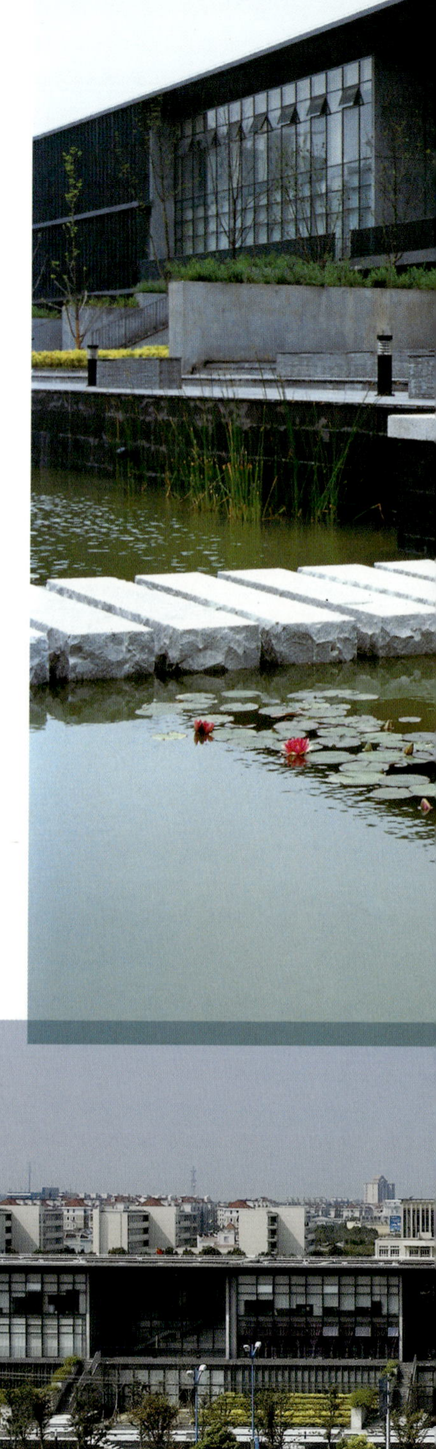

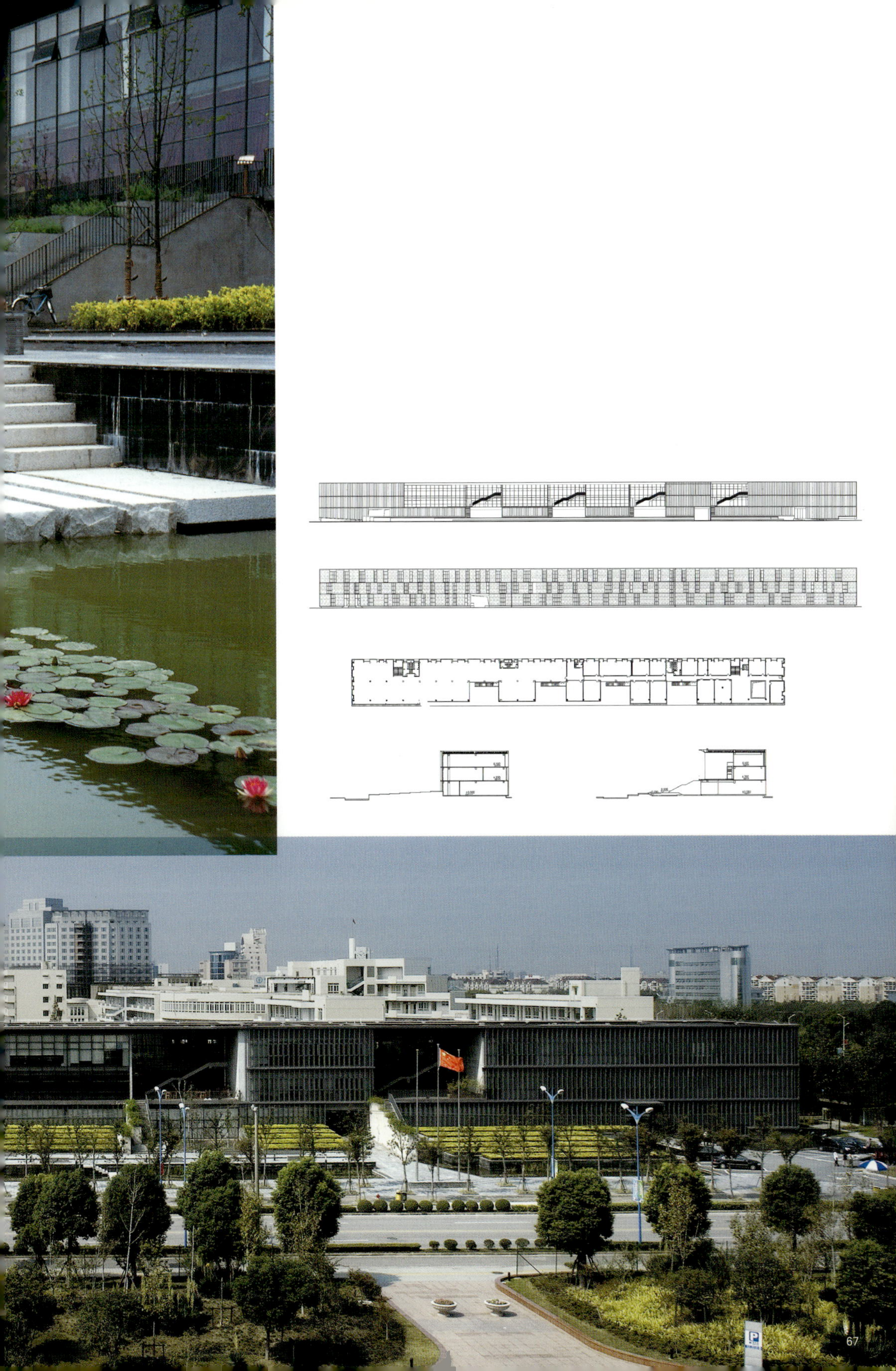

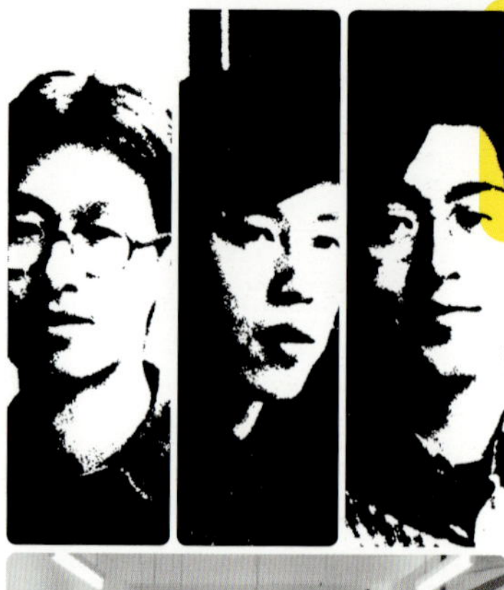

Deshaus 大舍建筑设计事务所
Liu Yichun 柳亦春, **Zhuang Shen** 庄慎, **Chen Yifeng** 陈屹峰

A certain Western tropism may doubtless mark the way in which we consider the achievements of the Chinese architects. Are they excessively influenced by their Western counterparts and by the reading of journals, or are they on the contrary virtuously attached to the contemporary restitution of traditional forms?

The adventure of the Deshaus studio ("dashe" in Chinese means "large dwelling") lets one imagine the emergence of a generation which finds its talent and roots first in the instinctive and then in the reflective cognition or recognition of what would form the components of today's China.

The three leading figures of the studio are Liu Yichun, 39 years, Zhuang Shen, 37 years, and Chen Yifeng, 36 years. At this point in their joint career, they appear indissociable and while Liu Yichun is often their spokesman, he effaces himself spontaneously before his two partners when the essence of their projects is evoked.

Their first undertaking was moreover their common home: three twin buildings in which they have gathered their families. It is perhaps there as well that these three former students of Tongji have abandoned their last references to the forum of classic modernity. All but nothing of their joint work would deserve to be left out of this presentation. A large part of it is assembled at Qingpu, thanks to the obstinacy of Sun Jiwei, who was then the deputy mayor of the city and who is also a Tongji graduate, just like the three architects. He gave them the chance there to express their talent in buildings with diverse functions: a branch of the Shanghai Chamber of Commerce, the Xiavu nursery school of Qingpu, and the clubhouse of the Renhengyunjie residential ensemble.

The first of the three buildings, with its hospital-like appearance, is completely closed to the public and forms what may be qualified as a sort of hardly agreeable "political office", while the second building prevents children from leaving before their parents arrive.

The third one reflects the new orders of the promoters: the clubhouse is inseparable from a large complex of dwellings (just as was the sales pavilion of the homes sold off plan at the beginning of the decade) and it is reserved for the members of the community of the residential ensemble and their close friends.

The fourth edifice which we present here is located in the south of the country, on the grounds of the immense Dongguan Technology Institute, a university campus where the architects have erected three major buildings.

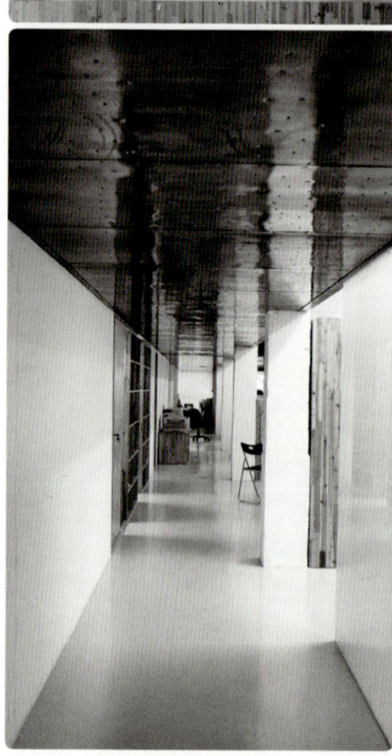

Partners
Liu Yichun 柳亦春
Born 1969
Master in architecture,
Tongji University, Shanghai, 1997
Zhuang Shen 庄慎
Born 1971
Master in architecture,
Tongji University, Shanghai, 1997
Chen Yifeng 陈屹峰
Born 1972
Master in architecture,
Tongji University, Shanghai, 1998
Office founded in 2001
Number of employees: 16
Turnover 2007: 500 000 € approx

Contact
Atelier Deshaus
C3-202 Red Town
N° 570 West Huaihai Rd
Shanghai 200052 China
T: +86 21 61 24 81 18
F: +86 21 61 24 81 19
info@deshaus.com
www.deshaus.com

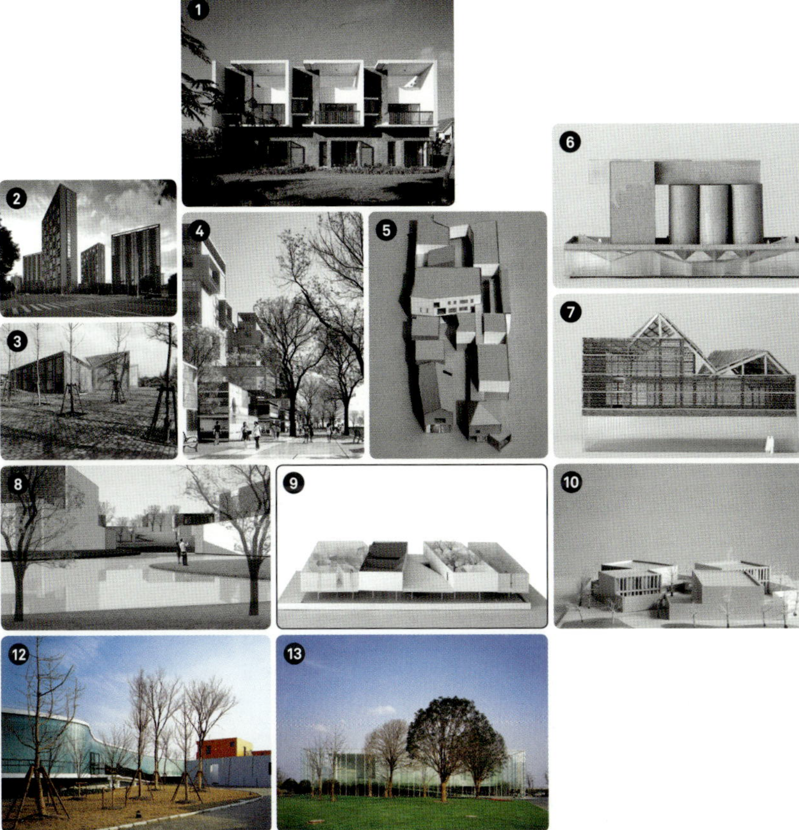

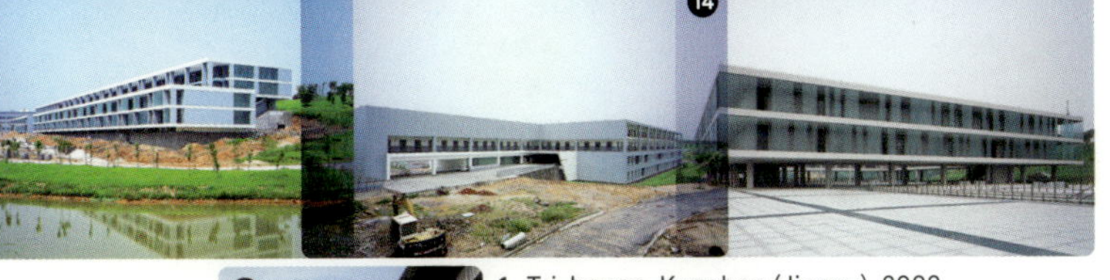

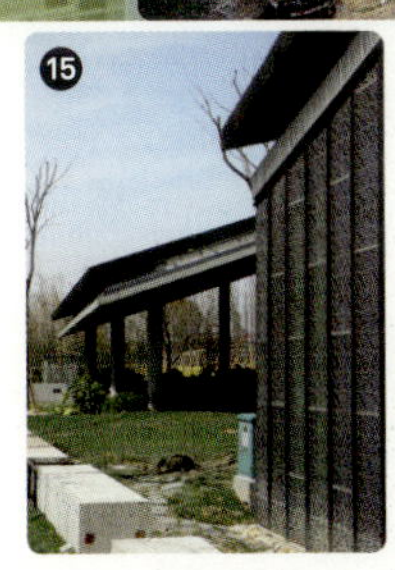

1 Tri-house, Kunshan (Jiansu), 2003.
2 Beyond City residential area,
   Hangzhou (Zhejiang), 2007.
3 Municipal Navigation Administration House of
   Zhujiajiao, Qingpu (Shanghai), 2004.
4 Han Lin Fu Di residential area,
   Jiaxing (Zhejiang), 2007.
5 Shang Du Li shopping centre, Qingpu, 2004.
6 National Museum, Qingpu, 2006.
7 Restaurant, Qingpu, 2006.
8 Bureau N park, Nankin (Jiangsu), 2006.
9 Zhu Clubhouse, Qingpu, 2006.
10 Hydrological research unit, Qingpu, 2007.
11 Qiuxia garden, Shanghai, 2008.
12 Xiayu nursery school, Qingpu, 2004.
13 Shanghai Business Association, Qingpu, 2005.
14 Dongguan Institute of Technology, information
   technology department, electronics department
   and human sciences department, Dongguan, 2004.
15 Clubhouse of the Renhengyunjie residential
   ensemble, Qingpu, 2008.

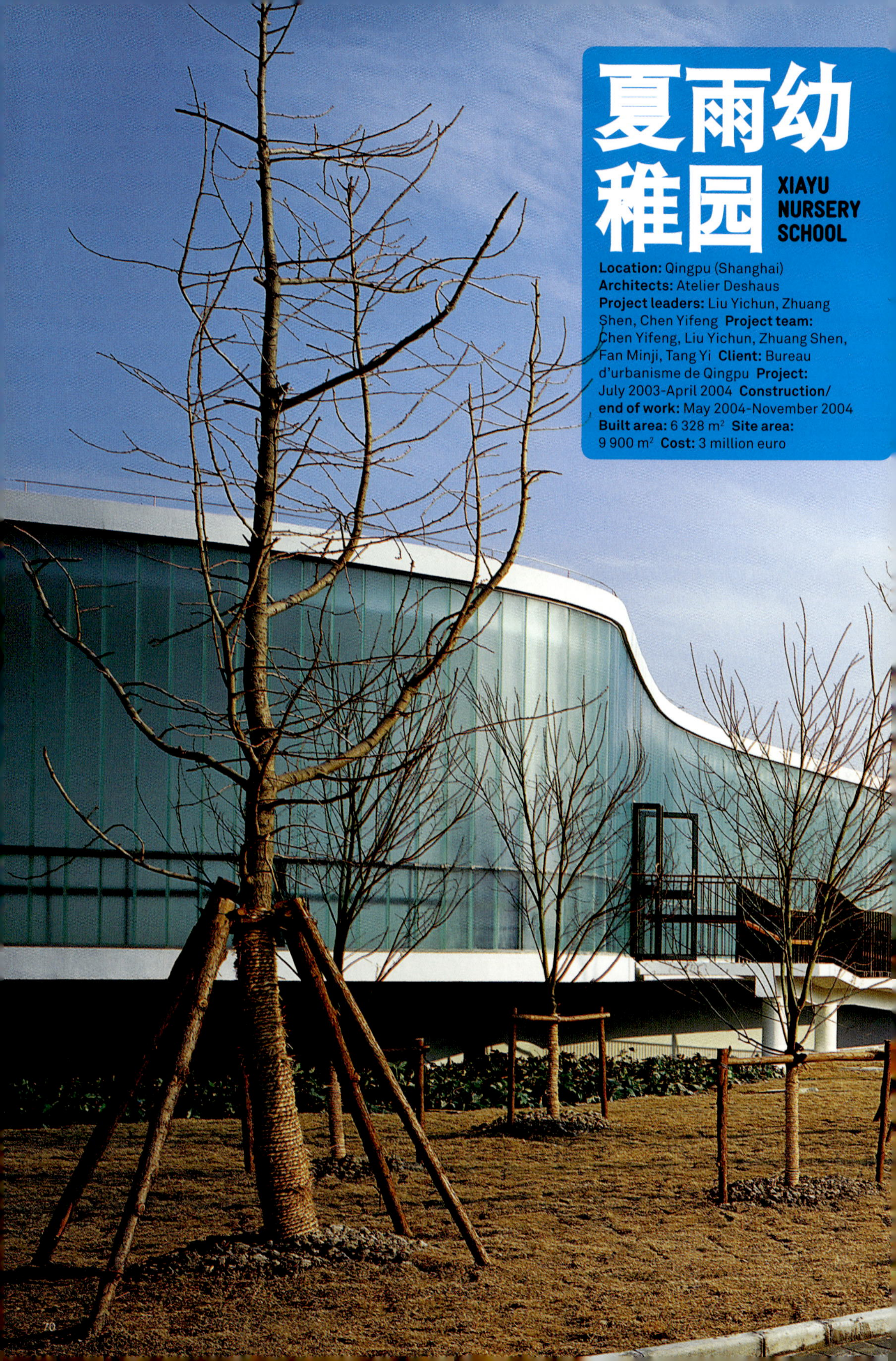

Location: Qingpu (Shanghai)
Architects: Atelier Deshaus
Project leaders: Liu Yichun, Zhuang Shen, Chen Yifeng **Project team:** Chen Yifeng, Liu Yichun, Zhuang Shen, Fan Minji, Tang Yi **Client:** Bureau d'urbanisme de Qingpu **Project:** July 2003–April 2004 **Construction/ end of work:** May 2004–November 2004 **Built area:** 6 328 m² **Site area:** 9 900 m² **Cost:** 3 million euro

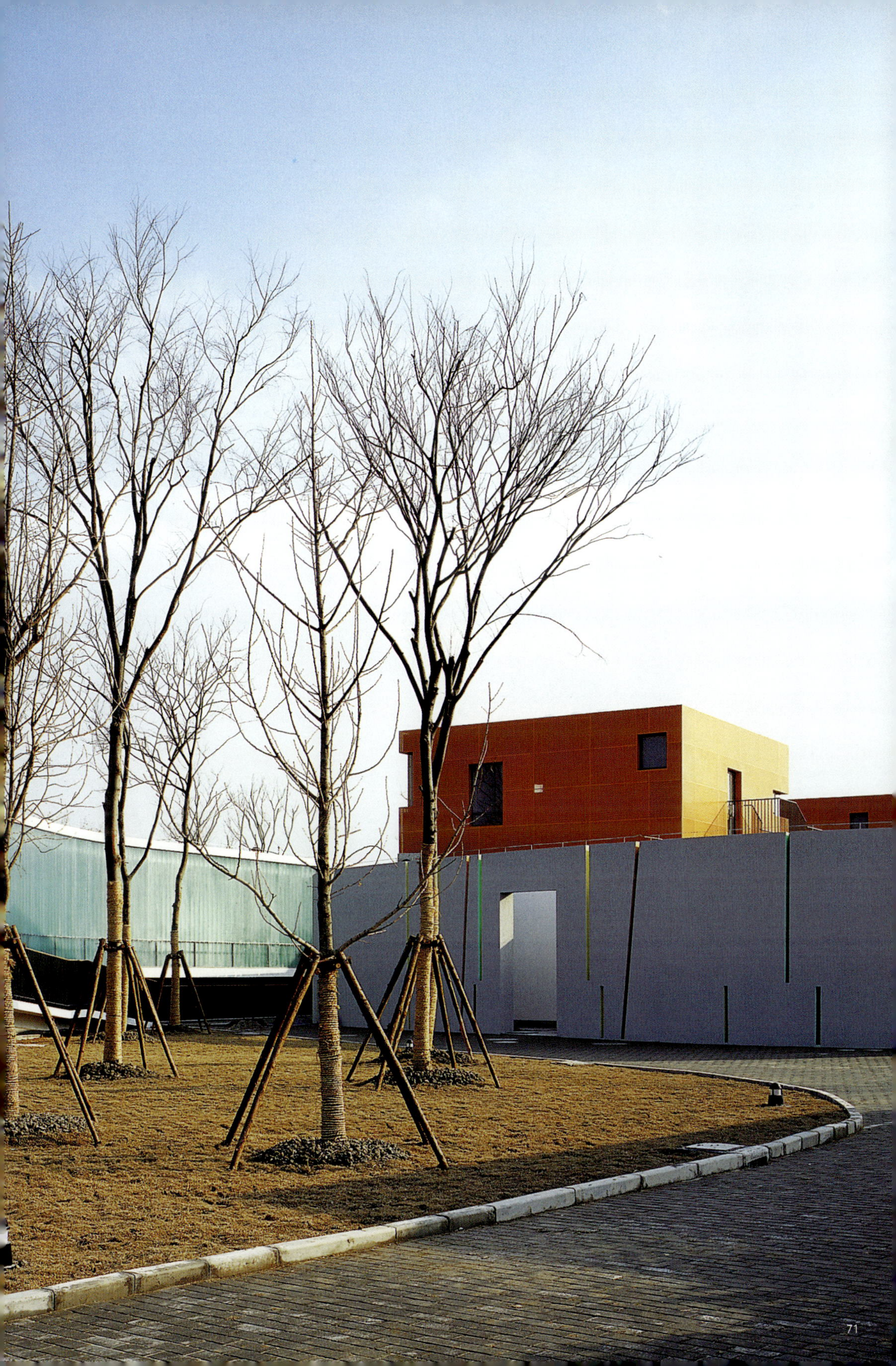

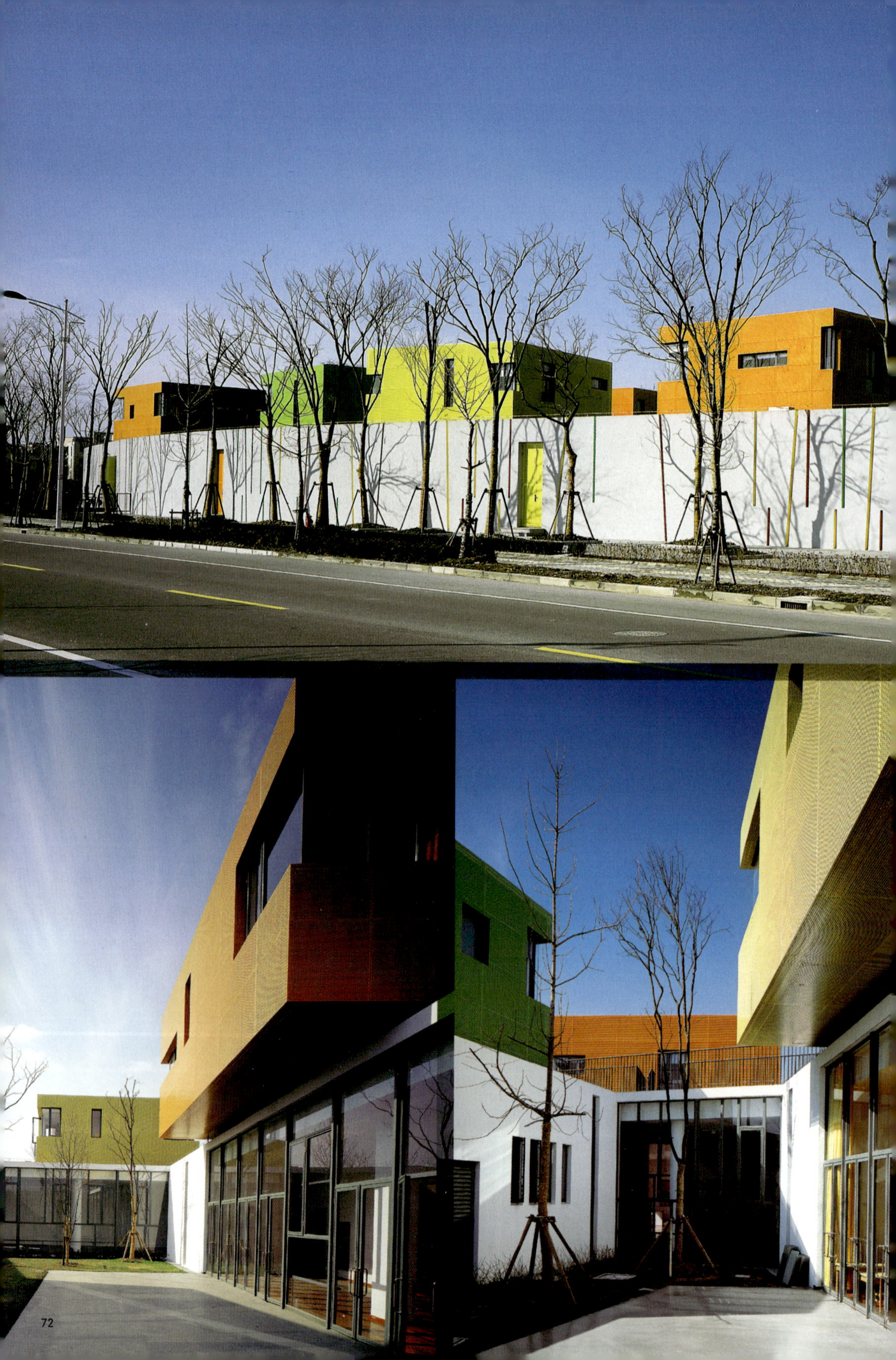

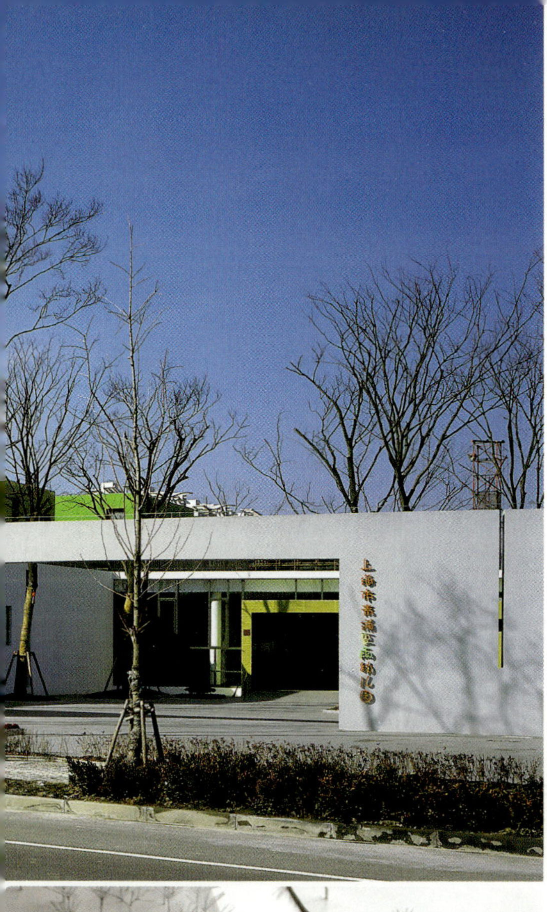

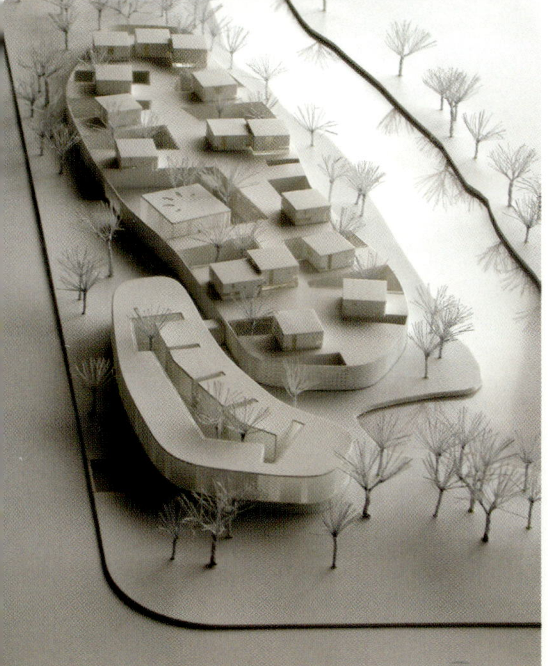

We are all acquainted with the way that adults, on visiting a nursery school, often ponder their own first steps and dream about a return to their childhood. This is a risky practice, however, which may lead to the rest-home.

Here Deshaus has designed a wonderful ensemble but it is one in which the proportions and circulations do away with this fusional phenomenon between children and adults. There is an adult universe here of course, which brings together the teachers according to spatial rules on their own scale. Likewise, there is a set of circulations which may be easily shared by adults and children, as well as a specific world for children, a different setting designed like something from a fairytale or a dream, distributing the elements of play at the height of the little ones, so as to allow them to climb up to the roofs as if they were playhouses.

The block plan of the whole, since here we must remain within the sphere of architecture, resembles a path through a forest in order to distance itself all the more from the structurally austere institutions, inherited for better from the decade of the Chinese reconstruction in the 1950s.

The numerous courtyards are planted with trees, the fronds of which, in the springtime, meet those of other trees growing round the nursery school. Each volume is coloured, more as a reference than to designate a function, giving the impression from afar of floating in the canopy of the trees.

The Qingpu nursery school stands by a canal, the last one before a vast extension which is as yet without an urban assignment. In the opposite direction lies lake Xiayang, which is the site of Ma Qingyun's Thumb Island, a promenade and a commercial and cultural centre. In the distance, Liu Jiakun's urban planning office and, a few steps from there, the branch of the Chamber of Commerce. All told, a still hollow landscape waiting to be filled by the children of Qingpu.

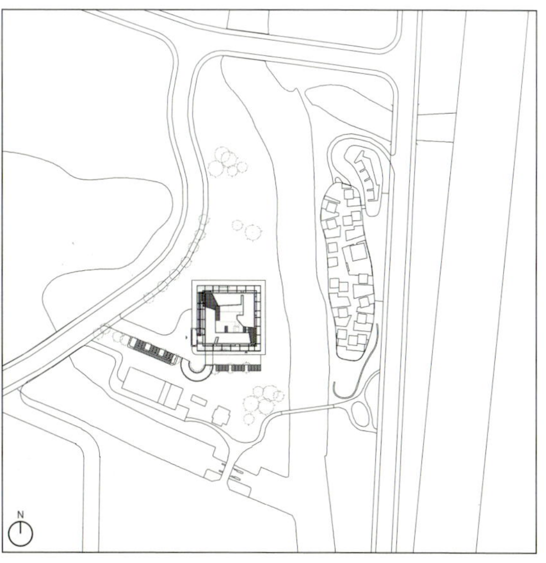

青浦私营企业协会办公楼

SHANGHAI BUSINESS ASSOCIATION QINGPU BRANCH OFFICE

Location: Qingpu (Shanghai) **Architects:** Deshaus **Project leaders:** Liu Yichun, Zhuang Shen, Chen Yifeng **Project team:** Zhuang Shen, Chen Yifeng, Liu Yichun, Tang Yi, Chen Jiang **Client:** Qingpu Business Association **Project:** August 2003-May 2004 **Construction/end of work:** January 2005-September 2005 **Built area:** 6 745 m² **Site area:** 8 773 m² **Cost:** 2 million euro

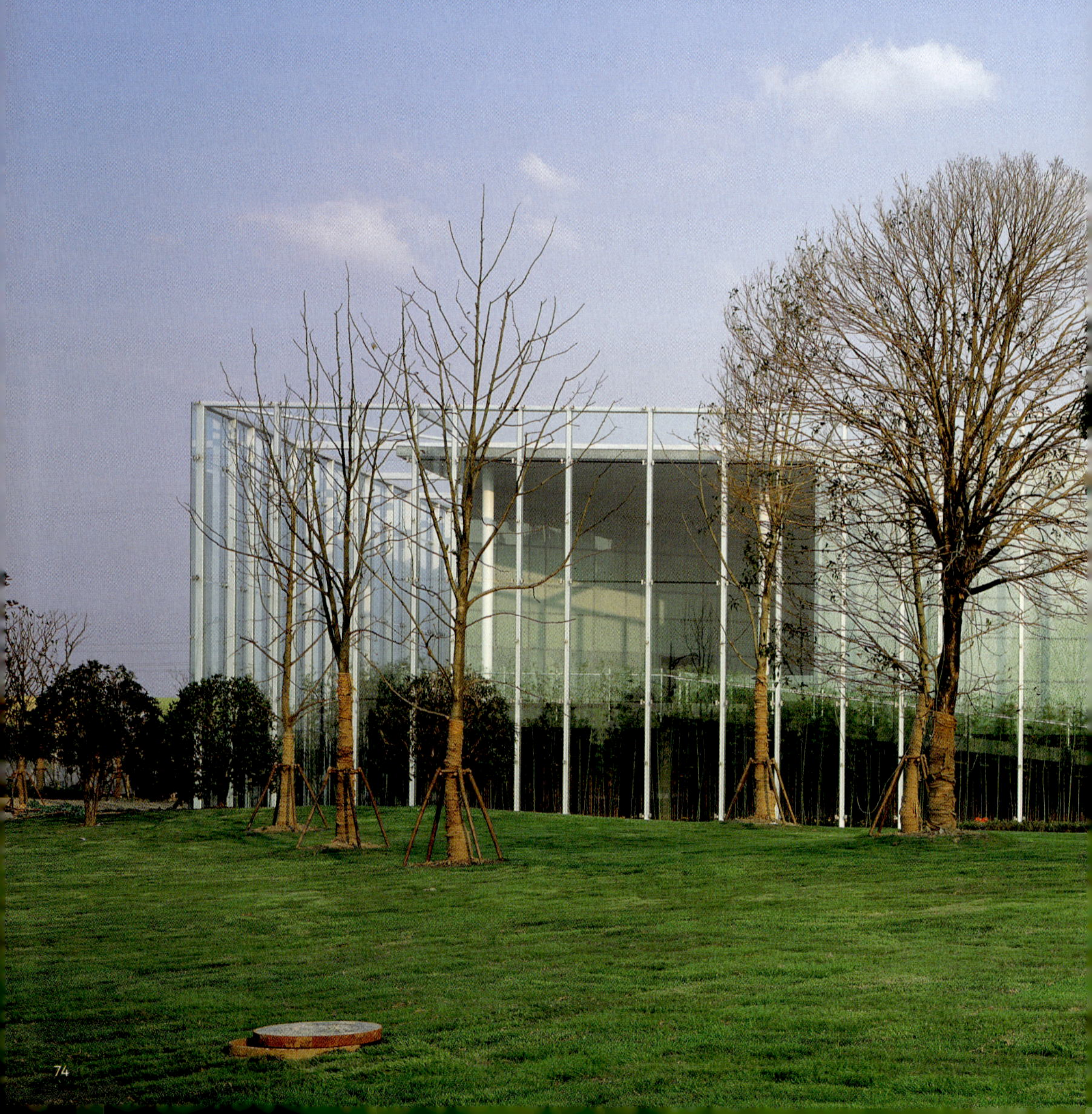

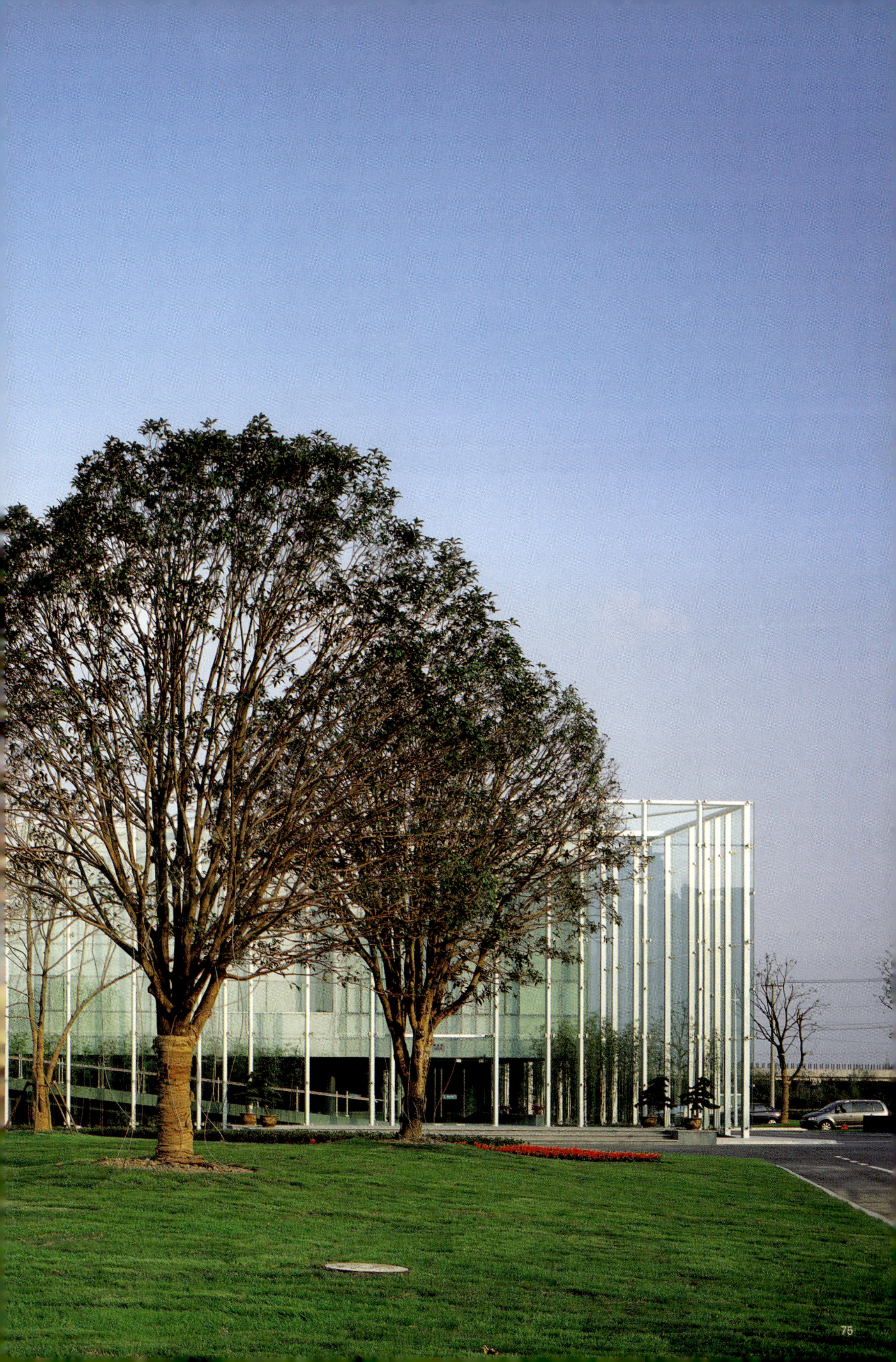

On the banks of the little lake Xiayang, near the nursery school, lies this large edifice on a square plan measuring sixty metres along each side, organised round a courtyard which is likewise square or nearly so, and partly occupied by a pond and a garden. A few stones placed here and there underscore its kinship with a garden of a more Japanese air than those of Suzhou or Jiangnan. The building stands entirely on piles, which does not prevent it from remaining partly opaque to the gaze from the outside since it is protected by a large glass panel, doubled by a bamboo curtain with the twofold advantage of isolating the structure from view while opening to the interior garden. It is also opaque in the interior courtyard, thanks to the falsely translucent glass of the façades which is declined according to a motif of random fragmentations, taken from the meticulously sculpted woodwork of the residences of the Jiangnan literati.

The whole of the building is surrounded by slender white steel columns, the choice of which may be perplexing, beyond their function of supporting the glass curtain behind which is concealed a set of offices with a less than welcoming appearance. Ill at ease between the model of the square courtyard space and a far-off reminiscence of Mies or Charreau, Deshaus appears a bit awkward on the inside. Benevolent spirits may see there an embryonic manifestation of feng shui: one part of the building which is cantilevered over the courtyard seems to be set to launch an assault on the old Qingpu (which is the reason for the free space left on the opposite side in an exterior corner of the building). The Western critic, however, may see more prosaically a vain effort of originality.

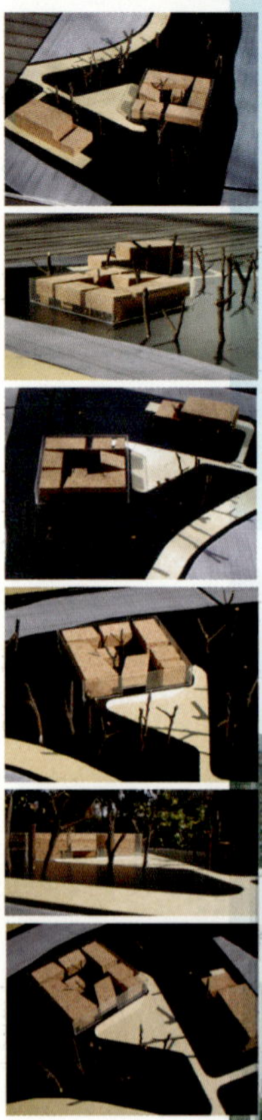

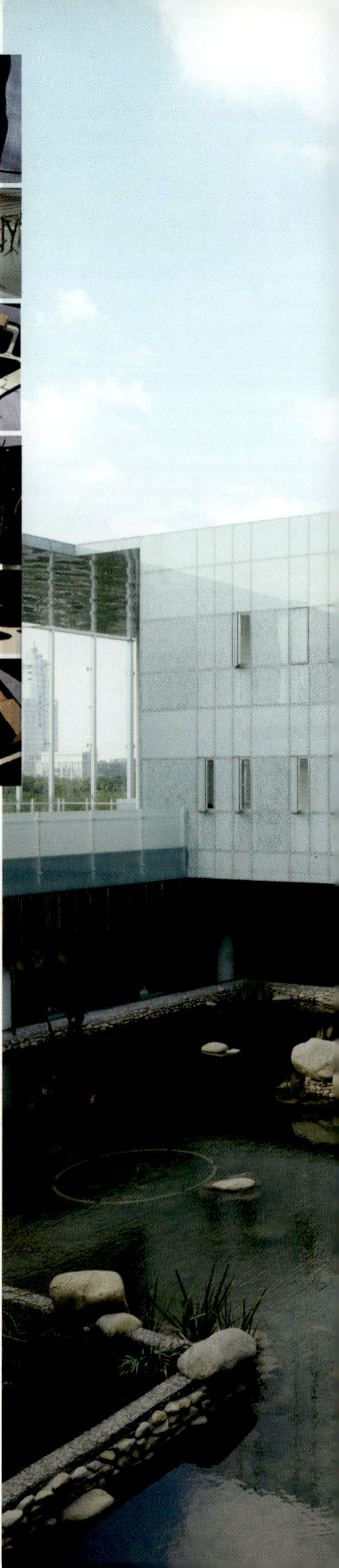

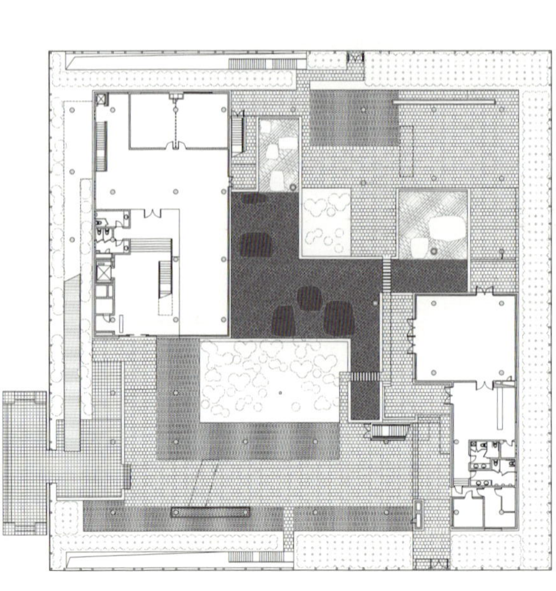

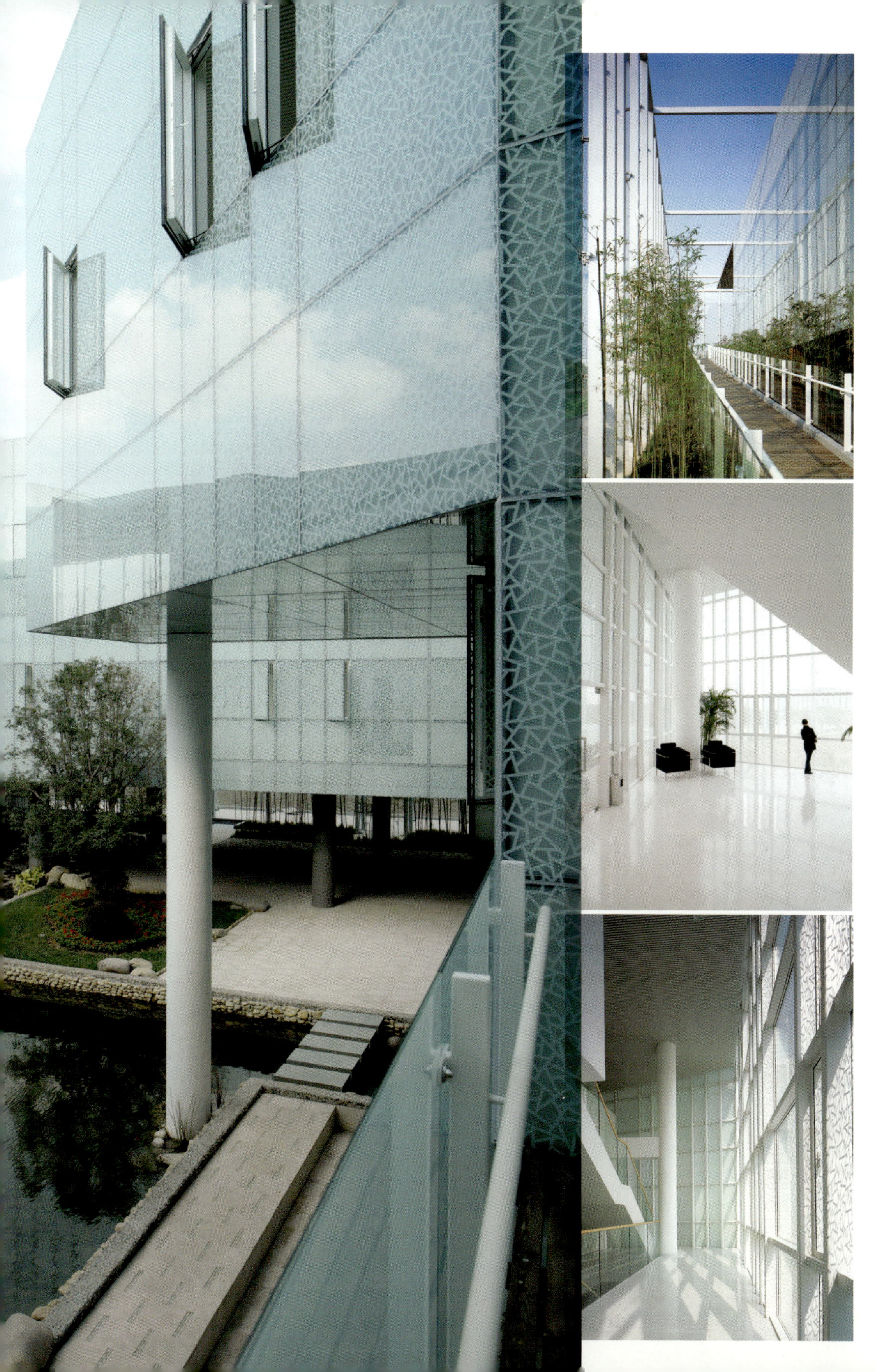

Location Dongguan (Guangdong) **Architects :** Atelier Deshaus **Project leaders:** Liu Yichun, Zhuang Shen, Chen Yifeng **Project team:** Tang Yi, He Yangsong **Client:** Management comittee of the new Songshanhu area **Project:** August 2002-March 2003 **Construction/end of work :** January 2003-August 2004 **Built area:** 45 320 m² **Site area:** 73 000 m² **Cost:** approximately 5 million euro

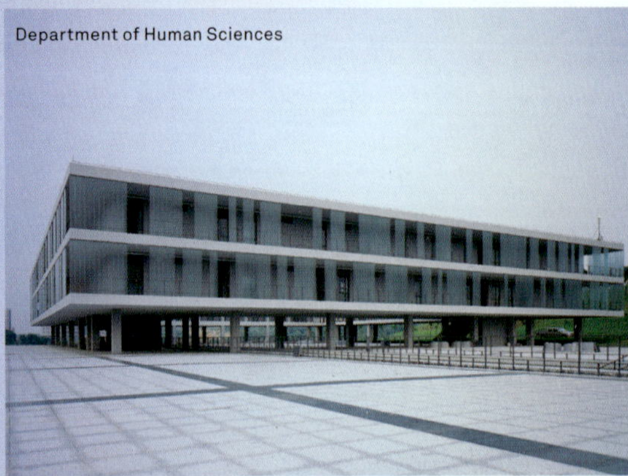
Department of Human Sciences

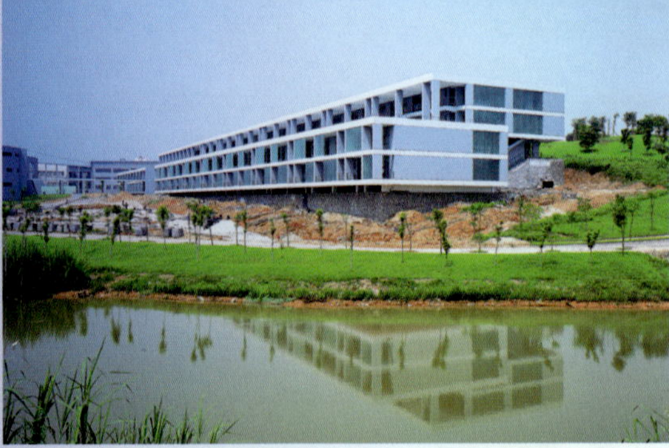
Department of Information Technology

Deshaus has made three buildings for the institute of technology of Dongguan (a city located between Canton and Shenzhen), comprising nearly forty-seven thousand square metres distributed on seven hectares of land. On beginning the project, the campus formed a strange desert where several well-known and lesser-known architecture studios of the new generation came to meet.

While one of the buildings, devoted to information technology (the Science and Computer Department) is a rectilinear volume closed off from the sun, the other two (the Liberal Arts Departments and the Electrical Engineering Technology Department) seem to play a more subtle game with the light, also imposed by the hot moist climate of southern China. Rooms with a dual orientation, opening onto high ventilated galleries providing protection from the sun and the rain, declined the constraints of the programme with simple implementations: speed of performance and delivery (a university building site to be delivered in one year) and a limitation and even prohibition of air conditioning in the structures. Closed or not, both types of buildings present the simple form of a rectangle or square around empty spaces which seem destined more to distribute the volumes without excess distances rather than to create truly enclosed spaces or courtyards. It is in the thickness and in the cladding of the buildings, and sometimes also in their depth, that the ingenuity of Deshaus is clearly manifested, alternating openings and translucent elements around and at a distance from a core or, more exactly, a skeleton of buildings, with hardly readable educational functions. It is probably the need for versatility in these places which leads to their appearance at once austere and refined.

Department of Electronics

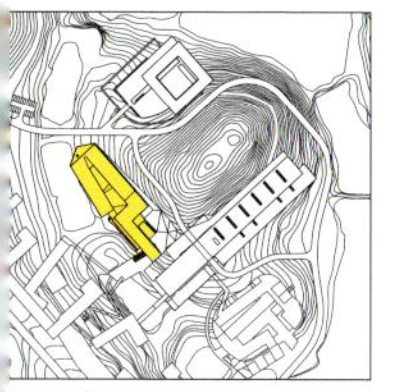

Department
of Electronics

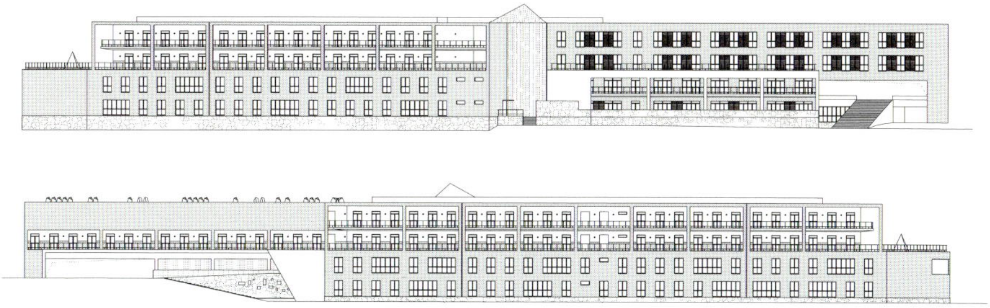

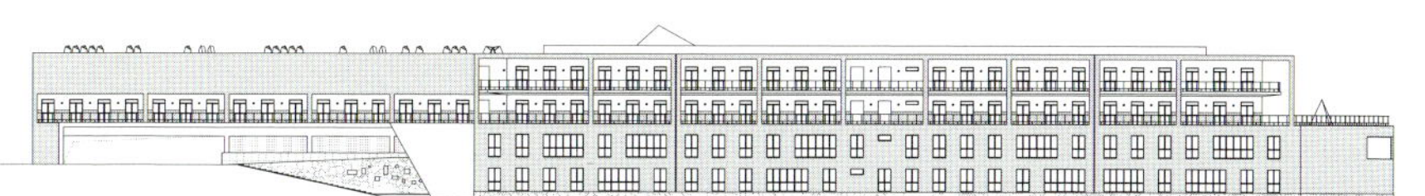

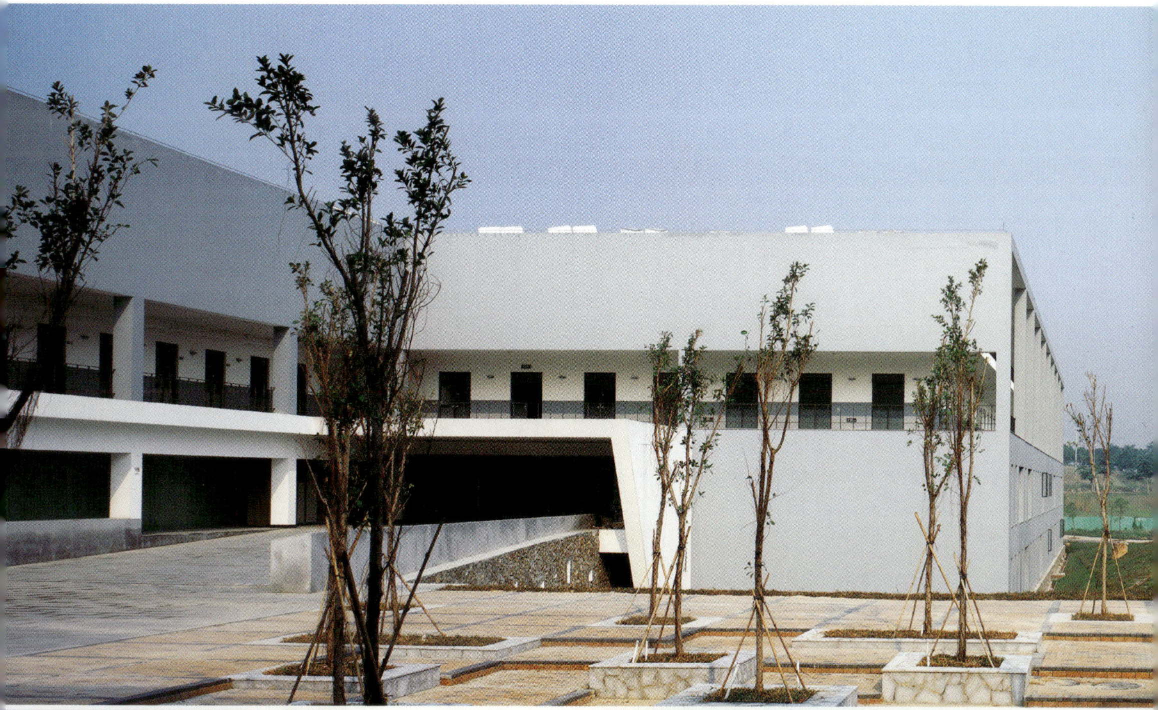

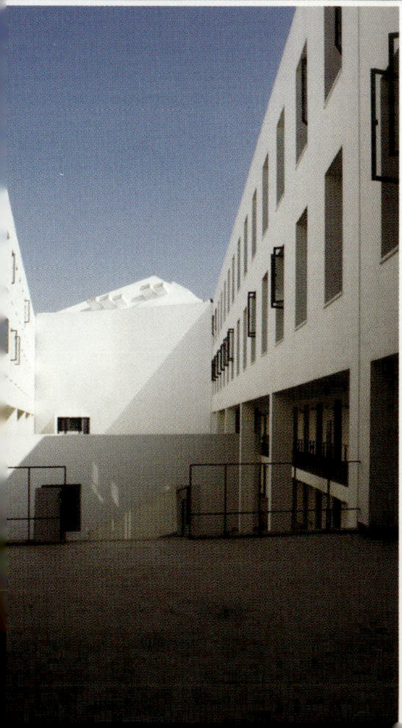

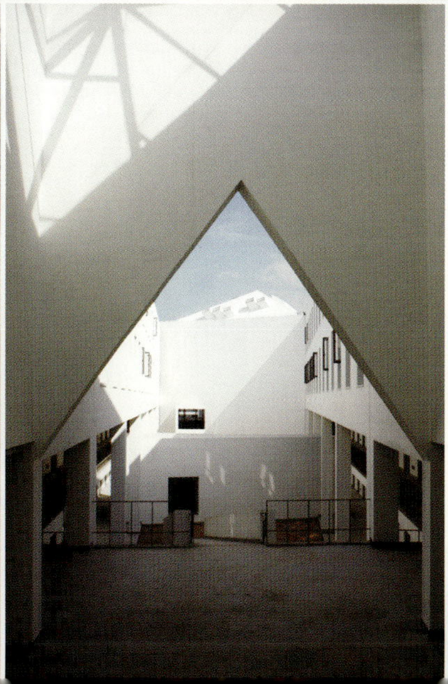

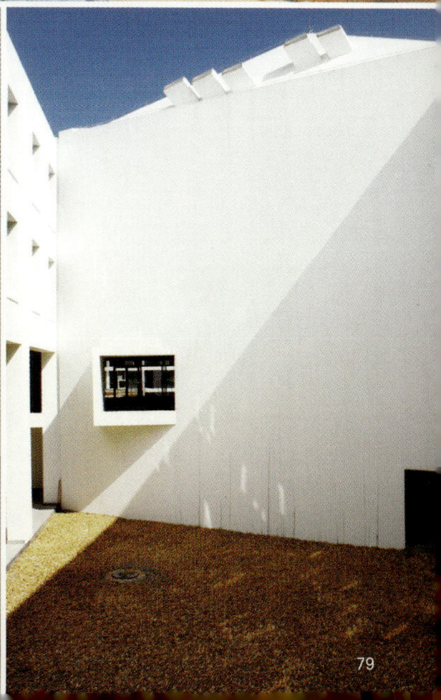

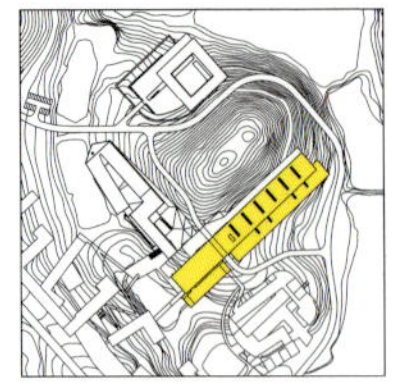

Department of
Information Technology

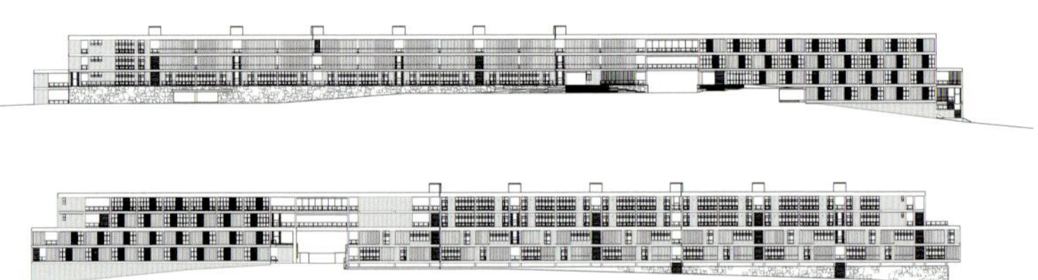

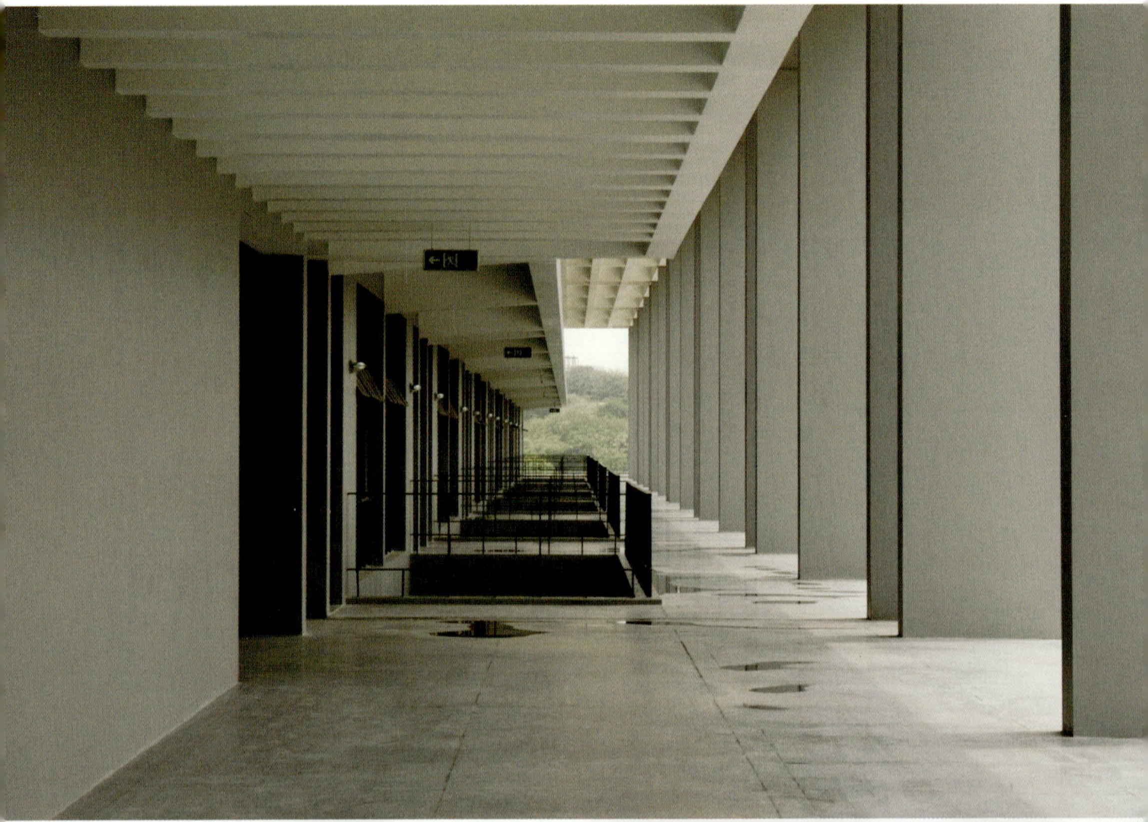

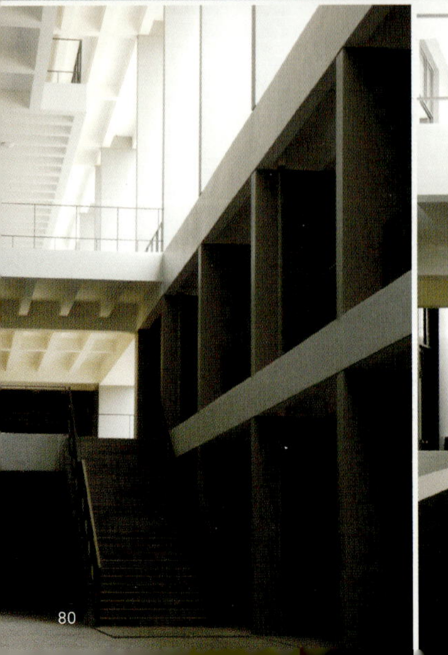

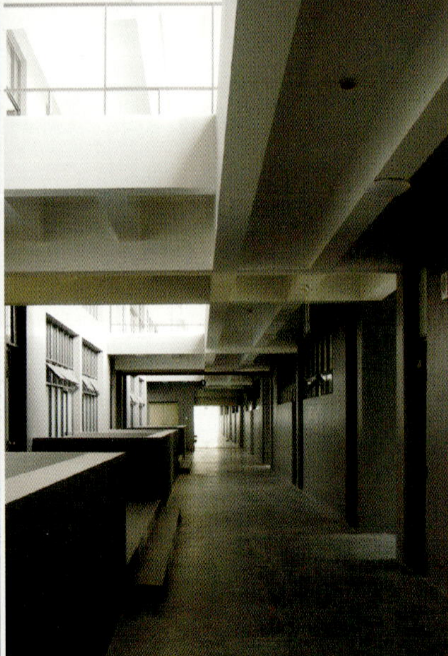

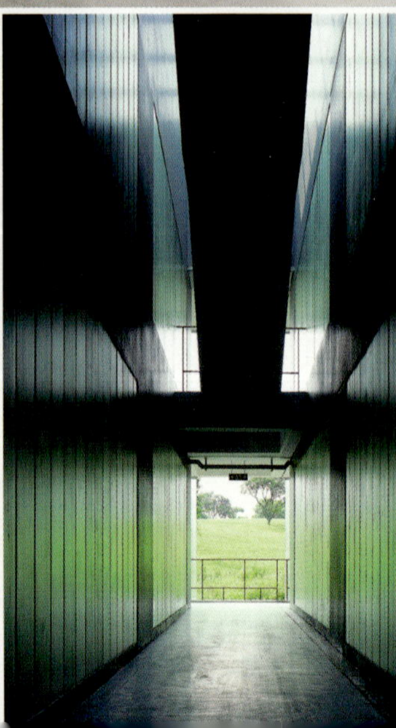

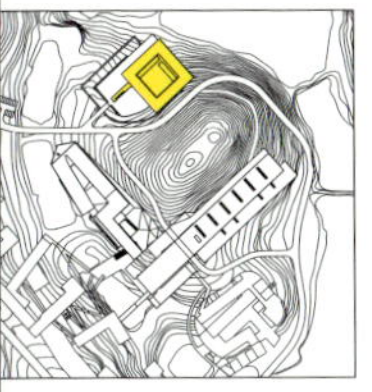

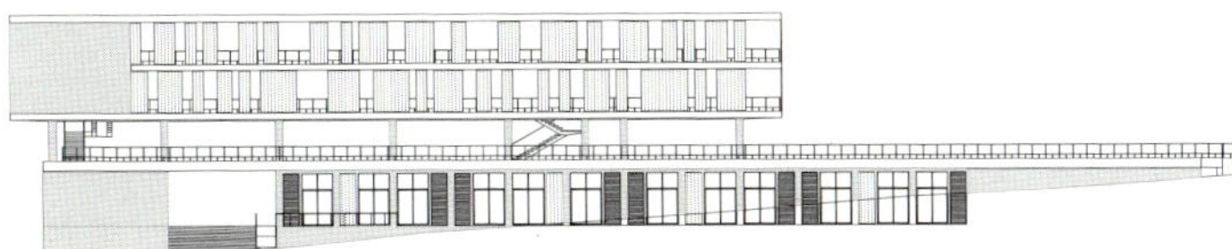

Department of
Human Sciences

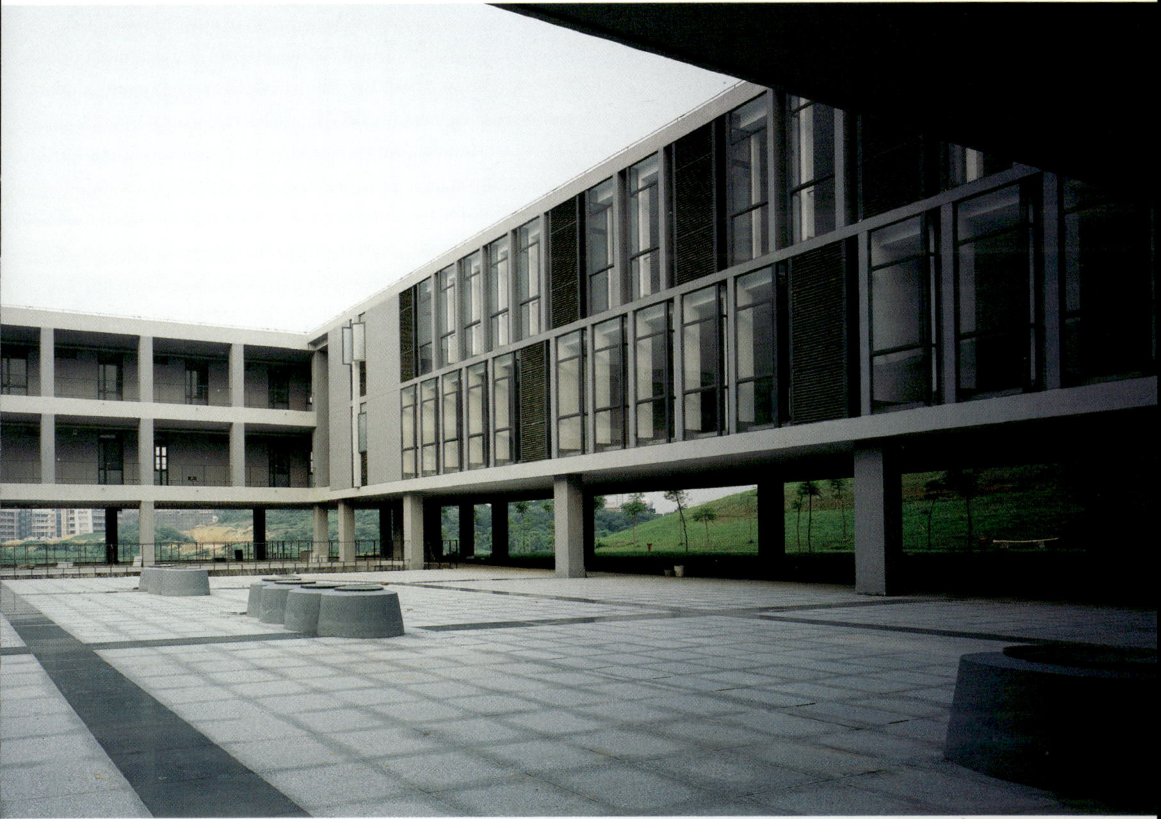

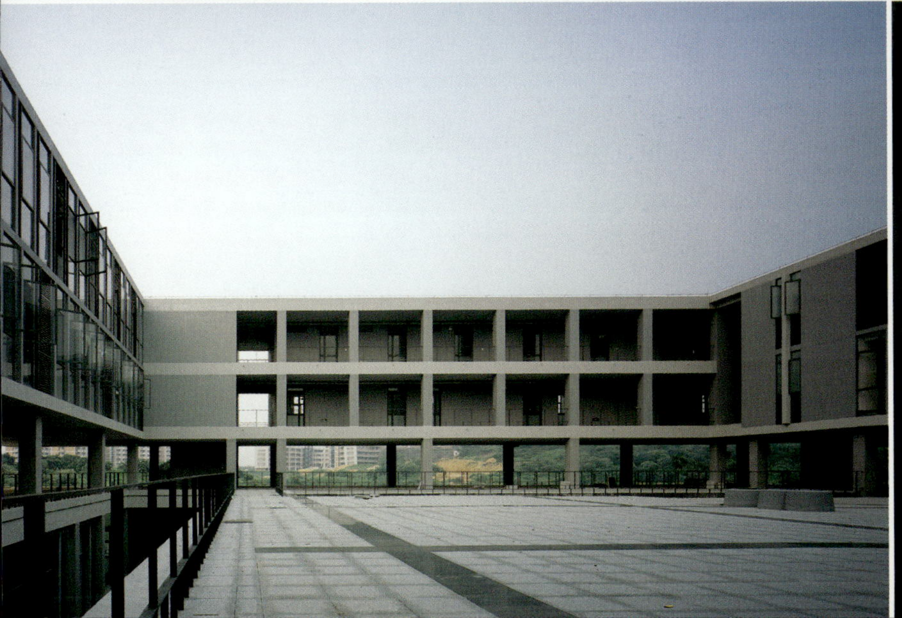

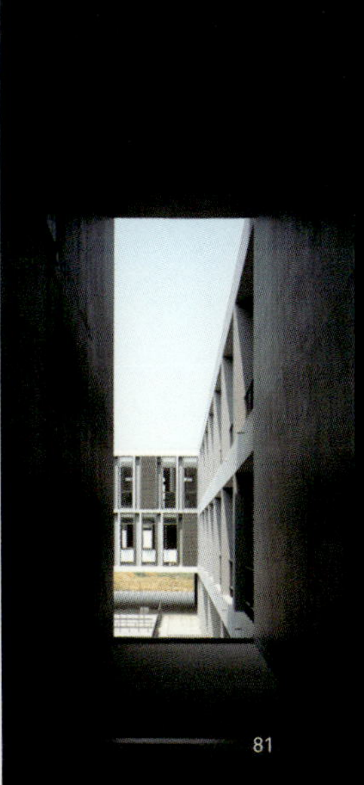

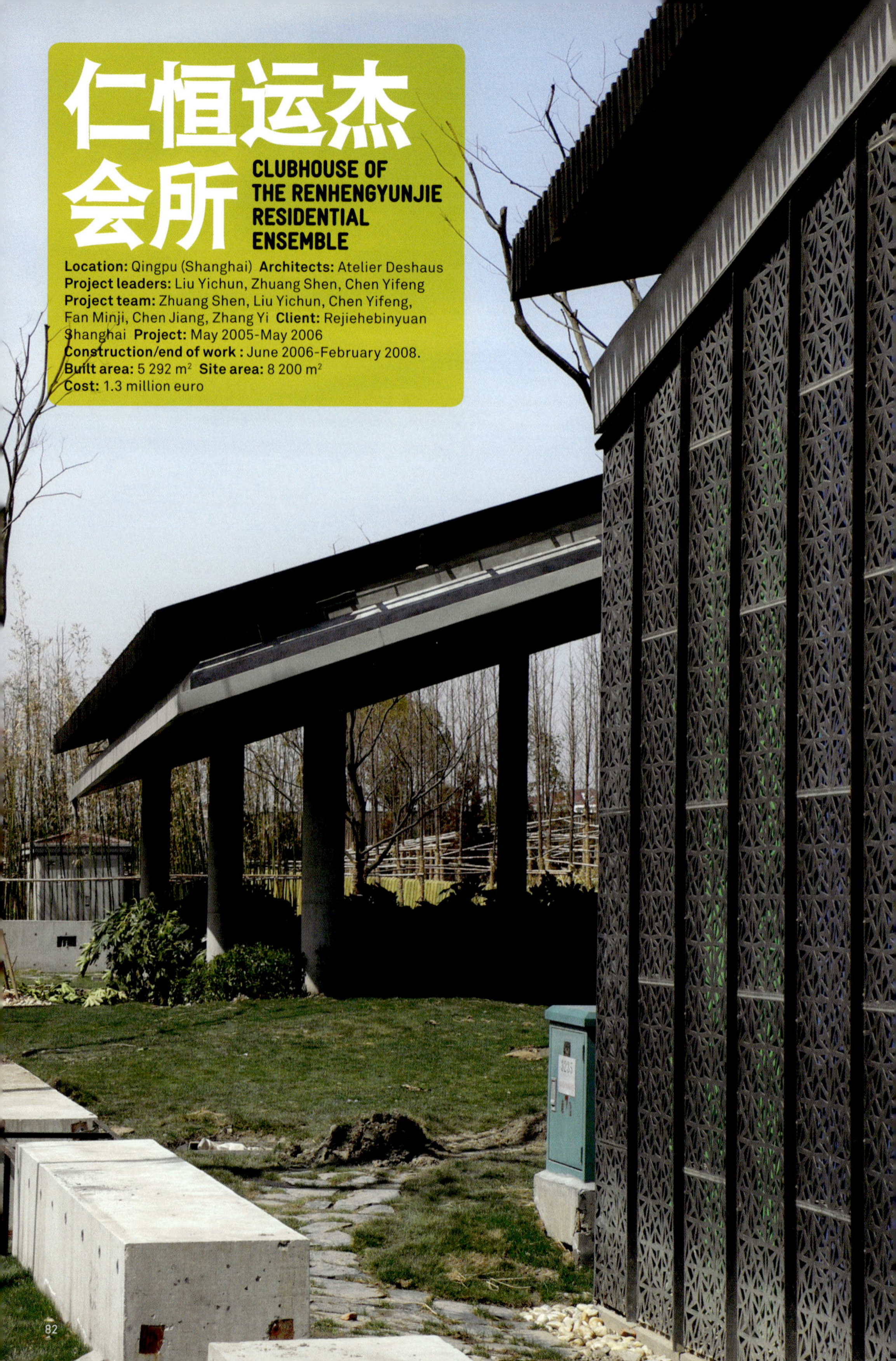

仁恒运杰
会所

CLUBHOUSE OF THE RENHENGYUNJIE RESIDENTIAL ENSEMBLE

Location: Qingpu (Shanghai) **Architects:** Atelier Deshaus
Project leaders: Liu Yichun, Zhuang Shen, Chen Yifeng
Project team: Zhuang Shen, Liu Yichun, Chen Yifeng, Fan Minji, Chen Jiang, Zhang Yi **Client:** Rejiehebinyuan Shanghai **Project:** May 2005-May 2006
Construction/end of work : June 2006-February 2008.
Built area: 5 292 m² **Site area:** 8 200 m²
Cost: 1.3 million euro

More than a unique building, for Deshaus it was a question of conceiving, by means of this double building, an ensemble of shelters which would be at once aesthetically homogeneous and distributed across a distance vast enough to allow irascible neighbours to avoid each other all year round or to permit the assembly, as is most often the case in China, of a friendly neighbourhood, with game-players of all ages, musicians, domino enthusiasts, tea or soda pop drinkers, contemplatives or tai-chi champions. These are all the functions which one finds in the parks of the big cities such as Beihai or Tiantan in Peking, Fuxing or the Bund in Shanghai. This translates into an alternation of open-air spaces, covered places without enclosures, closed halls and kiosks, which the Deshaus architects have laid out like a long segmented corridor not far from the river Dian. The Clubhouse, in effect, is linked to a set of dwellings intended for the community who have acquired a home there. Concealed in the frameworks, here one finds the soft colours of a nursery school designed by the same trio for the city. As if the present inhabitants of the residential ensemble, amid these vast volumes, could have to remember their first steps one day. The fragmentation recalls the tradition of covered alleys of the large and small gardens of the south and the north, but also, in a more modern way, the organisation of the public space on the banks of lake Hangzhou. This is a type of life and sharing which are almost unknown to our part of the world where these soul-supplements formed by common spaces are often forgotten. True enough, this type of residential ensemble is not the lot of all the Chinese, being accessible to relatively prosperous families of the cities alone. The architectural duty to which the promoter confines himself here is clearly pointed in the direction of a hope of social peace.

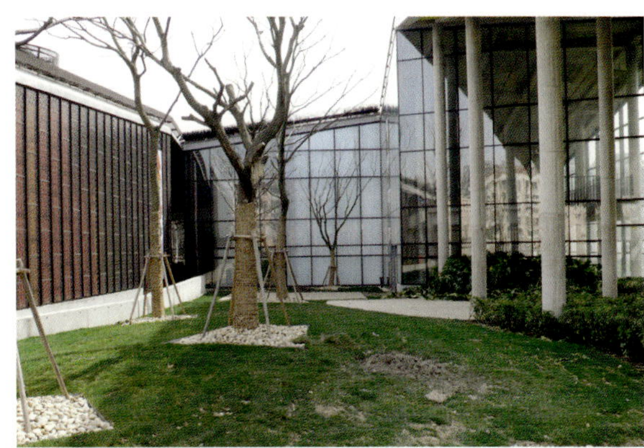

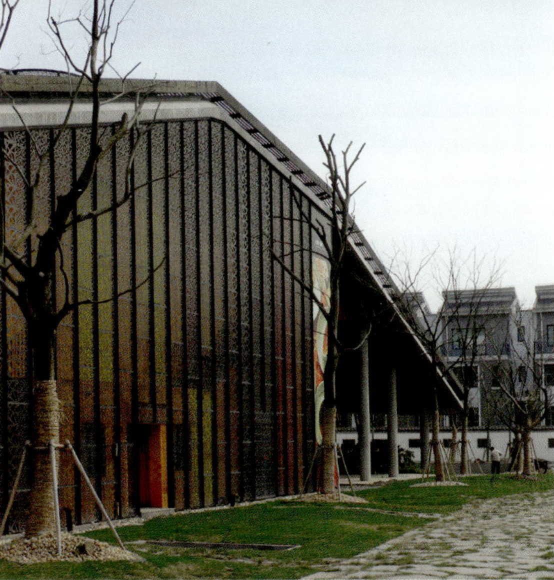

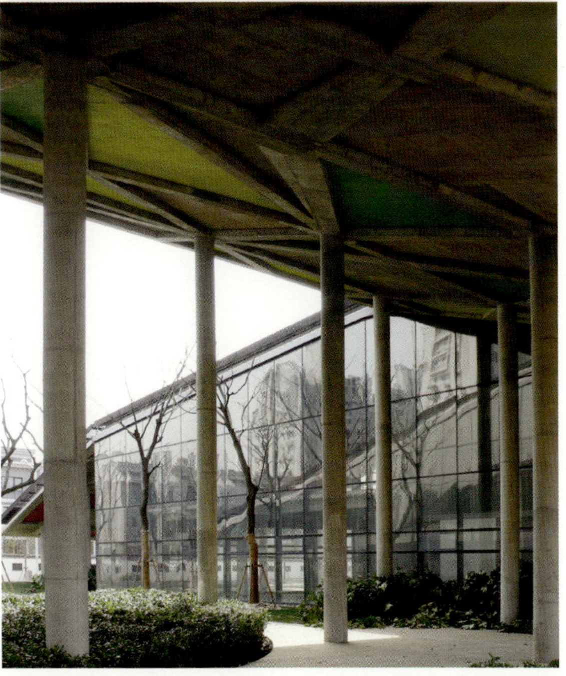

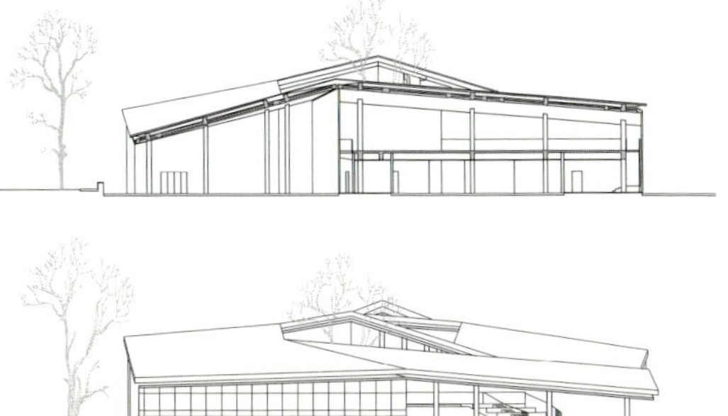

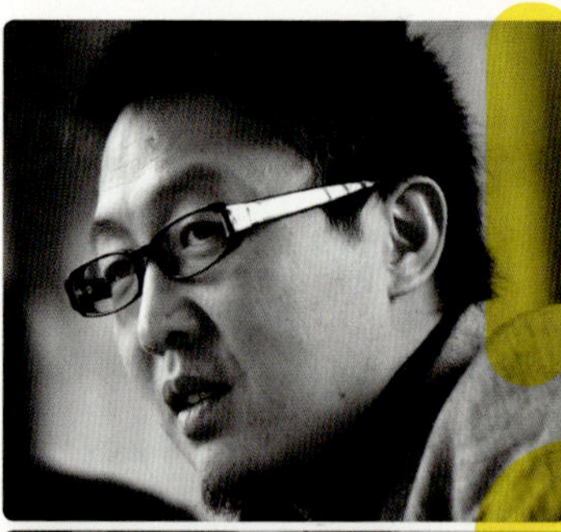

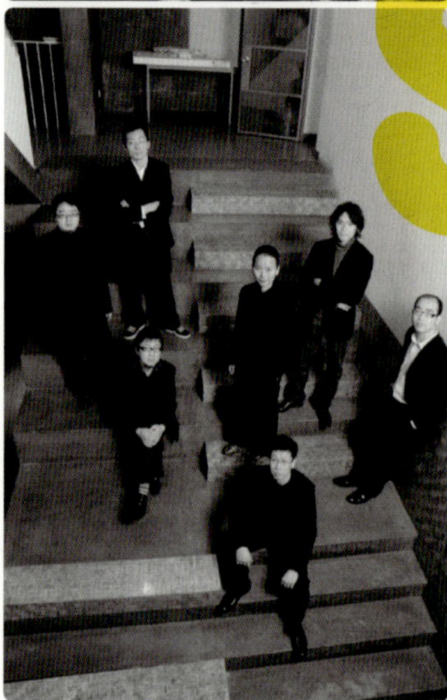

MADA s.p.a.m. 马达思班
MA Qingyun 马清运

Ma Qingyun comes from the heart of the ancient China, from Xi'an (Shaanxi province), where he was born in 1965. He recently stated in a conference at a Chinese university that he no longer knew very well to which reality his profession as an architect corresponds. A paradox of a renown too quickly achieved, or a provocation along the line of Rem Koolhas? Trained at the prestigious university of Tsinghua and a graduate of the University of Pennsylvania, he is indeed, like Koolhaas, a professor at Harvard.

Installed mainly in Shanghai today, he is building with his MADA Spam studio throughout the country. Deeply attached to his native land, this wine-lover is attempting to establish a vineyard in his father's village. In fact, it was for his father that he designed one of his first structures, a house in which he associated vigorously the vocabulary of tradition and the imaginary, at that time still highly reasoned, of modernity. Since then Ma has become specialised in interventions in ancient towns where, at the urban level, he takes up again the exercise carried out on his father's home.

At the Tianyi Centre in Ningbo, he has invented a commercial quarter, "CCD", which has become justifiably a reference thanks to its success. The city has also entrusted to him its urban planning museum near the old Bund and the art museum built by his colleague Wang Shu. While Wang Shu has proposed a timeless project, Ma has deployed a port vocabulary imbued with technical lyricism in his museum.

He does the same type of acrobatics at Qingpu. The immense shopping centre of this city near Shanghai associates a plurality of vocabulary tied to the traditions of walking in the hearts of the Chinese cities. In the same city, by the lake opposite the urban planning exhibition centre built by Liu Jiakun, Ma has made a building which is half-dragon and half-dock, of which the cultural and social calling has long survived. Nevertheless, remaining empty or unoccupied, this edifice with no precise name subsists as a demonstration of architecture on the limit of a construction toy. Since then Ma has not ceased to build, from Shanghai to Beijing, drawing on all the resources of contemporary vocabulary and especially techniques of diversely coloured glass, while always willingly preserving, in a somewhat playful way, the freedom to borrow from traditional techniques. Over the course of recent years, he has progressively acquired an international stature similar to that of his colleague Chang Yung Ho, but he also expresses a shadow of concern about the appearance on the Chinese scene of such personalities as Ma Yansong.

Partners
Ma Qingyun 马清运
Born 1965
Master in Architecture,
University of Pennsylvania, 1991
Chen Zhanhui 陈展辉
Born 1969
Master in Architecture,
Shenzhen University, 1992
Huang Rong 黃嶸
Born 1971
Bachelor in architecture,
Tongji University, Shanghai, 1994
Studio founded in 1990
Number of employees: 60

Contact
MADA s.p.a.m.
No. 2, Lane 134, Xinie Road, Xuhui District
Shanghai, China 200031
T: +86 (0) 21 5404 1166
F: +86 (0) 21 5404 6646
office@madaspam.com
www.madaspam.com

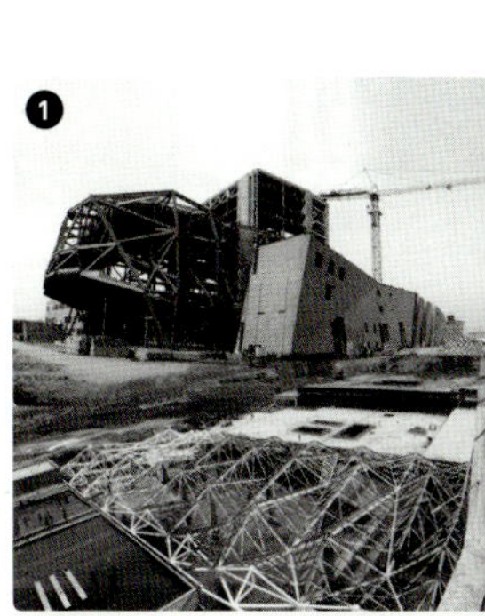
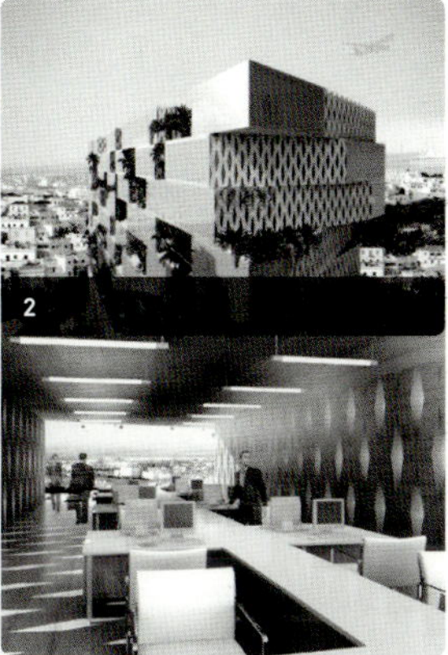
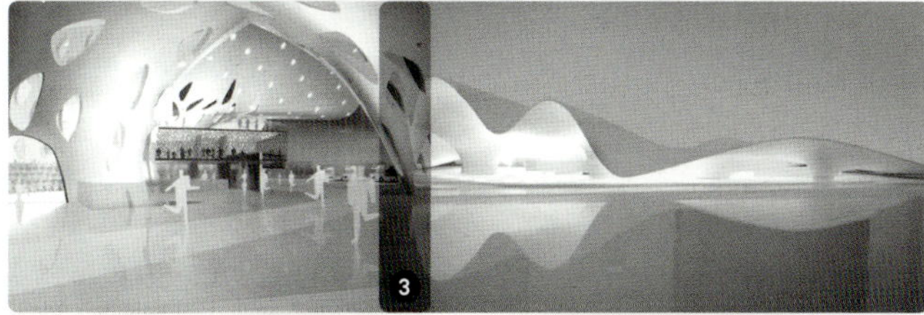
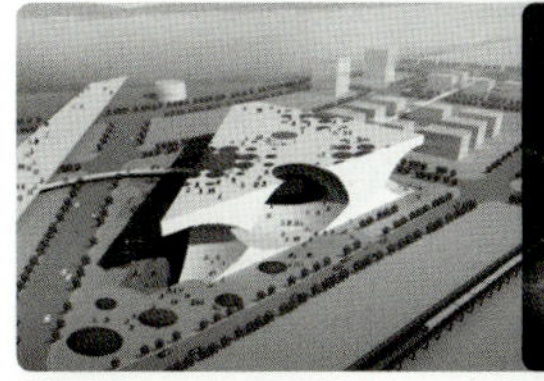
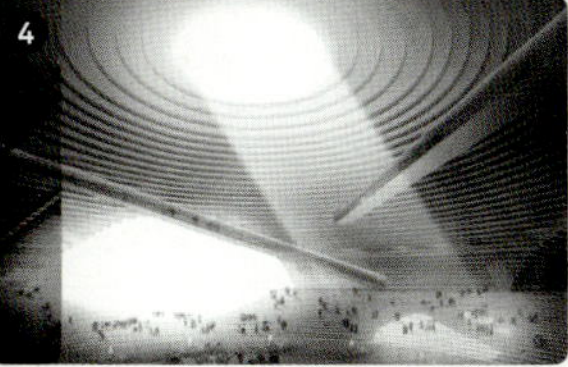
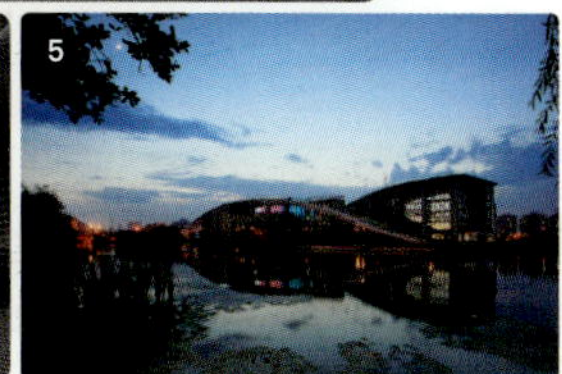
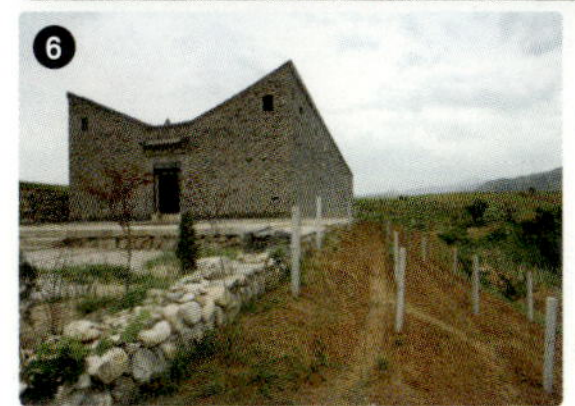
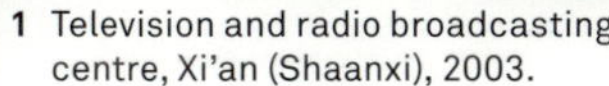
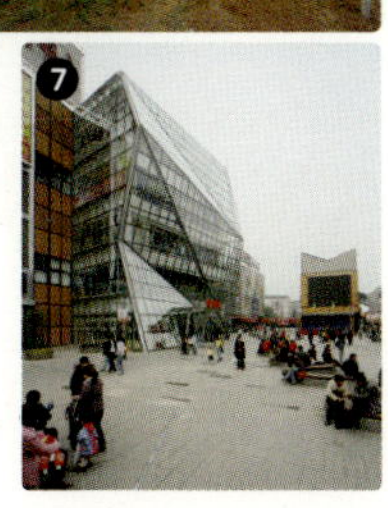

1 Television and radio broadcasting
centre, Xi'an (Shaanxi), 2003.
2 Airport office building
Hô-Chi-Minh-Ville (Vietnam),
2007 (unbuilt).
3 Renault Truckmon, Lyon, 2005
(unbuilt).
4 China pavillion for the World Exhibition
Shanghai 2010.
5 Thumb Island, Qingpu (Shanghai), 2006.
6 Jade Valley hotel-village,
Lantian (Xi'an), 2008.
7 Qiao Zi Wan shopping centre, Qingpu
(Shanghai), 2006.

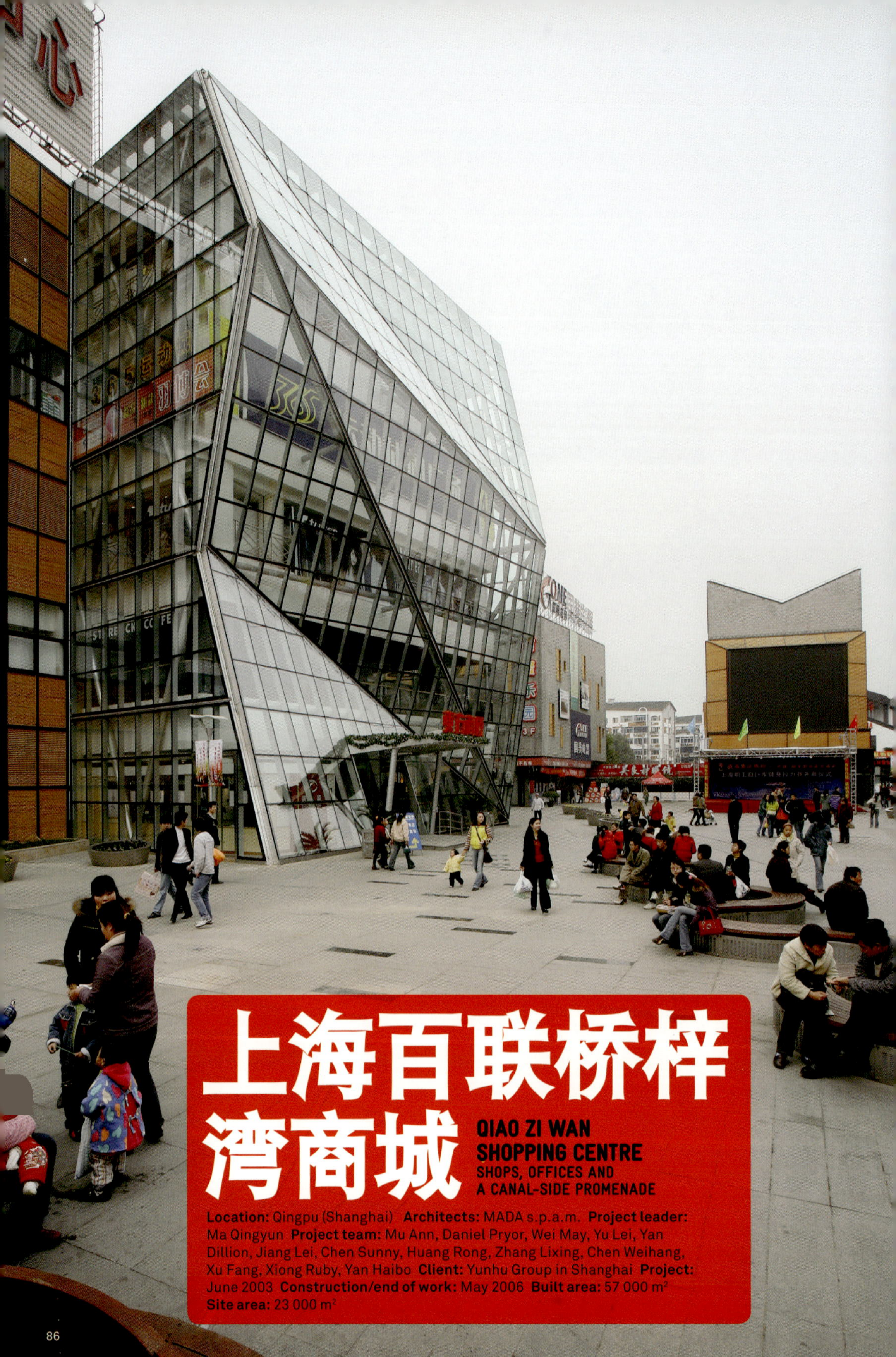

上海百联桥梓湾商城

QIAO ZI WAN SHOPPING CENTRE
SHOPS, OFFICES AND A CANAL-SIDE PROMENADE

Location: Qingpu (Shanghai) **Architects:** MADA s.p.a.m. **Project leader:** Ma Qingyun **Project team:** Mu Ann, Daniel Pryor, Wei May, Yu Lei, Yan Dillion, Jiang Lei, Chen Sunny, Huang Rong, Zhang Lixing, Chen Weihang, Xu Fang, Xiong Ruby, Yan Haibo **Client:** Yunhu Group in Shanghai **Project:** June 2003 **Construction/end of work:** May 2006 **Built area:** 57 000 m² **Site area:** 23 000 m²

To highlight the urban planning talents of Ma Qingyun and the MADA Spam studio, it would have been just as legitimate to present the Tianyi Shopping Centre in Ningbo, or even its branch in the heart of Shanghai. This branch is organised structurally as a place of reflection on architectural and urban form in relation to the city in a quarter where all the periods converge, from the times of the concessions and the *lilongs* to the crushing modernity of the condominiums, as well as the batteries of dwellings built in the 1970s and 1980s.

The interest of the Qingpu programme, however, is linked to the will of Mayor Sun Jiwei to move beyond an urban "system" based on chance, with no concern for coherence. This is indeed the essential aspect of the urban China, but it is clear that the population remains as if imbued with what was the ancient permanence of cities, preserved until the great convulsions of the 20th century.

Within this vast commercial quarter of Qingpu, the architect-urban planner came to compose with the ancient city, to create efficient modern spaces with a strongly marked structural appearance, and to propose, in short, a series of vocabularies to intermediate between the ancient and the modern, the whole with elegance, dignity and consequently with a practically constant respect for the inhabitants.

The overall design of the quarter preserves the virtue of all the components of a city: the habitat, commerce, services and even religion. One understands clearly here that the investment of Sun Jiwei, the man in charge of this city which has become a district attached to the municipality of Shanghai, has been able to play a major role, of the same type as that played by the Soho Group, in the general renewal of Chinese architecture.

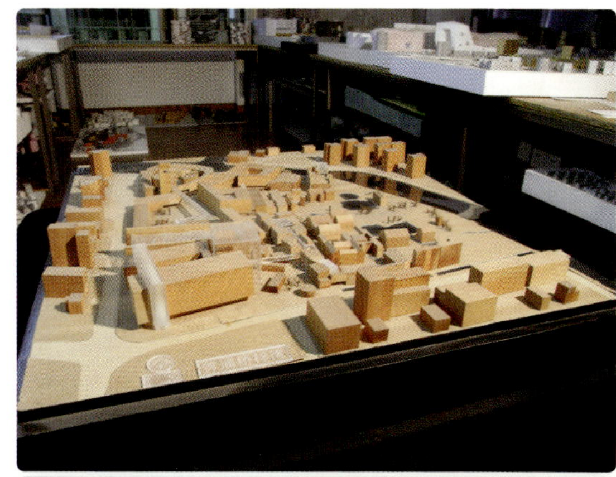

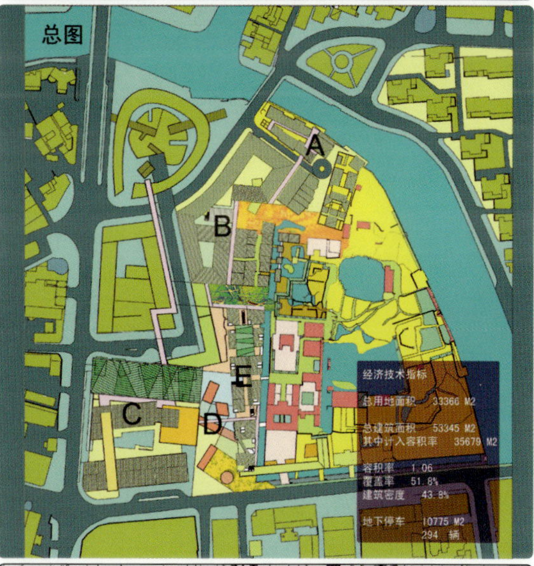

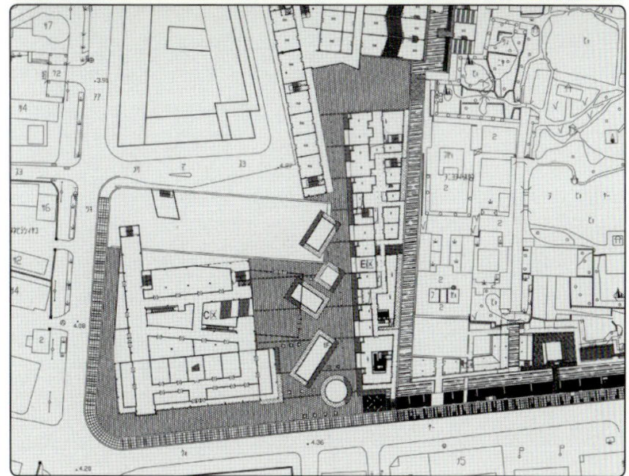

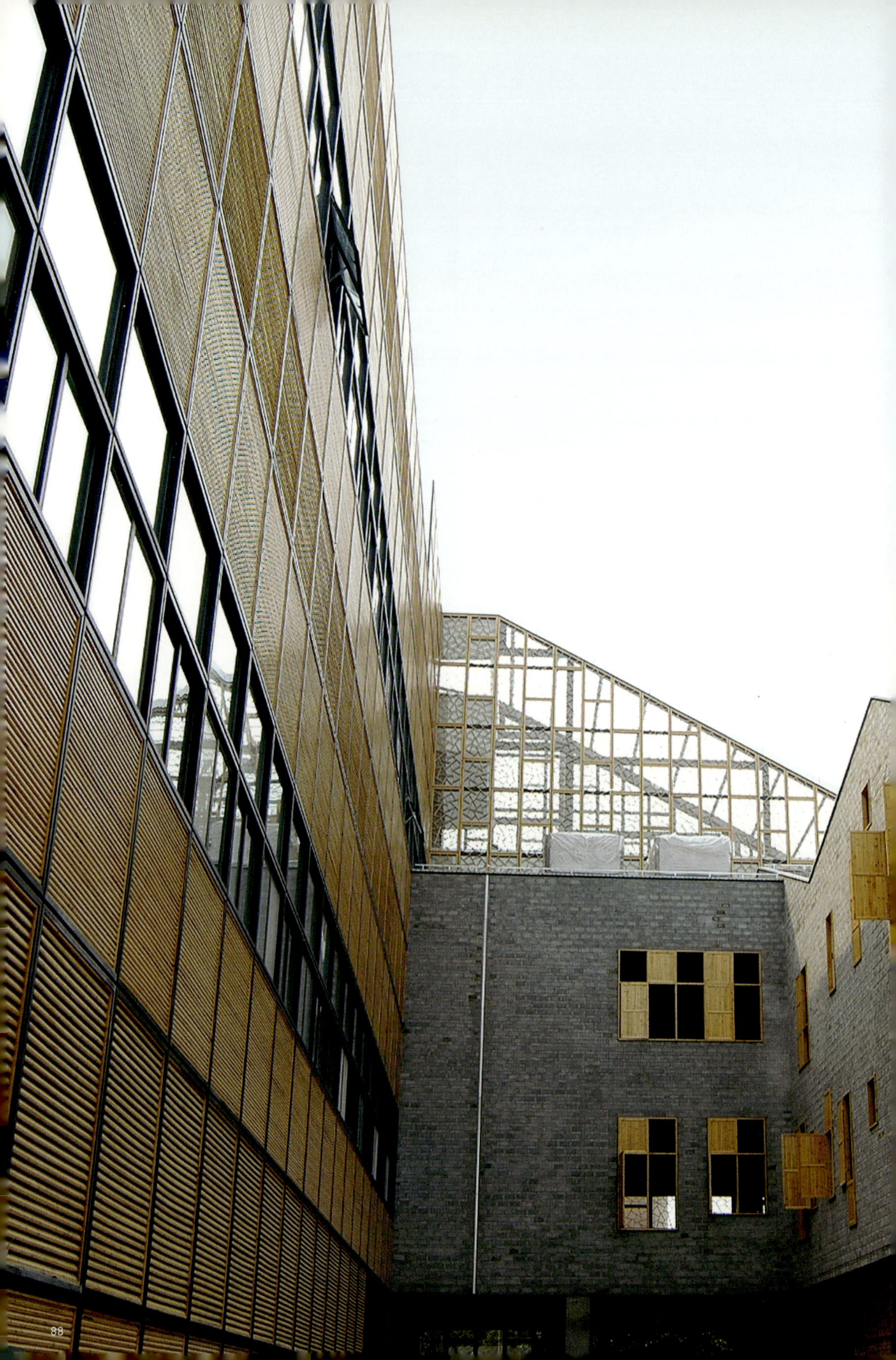

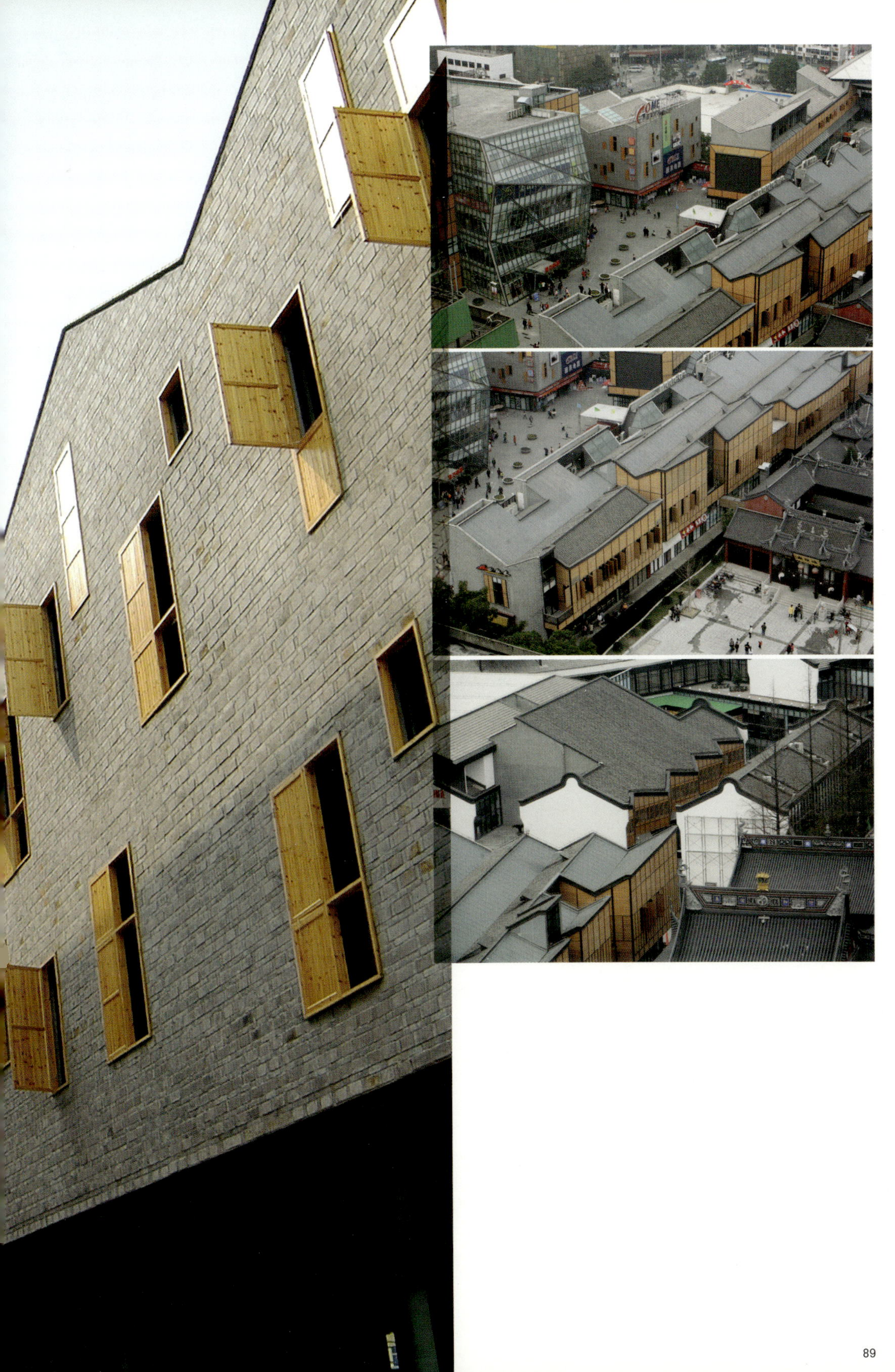

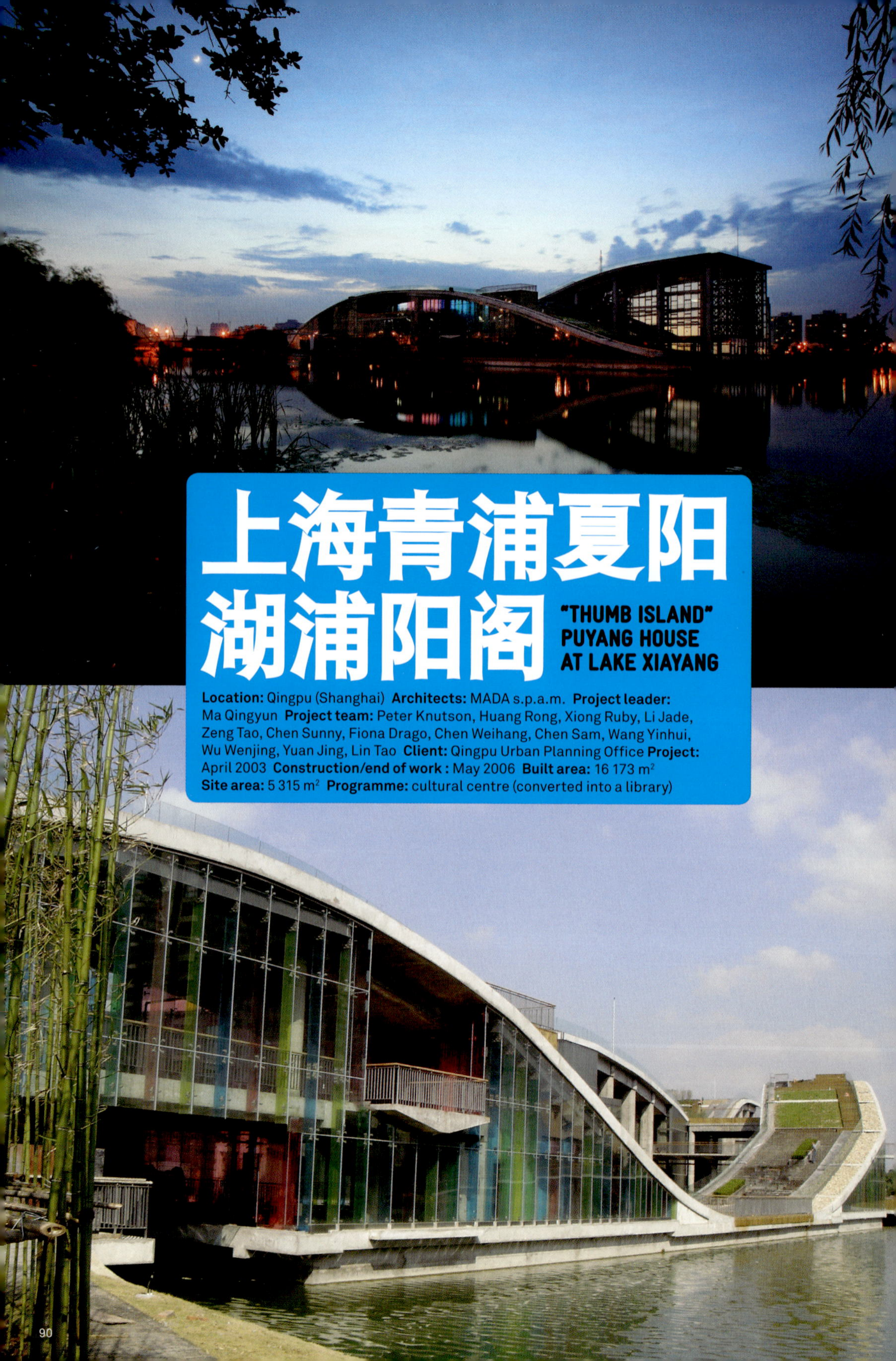

上海青浦夏阳湖浦阳阁

"THUMB ISLAND" PUYANG HOUSE AT LAKE XIAYANG

Location: Qingpu (Shanghai) **Architects:** MADA s.p.a.m. **Project leader:** Ma Qingyun **Project team:** Peter Knutson, Huang Rong, Xiong Ruby, Li Jade, Zeng Tao, Chen Sunny, Fiona Drago, Chen Weihang, Chen Sam, Wang Yinhui, Wu Wenjing, Yuan Jing, Lin Tao **Client:** Qingpu Urban Planning Office **Project:** April 2003 **Construction/end of work:** May 2006 **Built area:** 16 173 m² **Site area:** 5 315 m² **Programme:** cultural centre (converted into a library)

Here is Ma Qingyun of MADA Spam under the appearance of an energetic, free and fanciful architect.

For Qingpu, he has designed on the lake a "dragon building" which, thanks to the lake's reflections, arises from the water and returns to it again. Its function must have originally been that of a shopping centre of sorts, and it has been transformed to shelter cultural or leisure activities. Simply speaking, with respect to a form so complex that it has sometimes overshadowed the quality of the details, Ma has split the dragon, the undulations of which cross each other, sheltering all sorts of spaces with a convivial tone. To his way of thinking, this was to allow the inhabitants to pass freely from the inside to the outside, to do tai-chi, to sing an opera aria perhaps, to listen to poetry recitals or to play dice, all essential occupations. For reasons which are hard to understand, however (unless some kind of superstition keeps people away from the complicated belly of such an animal), the building has never really found its function and even its conversion into a library centre seems to be problematic.

This formal success doubling as a functional failure is not exceptional in China. One can play freely with forms when it is a question of a bar, a restaurant, or a building fated for changes or for destruction. The link with the land remains essential, even though water is present everywhere (as at Santanyinyue island in Hangzhou). Would the movement and the ephemeral, which are basic characteristics of this building strangely called "Thumb Island", have found their place more easily in the Japanese archipelago?

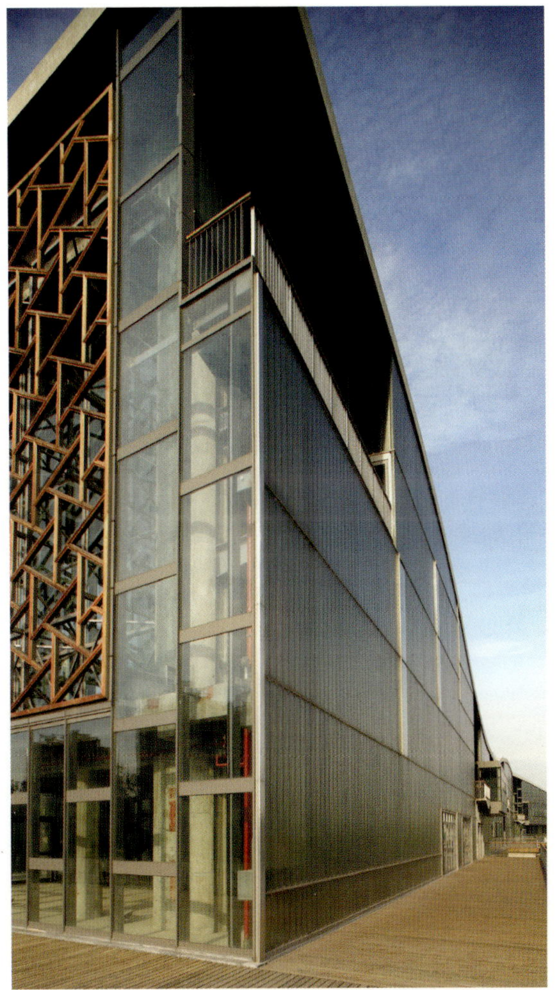

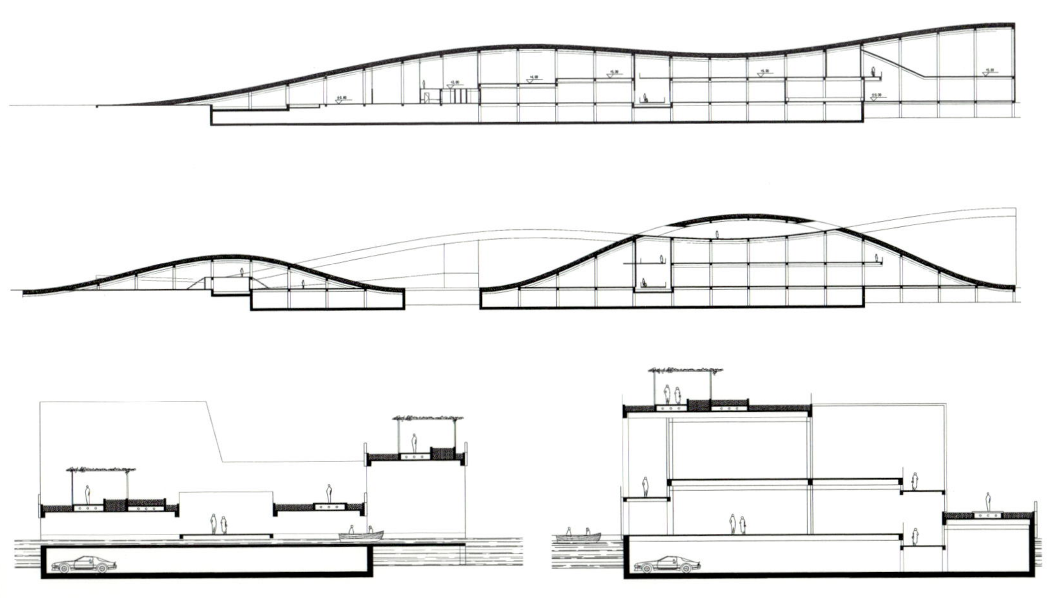

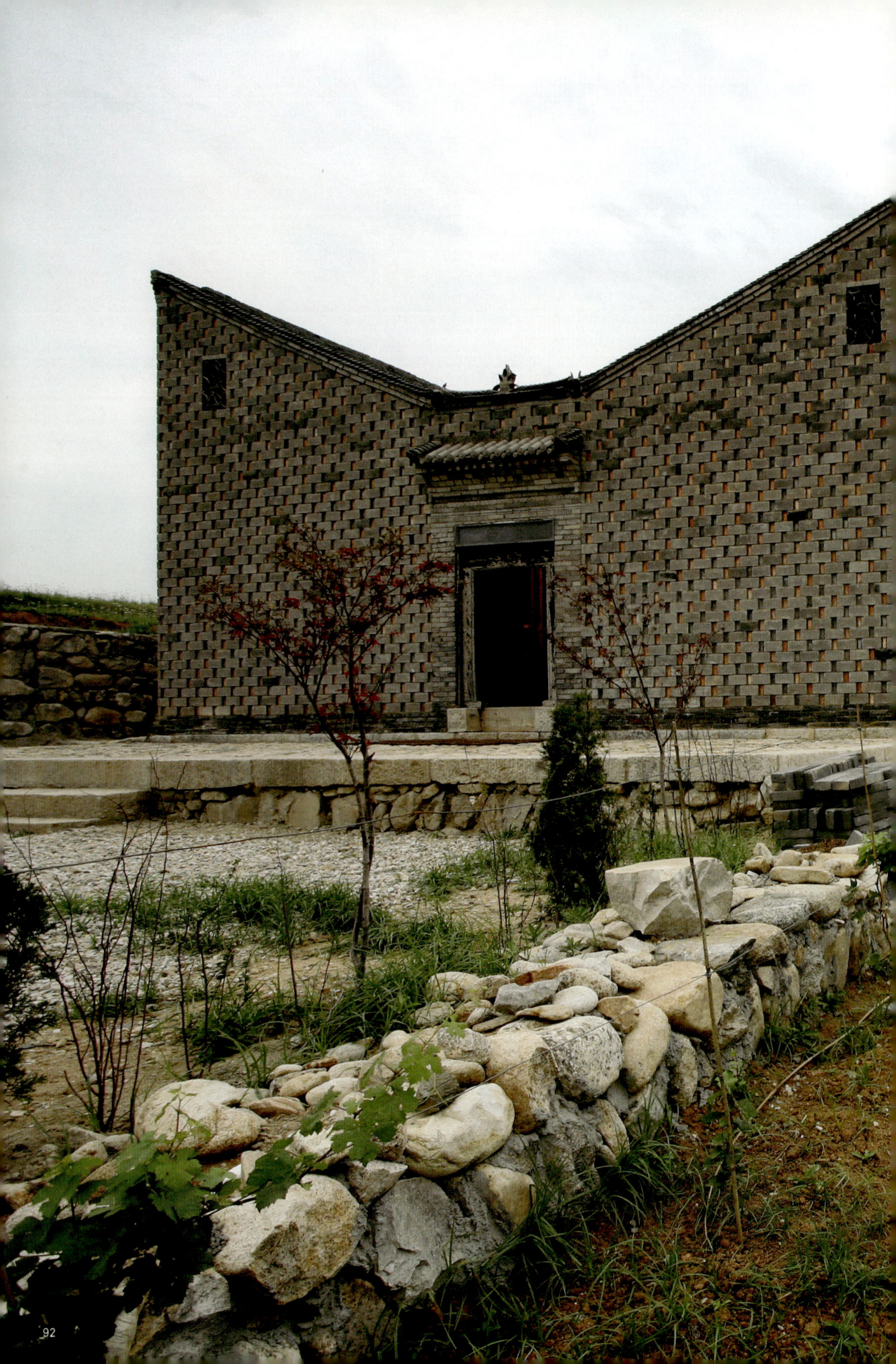

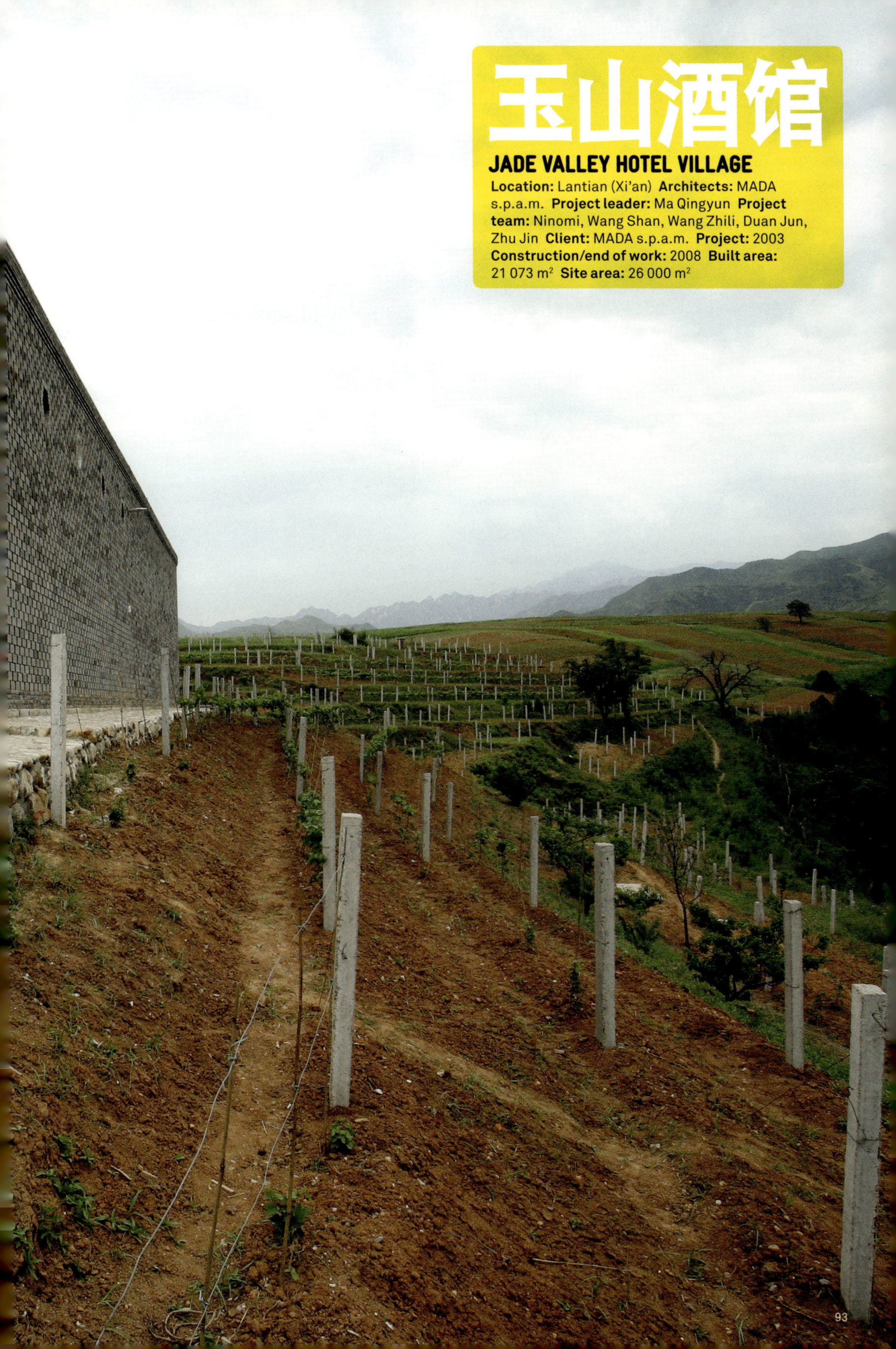
玉山酒馆
JADE VALLEY HOTEL VILLAGE
Location: Lantian (Xi'an) Architects: MADA s.p.a.m. Project leader: Ma Qingyun Project team: Ninomi, Wang Shan, Wang Zhili, Duan Jun, Zhu Jin Client: MADA s.p.a.m. Project: 2003 Construction/end of work: 2008 Built area: 21 073 m² Site area: 26 000 m²

Despite his appearance of a trendy architect,
Ma Qingyun remains a sentimental spirit attached
to his native Shaanxi. It is also a Chinese constant
to let oneself be carried by the winds, willingly or
not, to the other end of the country or the world
and then return to one's original area and rejoin
one's family.

As if he were growing weary of contemporary
rhetoric, but without abandoning its methods of
reflection, Ma plunges completely back into the
landscapes and building traditions of his area.
Here he is planting vines and producing his "Jade
Valley Wine", an appellation which will not be
controllable until a few years' time when the vines
are a few years older.

The principle is universal: wine cellars or a
château or some emblematic building is necessary
to carry the brand, and since the Jade Valley is not
on the most frequented routes of Shaanxi, Ma has
thought up the idea of developing here a sort of
hotel village, with a preliminary edifice containing
the rooms for guests, the indispensable wine
cellar and a farming museum.

His two main partners here are the simple bucolic
landscape and the craftsmen of the village of
Lantian, Zhang Qingcai and Zhou Qingtan. With
them he has developed a renewed utilisation of
brick, the spaced meshing of which gives the
illusion that the building is breathing, because
there is only a small number of hexagonal
openings on the exterior, a classical arrangement
in Chinese houses. The woodwork also belongs
to tradition.

The architect has almost concealed beneath
this appearance a structure which is actually
quite elaborate, in which the right angles can
efface themselves softly, allowing his Shanghai
computers to run once again. The interface
between the human gesture and the machines'
calculations, however, remains a mystery.

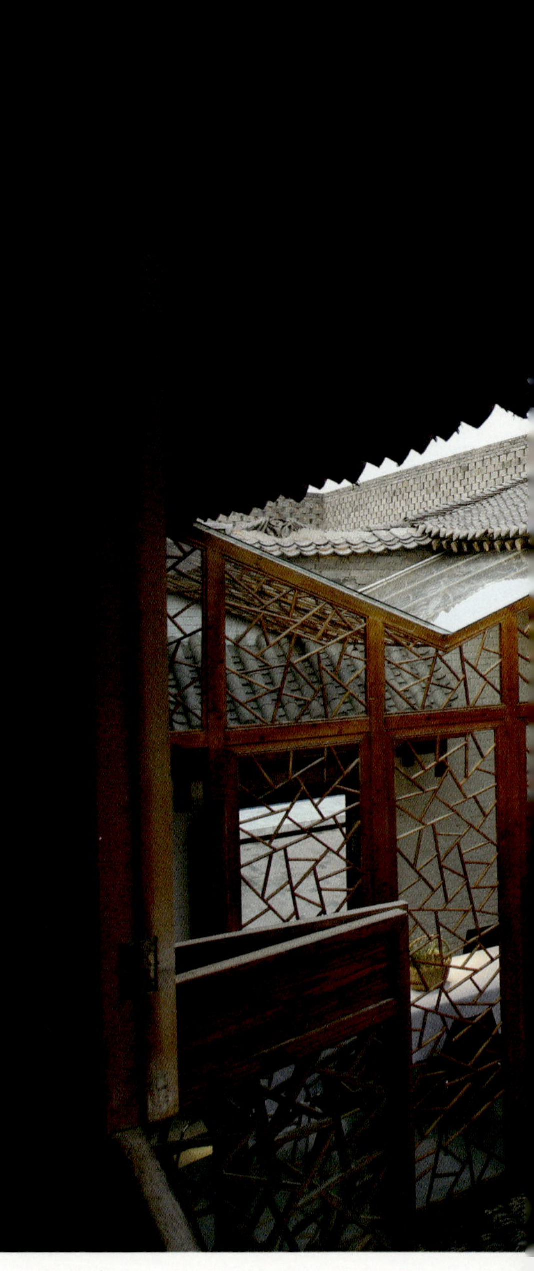

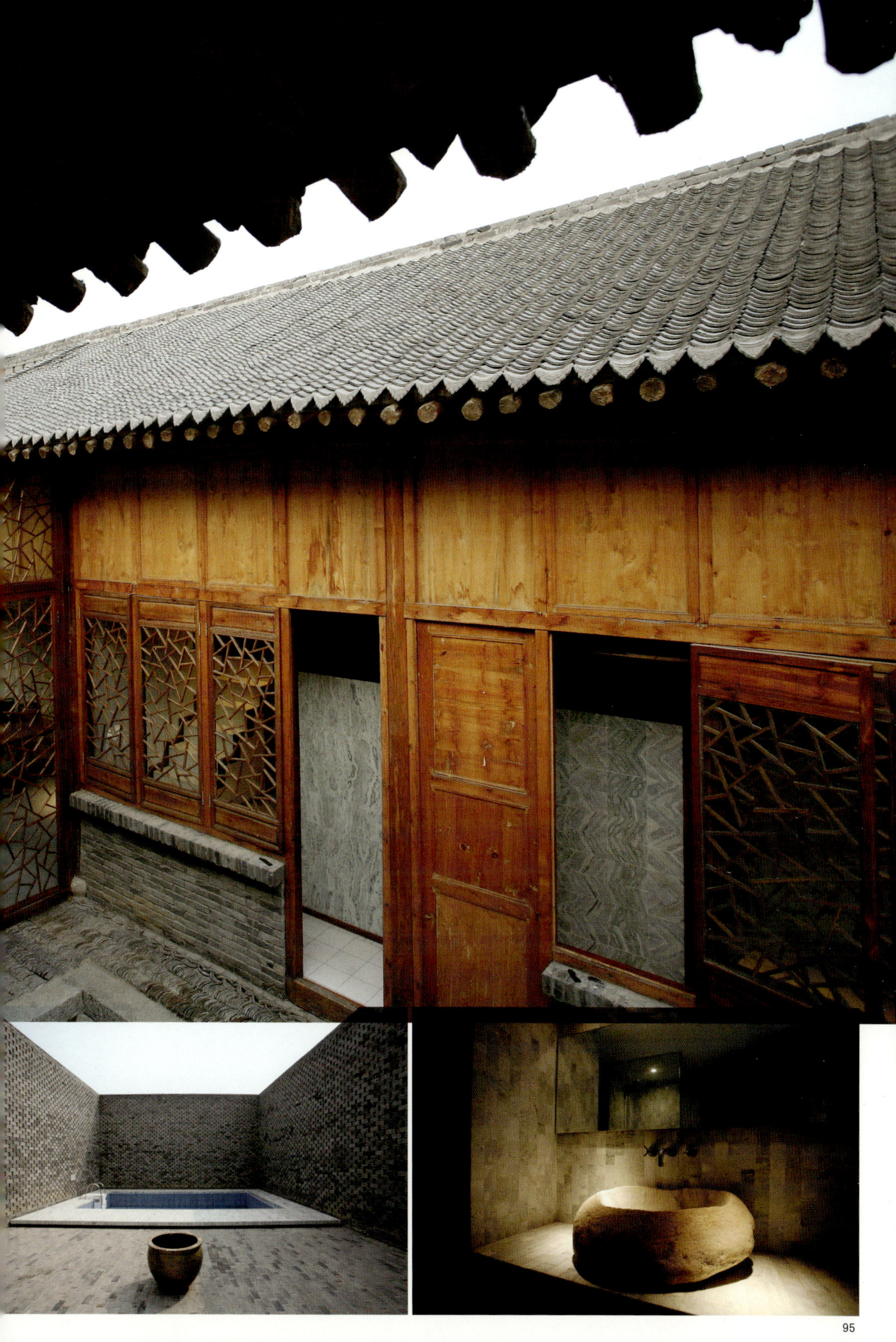

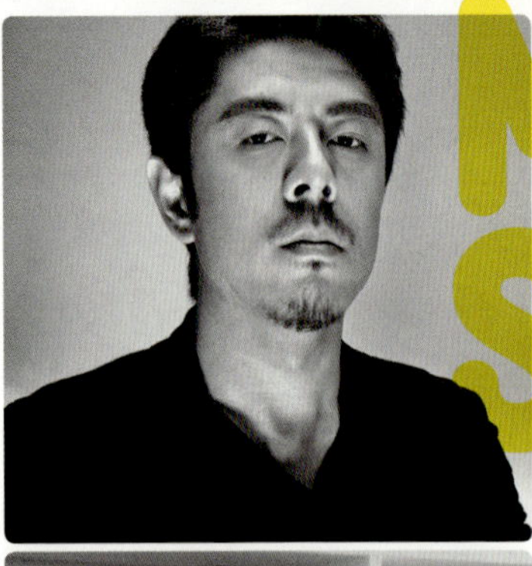

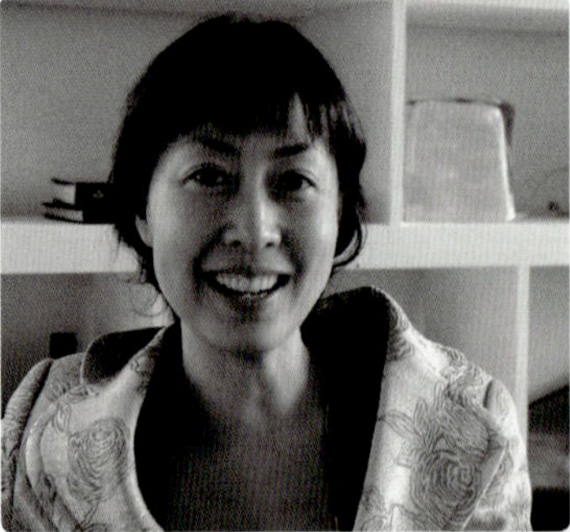

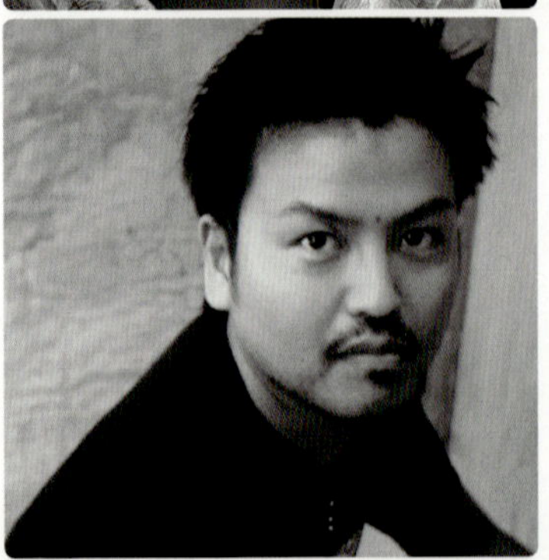

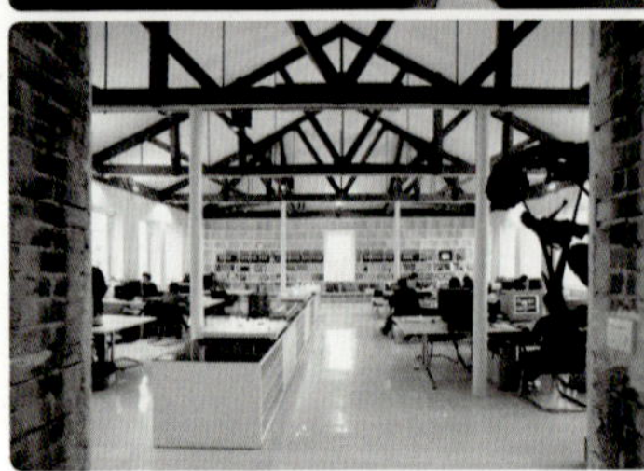

MAD Studio
Ma Yansong 马岩松

Born in 1975, Ma Yansong is the founder of the MAD studio which has been joined by two other partners, Yosuke Hayano from Japan and Dang Qun from Shanghai. It would be hard to be trendier in China at this time.

Ma is originally from Beijing but he carried out his studies at Yale University's School of Architecture, where he graduated in 2002, going to work successively for Zaha Hadid and Peter Eisenman, which assured his connections with London and New York. Yosuke, who has also worked for Zaha Hadid, forms the natural link to Tokyo while Dang, a University of Iowa graduate, worked in a series of American studios and made a stopover in Rome before joining MAD in Beijing.

If one were only to consider what it has really built in China (or elsewhere), aside from a multitude of futurist projects which have remained in limbo, this studio's place on these pages would not be so sure. What happens is that the international journals and the current fascination for China have propelled MAD into the limelight and it would be hard to ignore it.

Experts are no doubt acquainted with their tower project for Guangzhou (previously Canton): eight hundred metres long, an imposing contraption folding in on itself, with a height of four hundred metres – half scoubidou, half chewing-gum, which 3D techniques have finally made almost real. MAD has also proposed for the town of Mississauga, near Toronto, Canada, a fifty-floor tower drawing its inspiration from the eternal curves of Marylin Monroe (its name is the Absolute Tower). Since all that could appear sickly with respect to the perception which it has of its own talent, the studio has also proposed for Beijing a grandly ecological project formed by immense verdant platforms which are themselves resting on a forest of "stalks" which climb up to a height about four hundred metres.

For the time being, the only finished building is a clubhouse of five hundred square metres in Beijing's Miyun district. It is a safe bet, however, that the communication sense of Ma Yansong and his teammates will come to have the MAD studio inscribed in the future book of architectural records.

Partners
Ma Yansong 马岩松
Born 1975 (Beijing)
Master in architecture,
Yale University, Connecticut, 2002
Dang Qun 党群
Master in architecture,
Iowa University
Yosuke Hayano 早野洋介
Degree in Material Engineering,
Waseda University, Tokyo, 2000
Studio founded in 2004
Number of employees: 25

Contact
MAD
3rd floor West Tower, n°7 Banqiao
Nanxiang, Beixinqiao, Beijing,
China 100007
T: +86 10 64026632, 64031080
F: +86 10 64023940
mad@i-mad.com
www.i-mad.com

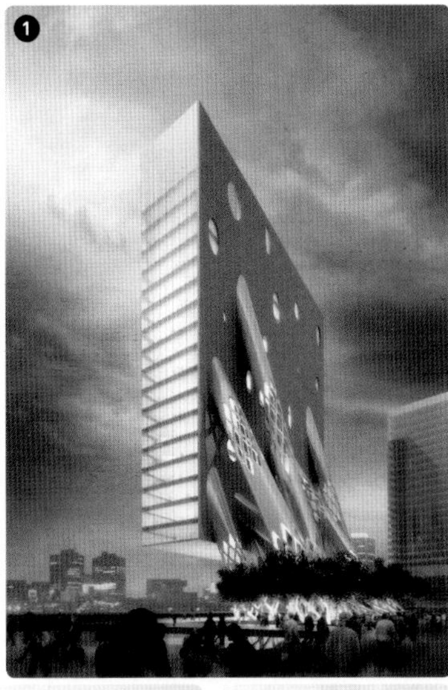
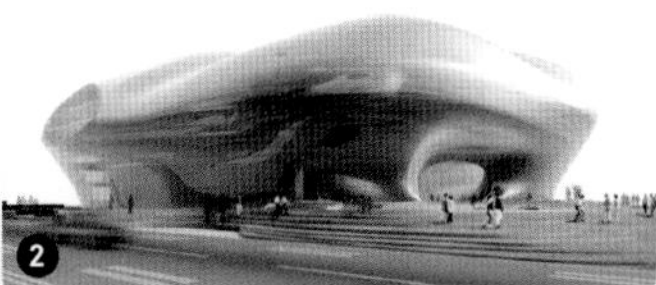
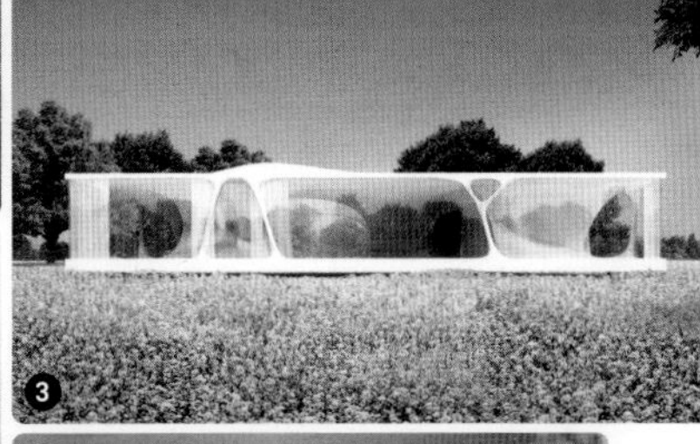
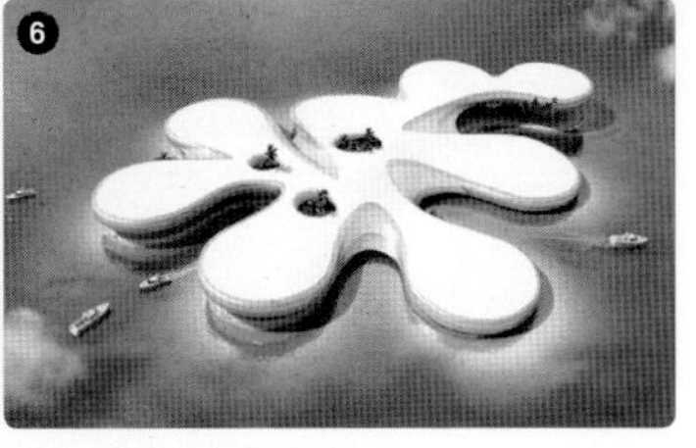
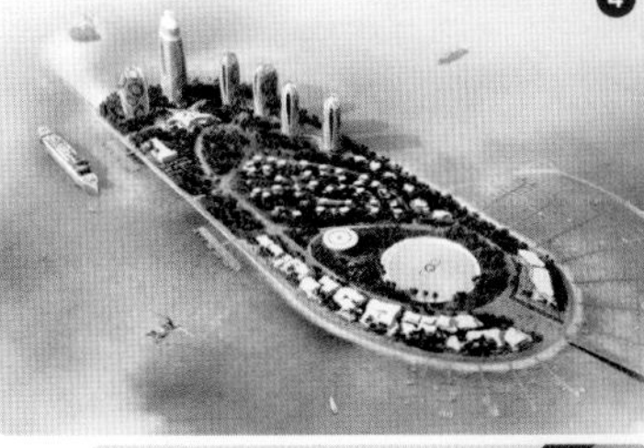
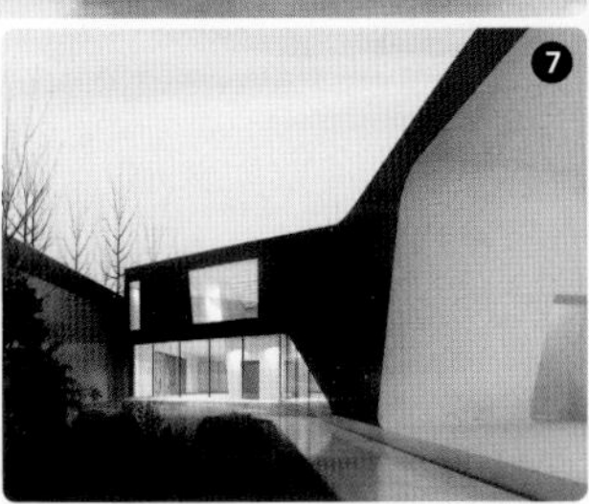
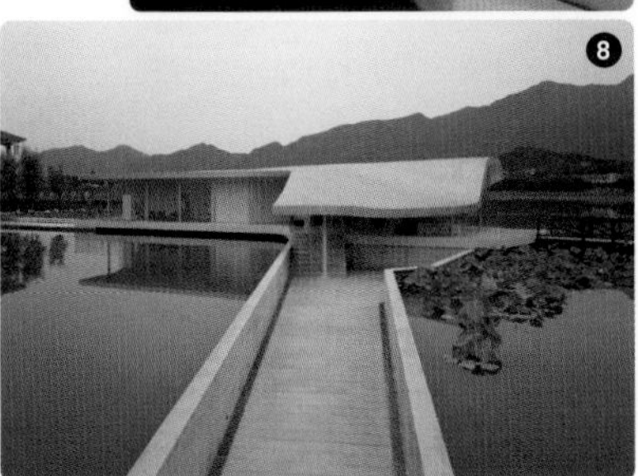

1 Head office of Al Rostamani group, Dubai,
  2007 (unbuilt).
2 Erdos Museum, inner Mongolia, under construction.
3 Pavilion in Denmark, 2007 (unbuilt).
4 Sanya Phœnix Island, China, 2007 (unbuilt).
5 Absolute Tower, Toronto, under construction.
6 Tokyo Island, Dubai, 2007 (unbuilt).
7 Rising House, Beijing, under construction.
8 Lake Hongluo Clubhouse, Beijing, 2006.

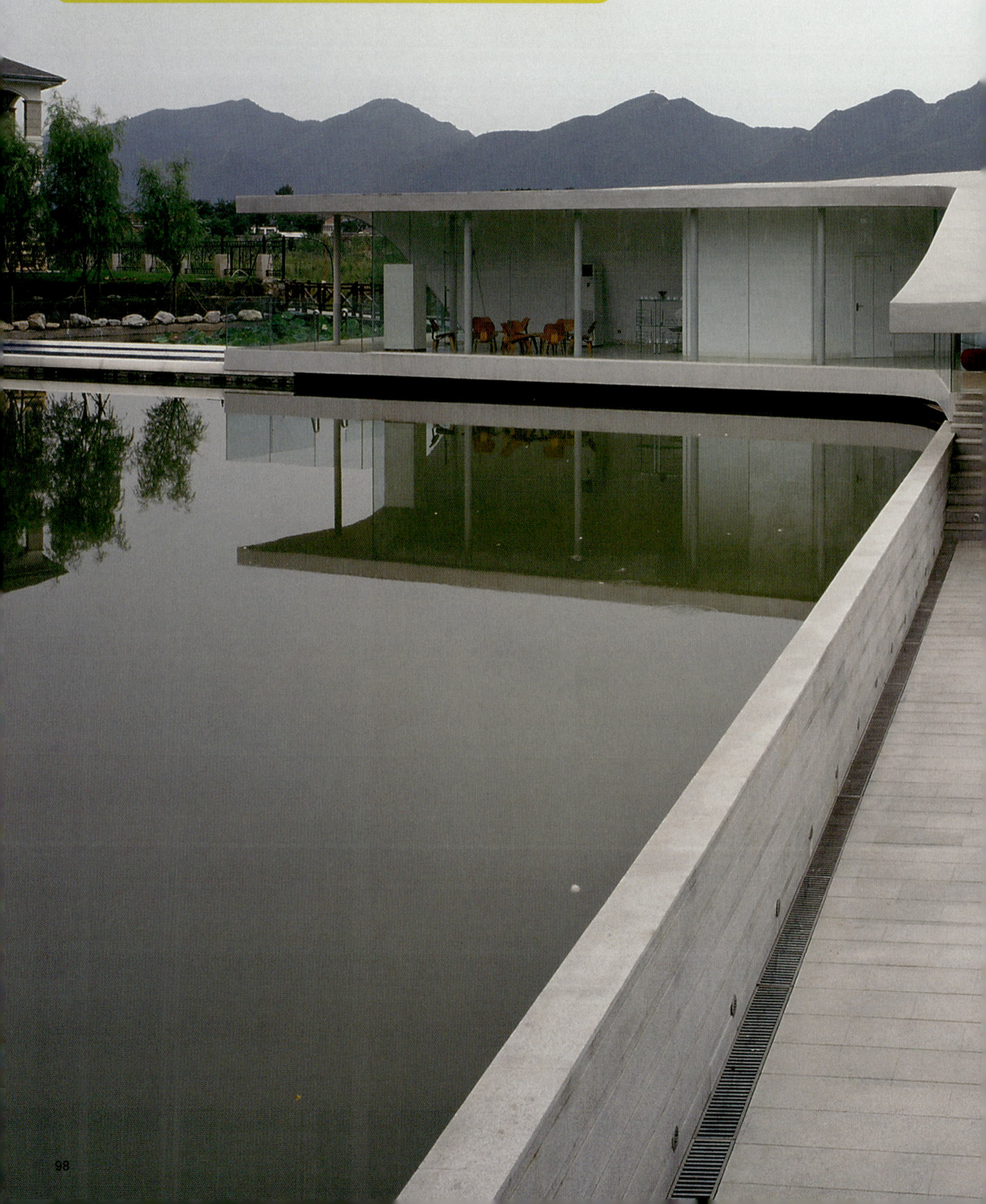

红螺会所 LAKE HONGLUO CLUBHOUSE

Location: Beijing **Architects:** MAD (Ma Yansong, Yosuke Hayano, Dang Qun) **Project leaders:** Yansong Ma, Yosuke Hayano **Project team:** Florian Pucher, Shen Jun, Christian Taubert, Marco Zuttioni, Yu Kui **Client:** Beijing Earth Real Estate Develops **Project:** May 2005 **Construction/end of work:** October 2005-May 2006 **Built area:** 487 m² **Photographs :** © Sun Xiangyu and She He

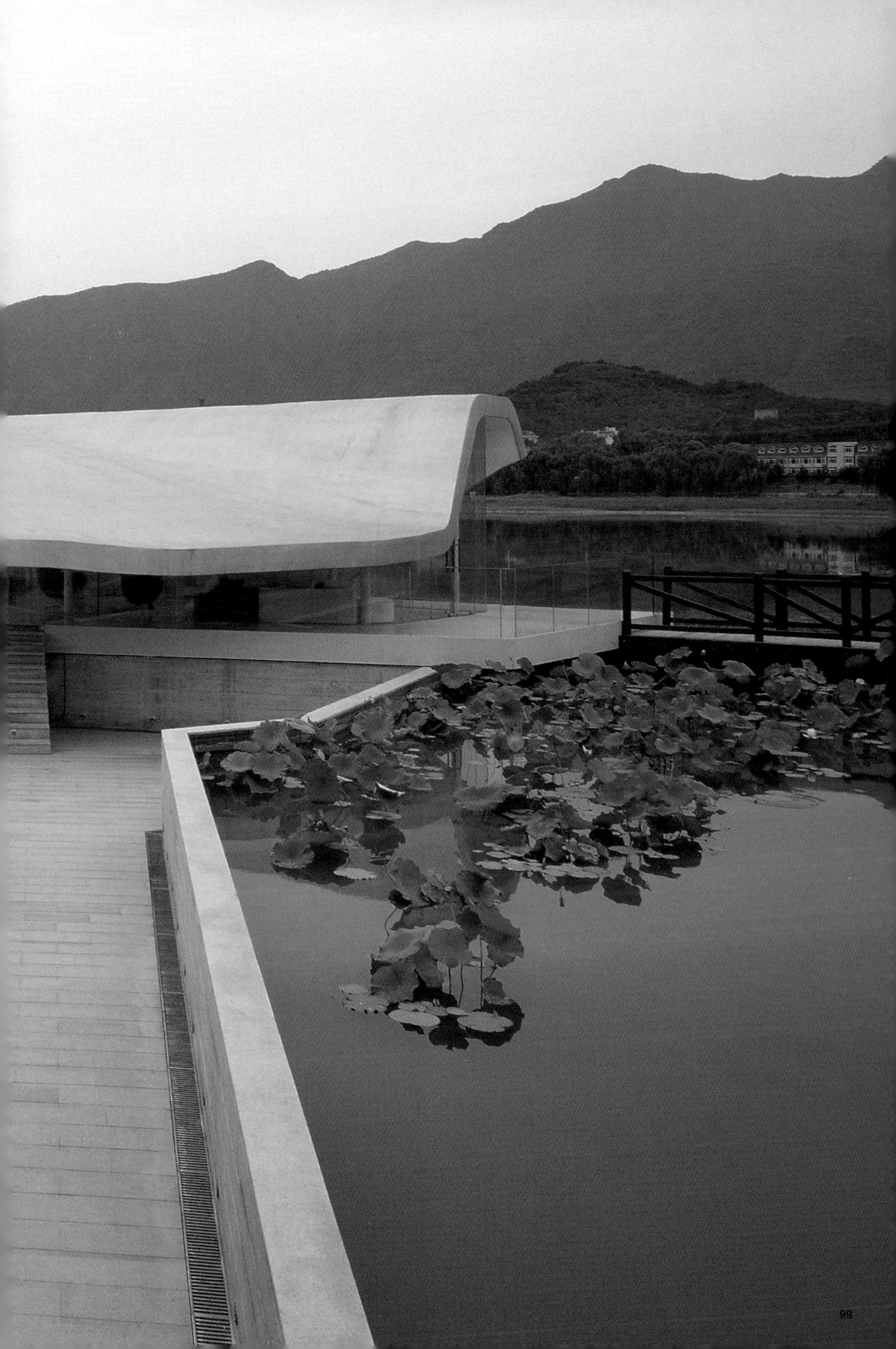

The Hongluo district presents itself as a sort
of ultra-chic village in the great north of the
municipality of Beijing, near the artificial Lake
Miyun. The villas of Hongluo are marked by an
ironclad classicism, evoking the stylish suburbs
of London, Rome or Berlin.
Within this context, the little clubhouse of five
hundred square metres conceived by MAD and
finished in 2006 looks like an intense and joyful
explosion of modernity. It has the appearance of
a mainsail of white concrete, undulating according
to formal principles familiar to Zaha Hadid, and
it offers diverse neighbourhood amenities for
enjoying a drink, playing mahjong, reading fashion
magazines, and eating three swallow's nests
or, more willingly, some sandwich or hamburger
combos, a culinary reference which would seem
to match the club members' tastes quite well.
A bit too thick, the concrete sail has to rest on
some posts which, for their part, are a bit too
numerous not to alter the desired feeling of grace.
Through the large bay-windows of this big white
bird alighting on the edge of the lake, there remains
a splendid view of the mountainous landscape
surrounding Beijing.

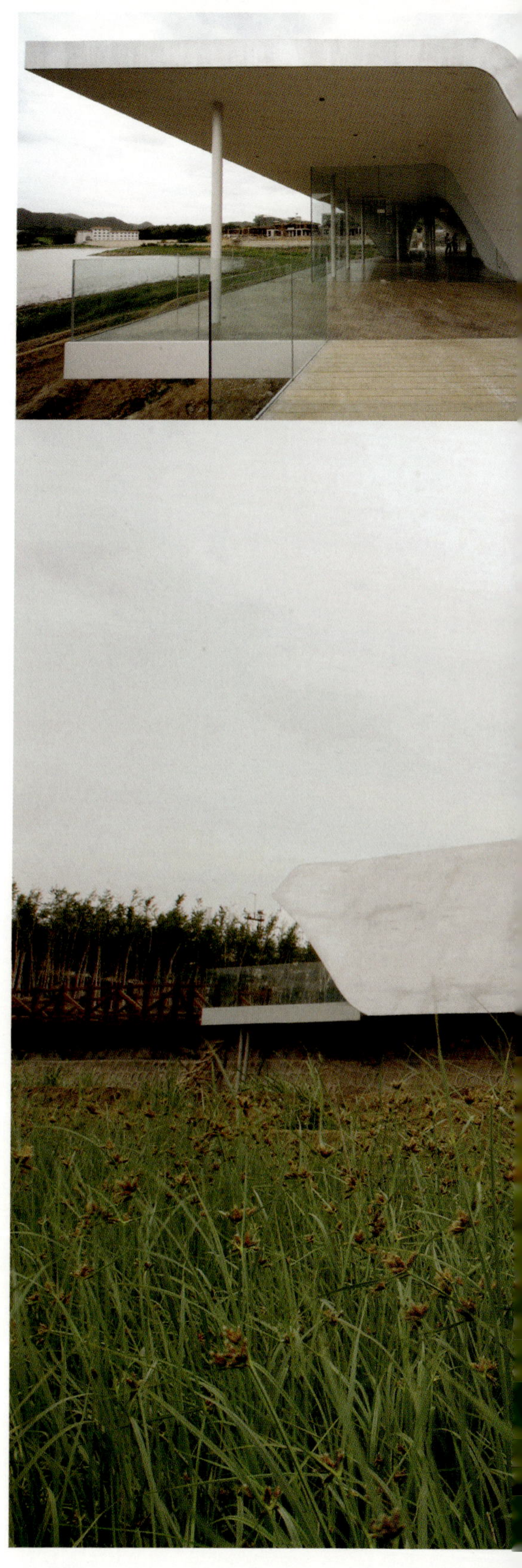

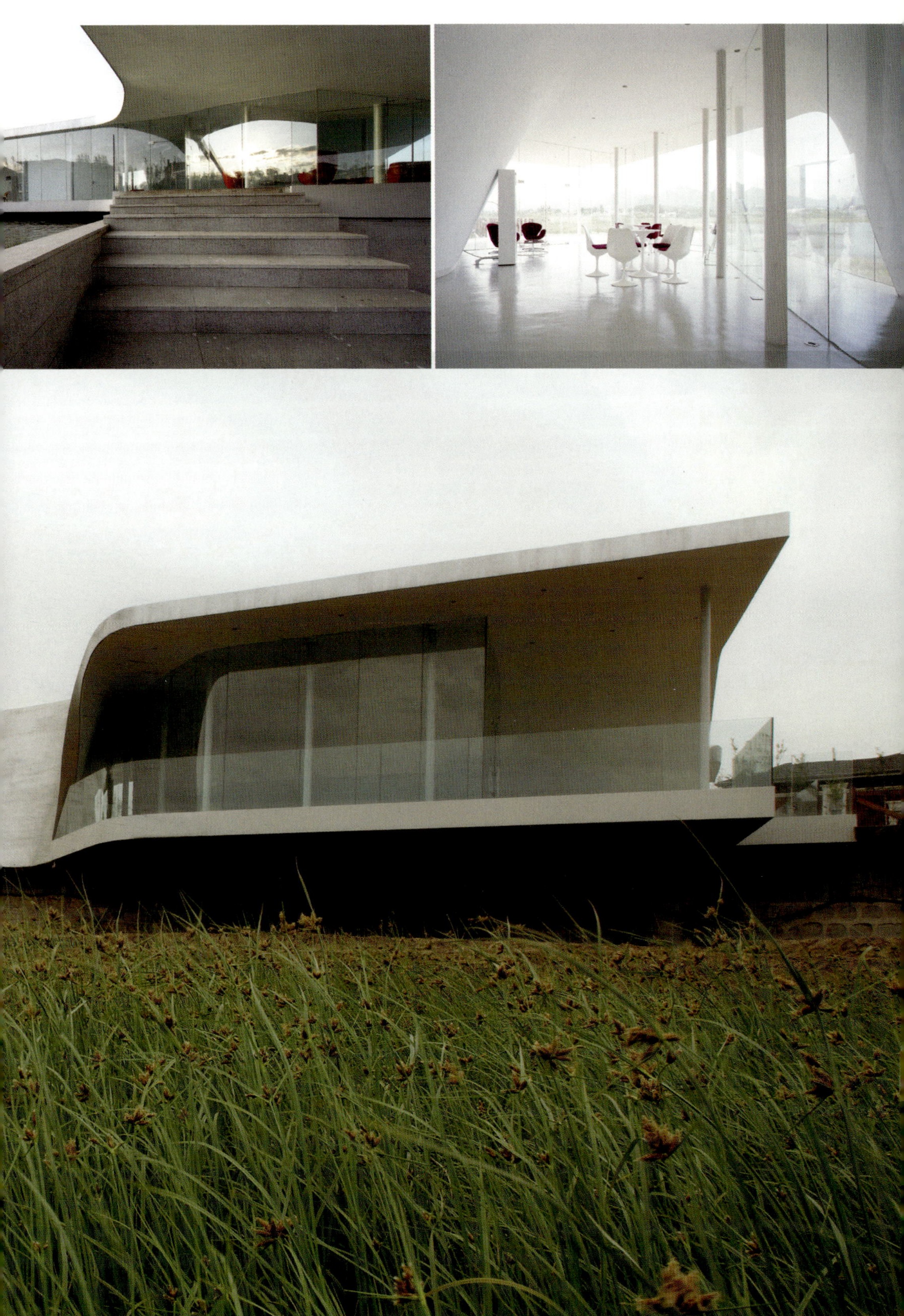

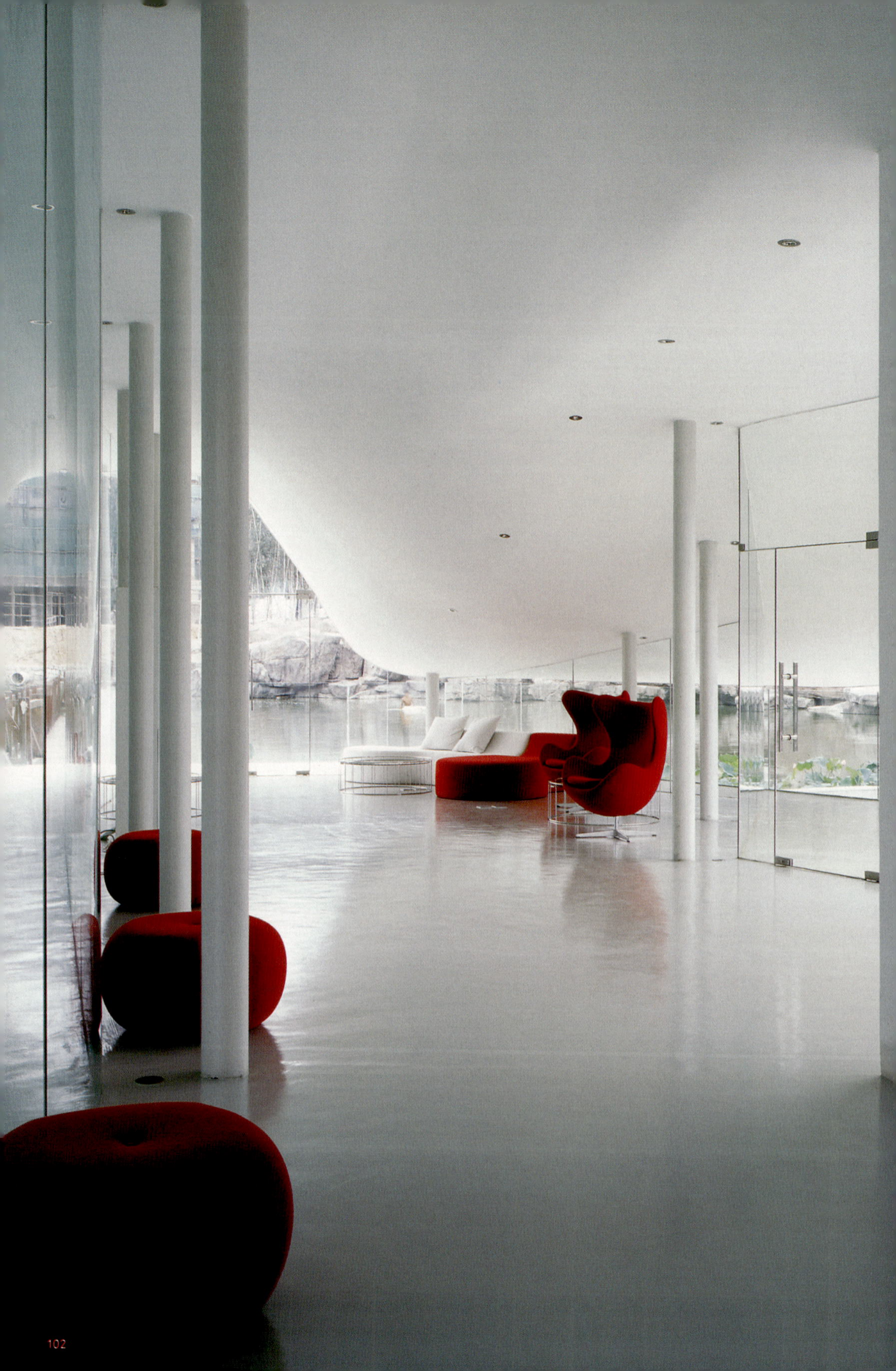

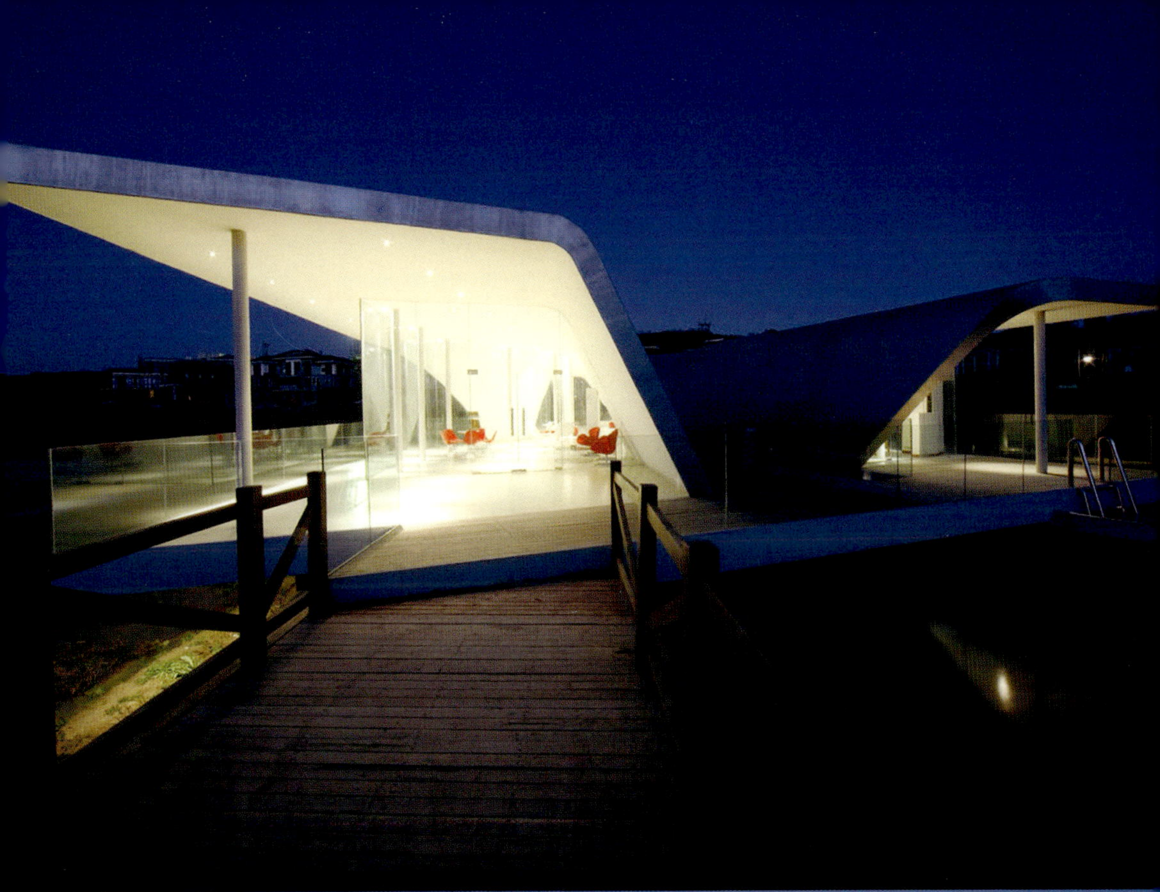

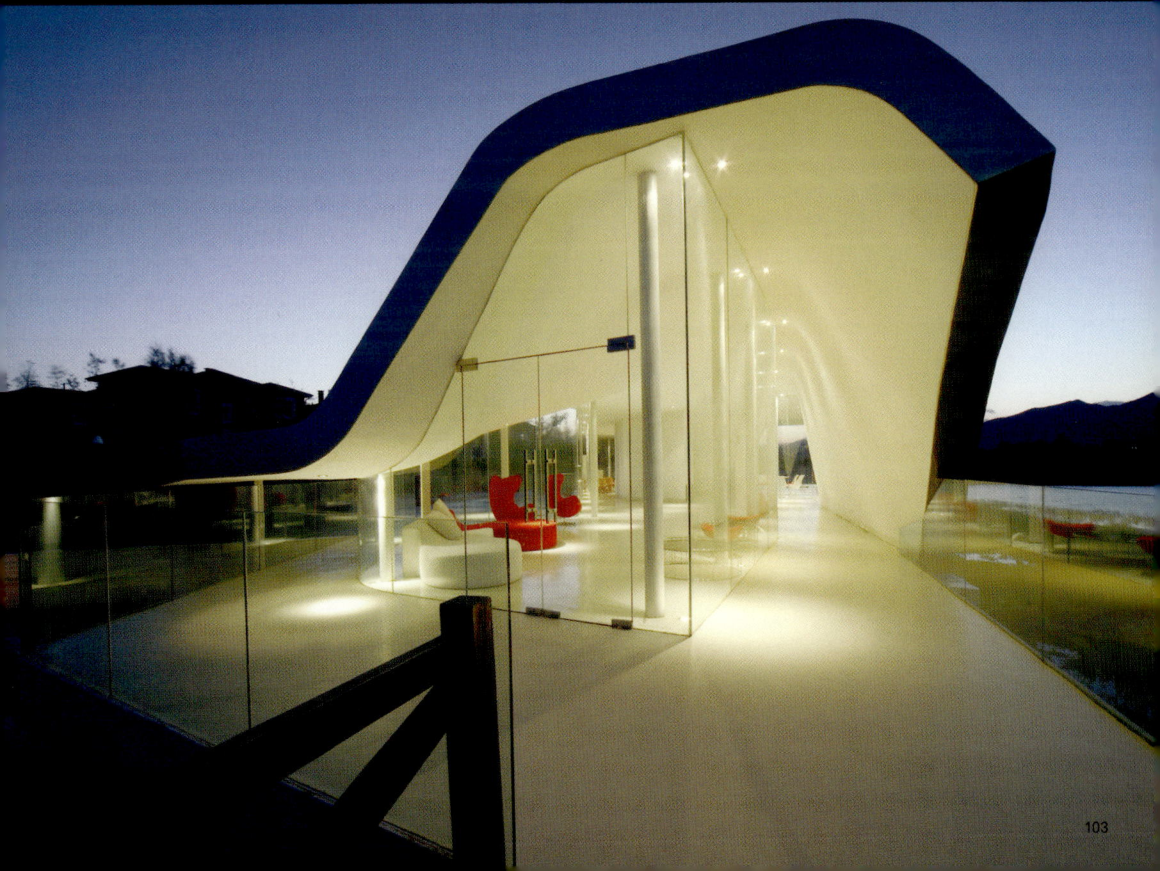

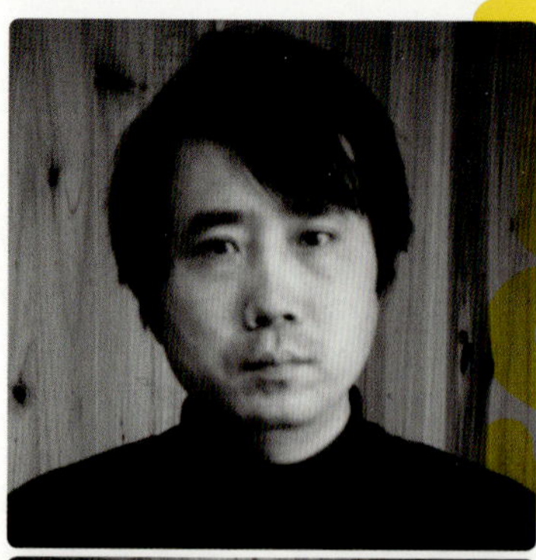

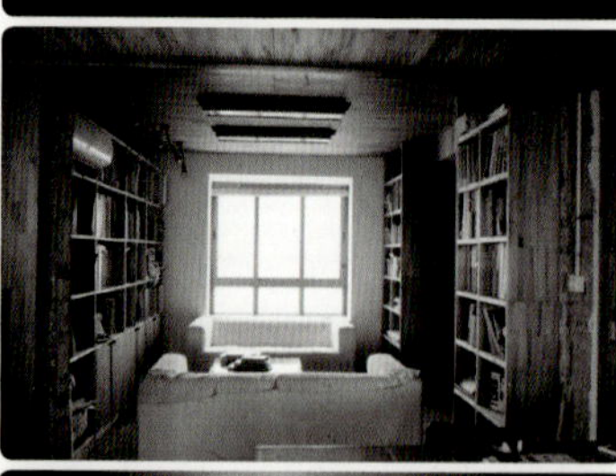

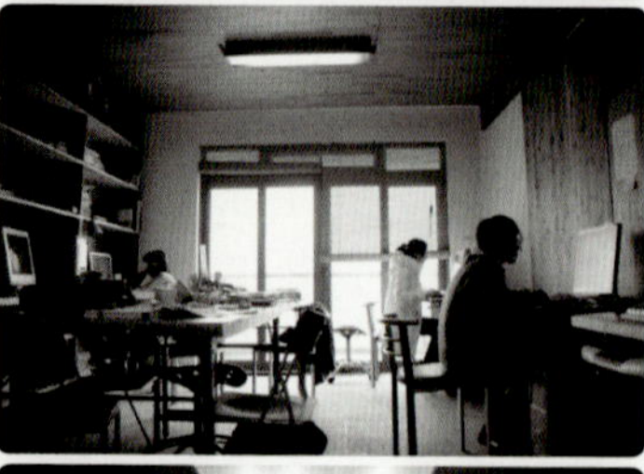

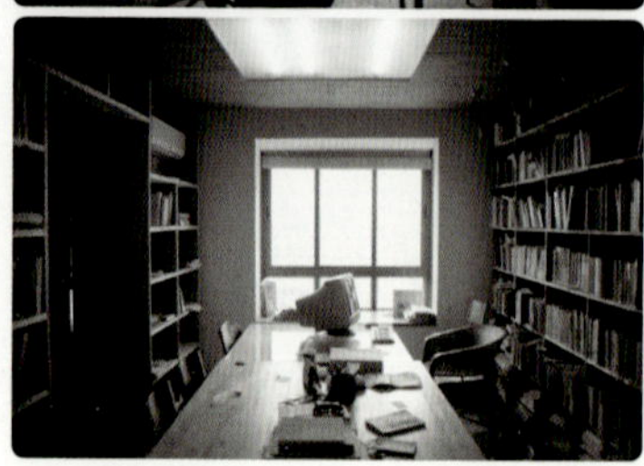

TM Studio
Tong Ming 童明

One can only think that Tong Ming is a discrete personality or perhaps the heir to a form of Chinese courtesy which causes him to move into the background when so many of his colleagues take a pronounced pleasure in rushing forth to meet the world which has opened up before them. Perhaps we did not knock at the right door to discover this figure, whose communication is limited to a few photographs. He is, however, an acknowledged professional, the true worth of whom has been valued since he set down to work in the year 2000. Accordingly, we are only acquainted with his studio through pictures which reveal a universe almost exclusively consecrated to wood (2003). Born in Shanghai in 1968, Tong Ming, who graduated in urban planning at Tongji University after obtaining his architect's degree in Nanking, has remained loyal up to now to Jiangsu province and the area around Shanghai.

For him each project means the chance to develop a new vocabulary but there where others would willingly depart towards the heterogeneous, Tong Ming makes each project a whole, a universe in which he attempts to raise the vocabulary to its highest point of perfection. In 2002 he worked on the Wenzhen College of Suzhou University. He conceives a serene urban landscape system dominated by whites and exchange spaces, especially outside or in passageways. Any awkwardness here is observed above all at what is today a still limited technical construction level, which is most likely quite frustrating for the architect himself.

He is consequently much more at ease on being called to erect two buildings in the old Pingjiang quarter in Suzhou. The first of these structures is the Dong bar and restaurant, forming an extension of the city's most beautiful hotel, which is indeed a transformed dwelling with the sense of refinement and luxury familiar to Suzhou. Along this same line, in 2007 he completed a shopping centre of 5,600 square metres called Suquan Yuan, where the essential aspect of the architecture is interiorised in existing structures. For this edifice he built a façade of "dominoes" which reflects a very subtle spirit.

In 2005, Tong Ming delivered an International Club for Nanking's hi-tech quarter. In this is a triple building inserted between two hills, the glasswork, plentiful on the façade, responds to a fine generosity of thought on the interior circulations. A sort of mystery or perhaps a secret seems to be the rule of the game, at least at the moment when the building was finished.

Tong Ming 童明
Born 1968
Doctor in urban planning,
Tongji University, Shanghai, 1999
Studio founded in 2000
Number of employees: 2

Contact
TM Studio
Room 1203, Unit 3
Guokang Road 46 Lane
200092 Shanghai, China
T: +86 21 65 98 86 10
F: +86 21 65 98 86 10
mtong@81890.net

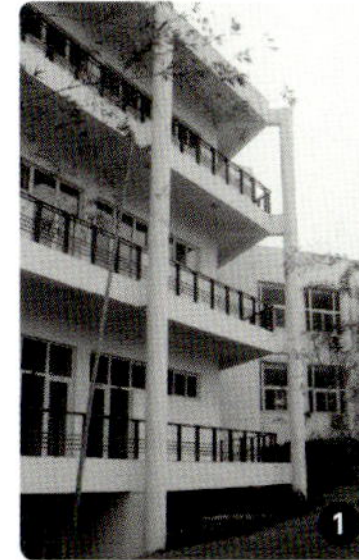
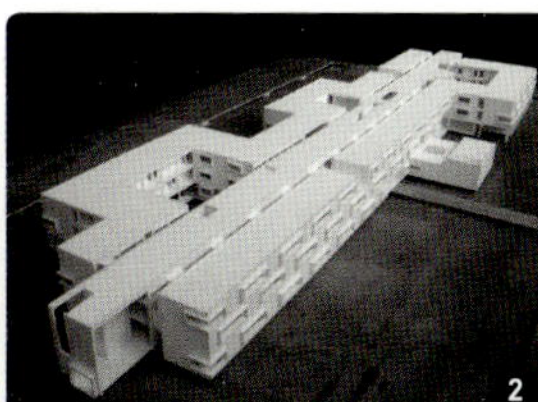
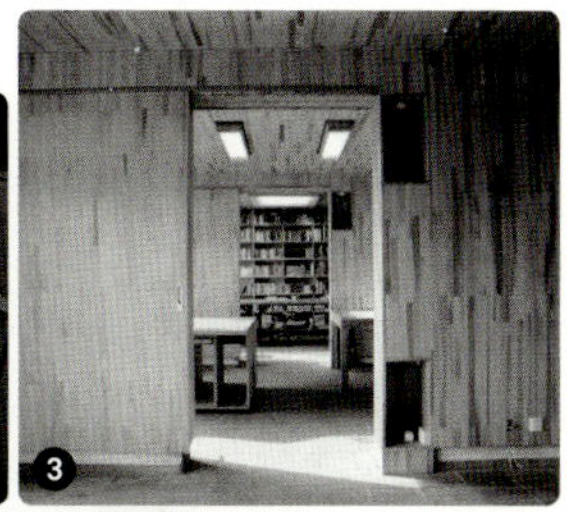
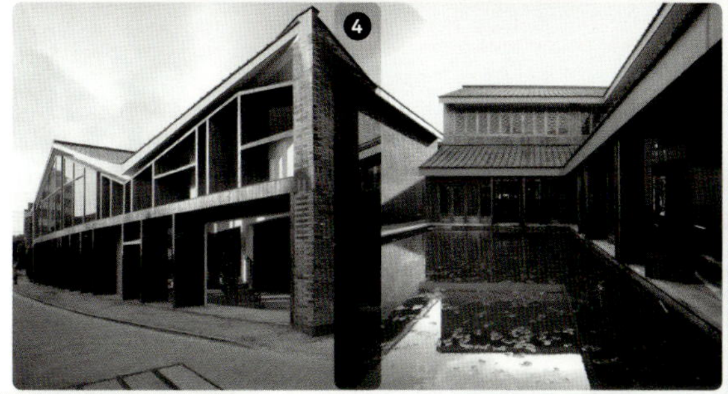
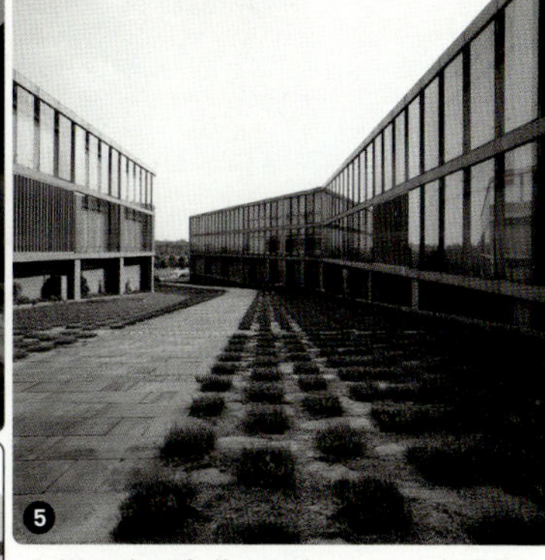
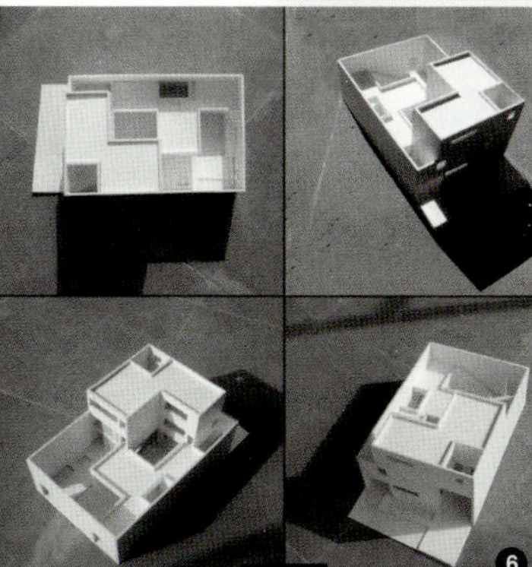

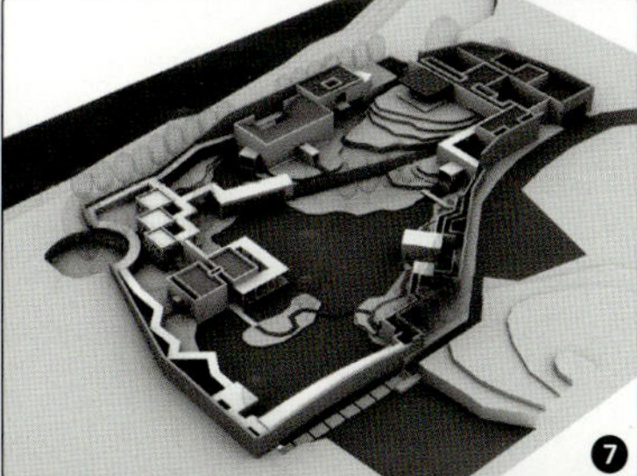
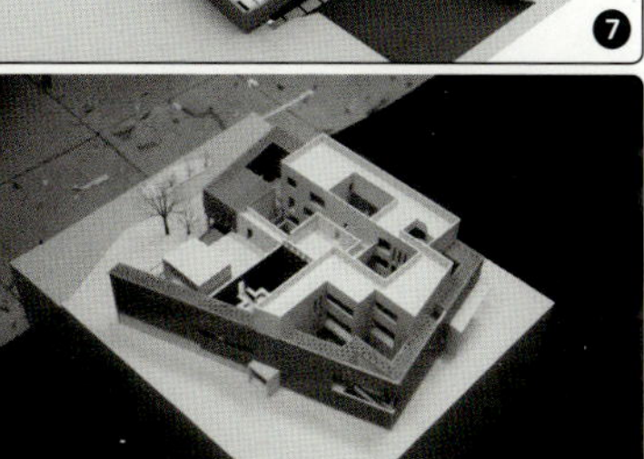
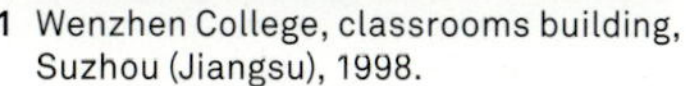
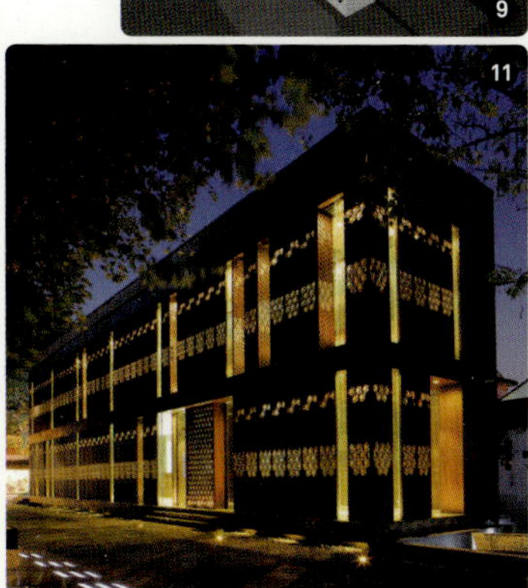
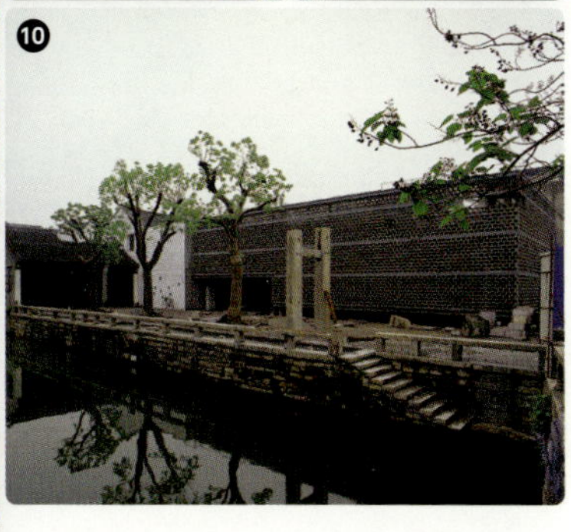

1 Wenzhen College, classrooms building,
  Suzhou (Jiangsu), 1998.
2 Wenzhen College, laboratory,
  Suzhou, 1998.
3 TM Studio offices, Shanghai, 2003.
4 Renovation of Park Luqiao building,
  Taizhou (Zhejiang), 2007.
5 Club international, Pukou district,
  Nankin, 2004.
6 Ten row houses Tianya,
  Suzhou, under construction.
7 House with garden, Nanning (Guangxi),
  under construction.
8 House "promenade", Suzhou,
  under construction.
9 Artist house, Shanghai,
  under construction.
10 Dong Tea house, Suzhou, 2004.
11 Suquan Yuan welcome building,
  Suzhou, 2007.

董氏茶庄改造茶室－平江客栈

EXTENSION OF THE PINGJIANG KEZHAN HOTEL-RESTAURANT AND THE DONG TEA HOUSE

Location: Suzhou (Jiangsu) **Architects:** TM Studio **Project leader:** Tong Ming **Project team:** Chen Hui, Du Shengming **Client:** Government of Pingjiang district, Suzhou **Project:** September 2003-November 2003 **Construction/end of work :** November 2003-July 2004 **Built area:** 1 800 m² **Site area:** 2 400 m² **Cost:** 20 million euro

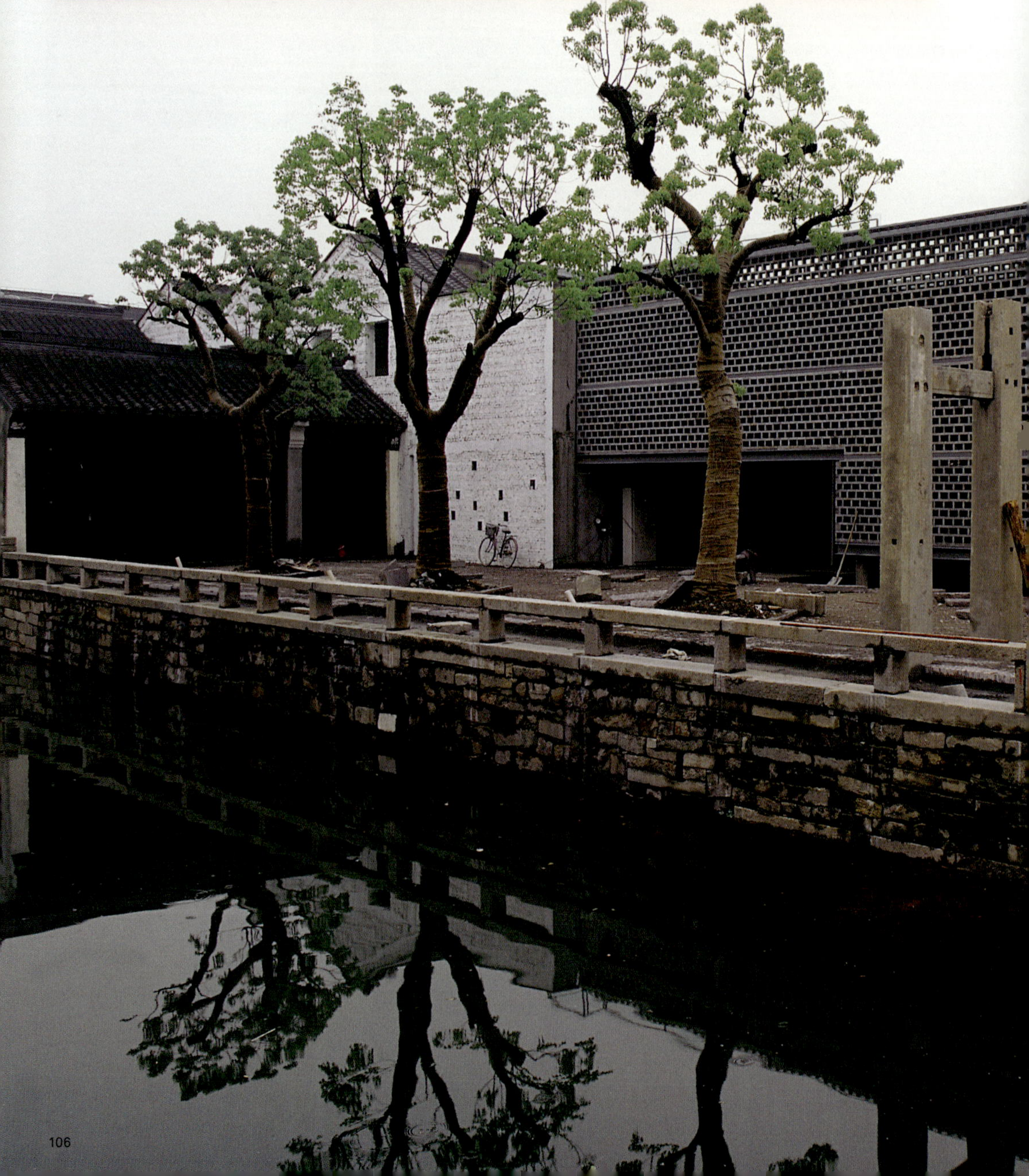

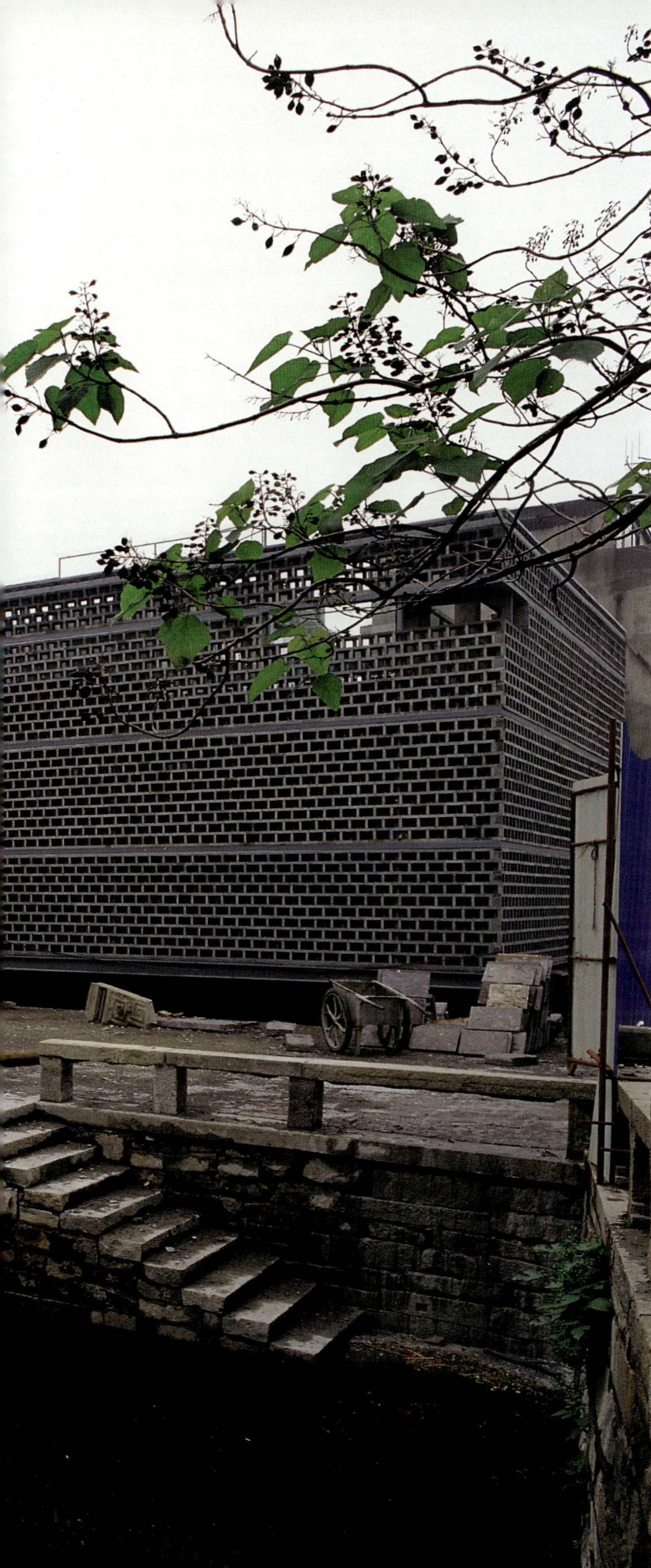

Almost concealed in what remains of the old quarters of the city of Suzhou, this tea house and restaurant signed by Tong Ming recalls, with its modernity, the little heritage centre built by Zhang Kai in Tongli, another of the water cities in this landscape of canals.

Just as Zhang Kai has counted on the quality and dignity of a contemporary writing without concessions, Tong Ming offers here, in Suzhou, a masterpiece which, if description and pastiche were not yet the rule, would put a definitive end to the false conflict between tradition and modernity. For the architect, who has freed the beneficial sigh of a diminutive square by a canal and the street, the façade seems to affirm itself simply as a long screen wall of bricks, without concessions and without aggression. Behind, along a regular slope, he develops a series of rooms which are private halls where the Chinese are particularly fond of gathering family or friends for a meal.

The whole hardly surpasses 1,800 square metres, but the fact is that the Pingjiang hotel and its new extension, set up in the large residence facing it, appropriately supplements at night the Dong house's daytime activities.

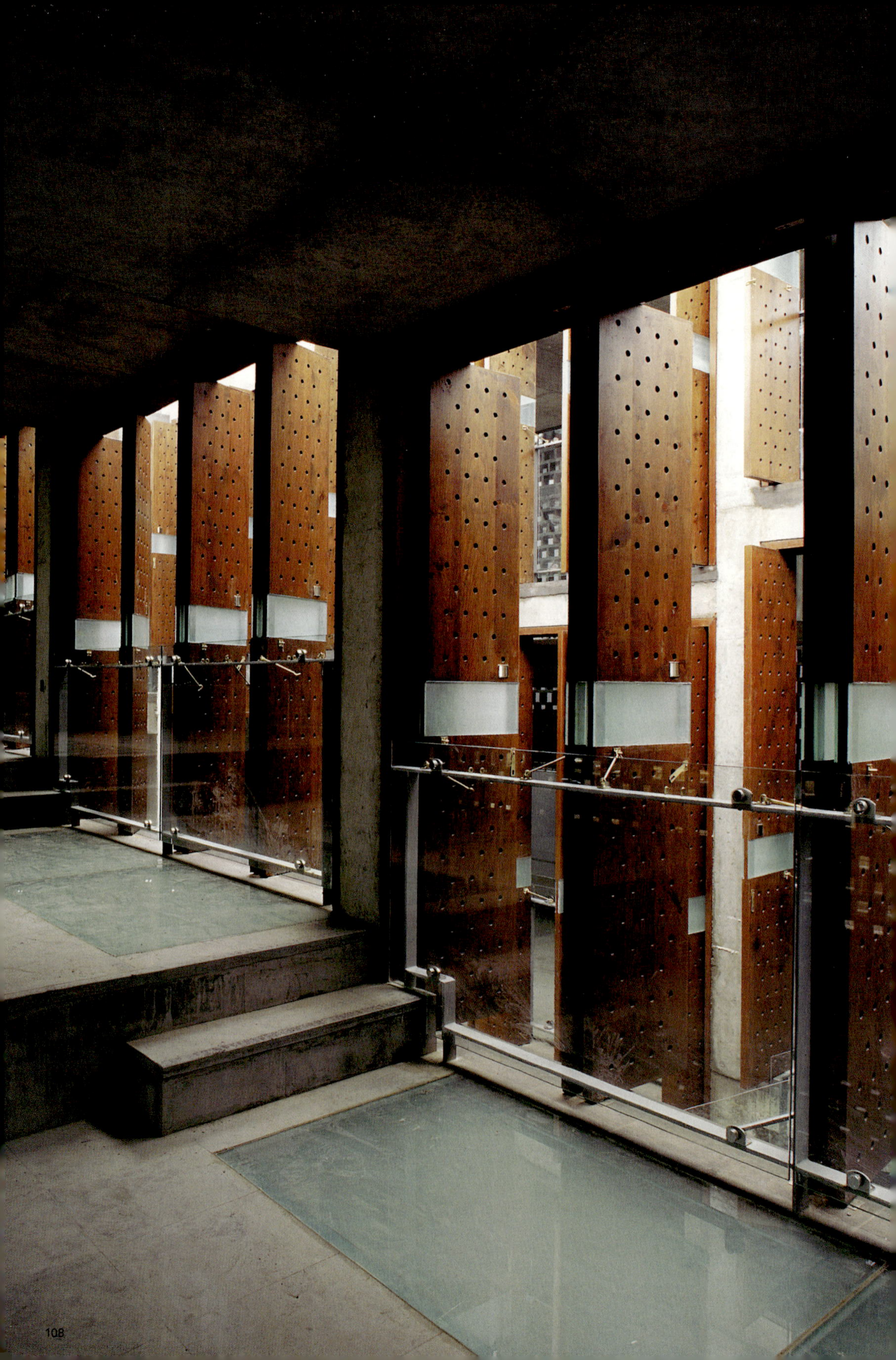

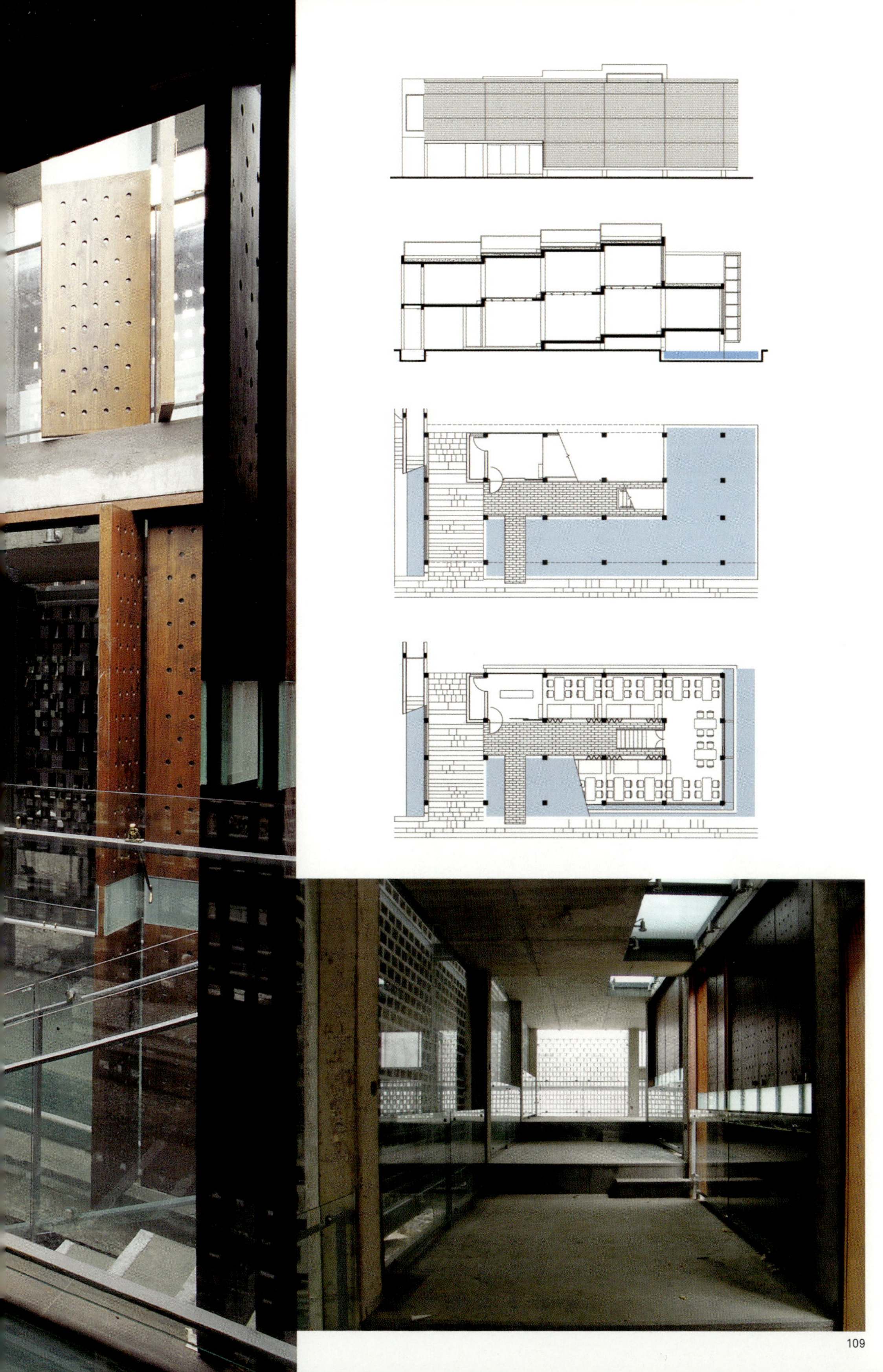

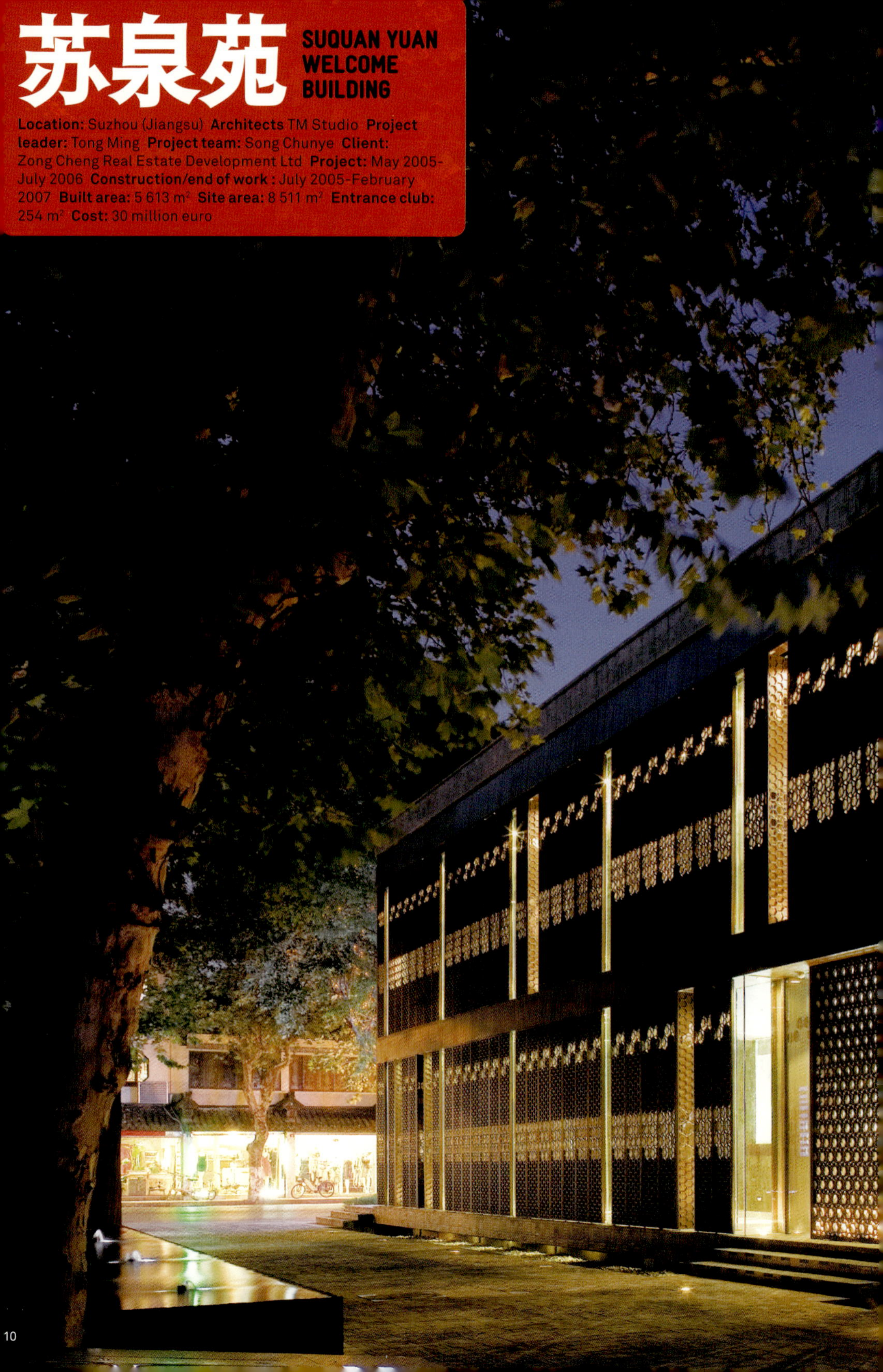

苏泉苑 SUQUAN YUAN WELCOME BUILDING

Location: Suzhou (Jiangsu) Architects TM Studio Project leader: Tong Ming Project team: Song Chunye Client: Zong Cheng Real Estate Development Ltd Project: May 2005-July 2006 Construction/end of work : July 2005-February 2007 Built area: 5 613 m² Site area: 8 511 m² Entrance club: 254 m² Cost: 30 million euro

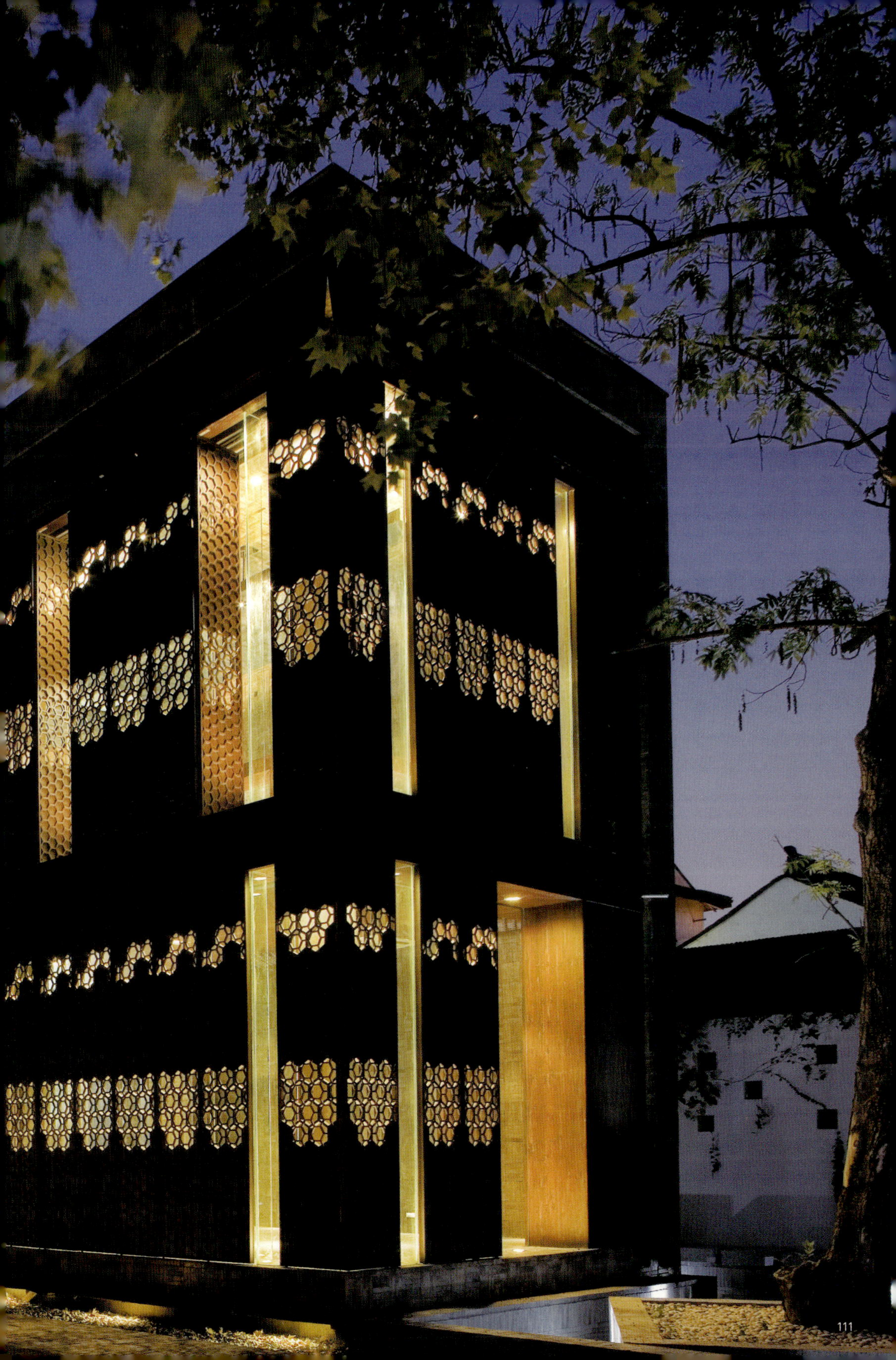

Suquan Avenue, one of the most touristic thoroughfares in the old Suzhou, has been renovated with a variable zeal. Near the Garden of the Master of the Nets, which is one of those gardens which have given the city its reputation as the Venice of the Orient, lies the Hotel Suzhou, the architecture of which shows a total indifference to the city's history, and there where Tong Ming has developed a shopping complex there was previously a parking lot. The Suquan garden site has been developed on over 8,500 square metres. Tong Ming has primarily been entrusted with designing the entrance, re-establishing the continuity between the commercial spaces and imparting the minimum dignity which one may expect in Suzhou.

In the urban disorder in which the façades of the boutiques spew out the fire of ten thousand dragons – but where magnificent plane trees have likewise survived – Tong Ming has conceived a building with a façade which may recall the principle of the Dong Tea House, but in a substantially more precious or even luxurious manner.

Tall mobile metal screens are reminiscent of the tradition of closures of carved wood. They serve here to create a rupture between the light from the street, a limpid clearness during the day and a garish yellow from the shops at night, thus contriving some volumes of exceptional purity in the interior. The whole, which adopts the shape of a great mah-jong tile, is placed slightly in suspension and is framed by a set of ponds which, without replicating uniformly the universe of canals of Suzhou, nevertheless perpetuates the link between the city and water.

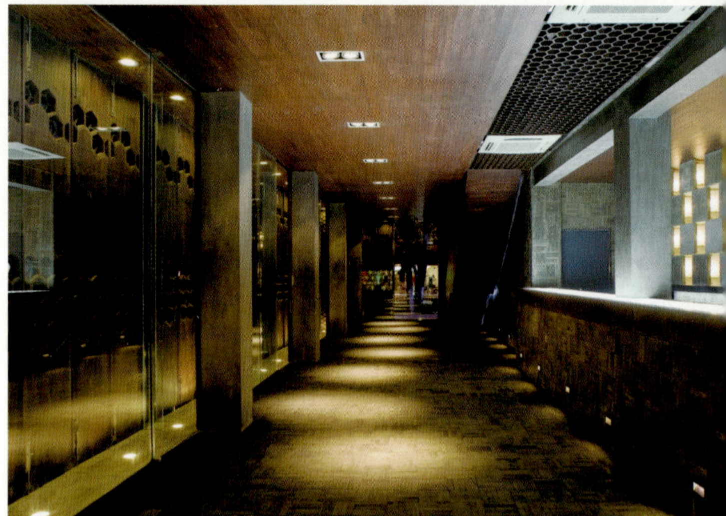

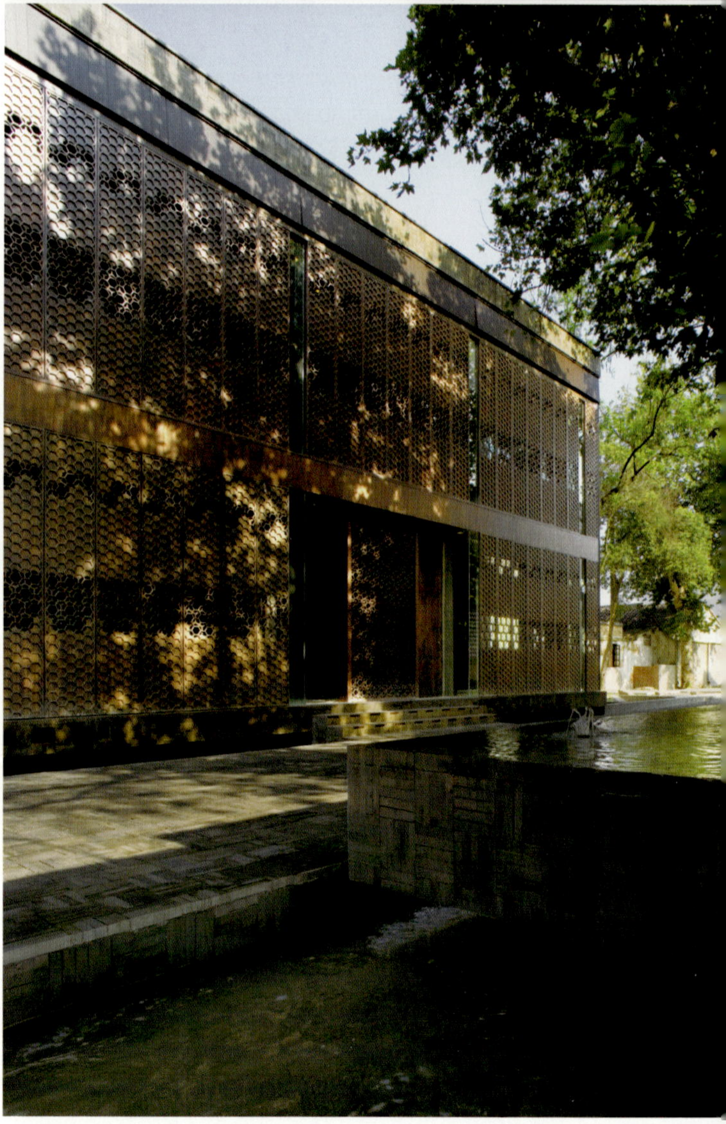

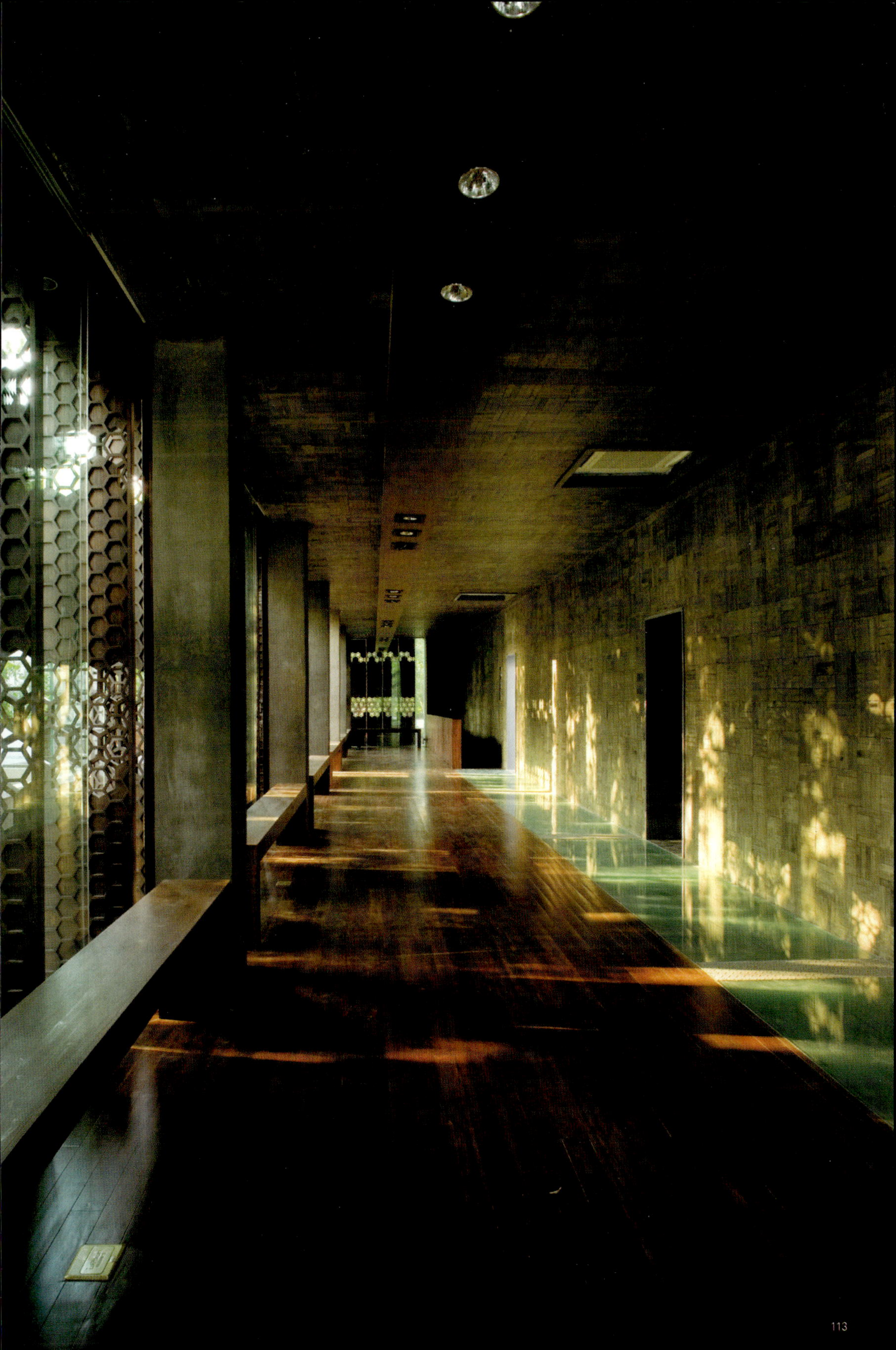

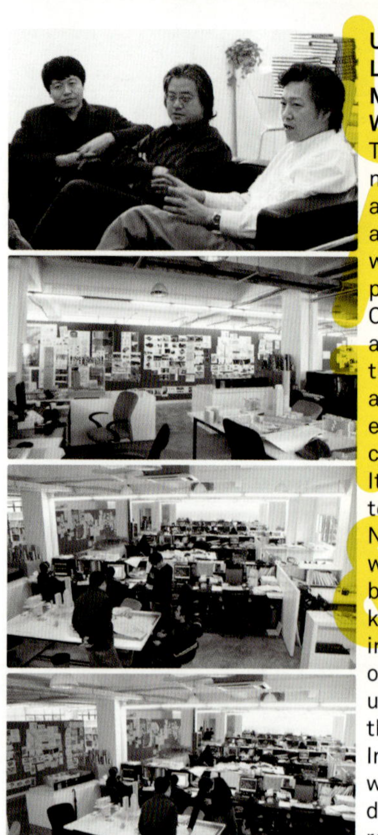

Urbanus Architecture & Design 都市实践
Liu Xiaodu 刘晓都
Meng Yan 孟岩
Wang Hui 王辉

The Urbanus studio, based in Beijing and Shenzhen (Hong Kong's non-identical twin), was formed by Liu Xiaodu, trained at Tsinghua and in the United States, Meng Yan, with a similar training, Wang Hui and Zhu Pei. The latter left the group in 2005 to create his own studio, which makes the legal paternity of their most important common project, Digital Beijing, a bit difficult to understand in a country, China, where the notion of intellectual property has long remained as relative as it is fluctuating. The other partners have also done their homework, however, and in depth at the American universities and studios, which gives them, in addition to a formidable technical efficiency, organisational habits which can strengthen their competences in juridical matters.

It is not easy just now to present here some projects subsequent to Zhu Pei's departure which are both significant and finished. Nevertheless, this detracts in no way from the vitality of the studio which, while remaining highly Americanised in the expression of its buildings or in the form adopted by its research, also reveals a rare knowledge of the topography of cities. The notion of topography must integrate an anthropological dimension, that is to say, a knowledge of lifestyles and of their contemporary mutation, and a more strictly urban and geographical dimension, which is particularly complex in the "new" city of Shenzhen.

In this respect, Urbanus is a name that is well suited to this team, which does not depart from architectural, urban and landscape dimensions and which knows how to integrate the issue of the reutilisation of the industrial spaces of recent decades, even if they are endowed with frail architectural qualities.

This is perhaps what separates Urbanus from Zhu Pei's studio. On the one hand, a way of adhering to the reality of the land, to the earth, such a fundamental element of Chinese thought, and on the other, a symbolic utilisation of the built-up dimension. For the time being, the projects of the two studios and of their figures remain too closely tied to distinguish strictly and objectively what may be attributed to the talent of one and the other.

Partners
Liu Xiaodu 刘晓都
Born 1961
Master in architecture,
Miami University, 1992
Meng Yan 孟岩
Born 1964
Master in architecture,
Miami University, 1995
Wang Hui 王辉
Born 1967
Master in architecture,
Miami University, 1997
Studio founded in 1999
Number of employees:
Shenzhen: 41
Beijing: 27

Contact
Urbanus

Shenzhen office
2nd Floor, E6 Building, OCT Loft
Nanshan District, Shenzhen 518053 China
T: +86 755 86 09 63 45
F: +86 755 86 10 63 36
office@urbanus.com.cn
urbanus@163.com
www.urbanus.com.cn

Beijing office
Beijing B302, Tian Hai Business Plaza
107#, Dong Si Bei Da Jie
Dongcheng District, Beijing 10007 China
T: +86 10 84 03 35 51
F: +86 10 84 03 35 61
office-bj@urbanus.com.cn
urbanus-bj@vip.163.com
www.urbanus.com.cn

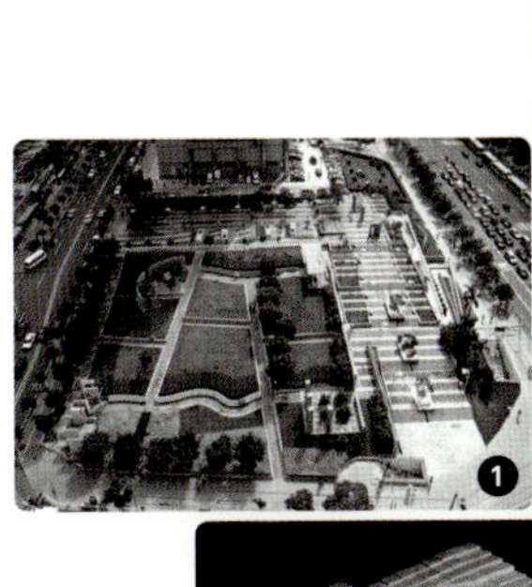
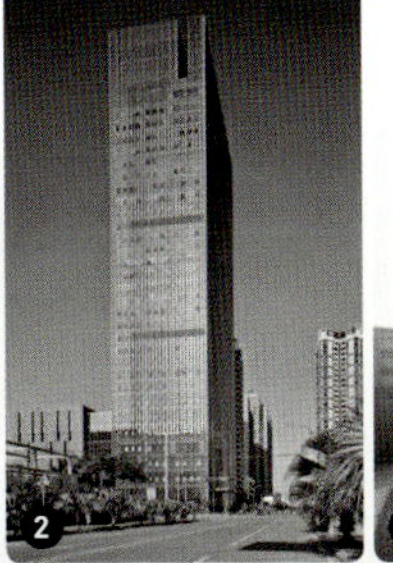
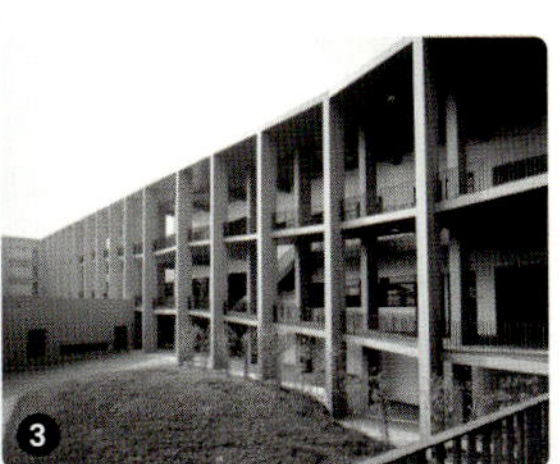
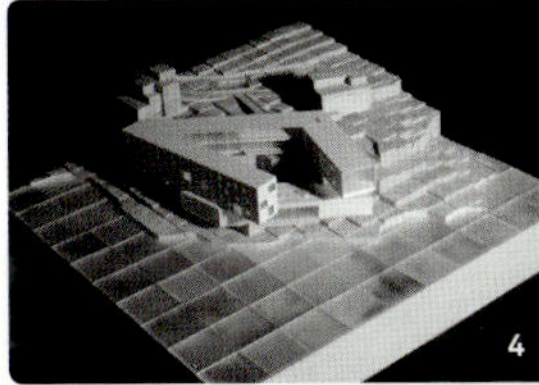
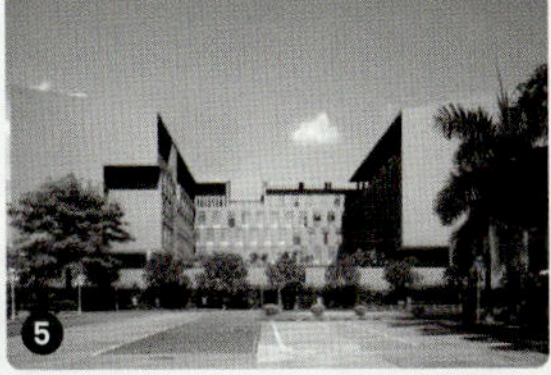
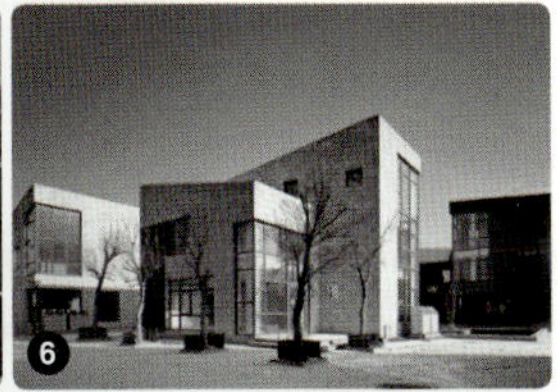
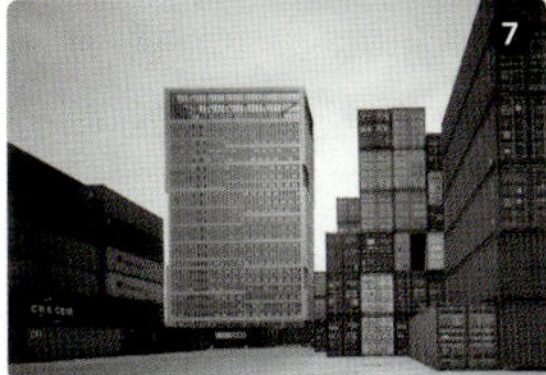
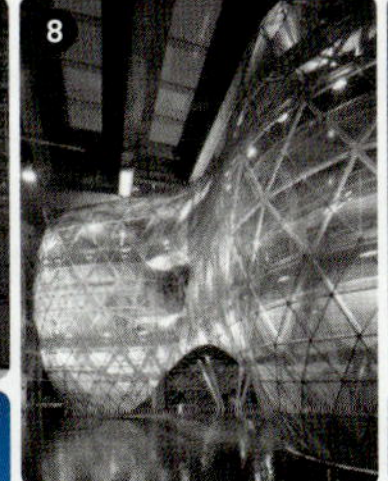
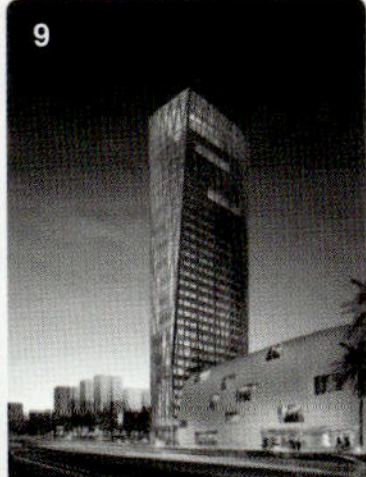
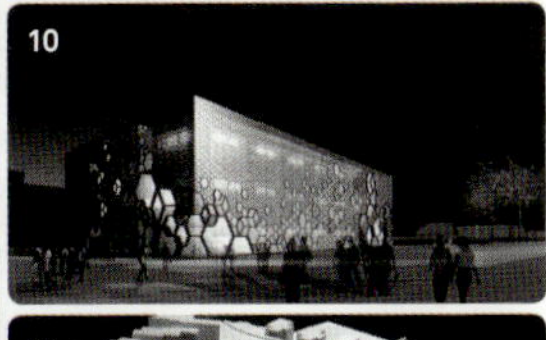
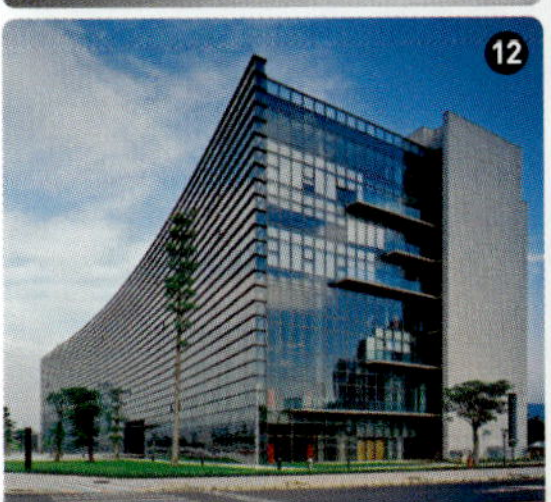
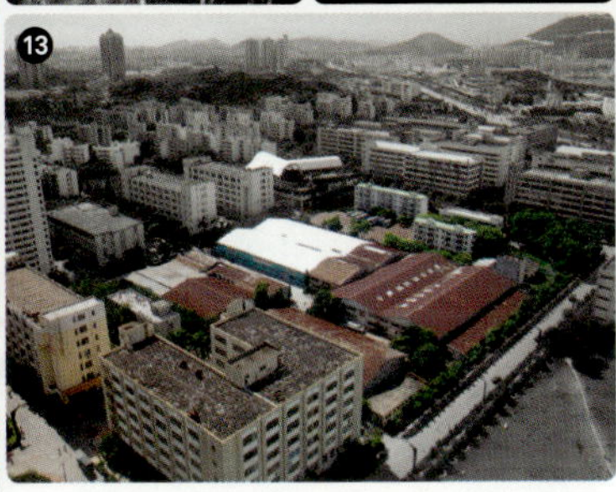
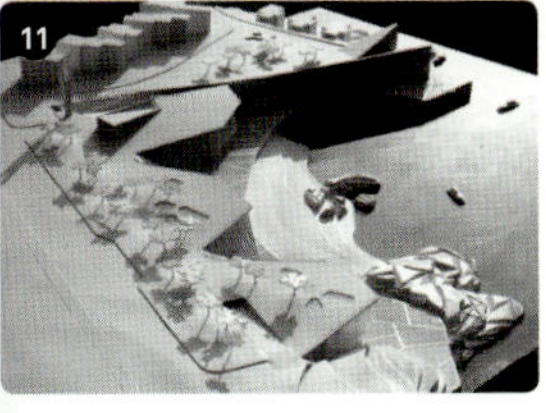
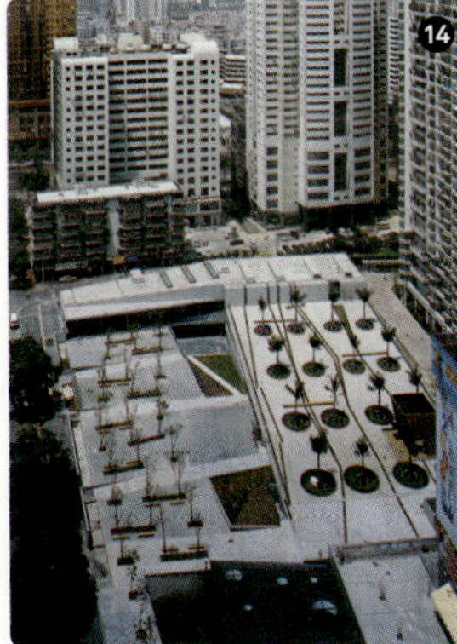
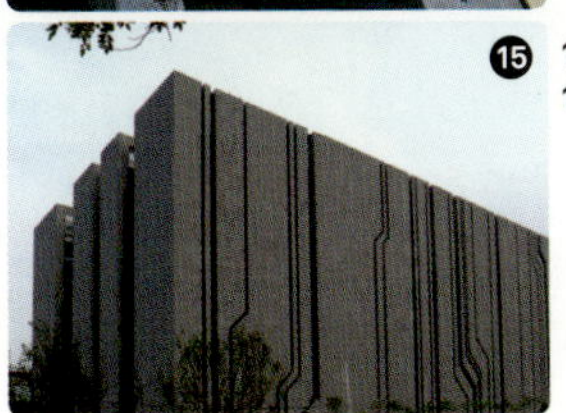

1 Diwang urban park, Shenzhen (Guangdong), 2000.
2 Tower of metro head office, Shenzhen, 2005.
3 Campus of the Polytechnical School, Dongguan (Guangdong), 2004.
4 Hotel by the sea Nanao, Shenzhen, 2002 (unbuilt).
5 Longgang formation centre, Shenzhen, 2005.
6 Drum Tower Lot 11#, Tianjin (Hebei), 2008.
7 Tour Maritime & Logistics Ltd., Shenzhen, 2007.
8 Vanke experimental centre, Shenzhen, 2006.
9 Xinghai building, phase 7, Shenzhen, 2006 (unbuilt).
10 Art gallery at the Intercontinental hotel OCT, Shenzhen, under construction.
11 Seaside Wedding Center, Tsingtao (Shandong), 2007.
12 Shenzhen Urban Planning Office, 2005.
13 Factory reconversion OCT Loft, Huaqiao Cheng,
   Shenzhen, 2007.
14 "Public Art Plaza", Guangdong, Shenzhen, 2007.
15 Digital Beijing (Urbanus & Zhu Pei), Olympic Games, Beijing, 2007.

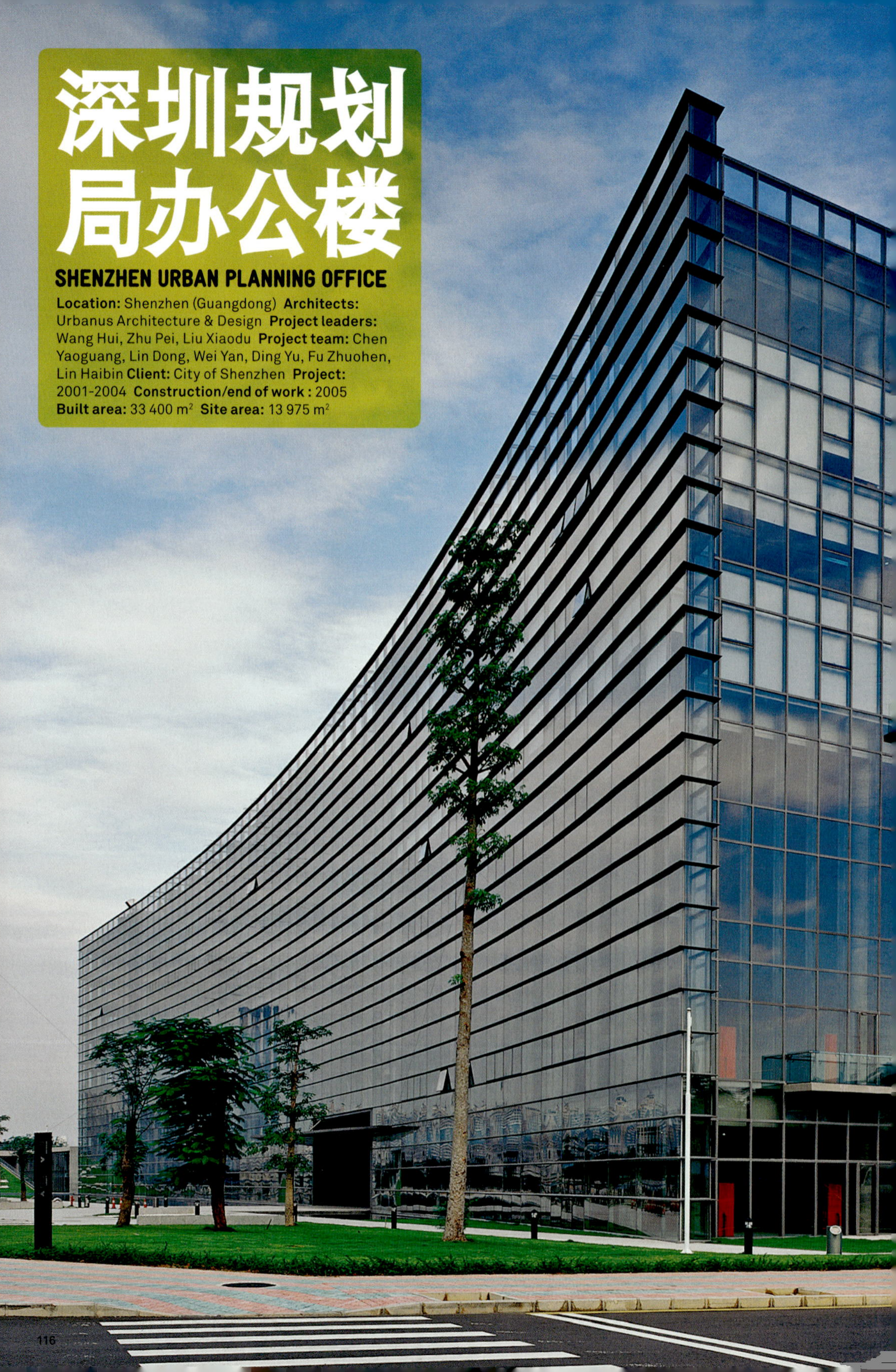

深圳规划局办公楼

SHENZHEN URBAN PLANNING OFFICE

Location: Shenzhen (Guangdong) **Architects:** Urbanus Architecture & Design **Project leaders:** Wang Hui, Zhu Pei, Liu Xiaodu **Project team:** Chen Yaoguang, Lin Dong, Wei Yan, Ding Yu, Fu Zhuohen, Lin Haibin **Client:** City of Shenzhen **Project:** 2001-2004 **Construction/end of work :** 2005 **Built area:** 33 400 m² **Site area:** 13 975 m²

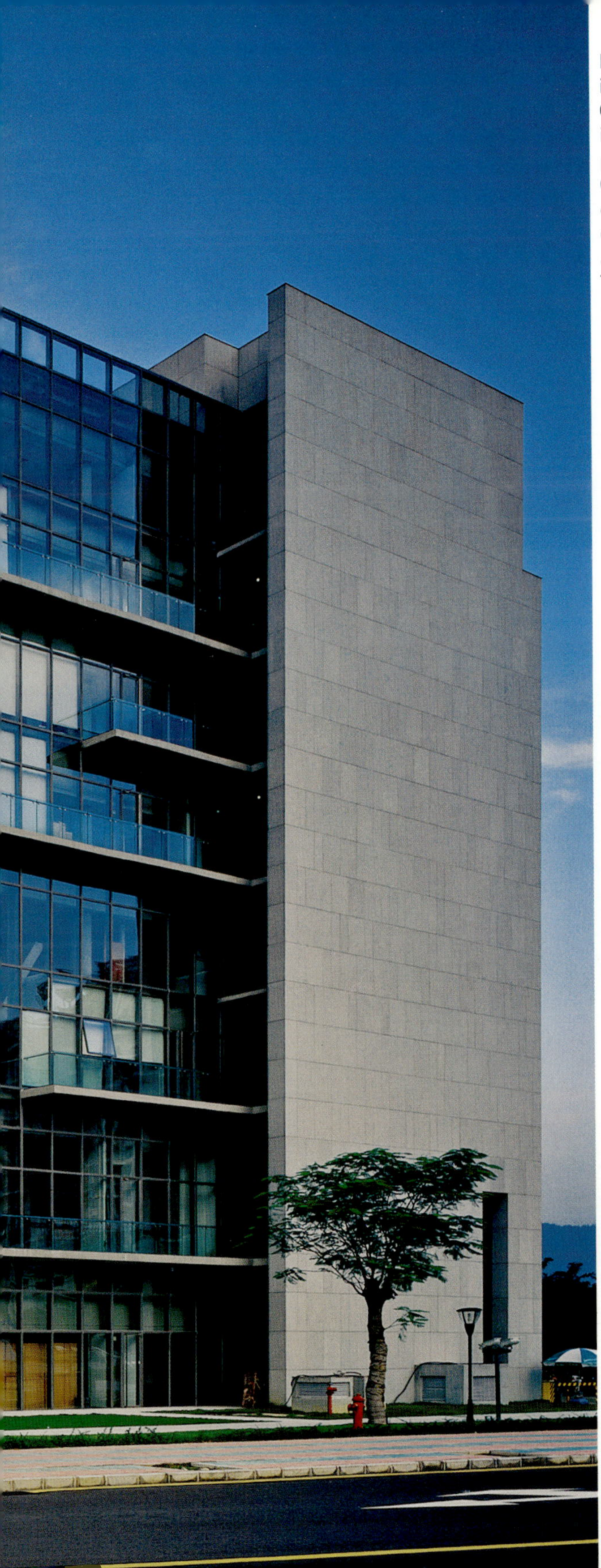

It would be hard to pinpoint what there is of specifically or even minimally Chinese to this building which draws its inspiration directly from the architecture practices of the big American firms. On the other hand, it is easier to distinguish the qualities of this construction, designed between 2001 and 2004.

The first of the qualities, which was difficult to obtain from the local companies, is that of its perfection or at least exactness of details, without which this type of construction loses the sacrosanct unction of the Miesian model and the International style: "God is in the details"... concrete, stone facing, glass, steel, etc. The exemplary work carried out by the various firms for this building with its strongly representative function, not only distinguishes itself from the production of the opening years of the 21st century in China but may moreover have helped to influence the demands set for other major structures.

Reduced to this alone, the building would actually be of only technical interest. Nevertheless, it presents many other qualities in its spatial distribution and in the manner in which it is inserted in the city, marking a sort of break with the instinctive megalomania displayed by the works managers of the big metropolises, while moreover offering Shenzhen a pronounced but pacified modernity in this way.

The composition all along the building (33,000 square metres) – one observes a similar process at the Qingpu Urban Planning Office – does not exclude a great address in the ruptures and the vertical devices. The structure, devoted to the management of local urban planning, operates like a city, without repetition, without boredom, and one can trust in Chinese spontaneity to bring a little fantasy into this initially sterile universe.

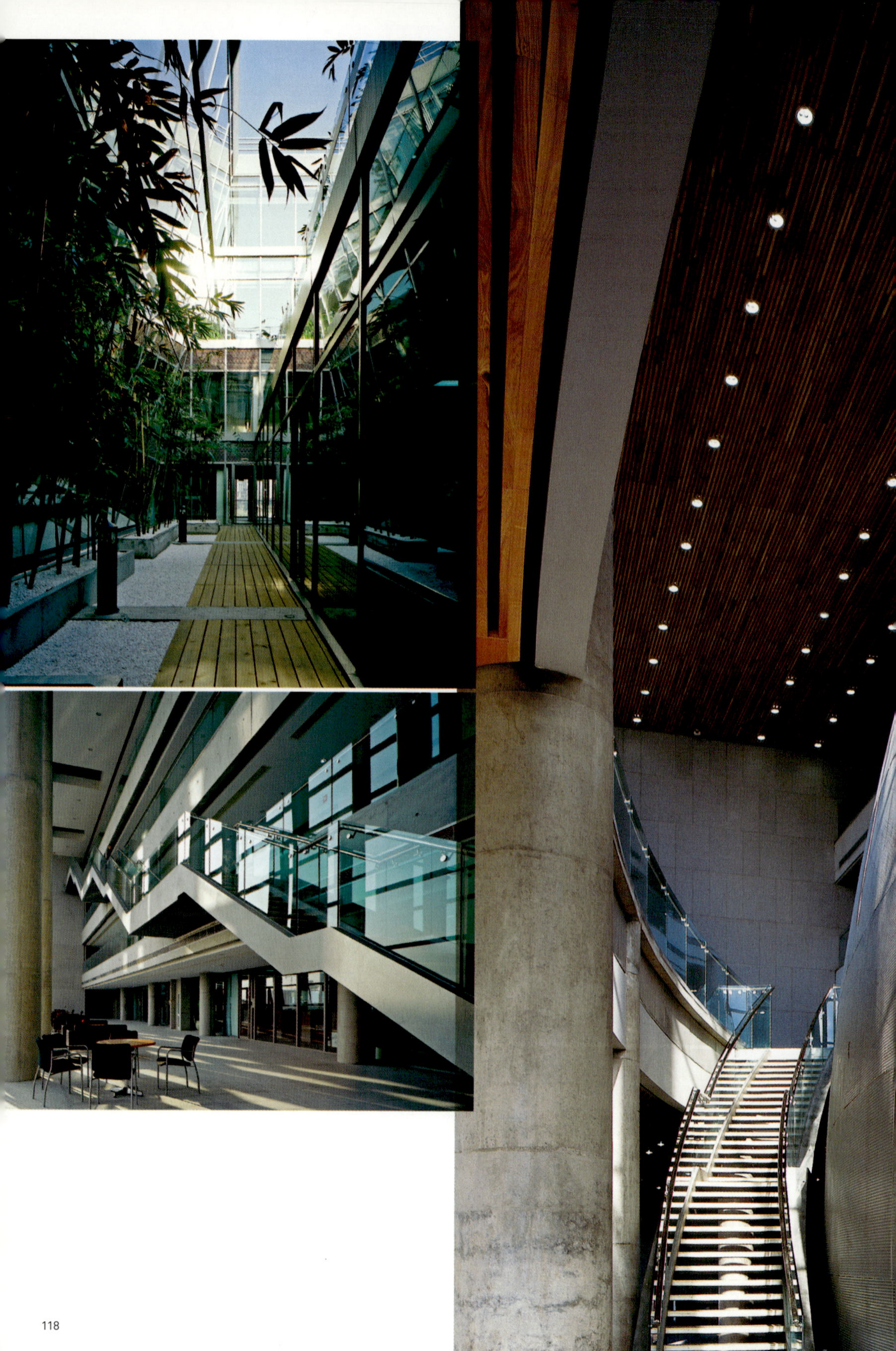

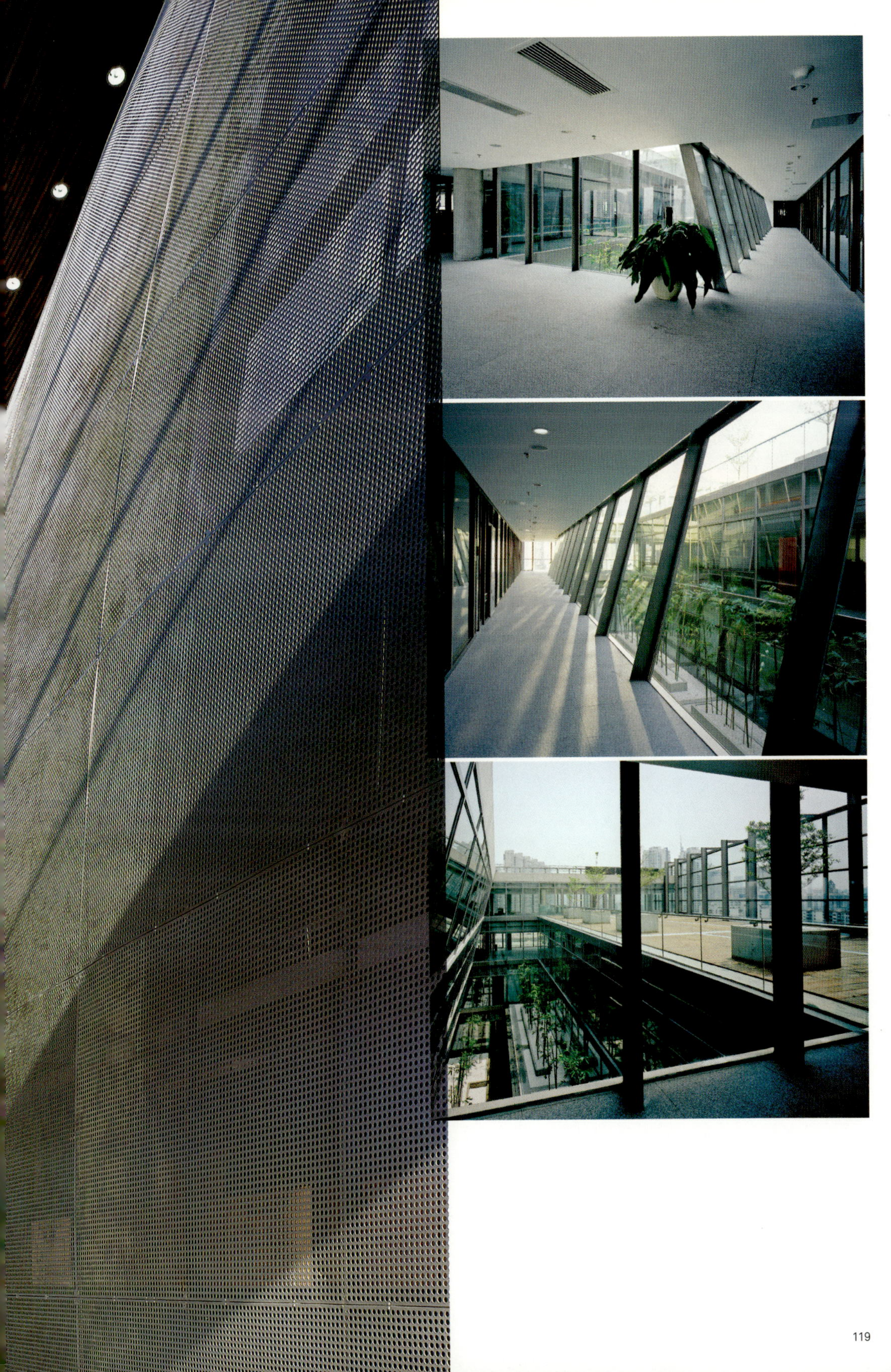

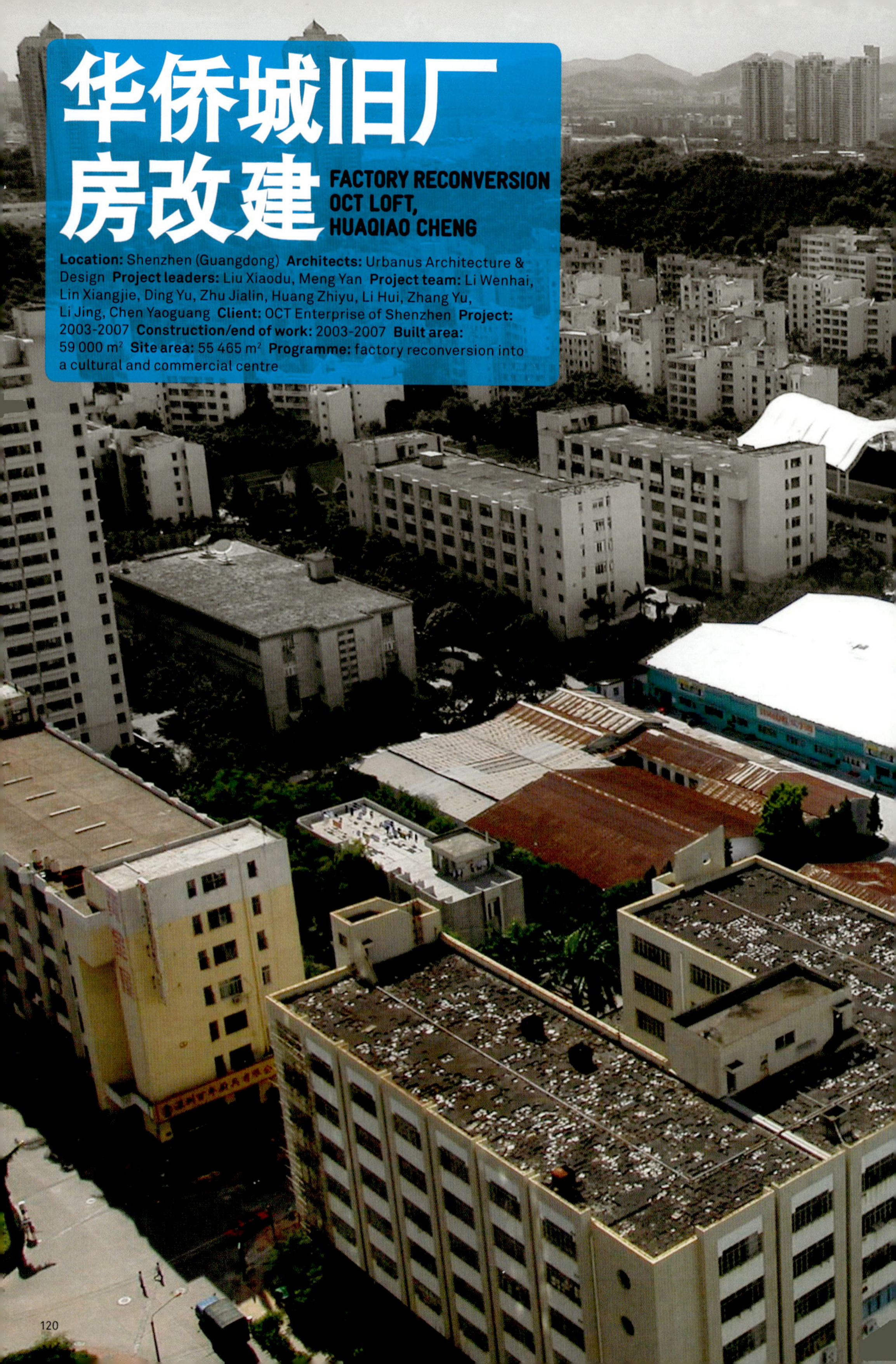

华侨城旧厂
房改建
FACTORY RECONVERSION
OCT LOFT,
HUAQIAO CHENG

Location: Shenzhen (Guangdong) Architects: Urbanus Architecture &
Design Project leaders: Liu Xiaodu, Meng Yan Project team: Li Wenhai,
Lin Xiangjie, Ding Yu, Zhu Jialin, Huang Zhiyu, Li Hui, Zhang Yu,
Li Jing, Chen Yaoguang Client: OCT Enterprise of Shenzhen Project:
2003-2007 Construction/end of work: 2003-2007 Built area:
59 000 m² Site area: 55 465 m² Programme: factory reconversion into
a cultural and commercial centre

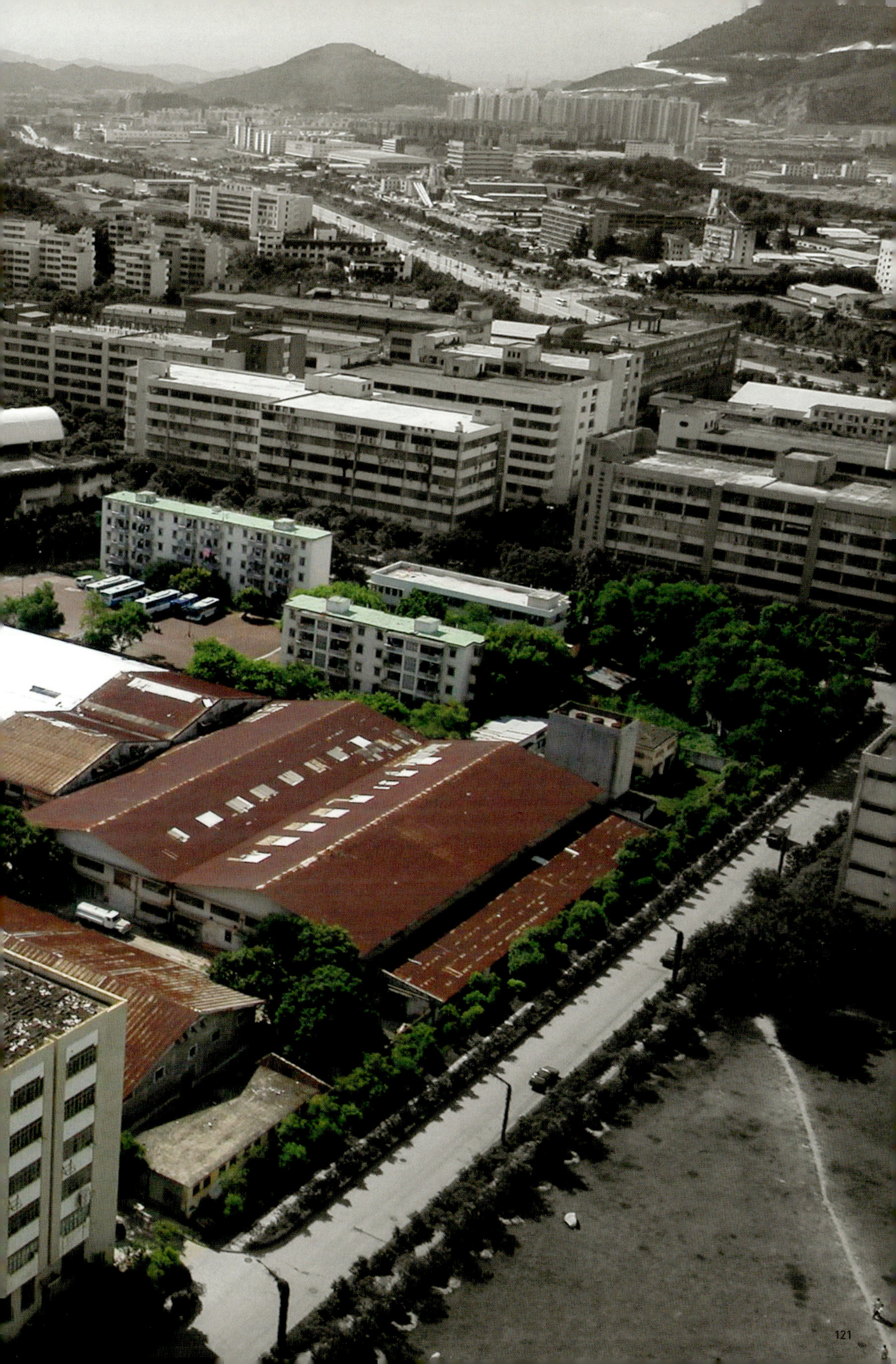

Maximalist by its size (150,000 interior square metres), this project involving the transformation of an old factory (including dormitories, offices and warehouses) unfolded in a minimalist way under the direction of Urbanus.

Like Dashanzi in Beijing, Urbanus has turned the site into a centre with galleries, cafés, trendy shops, and creation-related offices (graphic designers, architects...) near such amusement parks as Happy Valley and Window on the World, which form the basis of the city's success.

The old factory is located in a quarter known by its English abbreviation OCT (which stands for Overseas Chinese Town, the name of the promoter, derived from a national commission created to favour overseas investments in China). Urbanus has maintained the structure while adding strong elements to the façades, the dated character of which has been willingly preserved by the architecture studio. This intervention includes elements of graphics and micro-architecture as well as of added structural elements (of steel or wood), a departure from the unsophisticated materials of the original buildings.

Likewise, each space has preserved its particular virtues and disadvantages, and since this industrial ensemble has none of the qualities of Dashanzi's Beijing factories, designed by a Bauhaus disciple, the scenography of the exhibitions may prevail over the specification sheet of Urbanus, with the added pieces integrating themselves easily into a joyous patchwork.

Since 2005 this has been the venue of the Shenzhen Architecture Biennial, the first holding of which, under the supervision of Chang Yung Ho, was a model of elegance. On the contrary, the past edition, which was curated by Ma Qingyun, left each architecture to serve up its own image, sometimes for the better but not infrequently for the worst.

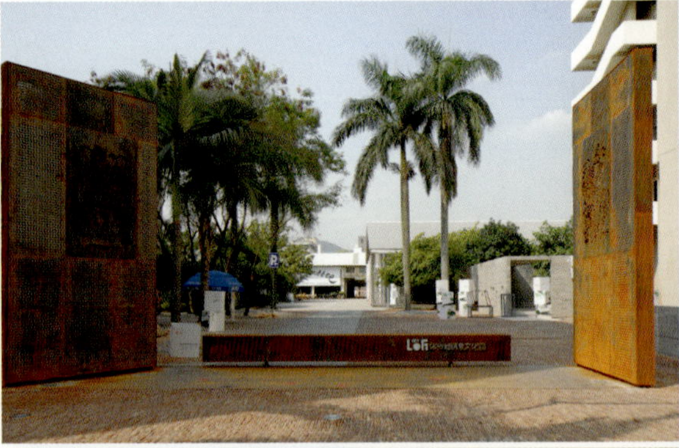

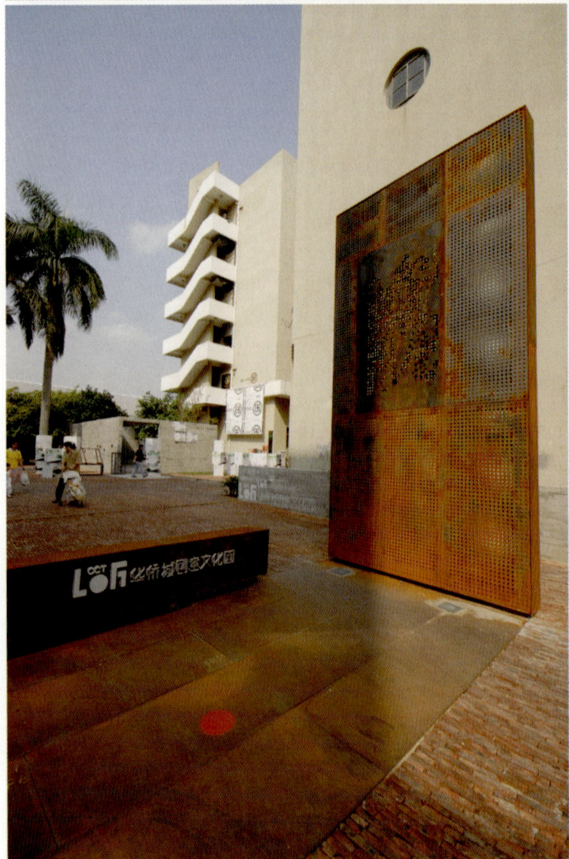

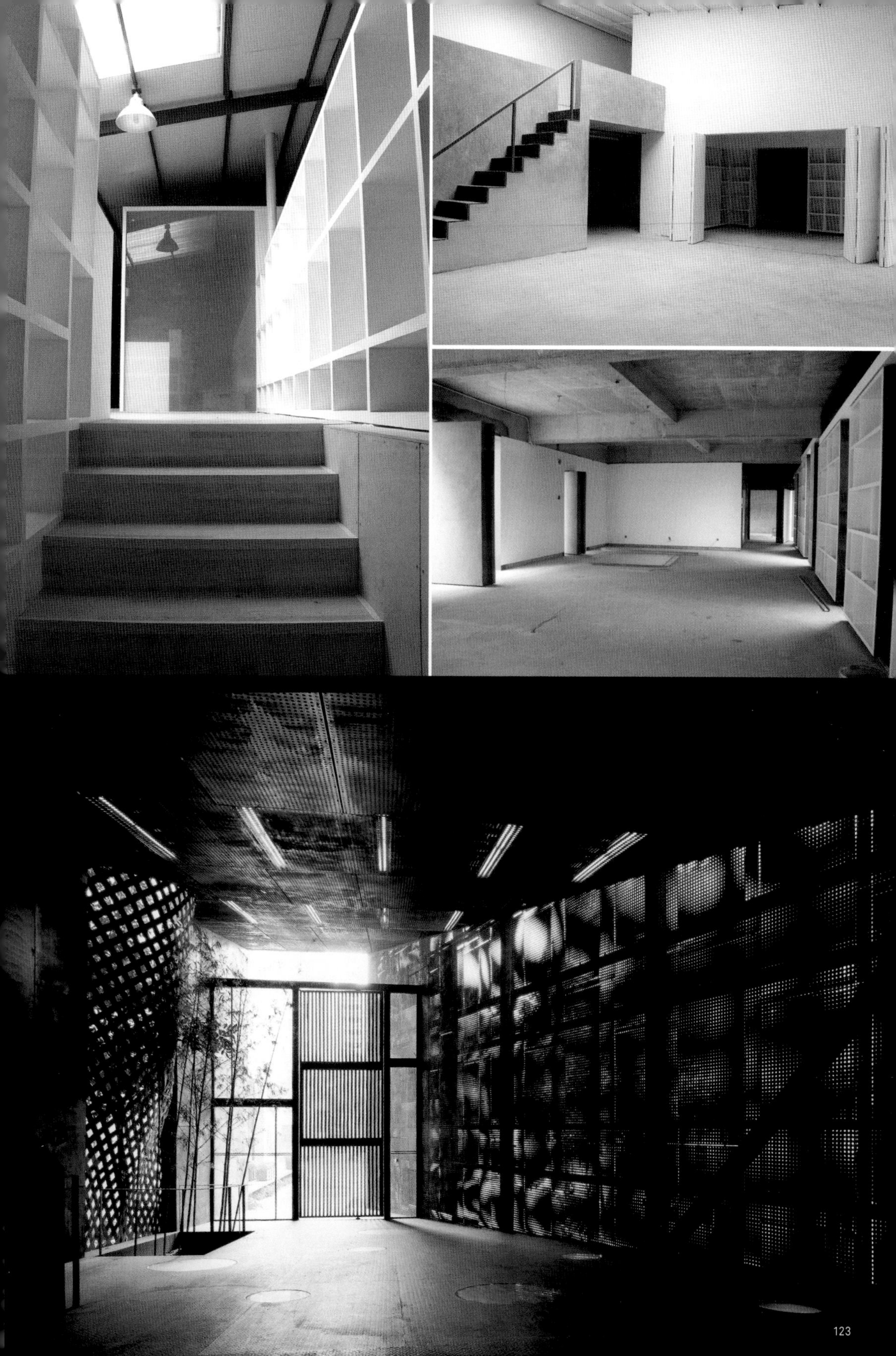

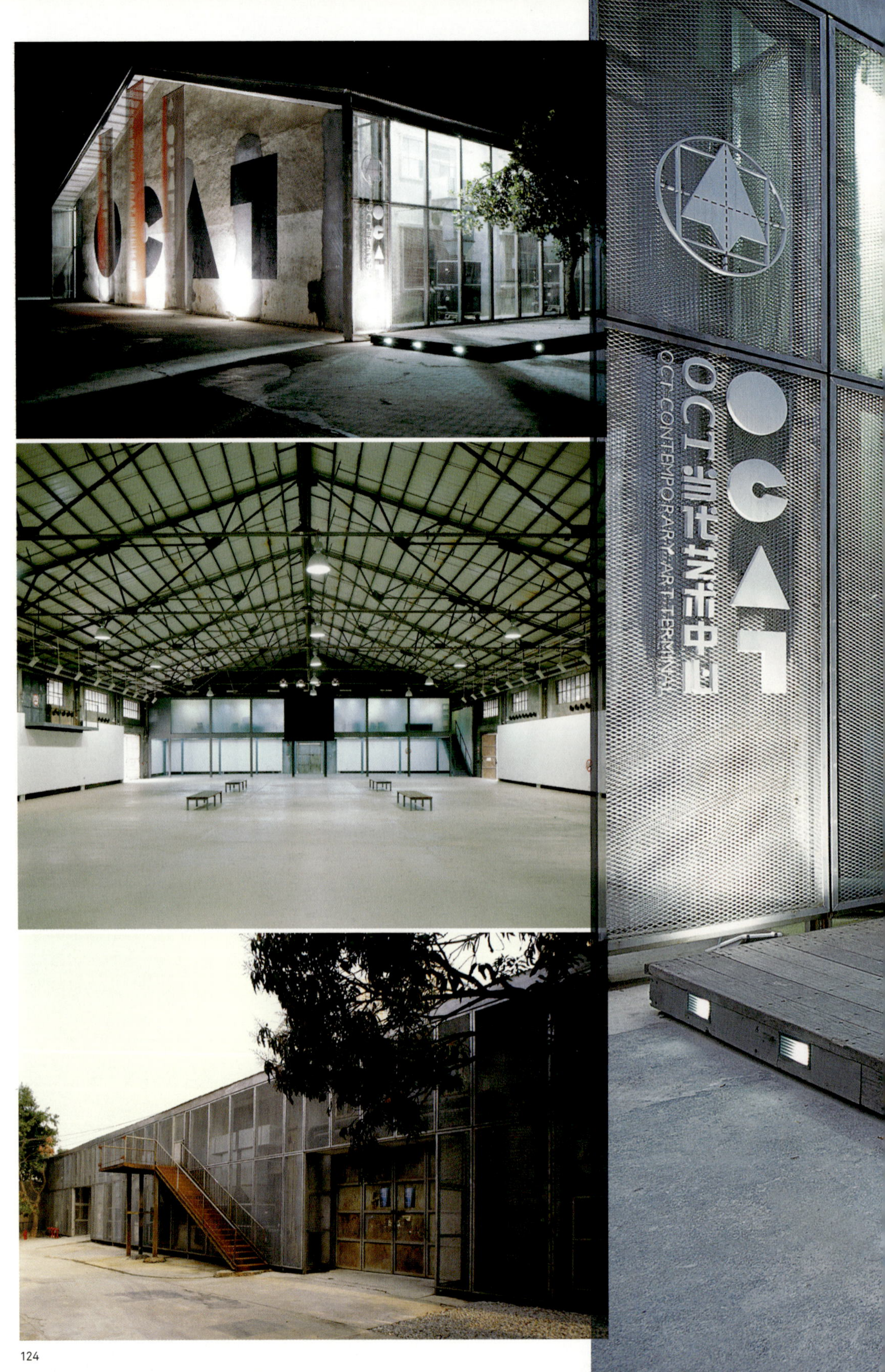
OCAT
OCT當代藝術中心
OCT CONTEMPORARY ART TERMINAL

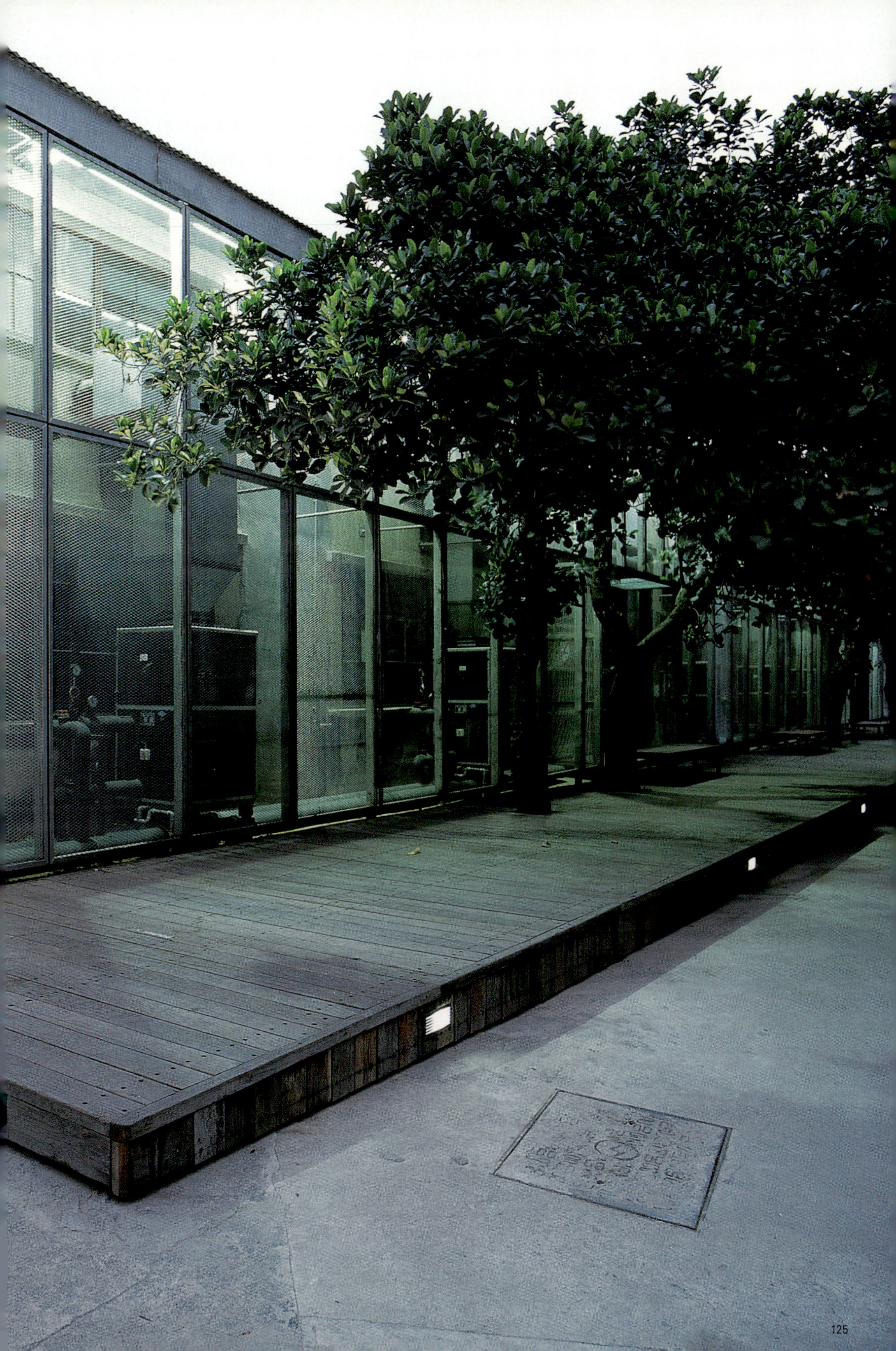

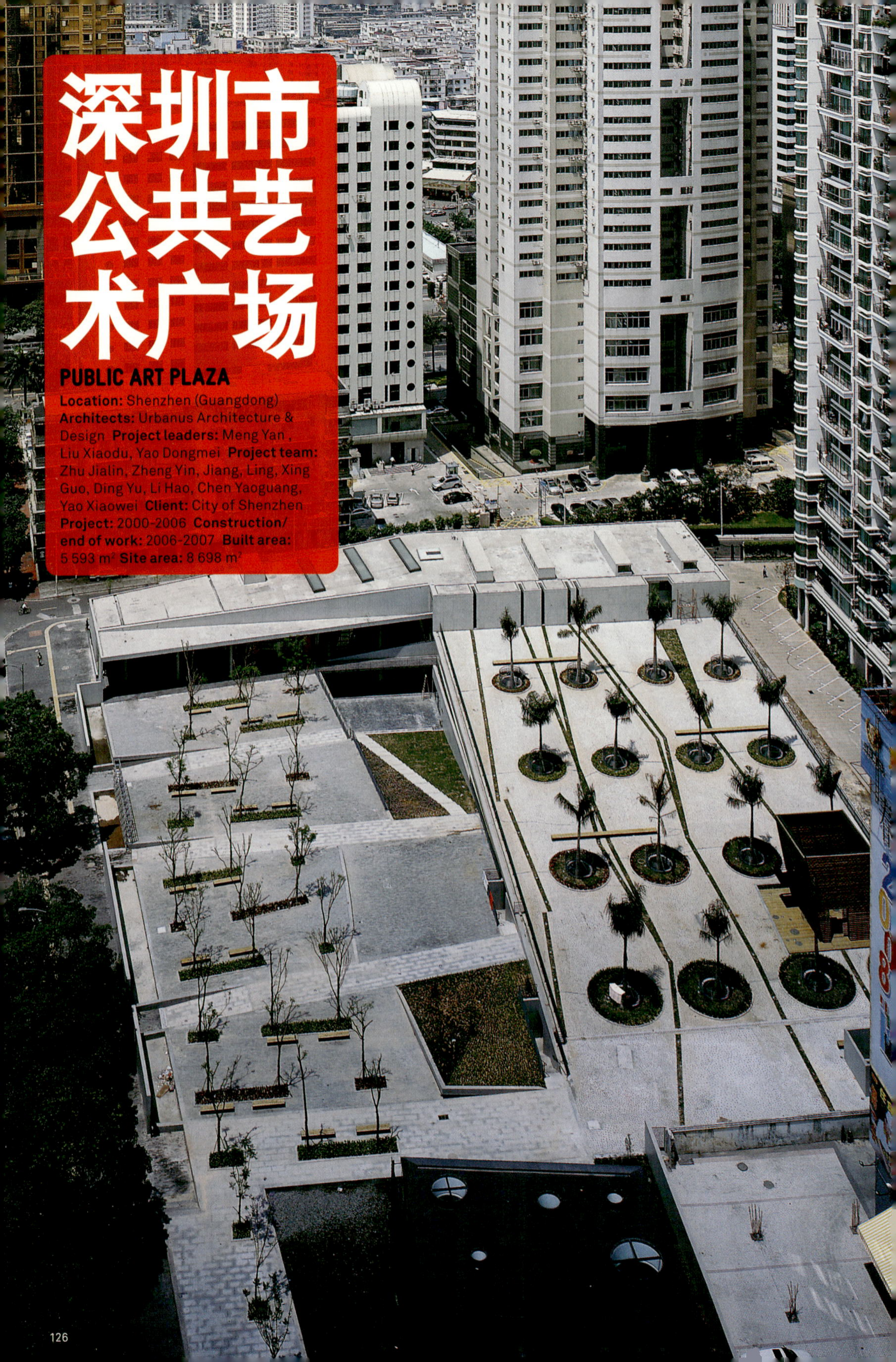

PUBLIC ART PLAZA

Location: Shenzhen (Guangdong)
Architects: Urbanus Architecture & Design **Project leaders:** Meng Yan , Liu Xiaodu, Yao Dongmei **Project team:** Zhu Jialin, Zheng Yin, Jiang, Ling, Xing Guo, Ding Yu, Li Hao, Chen Yaoguang, Yao Xiaowei **Client:** City of Shenzhen **Project:** 2000-2006 **Construction/ end of work:** 2006-2007 **Built area:** 5 593 m² **Site area:** 8 698 m²

This public pedestrian square of 5,000 sq m devoted to the arts and to walking, is located in the Luohu district.

It is bordered by a set of thoroughly heterogeneous buildings which Urbanus succeeds in making one forget, without hiding the sad reality, however. The square is presented as a landscape site which is strongly structured by a succession of concrete planes, from which emerges in a strictly ordered way a sort of musical score made of trees, benches, sandboxes and passages. So many elements, so many pitfalls which oblige walkers to observe carefully where they set their feet – a technique which is as good as any other to draw the gaze away from an unpleasant urban design. In the park, several buildings are conceived for art, without calling attention to themselves for any other reason than their architectural strength, among other structures leading to the car park or sheltering a café and a guard post. Here one may see exhibitions on what is generally a modest scale, without true plastic importance since the selfsame design of the architects of Urbanus has a pronounced artistic character. It is a genuine visual pleasure to see how their park succeeds in eliciting the smiles of the quarter's inhabitants.

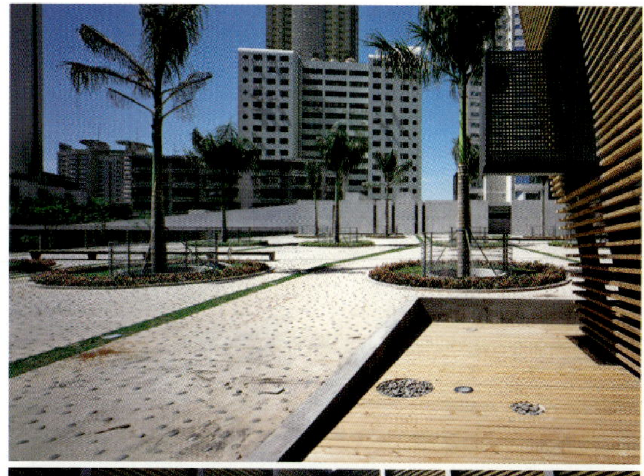

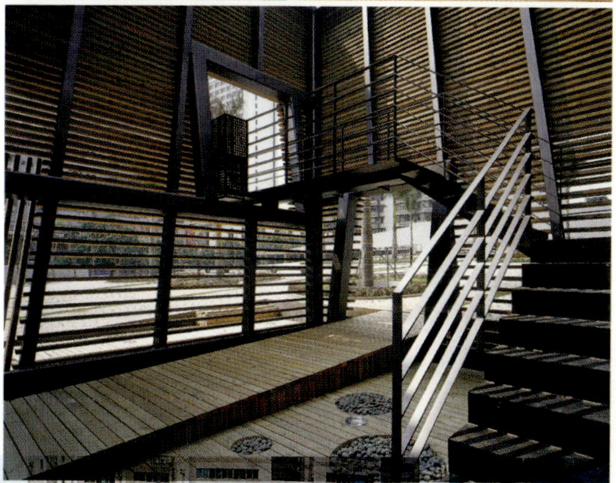

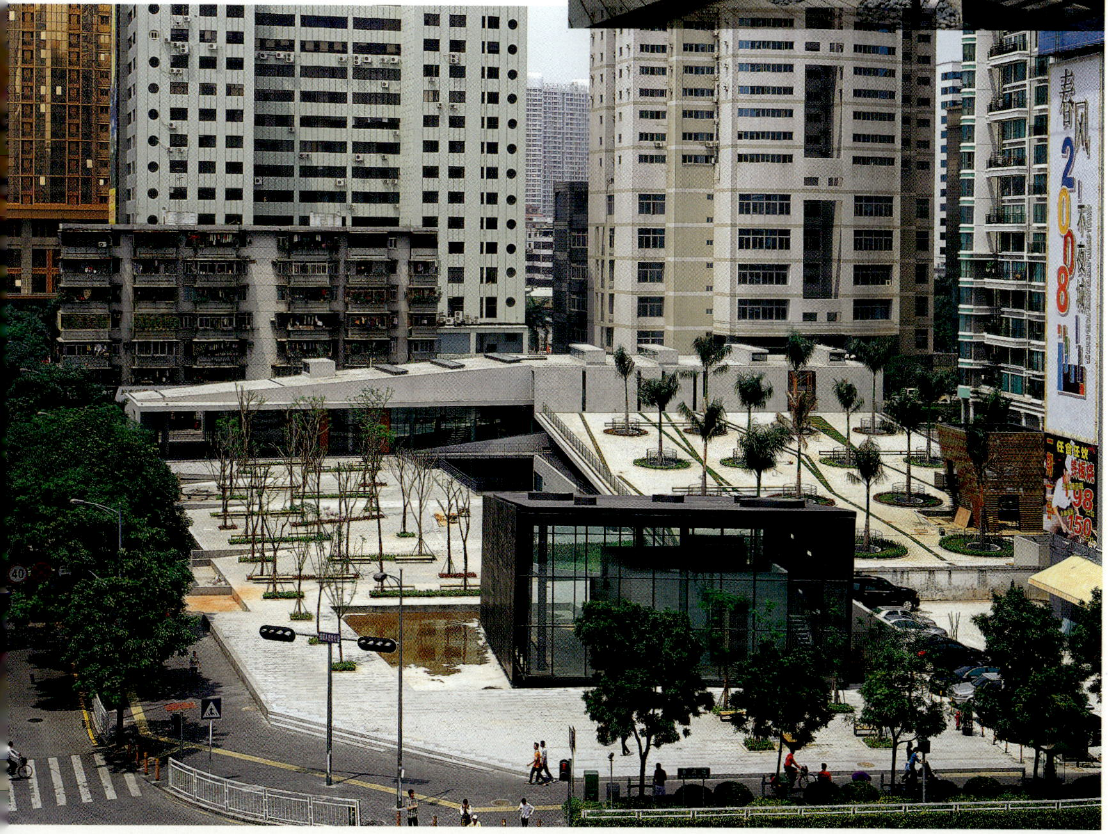

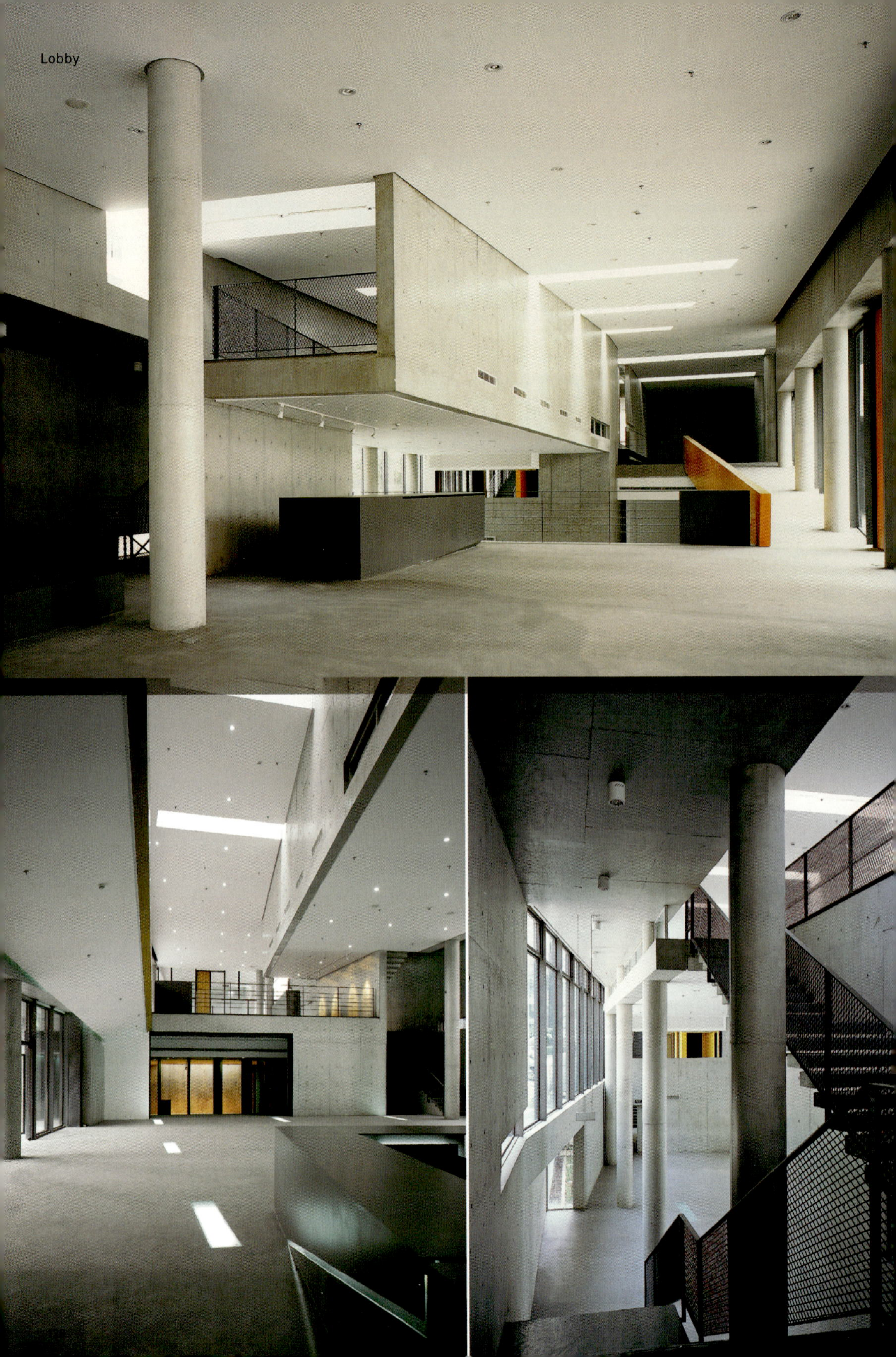
Lobby

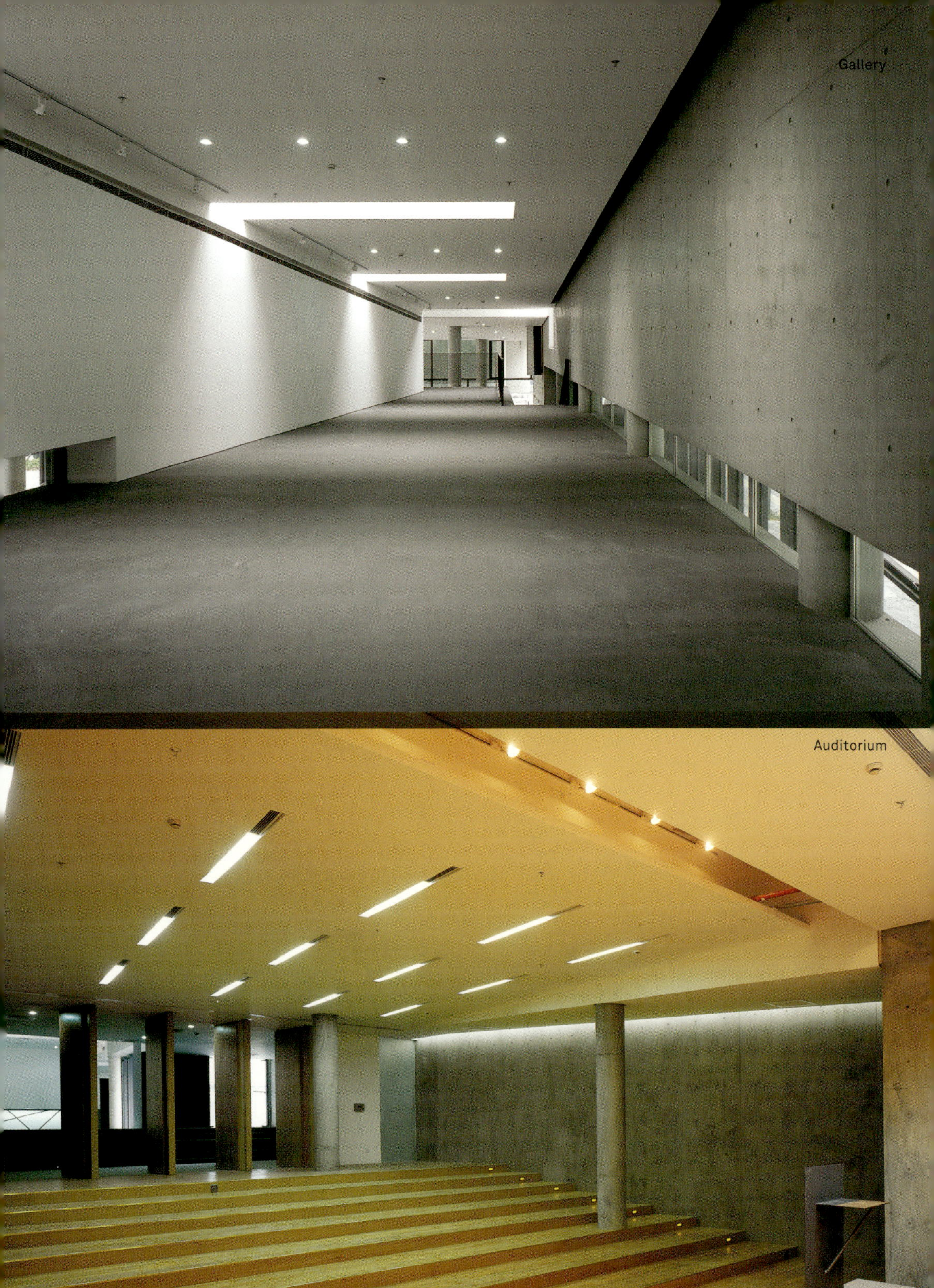

Gallery
Auditorium

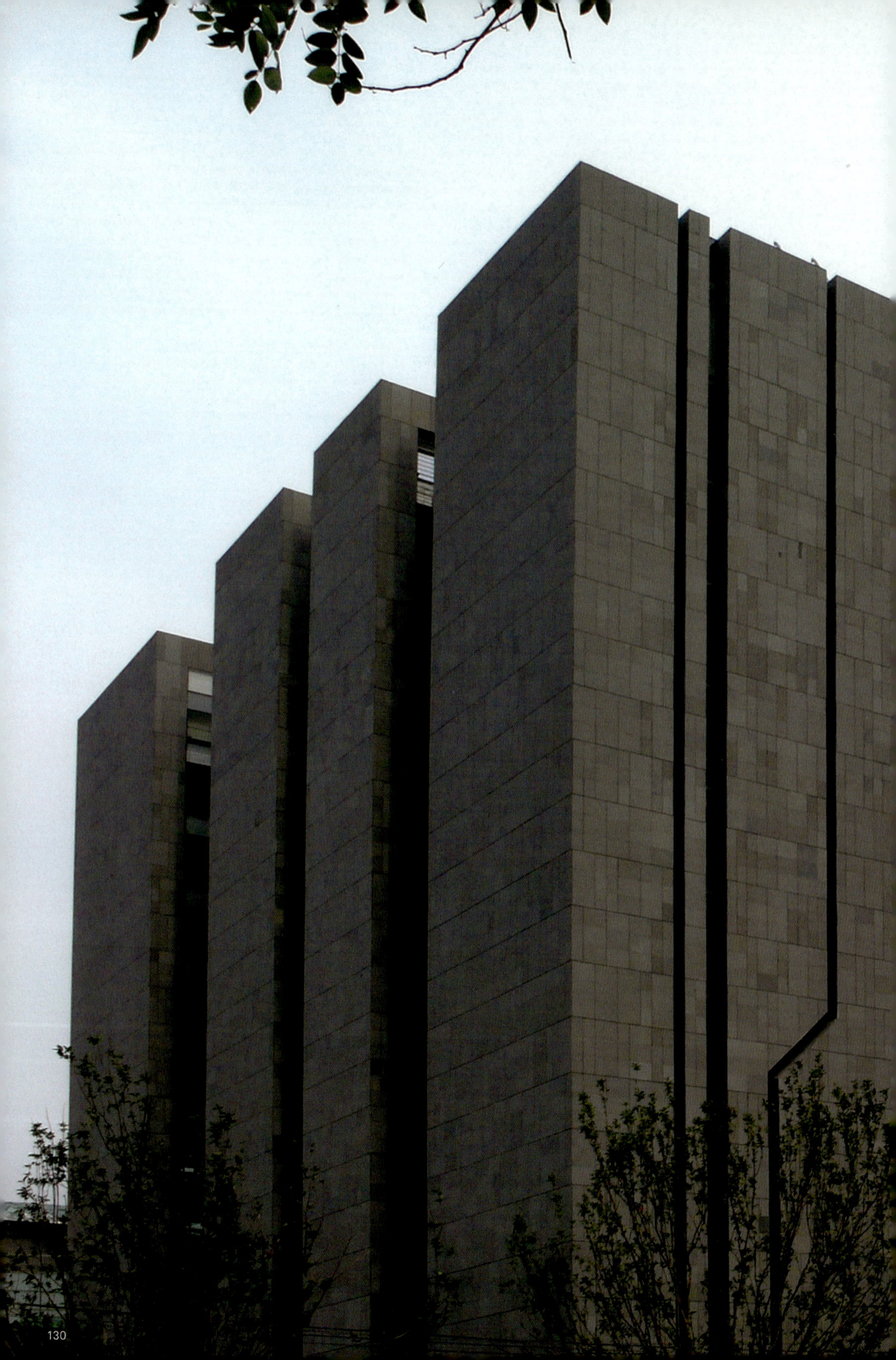

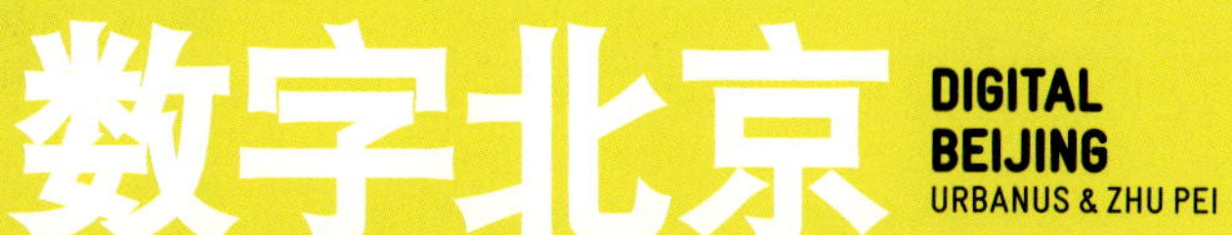

数字北京

DIGITAL BEIJING
URBANUS & ZHU PEI

Location: Olympic Park, Beijing **Agence :** Urbanus & Zhu Pei **Project leaders:** Zhu Pei, Wu Tong & Wang Hui **Project team:** Liu Wentian, Li Chuen, Lin Lin, Tian Qi **Client:** City of Beijing **Project:** 2004-2005 (international competition) **Construction/end of work:** 2005-2007 **Built area:** 98 000 m² **Site area:** 26 000 m² **Cost:** 76 million euro **Programme:** control centre of the computer systems during the Olympic Games and museum

The Digital Beijing Center (DBC) is the only
building commissioned, and for good reason,
to a Chinese project manager, Zhu Pei, trained
in part in the United States, who was one of the
associates of the Urbanus studio. This building,
drawing its inspiration with great elegance
from computer design, is also the edifice which
will concentrate, during the Olympic Games and
afterwards, all the computer systems allowing
the control of the smooth running of the Games,
and the harmony which should then reign in the
capital. It is the tool, the only tool about which no
one speaks, and which will continue to be used
once the Olympics have finished. It is not an easy
task to watch over a city like Beijing, or even to
observe it.
Called Digital Beijing, this structure is signed
jointly by Zhu Pei and Urbanus. Three of the
signatories have separated since then: Zhu Pei
on the one hand, and Wu Tong and Wang Hui on
the other, the latter two remaining the foremost
partners of Urbanus. The centre occupies a
strategic position beside large facilities of the
Olympic Park. Designed between 2004 and 2005,
it will have benefited from the improved skills in
Chinese construction, and especially those of
the engineers of the China Institute of Building
Standards, Design and Research. Its function
is to gather and dispatch all the data, images or
figures connected with the Olympic Games.
Without it being possible to know more about the
performance of the athletes, the various sites
and stadiums, traffic… in short, surveillance,
all these elements seem to be brought together
here. That is to say, it could also become a major
surveillance tool after the Olympic Games.
The whole is presented as four large
parallelepipeds, four large dark plates mounted
in parallel and separated by three rifts more
susceptible to emit light than to light up a
deliberately opaque interior. It thus evokes the
design of computer elements, four gigantic
"hard disks", a symbolic image reinforced on
the façade by a light network similar to the one
found on the computer experts' printed circuits.
From the opening of the Games, the ground
floor is to shelter an exhibition centre devoted
of course to information technology.
Zhu Pei and his team-mates have concentrated
there all their talent for the invention of spaces
and forms. The rest of the building remains a
mystery and closed to the public. This sombre
construction is made up of no less than 98,000
square metres.

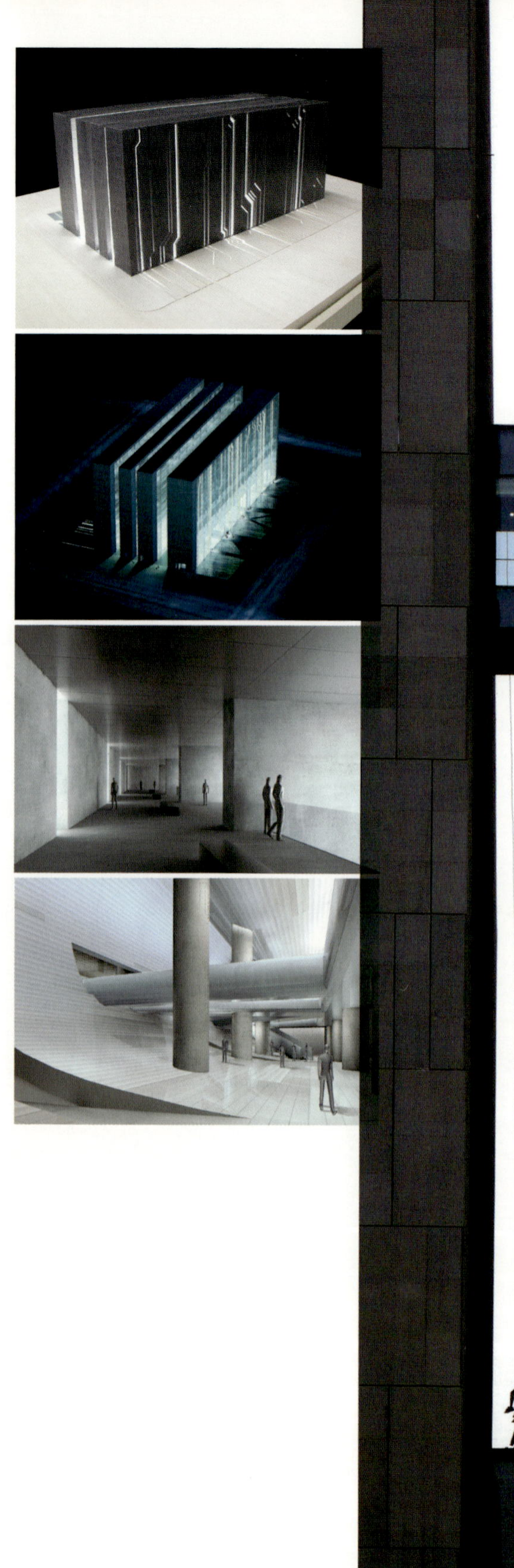

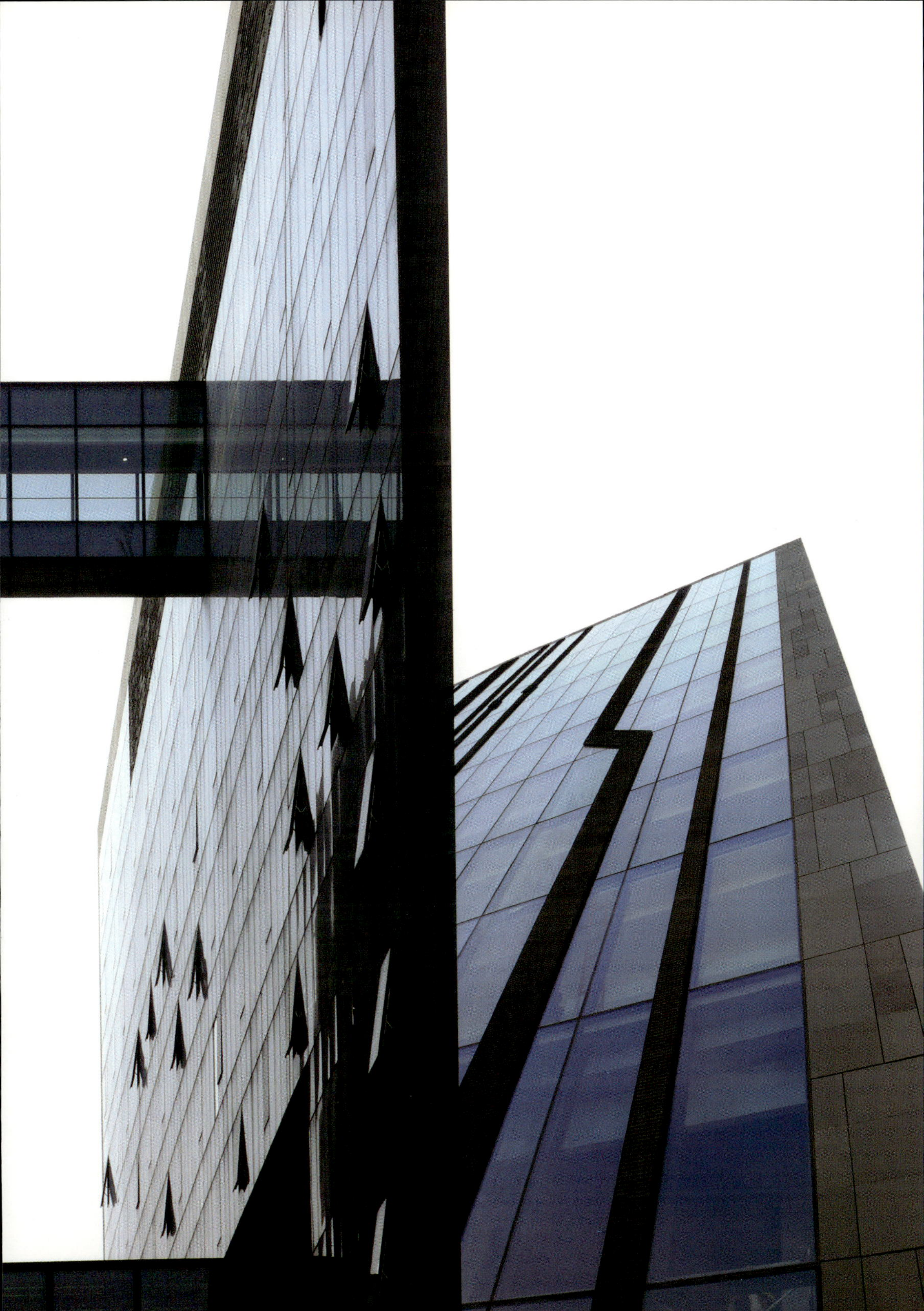

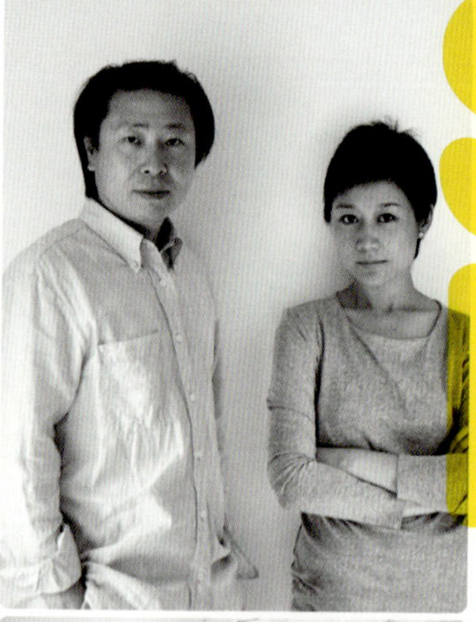

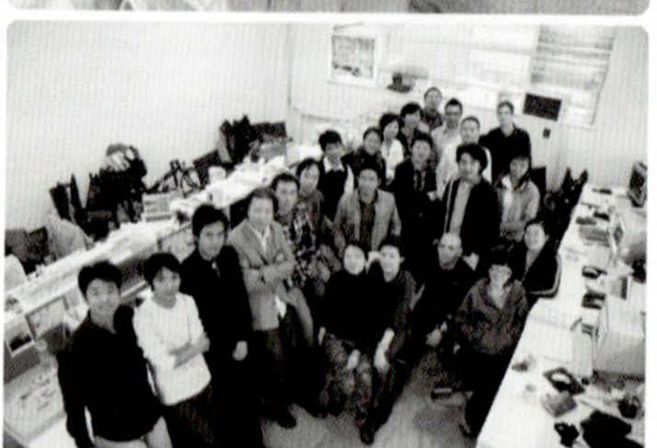

Studio Pei-Zhu 朱锫建筑事务所

Zhu Pei (朱锫) teaches at the Tsinghua School of Architecture. After leaving the Urbanus studio (Beijing and Shenzhen) not long ago, Zhu Pei, born in 1962, has opened his own practice in the heart of the capital, a few floors away from the office of the architect Qi Xin. A graduate of the Tsinghua school, Zhu Pei went away for eight years to the West Coast of the United States and became imbued with American methods, obtaining while he was there, a degree from the University of California, Berkeley. Perfectly bilingual, he has also succeeded in avoiding fashions and especially the system of imitating the big signatures, which is sometimes the cause of his Chinese colleagues' weakness. In this respect, it is not surprising that he has long been in harmony with his partners at Urbanus (Wang Hui, Meng Yan, Liu Xiaodu), proposing an ingenious adaptation of the international style to the dimension of the Chinese cities. While he co-signed the Digital Beijing Center (the only one of the Olympic Park's buildings which has not been commissioned to a foreign studio), he himself followed up the works, to the extent at least that this building practically classified as "top secret" (containing, as it does, all the instruments for the control and surveillance of the Summer Games) could escape the vigilance of the authorities.

In the immediate proximity of the Forbidden City, the Blur Hotel, Zhu Pei's first personal project, stands out with its realisation beyond the projects which he has subsequently developed. One has not gone beyond the competition stage, a project unfortunately lost for the transformation of Ningpo factories into a cultural centre and library, where Zhu Pei gave proof of a fine intuition in the establishment of multiple functional ties between heterogeneous structures. The other project, which is now in the course of construction and should be completed in 2008, has been designed for the publisher Beijing Publishing Group. These last two projects, lost or realised, bear witness to a great capacity to transform freely, with ingenuity and without inhibition, technically surpassed structures with a patrimonial dimension which is hard to establish in a country in the process of losing the urban dimension of its historical references. Zhu Pei remains a restless person, restless with his westernised image and restless perhaps with his own audacity. It would appear that his future career should unfold within this rich duality.

Partner
Zhu Pei 朱锫
Born 1962
Master in architecture, Berkeley University, California, 1997
Wu Tong 吴桐
Born 1968
Master in literature, Tsinghua University, Beijing, 1999
Studio founded in 2005
Number of employees: 30

Contact
Studio Pei-Zhu
B-413 Tiantai Business Center
N° 107 N. DongSi Street
100007, Beijing, China
T: +86 10 64 01 66 57
F: +86 10 64 03 89 67
office@studiozp.com
www.studiopeizhu.com

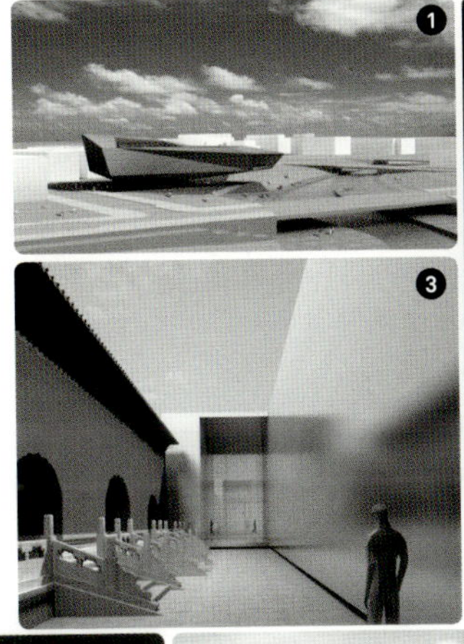
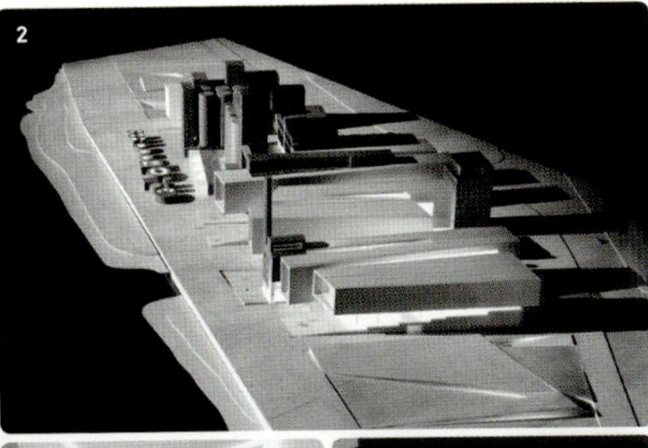
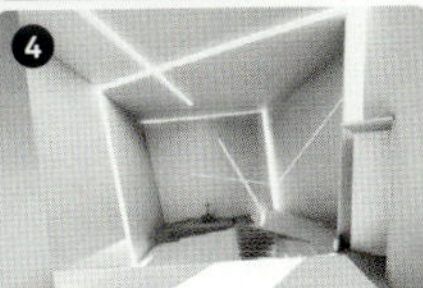
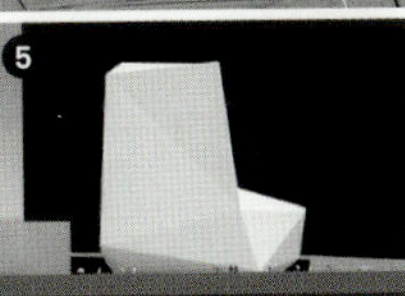
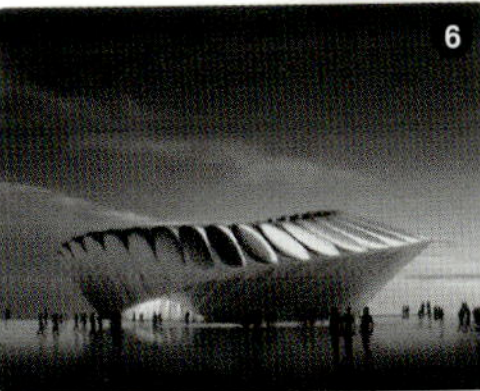
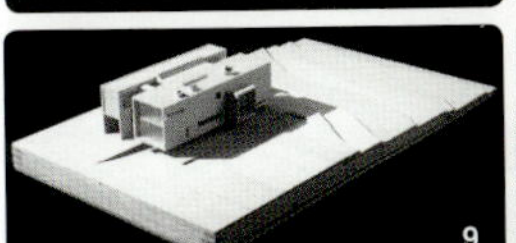
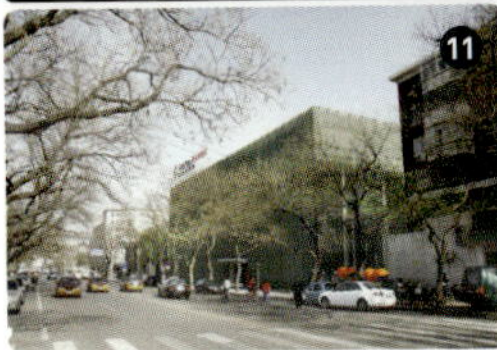
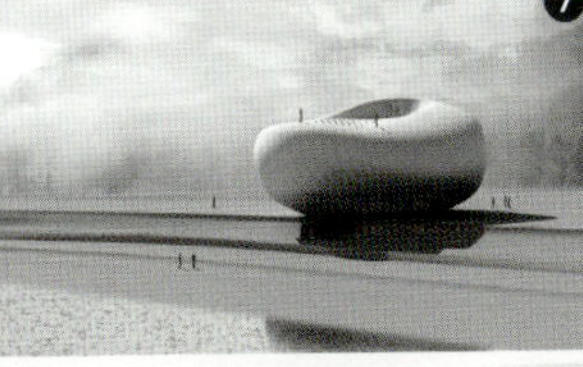
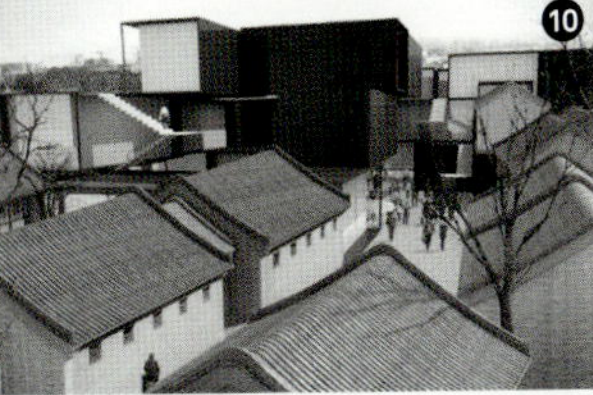
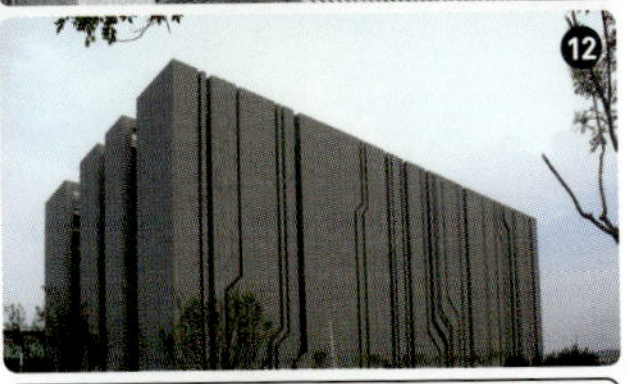
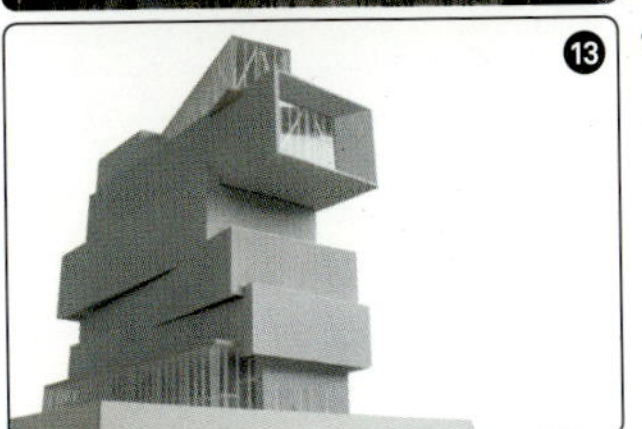
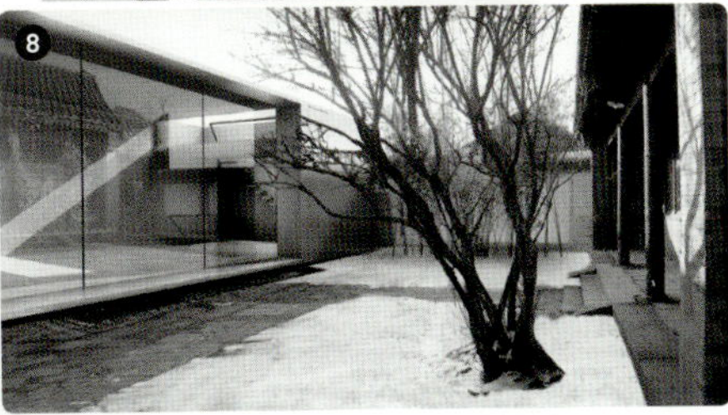

1 Guggenheim Art Pavilion, Abu Dhabi, under construction.
2 Book City, Ningbo (Zhejiang), under construction.
3 Guggenheim Museum, Beijing, 2007 (unbuilt).
4 Church, Ningbo, 2006 (unbuilt).
5 Hongxuan Centre, Beijing, 2006 (unbuilt).
6 Siemens pavilion, Shanghai, under construction.
7 Yue Minjun Art Pavilion, Sichuan, 2008.
8 House renovation, Cai Guoqing, Beijing, 2008.
9 N-House, Hainan (Guangdong), 2005.
10 Renovation of Xisi Bei area, Beijing, 2008 (unbuilt)
11 Blur Hotel, Beijing, 2006.
12 Digital Beijing (Urbanus and Zhu Pei), Olympic Games Park, Beijing, 2007
13 Beijing publishing group, under construction.

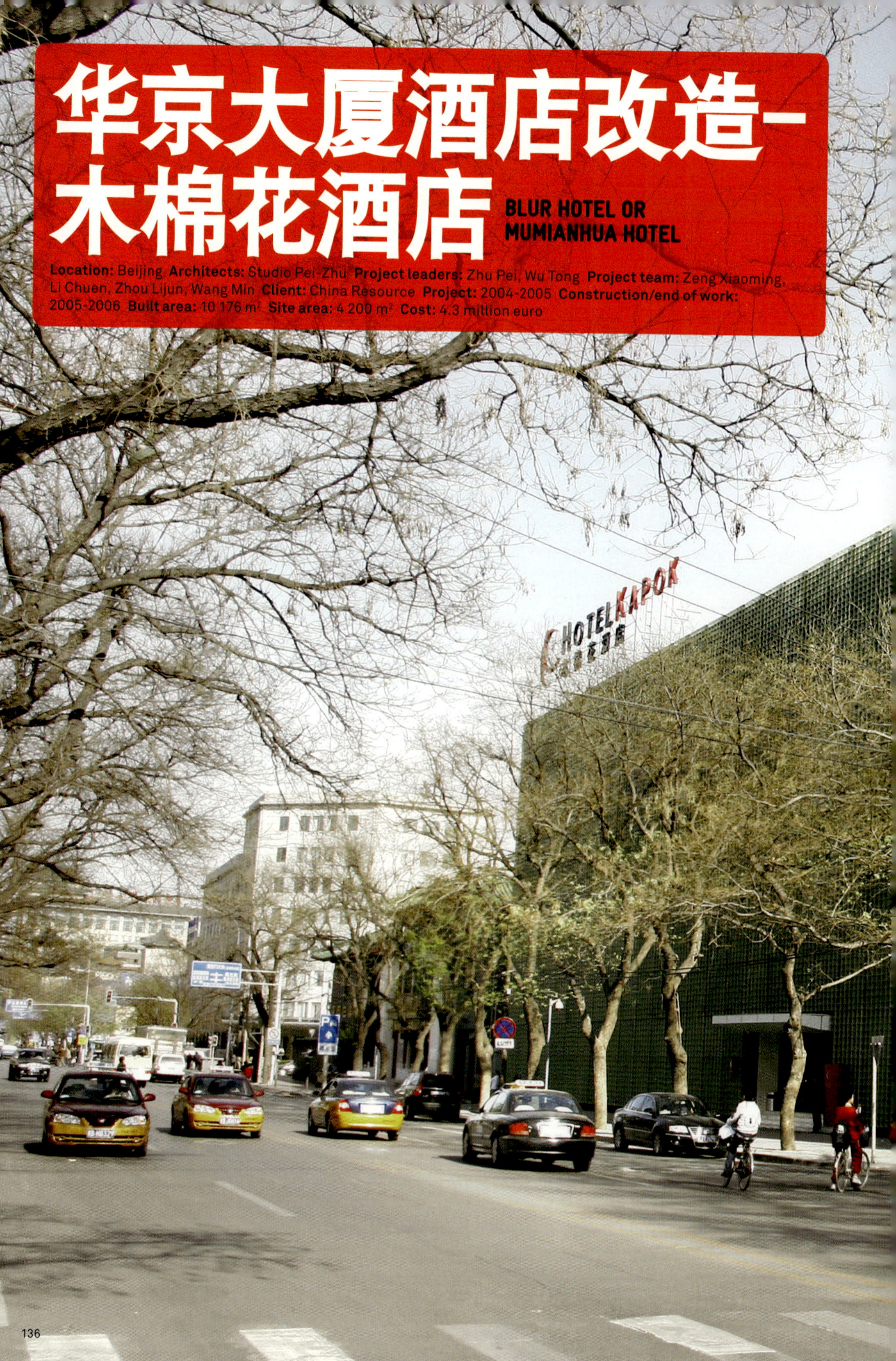

华京大厦酒店改造－
木棉花酒店

BLUR HOTEL OR
MUMIANHUA HOTEL

Location: Beijing **Architects:** Studio Pei-Zhu **Project leaders:** Zhu Pei, Wu Tong **Project team:** Zeng Xiaoming, Li Chuen, Zhou Lijun, Wang Min **Client:** China Resource **Project:** 2004-2005 **Construction/end of work:** 2005-2006 **Built area:** 10 176 m² **Site area:** 4 200 m² **Cost:** 4.3 million euro

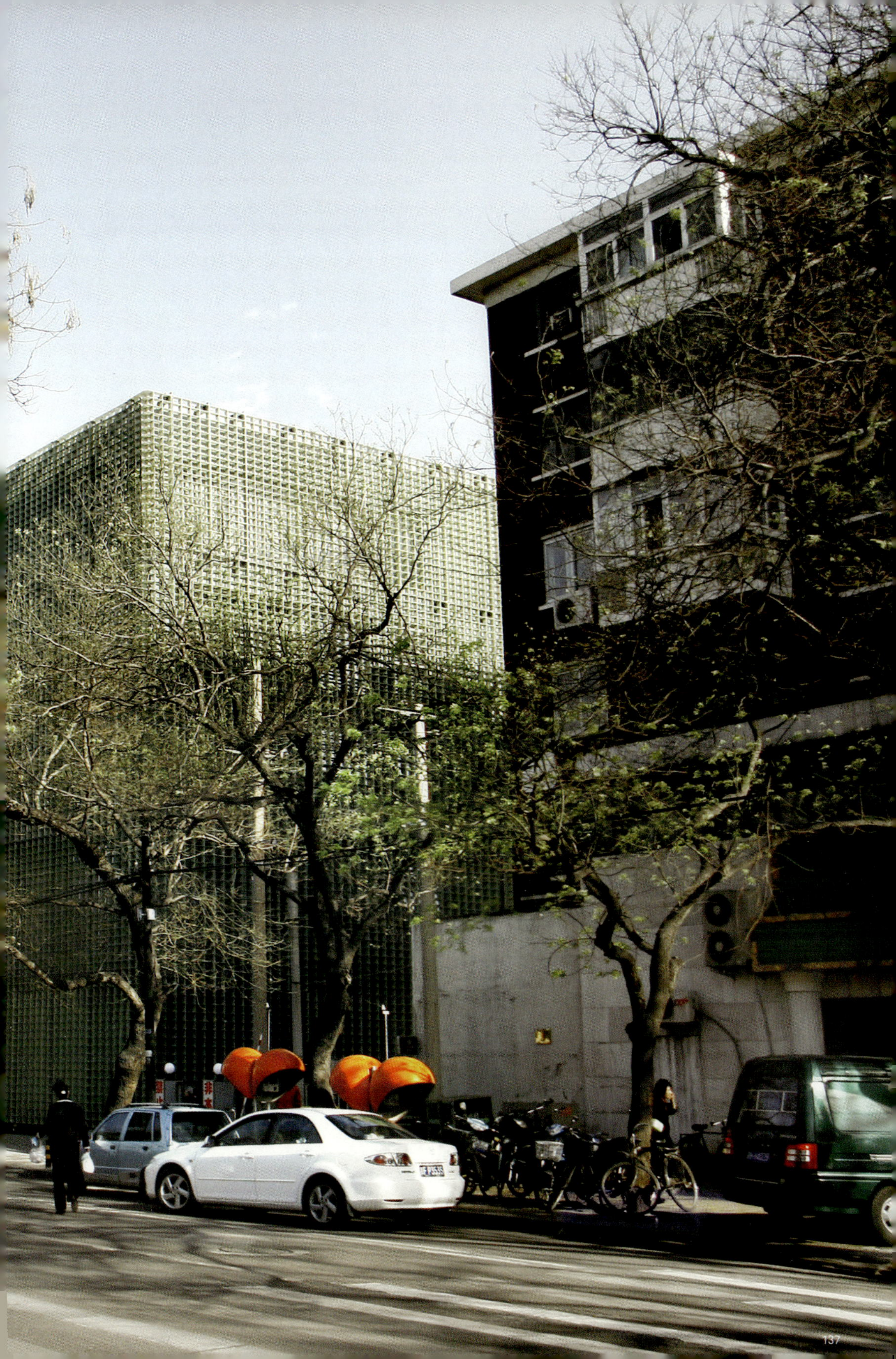

Located just a few steps away from the Forbidden City and two hundred metres from Wangfujing Avenue, the Blur Hotel (10,200 sq m) associates the signature of Wu Tong with that of Zhu Pei. Seeking to avoid both pastiche and formal aggressiveness, the architect has been led to adopt an envelope formed by a myriad of little glass-fibre honeycomb cells. Behind it there unfolds a hotel of international standing and standards, while accepting a sort of constriction and circulations which may recall the original complexity of this quarter of Beijing. Cut in five levels above the street and one basement level, several empty spaces may bring to mind the traditional courtyards, but as is the rule in this architect's works, it is more of a spiritual or symbolic parenthesis than a veritable transposition.

The Blur Hotel inscribes itself intelligently within a quarter which was supposedly protected according to the Unesco rules but which has been largely destroyed in order to be rebuilt "identically" with uneven skill. This is also its uniqueness, within such a context, that allows the acceptance of this object, opalescent by day and luminous like a lantern by night which, one might think, had been exported from Japan. Its height is the average for this small avenue, Donghua-men, which for that matter had already lost all memory of the original Beijing without, however, having lost its soul.

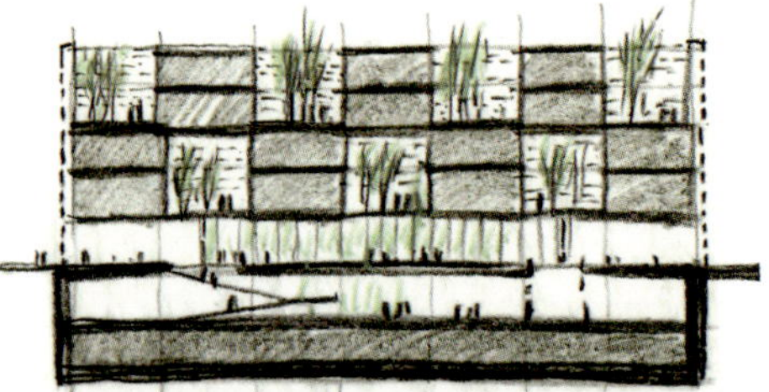

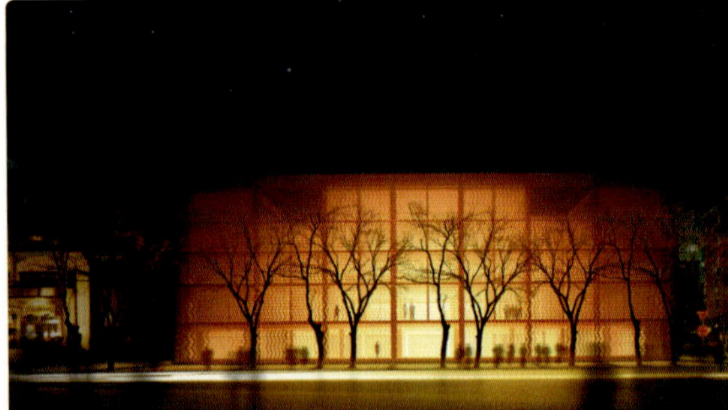

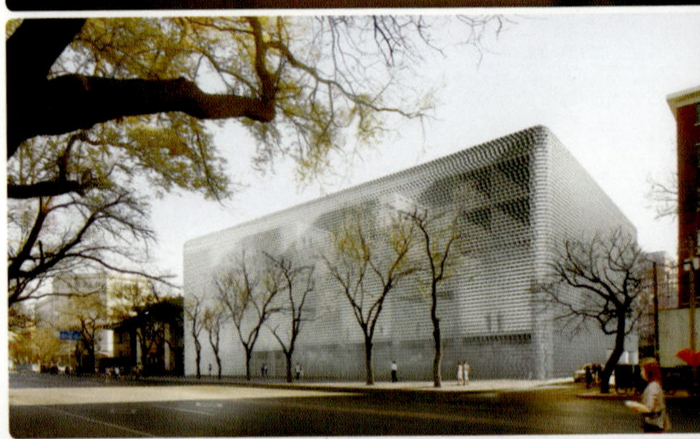

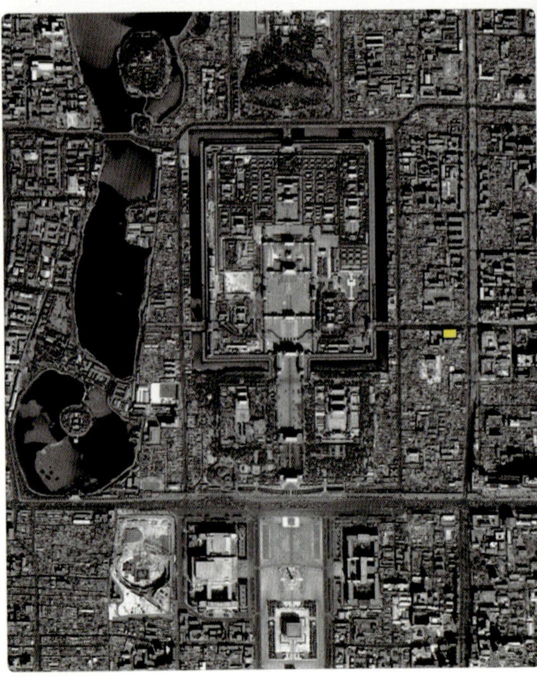

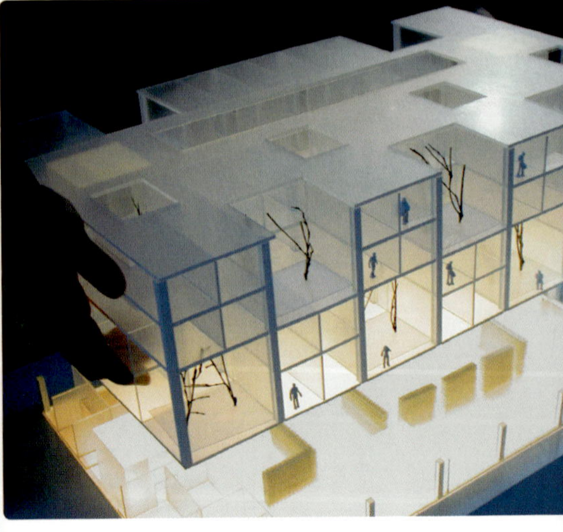

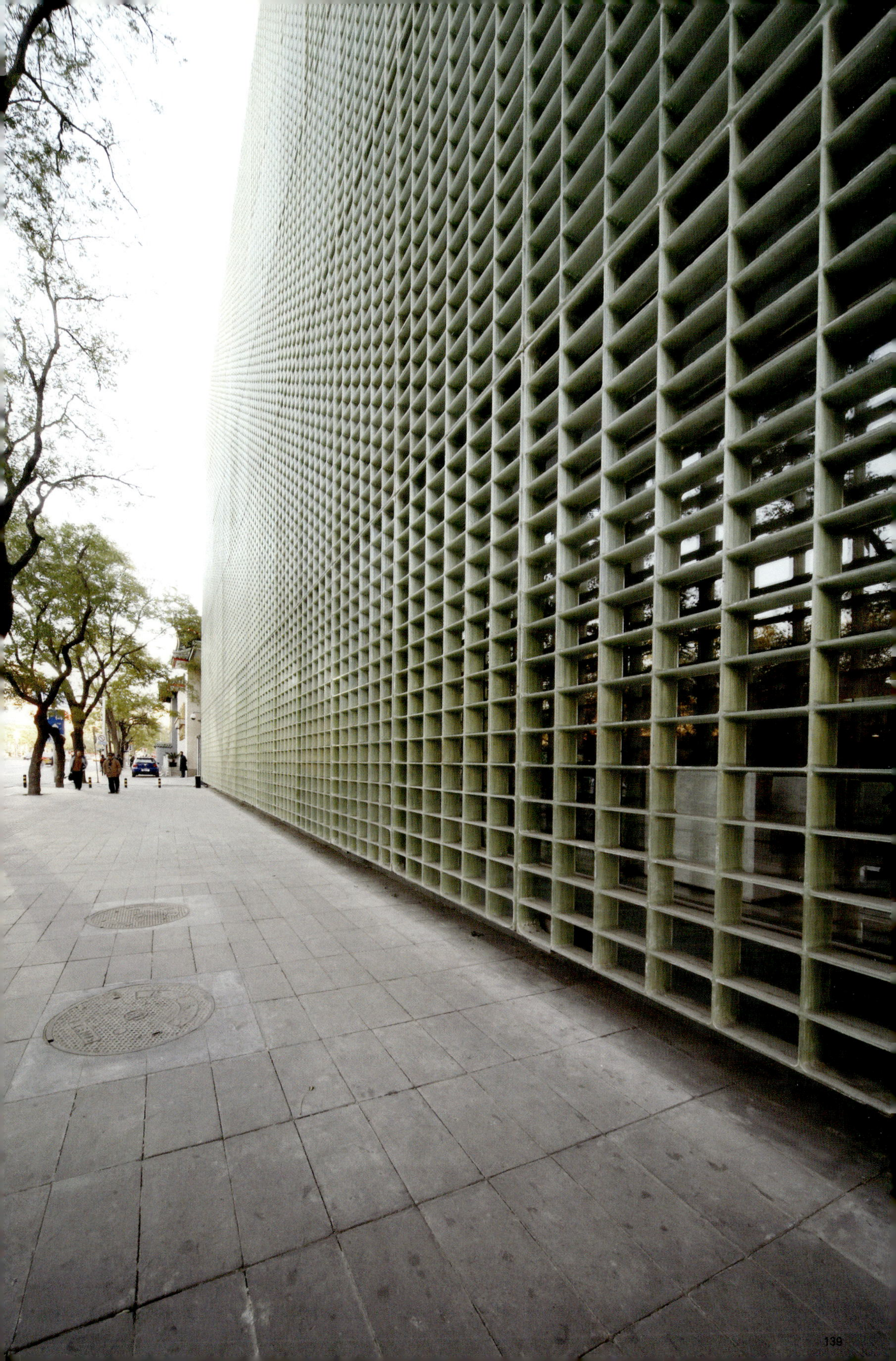

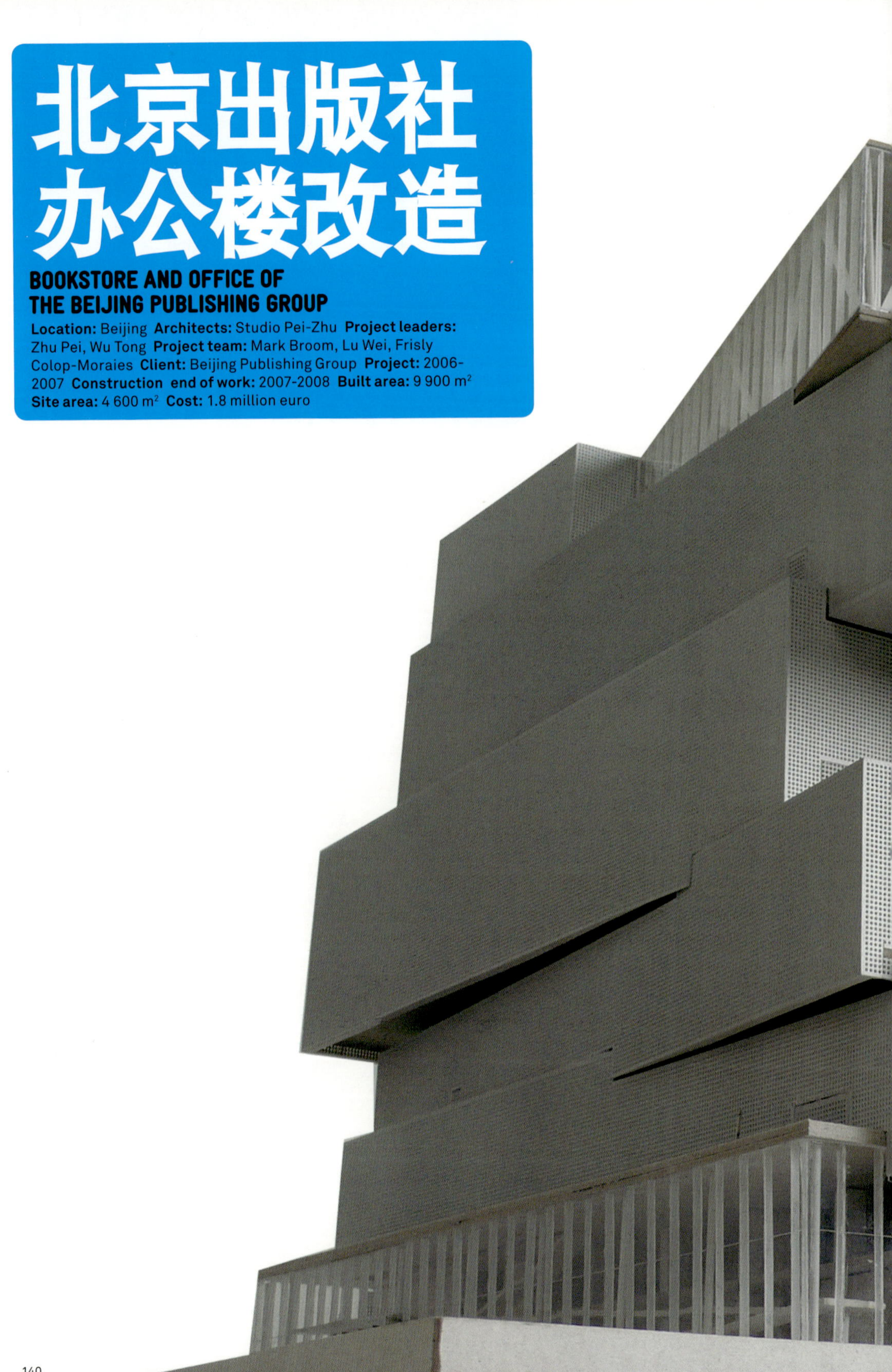

BOOKSTORE AND OFFICE OF THE BEIJING PUBLISHING GROUP

Location: Beijing **Architects:** Studio Pei-Zhu **Project leaders:** Zhu Pei, Wu Tong **Project team:** Mark Broom, Lu Wei, Frisly Colop-Moraies **Client:** Beijing Publishing Group **Project:** 2006-2007 **Construction end of work:** 2007-2008 **Built area:** 9 900 m² **Site area:** 4 600 m² **Cost:** 1.8 million euro

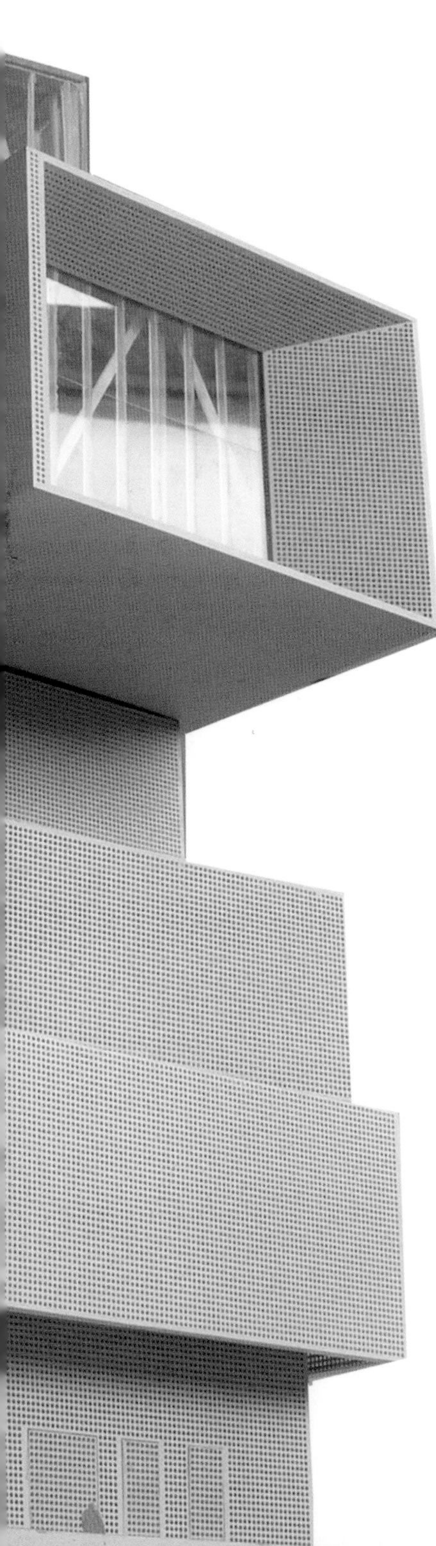

This is one of the very few projects which the curators have chosen without having seen the realisation and without being able to assure that it would in fact be completed in the course of the year 2008. It is nevertheless one of the projects in which Zhu Pei's originality is expressed most forcefully. This building was commissioned by a publishing house near the 3rd ring road on the city's north-south axis, not far from the Olympic Park. The architect was to take up work on a 12-story edifice of fairly recent construction but lacking in all quality. As may be seen at Beijing Digital (the reference to computer technology) or in the structural vocabulary of the Blur Hotel, this building devoted to publishing, to books and to all the life surrounding the printing processes invented in China six hundred years before Gutenberg, the design of this new building imitates the slightly disordered stacking of a half-dozen "large volumes" in the twofold sense of this term. It is a job of adding-on and cutting-away, very subtle in its original design which only the engineering work and the quality of the finishes will eventually lend significance. It may be noted here, without being truly ironic, that the building produces an effect of change of scale which seems to mock gently the difficulty of Zhu Pei's young colleagues in finding their just place in the city.

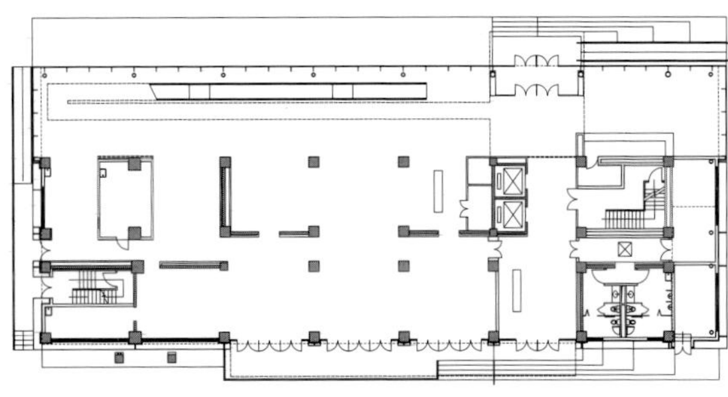

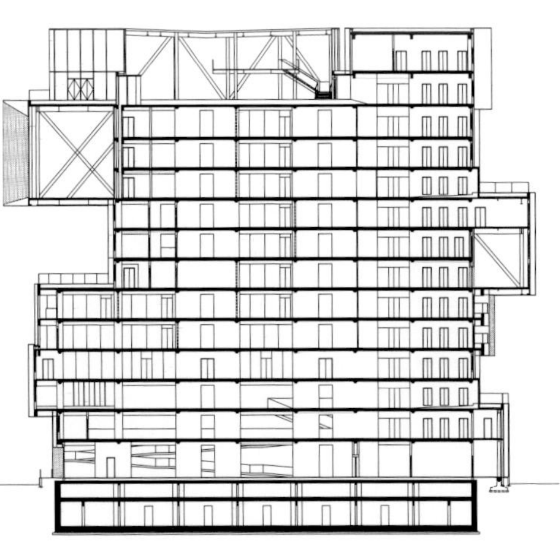

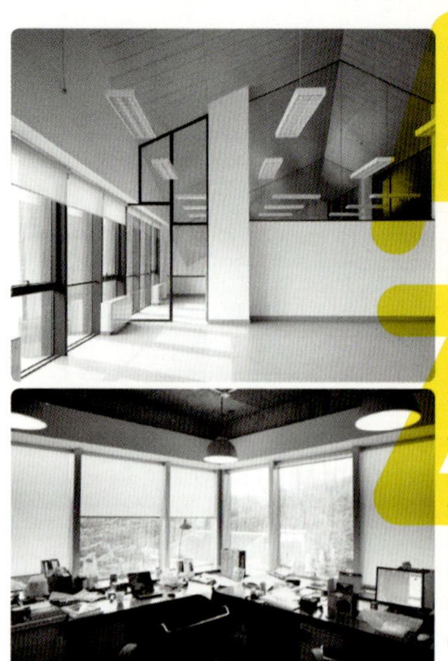

Atelier Z+
Zhang Bin 张斌, Zhou Wei 周蔚

Born in 1968, Zhang Bin is a pure product of Tongji University, where he obtained all his architecture and urban planning degrees before travelling to France, selected in the first groups of the presidential programme. In France he took the city projects courses at the Paris-Villemin school and did several internships, including one at the Architecture Studio. In his free time he visited Paris methodically, by streets and by districts, and saw the Europe that he could visit at week-ends and on university holidays.

In 2002, two years after his return to his native city, he and his companion and partner, Zhu Wei, founded the studio Z+. They strove to find their own writing even if, in the first building they carried out (for the Tongji Department of Architecture and Urban Planning), they remained quite close in the end to the vocabulary and materials used by Deshaus at Dongguan.

It was fairly natural that they would be entrusted the university's French-Chinese Centre, a project evoked at the time of Jacques Chirac's visit in 1997, moved by the wish to rival the German dynamic, which was all the more present in Tongji since it contributed to the creation of the university in 1907.

Before these two projects and even before creating the studio Z+, Zhang Bin had planned a square at Yangjiaping, one of the new urban centres of Chongqing, as well as some buildings which are not negligible for their size and complexity in Jiaxing (Zhejiang province) and Zouping (Shandong), even if they did not make the cover of the architecture journals.

The two buildings in Tongji have earned him a series of more modest orders, especially in Suzhou, which is perhaps proof of a more sensitive approach to scale, as well as on the fringes of Shanghai, with projects at Qingpu and at Jiading, the urban future of which has been redesigned by mayor Sun Jiwei, a figure already known for his architectural engagement and the new-found vitality of Qingpu, while he was its deputy mayor.

Partners
Zhang Bin 张斌
Born 1968
Master in architecture,
Tongji University, Shanghai, 1995
Zhou Wei 周蔚
Born 1972
Bachelor in architecture,
Tongji University, Shanghai, 1996
Studio founded in 2002
Number of employees: 6

Contact
Atelier Z+
2B 568 Ou'yang Rd.
200081 Shanghai, China
T: +86 21 5666 5987
F: +86 21 5666 7295
atelier_zplus@163.com

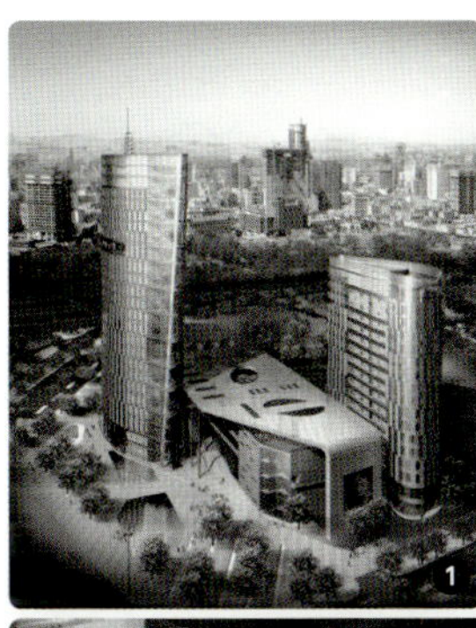
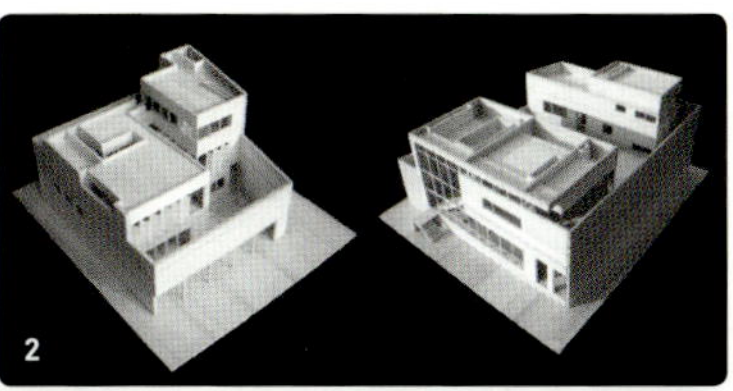
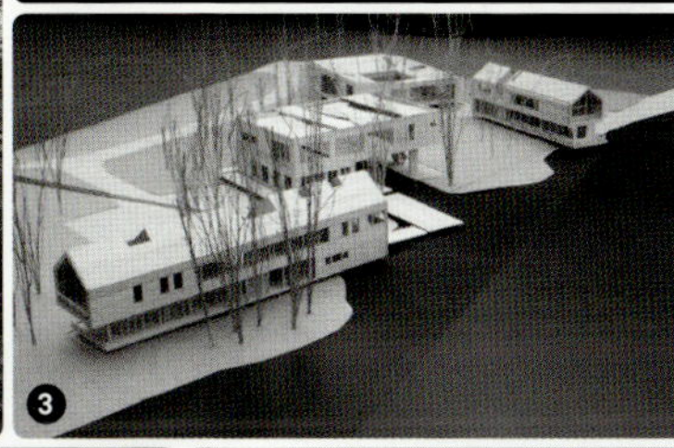
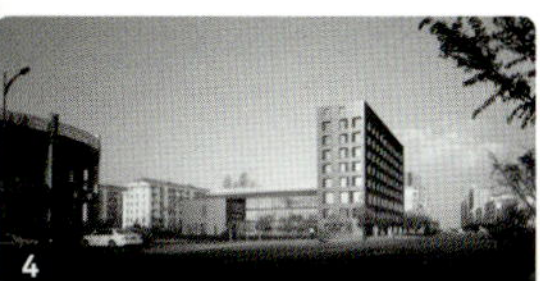
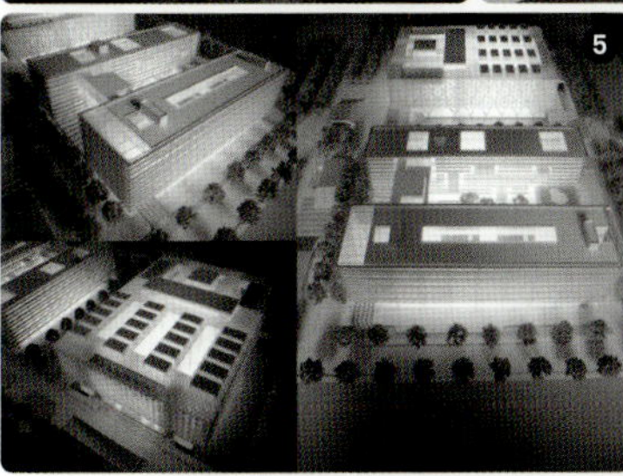
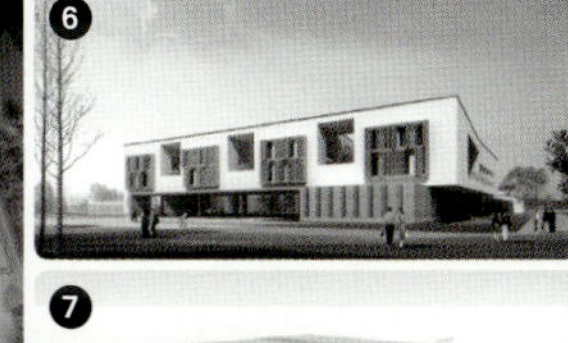
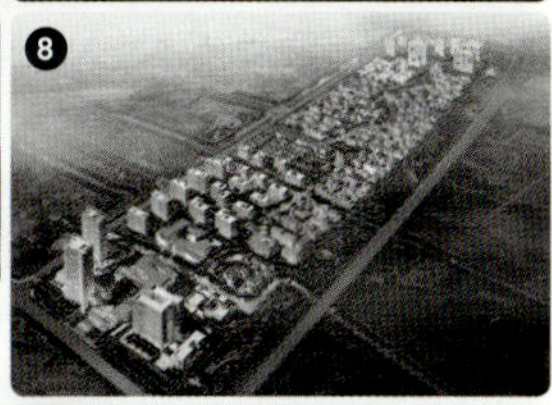
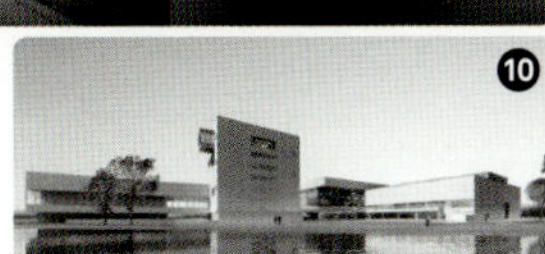
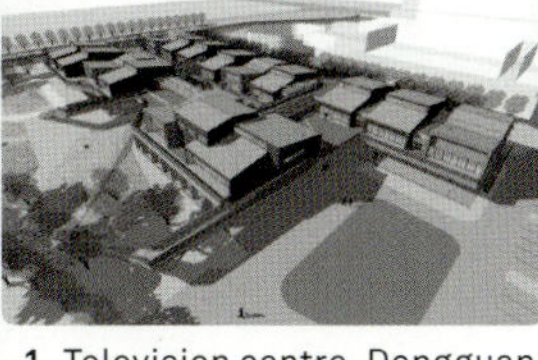
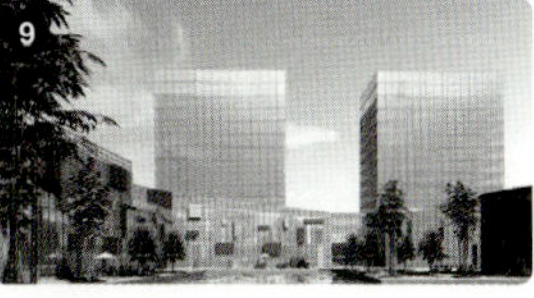
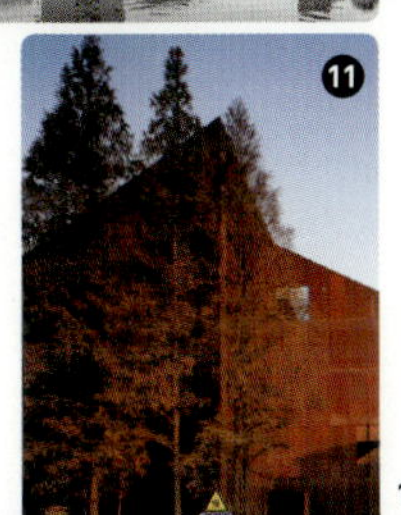
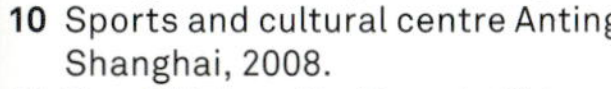
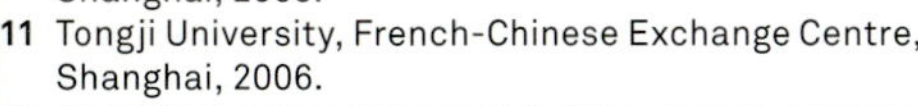
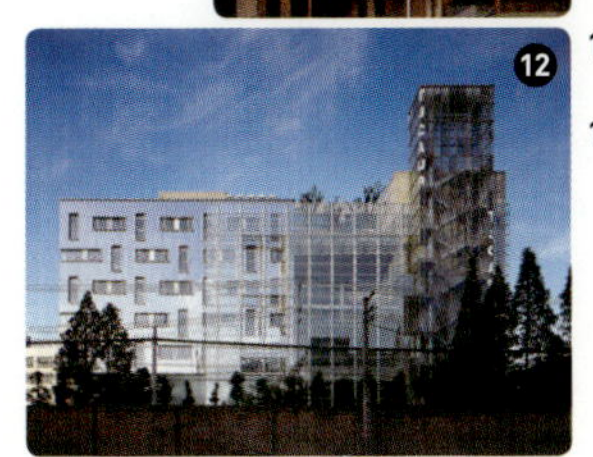

1 Television centre, Dongguan (Guangdong), 2004.
2 Row houses Tianya, Suzhou (Jiangsu), 2007.
3 Welcome building Dianshan Hu, Qingpu (Shanghai), 2005.
4 Business centre Xiayang, Qingpu, 2006.
5 Archive of Urban Constructon Centre, Zhenjiang (Jiangsu), 2006.
6 Liangtang Town Hall, Qingpu, 2007.
7 Jiangwan Nursery School, Shanghai, 2007.
8 Computer and Cultural Park, Shanghai, 2008.
9 Dongyun Leisure park, Shanghai, 2007.
10 Sports and cultural centre Anting, Shanghai, 2008.
11 Tongji University, French-Chinese Exchange Centre, Shanghai, 2006.
12 Tongji University, School of Architecture and Urban Planning, building 3, Shanghai, 2004.

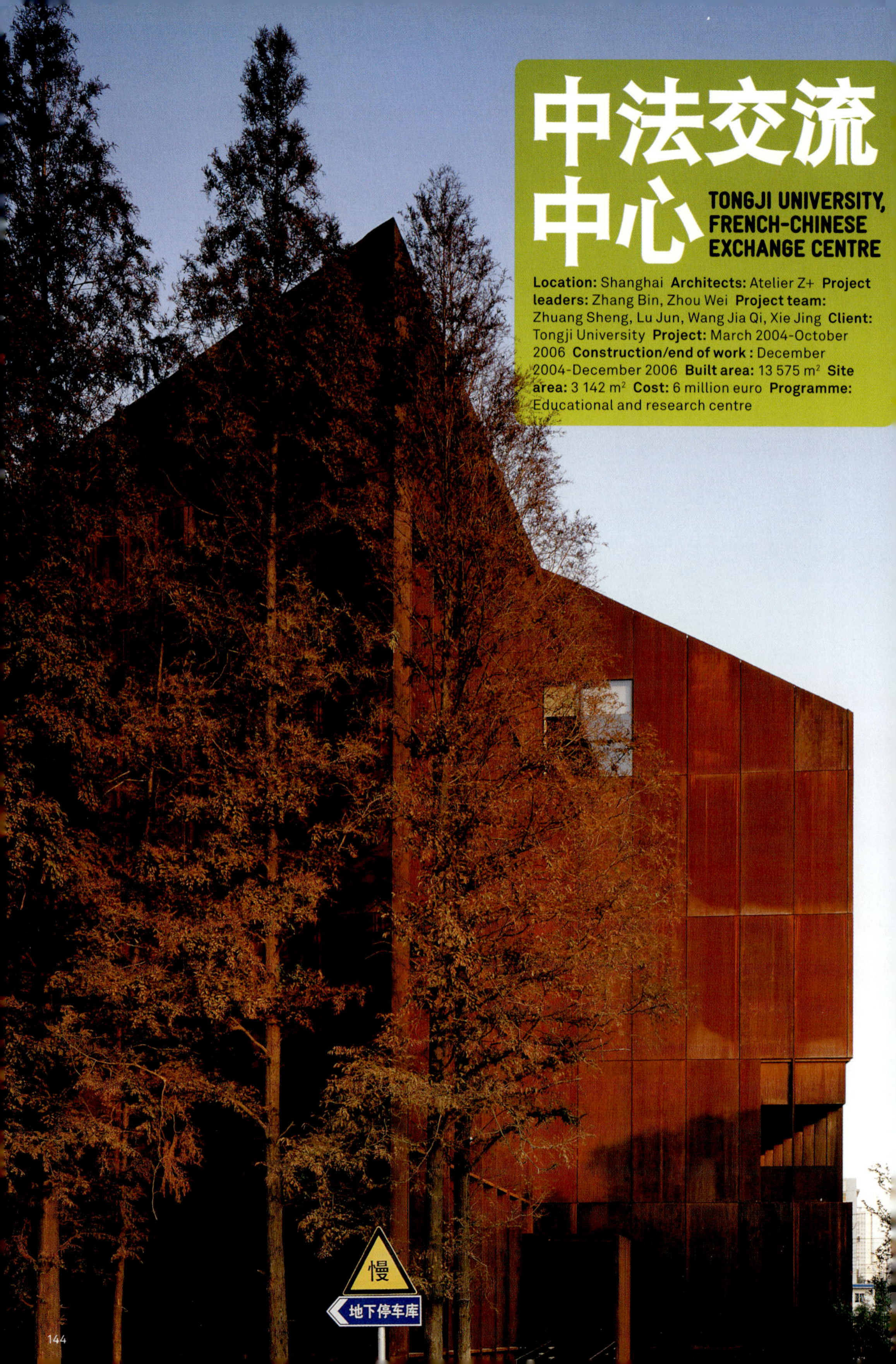

中法交流中心

TONGJI UNIVERSITY, FRENCH-CHINESE EXCHANGE CENTRE

Location: Shanghai **Architects:** Atelier Z+ **Project leaders:** Zhang Bin, Zhou Wei **Project team:** Zhuang Sheng, Lu Jun, Wang Jia Qi, Xie Jing **Client:** Tongji University **Project:** March 2004-October 2006 **Construction/end of work:** December 2004-December 2006 **Built area:** 13 575 m² **Site area:** 3 142 m² **Cost:** 6 million euro **Programme:** Educational and research centre

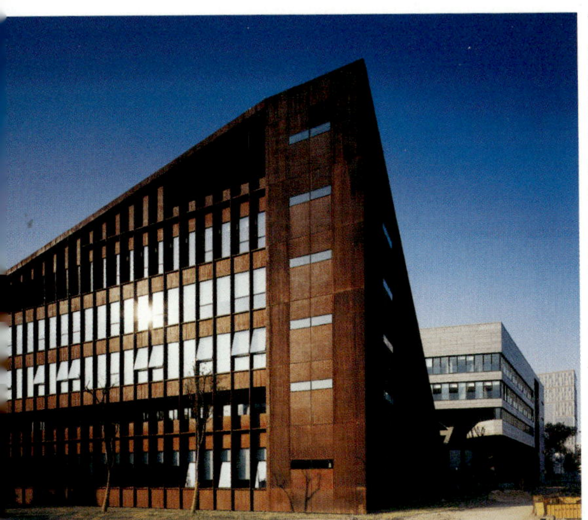

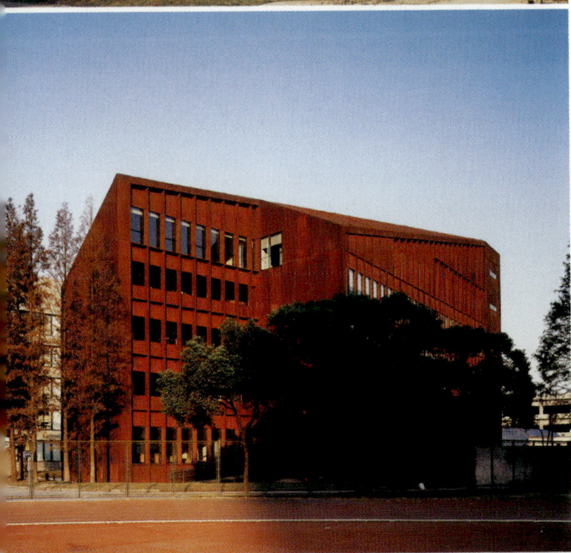

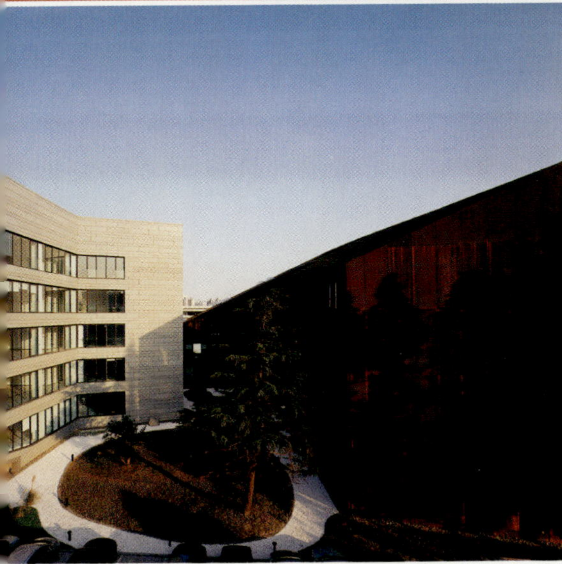

This rather mysterious and composite building takes its "French-Chinese" designation from a visit by President Jacques Chirac to Shanghai in 1997. The idea of a centre which would bring together the French enterprises around shared services, in the manner of the German practices, was deferred on several occasions because of a lack of common interests on the part of the company sector as well as a lack of financing. The university took up the project seven years later and entrusted it, *carte blanche* style, to Zhang Bin, on the plot established for this purpose. Meanwhile, the *grandes écoles* and the universities were interested in Tongji to carry out joint programmes and France had regained a certain aura.

It remained to define a programme for this French-Chinese Centre, which was in fact proposed by Zhang Bin, based on a principle of interlacings of volumes and of materials, with common spaces in the core, just as the architect's twofold personal path in China and in France has been able to intercross itself. Zhang Bin in person presented it in French in three minutes on the occasion of the presidential visit of 2004. The French calling still has some difficulty in expressly itself clearly in this place created to enhance exchanges, aside from the leasing of offices and the staging of technical exhibitions. In 2008, just part of the building reflected the educational, cultural and economic dimensions of the project. It is true that these dimensions are more difficult to associate because of the French context than in Anglo-Saxon projects, and that the notion of campus integrates this articulation of learning and investment from the start. As a reflection of this three-fold calling, the programme of the building comprised three parts: classrooms, offices and public spaces which the architect has "sewn together" by a zigzag system, the suitability of which will only be verified by the test of time. The plurality of materials in which Corten steel dominates with its sombre power, is presented as the reflection of the Centre's double nationality.

When it manages to become fully animated, the French-Chinese Centre of Tongji will be able to measure the strategic quality of its site on the campus, near one of the main entrances, and the quality of its landscape surroundings, where several metasequoias have been preserved as if to recall the cast shadow of the past century.

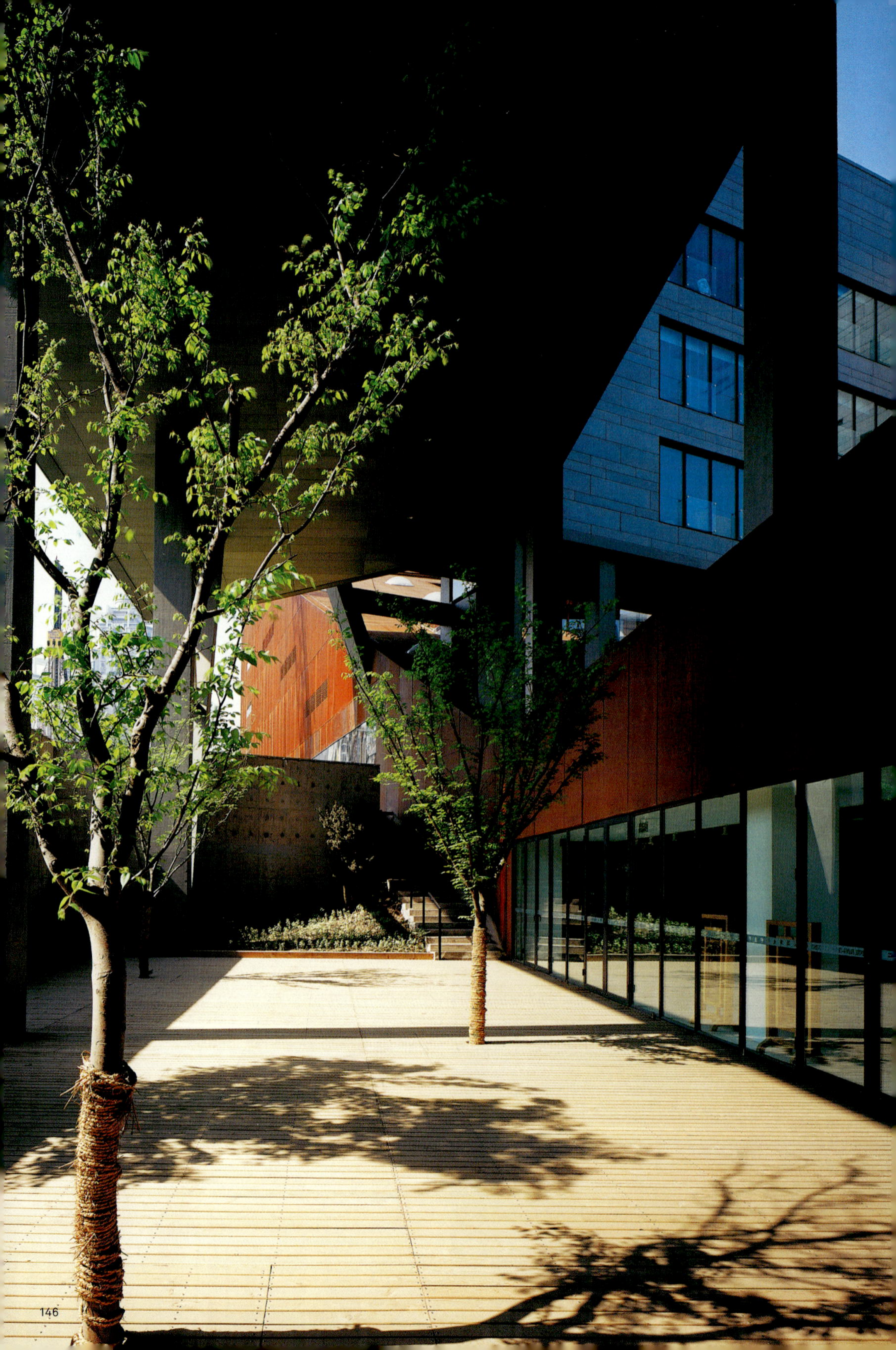

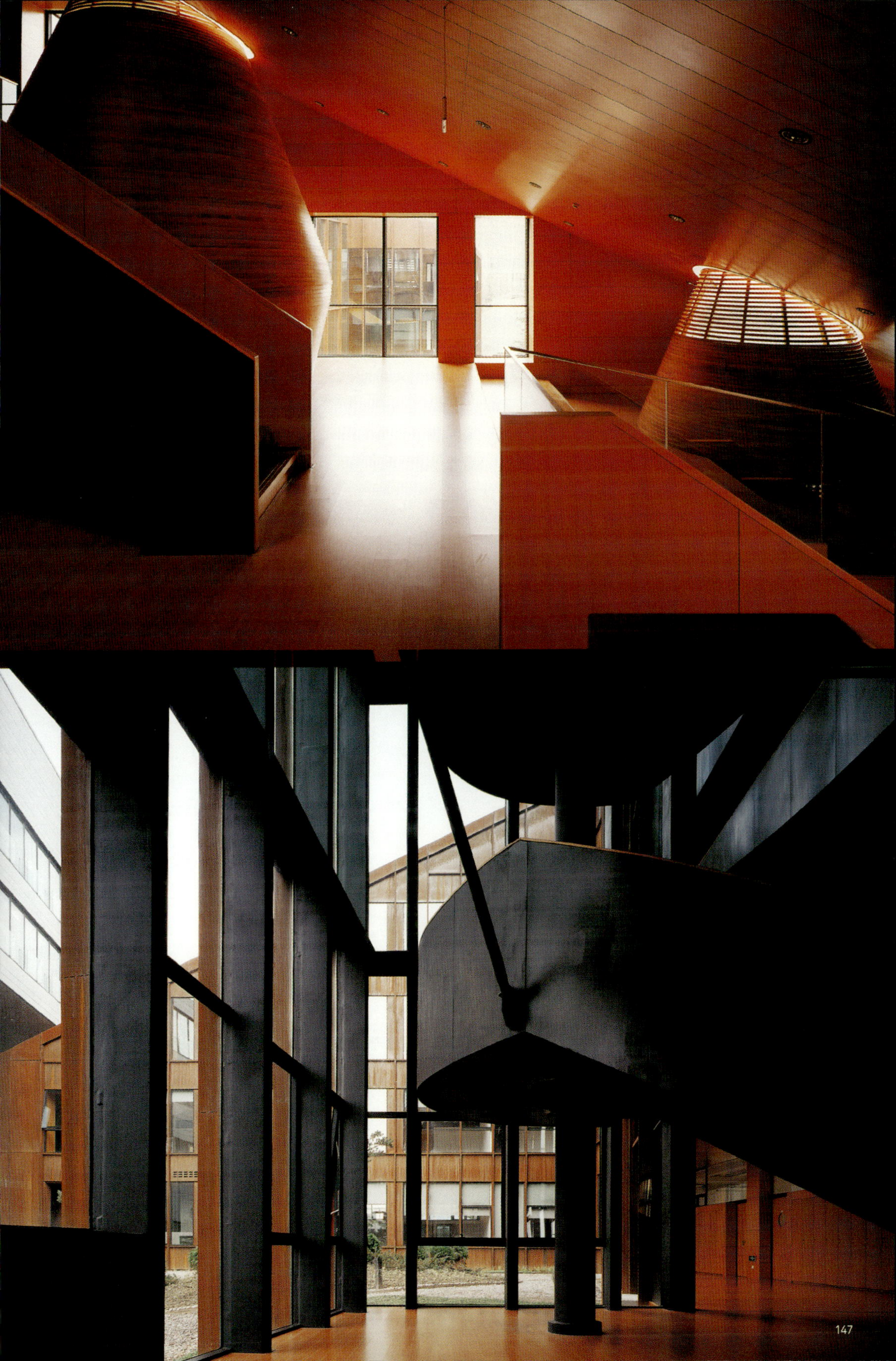

同济大学建筑与城市规划学院C楼

TONGJI UNIVERSITY, SCHOOL OF ARCHITECTURE AND URBAN PLANNING, BUILDING 3

Location: Shanghai **Architects:** Atelier Z+ **Project leader:** Zhang Bin, Zhou Wei **Landscape architect:** Zhou Xiangpin
Client: Tongji University **Project:** February 2002-May 2004 **Construction/end of work:** December 2002-May 2004
Built area: 9 672 m² **Site area:** 1 485 m² **Cost:** 4 million euro

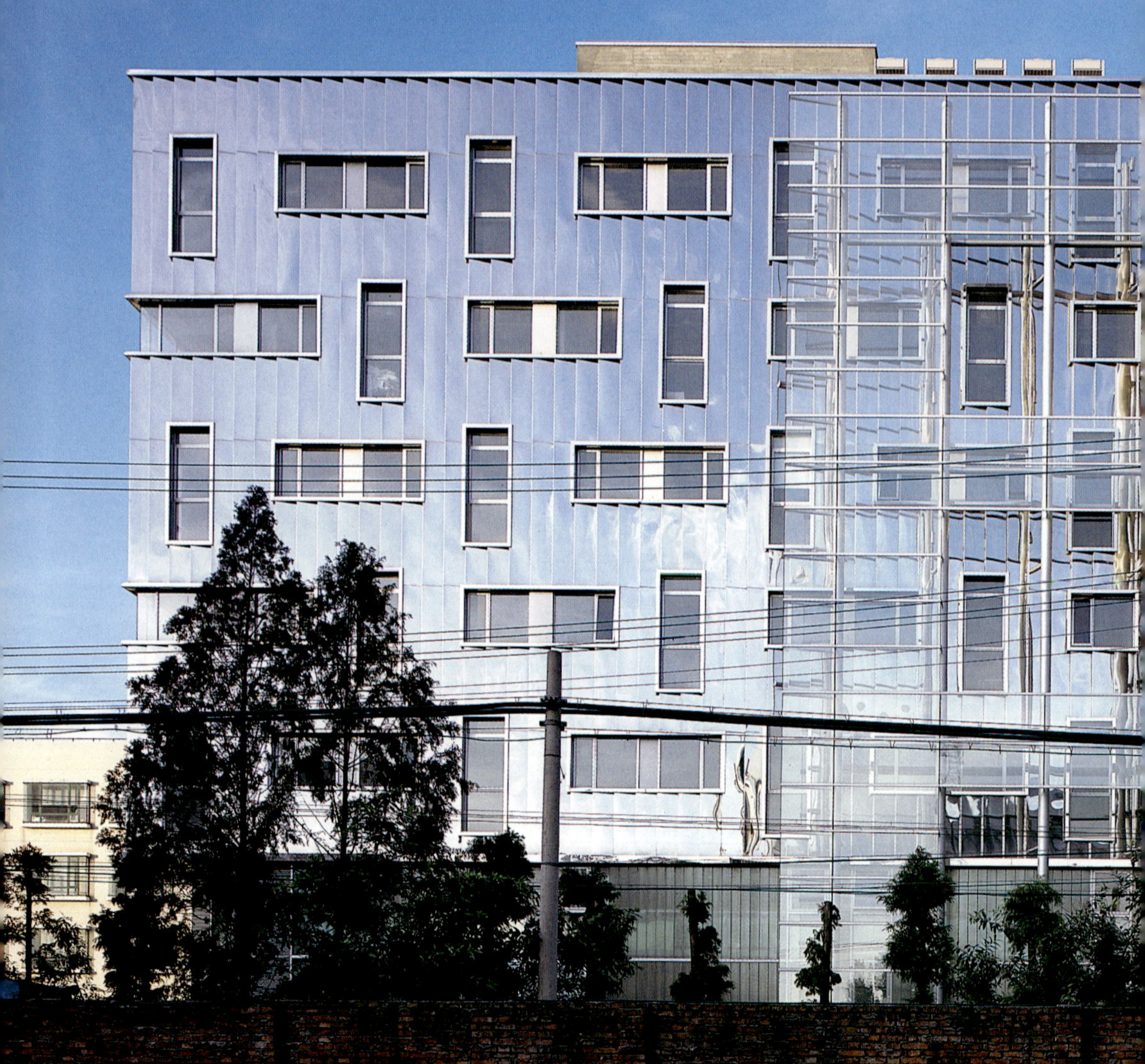

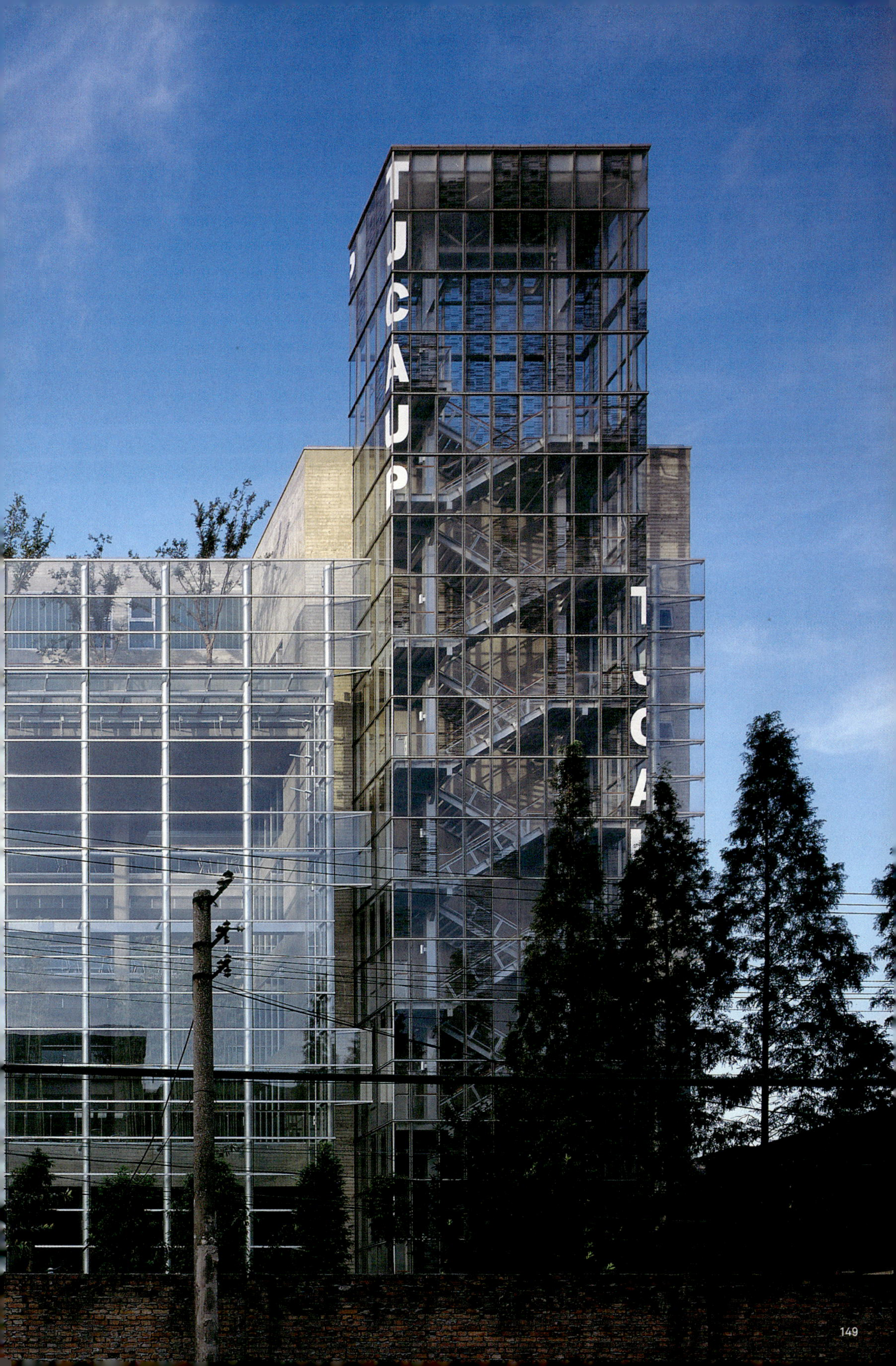
TJCAUP
TJCAUP
TJCA

Like all the Chinese universities, Tongji, until Deng
Xiaoping came to power, survived despite its
prestige in premises which had been left to it from
the pre-war period. This involved buildings which
were often reasonably well made but considerably
degraded and unsuitable for an educational system
which was being modernised like the economy
and the cities.

The teaching of architecture and urban planning
did not escape this rule, without suffering the
indifference which characterised the treatment
of schools in France until recent times. A new
building, by one of the deans of the School, was
erected towards the end of the 1980s to cope
with the increase in the number of students.
The modernity of that building, however, was soon
outdated by the improvement of construction
techniques and the circulations students had
to make as a result of each extension to the
university. At the end of the 1990s, the obligation
undertaken with the universities to find new
resources and to open up education to a larger
number of students, led numerous prestigious
institutions to profit from the real estate at
their disposal and, what was not a secondary
phenomenon, to invest massively in construction.
The engineering and architecture schools within
the universities thus became poles of excellence
and of building activity. Zhang Bin, one of the
youngest of the elders was chosen to design the
school's Building C, an edifice which was to act
as a link to its neighbour from the 1980s (which
was subsequently renovated) and to allow the
recasting of education there. The principle is
simple: an immense stairway which, starting from
the first floor, serves the six upper levels. A ground
floor conceived as a reception endowed with an
efficient bookstore and an enviable café. Lastly,
in the basement, which is brightened in an English
manner by a generous moat, there are exhibition
halls which are at once classic and versatile.
The central stairway forms a covered courtyard
where the calm is due more to the assiduousness
and silence of the students than to its specific
acoustic qualities. The classrooms benefit from
remarkable sunlight, while being protected in the
south by a double skin of glass which also lends
a beautiful depth to the façade. These rooms are
adapted to the multiple activities of the teachers
who are also researchers and practitioners,
whether this means the temporary installation
of international workshops or hosting the studios
of the Tongji Urban Planning Projects Institute,
which is directed by some of the professors.

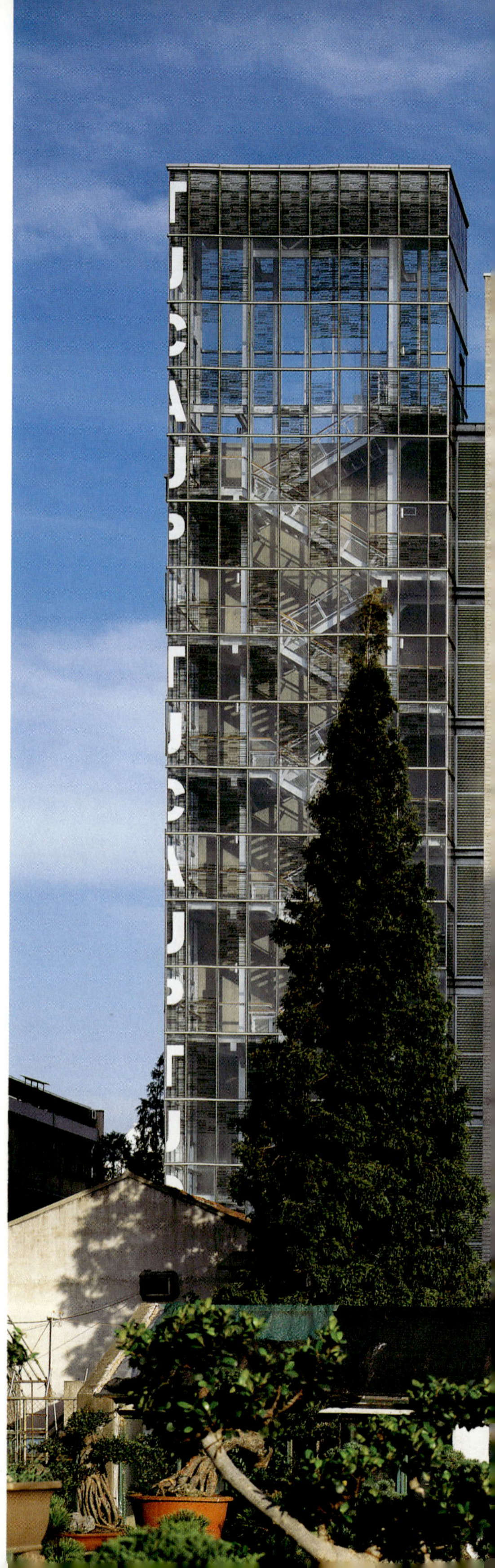

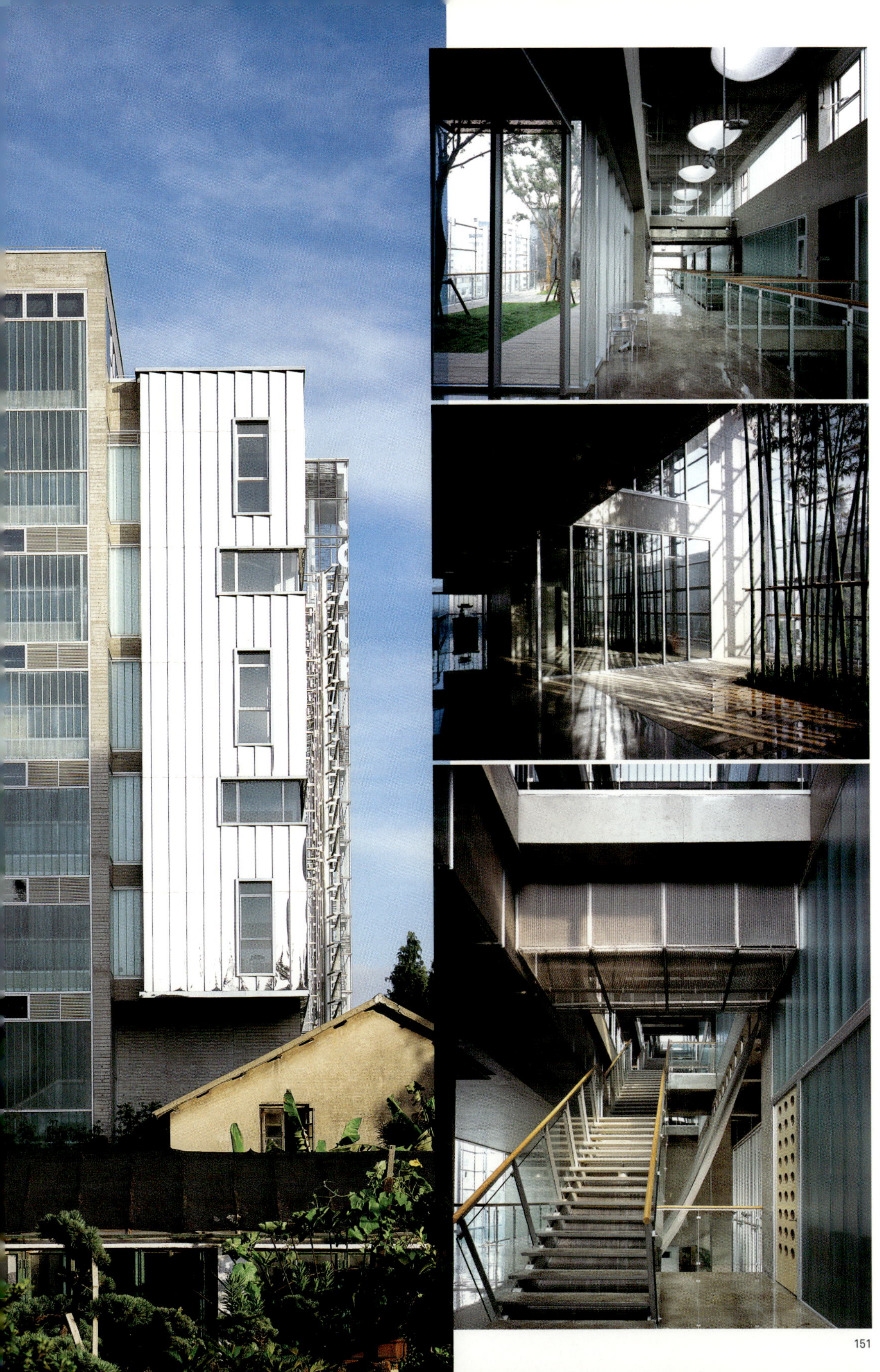

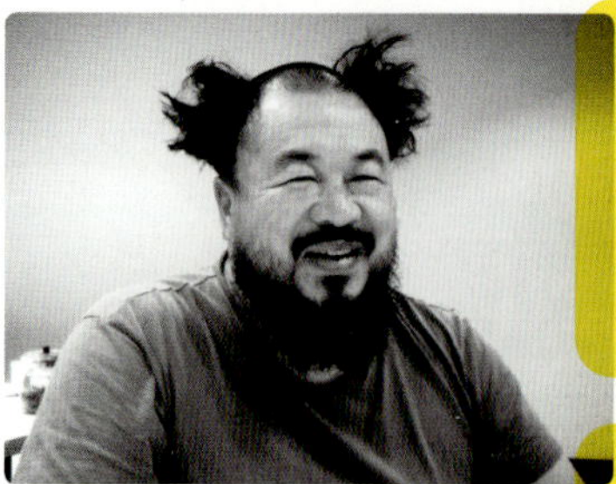

Fake Design 北京 **Fake** 设计
Ai Weiwei 艾未未

Ai Weiwei, born in 1957, son of the poet Ai Qing, is a very atypical personality in the world of architecture. Everything could lead him away but everything ceaselessly draws him back and in this respect he personifies the amazing porosity of the artistic universes which characterise China at present. He is first and foremost an artist with a conceptual and provocative style, a self-taught man who, as a member of the Group of the Stars at the end of the 1970s, left China like many of the others who had belonged to it. He chose the United States and, returning home at the beginning of the 1990s, he published three books, opened an art gallery in 1998 and an architecture studio the following year.

Closely tied to the intelligentsia of the major American schools, he plays the role, more or less, of the pope of modernity in his native country. There, he offers willingly to shelter artists in general and architects in particular, including Herzog & de Meuron who became associated with him from the start on the construction of the Grand Stadium, nicknamed the "Bird's Nest".

Ai Weiwei cultivates a provocateur aspect, both rowdy and ironic, and knows exactly how far he can overstep when expressing himself on public issues. His artistic work extends across a succession of periods which are hard to classify. His work as an architect is hardly more fathomable (he calls his architecture studio "Fake", for example). It may be read, however, as an intense will to create ties, to preserve the friendly and sometimes puzzling universe which has enveloped him since his stay in the United States.

This architect has built several homes in which it is difficult to define what part corresponds to the builder and what part to the designer, a little like the house of another artist, Gao Bo who, following a line similar to that of Ai Weiwei, has installed his creative base in the countryside surrounding Beijing. For his part, Ai Weiwei has chosen a site near Dashanzi, the factory renovated and transformed into an artistic centre close to Beijing's airport, which simplifies the comings and goings of this international star. The sixteen architects and artists which he has invited to work at Jinhua park, five hours by road from Shanghai in the heart of Zhejiang province, have found it easier to visit this illustrious grouch of Chinese contemporary art.

Ai Weiwei 艾未未
Born 1957
Studio founded in 2003
Number of employees: 9

Contact
FAKE Design
Caochangdi 258
Chaoyang District
Beijing, 100102 China
T: +86 10 84 56 41 94
F: +86 10 84 56 41 94
nobody@vip.sina.com
www.aiweiwei.com

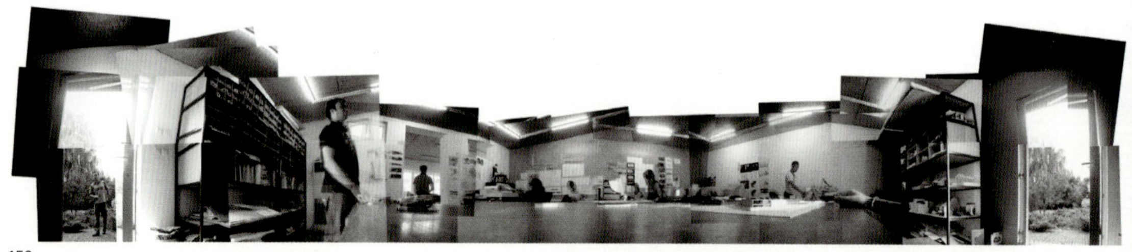

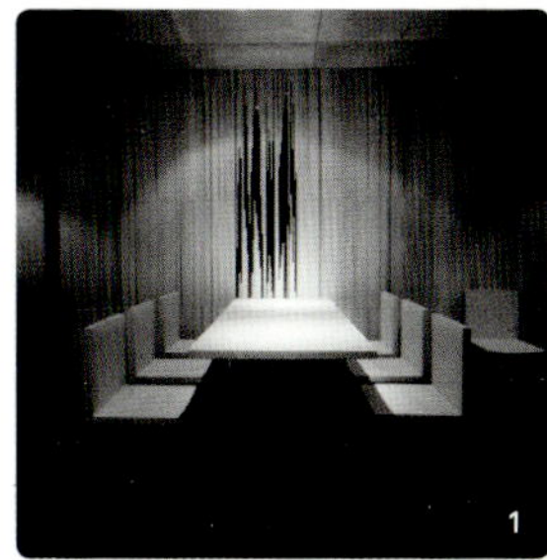

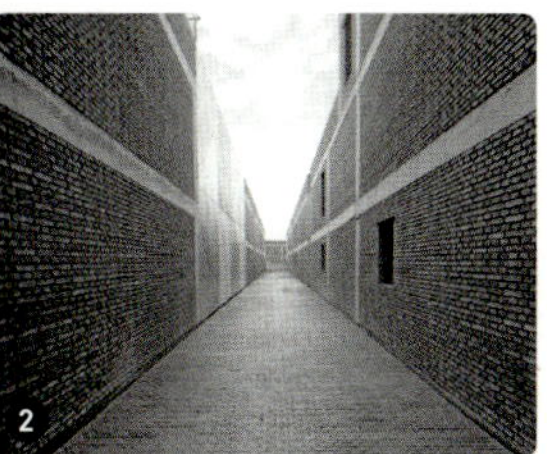

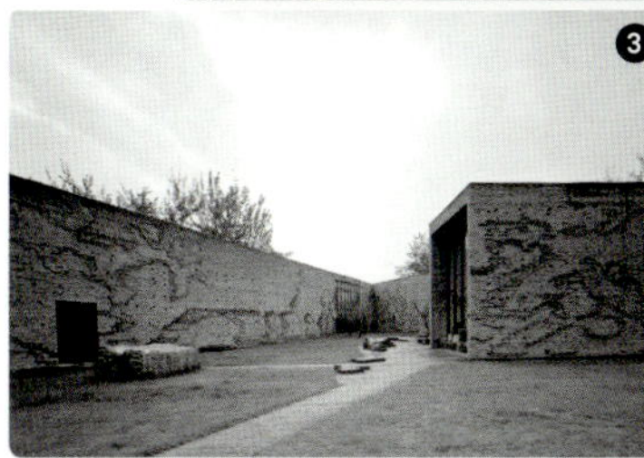

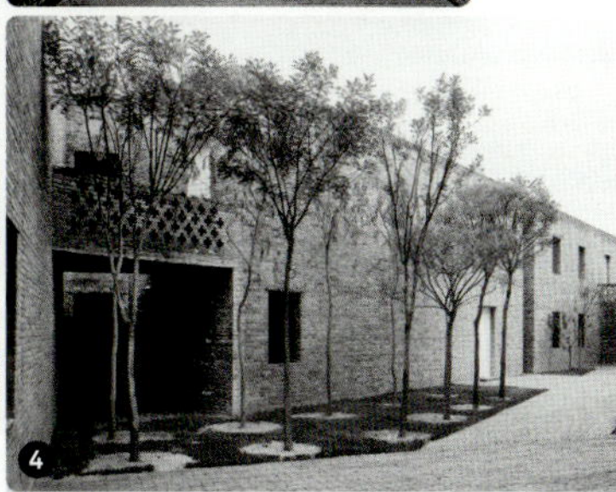

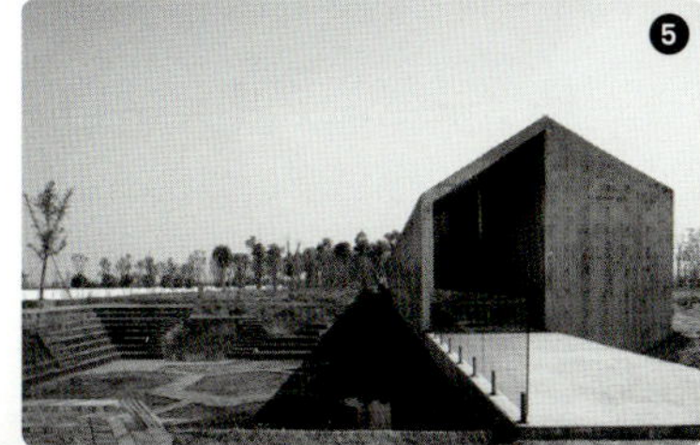

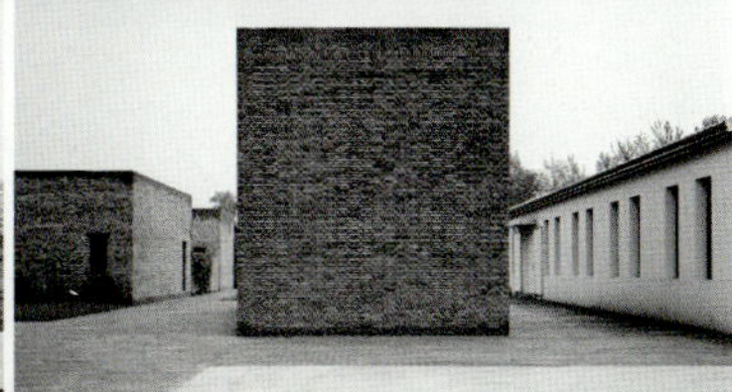

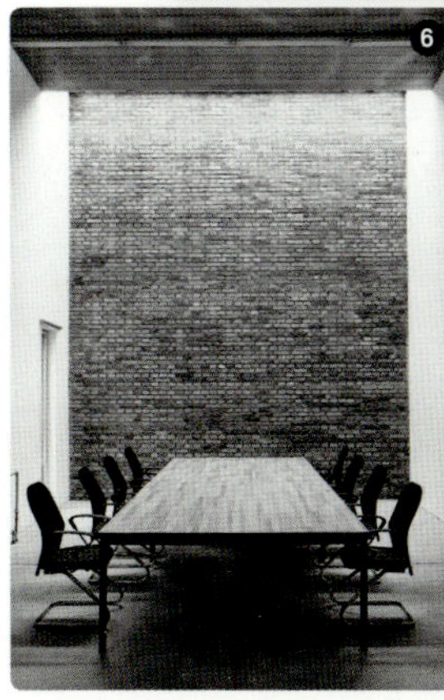

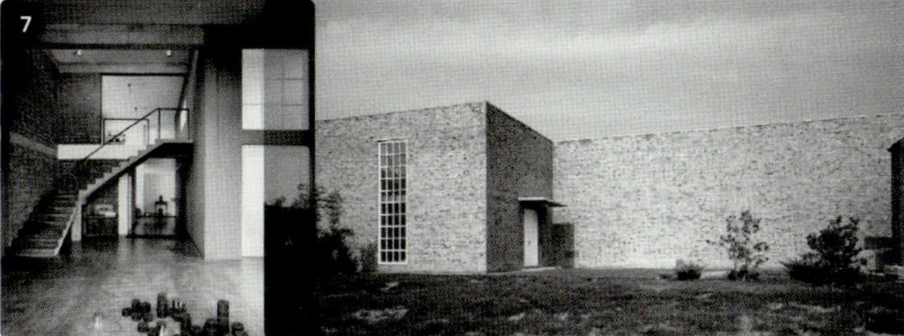

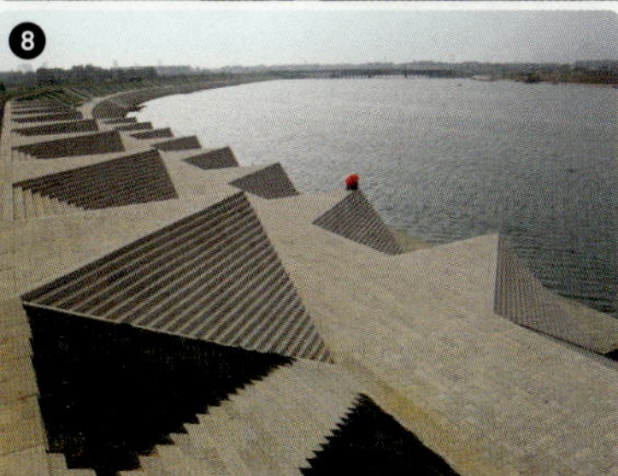

1 Go where Restaurant, Beijing, 2004.
2 Red N°1 Art Gallery, Caochangdi (Beijing), 2008.
3 Three Shadows, centre of photography, Caochangdi, 2007.
4 House with courtyard 104 (Urs Meile gallery), Caochangdi, 2004.
5 Museum of neolithic pottery, Jinhua (Zhejiang), 2007.
6 House with courtyard 105, Caochangdi, 2005.
7 Studiohouse, Caochangdi, 1999.
8 Development of the banks of the river Yiwu, Jinhua, 2004.

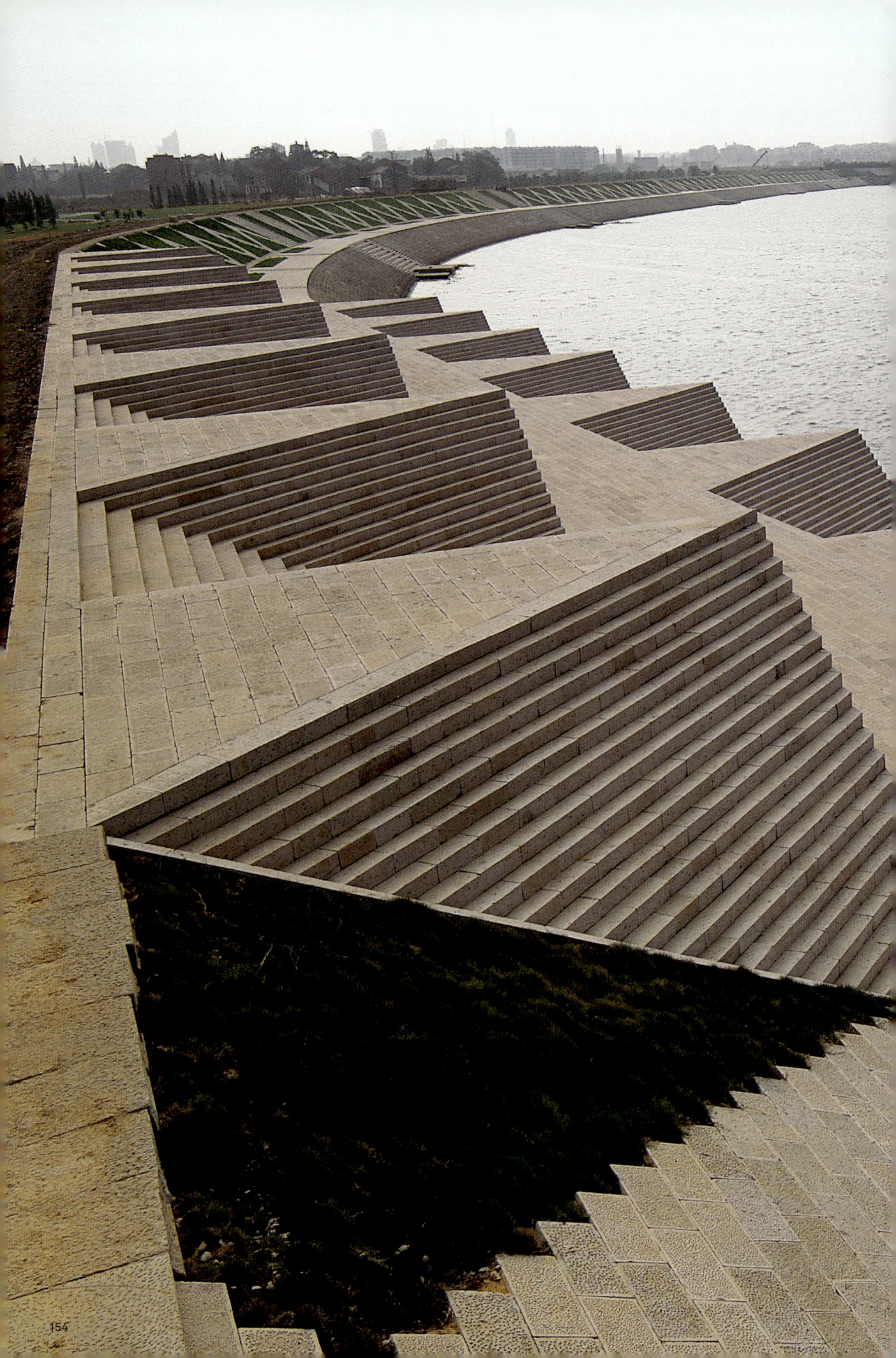

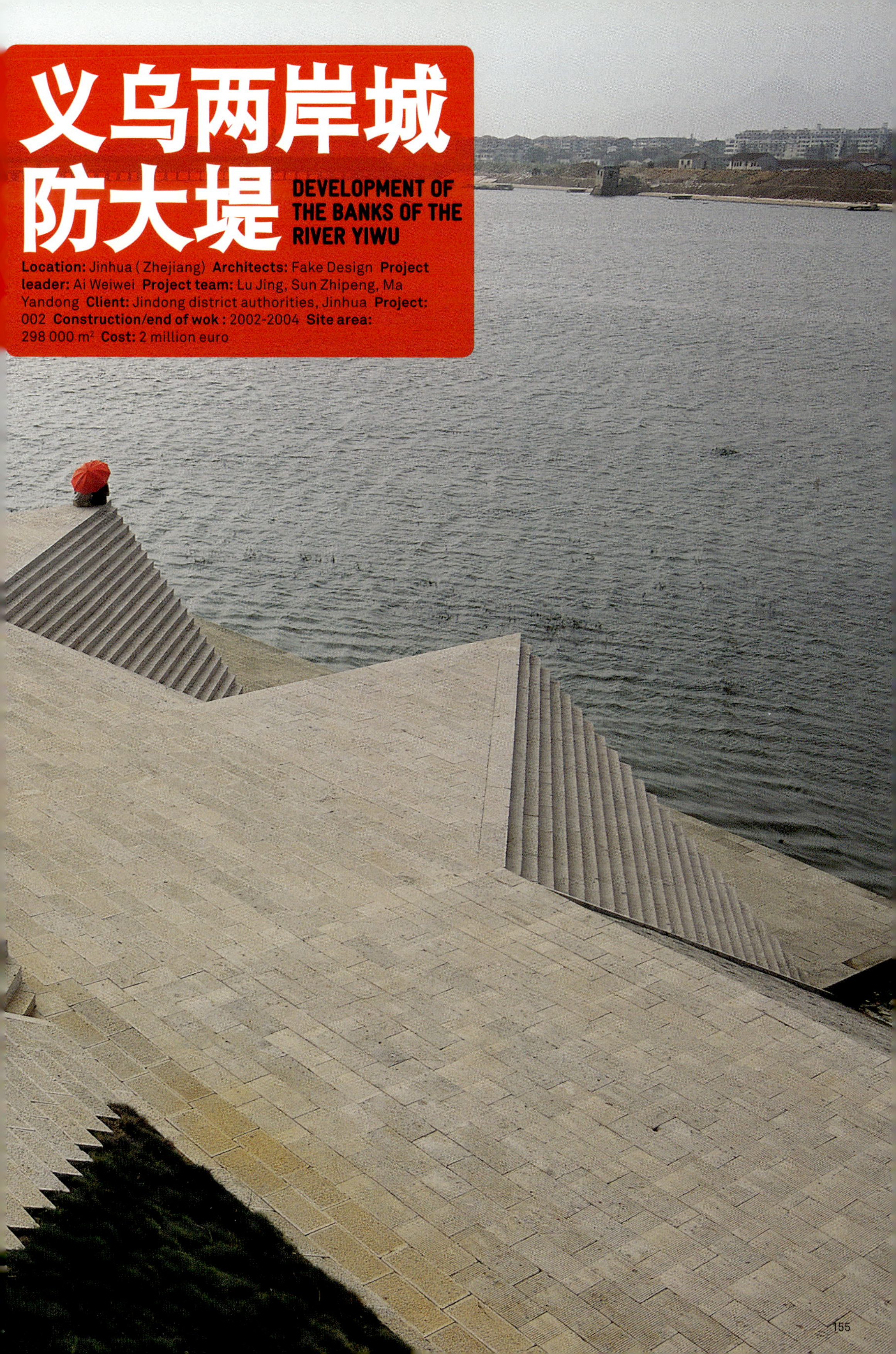

义乌两岸城
防大堤

DEVELOPMENT OF
THE BANKS OF THE
RIVER YIWU

Location: Jinhua (Zhejiang) Architects: Fake Design Project
leader: Ai Weiwei Project team: Lu Jing, Sun Zhipeng, Ma
Yandong Client: Jindong district authorities, Jinhua Project:
002 Construction/end of wok : 2002-2004 Site area:
298 000 m² Cost: 2 million euro

Ai Weiwei's most celebrated work involves a twofold project. It is located at Jinhua, in Zhejiang province, four or five hours by road to the south-east of Shanghai. It is the birthplace of the poet Ai Qing, the architect's father, in whose memory the town decided to build a monumental park. Indeed, this park extends all along the river Yiwu, for the opposite bank of which Ai Weiwei has conceived an unusually finely worked and very impressive quay made of meticulously cut stone blocks. Within the park itself he has invited sixteen artists or architects to design sculptures or structures in which the sculptural spirit in any case, or perhaps a playful intention, often prevails over the functional dimension. Here one finds the cream of the professors from Harvard and of the American galleries, Herzog & de Meuron of course, Toshiko Mori, the trio of David Gwimm with Nadine Quimbach and Tim Williams, Michael Maltzan, Till Sweitzer... and, less numerous, a few Chinese such as Liu Jiakun, Wang Shu, Chang Yung Ho and other personalities close to Ai Weiwei, including Wang Xingwei, Ding and Chen Shuyu.

More details at **http://iwan.com/photo_08_Chen_ShuYu.php** or at the artist's web site: **http://www.aiweiwei.com**

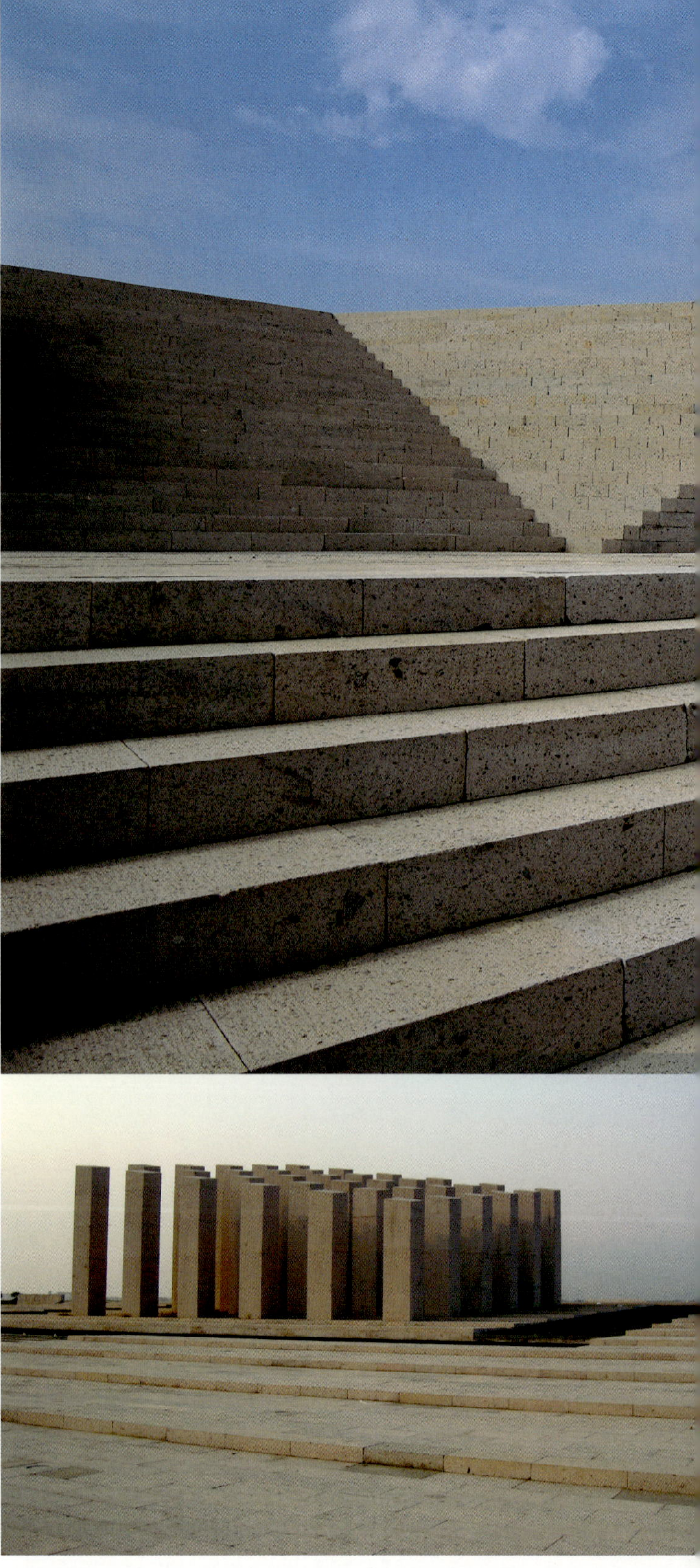

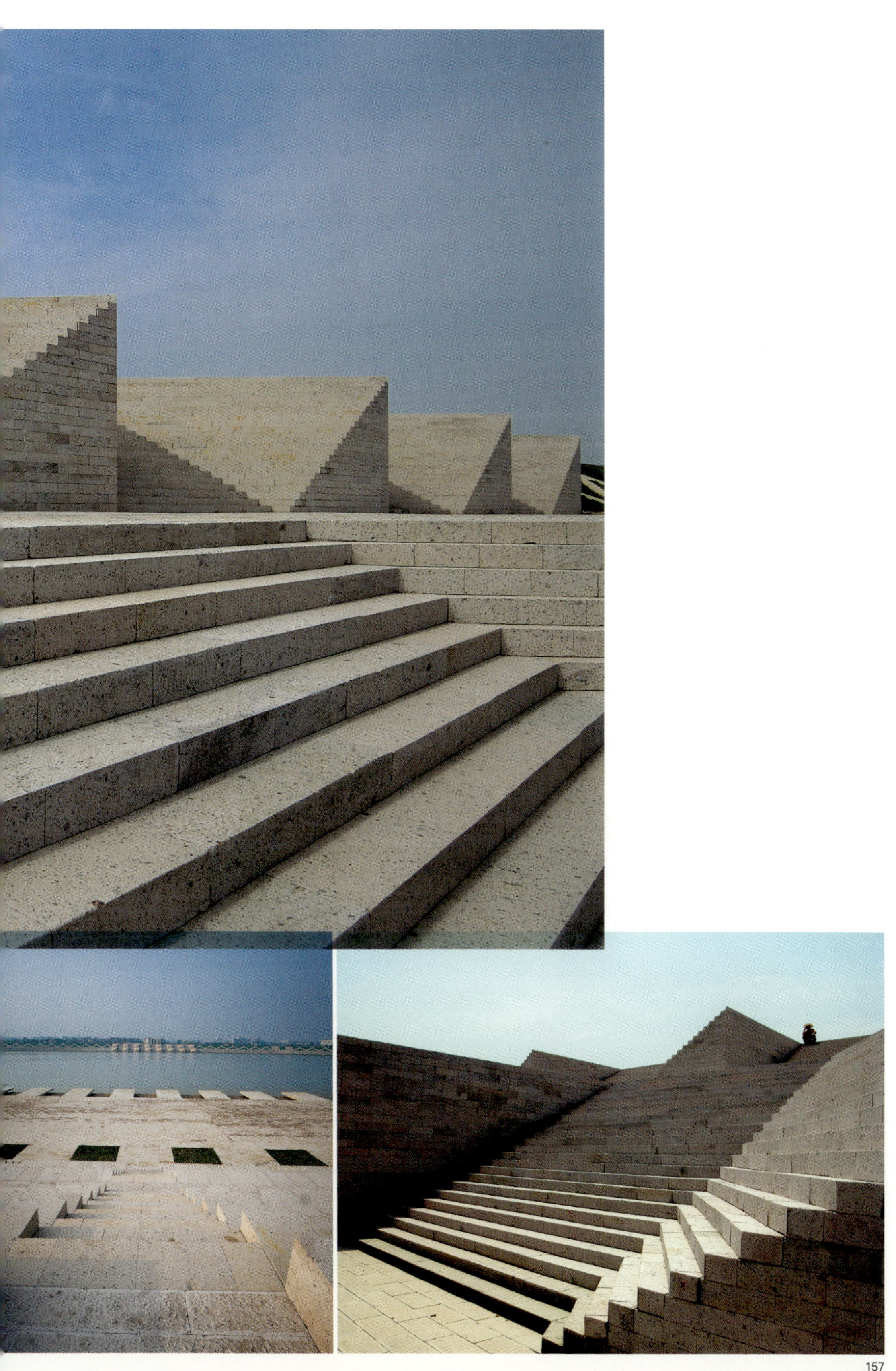

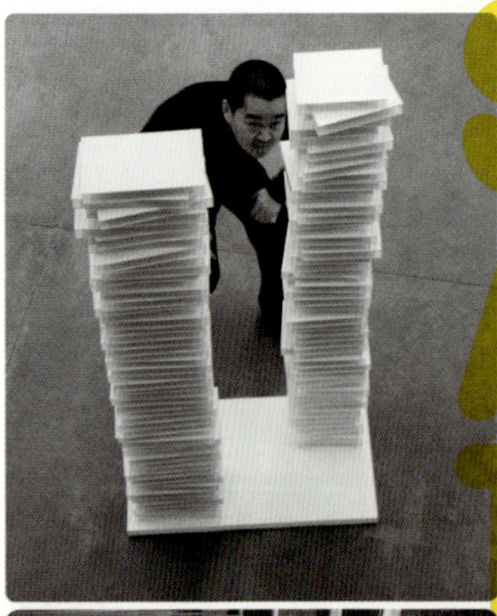
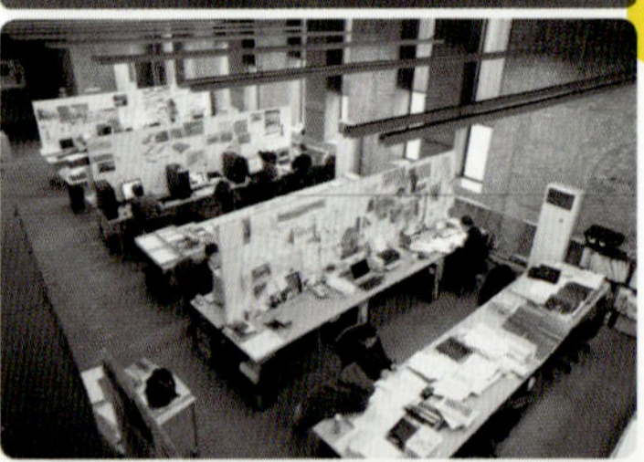
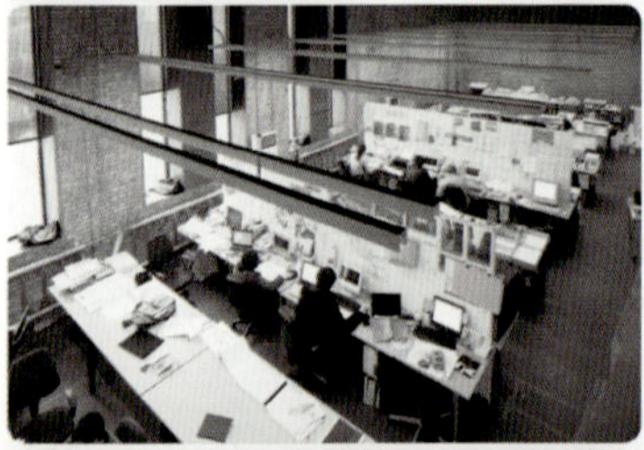
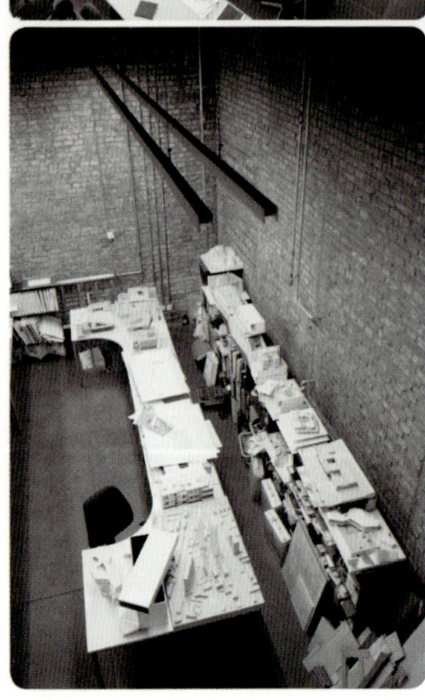

STANDARD ARCHITECTURE

Standardarchitecture 标准营造
Zhang Ke 张轲
Zhang Hong 张宏

The former, Zheng Ke (1970) is perhaps the most at ease because of his having added a degree from Harvard to one from Tsinghua University. The latter, Zhang Hong (1967), has also obtained degrees from two institutions: Tsinghua University and the architecture department of Nanking University. Their partners are Wu and a gifted Portuguese architect, Claudia Taborda.

The 20th century was reaching its end when they founded in New York the studio Standardarchitecture, which has nothing standard about it, however, and nothing conventional in its way of approaching architecture. Since 2001, the studio has been established in the Chinese capital, just a couple of steps away from the associates' common university, as if they could not yet stand wholly apart from this prestigious family.

They have installed their studio, a beautiful denuded space, on the first floor of a factory and, to supplement the classically laughable sum of their architects' fees, they have designed two terribly glamorous bars and restaurants where they also organise their lives, meals and even deliveries. One finds them commonly at Chengfu Lu, the street around which the university quarter is arranged.

In the image of their youth, their architecture is still quite heterogeneous. The auditorium of the school Wuyi (which doubtless means "1st May"), in the suburbs of Beijing, – a large structure of brick and concrete with dry jerky volumes – makes one imagine radical personalities. The shopping centre which they have designed in Yangshuo, near Guilin (Guangxi province), however, exposes them to the risk of being labelled as much more traditionalist.

If it were not for the fact that they built a French-Chinese Art Centre in Wuhan marked by a strong personality without concessions, one would have had to take into consideration their future projects, especially in Xi'an. The commission for the Art Centre evolved from a temporary exhibition building towards a cultural centre forming an emblematic anchorage in a city with quarters which are fairly dismembered.

One can only hope that their future urban projects will find the means required for their completion because this group of architects has talent in reserve.

Partners
Zhang Ke 张轲
Born 1970
Master in architecture, Harvard University, Massachusetts, 1998
Zhang Hong 张弘
Born 1967
Master in architecture,
Tsinghua University, Beijing, 1999
Hou Zhenghua 侯正华
Born 1975
Doctor in architecture,
Tsinghua University, Beijing, 2003
Claudia Taborda
Born 1965
Master in lansdcape architecture,
Harvard University,
Massachusetts, 1999
Studio founded in 2001
Number of employees: 25

Contact
Standardarchitecture
268 Chengfu Road, Room 203
Building #4, Haidian District
100080 Beijing, China
T +86 10 82 61 07 00
F +86 10 62 63 02 48
pro-sa@263.net
www.standardarchitecture.cn

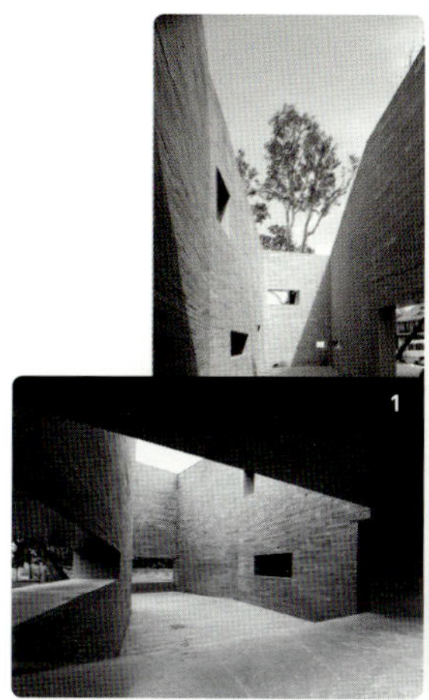
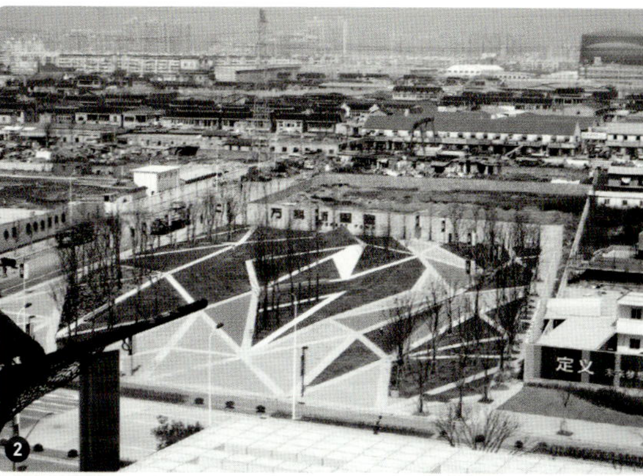
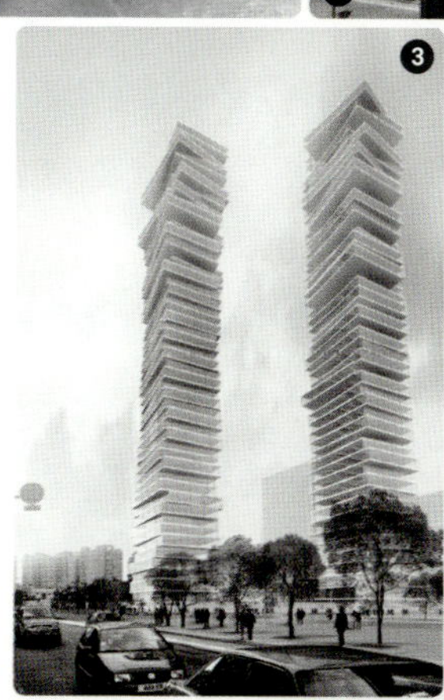
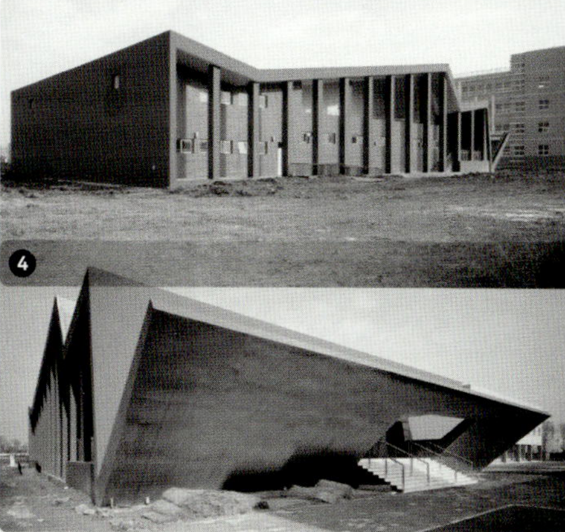
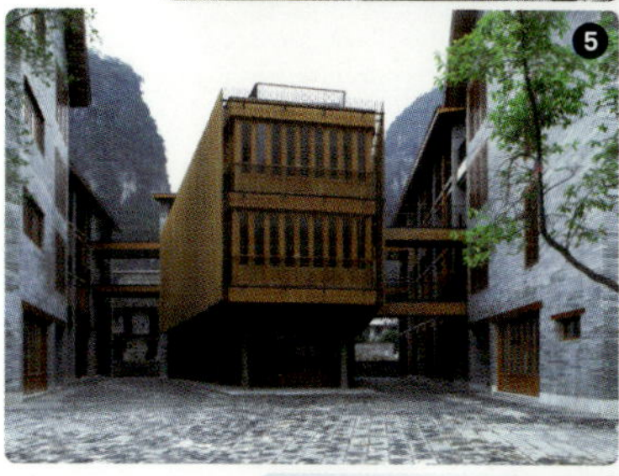
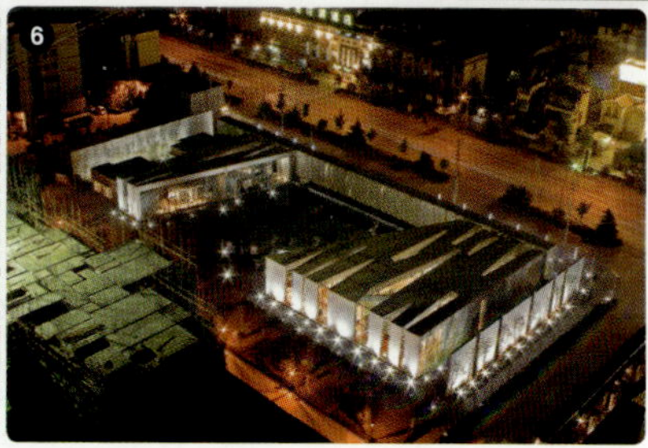
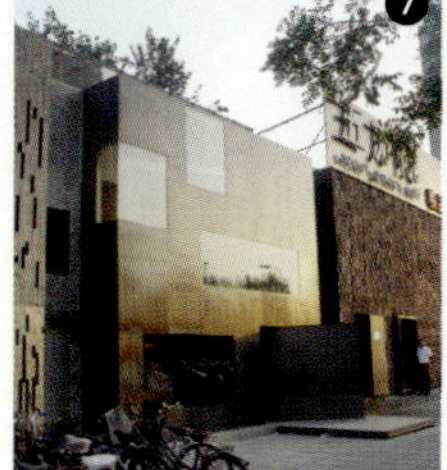

1 Tea house in Qingcheng mountain, Chengdu (Sichuan), 2007.
2 "Dancing Triangles" Park, Pudong (Shanghai), 2006.
3 "Dancing books" towers, Wuhan (Houbei), under construction.
4 Auditorium of Wuyi School, Beijing, 2003.
5 Yangshuo shopping centre (Guilin), 2005.
6 Wuhan French-Chinese Art Centre (Houbei), 2005.
7 Backyard bookstore, Beijing, 2007.

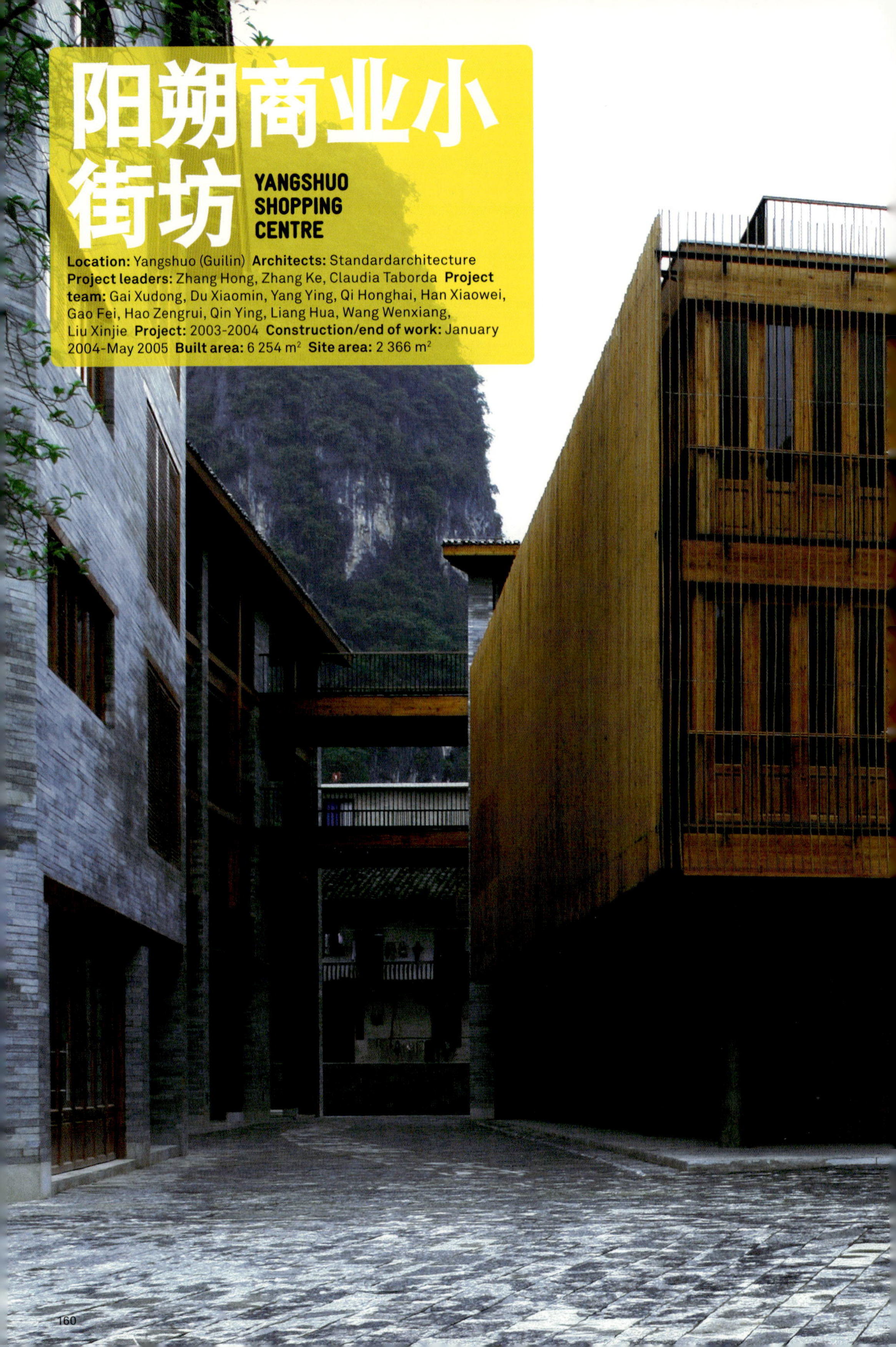

阳朔商业小街坊 YANGSHUO SHOPPING CENTRE

Location: Yangshuo (Guilin) **Architects:** Standardarchitecture
Project leaders: Zhang Hong, Zhang Ke, Claudia Taborda **Project team:** Gai Xudong, Du Xiaomin, Yang Ying, Qi Honghai, Han Xiaowei, Gao Fei, Hao Zengrui, Qin Ying, Liang Hua, Wang Wenxiang, Liu Xinjie **Project:** 2003-2004 **Construction/end of work:** January 2004-May 2005 **Built area:** 6 254 m² **Site area:** 2 366 m²

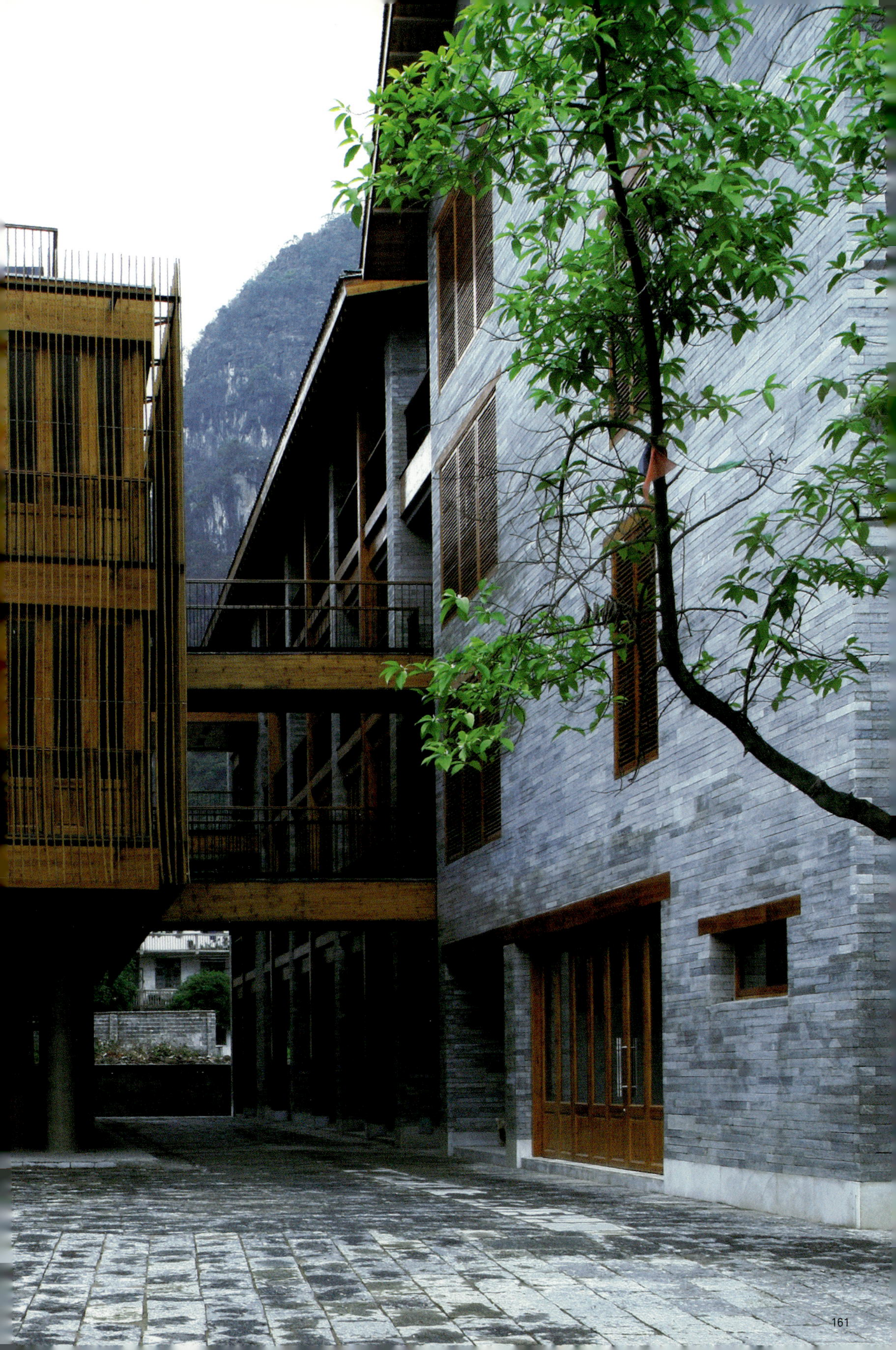

The Yangshuo complex near Guilin was completed
in 2005. It is located precisely in the historic and
tourism village of Yangshuo, on the west bank
of the river Jiang. While the composition and the
volumes of this building, in the old city,
obey a rigorously functional logic, the texture
of the materials, mainly including wood and brick,
evokes the local tradition.
Multi-floored dwellings (with three stories and
a commercial ground floor) recall the classic
operations which one finds in the Alpine stations,
except for the notable fact that only the materials
participate in the dialogue with the old town and,
if there is any connivance, it is found in the right
distance established between the old city and the
tourism ensemble.
An almost ascetic architectural quality acts
as the link here between the past and the
present, without complacency but also without
aggressiveness. On the contrary, the building
tends to highlight the old elements of Yangshuo
by framing them. The block plan of what is
presented, all told, as a self-standing quarter
with over thirty independent readable volumes,
lets one imagine a mode of transcription based
on the juxtaposition of typologies rather than
on mechanisms of random loans such as those
which define the classic mixtures of *fengmao*.

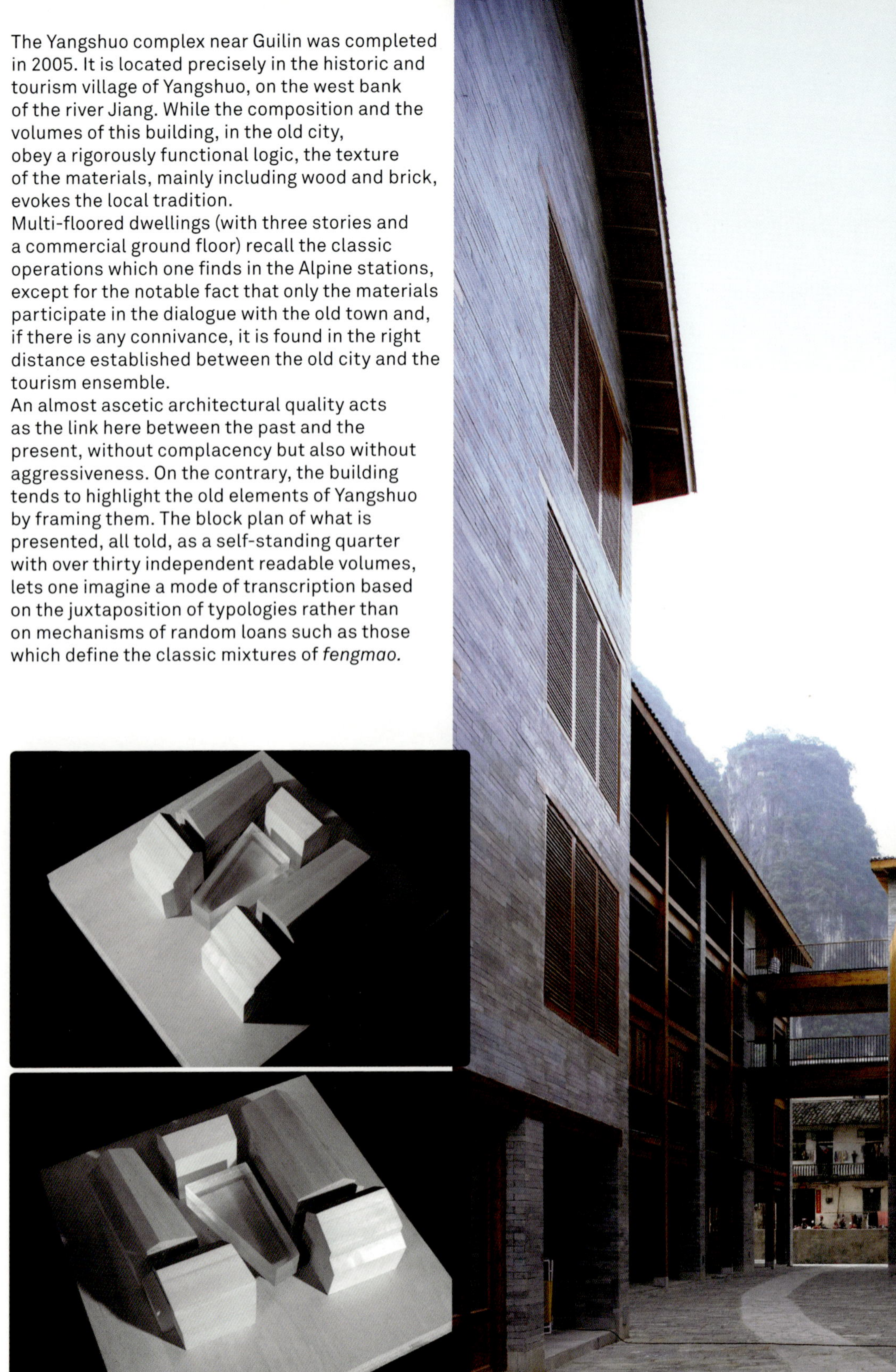

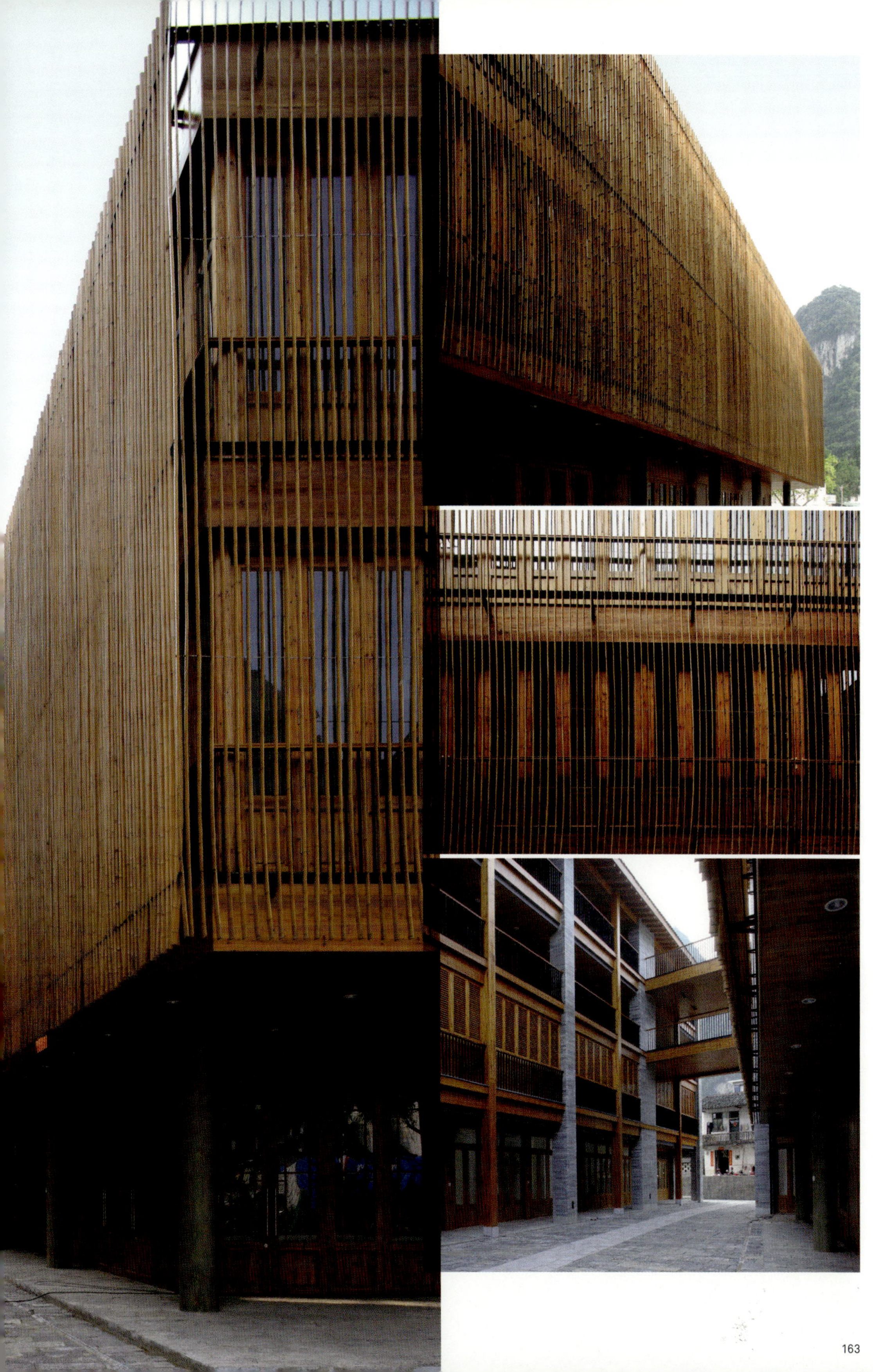

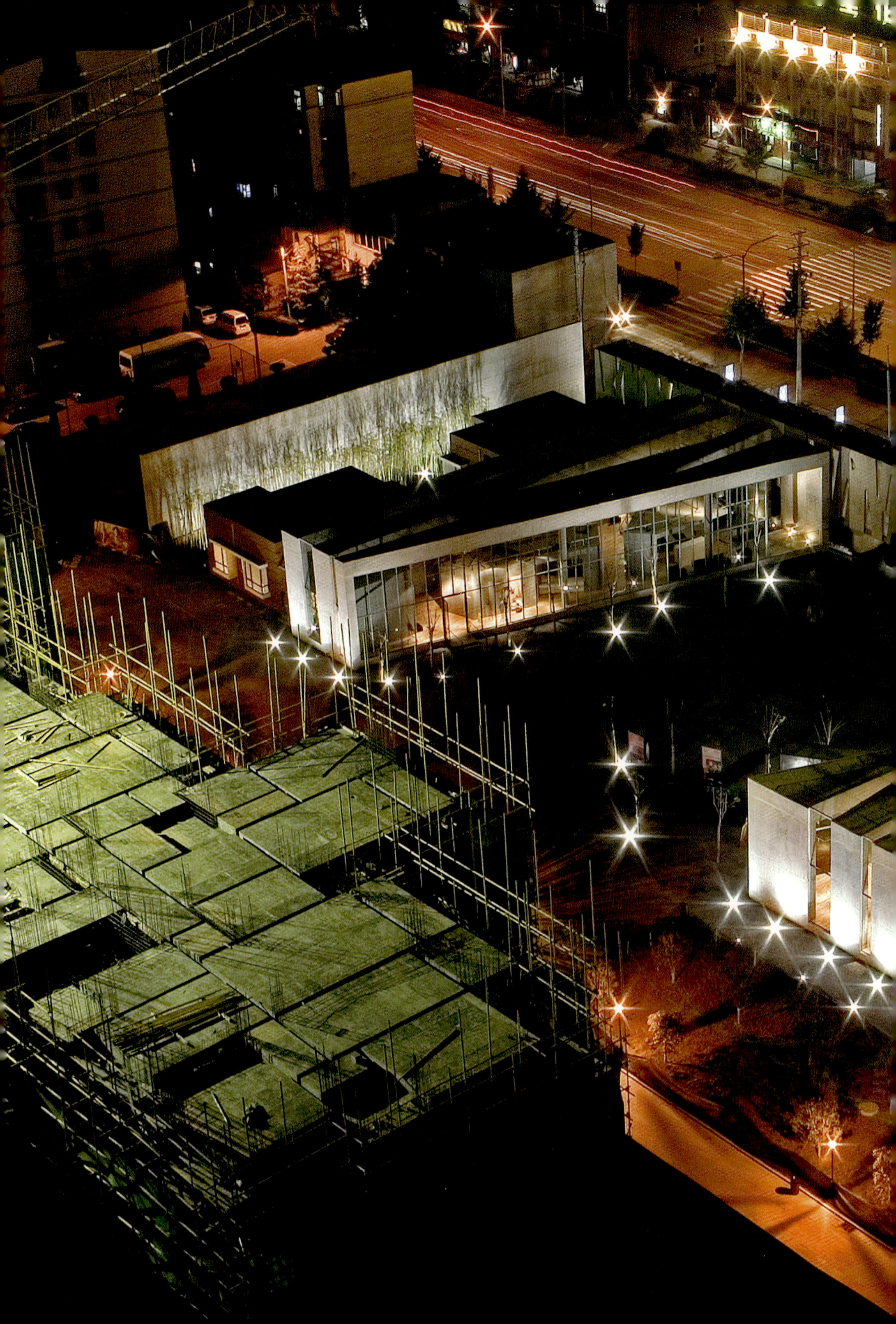

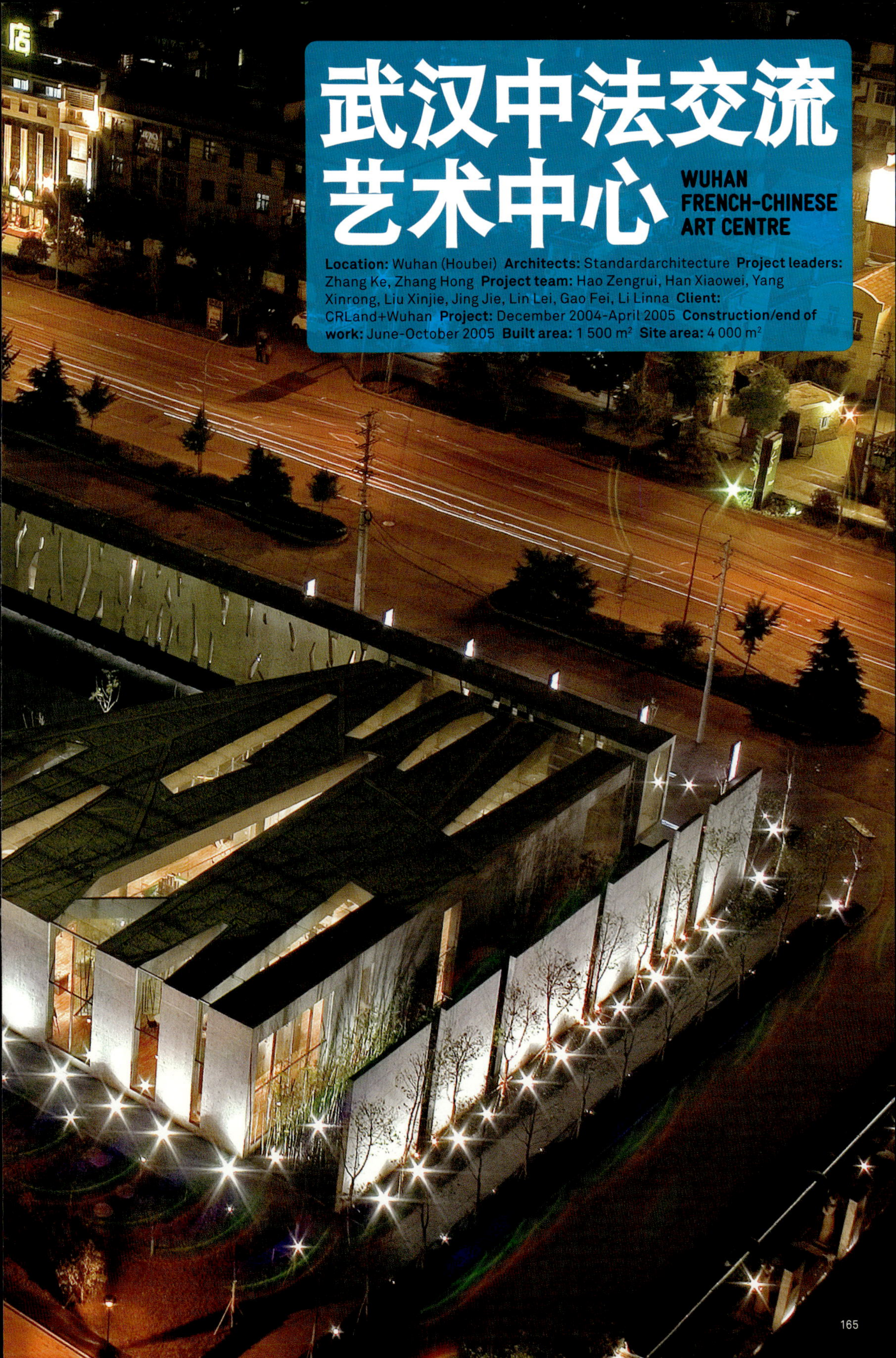

武汉中法交流
艺术中心

WUHAN
FRENCH-CHINESE
ART CENTRE

Location: Wuhan (Houbei) Architects: Standardarchitecture Project leaders: Zhang Ke, Zhang Hong Project team: Hao Zengrui, Han Xiaowei, Yang Xinrong, Liu Xinjie, Jing Jie, Lin Lei, Gao Fei, Li Linna Client: CRLand+Wuhan Project: December 2004-April 2005 Construction/end of work: June-October 2005 Built area: 1 500 m² Site area: 4 000 m²

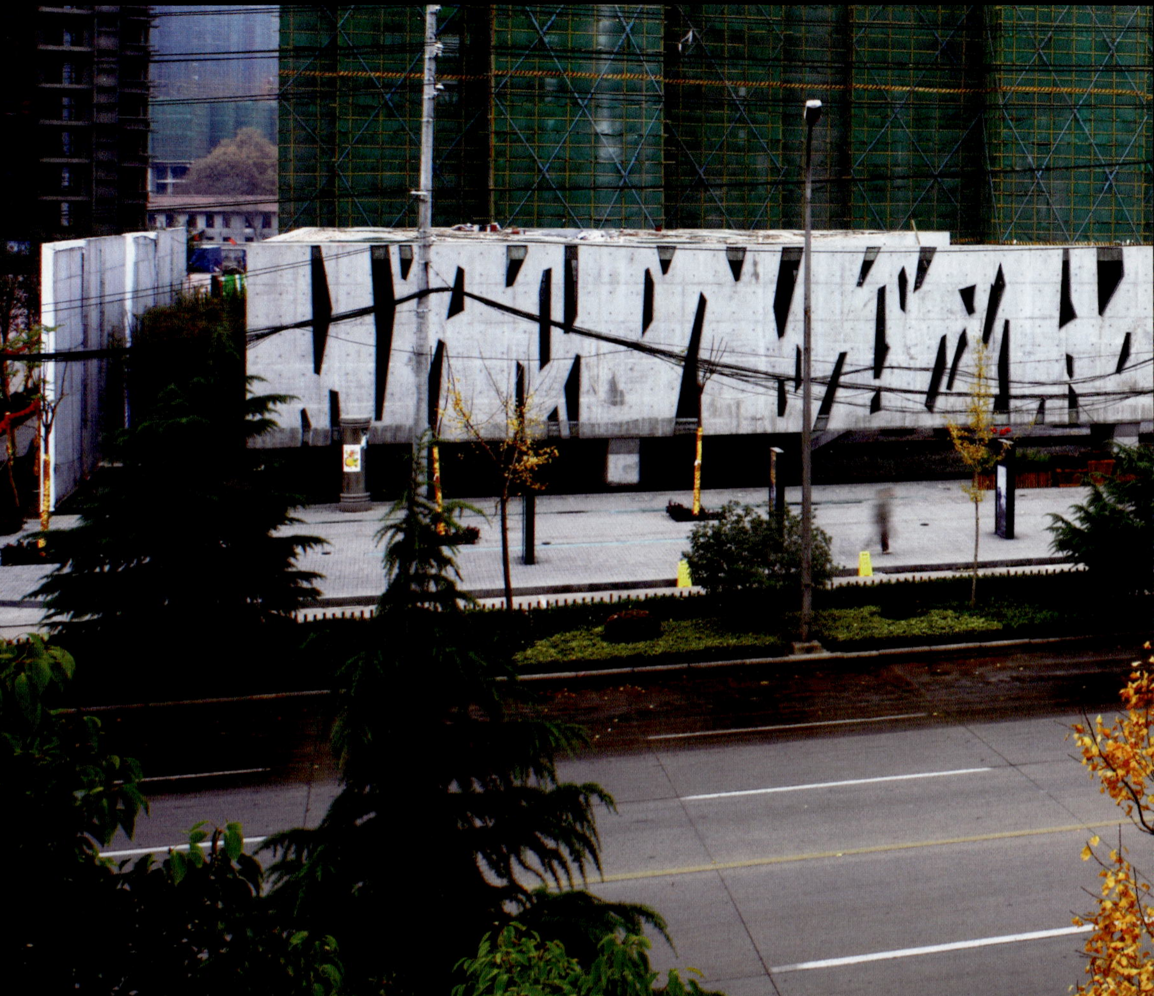

Wuhan is one of the Chinese cities where the French industries
are most solidly established. The French-Chinese Art Centre,
designed by Standardarchitecture, is consequently a place of
dialogue, where contemporary language was invited to express itself
forcefully and without concessions. The general design makes one
think that the architects were influenced to some degree by Daniel
Libeskind's gesturality (cf. the Berlin Jewish Museum), or by the
complex structure of the Swiss architects Herzog & de Meuron for
the Barcelona Forum.
Nevertheless, Standardarchitecture's project was hardly compatible
with the Chinese technical standards in 2004-2005. If the lateral
parts did not pose any particular difficulties, the façade – formed
by a footbridge measuring 80 m in length and 5.5 m in height – left
both the client and the engineers perplexed. From their studies there
remains a superb model which occupies the whole length of the
studio, serving as a highly demonstrative sign.
Libeskind, Herzog & de Meuron… such influence, however,
has nothing of a collage or sterile imitation to it. This building,
randomly striped with openings, can equally well be read as a mist
magnet, a suitable place for playing hide-and-seek or a pumpkin
lantern carved out with a knife for Halloween. The whole, of course,
is marked by a smile.

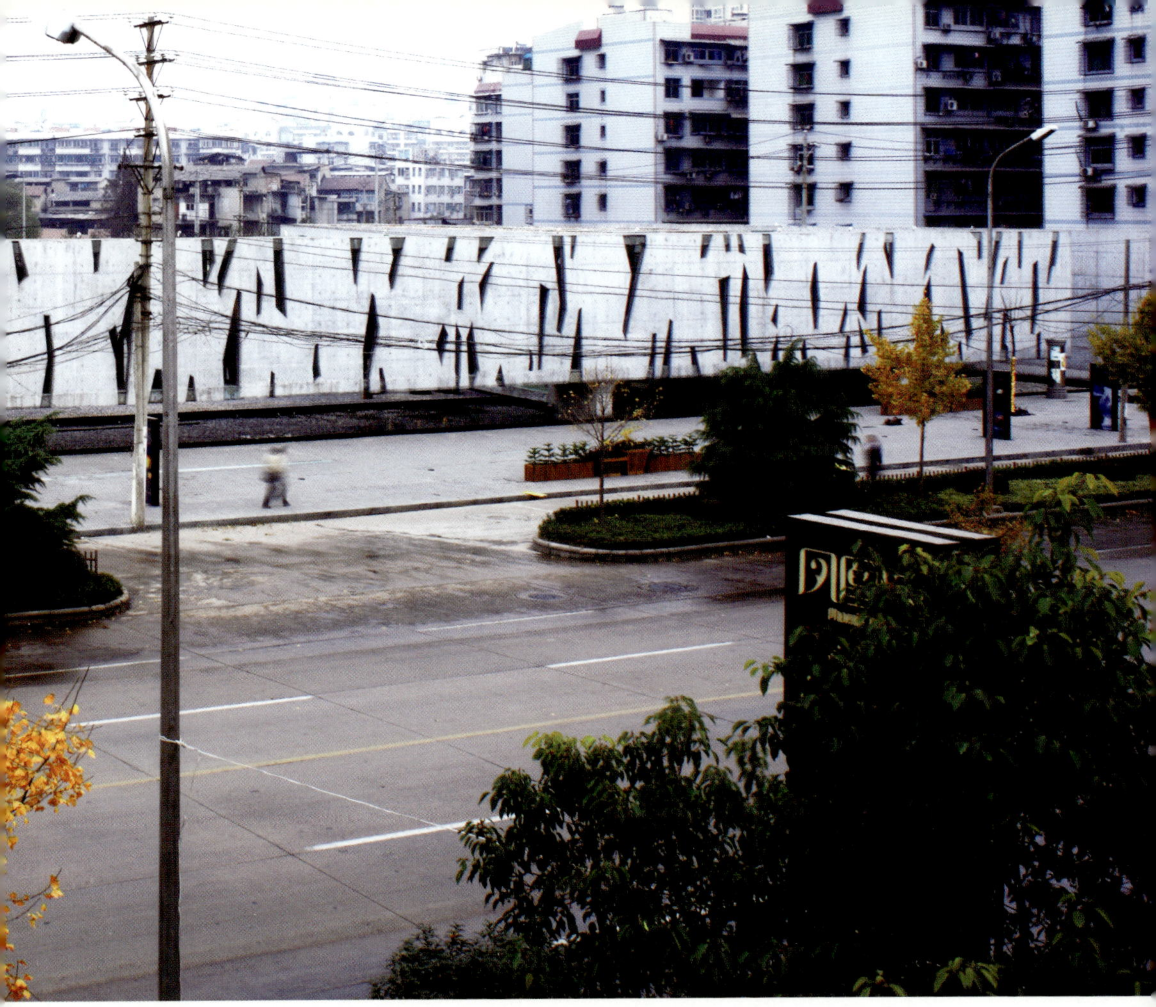

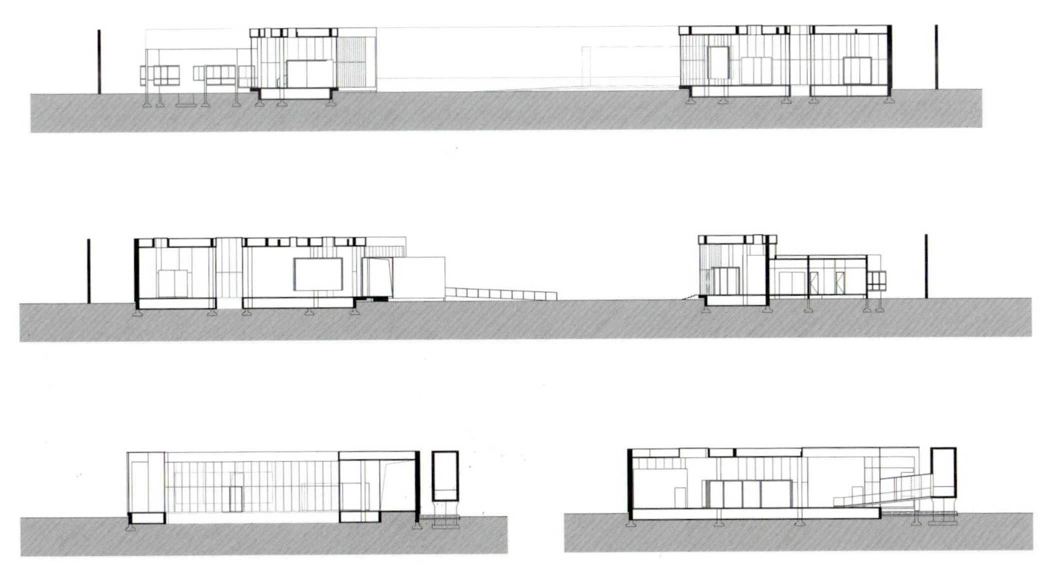

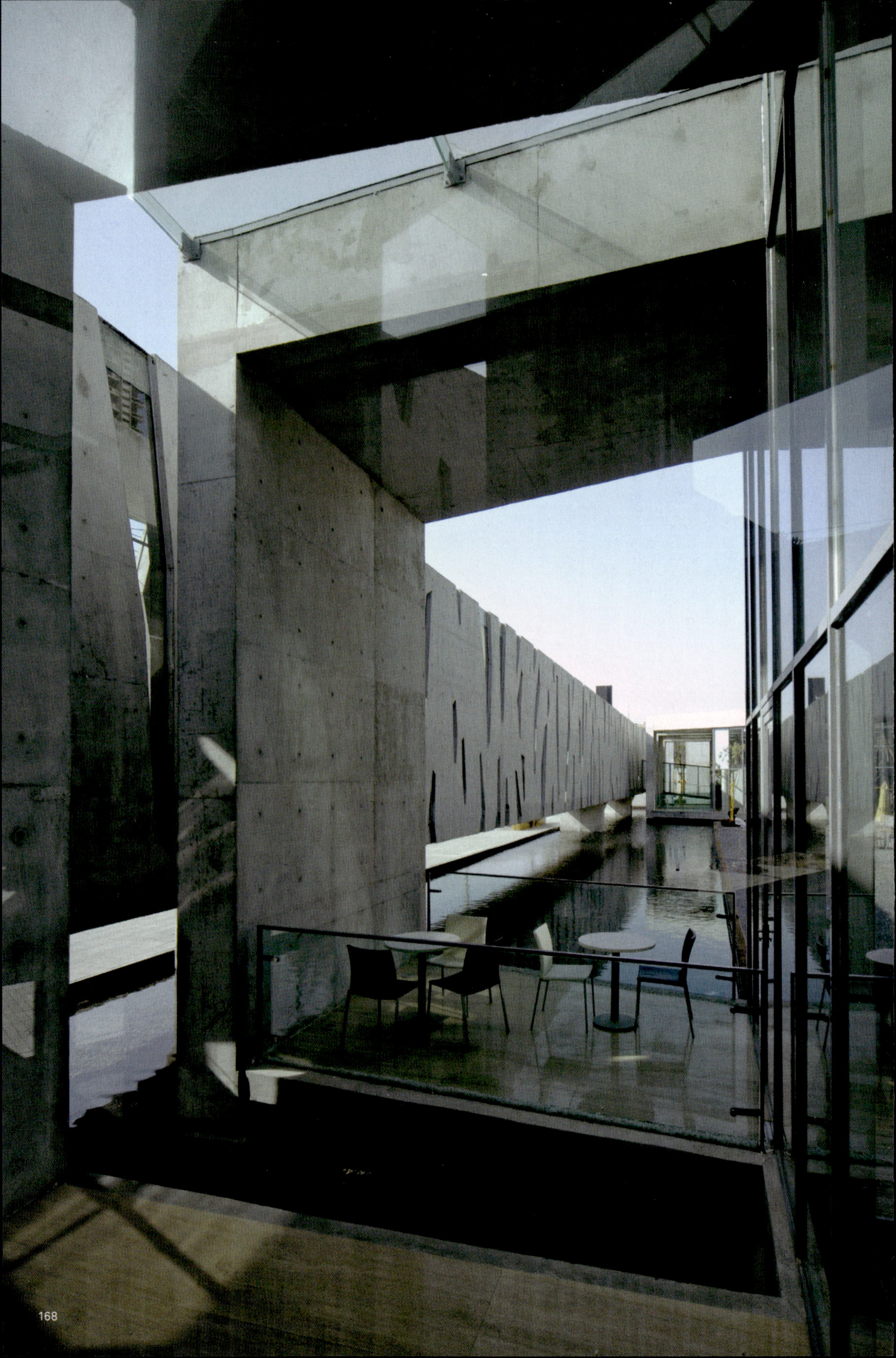

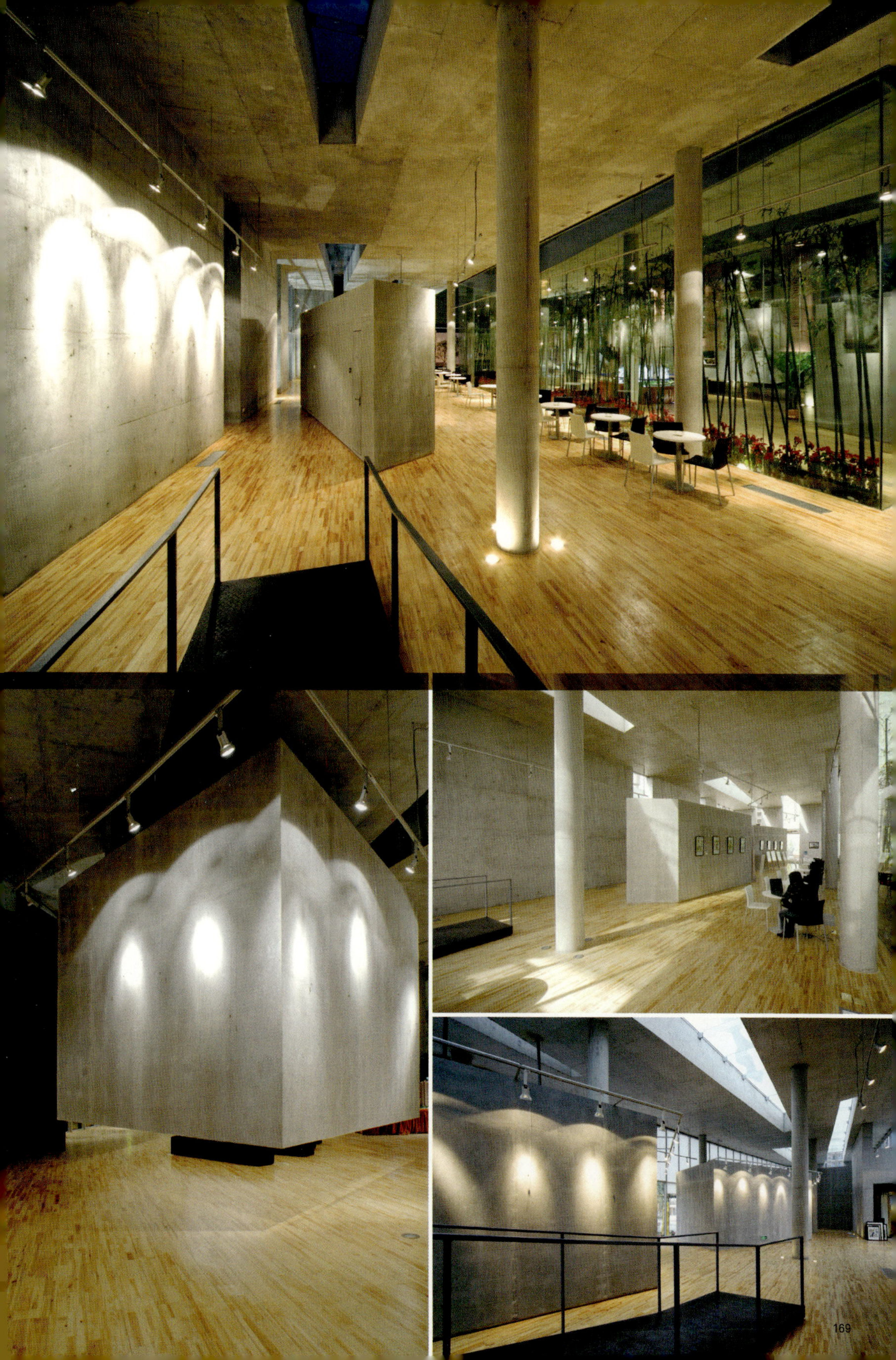

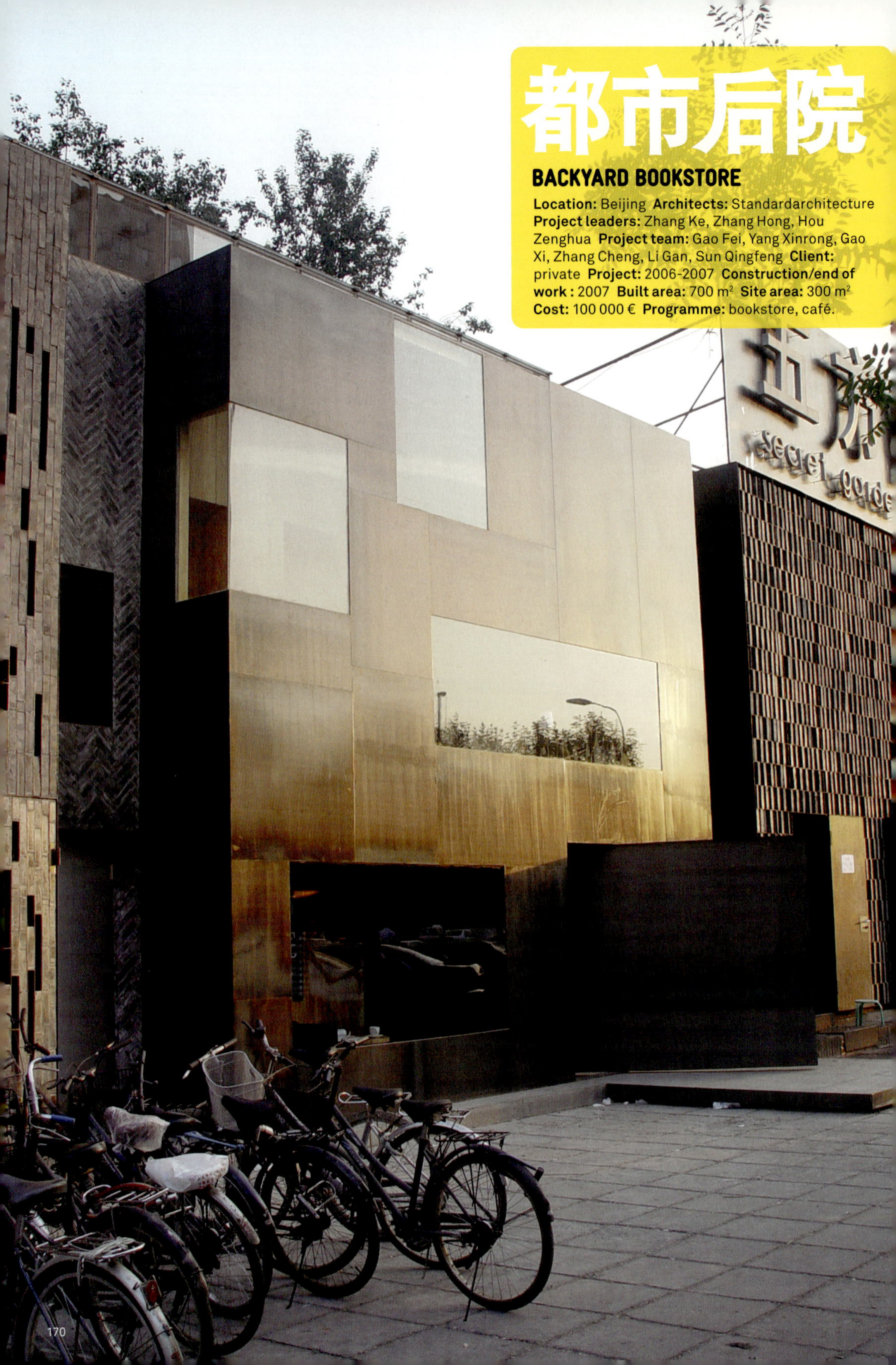
都市后院
BACKYARD BOOKSTORE
Location: Beijing Architects: Standardarchitecture
Project leaders: Zhang Ke, Zhang Hong, Hou
Zenghua Project team: Gao Fei, Yang Xinrong, Gao
Xi, Zhang Cheng, Li Gan, Sun Qingfeng Client:
private Project: 2006-2007 Construction/end of
work : 2007 Built area: 700 m² Site area: 300 m²
Cost: 100 000 € Programme: bookstore, café.

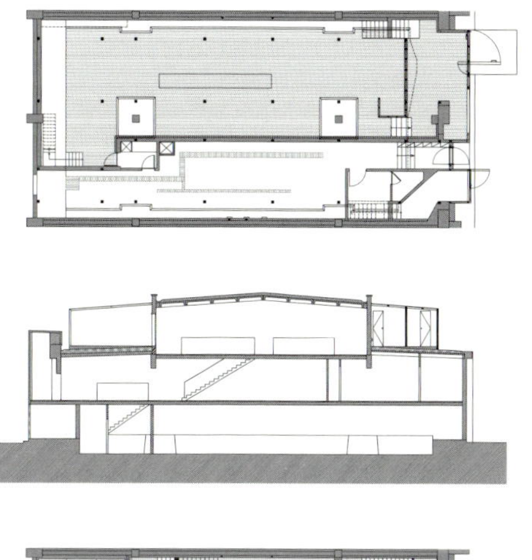

The Backyard Bookstore is a way of promoting one of the plural functions of these establishments which are blooming in China. Here shopkeepers seek to combine a wide range of pleasures for the spirit (a bookstore of variable geometry), the pleasures of discussion (at a bar with imaginative cocktails) and more worldly foods which are required by hard-working architects around Chengfu road. Aside from that, the narrow façade of this small building, which is all depth, is too plain and too carefully designed to let itself be muddled by even the smallest explicit sign. As at the French-Chinese Art Centre of Wuhan, this young architecture studio seeks to use materials here in the purest and most meticulous way, up to the point of making them vanish, and steel and glass borders, even in the interstice which designates a door, separating it from its frame and from what surrounds it. The keynote on the inside is set by brown and grey, changing in fact with the various floors and leading one to think more of an exercise in style destined to convince customers than of an ordinary shop. This type of shop often survives for just one season before a promoter comes to take possession of plots with a real estate value that is ceaselessly climbing.

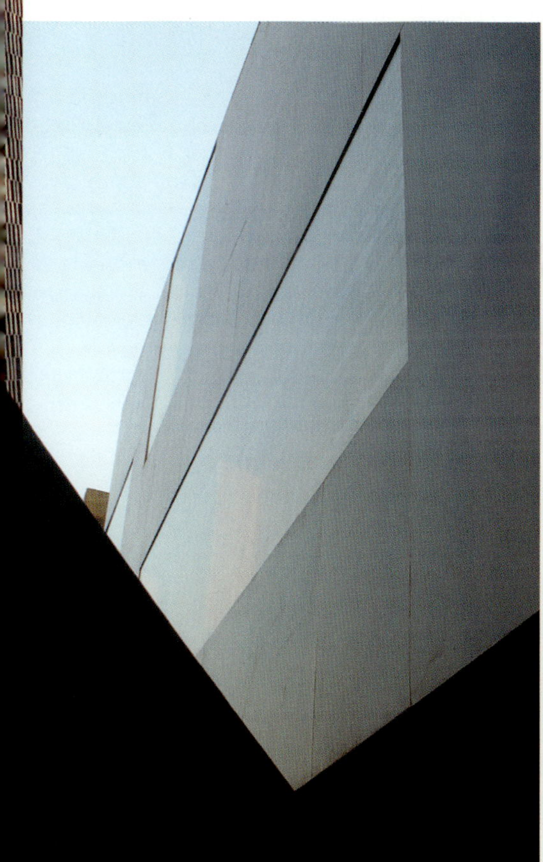

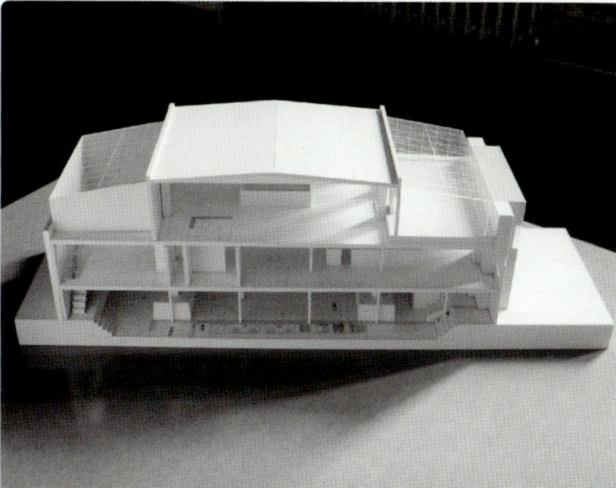

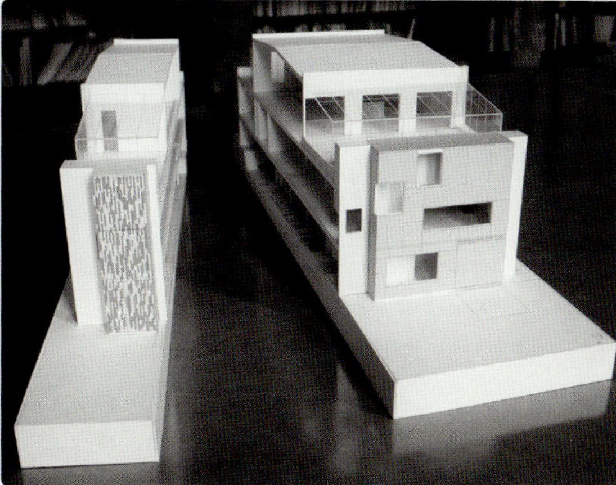

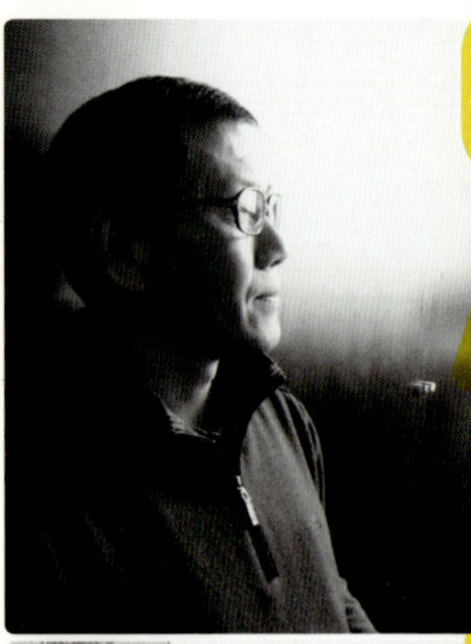

Qi Xin Architects and Engineers 齐欣建筑
Qi Xin 齐欣
Qin Yan 秦岩
He Wei 贺炜
Zhang Jiang 张江

Qi Xin is a unique figure, at least for the French, on the Chinese architectural scene. Born in 1959, he speaks fluent French since, after graduating from Tsinghua University, he went on to study in France, where he obtained degrees at Paris Villemin and later a DEA (Master of Advanced Studies) at the École Nationale Supérieure d'Architecture de Paris-La-Villette. Even so, his return to China would first translate into a three-year stay at Norman Foster's studio in Hong Kong before settling in Beijing.

The closeness of the French language allows him to explain sincerely the apprehension he felt, like so many of his colleagues, on returning to his native country armed with Western references. And there where others, such as his colleague Feng, from Shenzhen, also French-speaking, who had a very different background, took advantage immediately of this twofold perspective to develop their studios, Qi Xin showed himself to be amazingly reserved or hesitant. Sometimes he seems to be fettered by the reflexive slowness which he learned from the French culture, in a country where construction advances at the speed of light.

He has received important commissions since the creation of his studio in 1999 and after being appointed associate professor at Tsinghua, he was selected on the basis of a model to build a training centre near Beijing for the Ministry of Finance. In this building, Qi Xin seems to be fascinated by the symmetry of the plant kingdom, by the floral symmetry which one finds at work in the Administrative Centre of Dongguan, in the south of the country.

In his structures one perceives the mark of the models inherited from the project institutes, where he has never worked, and if he succeeds in lending more grace and skill to them, this is his link with the other actors of his generation who seem to have given him the greatest conceptual freedom. Generally speaking, for some years now he has never been so much at ease as when working on complex projects in which he can seek to associate his colleagues and to re-create the conditions of a welcome urbanity.

For the French Observatory of the Architecture of Contemporary China (OACC), directed by Françoise Ged, and for the numerous professionals who will have taken part in the presidential programme of exchange launched by Jacques Chirac, Qi Xin has always shown himself to be a precious friendly ally.

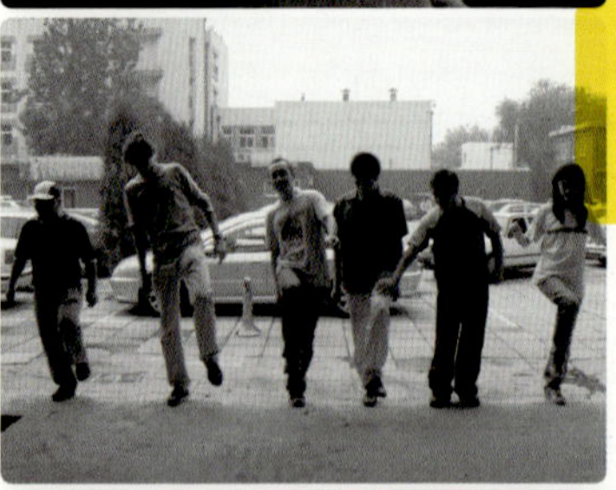

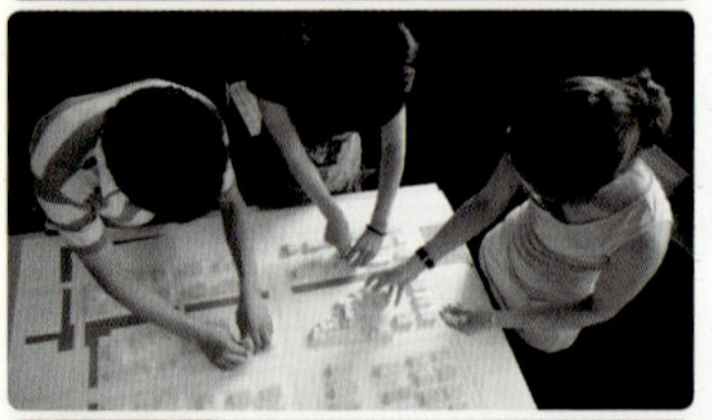

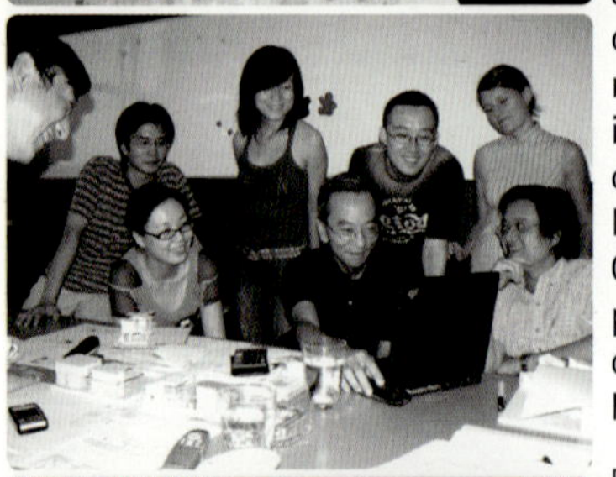

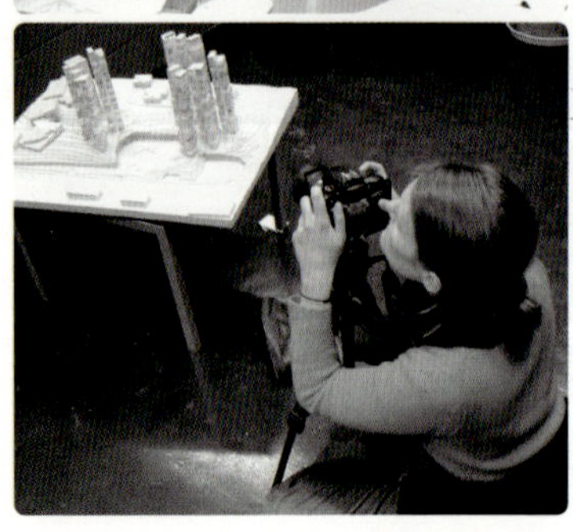

Partners
Qi Xin 齐欣
Born 1959
Degree in engineering,1983,
and architecture DPLG, Paris, 1992
Qin Yan 秦岩
Born 1961
Degree in engineering, 1983
He Wei 贺炜
Born 1964
Degree in engineering, 1983
Zhang Jiang 张江
Born 1971
Degree in economics, 1995
Studio founded in 2002
Number of employees: 14

Contact
Qi Xin Architects and Engineers
Rm. 602, Block B
Tianhai Bldg., 107, Dongsibei Rd.
Dongcheng District
100007 Beijing China
T: +86 10 64 07 33 18
F: +86 10 64 07 33 78
qixin@qixinatelier.com
www.qixinatelier.com

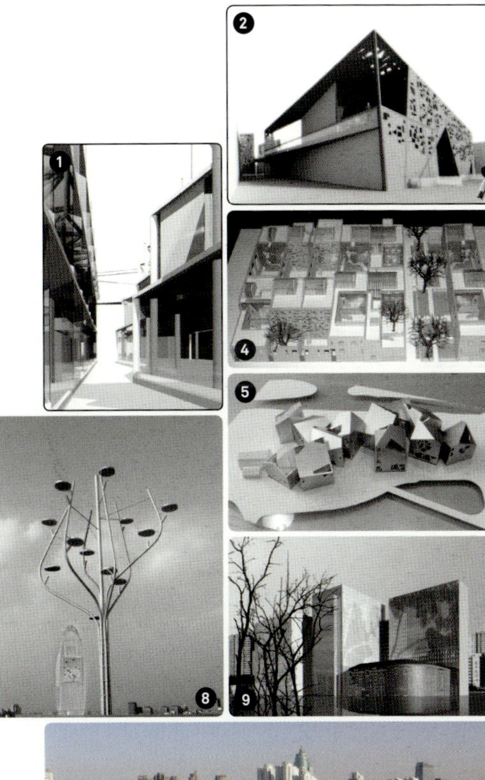

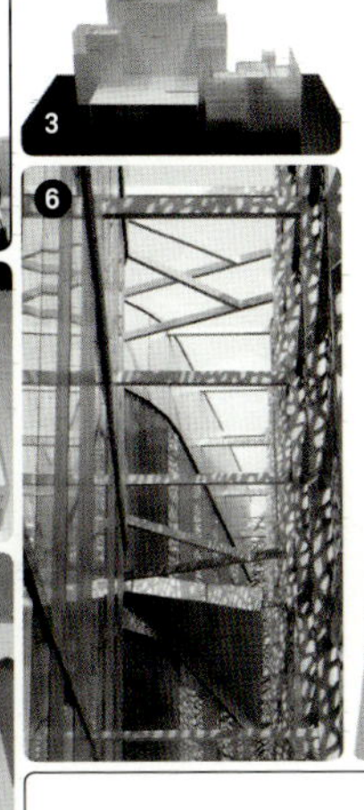

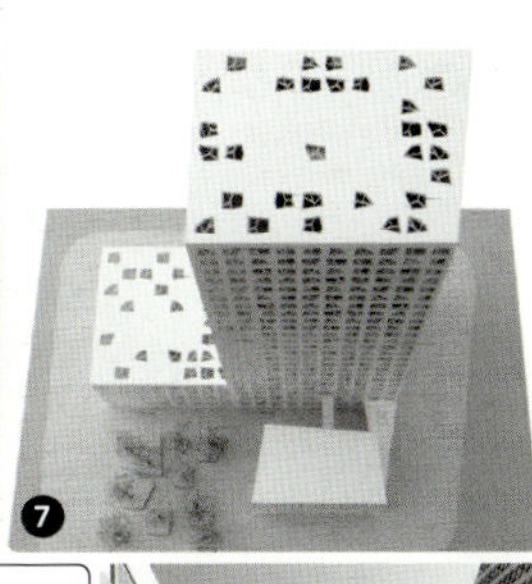

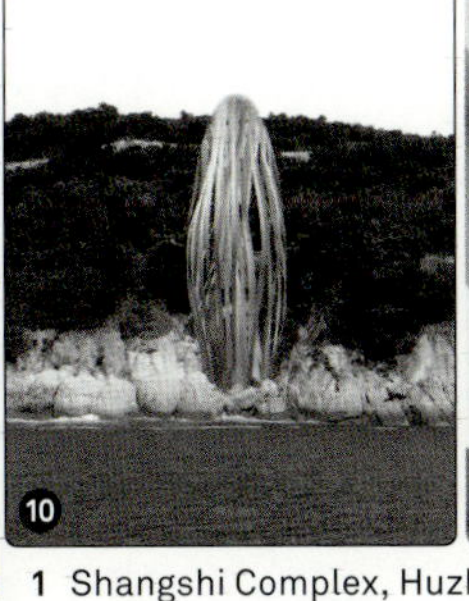

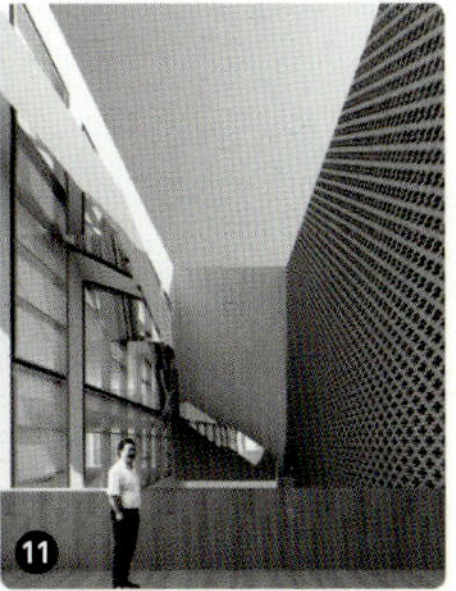

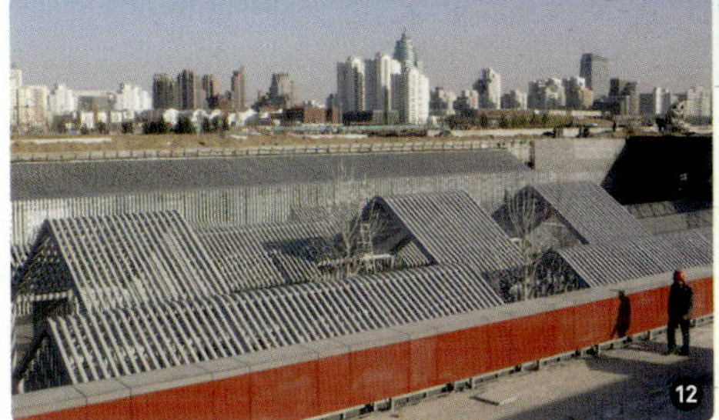

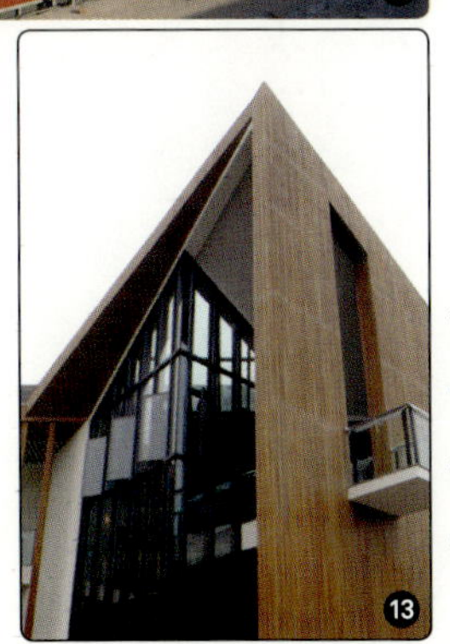

1 Shangshi Complex, Huzhou (Zhejiang), under construction.

2 Qinhuaifengqing bar and shops, Nanjing (Jiangsu), 2007 (unbuilt).

3 Façade renovation of the Gehua New Century Hotel, Beijing, 2006.

4 Xianshan housing scheme, Beijing, 2004 (unbuilt).

5 XiXi Clubhouses, Hangzhou (Zhejiang), under construction.

6 Rongketiancheng sales office, Wuhan (Hubei), 2006.

7 Zhonghai housing building, Tianjin (Hebei), 2007 (unbuilt).

8 Urban furniture, Beijing, 2007 (unbuilt).

9 Facades of Meilanfang opera, Beijing, 2005 (unbuilt)

10 Guanjingge panoramic viewpoint, Shenzhen (Guandong), 2005 (unbuilt)

11 Research centre, Qingchengshan (Sichuan), under construction

12 Siheyuan, Promenade and shopping area at the Olympic Games site, Beijing, 2007.

13 Yuniaoliusu, Liangzhu cultural village, 2008.

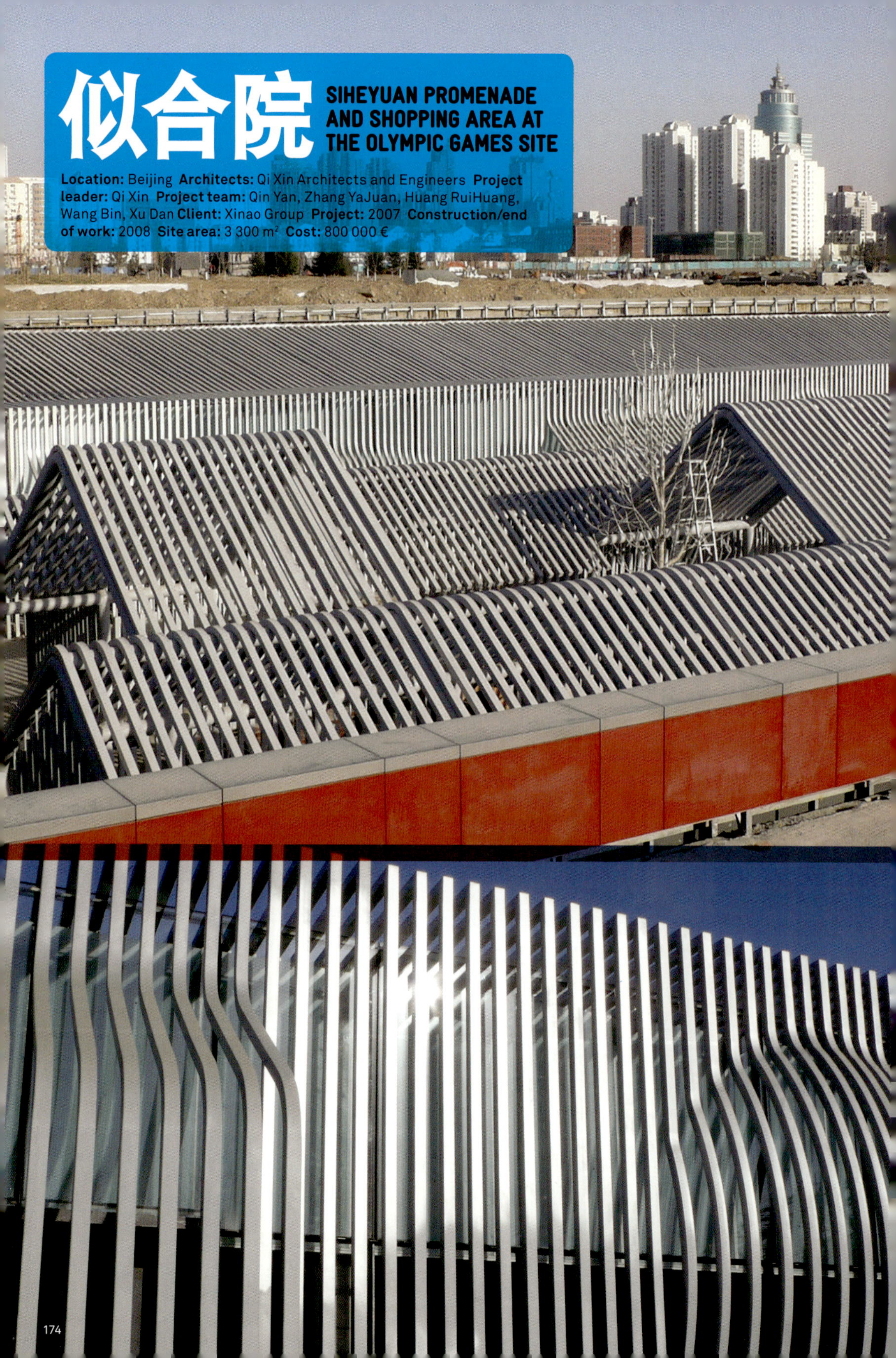

似合院
SIHEYUAN PROMENADE AND SHOPPING AREA AT THE OLYMPIC GAMES SITE
Location: Beijing Architects: Qi Xin Architects and Engineers Project leader: Qi Xin Project team: Qin Yan, Zhang YaJuan, Huang RuiHuang, Wang Bin, Xu Dan Client: Xinao Group Project: 2007 Construction/end of work: 2008 Site area: 3 300 m² Cost: 800 000 €

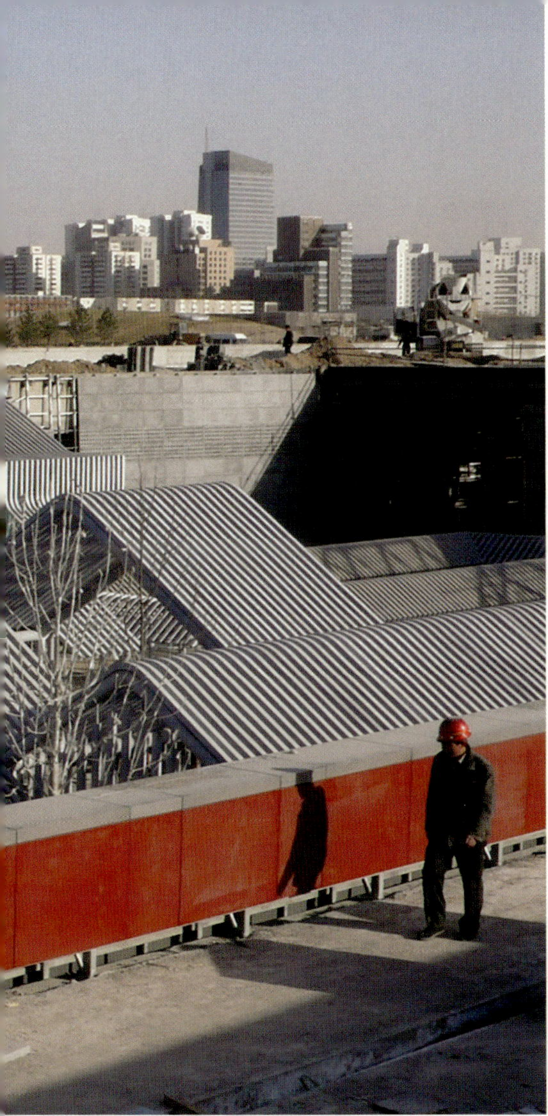

This structure is located in Beijing on the site of the Summer Olympics, just a short distance to the north of the great stadium and the national swimming pool, on the west side of the lake connecting the sports facilities to the freshly established Olympic Forest. Qi Xin has christened this outdoor area Siheyuan, a subtle play of homophony, evoking at one time the square courtyard of Beijing (四Si, "number 4") and its re-interpretation (似Si, "similar").

The plot of 3,300 sq m is integrated in a set of seven successive courtyards of variable area, sunken about ten metres into the ground and exposed to the open air. This long intermediate platform serves as the access level to the Metro and the basement shops. The block plan, imposed by the Project Institute of Beijing, provides a twofold cultural orientation: the plots shall be planned by Chinese architects, who are notably absent from the pharaonic workplace of the Olympic Games, and each shall restore the local culture in his project. Five local and national project institutes, Cui Kai's studio and that of Qi Xin have been invited to (re-)produce architectural elements recalling the traditional characteristics of the capital.

The programme is an uncovered outdoor promenade along the shop premises and leisure facilities. To lend homogeneity to the path, the courtyards are connected to each other by two "conducting walls", grey and red, which symbolise respectively the popular framework of Beijing and the Imperial City. Within this narrow sunken strip, Qi Xin chooses only to carry out an intervention on the landscape, a façade intervention, rather than to erect a strict and inevitably pastiche framework in response to the programme. He proposes a space planned around the principle of conviviality and transparency peculiar to Beijing's square courtyards. A gallery reminiscent of those of the traditional Chinese gardens winds along a pond. All along its east side runs an open façade sheltering shops, a sort of house truncated in its length.

A simple post-and-beam structure acts as a load-bearing wall. Hollow steel joists measuring 10 cm in diameter each are spaced in close regular strips, like a grey-blue filter acting transparently on the landscape. The joists writhe to redesign little by little the familiar contours of the courtyard house. The façade sheltering the shops is punctuated by openings and by some random "accidents", adding to the game some drop shadows and streaks of light. Twelve-metre tall masts carrying round light fixtures, platforms or frames, square off the space like the crossing points of the lines in the game of Go, and shine in fine slats on the esplanade level, only to melt into the super-urban landscape of northern Beijing.

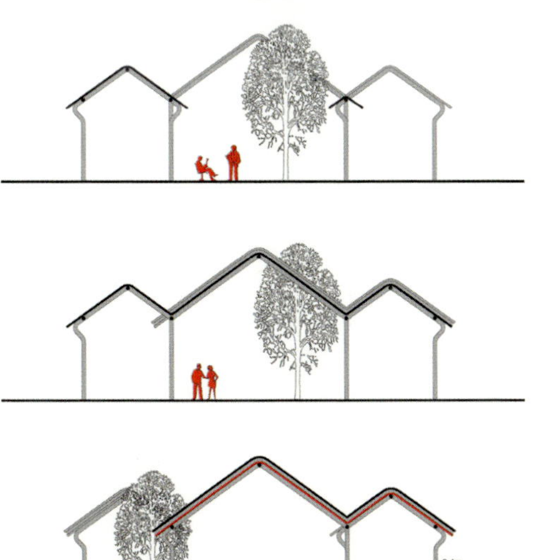

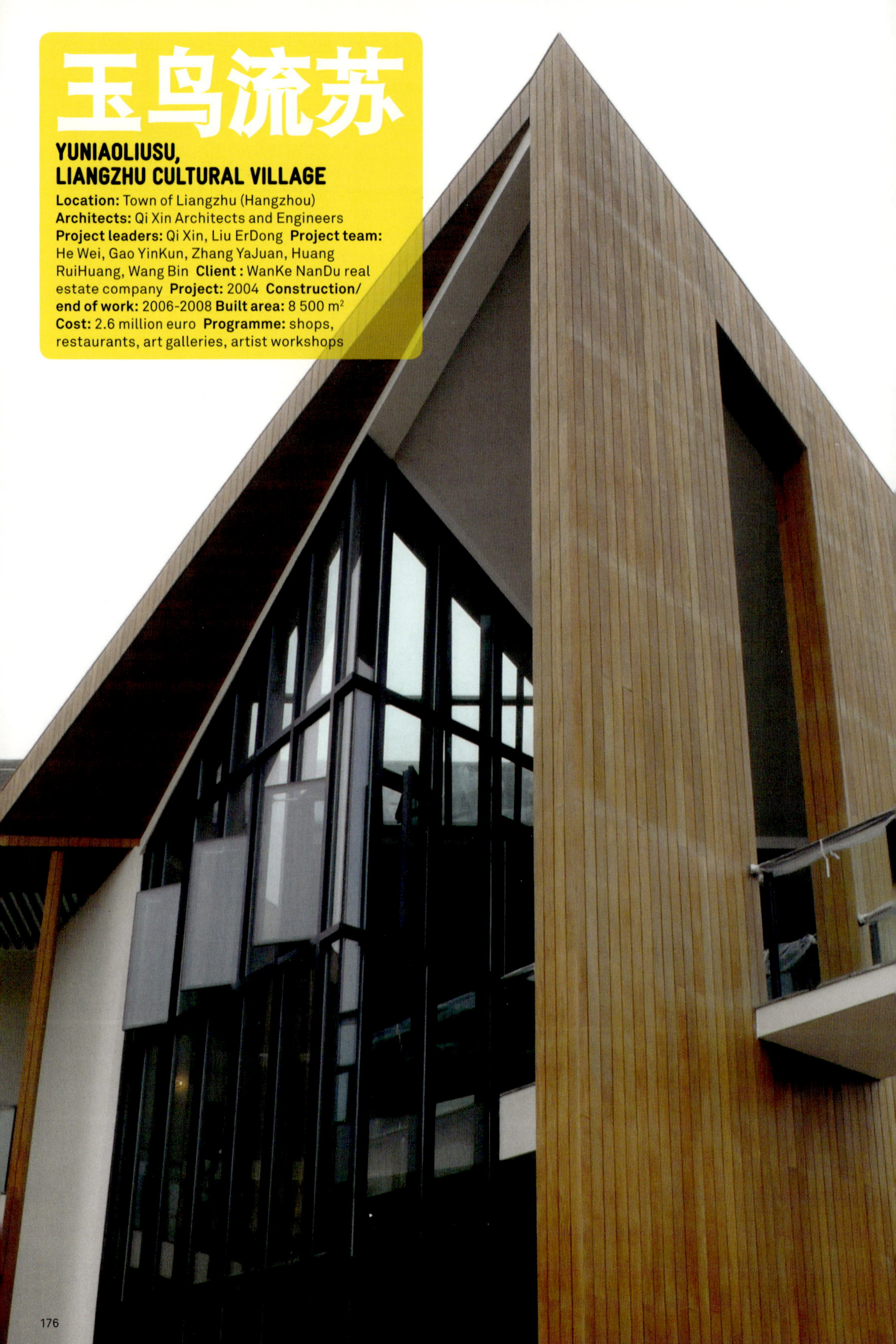

玉鸟流苏

YUNIAOLIUSU, LIANGZHU CULTURAL VILLAGE

Location: Town of Liangzhu (Hangzhou)
Architects: Qi Xin Architects and Engineers
Project leaders: Qi Xin, Liu ErDong **Project team:** He Wei, Gao YinKun, Zhang YaJuan, Huang RuiHuang, Wang Bin **Client :** WanKe NanDu real estate company **Project:** 2004 **Construction/ end of work:** 2006-2008 **Built area:** 8 500 m²
Cost: 2.6 million euro **Programme:** shops, restaurants, art galleries, artist workshops

This architectural ensemble brings together the projects of the studios of Qi Xin, Zhang Lei, Deshaus and WSP, in an area north of Hangzhou. The elegant forms of Qi Xin appear along the Nanking-Shanghai motorway, after kilometres of fairly gloomy urban implantation. With its name meaning "beautiful place surrounded by water", Liangzhu stands about one hundred *li* (about 50 km) from the centre of the provincial capital of Hangzhou. Together with Xisu, Liangzhu is a cradle of the local culture, with a history reaching back 4,000 years.

In 2004, a giant of the Chinese real estate sector was entrusted with providing some public tourism amenities for the city, in exchange for the development of a large part of the area. A programme of shops and leisure facilities has been defined on a site bounded by residential complexes under construction. The investor has called on four teams of Chinese and international architects to try to restore the local culture within the initial plan with its overly American look. They define together the rules of play and propose a counter-project, re-introducing the principle of "village, square and street", based especially on more local typologies.

The architects' aim of not imposing an excessively strict line on the overall project gives them a certain freedom of conception of the lot which they have drawn. It is within this agreeable blurriness that Qi Xin slides a building which is all length, on slightly uneven terrain, starting at the northern entrance of the site and extending the new shopping centre towards the south. In this first phase, this large covered gallery is formed by five independent modules connected by a continuous roof, footbridges and stairways.

On the western face, the large interior volumes open broadly on the street while in the east, the shops, restaurants or art galleries are protected by blind walls, surmounted outside by large compact tiles, designed to dampen the sound of the motorway. On the west side again, a filter of light-toned wood blocks out the heat of the sun and casts a timely shadow on the interior courtyards. On these 8,500 sq m of covered area, there is a strong link between the inside and the outside, creating the conditions for a welcome urbanity. The functioning of this new urban pole is still difficult to assess in the current state of the site, as yet too isolated socially and culturally. Moreover, the qualities of these projects, with their suitable proportions, irremediably highlight the shortcomings of surrounding works.

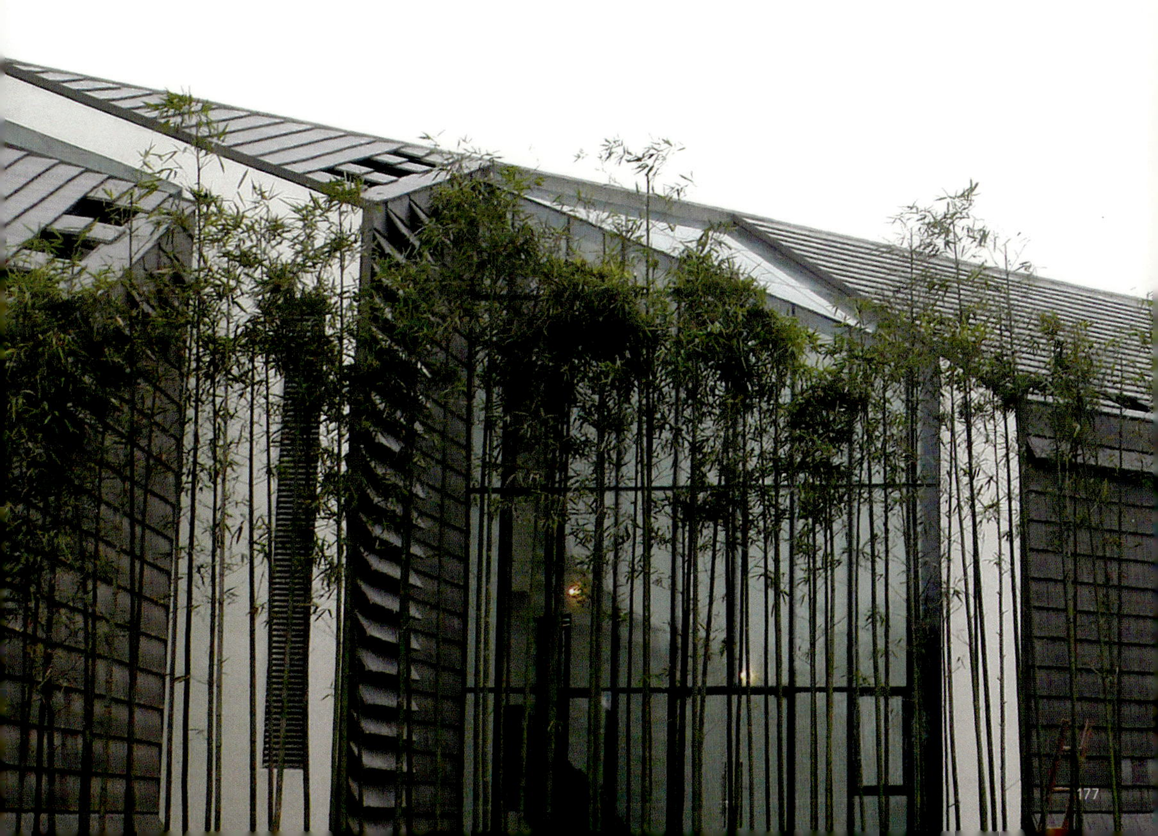

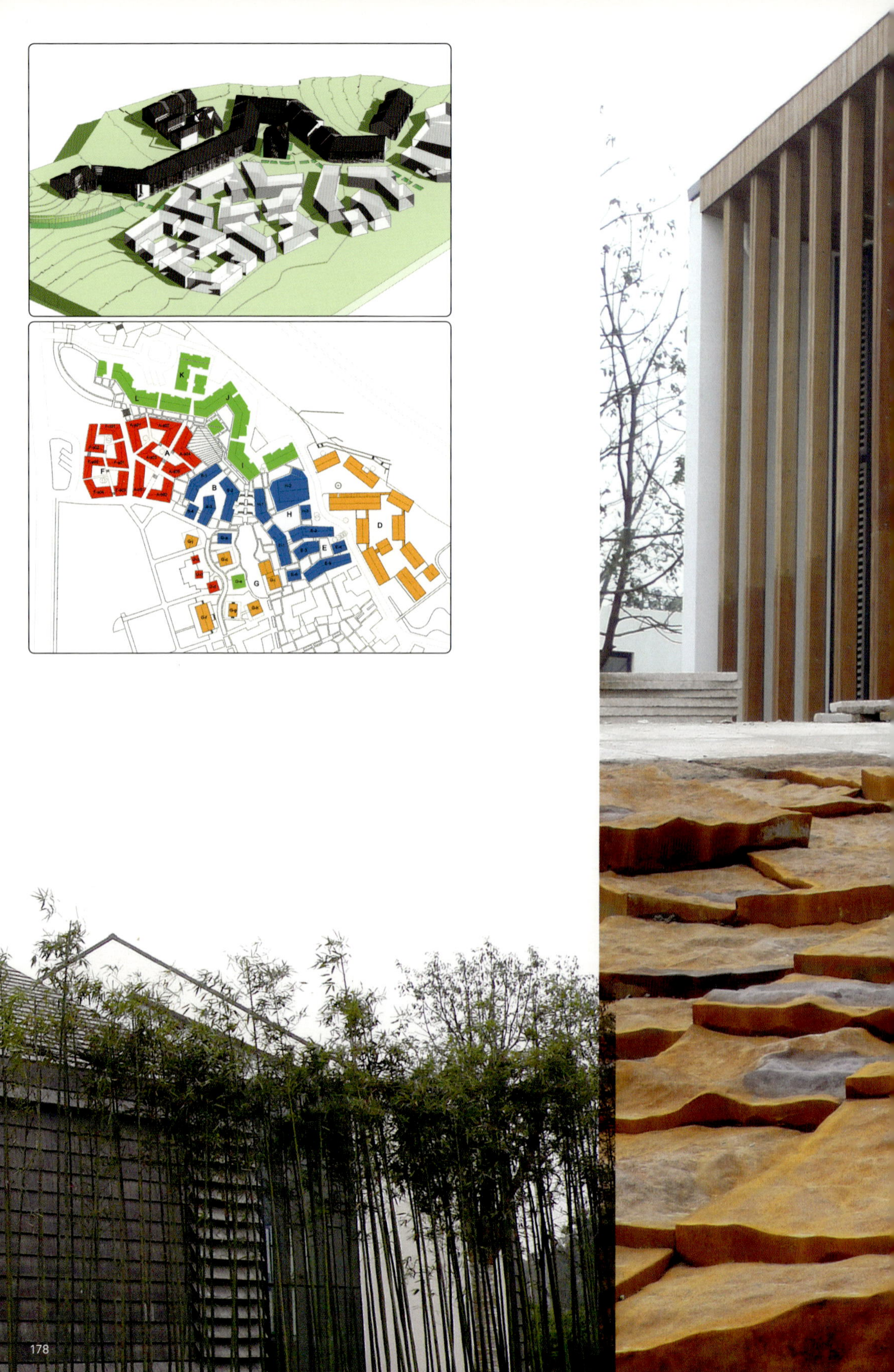

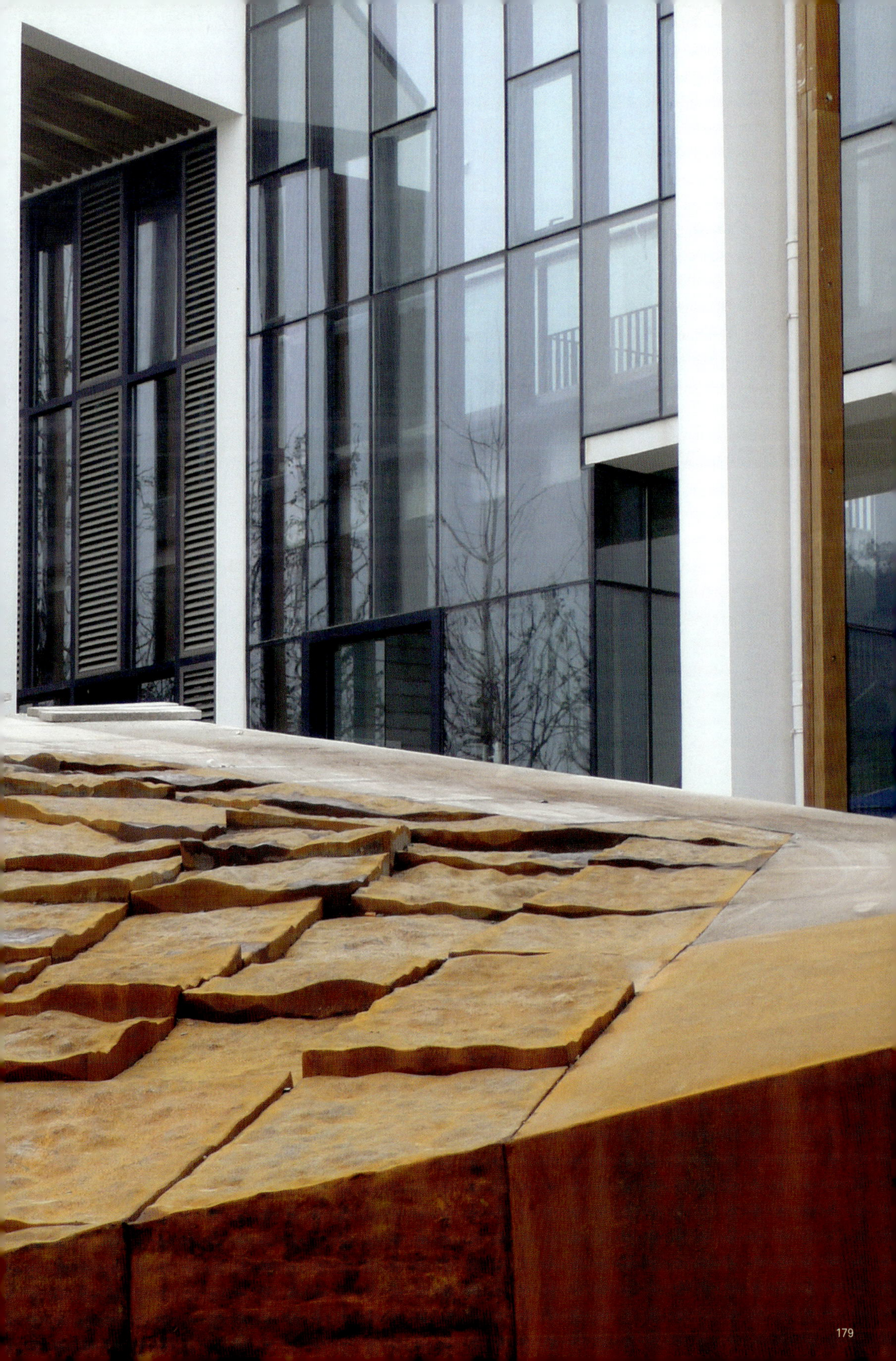

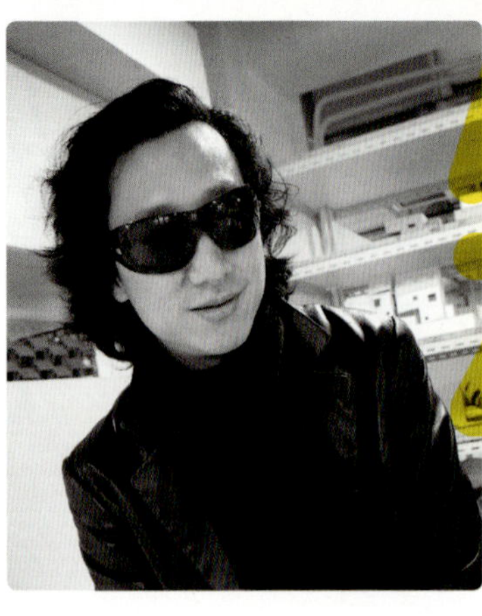

Atelier Zhanglei 张雷建筑设计事务所
Zhang Lei 张雷

Zhang Lei, born in 1963, a graduate of the school of Nanking, is characterised with respect to his generation by an extremely elaborate and constant architectural writing.

This constancy is not a style in itself, as could be said of such an architect as Wang Shu. It manifests itself by both a great rigour in the analysis of projects and by a capacity to remain open to all types of solutions and materials. The question of tradition and modernity has consequently been surpassed and, since he masters his profession to perfection, he delivers projects which have in common an apparent formal simplicity while in the details of each one is to be discovered the organisation of a complex thought.

His skill is evidently recognised by his colleagues. He is one of these personalities who, in a fairly systematic way, intervenes in shared projects, such as the Dongguan Campus, the city of Qingpu, or the museum of the history of the 10th army in Liyang near Chengdu.

To be fair, the Qingpu building, devoted to the local tax authority, does not have the elegance and simplicity of Zhang Lei's other structures. For this reason it will be preferable to see his work in the set of dormitories at Dongguan, and the little grey house which he has designed for a Nanjing intellectual.

Lastly, there are the two large houses built for two poets on the banks of a lake near Nanjing. Zhang Lei is still taking part in a common adventure in Nanjing, involving a new quarter for tertiary enterprises based on the theme of courtyard variations. This is a project for which several architects – Deshaus, Qi Xin and Zhang Lei himself – have been chosen to work together.

Zhang Lei 张雷
Born 1964
Master in architecture, Dongnan Unviersity, Nankin, 1988, PHD from École polytechnique fédérale in Zurich, 1993
Studio founded in 2000
Number of employees: 15

Contact
Atelier Zhanglei
Architecture Design Institute, NJU
Hankou Road 22
210093 Nanjing Jiangsu, China
T: +86 25 83 68 61 46
F: +86 25 83 59 56 73
atelierzhanglei@163.com
lzhang2000@vip.sina.com

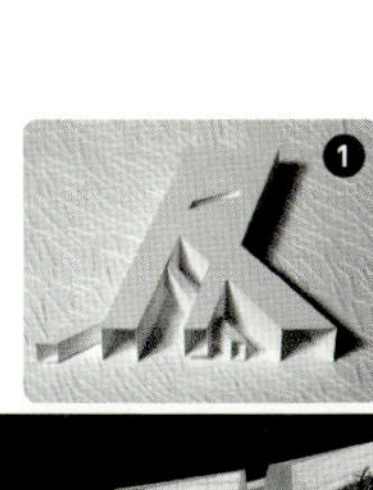
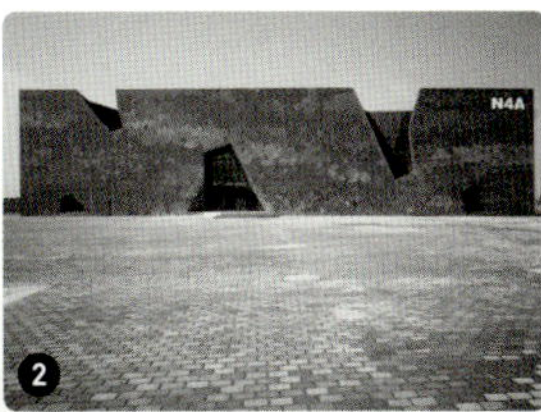
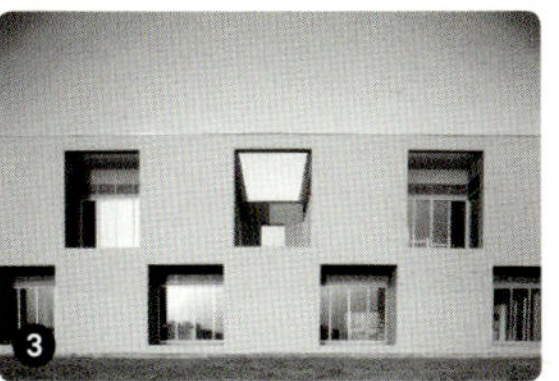
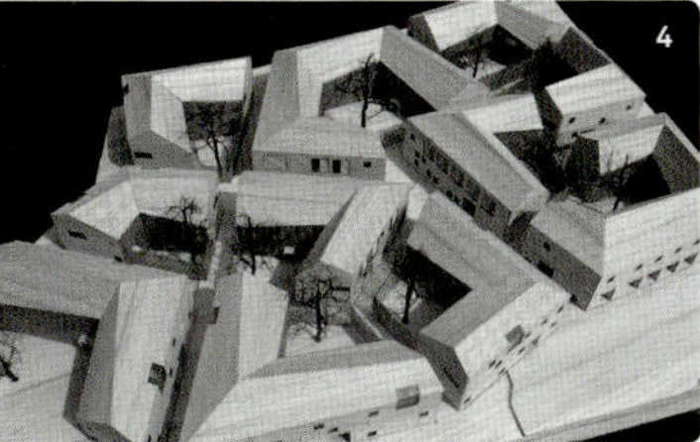
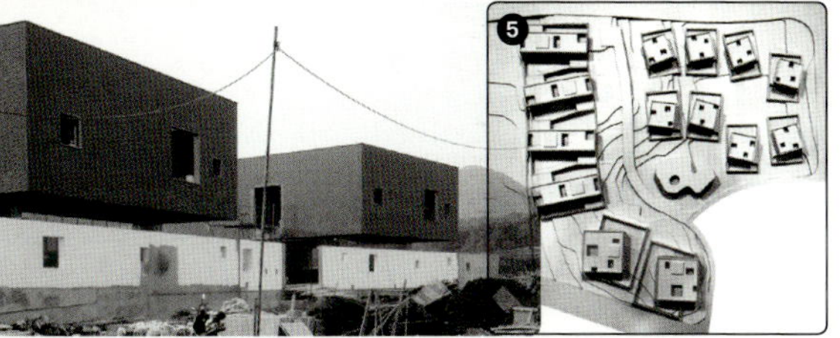
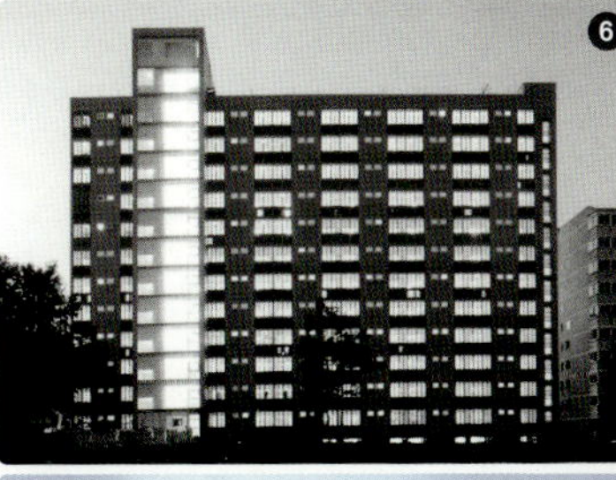
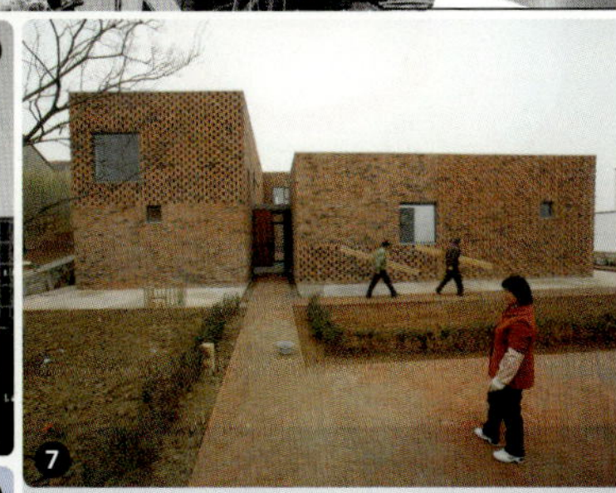
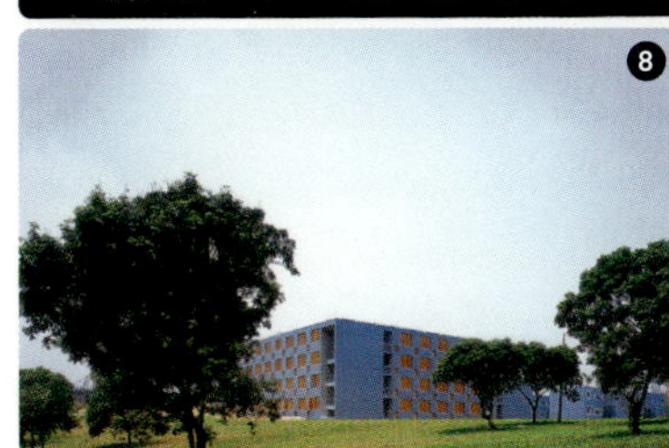
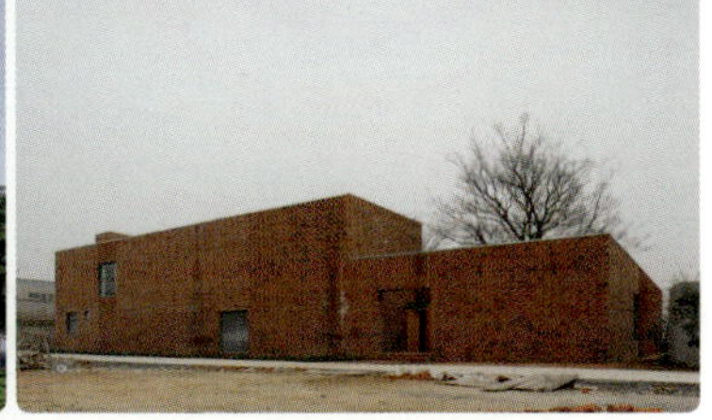
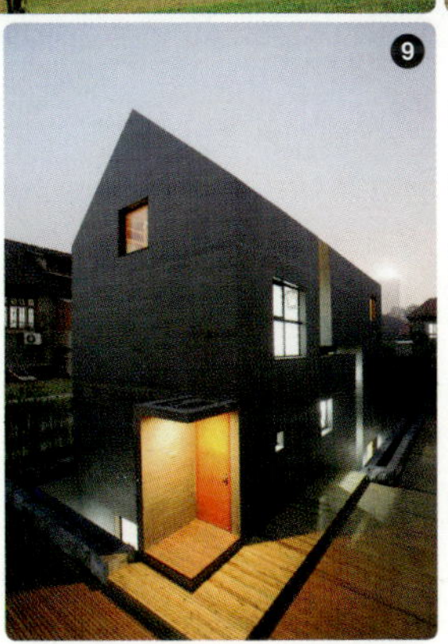

1 Fanglijun art gallery, Chengdu (Sichuan), under construction.
2 Xinsijun Army Museum in Jiangnan, Liyang (Jiangsu), 2007.
3 National laboratory of biological tests, Nankin (Jiangsu), 2003.
4 Yuniaoliusu, Hangzhou, 2008.
5 Jiangsu Computer Park, 2008.
6 Nankin University student dormitories, 2002.
7 Poet Houses, Nankin, 2007.
8 Dongguan Institute of Technology, staff residence, 2005.
9 Slit House, Nankin, 2007.

诗人之家 POET HOUSES

Location Nankin (Jiangsu) **Architects:** Atelier Zhanglei **Project leader:** Zhang Lei **Project team:** Zhang Ang, Ma Wenbin **Client:** Ye Hui, Wang Yongjun **Project:** August 2003-January 2004 **Construction/end of work:** October 2006-December 2007 **Built areas:** 680 m² + 850 m² **Site areas:** 1 500 m² + 1 650 m² **Cost:** 80 €/m² **Photographs** © Iwan Baan

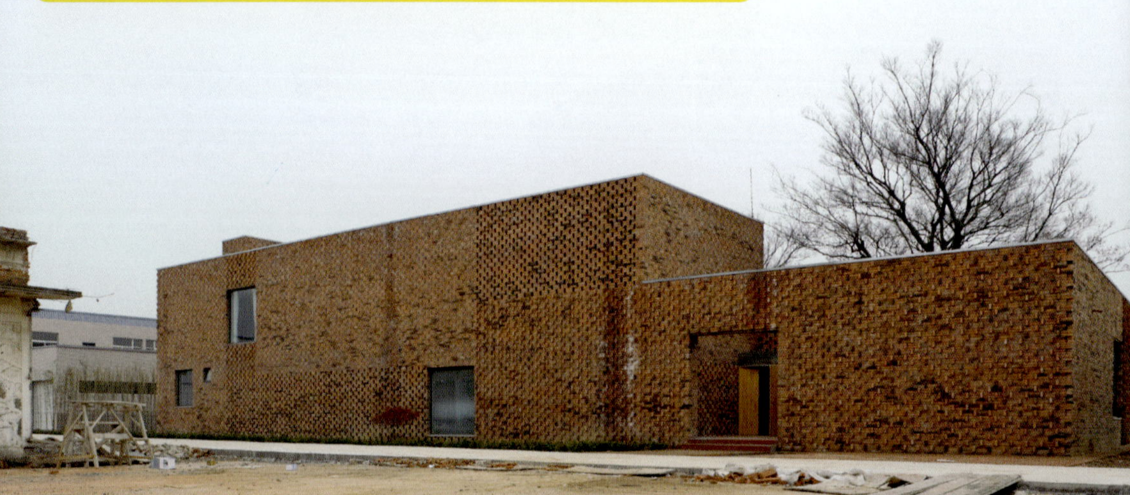

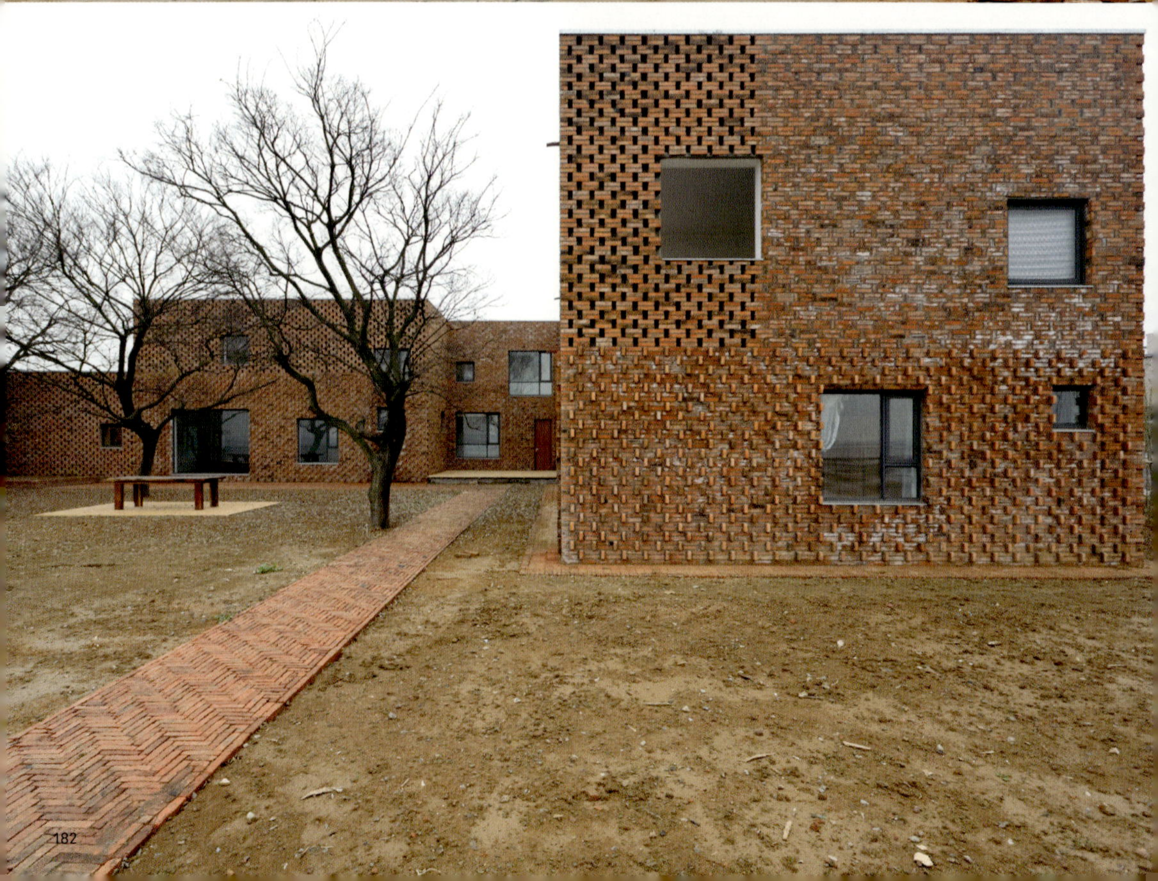

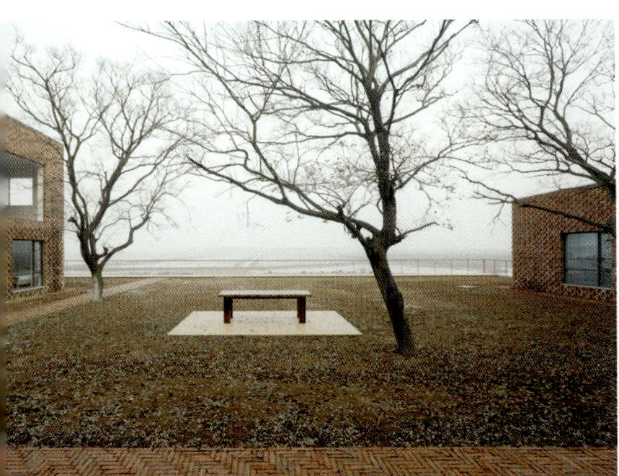

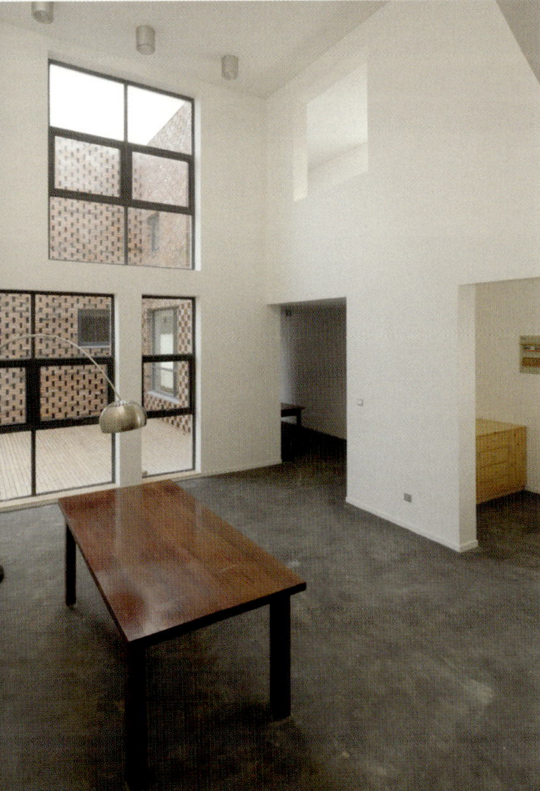

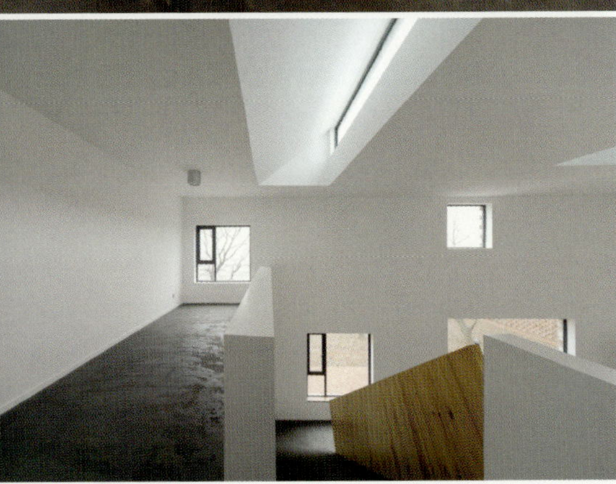

Zhang Lei's clients for these two houses on the banks of a lake in the Nanking region are singularly extroverted people and would appear to be just the opposite of the Slit House's owner. The site itself is exceptional, being an old factory of which one part subsists to be used without doubt as a common space for exhibitions or reading. Two other houses, marked by an indecisive architecture, are already installed there, with the formal arrogance which is sometimes authorized by wealth. The two poets for their part, together with Zhang Lei, have chosen to establish an intense relation with this site, its history and its lake.

A brickworks was found here and the architect makes full use of the possibilities which brick offers. Protective walls, animated walls, pierced walls... an unlimited declination of the varieties of fired clay and even overly fired clay used to draw one's attention to a particular point.

Very similar and very different, one and the other of very large dimensions, these houses are organised around courtyards, the fourth side of which becomes a stage overlooking the lake.

The interior, the reverse of the grey house at Nanking where the vanishing point is surely organised by the reading of books, is devoted to a sort of quest for space, a kind of forward-looking syndrome of the blank page. That lets one imagine times of reflection, Mallarméan whites followed by a unique brushstroke or by a frenetic casting of signs on leaves, reflections of the white of the walls. Of course, one could also be at the home of painters and clearly, considering the size of each of the houses, our two poets and their families do not have an ascetic calling. Both are houses for thinking, reflection, repose and work, and the two buildings are moreover built of the same materials.

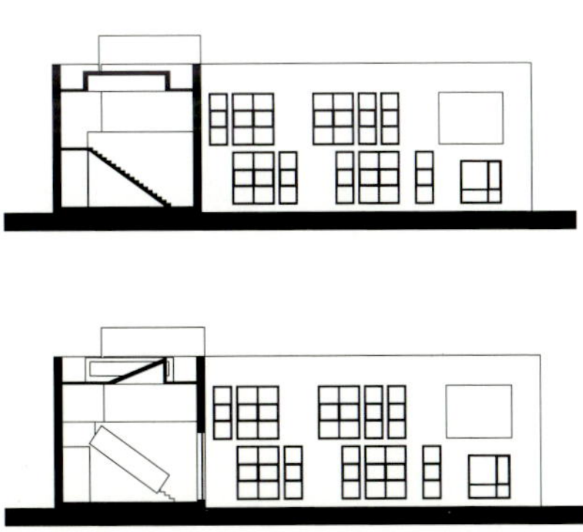

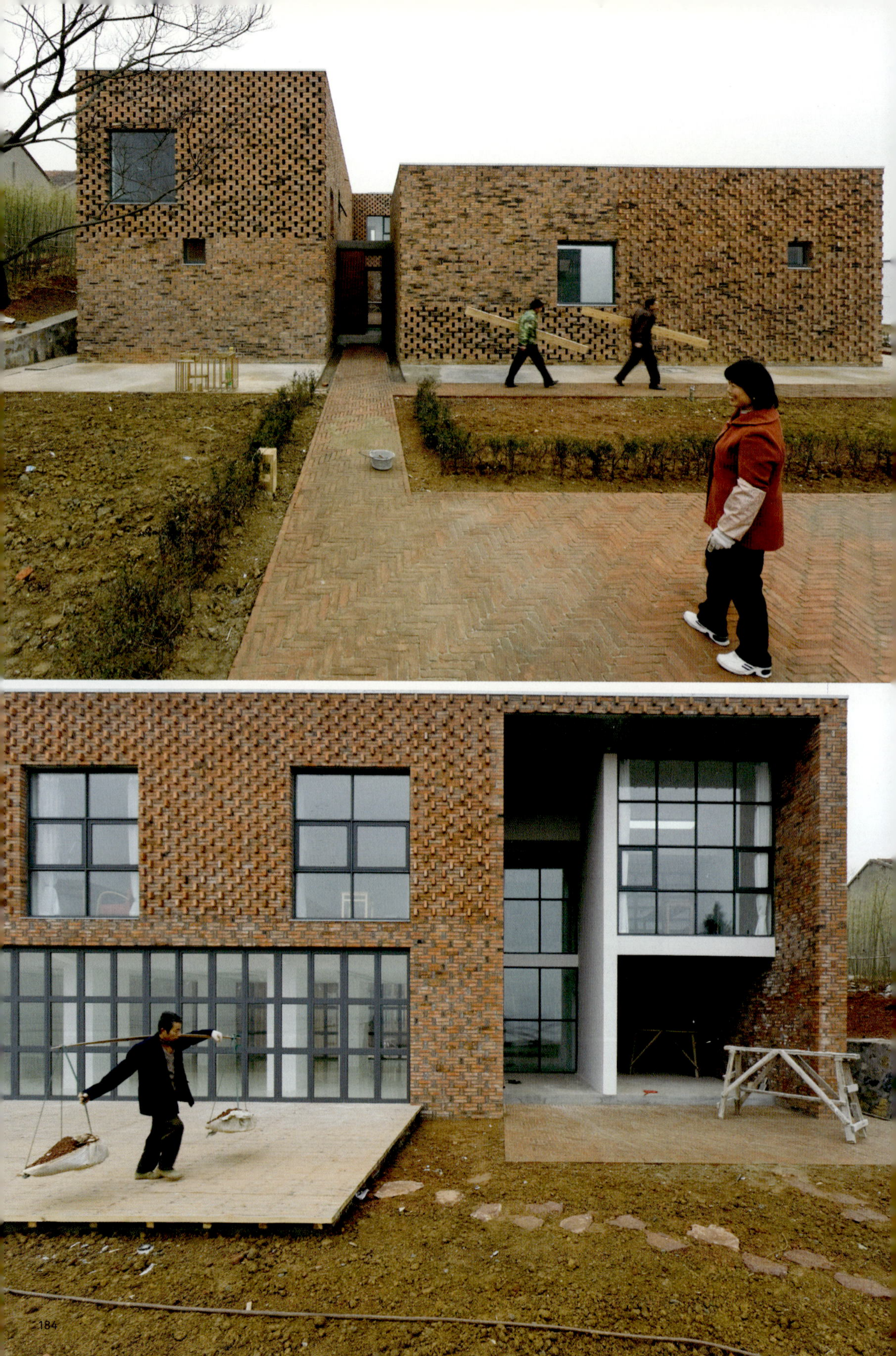

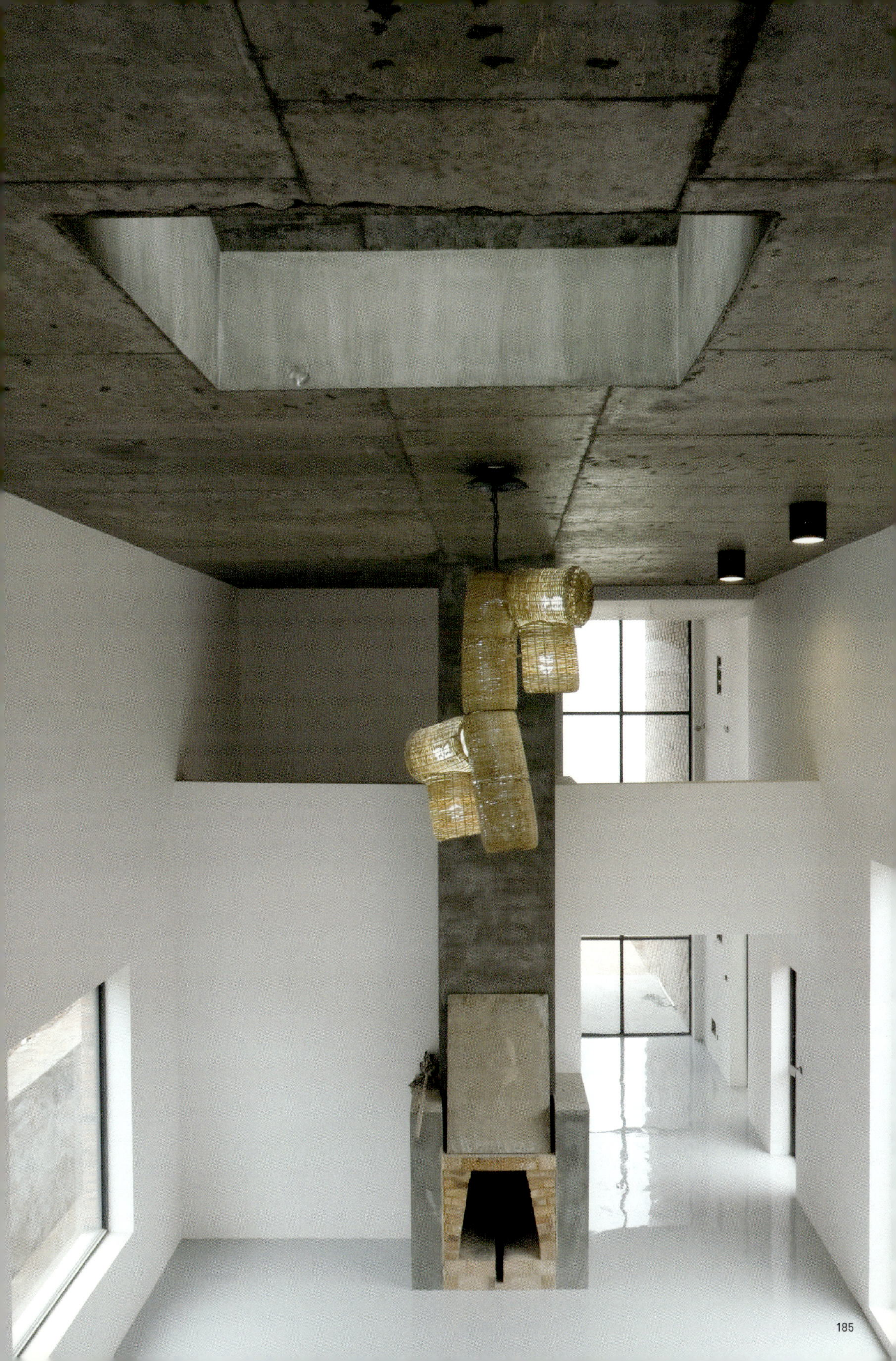

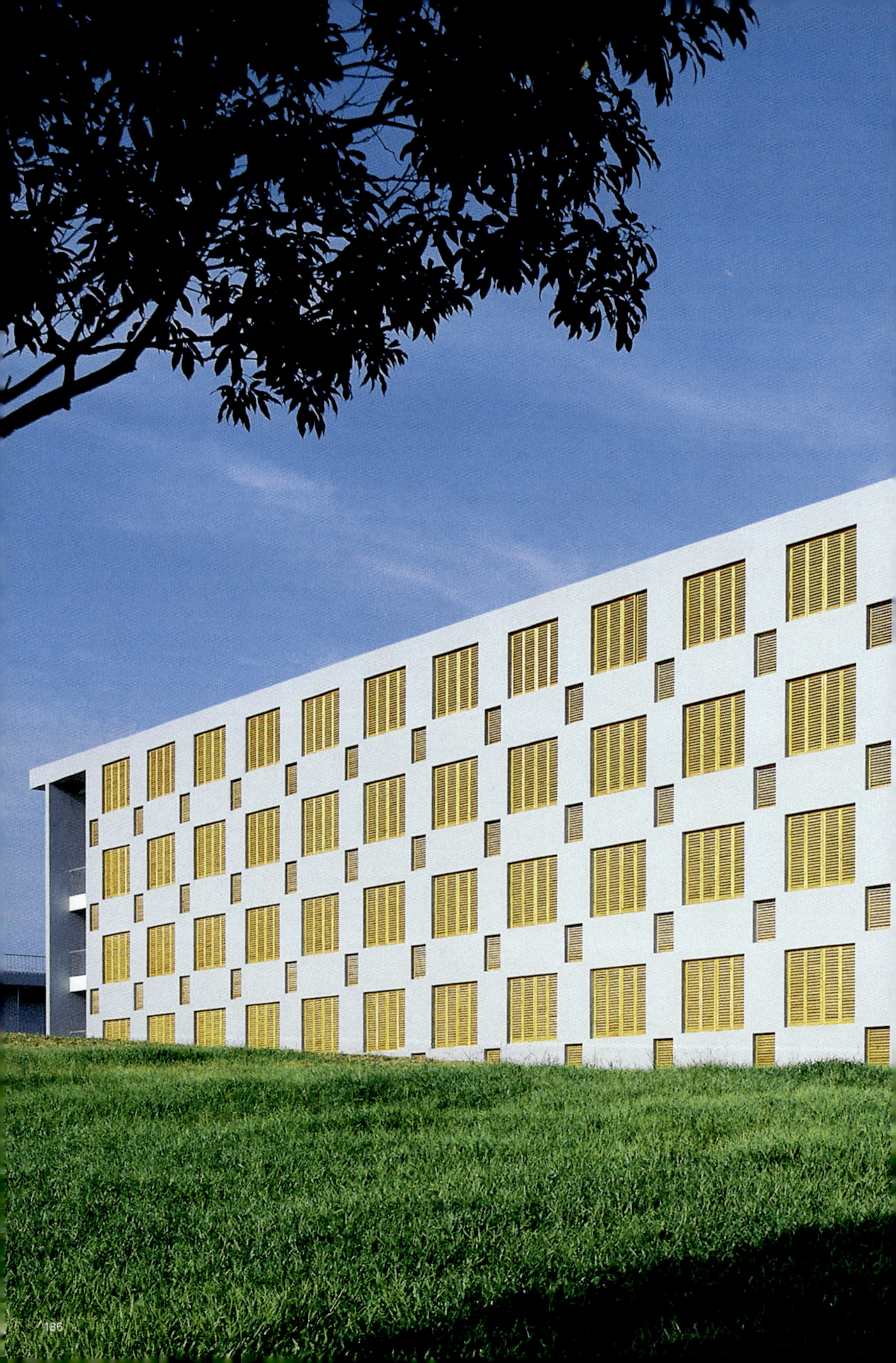

东莞理工学院教工生活区

DONGGUAN INSTITUTE OF TECHNOLOGY, STAFF RESIDENCE

Location: Dongguan (Guangdong) **Architects:** Atelier Zhanglei **Project leader:** Zhang Lei **Project team:** Dongxuan, Pan Juan **Client:** Dongguan Institute of Technology **Project:** July 2002–January 2003 **Construction/end of work:** April 2003–May 2005 **Built area:** 15 280 m² **Site area:** 20 000 m² **Cost:** 150 €/m²

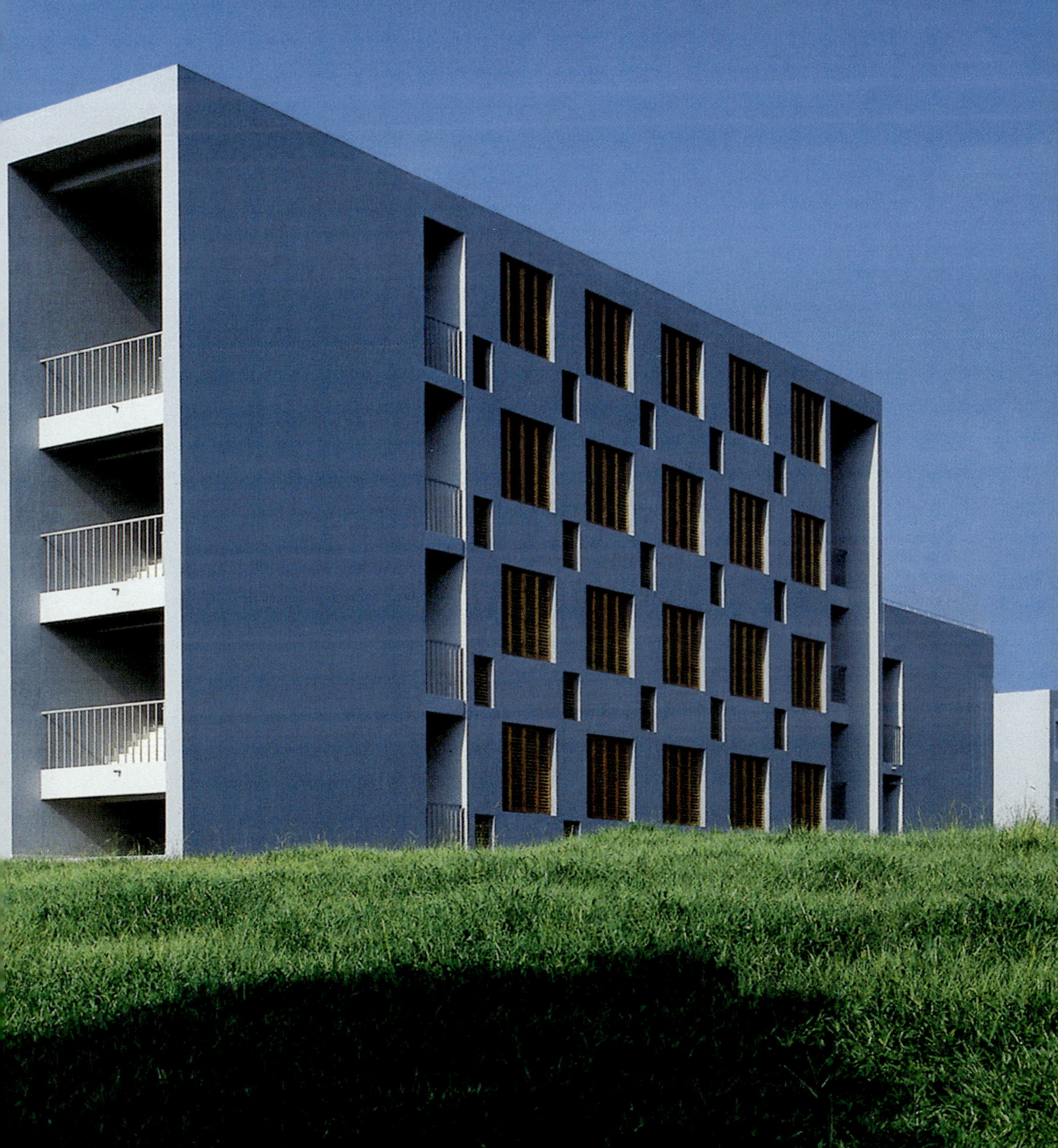

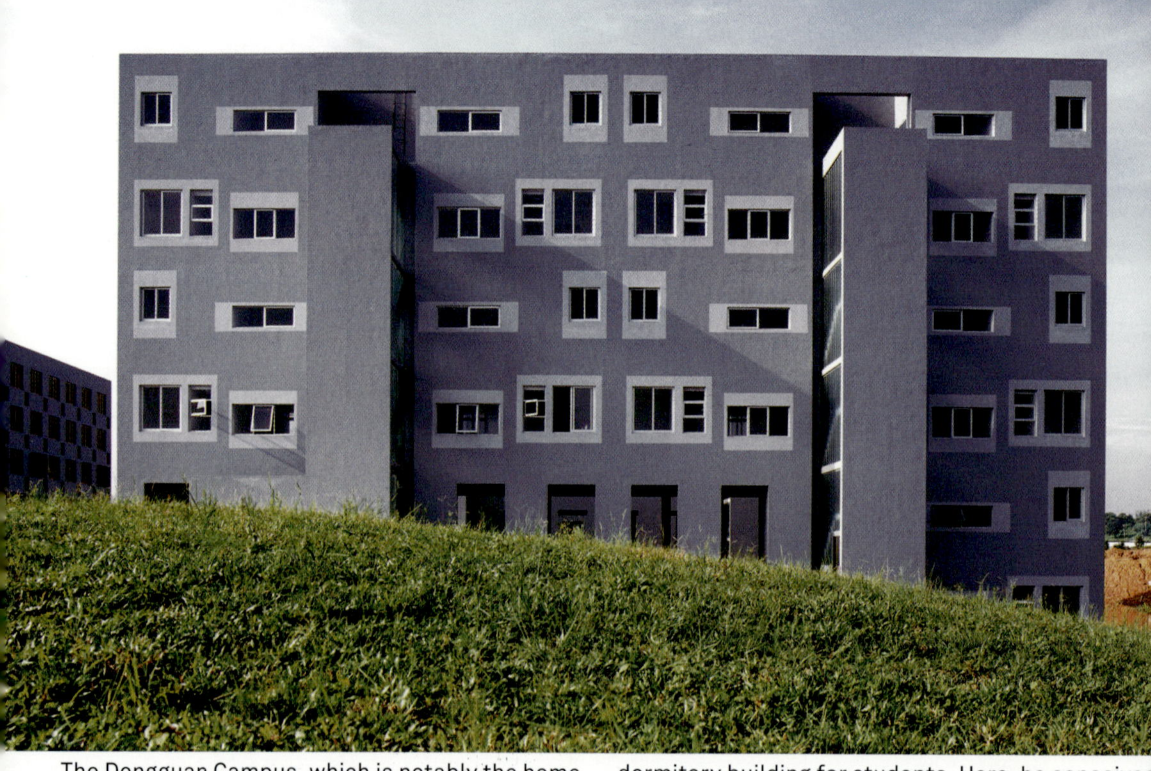

The Dongguan Campus, which is notably the home of the Deshaus studio, brings together about ten more or less well-known architects of the new generation. The campus site, immense and hardly accessible, has preserved its poetry... one would even be tempted to say that it has "confiscated" the original poetry of this region of fishermen and farmers of the Pearl River Delta.

The city of Dongguan itself, which is the region's administrative, scholastic and, above all, manufacturing centre, seems to be dispersed over a very vast territory which is crossed, pre-emptively, by a whole network of motorways and broad avenues. We are told that Dongguan is where seventy per cent of China's computers and electronic elements are manufactured, which is a statistic that is hard to verify on the spot. What can indeed be verified, on the other hand, is the importance lent here to higher education. The students of the technology institute benefit from fairly exceptional accommodation and living conditions, even if the heat of southern China is not something to make them rejoice in the summer. To draw teachers to this institution (all the banks of the Delta, from Zhuhai to Shenzhen and from Shenzhen to Canton are teeming with such centres), its architecture becomes an added value. Zhang Lei had already designed at Nanking a large dormitory building for students. Here, he conceived an ensemble which was to accommodate, according to an elaborate hierarchy, the young professors and the teaching staff's notables as well as the guest teachers.

As opposed to the educational poles (see Deshaus), Zhang Lei has had to think up a residential building that would allow people to live autonomously while maintaining a link with the educational centres. This exercise, which is simple on the American campuses or near the old cities, runs up against a lack of neighbours here, unless one imagines that the educators and their families would start to share their lives day and night with their students. Consequently, the architect uses such calculated surprises as a sloping lawn. Opposite the student dormitories, the balconies of which present a joyful disorder of bicycles and clothes hung out to dry, he creates an extremely clear-cut volume in which the dwellings are interiorised and in which the greater part of the façades declines the rhythm of wood and concrete like a Baroque melody. Aside from that, this ensemble does not allow itself to be read immediately. Behind its almost impenetrable façades is organised a network of courtyards and even cottages... all the scales, in short, of a small city but without the flytrap character of a hotel structure.

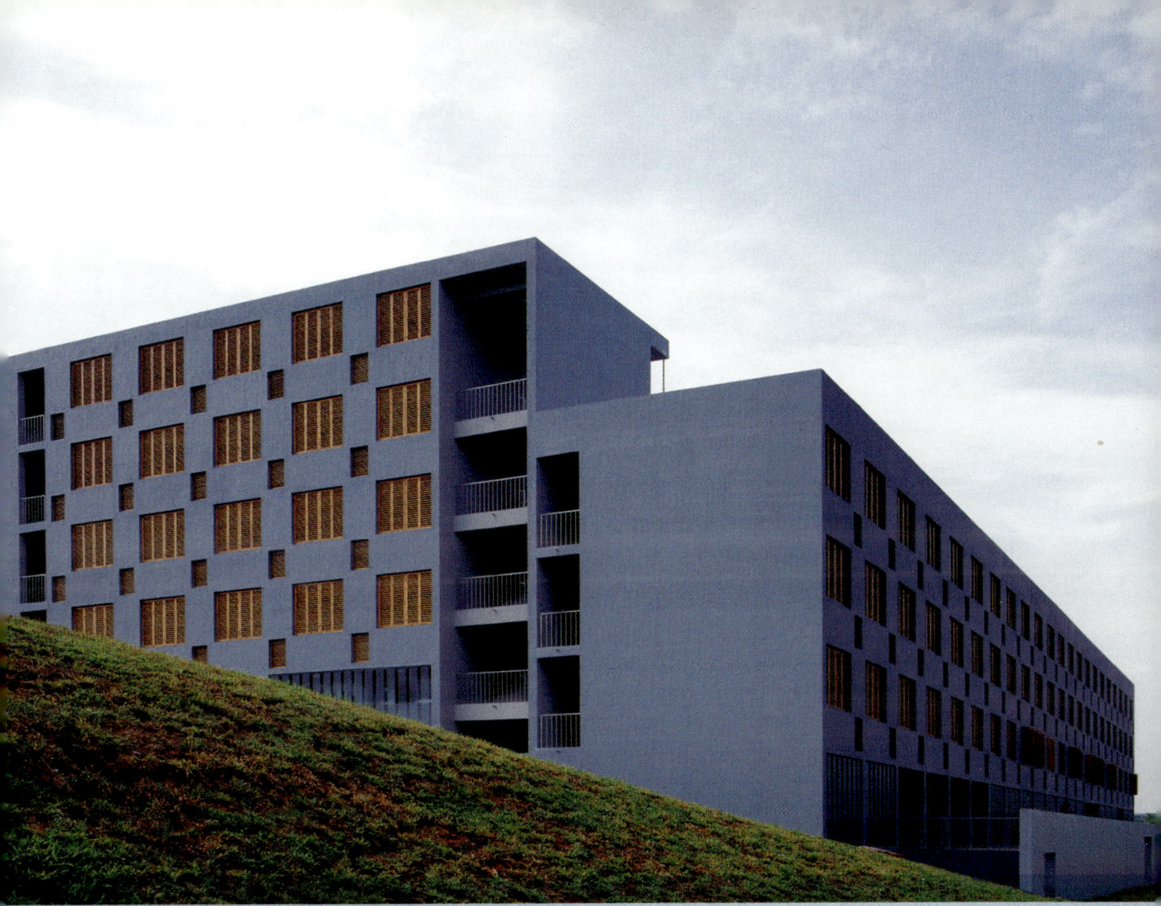

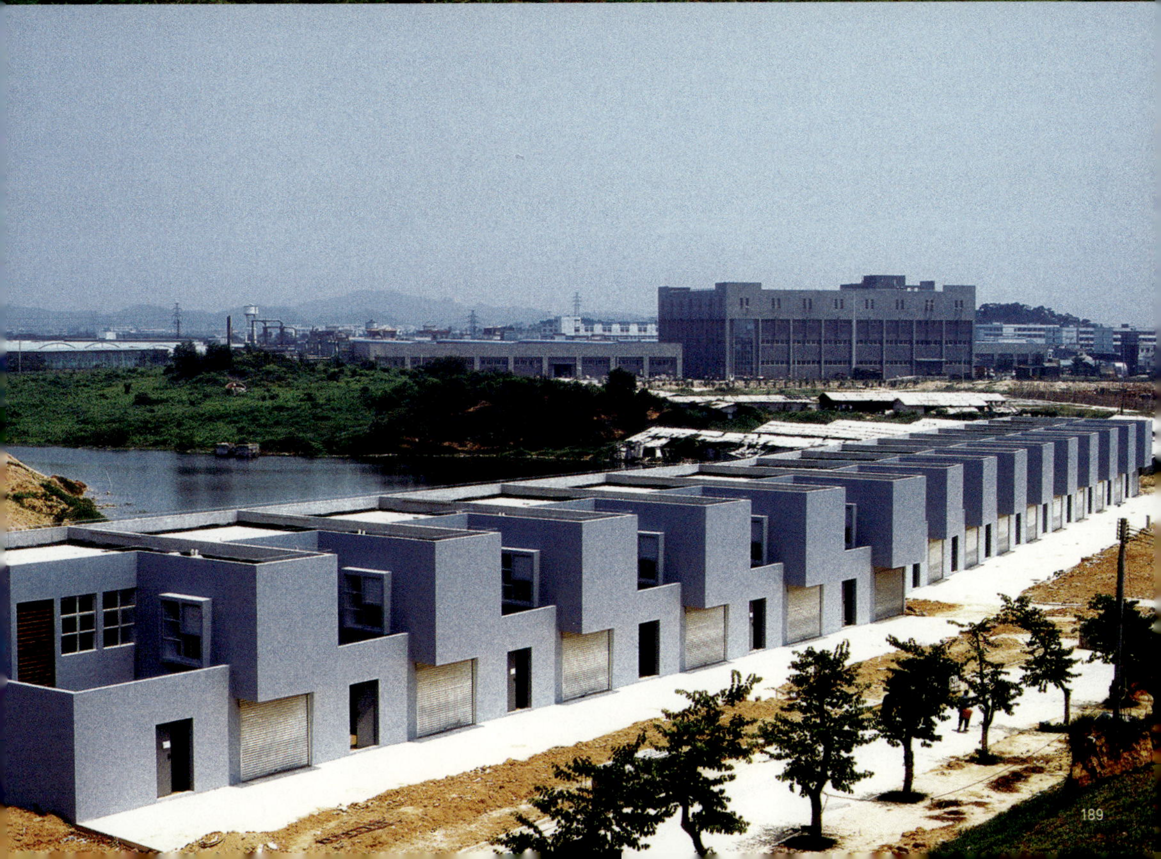

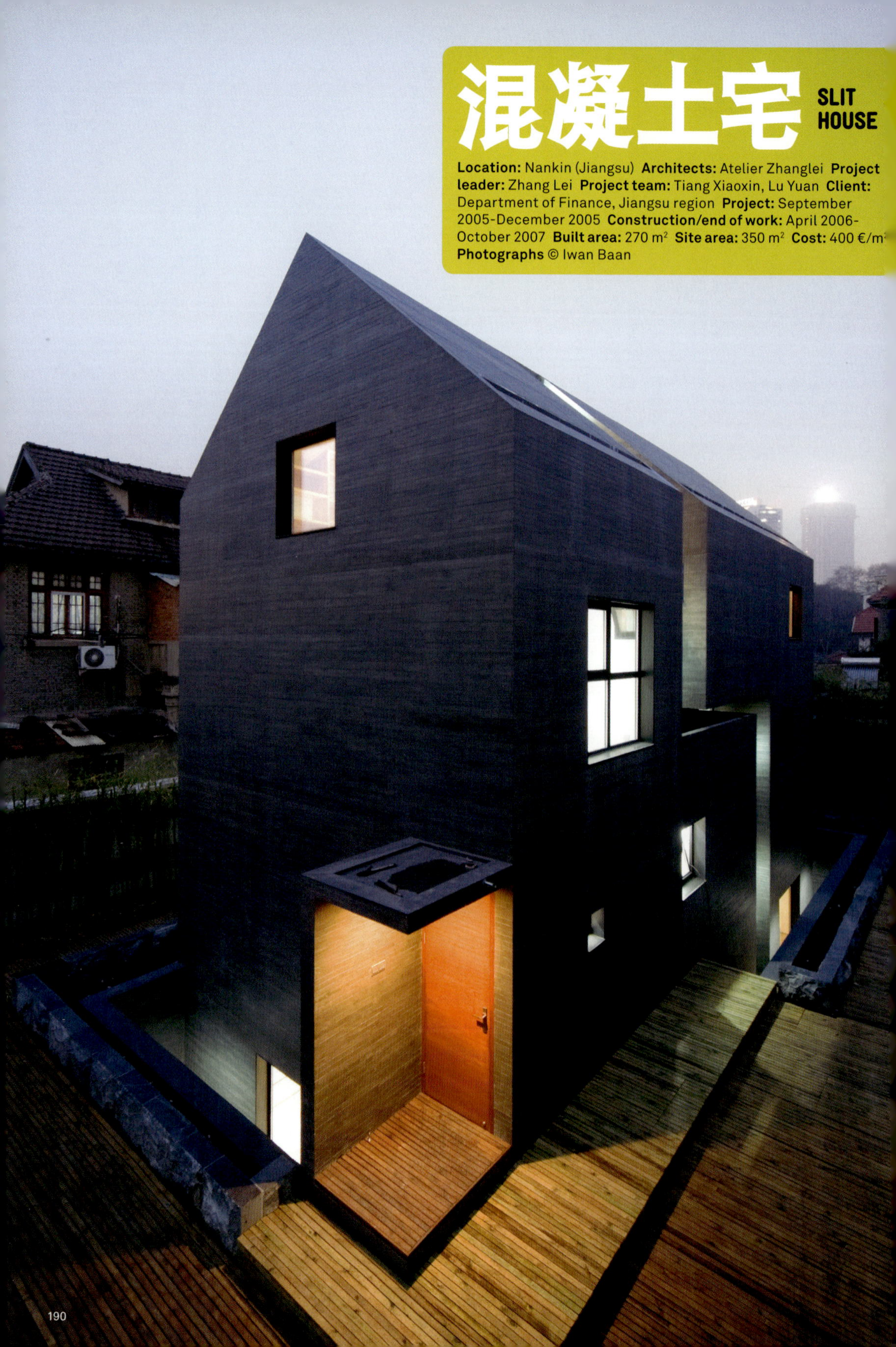

混凝土宅 SLIT HOUSE
Location: Nankin (Jiangsu) Architects: Atelier Zhanglei Project leader: Zhang Lei Project team: Tiang Xiaoxin, Lu Yuan Client: Department of Finance, Jiangsu region Project: September 2005-December 2005 Construction/end of work: April 2006-October 2007 Built area: 270 m² Site area: 350 m² Cost: 400 €/m² Photographs © Iwan Baan

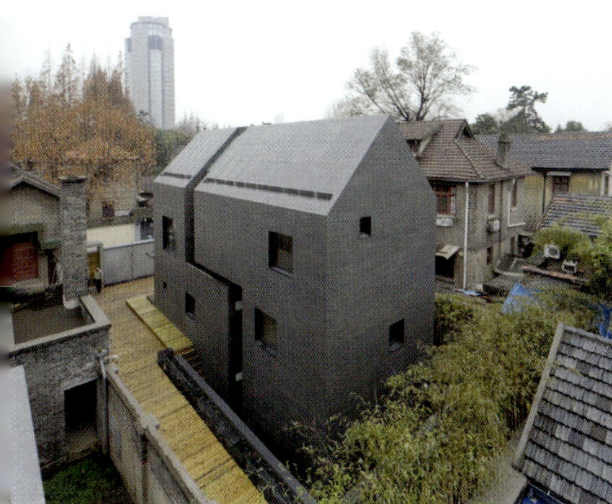

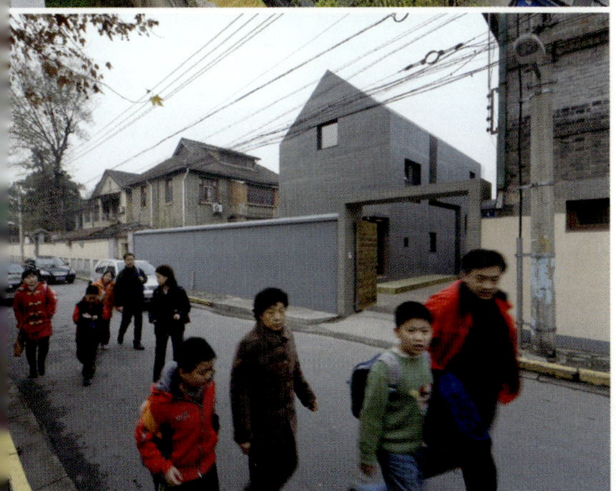

We are in a quarter of Nanking with a rather Western air, a sheltered quarter subject to strict urban constraints, even if some signs indicate the proximity of Jiangsu. Zhang Lei's client, an intellectual, is of the ideal type. He accepts a formal radicalism on society's boundary line. In this house, "slit" refers to the long narrow opening, the interstice; a geometrical cut-out in a house made of a single block of concrete, grey in colour, a colour of principle which starts from the foundations and reaches all the way to the roof. Almost none of the windows open except to let in a little air. Everything indicates here, in a Chinese manner if there ever was one, that the mystery of life and of the family is organised within the shelter of the walls. The client family has not sought shelter from modernity, however. If the materials are soft and worked with an extreme attention to detail, if in short they are simple (the alternation of wood and of white walls of a soft tone), no concessions are shown in the design of the rooms, a design marked by this same hardness which one finds in certain houses by Le Corbusier or, more recently, by Koolhaas.

The owner has made the tyranny of the architect his own and it is hard to see what type of furniture will have its place in this encoded universe. Perhaps tomorrow one will visit this house like the standard apartments of the Cité Radieuse, Johnson's glass house or even the house by Koolhaas in Bordeaux.

Asians, in particular Japanese or Koreans, also find here a vocabulary different from the radicalism of their best architects, coupled with the principle of the minimal surface which is rather amazing in modern China.

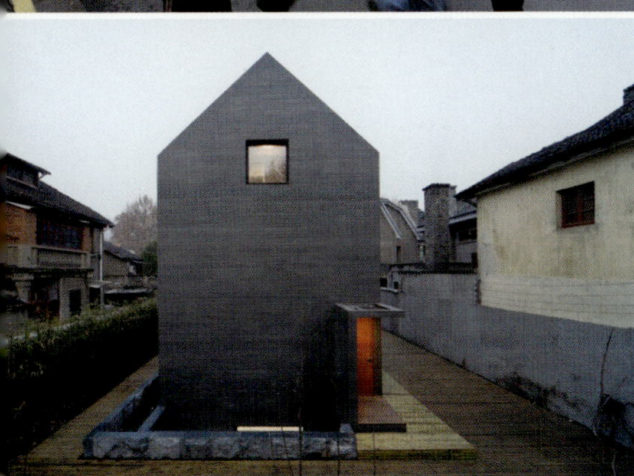

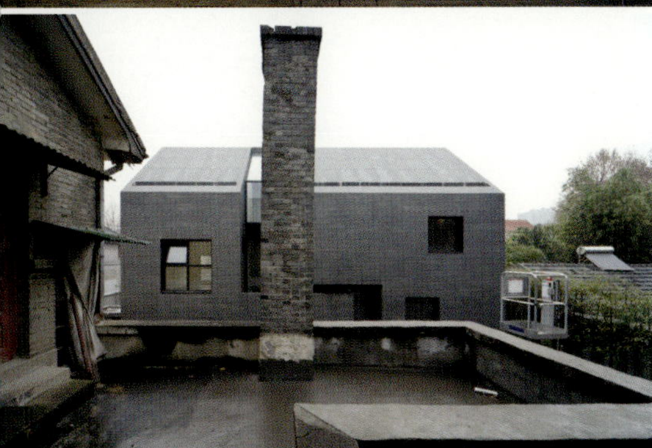

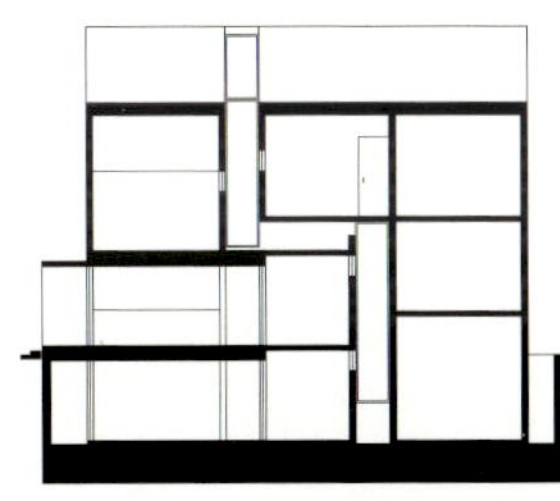

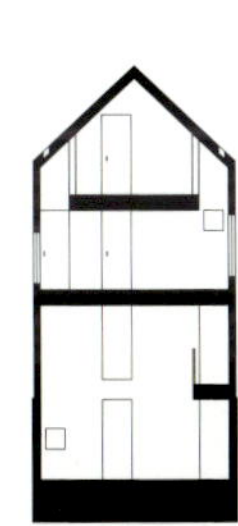

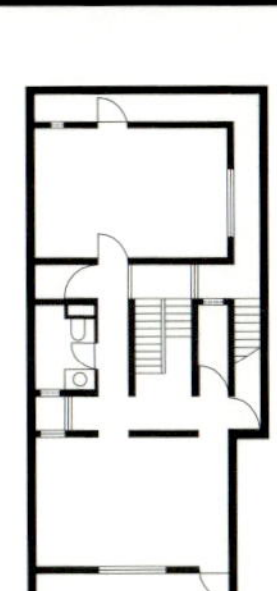

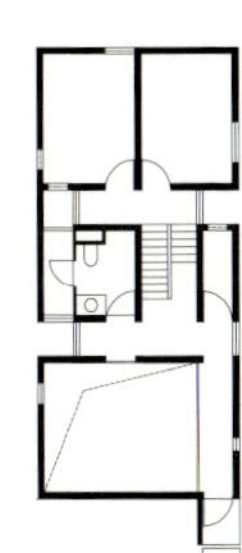

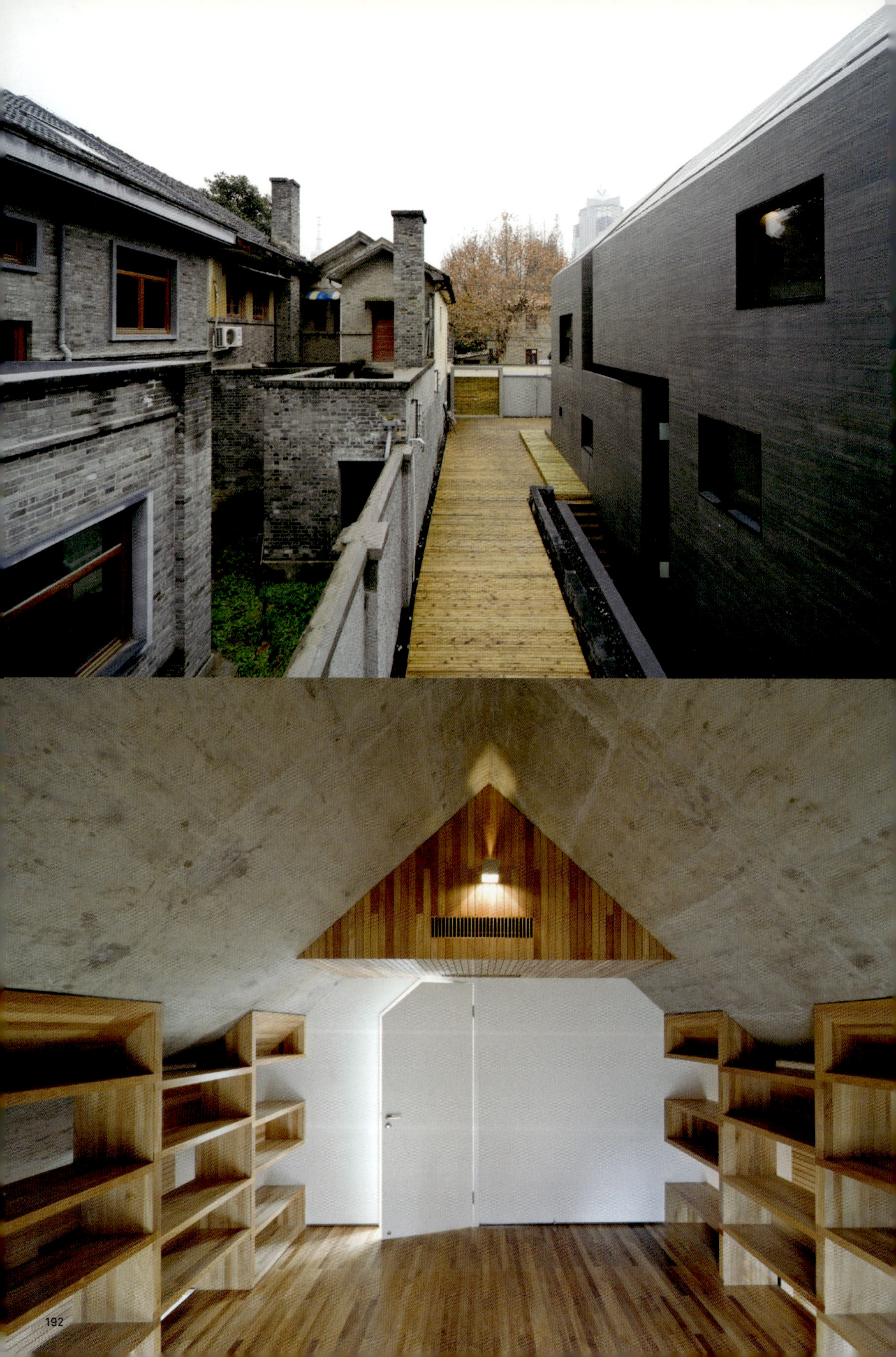

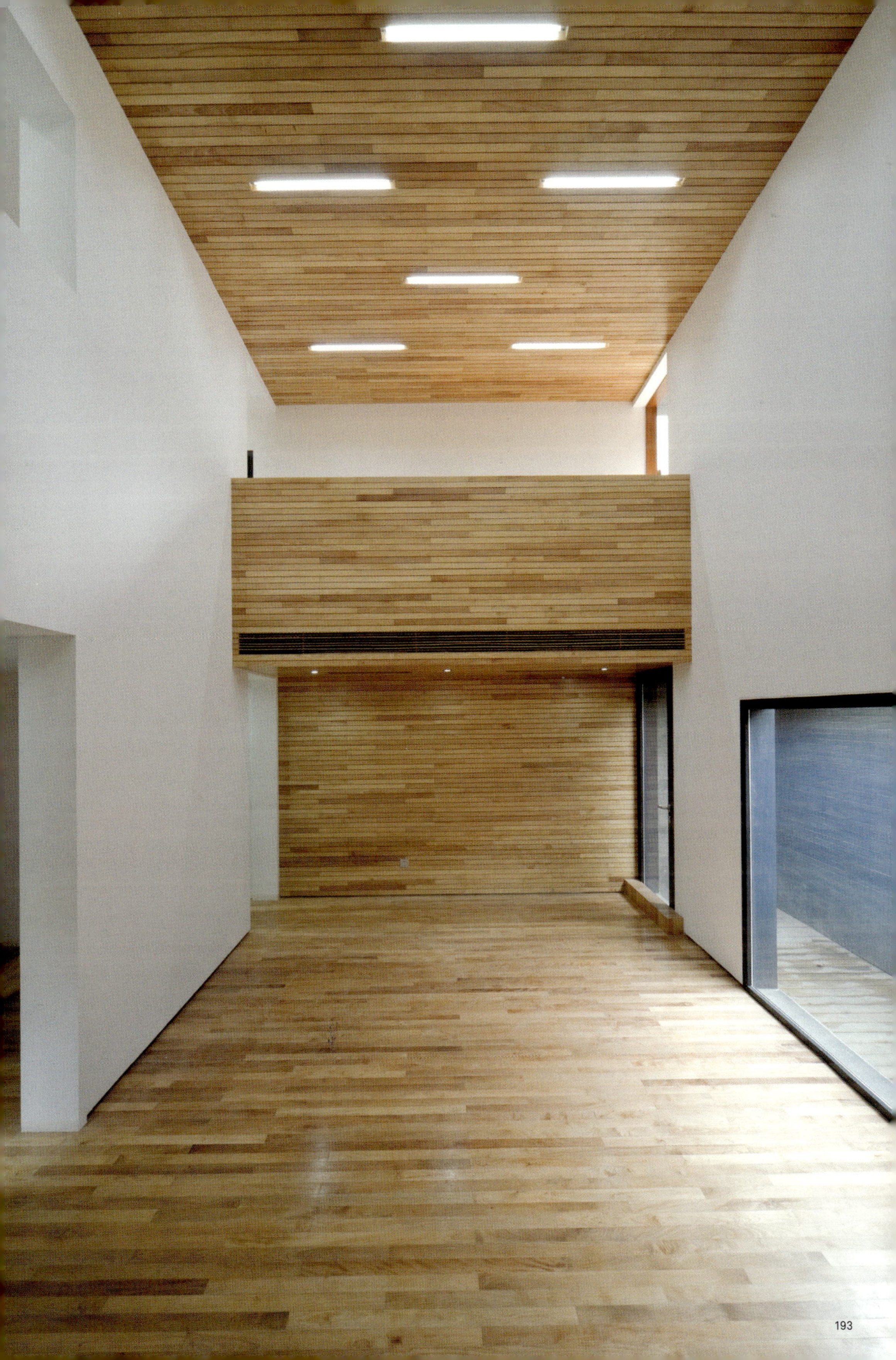

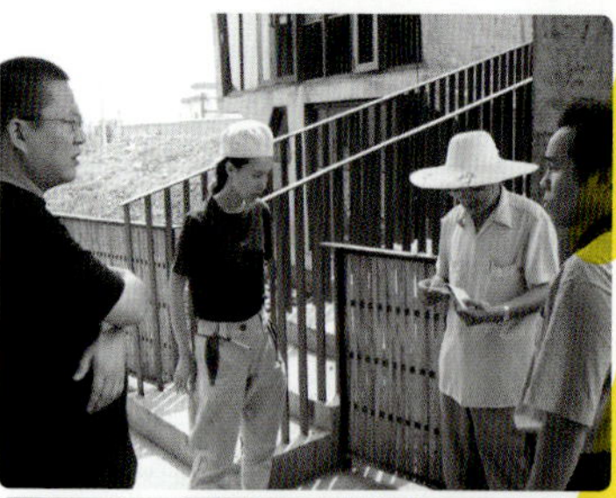

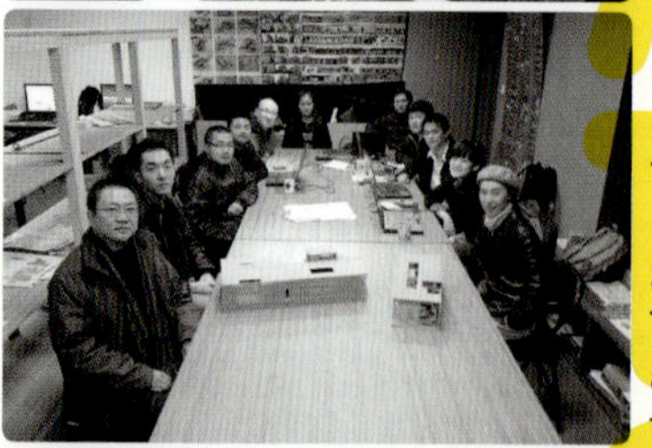

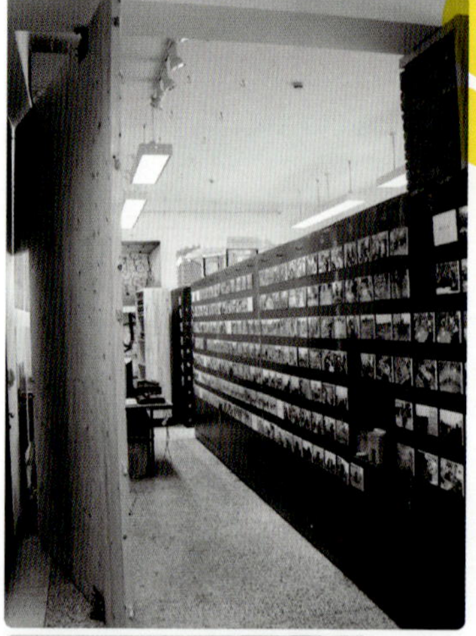

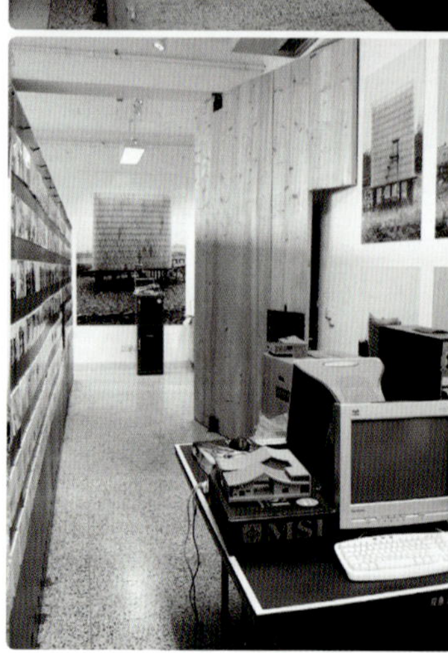

Amateur Architecture Studio 业余建筑工作室
Wang Shu 王澍
Lu Wenyu 陆文宇

Wang Shu, born in 1963, is one of the easiest architects to grasp from the Western standpoint. His country's authorities have understood this clearly and chose him to represent Chinese architecture at the Venice Biennale in 2006. He was born in Hangzhou and brought up during the cultural revolution in Urumqi in Xinjiang province, the "new territories in the country's west" where the landscape is marked by austerity, rigour and sometimes silence. He left to carry out his studies in Nanking and Shanghai before returning to the blissful city of Hangzhou, skirted by the "Great Lake of the West", so dear to poets.

The School of Fine Arts of Hangzhou is one of the oldest and the most celebrated in China. After founding his studio in 1997, Wang Shu took charge of the School's architecture department in 2003. The School of Fine Arts is presided over by the artist Xu Jiang, a friend of long standing of the architect, with all which this means in terms of solidarity in a China where the most innovative creators may sometimes feel isolated.

Spontaneously, he presents himself with a smile, a distended version of the Chinese smile, and it is in this same spirit that he seems to look upon the vestiges of the cities of his country. He loves its simple materials. He discovers with pleasure the countless Chinese building techniques, from stone to wood, from brick to tiles, from the running water of the fountains to the ridgepoles of the houses. Above all, however, he knows how to respond as an efficient works manager when a commission arrives. Whether it is for the Ningbo Fine Arts Museum (2005) in Zhejiang or the new Hangzhou Fine Arts Campus in Xiangshan, he stands out, with his wife and partner Lu Wenyu, above all as a master of the landscape and of urban composition. Each building then finds its place to welcome the sun or to make use of the vibrations of the air when the mist comes to limit the horizon. This master of the landscape then becomes the inventor of an architecture which is both personal and magical in that it remains deeply attached to nature. In this respect, Wang Shu is a spontaneous ecologist who is all the more enthralling since, between their construction and upkeep, his buildings are born and remain cost-efficient.

He uses with equal skill brick, tile, stone, the various expressions of concrete, and also steel, but only when the strength of this material proves necessary. For Wang Shu, it is as if tradition and modernity were natural partners in contemporary writing. At the University of Suzhou, he has delivered a more classically modern library which, because of its relation to the lake, may recall Ciriani's Péronne museum. In brief, near the river Qiantang, in Hangzhou, he has completed an ensemble of towers with a structural appearance that succeeds in avoiding the obsessed regularity shown by most of the condominiums in China.

Partners
Wang Shu 王澍
Born 1963
Doctorate in architecture,
Tongji University, Shanghai, 2000
Lu Wenyu 陆文宇
Born 1967
Bachelor in architecture,
Dongnan University, Nankin, 1989
Studio founded 1997
Number of employees: 5-8

Contact
Amateur Architecture Studio
N°3-1-109, 222 Nanshan road,
310002 Hangzhou, China
T/F: + 86 571 871 64708
wangshu@caa.edu.cn

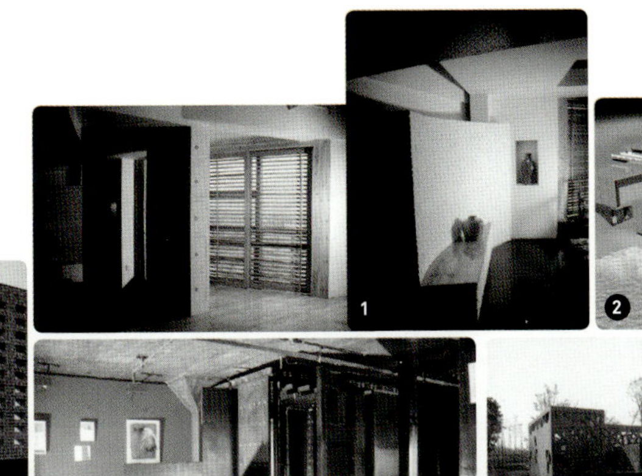
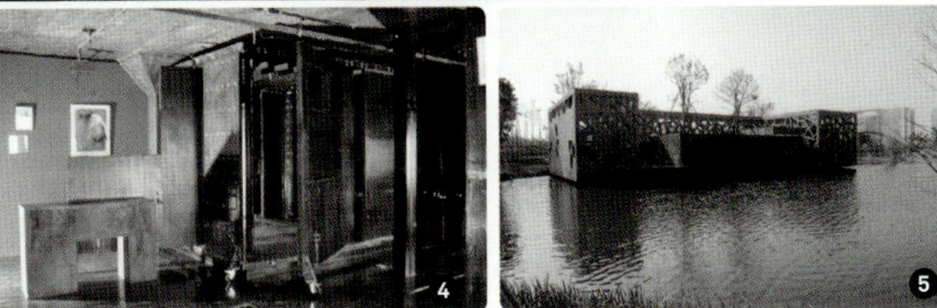
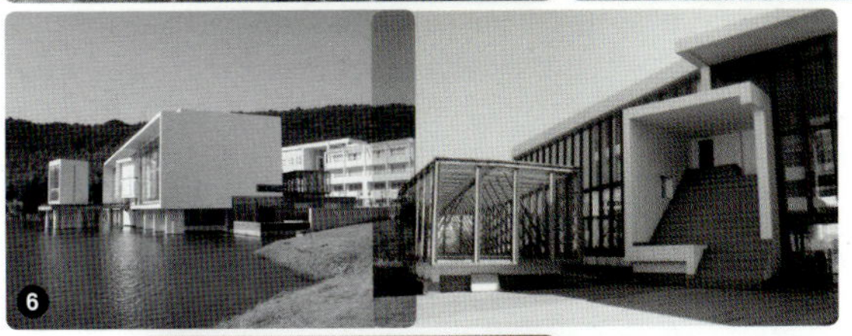
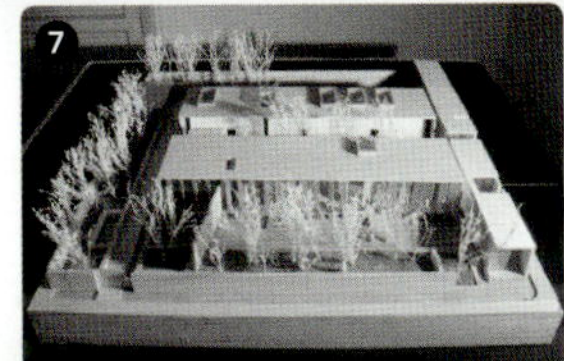
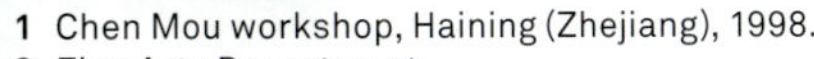
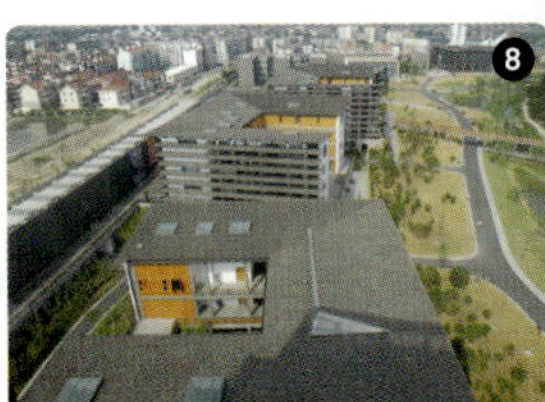
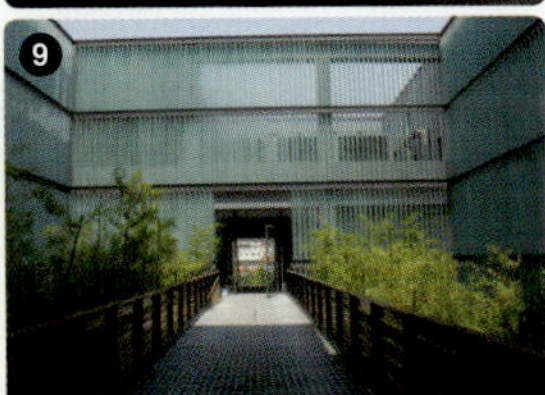
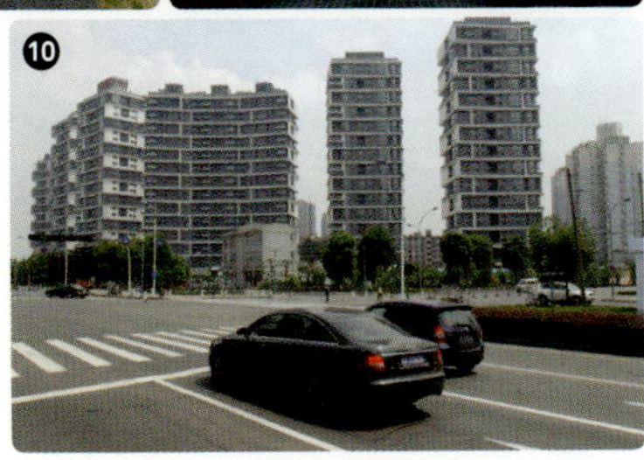

1 Chen Mou workshop, Haining (Zhejiang), 1998.
2 Fine Arts Department,
Dongguan Institute (Guangdong), 2005
3 House of Porcelain, Jinhua (Zhejiang), 2007.
4 "Below roof" Gallery, Shanghai, 2000.
5 Wusan House, Ningbo (Zhejiang), 2006.
6 Library in Suzhou University
(Jiangsu), 2000.
7 Zhangyuan House, Haining (Zhejiang),
2000 (unbuilt).
8 Xiangshan Campus of the Higher School of Fine
Arts of China, Hangzhou (Zhejiang), 2007.
9 Fine Arts Museum, Ningbo, 2005.
10 Housing towers, Hangzhou, 2007.

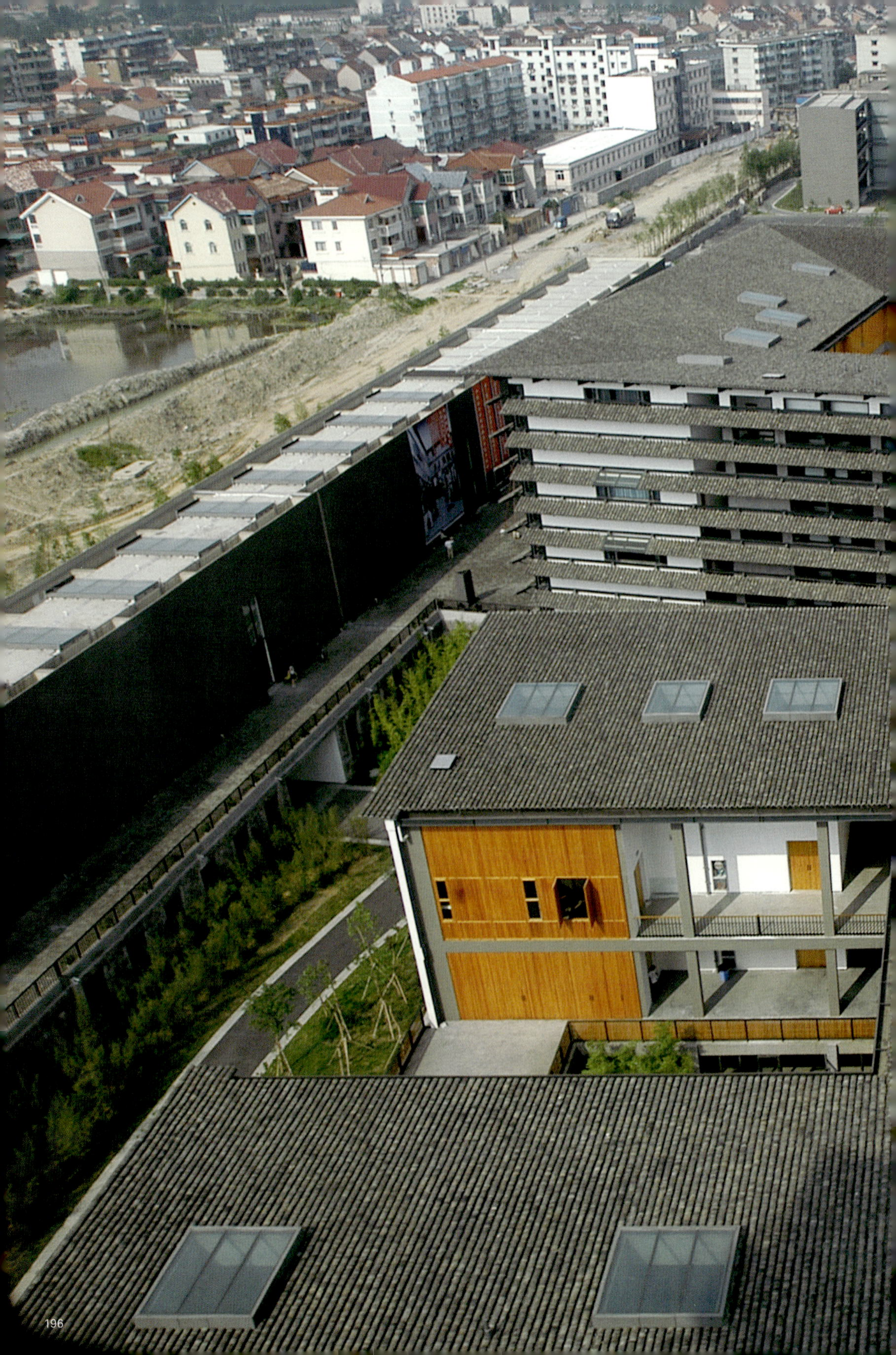

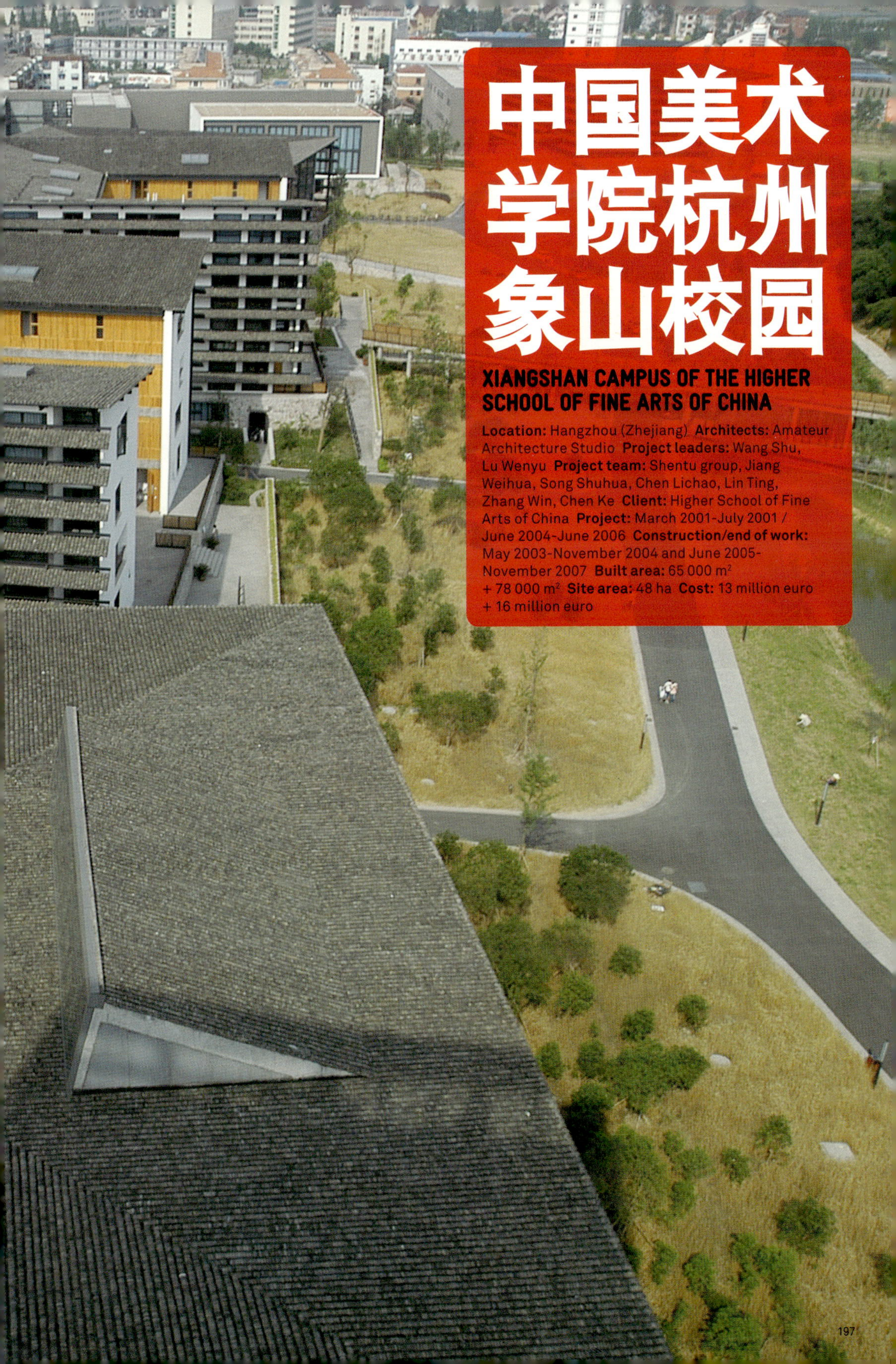

XIANGSHAN CAMPUS OF THE HIGHER SCHOOL OF FINE ARTS OF CHINA

Location: Hangzhou (Zhejiang) **Architects:** Amateur Architecture Studio **Project leaders:** Wang Shu, Lu Wenyu **Project team:** Shentu group, Jiang Weihua, Song Shuhua, Chen Lichao, Lin Ting, Zhang Win, Chen Ke **Client:** Higher School of Fine Arts of China **Project:** March 2001-July 2001 / June 2004-June 2006 **Construction/end of work:** May 2003-November 2004 and June 2005-November 2007 **Built area:** 65 000 m² + 78 000 m² **Site area:** 48 ha **Cost:** 13 million euro + 16 million euro

The new campus of the School of Fine Arts at Hangzhou, considered the country's most prestigious institution of its type and one of the oldest, has been installed in an industrial area near the river Qiantang. The landscape here was substantially ravaged during the Communist period and even more in the course of the last two decades. On the other hand, it benefits from the presence of mount Xiangshan (Elephant Mountain), a homophone of Beijing's "Fragrant Hills" but above all celebrated for sheltering a still wild variety of Longjing tea.

Wang Shu's work has never been dissociated from that of a team in which he includes the masons as well as the works managers. With his wife Lu Wenyu, he follows closely the progress of constructions and the care devoted to details. The campus is formed by about twenty main buildings (erected in two successive and formally distinct phases), all of which differ in their structures and their materials although they are similar in their common writing.

Library or classrooms, dormitories, offices, gymnasiums or amphitheatres, everything is integrated in modules which are more regular than it would seem, the floor plan of which is usually a rectangle approaching a square.

In the heart of the buildings or sometimes on the edge, the architect has designed a large square courtyard where one rediscovers the spirit of the Chinese tradition fortified by the use of large panels of wood, which allow the modulation of the irrupting light while providing a reassuring solidity on each level.

The wise simplicity of the volumes and the pathways gives one a feeling of timelessness here, or of being in the soothing temporality of some monastery. This feeling is strengthened by the link with nature, which is the fruit of an impressive landscape job if one compares it with the majority of the European universities.

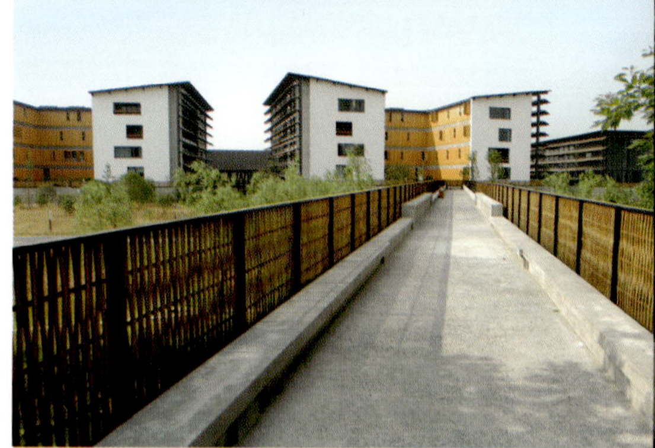

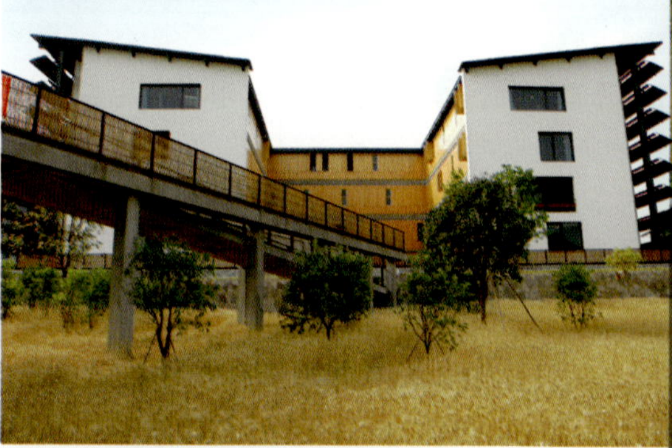

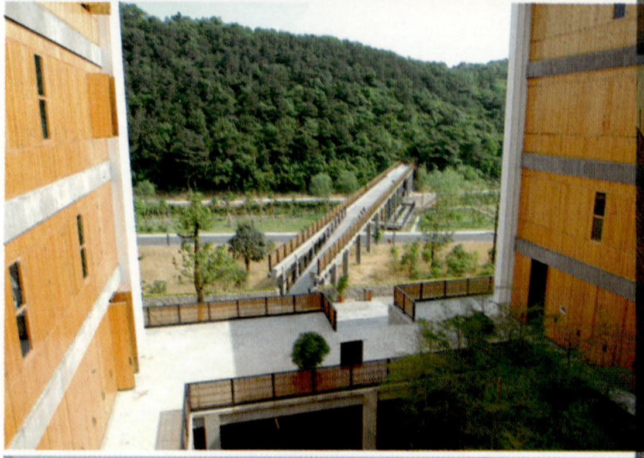

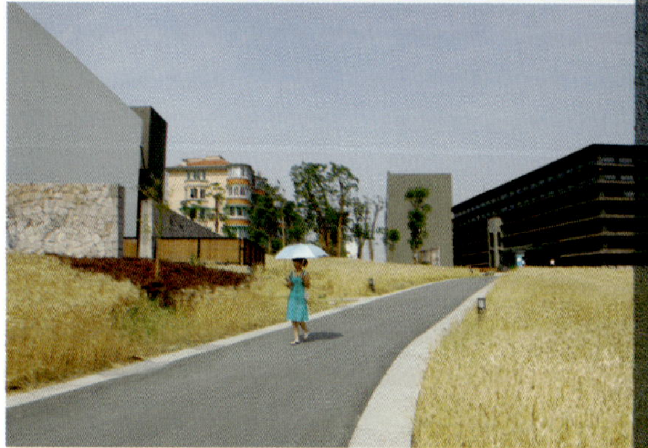

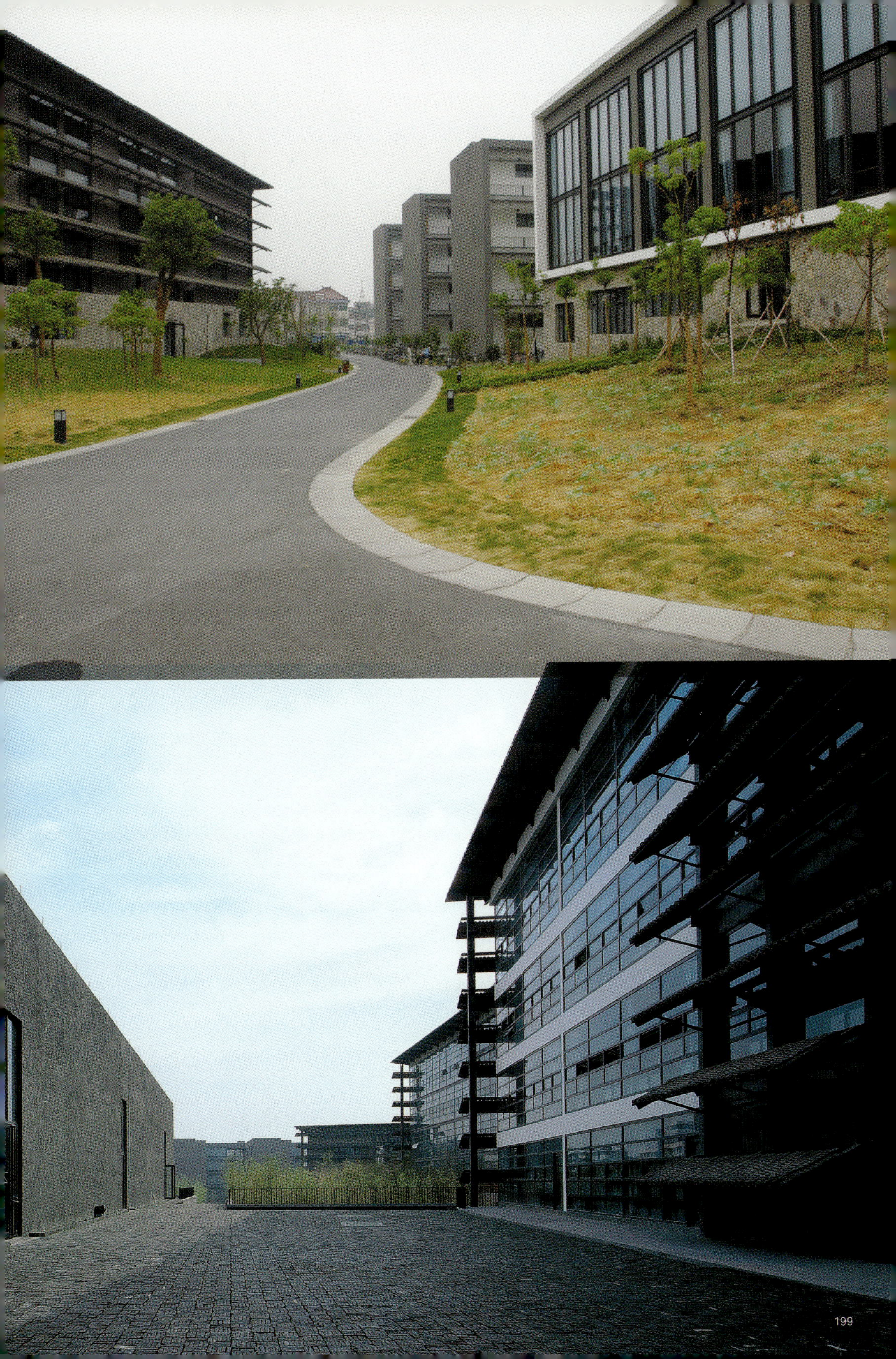

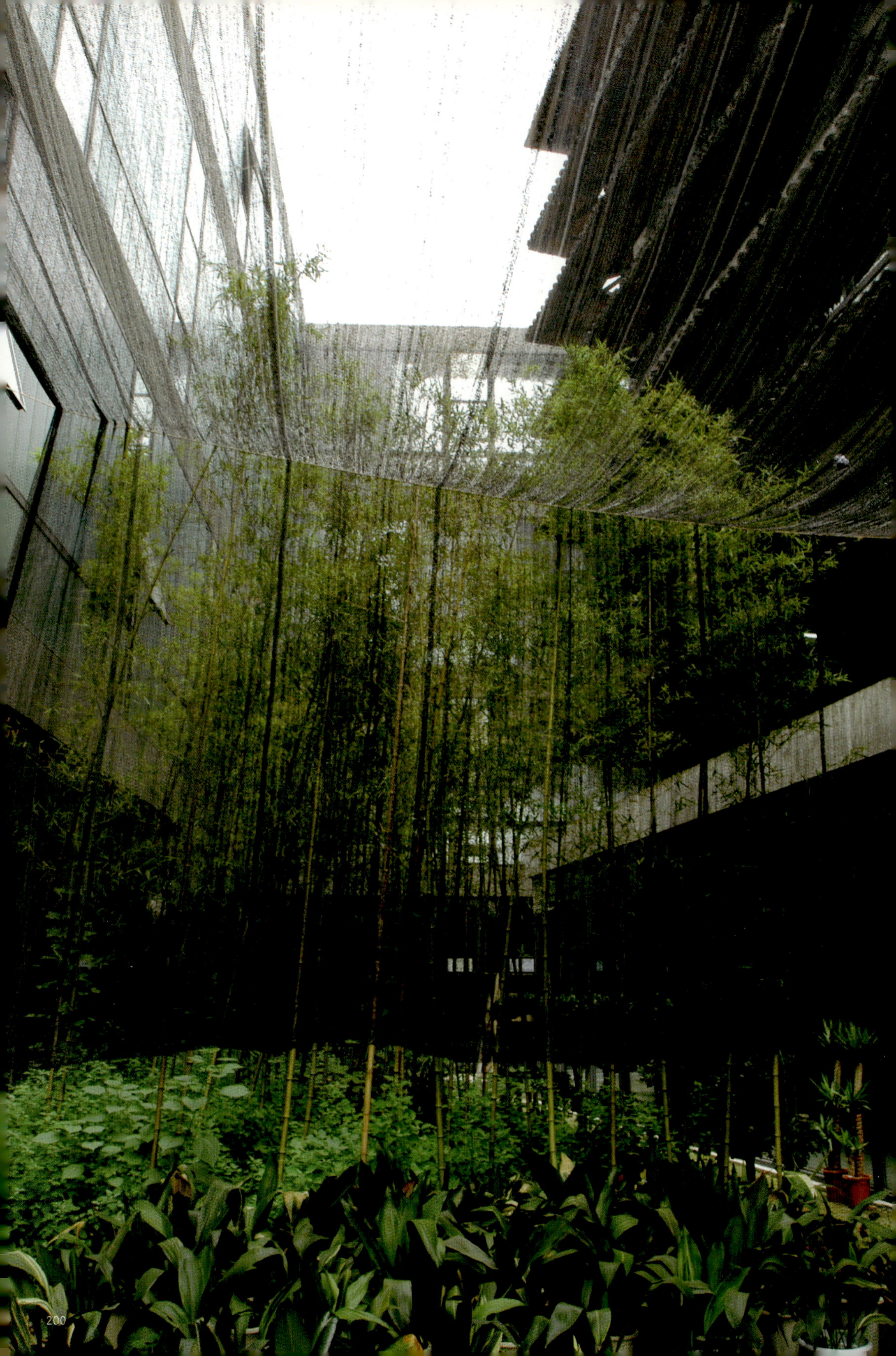

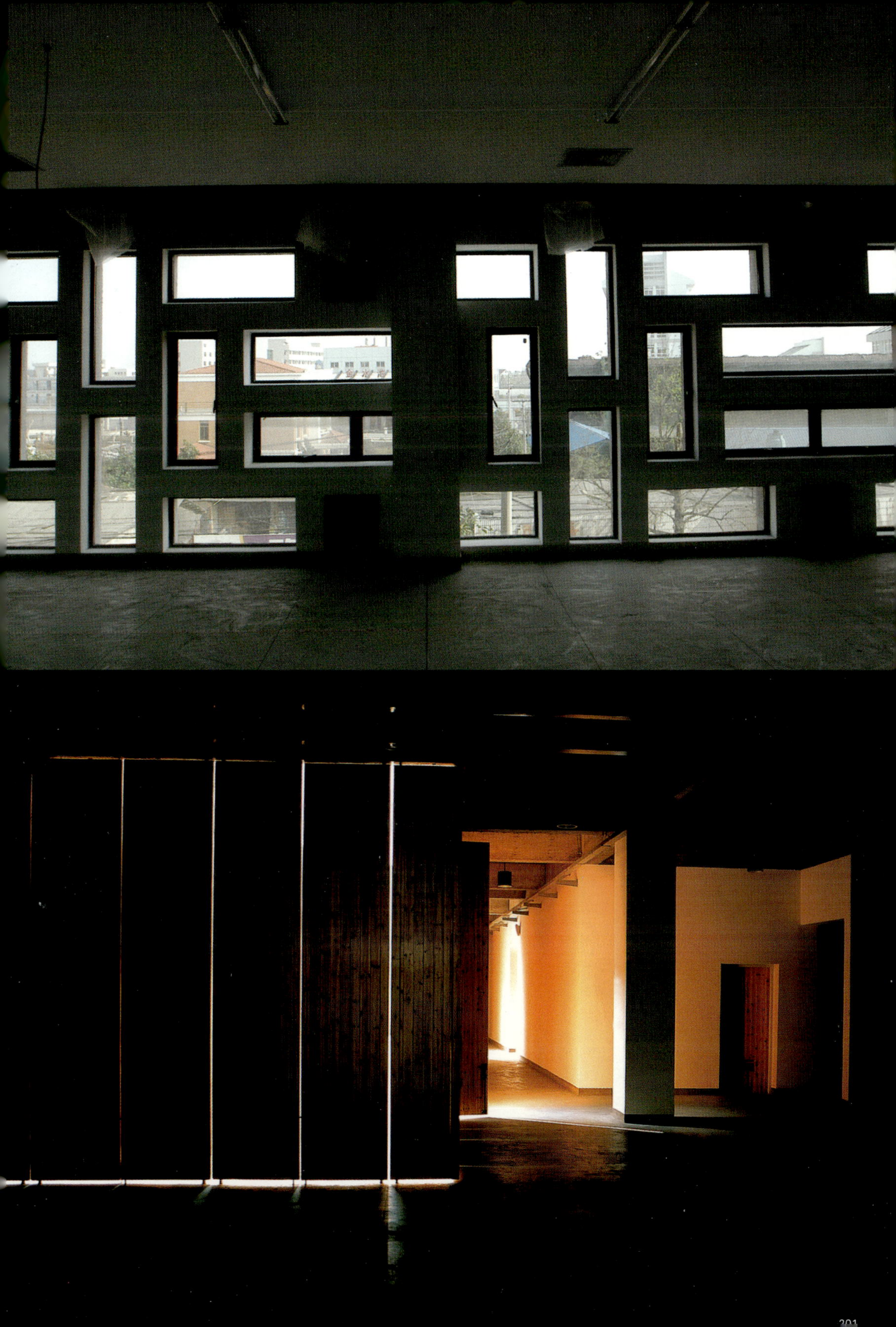

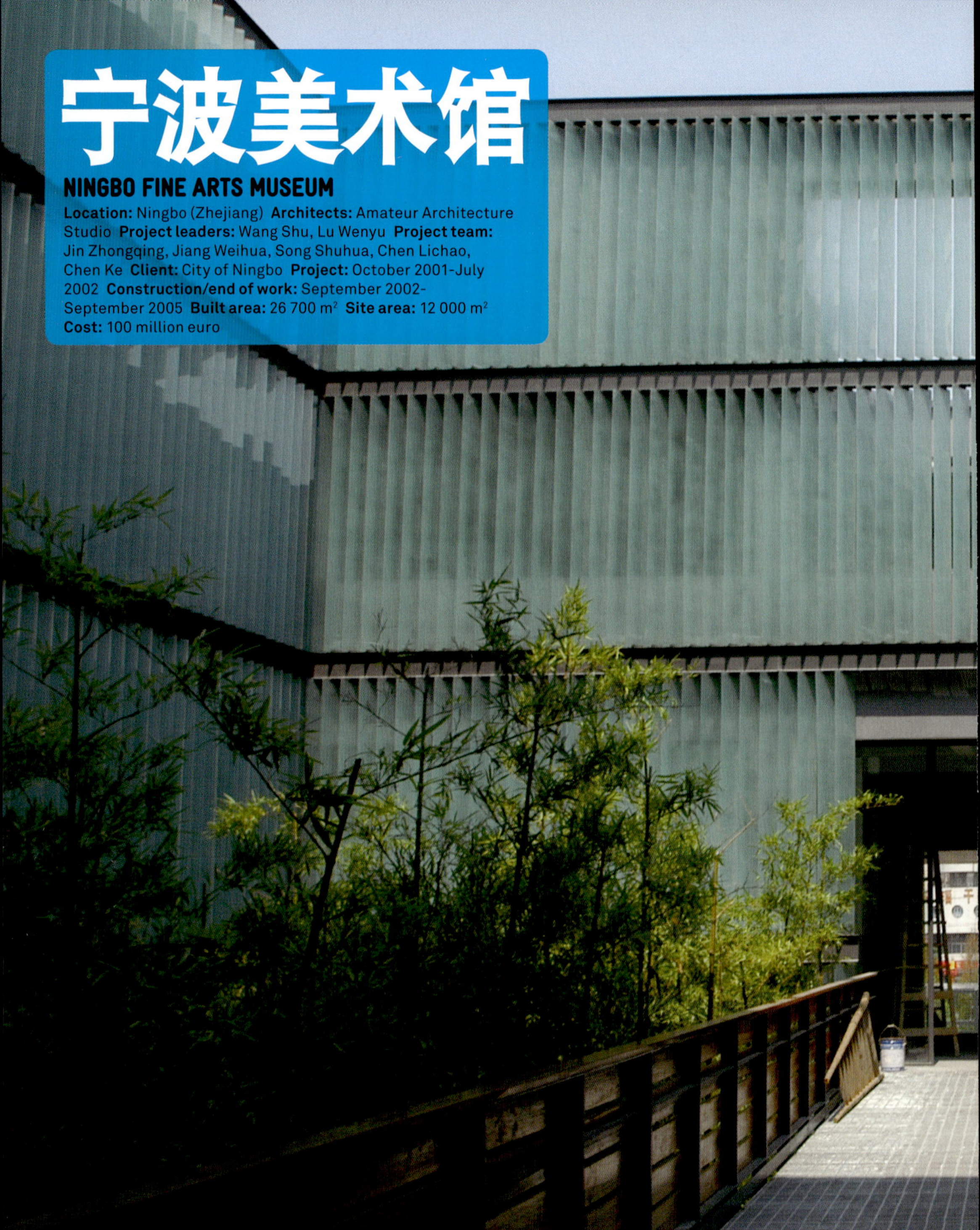

宁波美术馆

NINGBO FINE ARTS MUSEUM

Location: Ningbo (Zhejiang) **Architects:** Amateur Architecture Studio **Project leaders:** Wang Shu, Lu Wenyu **Project team:** Jin Zhongqing, Jiang Weihua, Song Shuhua, Chen Lichao, Chen Ke **Client:** City of Ningbo **Project:** October 2001-July 2002 **Construction/end of work:** September 2002-September 2005 **Built area:** 26 700 m² **Site area:** 12 000 m² **Cost:** 100 million euro

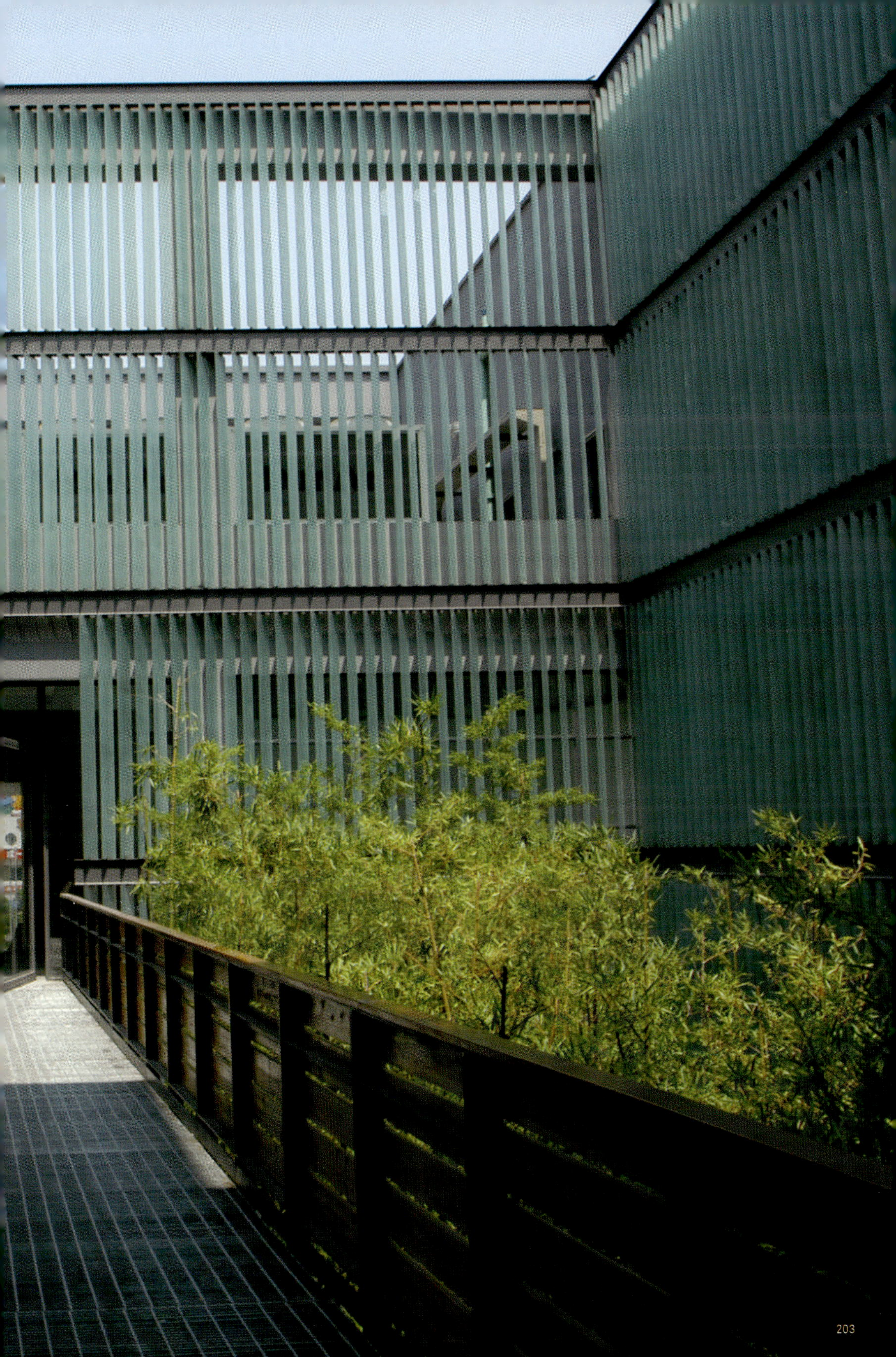

Together with Qingpu, Ningbo is one of the cities
which has made the greatest efforts to enhance
the appreciation of what remains of its heritage
(here one finds a fragment of a Bund, like the one in
Shanghai, which is correctly valued) and to favour
the call to talented architects. The city overlooks
a river which empties into the vast bay extending
from Hangzhou to the south of the municipality of
Shanghai. About one hundred kilometres separate
this port from Wang Shu's native city. As the crow
flies, the same distance separates Ningbo from
Shanghai across the bay. All this explains why the
local clients often take recourse to the architects
of the region, mainly including Ma Qingyun
(Shanghai) and the national treasure which is
now represented for Hangzhou by Wang Shu.
While Ma Qingyun has deployed here an address
more urban than architectural, Wang Shu –
to whom has been commissioned the Fine Arts
Museum, a former wharf which was transferred
down –, has chosen to propose a clearly signed,
sharply styled building, which could have left it ill
at ease with the rather harsh quarter extending
along the river in Ningbo. In the end, all this lends
a clear singularity while creating a sort of peaceful
sanctuary for works which, in China, often play
(in their contemporary version) with the roughest
and even cruellest representations.
The museum stands along the lines of a pacified
architecture. That translates, as at the Hangzhou
School of Fine Arts, into large wooden platforms
on a stone plinth. On the river side, the plinth has
provided the opportunity to highlight and to protect
a set of ancient Buddhist sculptures. On the city
side, the architect, who has rejected the fatal
principle of tiering which is characteristic of so
many Chinese monuments, has chosen to build
a broad platform (including a basement car park)
which creates distance and elicits the respect
demanded by all museum institutions.
The main floor of the museum is partitioned
and fractioned like a Chinese temple, while the
principal courtyard is covered by a grill which
is more theatrical than museal. It must be
recognised, however, that the usual dimensions
of works of art in China, whether they involve
sculptures or photographs, often adopt a
considerable scale within the tradition of these
statues whose heads disappear in the shadow
of the roofing.

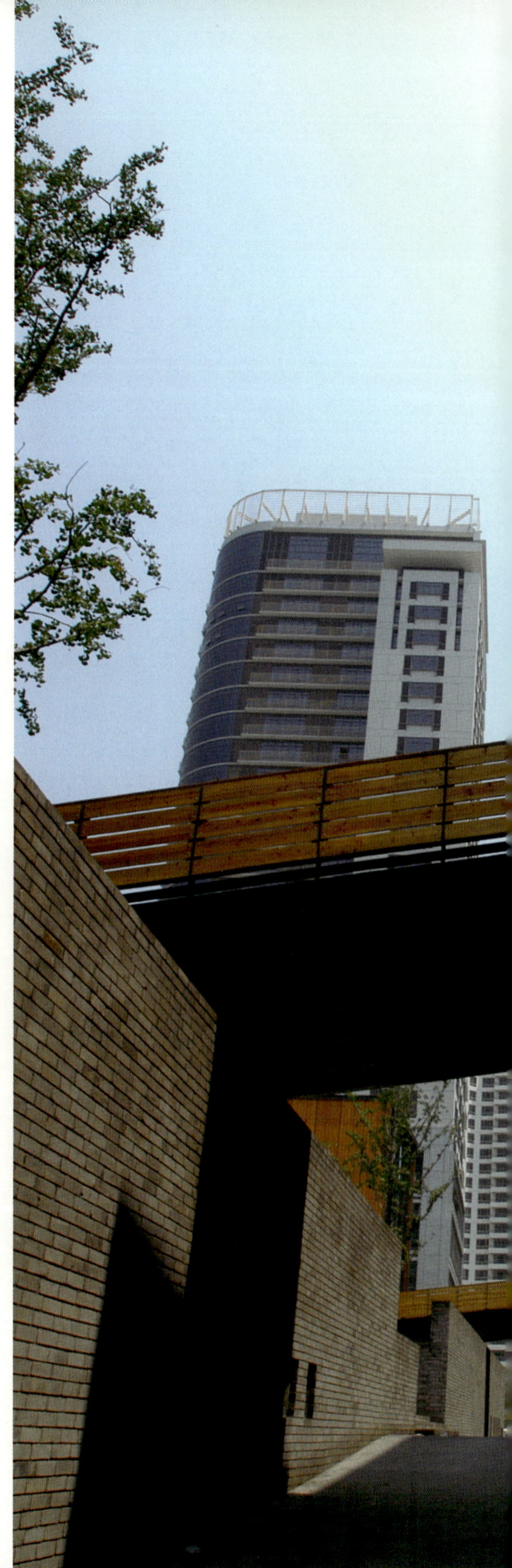

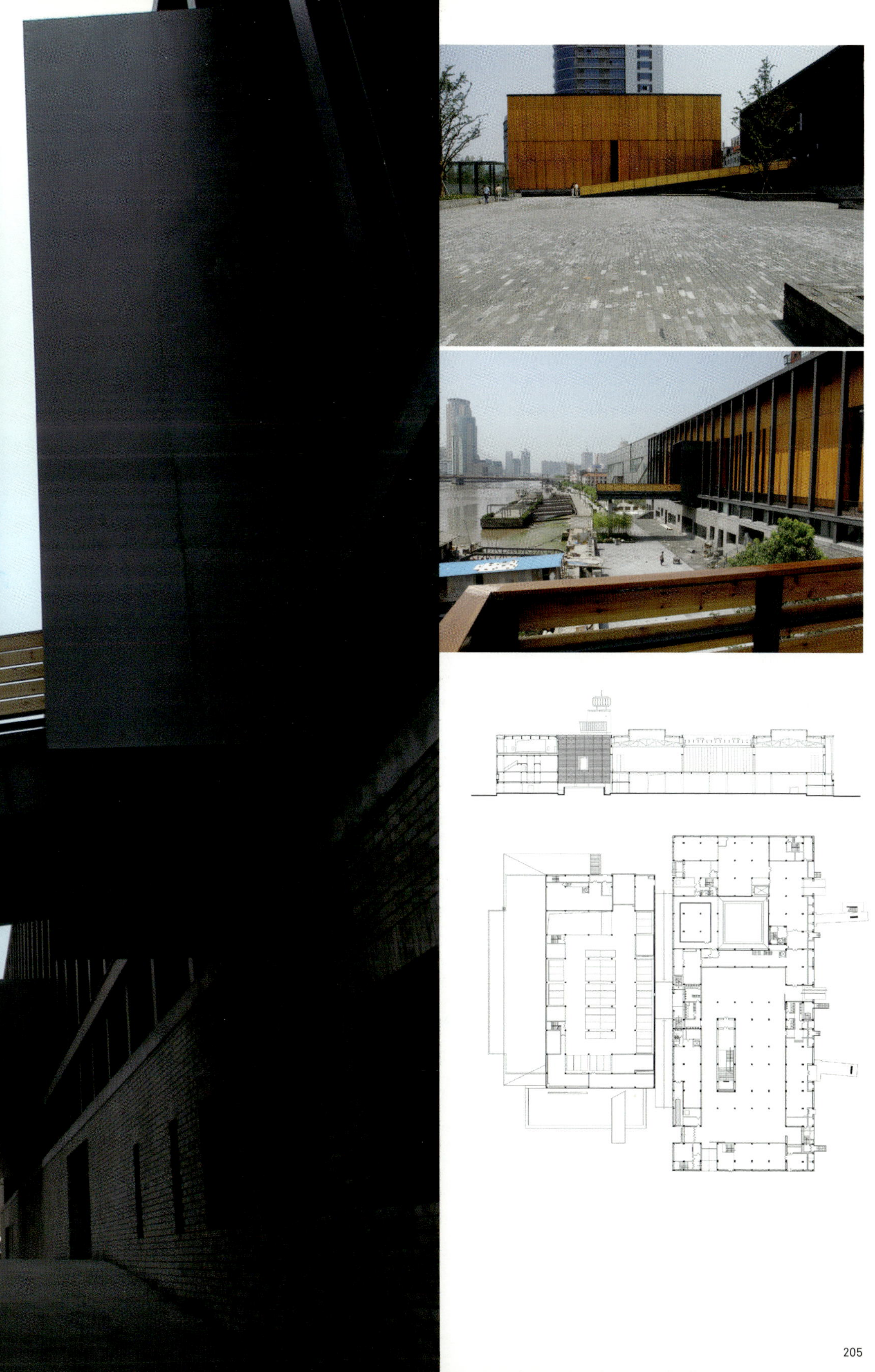

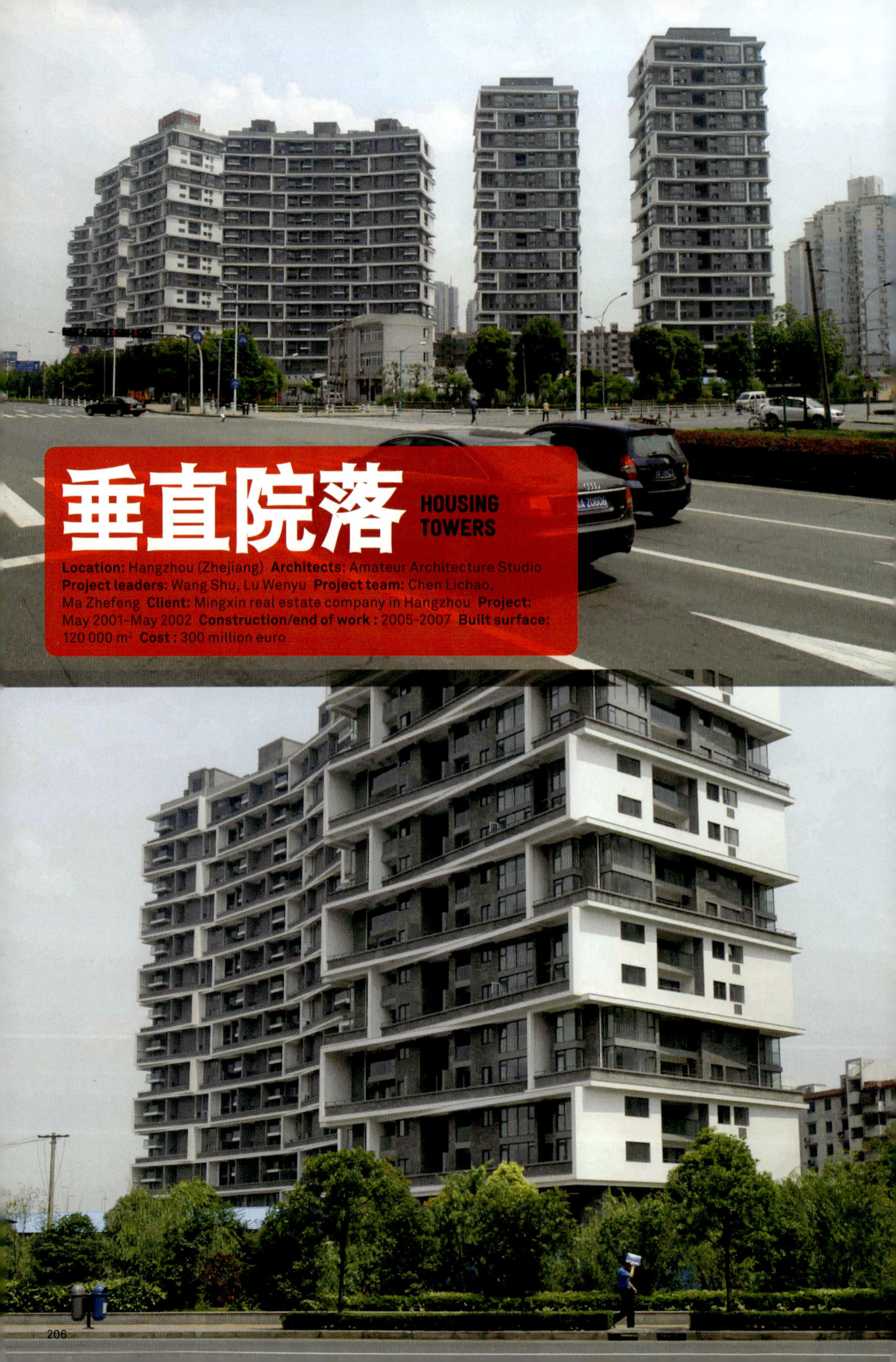

垂直院落 HOUSING TOWERS
Location: Hangzhou (Zhejiang) Architects: Amateur Architecture Studio
Project leaders: Wang Shu, Lu Wenyu Project team: Chen Lichao,
Ma Zhefeng Client: Mingxin real estate company in Hangzhou Project:
May 2001-May 2002 Construction/end of work : 2005-2007 Built surface:
120 000 m² Cost : 300 million euro

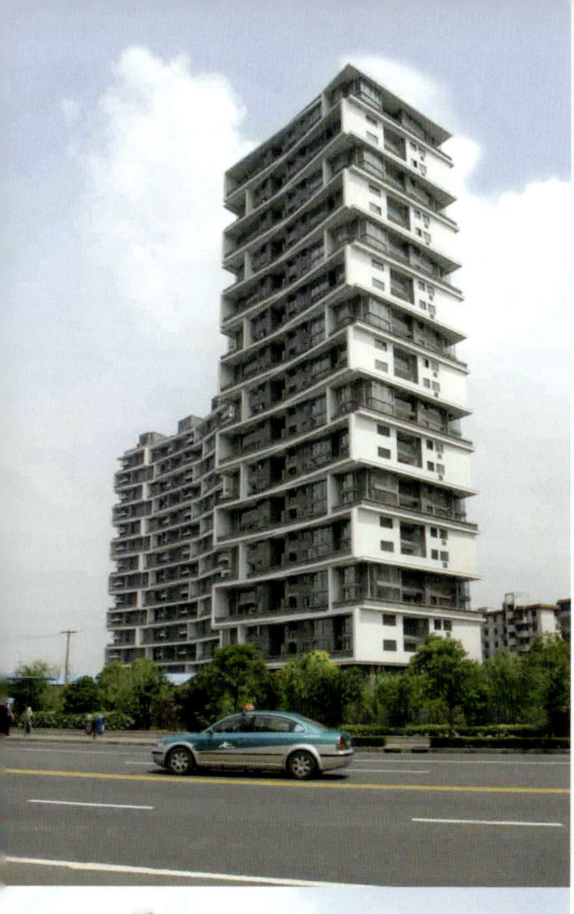

The set of dwellings which Wang Shu and Lu Wenyu have just finished in Hangzhou is a commission from a private promoter. It took longer to complete than is usual in China, partly because of the complexity of the project and partly because the real estate opportunities had to wait for the construction of important road infrastructures, in particular a suspension bridge connecting the eastern part of the city to the economic and industrial southern area. The structural appearance of the six towers breaks away from the obsessive regularity of the majority of China's condominiums. White and grey, the traditional colours of Jiangnan, predominate. The design of this ensemble of six buildings seems to associate strangely the warlike merits of watch towers with the more pacific virtues of pagodas. It is above all in the interior organisation of each of these towers that one discovers Wang Shu's originality.

The towers function as if they formed a stack of two-story dwellings, and each block seems strongly independent, presenting an image which is indeed quite distant from that of the traditional dwellings which could exist in the old cities with their fragments of courtyards, their facing neighbours and, in short, their complicities, at least if the new generation does not change radically its forms of relation.

In this respect, it seems rather pleasant to wander on the common landings, as if the interior and exterior of the apartments stemmed from one same community.

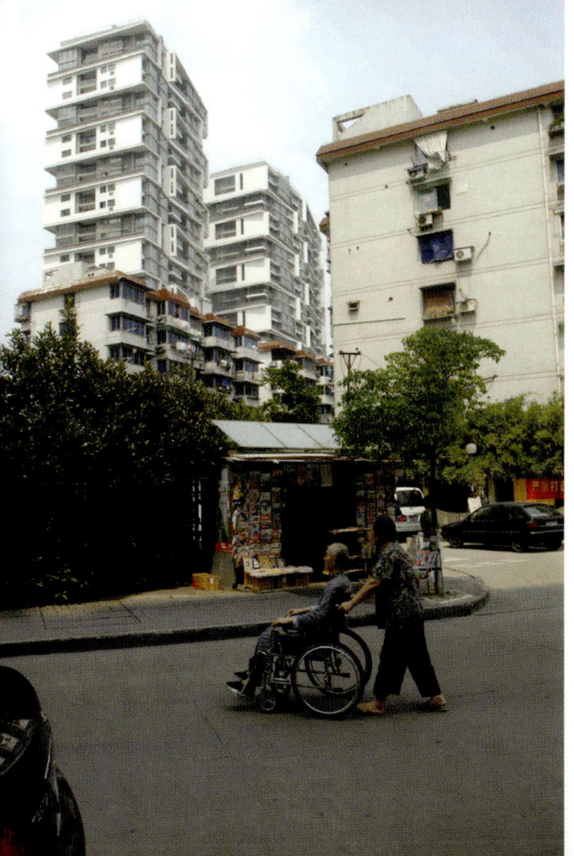

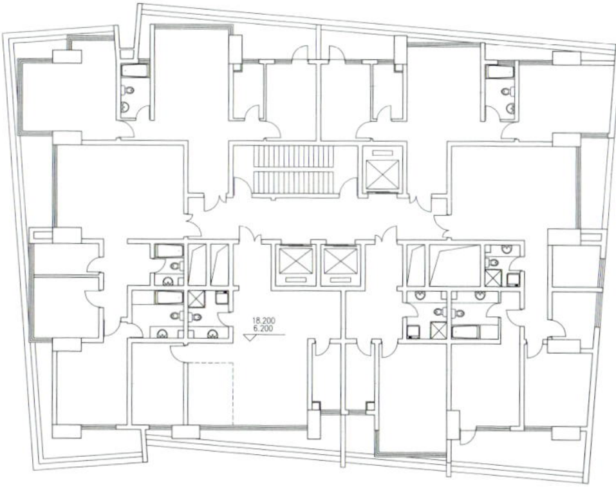

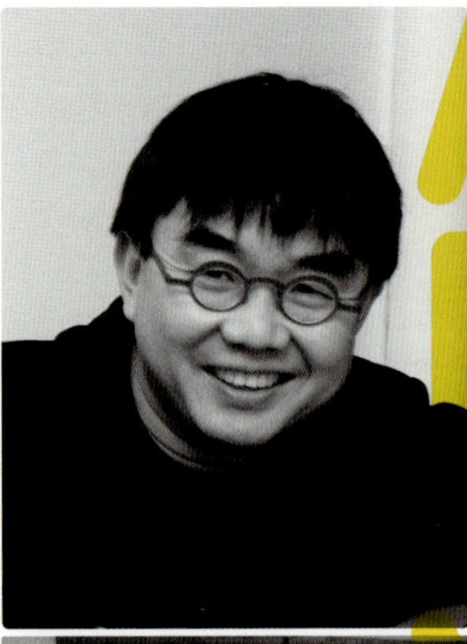

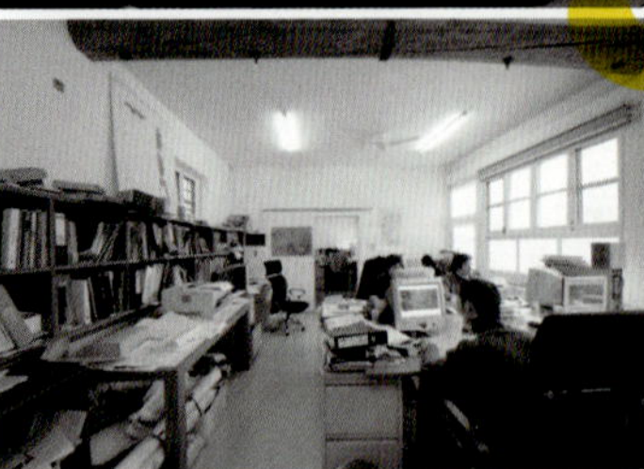

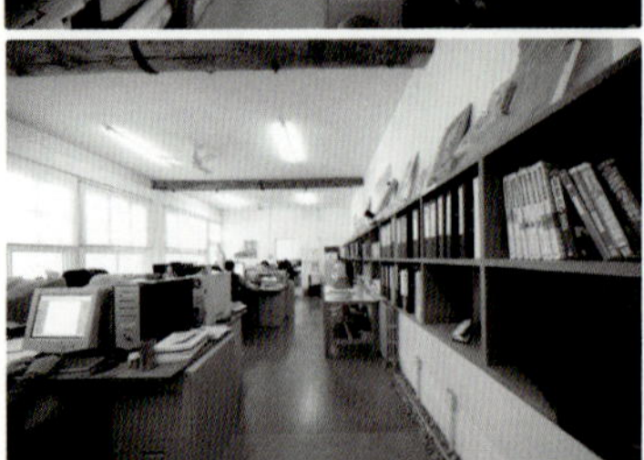

Atelier Feichang Jianzhu 北京非常建筑设计研究所
Chang Yung Ho 张永和

Chang Yung Ho is the Americanised version of Zhang Yonghe.
Born in Beijing in 1956, Chang took his degree at the University of
Nanking before going on to obtain a master's in Berkeley, California
(US). Back in China, where he founded the Feichang Jianzhu Studio,
the young architect succeeded in making people forget that he is
the son of one of the country's most celebrated master builders,
Zhang Kaiji, the author of the famous Museum of Chinese History
and of the Chinese Revolution, one of the ten buildings erected in
ten months for the tenth anniversary of the People's Republic of
China, as well as of lesser known ensembles of dwellings organised
around common gardens, or the beautiful exhibition presented in
Paris in 1982 on the everyday environment in China.
It is likely that this family background did not harm Chang, whose
lively intelligence addressed itself to the field of the renovation
of architecture. There he broke away from the heroic dimension of
the buildings presented by his illustrious father, while remaining
in continuity with his concerns for the quality of everyday life.
A theorist of micro-urbanism, he practised on a "bike-library"
(demolished in 1996) and obtained his first serious commission
thanks to the Soho group. He was one of the architects chosen
to build one of the prototype houses of the Commune by the
Great Wall. Called the Split House in English, it was presented
at the Venice Biennale in 2002. The structure is formed by two
bodies of similar shapes, according to the Chinese tradition,
which present the subtle feature of forming an acute angle rather
than a right angle.
This mark of independence, which has been renewed in a perhaps
more energetic manner in recent projects, has led Chang to publish
his ideas and to disseminate them in public conferences, as well as
to accept to head the prestigious architecture department of MIT
in Cambridge, Massachusetts (US).
Although he does not always say so, his production is considered
extremely important among his younger colleagues and he helps
them as much as he can. For example it was Chang who conceived
the first Shenzhen Biennial in 2005, a remarkable manifestation of
open-mindedness and intelligence which was highlighted without
detriment by a strong simple scenography.
In Chinese, "Feichang Jianzhu" means extraordinary, uncommon or
in any case non-standard architecture. This expression could seem
more appropriate to an initiative based on both polite discretion and
a singular will or ambition in China, focusing on quality as a constant
demand. In reality, Chang's architecture is rather sensible and
his hallmark, perhaps, is his capacity to integrate the improvement
and renewal of the building technologies of a country which was
bankrupt when he was beginning his career. Among his foremost
works and his recent accomplishments, Chang has carried out the
"great swerve", a term that could be the most suitable translation
of the expression *feichang*.

Chang Yung Ho
Born 1956
Master in architecture,
Berkeley University, California, 1984
Studio founded in 1993
Number of employees: 20

Contact
Atelier Feichang Jianzhu
Yuan Ming Yuan East Gate
Nei Yard N°1
Yuan Ming Yuan East Road
100084 Haidian District, Beijing, China
T: +86 10 82 62 61 23
F: +86 10 82 62 27 12
fcjz@fcjz.com
www.fcjz.com

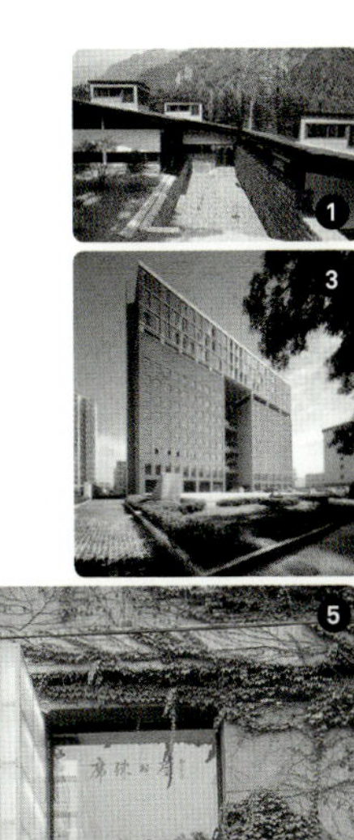
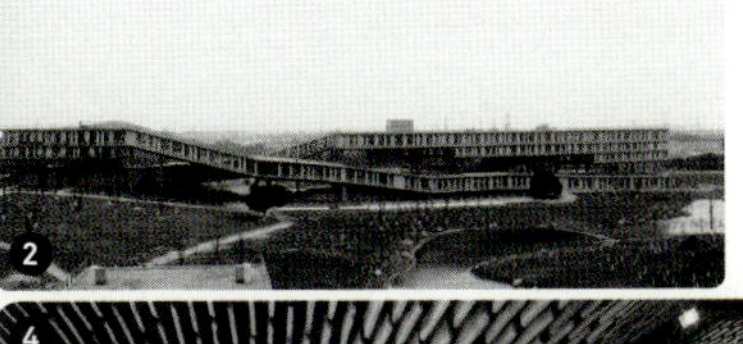
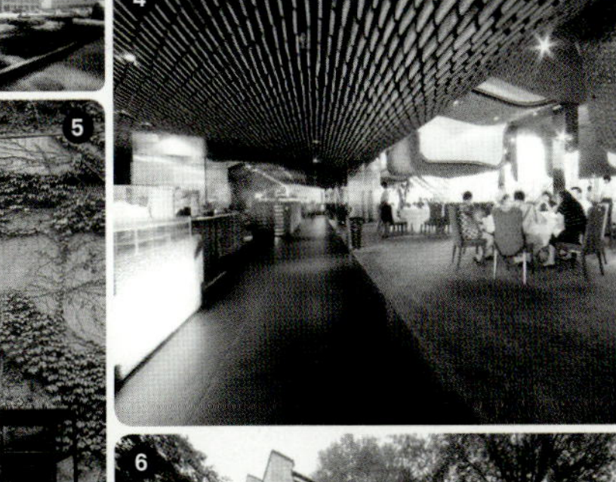
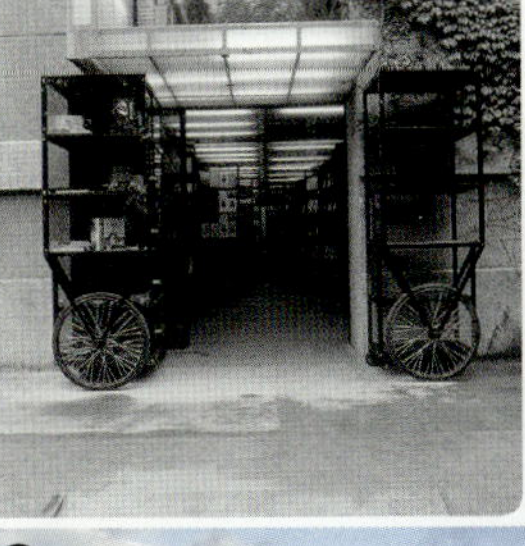
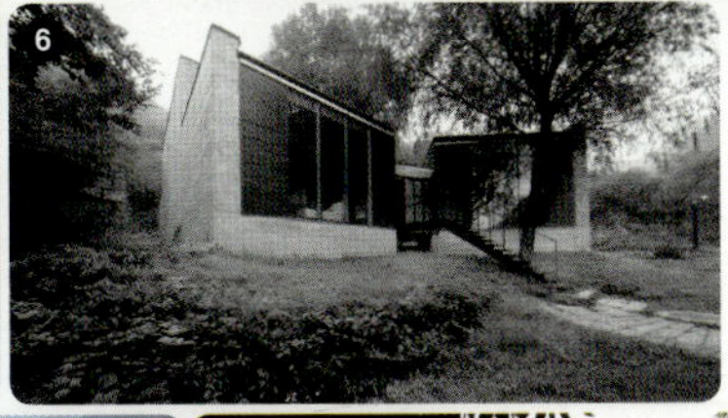
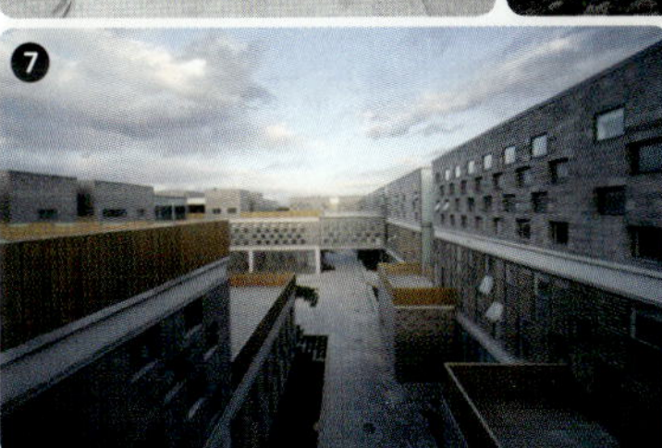
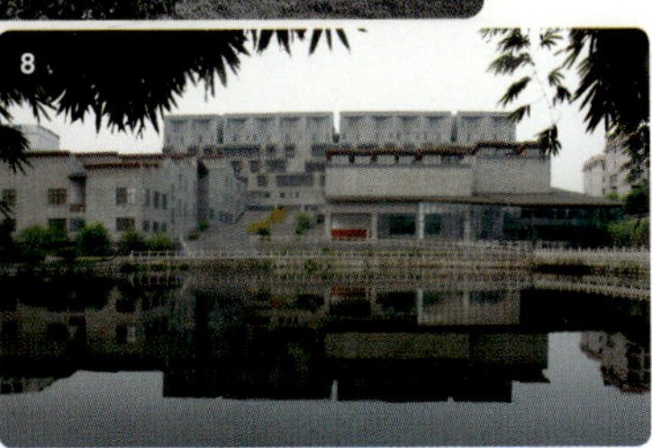
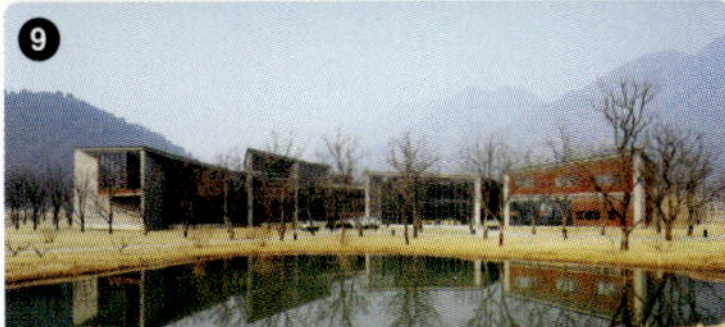

1 Villa Shanyujian, Beijing, 1998.
2 Songshanhu office building, Dongguan (Guangdong), 2005.
3 Hebei Publishing House, Shijiazhuang, 2004.
4 Beijing University Conference Hall,
  Qingdao (Shandong), 2001.
5 Xishu Library, Beijing, 1996.
6 Split House, Commune by the Great Wall, Beijing, 2002.
7 UFIDA Research and Development Centre, Beijing, 2007
8 Jishou University, educational and research buildings, and
  Huang Yongyu Museum, Jishou, 2006.
9 Villa Shizilin, Beijing, 2004.

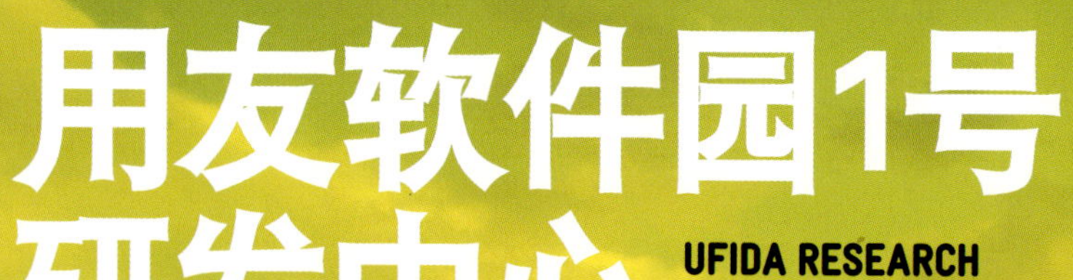

Location: Beijing **Architects:** Atelier Feichang Jianzhu **Project leader:** Chang Yung Ho **Project team:** Jia Lianna, Chen Long, Liu Yang, Bai Chen, Hao Shuang, Zang Feng, Yang Jing **Client:** Ufida corporation **Project:** November 2003-May 2005 **Construction end of work:** April 2005-January 2007 **Built area:** 46 122 m² **Site area:** 15 346 m² **Cost:** 14.3 million euro

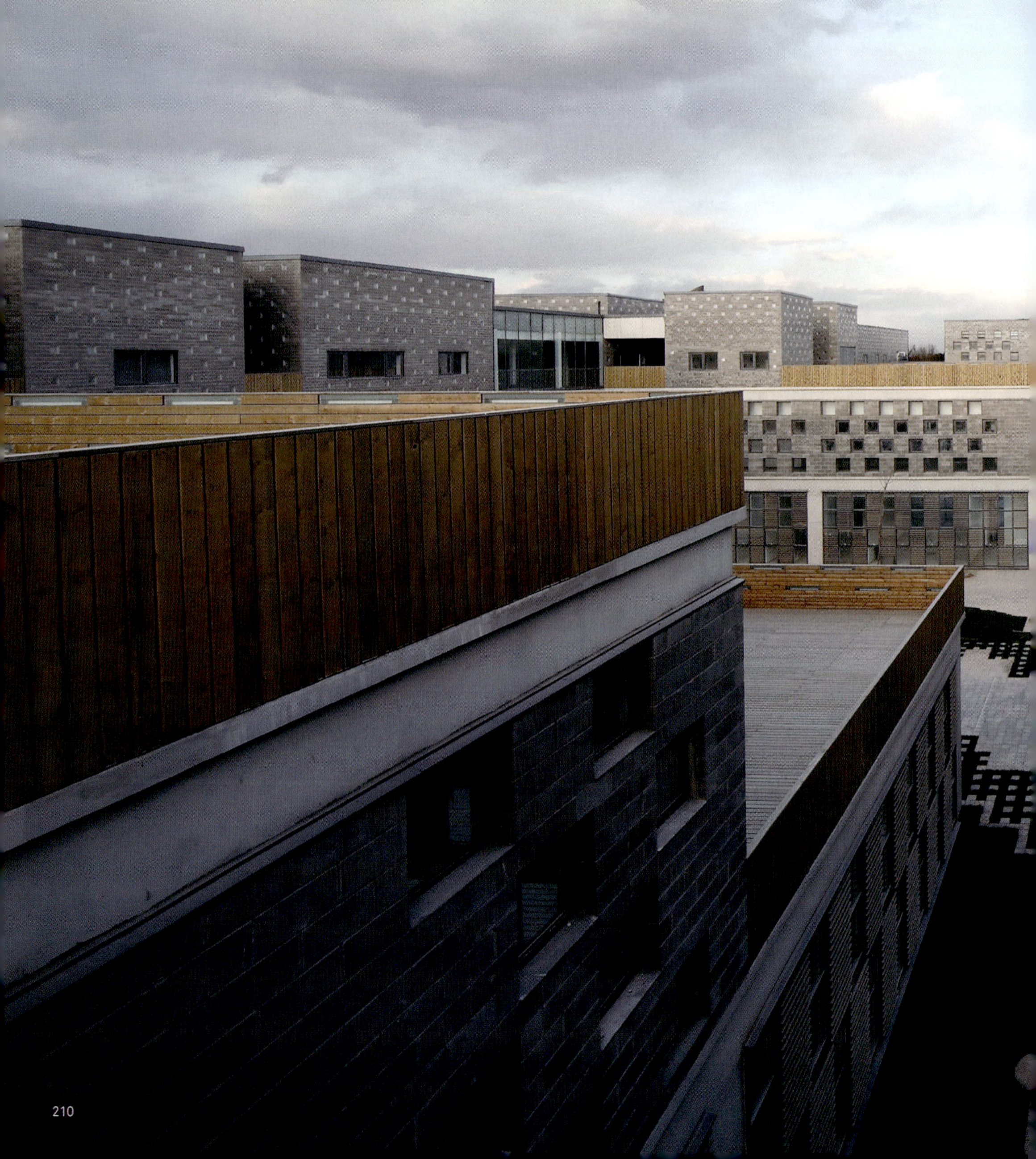

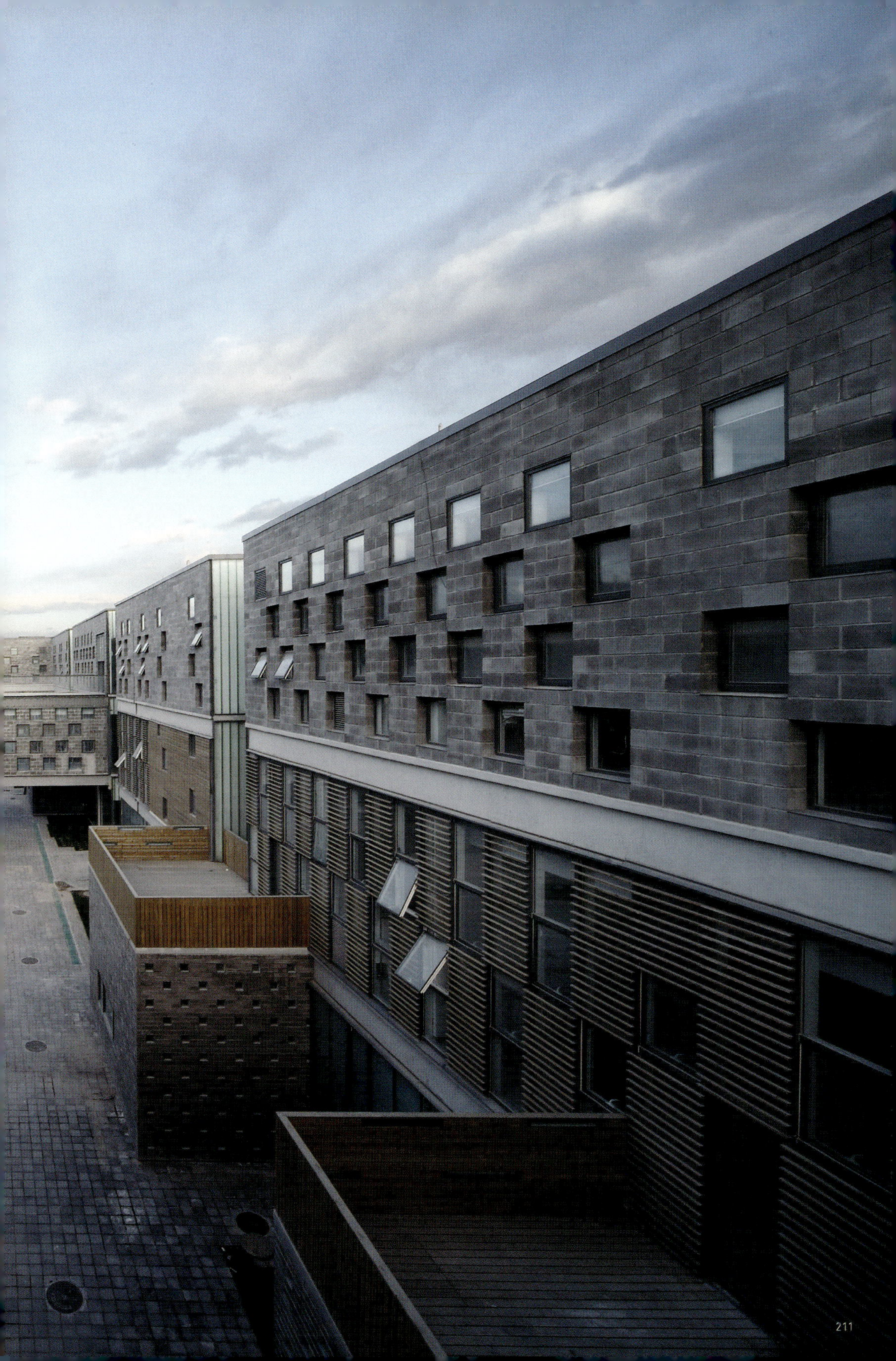

Ufida is one of China's most important IT companies. It has undertaken the construction of the equivalent of an "industrial city" in the suburbs of Beijing, entrusting the various elements of this wide-ranging programme to three architects, including Chang Yung Ho, whose project was the first to be completed, as well as Qi Xin and Zhu Pei, X, Y, Z. With each one working in his own style, this means, if the overall project comes to be carried out, that it will form one of the collections of architecture that represent a characteristic form of contemporary creativity in China as exemplified by the Anren museums, of which Chang Yung Ho was initially the coordinator. Whether it is at Anren or for the headquarters of Ufida, Yung Ho Chang works deftly to support the best of his contemporaries. How does this theorist of "micro-urbanism" express himself in such a vast and complex edifice as this research centre measuring forty-six thousand square metres? Perhaps it is by a cascading fragmentation of the overall project. Indeed, he has begun by fragmenting it in three large parallel wings which will present a unified appearance thanks to the recurrent use of simple materials, the installation of which is mastered by Chinese companies. These materials mainly include brick but now also concrete and glass. To all this must be added the landscaping dimension, which affects both the ensemble of the site and the two long courtyards which "couple" three buildings of Centre No. 1. Each of these three blocks is fractioned in turn into vast modules in which Chang Yung Ho ingeniously multiplies the possible declinations of the basic materials. The size of the openings, mainly comprising standard windows and picture windows, means that even the empty spaces become living materials since each piercing allows a calculated, changing light to penetrate depending on its level and orientation.
The colours of the brick which is used – a grey tone tending towards brown – could make this building look a bit sad to the Western eye, in which these materials and colours evoke an industrial vocabulary which is more a thing of the past than the present. In China and particularly in Beijing, however, these variations on the colour of brick correspond to a sort of musical score of architecture, a type of scale, and the public will perceive instinctively a savoir-faire, a form of luxury or simply a dignity and earnestness. It will perceive, in short, all that is appropriate in a demanding and solidly established firm. Ufida, also known by the name of UF SOFT R&D, has only been in existence for a few years but its very rapid development and youth now acquire, thanks to this architecture, the dimension of respectability which is generally attributed to enterprises of much longer standing.

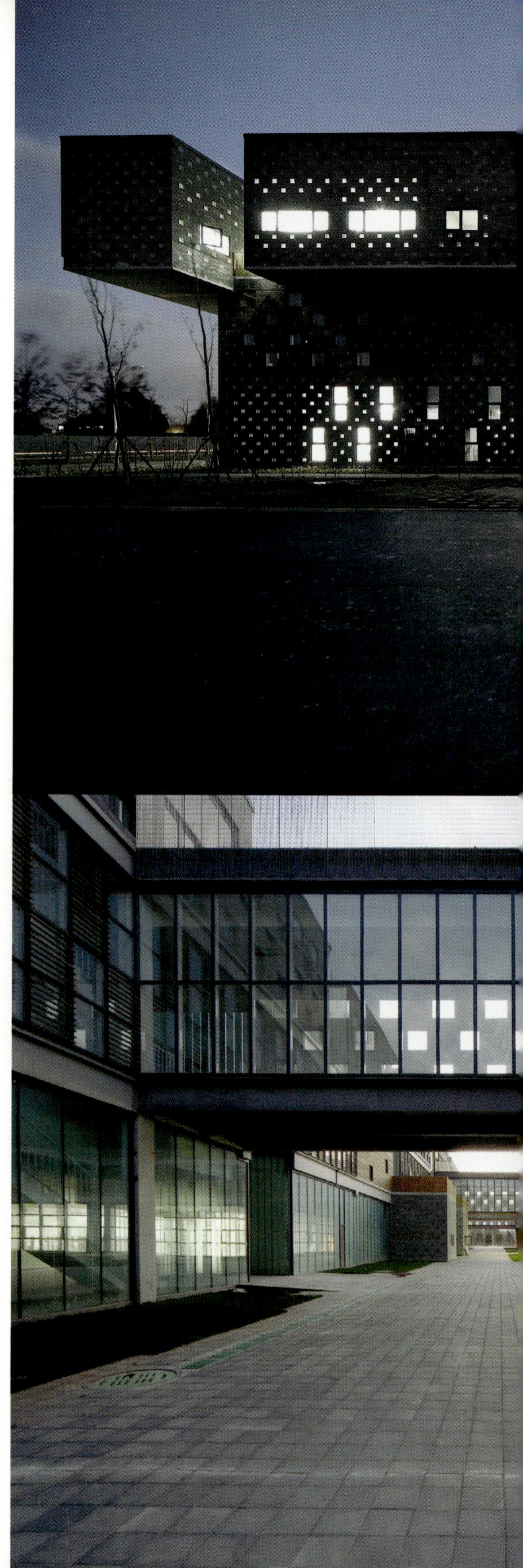

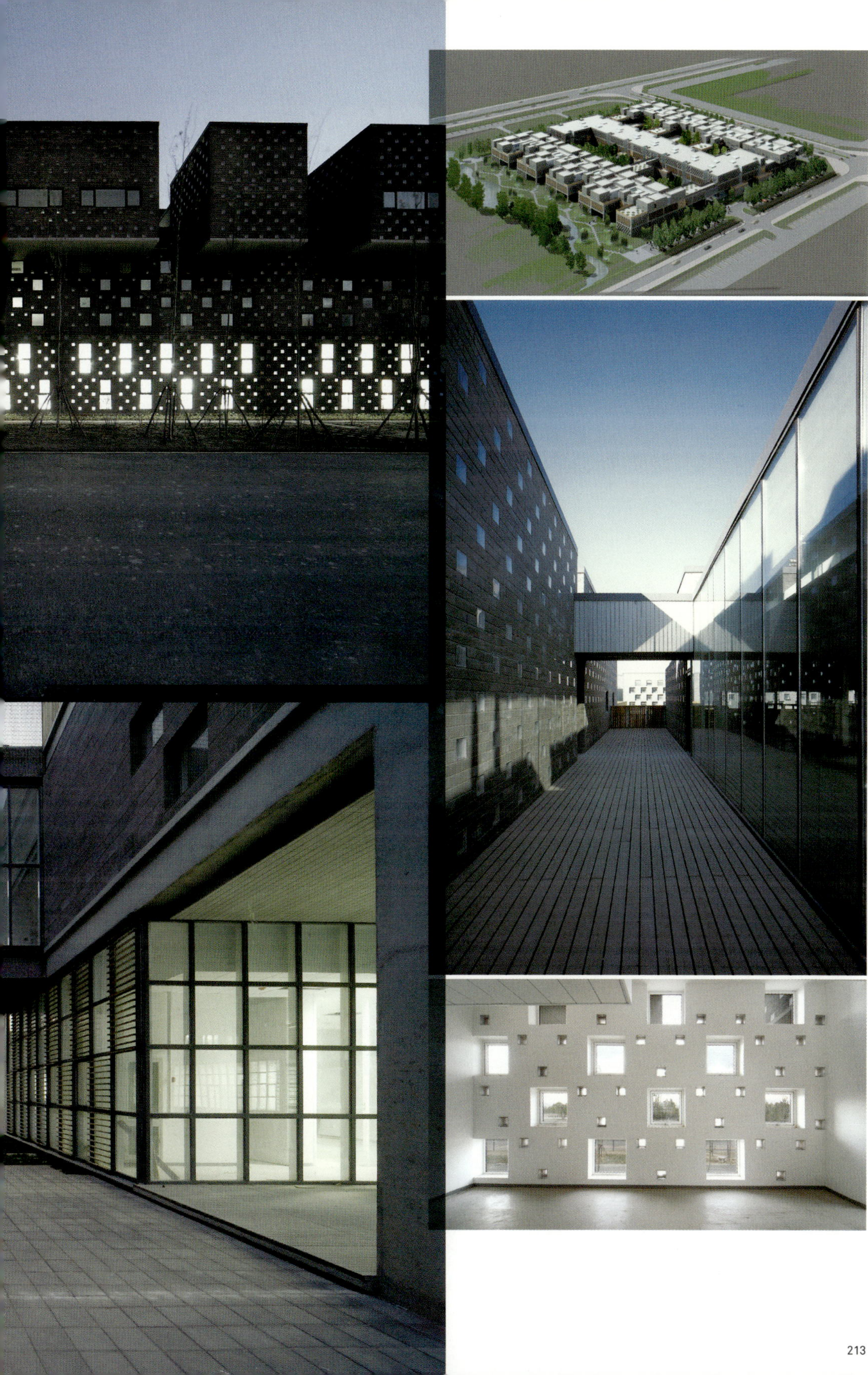

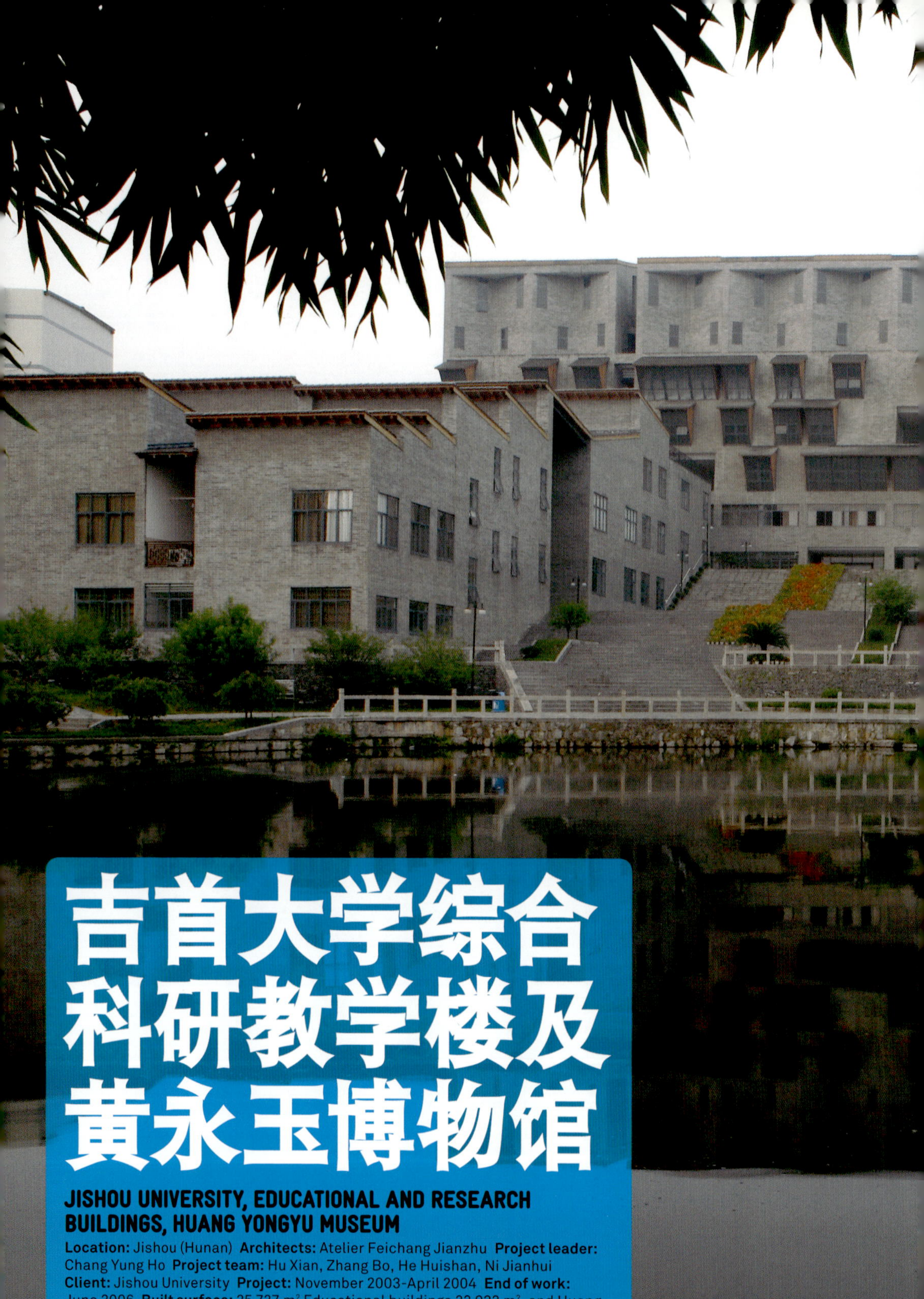

JISHOU UNIVERSITY, EDUCATIONAL AND RESEARCH BUILDINGS, HUANG YONGYU MUSEUM

Location: Jishou (Hunan) **Architects:** Atelier Feichang Jianzhu **Project leader:** Chang Yung Ho **Project team:** Hu Xian, Zhang Bo, He Huishan, Ni Jianhui
Client: Jishou University **Project:** November 2003-April 2004 **End of work:** June 2006 **Built surface:** 25 727 m² Educational buildings 22 032 m², and Huang Yongyu museum 3 688 m² **Cost:** 4.6 million euro

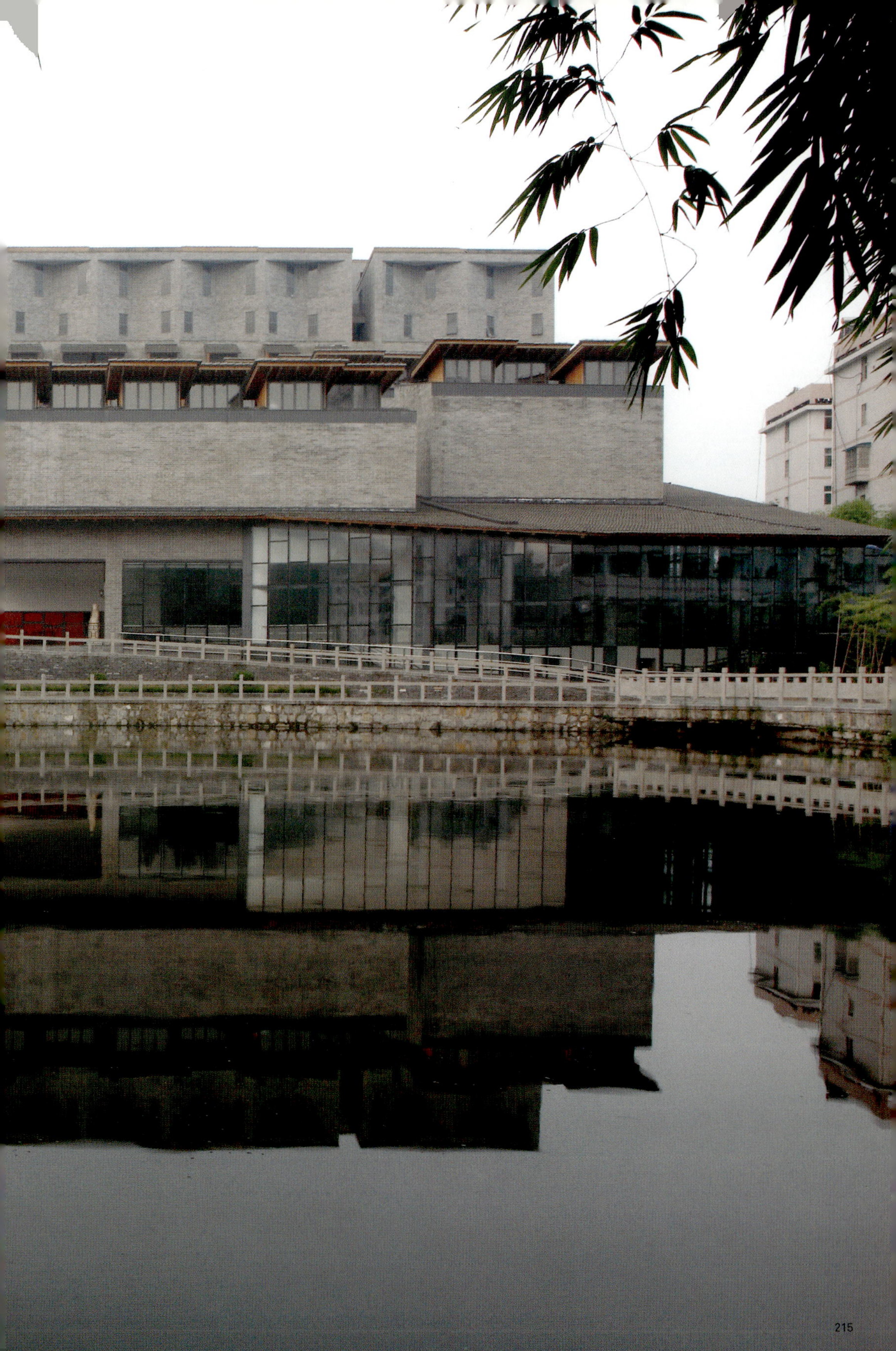

In this dual building, Chang Yung Ho has displayed unquestionably the best of his inventiveness. The city of Jishou, in the Hunan region (southern China), one of the most ancient and most "modernised" towns in the area (and one that has been spared from mass tourism for this reason), is the site of the Miao ethnic group prefecture. For the architect, it was a question of creating a strong tie to the landscape with its mountains in the distance, close to the lake of the university founded in 1958.

Second objective: to offer a contemporary vocabulary anchored in the local tradition and culture. Brick, or veneer brick, play a role here which is different from that of the Ufida Research Centre. These materials allow the Jishou cultural and university ensemble to become imbued with the city's history and almost to invent one.

In a much more forceful way than at the research centre, Chang Yung Ho has modulated the antagonistic expression of the volumes. The ensemble is devoted to education and research, presenting itself as a block of near ten levels in height (22,000 square metres), which is fragmented vertically in four elements and marked horizontally by three types of radically different openings, the unity of which (without going into details here) reflects Chang's natural elegance. At the foot of this building, the Huang Yongyu Museum (3,700 square metres) takes the appearance of a village with a complexity of roofs, something which does not prevent the creation of the large halls required for such a museum facility.

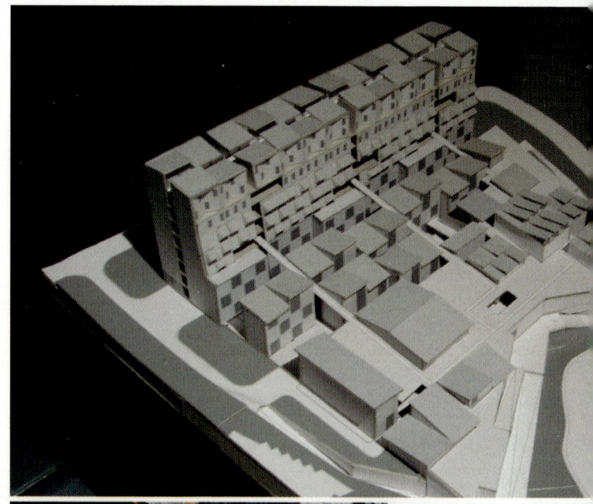

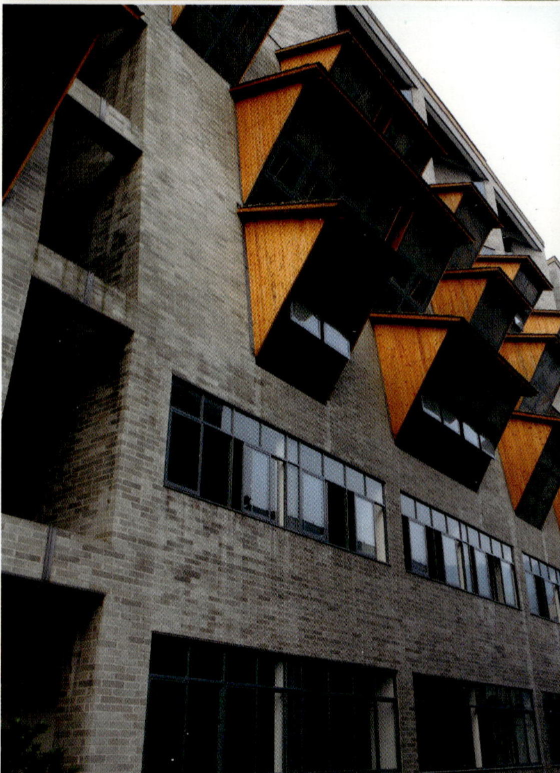

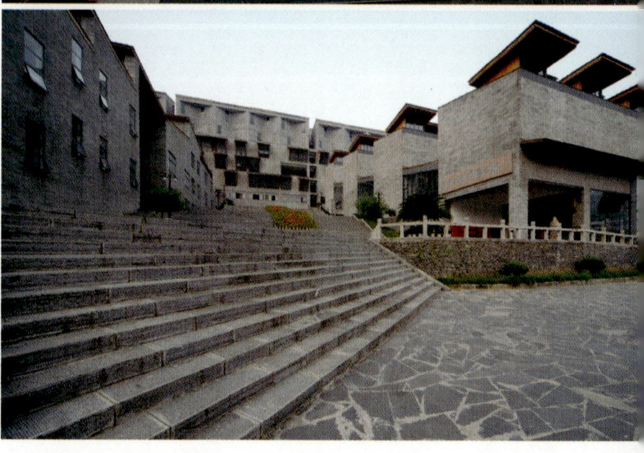

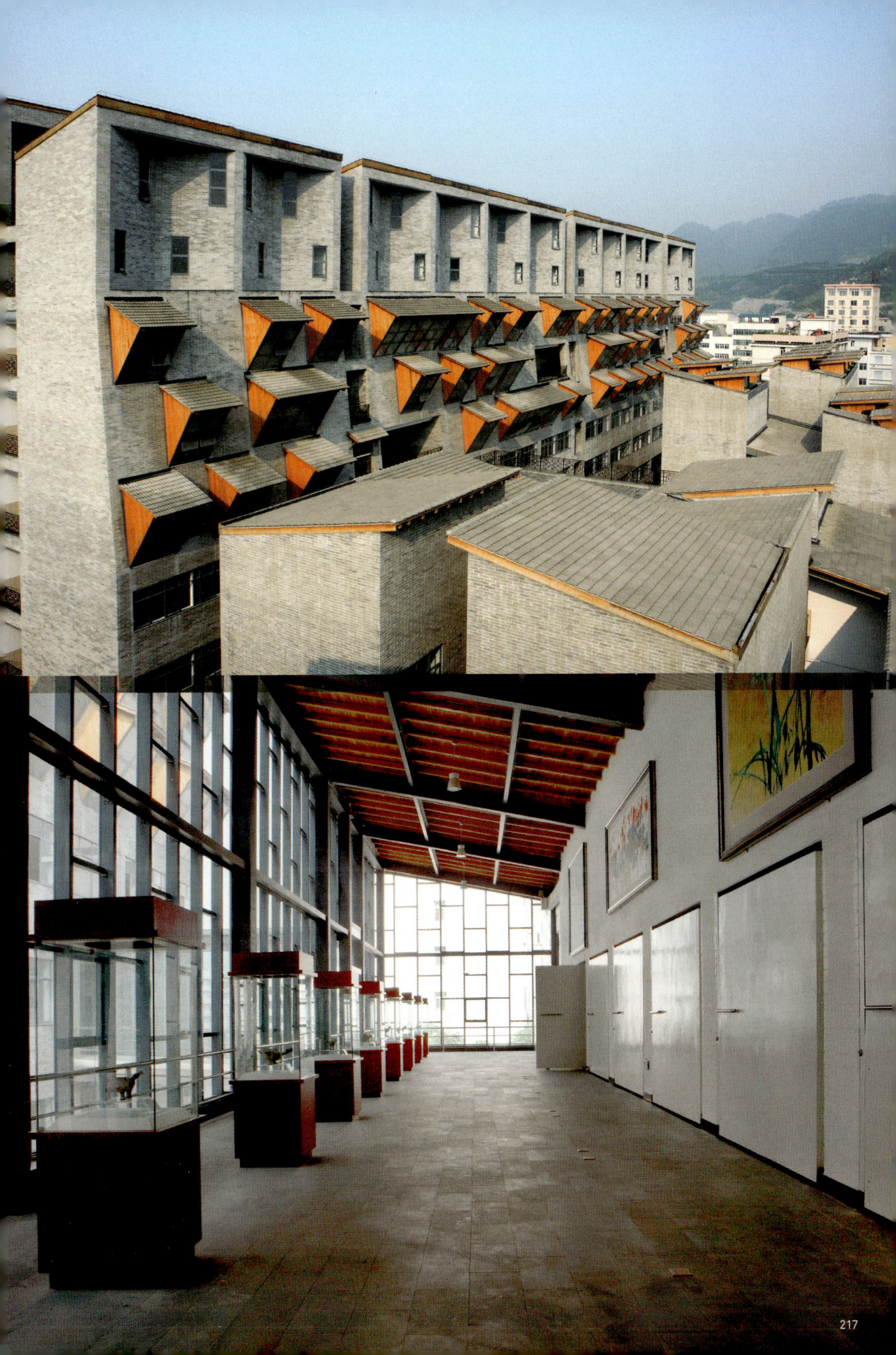

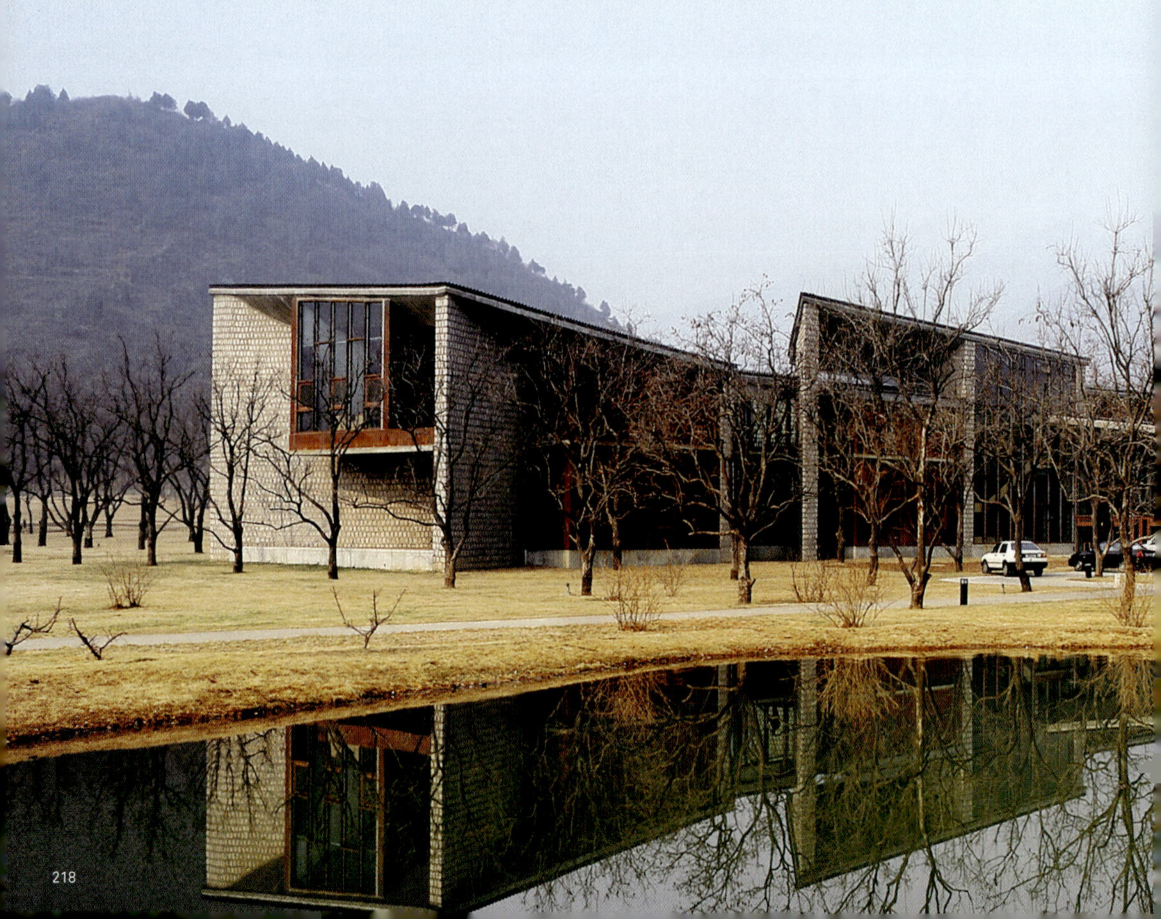

柿子林 VILLA SHIZILIN

Location: Beijing Architects: Atelier Feichang Jianzhu Project leaders: Chang Yung Ho, Wang Hui Project team: Wang Xin, Jing Yong, Zhong Peng, Yu Lu, Dai Changqing Client: Jindian Group Project: June 2001-June 2003 Construction/end of work: June 2003-May 2004 Built area: 4 800 m² Site area: 200 100 m² Cost: 4 million euro Programme: single-family house

The Villa Shizilin is located about sixty kilometres from the centre of Beijing (along the 2nd ring road), in Changping district, a vast peripheral urban and rural area north of the municipality. Built in a farming village formed by houses with square courtyards, the ensemble comprises a villa of 4,800 sq m in a park of 20 hectares, protected by a wall. The property extends across a rocky plain with kaki persimmon trees in the piedmont area of a chain of mountains stretching to the north. In 2001 the architects Yung Ho Chang and Wang Hui were chosen by the director of an important Chinese real estate group, Antaeus, to design a private villa and landscape park. It is a place where the promoter can welcome family, guests and clients to relax. Its construction began in 2003 and it was completed one year later.

At the beginning of the year 2000, the enlightened promoter, a lover of open-air sports and a participant in colloquiums on contemporary Chinese art, collaborated regularly with Atelier Feichang Jianzhu on real estate programmes in the capital. At that time, this singular businessman took an interest in the changes of living conditions generated by the rapid development of the Chinese cities. He considered architecture to be an authentic lever for improving the frame of life of urban inhabitants.

It was within this context that he placed his trust in the architects of Atelier Feichang Jianzhu, a trust which simplified the implementation of this decomplexed and very well planned project in which the designers kept control of the works all the way to the end.

The programme envisages a park and an artificial lake opposite the villa, which turns its back on the mountains, combining several categories of spaces and recreations – a club house with a spa and an indoor swimming pool, film-viewing and reception rooms, as well as private spaces, which are mainly situated on the upper floor, including the office where the promoter does calligraphy exercises. On the ground floor, a thick ceiling of concrete casings acts as the link between the nine architectural "modules" which form the overall framework.

At the crossroads of cultures and influences, Yung Ho Chang loves articulations: the articulation between the planned space – structural and landscape – and its natural site (indeed, the operation is inscribed forcefully within this vast site with its irregular terrain); the articulation of the various architectural modules, which offer the user a great variety of view points, and the articulation between the resolutely contemporary structural materials and architectural design. The use of stone, brick and wood is tied to that of traditional building elements.

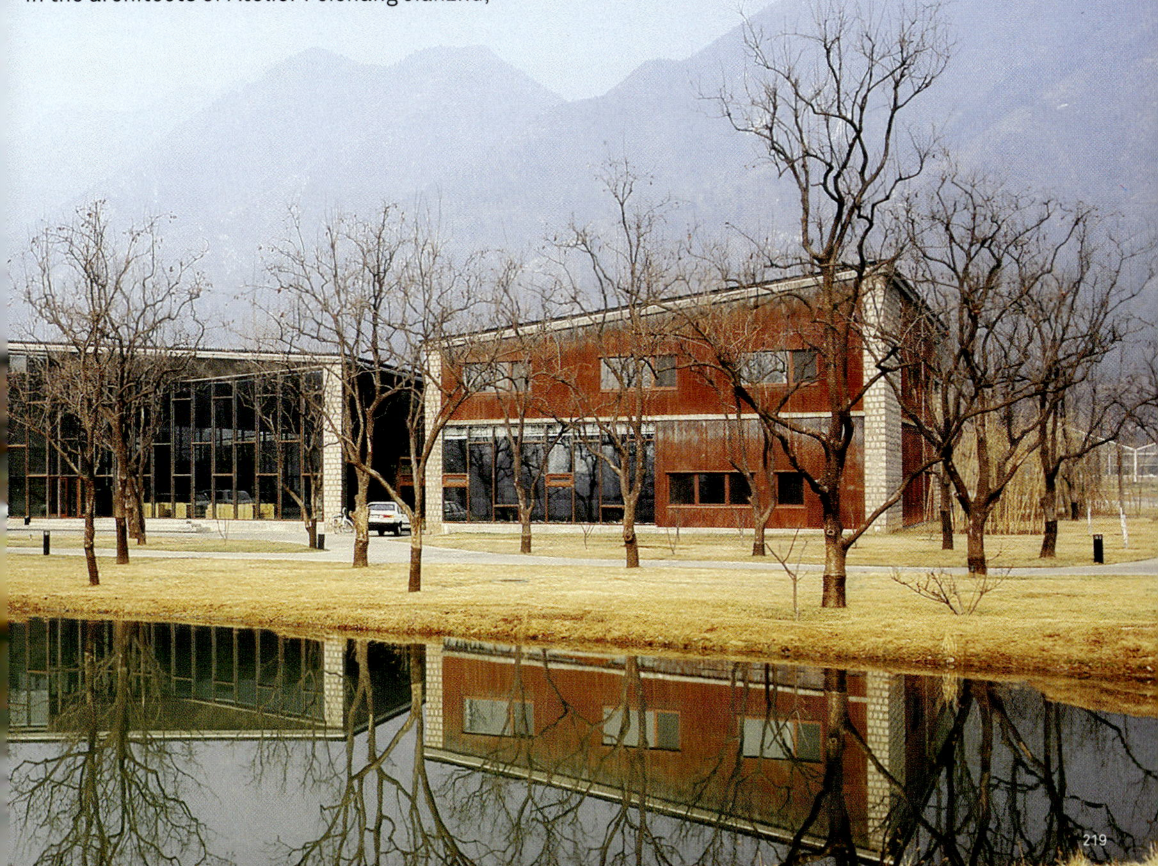

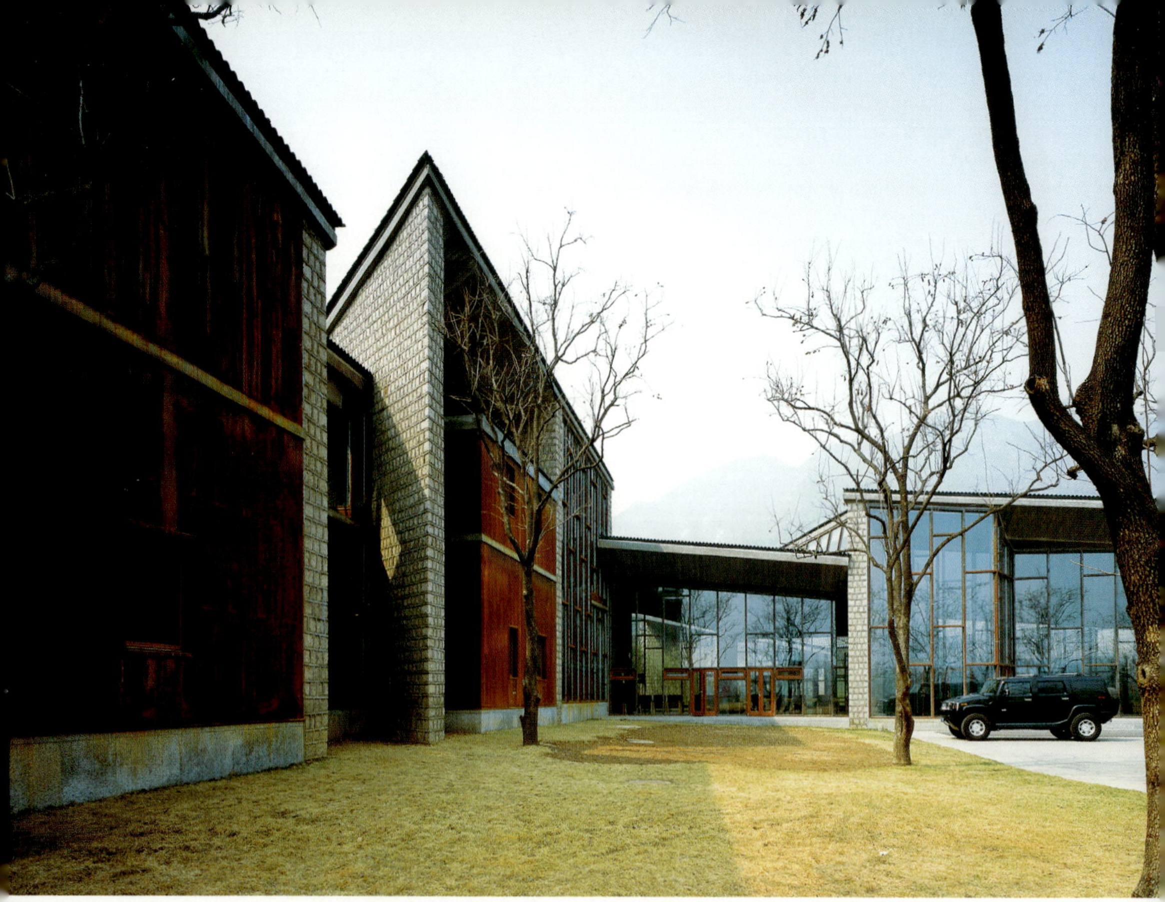

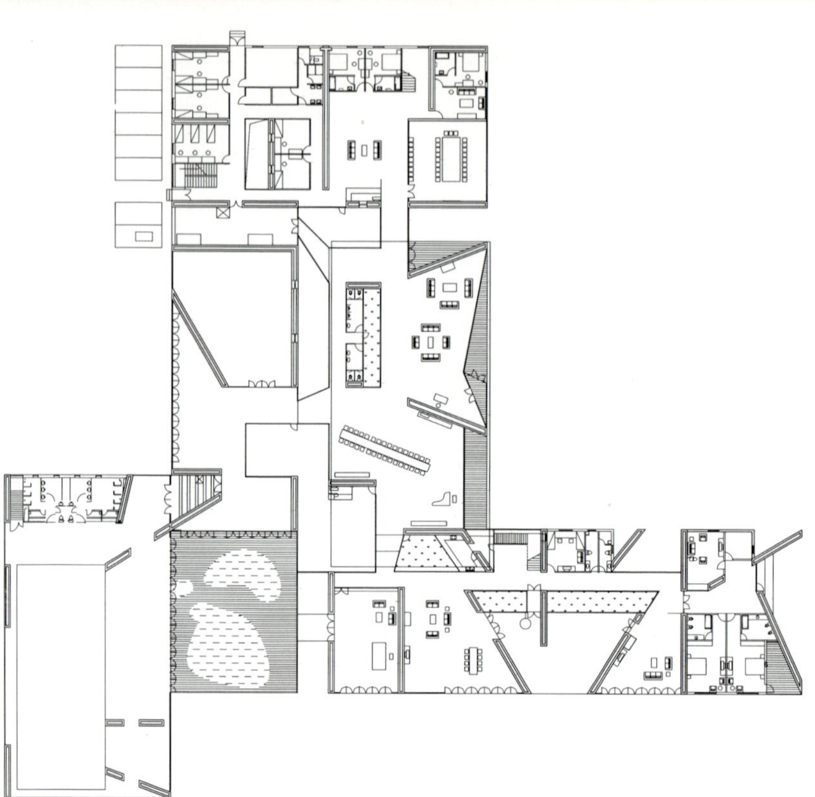

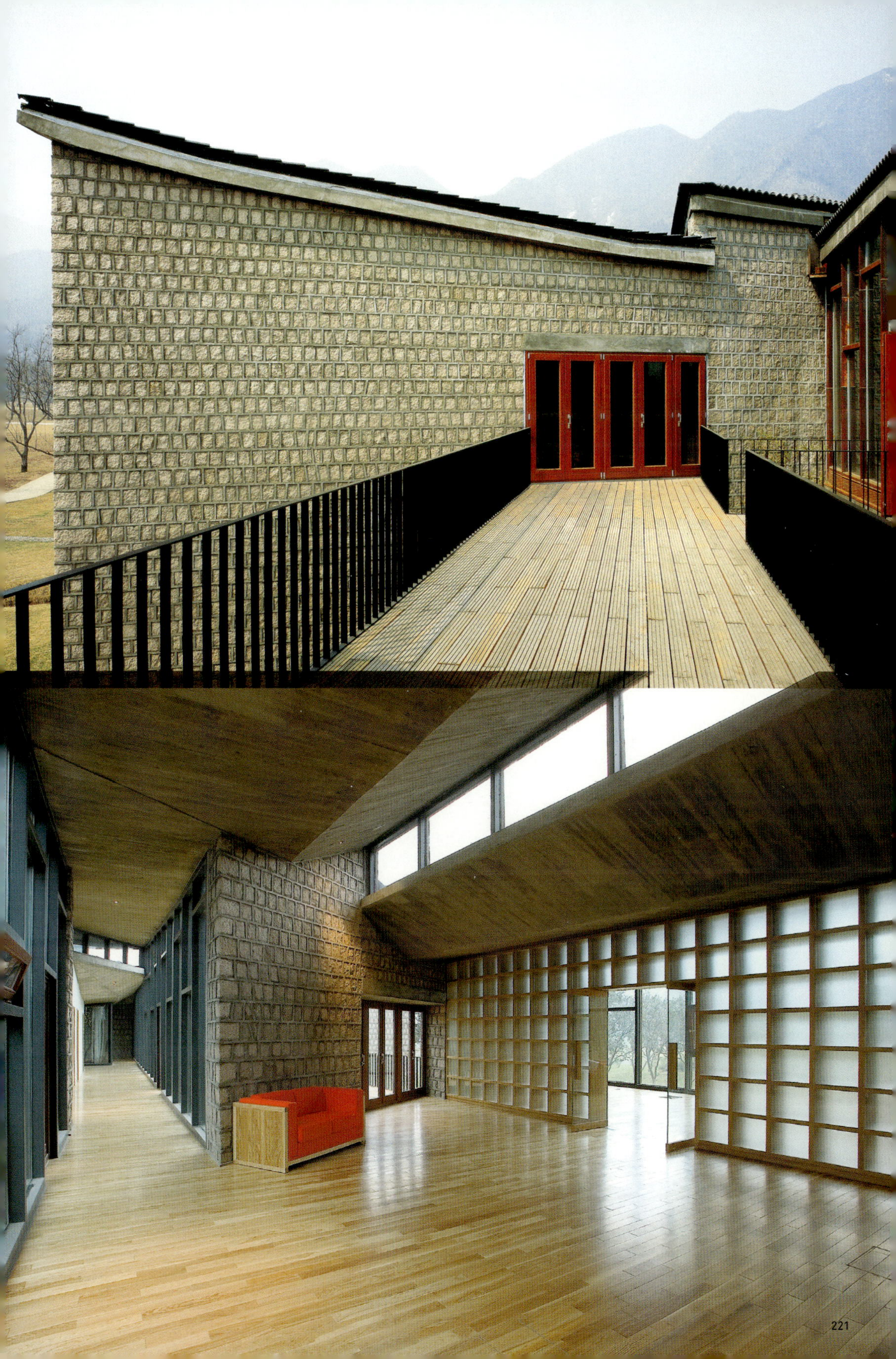

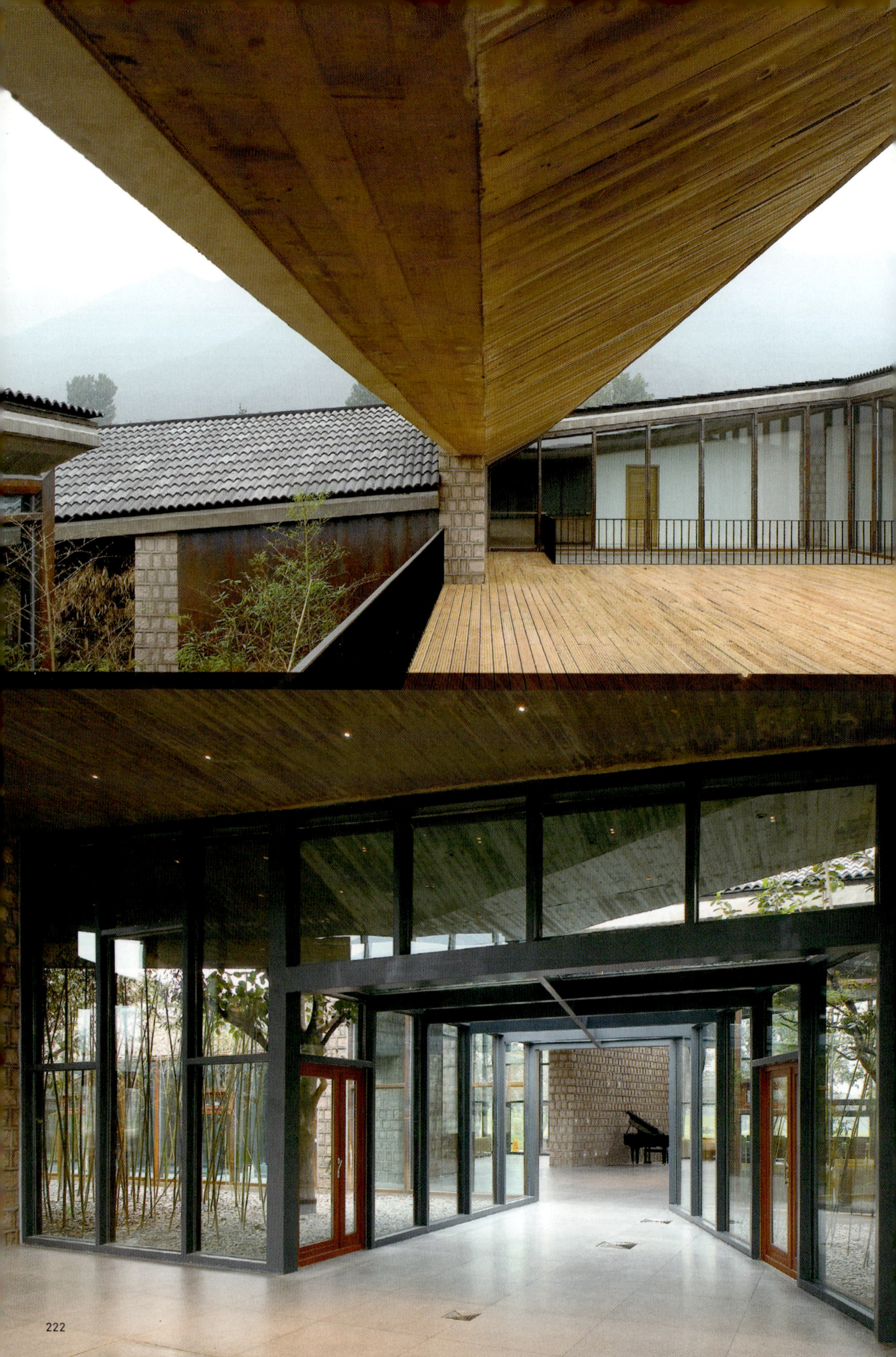

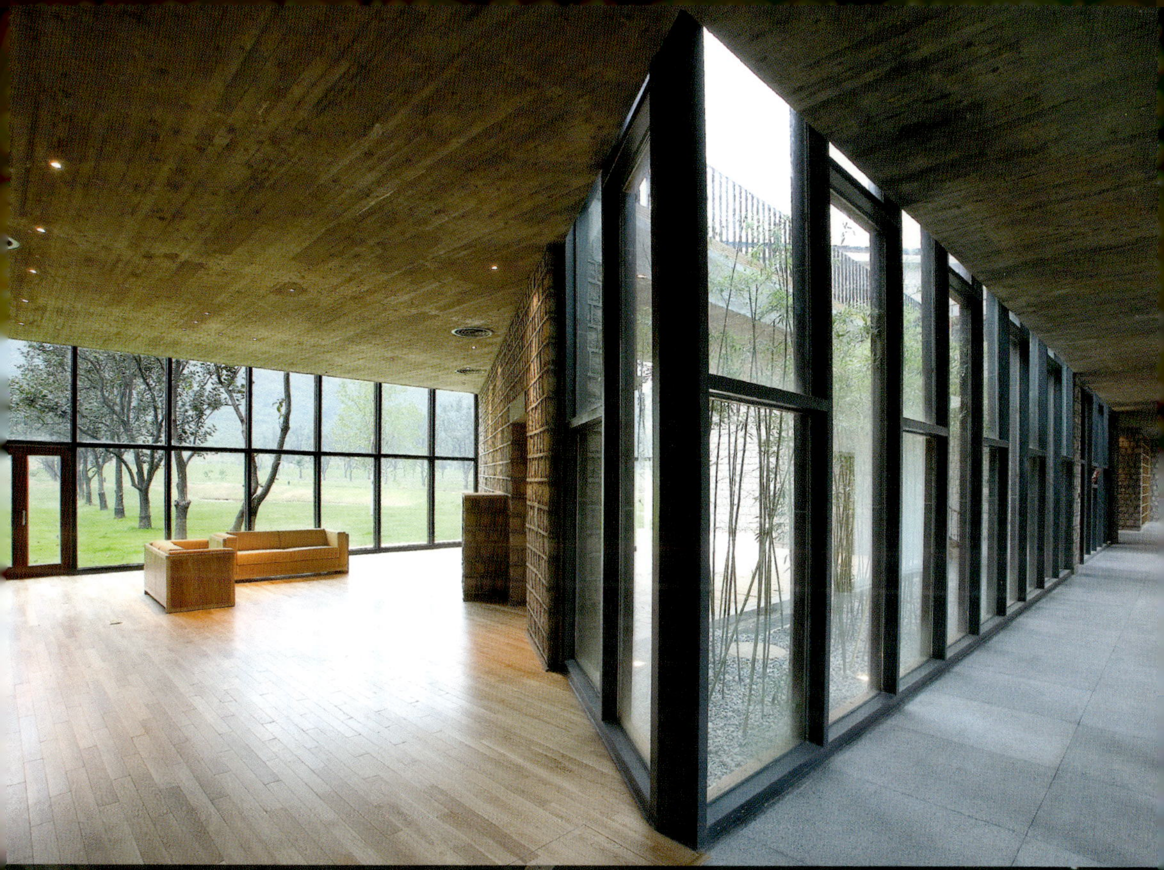

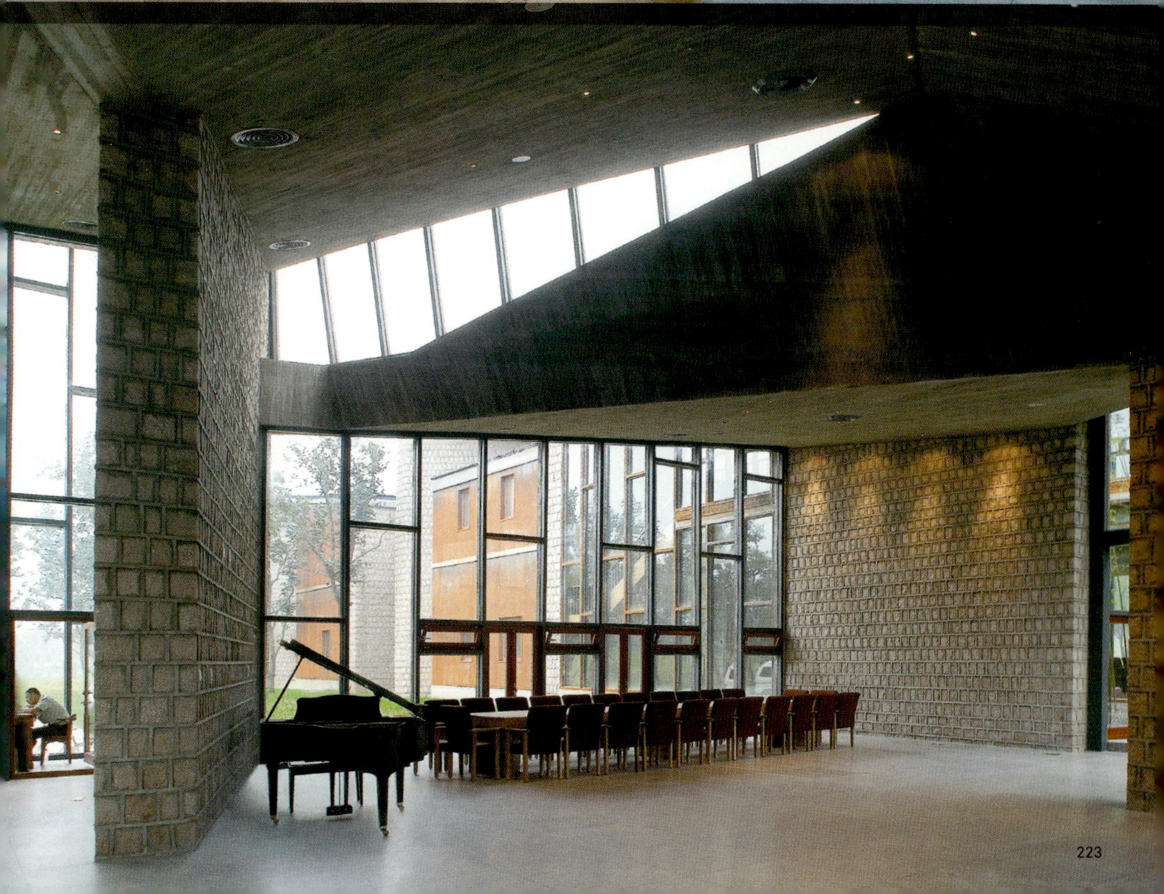

Positions, portrait of a new generation of Chinese architects

An exhibition conceived and realised by the Cité de l'architecture & du patrimoine / Institut français d'architecture (Ifa)

Cité de l'architecture & du patrimoine

François de Mazières, President
Francis Rambert, Director of Ifa

Curators

Frédéric Edelmann
Françoise Ged, in charge of the Observatoire de l'architecture de la Chine contemporaine, Ifa

Assistant curator and coordinators of graphic content

Chung Chih-Chia, Delphine Dollfus, Lucie Haguenauer-Caceres, Ifa
In China, Jérémie Descamps

Production and general coordination

Myriam Feuchot, Chung Chih-Chia, Delphine Dollfus,
Lucie Haguenauer-Caceres, Marion Zirk, Production Ifa service
Tien-Hung Hwang, Ségolène Dubernet, Émilie Rousseau,
Observatoire de l'architecture de la Chine contemporaine, Ifa
In China, Société 8th Ring Road / Jérémie Descamps

Texts

Authors: Frédéric Edelmann and Jérémie Descamps,
with the assistance of Marie-Françoise Georges
Translations: Chung Chih-Chia, Liu Ning, Emmanuelle Péchenart,
Wong Wenyan, Discobole, Serveis lingüístics (Chinese/French)
and John Crisp, Phillip-Victor Ortega for Manners (French/English)

Exhibition design

Myriam Feuchot, production Ifa service, with Serge Barto, designer

Graphic designer

Serge Barto

Interviews

Realisation and editing: José-Antonio Soria and Cristina Brossa, CCCB
Realisation (interview Qi Xin): Jean Sébastien Lallemand
Editing: Charles Gallois, Cité

Photographic credits

Panoramic photography of the exhibition: Aurélien Chen
Unless otherwise indicated, all the illustrations are from the architecture studios

Production manager

Éric Michaux, Production Ifa service

Exhibition contractor

In partnership with Thyssenkrupp Cadillac Plastic
Printing: Studio 3B

Communication

Jean-Marie Guinebert, Director of communication and partnerships,
Cité de l'architecture & du patrimoine
Guillaume Lebigre, graphic designer, Cité
Agostina Pinon, press relations, Cité
Valérie Samuel et Arnaud Pain, press relations, Opus 64

Catalogue

Coedition published by the Cité de l'architecture & du patrimoine, Paris, and Actar, Barcelona/New York

Director

Frédéric Edelmann

Authors

Frédéric Edelmann and Jérémie Descamps

Editorial director

Yves Kirchner

Editorial coordinators

Chung Chih-Chia, Martine Colombet, Ifa

Actar (www.actar.com)

Ramon Prat, director
Anna Tetas, editorial coordinator

Graphic design

Reinhard Steger

Digital production

Oriol Rigat

Printing

Ingoprint SL

Distribution

Actar-D
Roca i Batlle 2
08023 Barcelona
Spain
Tel: +34 93 417 49 93
Fax: +34 93 418 67 07
office@actar-d.com
www.actar-d.com

Actar-D USA
158 Lafayette Street, 5th Fl.
New York
NY 10013
Tel: +1 212-966-2207
Fax: +1 212-966-2214
officeusa@actar-d.com
www.actar-d.com

ISBN: 978-84-96954-50-2
DL: B-27076-08

The curators of the exhibition, the Cité de l'architecture & du patrimoine and the Observatoire de l'architecture de la Chine contemporaine wish to acknowledge the Chinese architecture studios for their contribution to the exhibition:

Amateur Architecture Studio; Atelier Deshaus; Atelier Feichang Jianzhu; Atelier Z+; Atelier Zhanglei; Aube Conception; China Architecture Design & Research Group (Cui Kai); Fake Design; Jiakun Architects; Mada s.p.a.m.; MAD; Qi Xin Architects & Engineers; Standardarchitecture; Studio Pei-Zhu; TM Studio; Urbanus Architecture & Design

The curators also wish to express their gratitude for the assistance of the photographers Tristan Chapuis, Philippe Ruault and Gilles Sabrie;
of the promoter SOHO China;
of the universities Tongji in Shanghai, Tsinghua in Beijing ;
and those of Chongqing, Canton, Tianjing and Nankin;
as well as ofAugustin Cornet, Zhou Jian, Feng Yueqiang, Qi Xin and Diana Chan Chieng

© Cité de l'architecture & du patrimoine, Paris, and Actar, Barcelona/New York

Printed & bound in the European Union

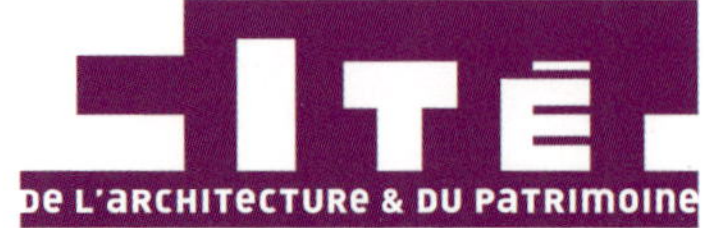
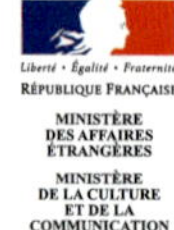